The West German Social Democrats, 1969–1982

About the Book and Author

The West German Social Democrats, 1969–1982: Profile of a Party in Power

Gerard Braunthal

The fall of the West German government in 1982 ended the 13-year rule of the Social Democratic Party (SPD) as the senior coalition partner under Chancellors Willy Brandt and Helmut Schmidt. In perpetual opposition from 1949 to 1966, the Social Democrats finally entered the government as the junior coalition party in 1966; three years later they assumed primary responsibility for guiding the nation.

The central theme of this detailed examination of the SPD during its years of governance is that social and economic forces in the nation had a major effect, often unsettling, on the party at a time when it had achieved the pinnacle of political power. Significant changes in the party's organization, membership, leadership, factionalism, ideology, and voter support limited its role within the political system (in the executive and legislative branches) and its influence on domestic and foreign policies. Yet, its ability to remain in power for a comparatively long period attests to its strength and respectability among the voting public.

Dr. Braunthal draws on a wealth of documentation, some unpublished, located primarily in German archives and libraries. In addition, he interviewed more than 120 persons, ranging from the top SPD leaders to staff officials, members, and other specialists, to gain a greater understanding of a party that is one of the most powerful in Western Europe and in the social democratic world, and whose organization has been a model of the twentieth-century mass party.

Dr. Gerard Braunthal is professor of political science at the University of Massachusetts, Amherst.

The West German Social Democrats, 1969–1982

Profile of a Party in Power

Gerard Braunthal

Westview Press / Boulder, Colorado

A Westview Replica Edition

Published in 1983 in the United States of America by
Westview Press, Inc.
5500 Central Avenue
Boulder, Colorado 80301
Frederick A. Praeger, President and Publisher

Library of Congress Cataloging in Publications Data
Braunthal, Gerard, 1923-
The West German Social Democrats, 1969-1982.
(A Westview Replica Edition)
Bibliography: p.
Includes index.
1. Sozialdemokratische Partei Deutschlands. I. Title
JN3971.A98S57443 1983 324.243'072 82-3464
ISBN 0-86531-958-8

Composition for this book was provided by the author.
Printed and bound in the United States of America.

10 9 8 7 6 5 4 3

Contents

Tables and Figures

Tables

Figures

Preface

This is a study of the West German Social Democratic Party (SPD) from 1969 to 1982, a period of thirteen years in which it governed the Federal Republic as the senior member of coalition cabinets. During this time the party held the chancellorship, first under Willy Brandt and then under Helmut Schmidt, and played an important role during four successive legislative periods. In 1982, its coalition with the small neoliberal Free Democratic Party (FDP) fell apart, leading to the sudden but not unexpected end of its rule. Although thirteen years in power, preceded by three years (1966-1969) as the junior coalition partner of the conservative Christian Democratic Union and its Bavarian ally, the Christian Social Union (CDU/CSU), seems like a short time when compared with the reigns of the Social Democrats in Scandinavia, it is a record of longevity for the SPD, which governed only briefly during the Weimar period and was in perpetual opposition during the Empire period.

Innumerable volumes have been published on the SPD since its official birth in 1875. The present volume seeks to fill one gap by providing a survey of the party during its recent years of governance. [1] This survey has two major themes: one, new social and economic forces within the nation, reflecting changes in the external environment, had a major and often unsettling effect on the party during its period in power; two, the party's role within the political system and its influence on domestic and foreign policies were limited. Before turning to these themes, it is important to note that the SPD has been one of the most powerful parties in Western Europe and in the social democratic world because of the size of its vote and membership support. The number of its members (matched only by the Swedish party) and its vote in national elections exceed by far that of any other social democratic party. [2] Its organization has been the model of the modern mass party. Moreover, from 1969 to 1982 the SPD was the governing party in a state with significant strength in Europe and internationally. Foreign policy decisions made by a Social Democratic chancellor reflected to some extent the views of his party, although he operated under a number of constraints, including the coalition with the FDP.

To understand the SPD's recent governing role, let us look at the historical context within which the party system developed in Germany. The authoritarian state of the Empire era provided only limited scope for parties to function; during the Weimar era the democratic parties were derided by their many opponents who remained safely ensconced within the bureaucratic, military, and judicial establishments. Only since 1949 have the parties received constitutional and statutory recognition. Article 21 of the Basic Law states that "the parties shall participate in forming the political will of the people." [3] The Party Law of 1967 provides for some state financing of parties and recognizes their right to engage in political education and influence political developments.

As a result of this recognition, some specialists on Germany have labeled the Federal Republic a "party state" (comparable to "party government" in Britain), in which two major parties and one minor party have played a key role in the establishment of the state; have popular mandates to carry out policies; have penetrated the administration (leading to substantial political patronage), the mass media, and education; and have mediated between government authorities and the citizenry. [4] Political scientist Kurt Sontheimer claims: "In fact, all political decisions in the Federal Republic are made by the parties and their representatives. There are no political decisions of importance in the German democracy which have not been brought to the parties, prepared by them and finally taken by them. This does not mean that other social groups have no power but that they have to realize their power within the party state." [5] Samuel Eldersveld, too, in a pioneering study on American party politics, argues that "party is king," and that parties are central to a democratic political system and provide the moving force for the governmental process. [6]

Other specialists disagree about the role of parties in political systems. Anthony King questions the centrality of parties in government decision making, although acknowledging that parties are the vehicle for leadership recruitment into government positions once they gain control of the executive branch. [7] Alessandro Pizzorno sees the necessity of parties but contends that given their lack of ideological differentiation, they provide citizens at election time with only an illusion of choice. [8] By focusing on the SPD during its period of rule, this study, in one of its themes, attempts to answer these questions: How important are parties in democratic political systems and do parties matter in government decision making? [9]

A related question must be asked: Are the parties able to cope with the increasingly intractable economic problems faced by all advanced industrial countries, or are other political forces, ranging from bureaucrats to interest group leaders, making the crucial decisions? In writing about the United States in 1980, William J. Keefe implies the latter: "The American party system is in serious trouble. Its loss of vitality appears both in government and in the electorate. Voters ignore parties, politicians dismiss them, and activists bypass them." [10] Does his observation apply to the Federal Republic as well?

If activists bypass parties or form new ones, the claim of West German parties (SPD and CDU/CSU) that they have increasingly assumed the characteristics of "catch-all" or people's parties with a large and diverse membership and voting base must be reexamined. How successful has the SPD been in gaining the support of and integrating diverse social groups within the framework of moderate pluralism? Why has the SPD been unable to capture more than 50 percent of the vote in any national election, unlike the British Labour and Scandinavian Social Democratic parties, which have often been more successful in their integrative and aggregative functions? [11]

In seeking answers to these questions, the political milieu in which the

SPD operates must be considered. In the early decades of the Federal Republic, parties were numerous (ten were represented in the first Bundestag in 1949), but from 1961 on, only the SPD, CDU/CSU, and FDP obtained enough votes to gain parliamentary seats. Despite receiving more than 50 percent of the vote in one election, the CDU/CSU always chose to form a coalition cabinet, as did the SPD when its votes exceeded 40 percent, normally the minimum needed to form a coalition government. Hence the West German party system fits into what Giovanni Sartori calls, in his typology of political parties, a bipolar alignment of alternative coalitions. [12] In this spectrum of parties, the SPD lies slightly to the left of center, the FDP in the center, the CDU slightly to the right of center, and the CSU to the right, with each party's field of gravity overlapping those of its neighbors.

These parties operate within a stable political system reflecting changed socioeconomic conditions in which antisystem parties on both left and right have remained weak. Such stability reflects the relative homogeneity of the population; decreasing national, religious, and social-class cleavages (except for foreign workers and their families); and the continuing decline of blue-collar and rise of white-collar workers—typical characteristics of states moving into a postindustrial or advanced industrial stage. [13] The result has been a moderate level of interparty competition in which ideological schisms are increasingly less visible. Yet because they have not vanished entirely, Sigmund Neumann's observation, made in 1956, of the importance of party doctrine and choice still held true to some extent in the 1970s. He wrote that parties remain "brokers of ideas, constantly clarifying, systematizing and expounding the party's doctrine. They maximize the voters' education in the competitive scheme of at least a two party system and sharpen his free choice." [14]

One central theme of this study is that social and economic forces produced significant changes in the SPD, often with destabilizing effects, just when the party was assuming a major governing role in 1969. Such forces will always affect many institutions in a polity, but in this instance the SPD was the primary organization subject to important changes. These tend to occur cyclically—the SPD (and other socialist parties), after all, emerged during the nineteenth century in response to the social and economic consequences of the industrial revolution. [15] External and historical forces produce not only changes but also constraints. As Jean Blondel notes: "Social and economic forces constrain parties; so do individuals, habits of thought, images, associations, in short the various aspects of the political culture of the country." [16]

In West Germany, the SPD and other major organizations were buffeted by change emanating primarily from youth rebelling against establishment politics, an emergency decree that could restrict civil liberties, the Vietnam war, the rise of a neo-Nazi movement, the hierarchies of ossified universities, and the materialistic aspirations of a bourgeois society. Such protests from an important neo-Marxist segment of society were bound to create a new political subculture that would inevitably conflict with the country's traditional reliance on technology and economic growth. Anthony Giddens' observation on conflict is surely appropriate to the strife-torn SPD of the 1970s: "Conflict is the irremediable fact of the human condition, the inescapable source of much that is creative, as well as destructive, in human society." [17]

The tradition-laden SPD, especially, could not escape this dramatic youth rebellion that represented perhaps the first major societal conflict and challenge to the system since the founding of the Federal Republic two decades earlier. The party responded with a strong attempt to integrate the youth, who had gathered forces in an extraparliamentary opposition, into its organization. It succeeded in this effort—but at heavy cost.

I argue in the chapters to follow that the integration of the New Left affected both positively and negatively the party's internal developments and its external relations. The New Left challenged the party's oligarchical organization and caused significant changes in the membership's socioeconomic base, leadership, and left-right factional cleavages; an increase in intraparty democracy (challenging the iron law of oligarchy propounded by Robert Michels), and the activation of its constituent organizations. [18] The left, mirroring the ideological ferment of the 1970s, revived the dormant ideological debates within the SPD that in their wake caused friction with a more pragmatic leadership.

The party not only acted as a magnet to the left in the late 1960s and early 1970s but also courted workers, salaried employees, civil servants, and other groups for membership and voting support in the frequent national, state, and local elections. By the late 1970s, however, some of the SPD's attraction had worn off as parties were confronted by the new divisive issues of ecology, nuclear energy, and national defense. By then, increasing numbers of people, especially the young, had become disenchanted with the parties' seeming inability to cope with the major crises that have shaken the advanced industrial states. When a portion of the population begins to challenge the legitimacy of the party system, the parties must question their integrative role in policymaking. Thus, once again, the SPD was not spared the external developments that produced new divisions—not always left versus right—within its organization.

This study also examines the SPD's relations with the other two segments of the Social Democratic triad—its parliamentary group and the SPD-led government. Questions must be posed about the effect of the change in the party's profile on the parliamentary group's factional struggles and—to return to the second theme of this study—on selected domestic and foreign policies of the government. At the pinnacle of power as a member of the governing coalition, to what extent was the party able to transform its policy planks into government policy and leave its imprint on the country's development? Given systemic, institutional, and political constraints and the conservative viewpoint of many key SPD leaders, did the party produce more social democracy or socialism in the Federal Republic? Or was it restricted to making gradual reforms within the neocapitalist system by planting a few more grains of social welfare in the country's soil? Even though the SPD shared in governmental power, did its cleavage-ridden organization or the general decline of parties signify that its importance had diminished vis-à-vis the government?

These questions indicate that a party cannot operate autonomously, but interacts constantly with other forces impinging on its freedom of action. The types of constraints need to be assessed in order to determine the nature and extent of reforms. One newspaper, surveying the SPD and social democratic parties in other countries, noted aptly: "What do social democrats do for an encore after 100 years of pioneering social reforms? They are still adept at outmaneuvering the West's communist parties. But with voters burdened by the welfare state's tax bill and the West's economic slowdown, some of the bloom has worn off the previously accepted appeal of social democracy." [19] If the social democrats are in a cul-de-sac, can they in the long run become a powerful third force between capitalism and communism? A positive answer to that question may depend on the SPD. In 1975, Chancellor Bruno Kreisky of Austria told the SPD delegates at their convention that the "strength of social democracy in Europe and the world depends to a great extent on how strong social democracy is in Germany." [20]

Thus, my intention in this examination of the SPD from 1969 to 1982 is to provide a general (but certainly not all-inclusive) view of a major party in Western Europe in an unsettled period during which storm clouds keep reemerging on the horizon. I abandoned the original plan of surveying the party from 1969 to 1980 (marking the end of three successive legislative periods during which the SPD was in power) when the SPD-led government fell prematurely in 1982—just after the manuscript was completed. Because it then seemed appropriate to cover the SPD's entire reign, I have made additions for the period from 1980 to 1982. Needless to say, the new coverage is not as extensive as that for the 1969-1980 period.

For financial support for this study, I owe thanks to the German Academic Exchange Service (DAAD) for two grants in 1975 and 1977, the Inter Nationes for my participation on a team of scholars observing the 1976 election, the University of Massachusetts for providing a research grant in 1977-1978, and the American Council of Learned Societies for a Grant-in-Aid for 1979-1980.

I am especially thankful to the staffs of the SPD archive and press documentation center, the Friedrich Ebert archive, the Bundeshaus library and press documentation center, the Deutsche Gesellschaft für Auswärtige Politik library, all located in Bonn, the Zentralarchiv für empirische Sozialforschung in Cologne, and the German Information Center in New York for making available their extensive holdings, some unpublished.

To gain a better understanding of the dynamics and profile of the party, I interviewed, usually at length, 128 persons, primarily in 1971, 1975, 1977, and 1980. Most of the respondents were officials and staff members in the Bonn national SPD headquarters and in Munich, Frankfurt, Bonn, Dortmund, and Hamburg SPD offices. To view the party from the bottom up, I also interviewed rank and file in a number of cities. In addition, I interviewed trade union officials and workers, journalists, CDU/CSU and FDP officials and staff members, and professors about their opinions of the SPD. Some persons were interviewed twice over the course of years in order to gain a perspective over time. To all respondents, to some of whom I promised anonymity, my heartfelt thanks.

I am also grateful to Hans-Eberhard Dingels, head of the SPD international division, for invitations to a 1975 party foreign policy conference in Bonn and the 1979 national convention in Berlin and for facilitating my contacts with SPD officials and staff members. Among the many others who were especially helpful were Peter Munkelt (SPD headquarters), Hermann Volle (Deutsche Gesellschaft für Auswärtige Politik), Franklin Schultheiss (Bundeszentrale für Politische Bildung), Sigrid Lanzrath and Elisabeth Pieper (Inter Nationes), Werner Blischke (Bundeshaus), and Hannelore Koehler and Inge Godenschweger (German Information Center, New York).

Finally, I am indebted to many persons who helped to shape this volume: David P. Conradt and Lewis J. Edinger for their numerous constructive criticisms of the first draft of the manuscript; Hans-Eberhard Dingels, Hilda Golden, Dietrich Schuster, and Joel Wolfe for their comments on all or parts of the manuscript; Janet Colombo for her invaluable editorial assistance; Vera Smith and Richard Spates for their typing; and Mareile Fenner for the art work. Special thanks go to my wife, Sabina, for her aid and patience in seeing the manuscript through to completion.

Gerard Braunthal

NOTES

1. For bibliographies, see Hans-Josef Steinberg, Die deutsche sozialistische Arbeiterbewegung bis 1914: Eine bibliographische Einführung (Frankfurt/M.: Campus, 1945); Kurt Klotzbach, Bibliographie zur Geschichte der deutschen Arbeiterbewegung, 1914-1945 (2d ed., Bonn-Bad Godesberg: Neue Gesellschaft, 1974); Klaus Günther and Kurt Thomas Schmitz, SPD, KPD/DKP, DGB in den Westzonen und in der Bundesrepublik Deutschland, 1945-1973: Eine Bibliographie (Bonn: Neue Gesellschaft, 1976). For citations to individual volumes for Empire, Weimar, and Federal Republic periods, see notes in chapter 1.

2. For a 1975 tabulation of membership and voting support for parties in the Socialist International, see Werner Kowalski and Johannes Glasneck, Die Sozialistische Internationale: Ihre Geschichte und Politik (Berlin: VEB Deutscher Verlag der Wissenschaften, 1977), p. 299.

3. Hans Lechner and Klaus Hülshoff, Parlament und Regierung (2d ed., Munich and Berlin: C. H. Beck'sche Verlagsbuchhandlung, 1958), p. 8. See also Kenneth H.F. Dyson, Party, State and Bureaucracy in Western Germany (Beverly Hills, Calif.: Sage, 1977).

4. Among them is Gerhard Leibholz. See, for instance, his Strukturprobleme der modernen Demokratie (3d ed., Karlsruhe: C. F. Müller, 1967). For commentaries, see Peter Haungs, "Die Bundesrepublik—ein Parteienstaat: Kritische Anmerkungen zu einem wissenschaftlichen Mythos," Zeitschrift für Parlamentsfragen, IV, No. 4 (Dec. 1973), 502-524; Dyson, "The Ambiguous Politics of Western Germany: Politicization in a 'State' Society," European Journal of Political Research, VII, No. 4 (1979), 375-396.

5. Kurt Sontheimer, The Government and Politics of West Germany (New York: Praeger, 1973), p. 95.

6. Samuel J. Eldersveld, Political Parties: A Behavioral Analysis (Chicago: Rand McNally, 1964), p. 21.

7. Anthony King, "Political Parties in Western Democracies," Polity, II (Winter 1969), 118.

8. Alessandro Pizzorno, "Interests and Parties in Pluralism," Organizing Interests in Western Europe: Pluralism, Corporatism and the Transformation of Politics, ed. Suzanne Berger (Cambridge, England: Cambridge University Press, 1981), pp. 274-275.

9. Richard Rose, Do Parties Make a Difference? (Chatham, N.J.: Chatham House Publishers, 1980).

10. William J. Keefe, Parties, Politics, and Public Policy in America (3d ed., New York: Holt, Rinehart and Winston, 1980), p. iii.

11. Francis G. Castles, The Social Democratic Image of Society: A Study of the Achievements and Origins of Scandinavian Social Democracy in Comparative Perspective (London: Routledge and Kegan Paul, 1978), p. 10.

12. Giovanni Sartori, Parties and Party Systems: A Framework for Analysis (Cambridge, England: Cambridge University Press, 1976), p. 179.

13. See Otto Kirchheimer, "Germany: The Vanishing Opposition," Political Oppositions in Western Democracies, ed. Robert A. Dahl (New Haven: Yale University Press, 1966), pp. 237-259; Gerhard Loewenberg, "The Remaking of the German Party System," Polity, I, No. 1 (1968), 87-113.

14. Sigmund Neumann, Modern Political Parties (Chicago: University of Chicago Press, 1956), p. 396.

15. On the theme of change, see Frank L. Wilson, The French Democratic Left, 1963-1969: Toward a Modern Party System (Stanford, Calif.: Stanford University Press, 1971), p. 4 ff.

16. Jean Blondel, Political Parties: A Genuine Case for Discontent (London: Wildwood House, 1978), p. 25.

17. Anthony Giddens, The Class Structure of the Advanced Societies (New York: Harper and Row, 1975), p. 238.

18. Robert Michels, Political Parties: A Sociological Study of the Oligarchical Tendencies of Modern Democracy (New York: Collier Books, 1962). Reprint of Zur Soziologie des Parteiwesens in der modernen Demokratie (Leipzig: W. Klinkhardt, 1911).

19. Christian Science Monitor, Apr. 17, 1979.

20. Vorwärts, Nov. 20, 1975.

Abbreviations

AfA	Arbeitsgemeinschaft für Arbeitnehmerfragen (Association of Workers)
AfB	Arbeitsgemeinschaft für Sozialdemokraten im Bildungsbereich (Association for Social Democrats in the Educational Sector)
AGS	Arbeitsgemeinschaft Selbständige (Association of Self-Employed)
APO	Ausserparlamentarische Opposition (Extraparliamentary Opposition)
ASF	Arbeitsgemeinschaft Sozialdemokratischer Frauen (Association of Social Democratic Women)
CDU/CSU	Christlich-Demokratische Union/Christlich-Soziale Union (Christian Democratic Union—Christian Social Union)
DAG	Deutsche Angestellten-Gewerkschaft (German Salaried Employees Union)
DBB	Deutscher Beamtenbund (German Federation of Civil Servants)
DGB	Deutscher Gewerkschaftsbund (German Trade Union Federation)
EC	European Community
FDP	Freie Demokratische Partei (Free Democratic Party)
GEW	Gewerkschaft Erziehung und Wissenschaft (Union of Teachers and Scientists)
Jusos	Jungsozialisten in der SPD (Young Socialists in the SPD)
KPD	Kommunistische Partei Deutschlands (Communist Party of Germany)
MBFR	Mutual Balanced Force Reductions
NATO	North Atlantic Treaty Organization
OR '85	Orientation Framework for 1985
ÖTV	Gewerkschaft Öffentliche Dienste, Transport und Verkehr (Public Service and Transport Workers Union)
PSF	Parti Socialiste Français (French Socialist Party)
SDS	Sozialistische Deutsche Studentenbund (German Socialist Student Federation)
SED	Sozialistische Einheitspartei Deutschlands (Socialist Unity Party of Germany
SHB	Sozialdemokratischer Hochschulbund (Social Democratic University League)
SI	Socialist International
SPD	Sozialdemokratische Partei Deutschlands (Social Democratic Party of Germany)
USPD	Unabhängige Sozialdemokratische Partei Deutschlands (Independent Social Democratic Party of Germany)

1
Historical Overview

A survey of the Social Democratic Party from 1969 to 1982 must be preceded by an account of its development since its inception in the middle of the nineteenth century. Only then can one gain the necessary perspective to understand the roots of contemporary problems facing the party. Its ideological schisms, its factional cleavages, its leadership struggles, its difficult relationship with an SPD-led government—these problems have their antecedents or parallels in the past. If current difficulties seem to be of major proportions, a look back will show that the party has always been faced by problems and yet sooner or later was able to surmount them—only to be faced by new ones. But despite such difficulties, occurring regardless of whether it was in political opposition or in power, the SPD has shown remarkable longevity as an organization dedicated to the betterment of the less privileged classes in German society.

The plight of exploited factory workers and their families in the aftermath of the nineteenth century industrial revolution precipitated the rise of socialist parties and trade unions throughout Europe. Such organizations sought to recruit workers who had to work long hours at low wages in sweatshop conditions and to live in miserable slums, in poor health, with a bleak future. In 1848, Karl Marx and Friedrich Engels published the Communist Manifesto providing doctrinal support to the growing urban proletariat becoming increasingly restive against the exploiting entrepreneurial class.

As the industrial revolution gained momentum in Germany, Ferdinand Lassalle, formerly a liberal leader who had turned socialist but not Marxist, founded in May 1863 the General German Workers' Association (Allgemeiner Deutscher Arbeiterverein). Workers joined it who in earlier decades would have formed secret local political associations, officially disguised as being devoted to education and recreation in order to circumvent decrees prohibiting the formation of radical groups. The new organization, representing the beginning of the social democratic movement, sought first to extend the limited suffrage and then to build socialism by creating a network of producers' cooperatives that would eventually supplant capitalist enterprises. With the death of Lassalle in 1864, Jean Baptiste von Schweitzer became president. By 1875, he was instrumental in tripling the association's membership to over 16,000. But he had to compete with a new rival organization, the Social Democratic Workers Party (Sozialdemokratische Arbeiterpartei), founded at Eisenach in

August 1869 by two Marxist leaders, August Bebel and Wilhelm Liebknecht. The new party supported the program of the short-lived International Workers Association, calling on workers in all countries to unite in a class struggle against the bourgeoisie and eliminate the capitalist states. Yet for Germany it opted for evolutionary rather than revolutionary change to gain its objective of economic and social justice within a socialist state.

BIRTH OF THE PARTY

The two rival organizations fought each other bitterly over such issues as centralization of state power but soon realized that their schism only benefited the hostile business and political elites. In May 1875, at a conference in Gotha, they merged forces and founded the Socialist Workers' Party of Germany (in 1891, renamed the Social Democratic Party of Germany—Sozialdemokratische Partei Deutschlands). [1] Gotha Conference delegates adopted unanimously a Marxist program drafted primarily by Liebknecht, which, according to a critical Marx, made some concessions to Lassalle's reformist theories. [2]

Three years after Gotha, Chancellor Bismarck, heading the unified Reich, launched his antisocialist campaign. His first move was to outlaw the party as a national organization by forbidding it to meet or to distribute its literature. On the other hand, its candidates were allowed to stand for election to the Reichstag (the lower house of Parliament) and its deputies were permitted to retain their seats. The outlawed party maintained a flourishing underground existence, not affected by Bismarck's preemptive introduction in 1881 of pioneering social welfare measures. By 1890, when the antisocialist legislation expired, the party was able to capture 20 percent of the vote for Reichstag candidates.

The period of repression radicalized many party adherents, who became increasingly dissatisfied with unsuccessful parliamentary means of achieving their objectives. In 1891 (one year after Bismarck's ouster from the chancellorship), Erfurt party convention delegates adopted a program, drafted by Karl Kautsky and Eduard Bernstein, that blended Marxism and reformism. In the Marxist section, it noted the growth of monopolies, the increasing exploitation of the workers, and the gradual proletarianization of the middle class, as a consequence of which, workers would intensify the class struggle during mounting economic crises, seize political power, and then transform capitalist private property into public ownership. In the reformist section, the program dealt with goals to be achieved within the existing capitalist order—among them, a progressive income tax, an eight-hour day, universal suffrage, proportional representation for Reichstag elections, referendums and recall of deputies, and equal rights for women. [3]

The programmatic mix of orthodox Marxism and reformism, designed to please different party groups, did not just reflect the 1891 scene but was included in party programs throughout the Empire, Weimar, and early Federal Republic eras. In its day-to-day actions around the turn of the century, however, the party moved increasingly toward reformism. In analyzing the Erfurt program, Bertrand Russell in 1896 predicted accurately: ". . . it seems indubitable that, if the party has a future of power at all, it must purchase power by a practical, if not a theoretical abandonment of some portions of Marx's doctrines. His influence is now almost omnipotent, but this omnipotence must, sooner or later, be conquered by practical necessity, if the Party is not to remain forever a struggling minority." [4]

The party's reformist wing was strengthened at the time by the emergence of a socialist trade union movement. (As in other European countries trade union federations were split along ideological lines; in Germany liberal and Christian unions were the chief, but weaker, competitors of the socialist unions.) A fraternal linkage did not emerge immediately between the twin pillars of the labor movement. The weak unions, not formed until the 1860s and not centrally organized until 1890, were at first subsidiary to the party, but by 1890 they were strong enough to claim equality—a relationship formalized in the Mannheim Agreement of 1906. Formalization aside, the unions' numbers had already given them de facto veto power over SPD decisions inimical to their interests. Union leaders were more concerned with reforms to gain immediate benefits for their members than in Marxist theory; hence they had a moderating, conservative influence on the party.

Party reformists strengthened their case for working within the existing capitalist system by pointing to striking gains made by the SPD in successive Reichstag elections. In 1893, 1.8 million voters cast their ballots for the SPD, but one decade later the total had risen to 3 million (an increase from 23.3 to 32 percent of the total vote). As a result of its sizable Reichstag group, the party sought through legislation to improve the workers' economic and social conditions.

These reformist policies were based on the writings of Eduard Bernstein, whose Marxist views were moderated by exposure to the British Fabians while in London exile in the late eighties. On his return to Germany, he called on the SPD "to find the courage to free itself from a phraseology which is indeed outdated; and to appear as what it really is today—a democratic, socialist reform party." [5] He noted that some of Marx's predictions were not accurate: The working class was improving economically, rather than becoming impoverished, and increasing its political power; the middle class was growing rather than shrinking; major economic crises had not occurred; and the capitalist system was well entrenched. Hence it was important for the party to press for gradual economic and political reforms which eventually would lead to socialism.

Bernstein presented his views at a number of party conventions, but the reformist wing could not convince its critics in the radical and centrist wings of the soundness of its position, except for its opposition at the 1906 convention to the call for political strikes for political purposes. The emergent radical wing, led by Karl Liebknecht (the son of Wilhelm Liebknecht) and Rosa Luxemburg, gained many adherents among SPD members as a result of radicalization among the unorganized urban proletariat, minor political strikes, an economic recession, and the Russian Revolution of 1905. The two leaders, holding fast to orthodox Marxist doctrine, considered the situation ripe for a general strike and other revolutionary tactics. But with no more than one-third support at the 1906 convention, the radicals, like the reformists, could not gain a majority for their position.

A centrist wing, led by Bebel and Kautsky, was initially sympathetic to the radicals, because the party, it argued, could rob the workers of their faith in and enthusiasm for a socialist future. But after 1903, still using Marxist rhetoric, the centrists increasingly sided with the reformists in their demand for parliamentary and other reforms.

The fratricidal disputes over theory and tactics did not preclude a further swift rise in the party's membership support. By 1914, it numbered over 1 million (twice as many as in 1907) and had a circulation of 1.4 million subscribers for its 90 newspapers; diverse holdings worth more than 20 million marks in capital assets; and a thriving network of youth, women's, sports, adult education, and other ancillary groups. In the 1912 Reichstag election, it received more than 4.2 million votes (nearly 35 percent of the total). Its bloc of 110 deputies was the largest in the 396-member Reichstag. [6]

In the face of political opposition from the Imperial regime and the solidly established capitalist elite, the party's growth to become the best organized in the Western world was remarkable. The explanation lay in a dedicated corps of officials and loyal members whose worlds revolved around their own organizations. At odds with the prevailing cultural norms, they had no choice but to form a distinct subculture that provided a home for their diverse activities.

The SPD organization, a model for many other European socialist parties, consisted of a hierarchical structure of national, regional, and local organs. Policymaking was centered in the party executive, whose members were elected indirectly by the local organizations. A large bureaucracy blossomed to schedule meetings, enroll members, engage in political agitation, and organize campaigns and educational and cultural activities.

When World War I erupted, party leaders abruptly abandoned their pledge to promote international peace and working class solidarity and to fight nationalism; they supported the war effort instead. In defense of their prowar position, they claimed that their members might not support them otherwise and that the war could lead to the overthrow of the reactionary czarist regime in Russia. In reality, they had become more cautious, afraid that government leaders would crush their organization. Although on August 3, 1914, left-wing leaders voted against the new policy in a Reichstag group meeting, on the next day, bowing to party discipline, they voted for war credits in the Reichstag plenary session. [7]

In March 1916, the dissident leaders broke with the party and established their own parliamentary group. One year later (April 1917), they formed the Independent Social Democratic Party (USPD), consisting of a number of ideologically disparate wings held together by their opposition to the war. Among the radical groups were the Spartacists, led by Liebknecht and Luxemburg, demanding mass action and revolution as means of stopping the war. The bulk of the USPD consisted of former SPD left-centrists led by Hugo Haase and Kautsky, along with a few reformist intellectuals, such as Bernstein, who wanted the German government to drop its annexationist war aims. The USPD succeeded in capturing control of a number of SPD organizations in Berlin, Leipzig, Halle, and other cities.

In 1917 and 1918, under USPD and left-wing union initiatives, an increasing number of war-weary and hungry workers, dissatisfied by the SPD prowar stance and angry at the government's failure to make democratic reforms, staged widespread strikes. By November 1918 the strikes, added to military defeats, contributed to the downfall of the Imperial regime.

THE WEIMAR ERA

With the war's end and the Kaiser's removal, the political left (SPD and USPD) was catapulted by the spontaneous revolutionary fervor sweeping Germany into governing the nation. But SPD leaders had no blueprint prepared for taking over power in a republican regime. Indeed, afraid of a revolution, they would have been willing to govern under a democratic constitutional monarch. Friedrich Ebert, SPD chairman, assumed control of a six-person (three SPD and three USPD) provisional government, then known as the Council of People's Delegates. After a period of initial turmoil, the SPD leaders gained control of workers' and soldiers' councils set up spontaneously at local levels and modeled partly on the soviets in the Soviet Union.

The USPD left wing, including Spartacists (the forerunners of the German Communist Party [KPD] established in December 1918), demanded the immediate nationalization of industry, the expropriation of Junker agricultural estates in East Prussia, and the purge of conservative army officers, civil servants, and judges. The SPD did not dare to endorse these bold demands for fear that political agitation and a dictatorship of the proletariat might result. Its fears and its opposition to a radical change of the old order were not entirely unfounded, as in late 1918 and early 1919 left forces sought to overthrow the transitional SPD-controlled government by means of strikes, riots, and an uprising. Reluctantly, the SPD leaders ordered the conservative Reichswehr and the antirepublican Free Corps units to quell the widespread disturbances. In their aftermath, the right murdered Liebknecht and Luxemburg. The embittered left wing in the USPD and the KPD never forgave the SPD for allying itself with the conservative forces to crush the left, thereby blocking fundamental political, economic, and social reforms. [8]

During this period of major civil disturbances, the SPD pressed for the establishment of a parliamentary system. It received the support of the nonleft parties to convene a national assembly in Weimar to draft a constitution. In January 1919, the vote for delegates to the National Assembly totaled 37.9 percent for the SPD and 7.6 percent for the USPD. Although the two left parties failed to obtain a majority, other democratic parties won enough seats in the National Assembly to help draft and enact a constitution then considered one of the most democratic in the world.

When the parliamentary system was established in 1919, Ebert became president. As the largest party, the SPD sought the USPD's support in forming a coalition cabinet, but the USPD declined. It was unwilling to join a cabinet that would have to include members of the bourgeois parties (Catholic and liberal) to gain majority support from the Reichstag. Thus the SPD had to seek allies among the nonsocialist parties in order to produce viable governments. From February 1919 to June 1920 and from June 1928 to March 1930, SPD leaders formed coalition cabinets, but in other periods, as SPD electoral strength dipped, nonsocialist chancellors were at the helm, with occasional SPD representation. [9]

In the meantime the USPD, although gaining almost as many votes as the SPD in the June 1920 Reichstag election, split over the issue of supporting the parliamentary system. At its October 1920 convention, the left-wing majority, favoring a workers' council system, decided to join the KPD and the communist Third International. The right-wing minority attempted to keep the rump party alive, but by September 1922 it had rejoined the SPD. From then on it became the left wing of the SPD.

When the SPD governed, it failed to enact radical economic and social reforms not only demanded earlier by the USPD but also enunciated in previous party programs. True, the SPD and the unions achieved moderate reforms (collective bargaining was institutionalized, works councils in the shops were established, and welfare legislation was passed), but no industries were socialized, other than electric power—ironically, taken over by a nonsocialist government. To justify preserving the status quo, the SPD argued that immediate material needs had to be met through higher production, reparations had to be paid, and the opposition of other parties had to be considered.

Paradoxically, the SPD reformist policies did not produce more moderate party programs. At two conventions (Görlitz, 1921; Heidelberg, 1925), Marxist calls for class struggle and nationalization remained imbedded in the programs. Such a stance obviously alienated more moderate voters (salaried employees and the small bourgeoisie), whose electoral support the party desperately needed. The SPD also had difficulty attracting enough women and young voters. To many of the latter, the party's leaders lacked dynamism and élan.

The SPD had to worry not only about electoral reverses at the national level but also about the repeated crises shaking the fragile Weimar parliamentary system. In the initial years, uprisings from the left and the right, political assassinations, foreign intervention, and inflation led to extreme instability. After a few short years of consolidation (1925-1928), the Great Depression and political authoritarianism greatly contributed to Adolf Hitler's rise to chancellorship in January 1933.

THE NAZI INTERLUDE

Neither the SPD nor the unions were able to halt the Nazi engulfment of the nation. They feared calling a general strike that might have led to a ruinous civil war. The dispirited leaders viewed any resistance against the swiftly entrenched government as useless, especially because millions of unemployed would not back them. Instead, upon Hitler's accession, they requested party and union members to remain calm and to follow orders.

Resistance soon became dangerous when the Nazis instituted a reign of terror against all democratic forces. To the credit of the SPD, its officials instructed their deputies in the Reichstag to vote on March 23 against the Enabling Act granting Hitler dictatorial powers. By then, other parties, except for the KPD, were too cowed to take similar action. (KPD deputies, however, had not been allowed to take their seats.) By summer 1933, Hitler disbanded all union federations. On June 22, he banned the SPD and had 3,000 leaders arrested. Another 3,000 Social Democrats went into exile, many of them to Great Britain, Sweden, and the United States. The party executive moved to Prague, from where it smuggled literature into Germany and encouraged resistance against the regime. [10] In the resistance movement were primarily social democrats, communists, and other leftists, but also numerous church, army, and other leaders. Many perished in the concentration camps, but those who did not formed the cadres for the country's postwar reconstruction.

THE POSTWAR ERA

Soon after the Nazi regime collapsed in May 1945, former SPD officials requested permission from Allied occupation authorities to rebuild their party. But the schisms within party ranks and among the occupation powers made the task difficult. Three centers of SPD strength emerged: one in Hannover—known as Büro Dr. Schumacher for its founder, Kurt Schumacher, a veteran leader whom the Nazis had imprisoned for years; a second in London, consisting of the remnant of the party executive in exile, headed by Erich Ollenhauer, which was isolated by its distance from Germany and did not receive permission to move back to Germany until February 1946; and a third in Berlin, a "Central Committee" led by Otto Grotewohl, which claimed to be the legal heir of the party suppressed in 1933. [11]

The Berlin Central Committee soon became the center of intense dispute within party ranks. Schumacher refused to recognize its claim to represent the SPD in all of Germany, accepting it only in the Soviet zone of occupation. He won this struggle; indeed, by April 1946 the SPD vanished in the Soviet zone when Grotewohl agreed to a merger of the SPD and KPD into the Socialist Unity Party (SED), whose formation the Soviet Union had encouraged. Many former SPD officials received posts in the SED, but it was not long before more reliable communists eased them out. The failure of the SPD to survive in the Soviet zone was a bitter disappointment for West German SPD chiefs, because the SPD's greatest strength before 1933 had been in the East German area.

Schumacher and other SPD leaders in the Western zones of occupation did not want to see a repetition of the East German merger in their area. Schumacher was sympathetic to a united workers' party, but not on the basis of unity with the KPD, considered to be a tool of the Soviet Union. Some unity committees were formed in West German cities, but they were short-lived once the Social Democratic members heard about developments in East Germany. In West Berlin, 82 percent of the SPD members voted against a merger in a referendum (forbidden by Soviet authorities in their Berlin sector). Hence the SPD in West Berlin remained in existence.

In the meantime Schumacher became undisputed party leader in West Germany. At the first official convention in Hannover (May 1946) he was elected chairman, and Ollenhauer, who by then had returned from London, became deputy chairman. The party was reconstructed on the foundations set before 1933. A statute was adopted; ancillary organizations, ranging from youth and women to sports, were reestablished; a party press emerged; and members flocked in (by 1947 more than 875,000, although three years later, membership had dropped to 683,000). [12]

Once again the party adopted the mixture of Marxist doctrine and reformist practice. In his speeches and writings, Schumacher cited the need to develop an economy based on planning rather than private profit. [13] He recalled that monopoly capital had helped Hitler to power and said that democracy could be assured only by transferring ownership of the major means of production. On the other hand, he did not call for total nationalization nor did he issue appeals addressed solely to the working class. Rather, he insisted that the party must be open to all those who "share a concern for the free development of the individual." [14] Thus Schumacher set the stage for a gradual evolution of the SPD into a people's party.

The SPD call for limited nationalization was incorporated into the constitutions of the states (Länder) of Hesse and Bremen, two strongholds of the SPD, and North Rhine-Westphalia but could not be implemented because of Allied opposition. The Christian Democratic Union (CDU), the chief rival of the SPD, in its Ahlen program of 1947 also supported nationalization of industry, but as the business community increased its power in the CDU in succeeding years, that proposal was quietly put aside.

Schumacher also emphasized foreign policy objectives, hitherto neglected by the party. To him, reunification of the divided country was one important way to ensure peace in Europe (as well as to ensure the party becoming the strongest in Germany). A united Germany, based on the borders of 1937, should receive back the Saar and not recognize the Oder-Neisse line as the final boundary with Poland. The SPD leader's accent on nationalism was intended to erase the image drawn during the Weimar period by the party's opponents, who had then accused the SPD of stabbing Germany in the back by accepting the Versailles treaty. Ironically, the emphasis on nationalism at a time when supranationalism was the rallying cry among European, including German, youth, put the party out of tune with this important group.

THE FEDERAL REPUBLIC

SPD hopes that it would become the governing party once the new West German Republic was created were dashed when election returns were tabulated during the night of August 14, 1949. The CDU/CSU defeated the SPD by less than 2 percent (31 to 29.2). Chancellor Konrad Adenauer (CDU) formed a coalition cabinet of conservative parties, and the SPD became the major opposition party—and remained so until 1966.

The SPD defeat was caused primarily by the successful economic revival of the western zones under the tutelage of Ludwig Erhard (CDU head of the Economic Council), Adenauer's strong anticommunist and pro-West stance in the face of tight Soviet control in the East zone, the loss to the SPD of its Protestant bastion in East Germany, and the voters' failure to respond to its neo-Marxist campaign speeches.

In the following four federal elections (1953, 1957, 1961, 1965) the SPD gradually gained voter support but was barely able to surmount the one-third barrier. The party faced a magnitude of problems in the quadrennial elections. An opposition party in the legislature needs to present alternatives to government policy that will appeal to the electorate. Schumacher's foreign policy alternatives to Adenauer's lacked broad support. The SPD chairman opposed West Germany's entrance into the Council of Europe and the European Coal and Steel Community because he feared that capitalist countries would dominate these organizations and that the more West Germany was drawn into West European organizations the more difficult it would be for the two Germanys to be reunited. Schumacher's negative position did not match the party's professed internationalist orientation.

In the 1950s, the SPD also opposed West German rearmament within the framework of a Western alliance system, again because such a policy would torpedo any chance for German reunification, to which the Soviets would have to give assent. At the 1954 convention, the party veered toward acceptance of a West German numerically limited volunteer army if a number of conditions were met. But these were not acceptable to the Adenauer government, and the SPD maintained its opposition. In 1958, the party joined trade unionists, academicians, and religious leaders in a campaign against arming the Bundeswehr with weapons capable of carrying nuclear warheads, and in 1959 it announced a "Germany Plan," advocating a militarily thinned-out zone in central Europe and a political and economic rapprochement of the two Germanys in advance of free elections in both states. The government never seriously considered the plan; the party soon shelved it when the hoped-for support in the nation or from other Western and Eastern governments failed to materialize.

Policy differences between SPD and CDU/CSU were sharp in foreign affairs but less acute in domestic policy. Competitive interparty opposition soon turned into cooperative opposition in which the SPD increasingly adapted itself to government initiatives, making only minor changes to or voting pro forma against many government bills. [15] Even though the SPD publicized its positive legislative contributions, the public could not easily perceive the nuances of which party was responsible for which revisions. It was hard for the SPD to rid itself of its image of being always on the negative side or even disloyal to the state.

In short, although the party contributed its share to policy input and output during its seventeen years of opposition in Bonn, the governing coalition parties shaped the grand design of domestic and foreign policies. In many Länder and cities, SPD officials were in policymaking positions, but their achievements did not get the same publicity as did those of the CDU/CSU-dominated federal government, which took credit for generating economic prosperity and for putting the country solidly in the Western camp.

What policy alternatives to present to the citizenry was but one of several difficult questions facing the SPD. Another was how to widen its electoral base in order to exceed the one-third national vote which it had seemed unable to surpass. This issue became more pressing as the socioeconomic composition of the population changed. In the labor force, the percentage of blue-collar workers, the traditional source of SPD strength, was decreasing and that of white-collar workers was increasing. Still tainted with Marxism the party could not easily win white-collar support or that of small shopkeepers and professionals. Nor could it be assured of automatic support from blue-collar workers, who did not necessarily consider themselves as the exploited class in the Marxist sense but increasingly as part of the middle class.

The initial attempt by SPD officials to recreate the party in the Weimar mold, with pride in tradition; loyalty to its leaders; and mistrust of the state, employers, the churches, and the intelligentsia produced an aura of pseudorevolutionary radicalism but led to a 25 percent decline in membership from 1947 to 1950. As a result, a group, led by reformist and pragmatic mayors in the SPD strongholds of Hamburg, Bremen, and West Berlin, later joined by many SPD Bundestag deputies, called for a change in the direction of party policy. Chairman Ollenhauer, who succeeded Schumacher upon his death in 1952, was partly receptive, unlike most party functionaries, who clung to past traditions and doctrines and were offended by the reformist group's assault on the "entrenched party bureaucracy" and the call on the party to throw overboard its ideological Marxist ballast, including the red flag and the term "comrade" when addressing one another.

Continuing electoral defeats made Ollenhauer aware that changes had to be made. In 1955, he set up a program commission under the direction of Willi Eichler. After years of preparatory work, the commission's draft proposal for a new reformist program was circulated throughout party ranks and then approved at the 1959 Bad Godesberg convention with only a few dissenting votes from a neo-Marxist group. [16]

Passage of the Godesberg program marked the historic turning to reformist ideology by a party committed until then to a mixture of Marxist ideology and reformist practice. The program abandoned Marxist determinism and affirmed the religious and philosophical roots of democratic socialism as well as the principles of freedom, justice, and solidarity in a parliamentary, democratic system. Nationalization was considered no longer the major principle of a socialist economy but only one of several, and then only the last, means of controlling and preventing economic concentration and power. The program assented to as much free competition as possible with only as much planning as necessary. In other areas, it committed the party to the defense of the country and support of the army. It called for respect and cooperation with churches on the basis of a free partnership with them.

The program reflected not only the views of many former émigré leaders who were impressed by the British and Scandinavian pluralist and welfare systems but also their conviction that the West German population was wary of any "experiments" that might undermine the neocapitalist system (a regulated economic system infused with social welfare measures). Although the Godesberg program seemed to mark a radical change to reformism, it represented the culmination of gradual deideologization within the party, as exemplified by the 1952 Action Program, revised in 1954. The SPD was not alone in espousing a reformist doctrinal position; other European socialist parties and the Socialist International (in 1951) had already taken or were adopting a similar position. Thus these parties turned from being workers' parties to becoming people's parties, in the hope of widening their voter base.

In the Federal Republic, such a doctrinal shift meant that the SPD no longer presented an alternative governmental program with limited appeal but had embarked on an "embracement" policy with its political opponent. Periodically, from 1961 to 1966, Herbert Wehner, a leading SPD official, discreetly probed the possibilities for a grand coalition with the CDU/CSU. He considered this the only practical strategy for the SPD to gain respectability and share in governing the state.

Until 1966 all such efforts failed, despite the nomination of Willy Brandt, mayor of West Berlin, as chancellor candidate in 1961 and 1965. Brandt had strongly supported the reformist wing of the party, the Western alliance system, and a strong anticommunist policy. But in the first election campaign, especially, the party emphasized the virtues of its top candidate rather than issues. Once again the election results were disappointing to the party, although it received more votes than previously from urban residents and young people.

The break for the SPD came in late 1966 when Chancellor Ludwig Erhard (who had succeeded Adenauer in 1963) suddenly resigned. A national economic recession compounded by difficulties with the United States and France over financial matters, economic cooperation, and the Common Market caused the crisis. On November 10, the CDU/CSU nominated Kurt Georg Kiesinger, Minister-President of Baden-Wuerttemberg, as their candidate for chancellor. Unable to set up another governing alliance with the Free Democratic Party (FDP), he formed a grand coalition with the SPD. The FDP, with only 8 percent of the Bundestag seats, was relegated to the opposition bench. [17]

Within the SPD, the advisability of joining a cabinet with the erstwhile foe was debated heatedly then and in later years. The proponents, led by Wehner, argued that the party had been in opposition long enough and had to demonstrate to the voters its ability to govern the state. The opponents, primarily the left wing, resented an alliance with the conservative CDU/CSU and were worried about the lack of an effective parliamentary opposition. Their views did not prevail.

On December 1, 1966, the new government was sworn in, the first SPD participation in a national government since 1930. Among the nine SPD cabinet members (the CDU/CSU had ten) were Brandt, Vice Chancellor and Foreign Minister; Karl Schiller, Minister of Economic Affairs; and Wehner, Minister of All-German Affairs. Within the constraints of coalition bargaining, the SPD was eager to make its mark on domestic and foreign policy. Brandt wanted to establish closer relations with Eastern bloc states, and Schiller pushed hard for a Keynesian pump-priming program in order to get the economy moving again. These efforts were partly successful, and other SPD-controlled ministries also initiated a number of legislative reforms. [18]

In 1969, the Grand Coalition neared the end of the parliamentary four-year term. The SPD, not eager to renew its strained alliance with the CDU/CSU, emphasized in its electoral strategy its discords with the CDU/CSU over enactment of the government program. To convince the voters that the two parties did not agree on all fundamental policies, it stressed its responsibility for economic expansion and a more flexible foreign policy. It gained at the polls, but not enough to outpace the CDU/CSU as the party with the highest plurality. The latter, however, could not get SPD or FDP support for another coalition. Hence the SPD requested the FDP to join it in a coalition cabinet.

After protracted negotiations, Brandt was sworn in as chancellor, the first SPD chief executive since 1930. [19] In the government declaration, Brandt mentioned "continuity and renewal," indicating that drastic policy changes were not contemplated. In the succeeding three years, modest labor, social, and economic reforms were enacted, but not enough for many SPD members, whose reform euphoria dissipated into bitterness about electoral promises not having been kept. The limits on reforms reflected the lack of accord between SPD and FDP, budgetary restraints, and the complexity of some issues.

Paradoxically, not the tortoise pace of domestic reforms but the successful pace of Ostpolitik produced a major governmental crisis in 1972. From 1969 until then, Brandt and Foreign Minister Walter Scheel (FDP) acted swiftly to normalize relations with East bloc states. The two leaders signed treaties, highlighted by the renunciation of force, with the Soviet Union, Poland, and the German Democratic Republic. But a few conservative Bundestag deputies in the SPD and FDP, considering this policy a sellout to the Communists, crossed over to the CDU/CSU. Consequently, the coalition lost its governing majority and was forced prematurely to call a national election, held on November 19,1972.

The SPD and FDP gained a clear-cut victory. For the first time since 1949, the SPD outpolled the CDU/CSU (by less than 1 percent). With a comfortable forty-six-seat majority, the governing coalition had a popular mandate to continue its policies. After the government chiefs concurred on a government program and on the distribution of cabinet seats, Brandt promised to speed up the slow pace of reforms. He called for changes in taxation, social welfare, labor, land, education, and environmental protection. In foreign policy, he tried to consolidate his gains in the Ostpolitik but encountered difficulties in normalizing relations with Czechoslovakia, Hungary, and Bulgaria.

In late 1973 and early 1974, the Chancellor ran into other roadblocks. Within the SPD, the Young Socialists clashed with their elders on ideological and pragmatic issues; Wehner, head of the SPD parliamentary group (Fraktion), publicly criticized his government's stand on Berlin while on a visit to Moscow; new economic and financial problems arose from the international oil crisis; and some public service workers went on strike. To compound Brandt's difficulties, in April 1974 a spy scandal broke in the Chancellor's Office. Günter Guillaume, a secret agent of the German Democratic Republic who had made his way up the ladder of the SPD to become one of Brandt's personal assistants, was arrested, which, along with subsequent revelations about the Chancellor's personal life, caused Brandt's resignation on May 5. After consultations with SPD chiefs, Brandt requested the appointment of Helmut Schmidt, then Minister of Finance, as his successor.

On May 16 Schmidt was sworn in as chancellor and formed another SPD-FDP cabinet. It contained a few new members who were technocrats and pragmatists rather than intellectuals. In the government policy statement, the chancellor pledged to continue Brandt's social-liberal coalition program. He lauded Brandt's determination to win for West Germany a position of respect in the world community and noted that Brandt's domestic reform program from 1969 to 1974 had accomplished more than any previous program for a comparable period.

Brandt remained party chairman and was reelected to this post at succeeding conventions. The collective leadership of Brandt and Schmidt was unusual; normally, in West Germany the chancellor is simultaneously head of the party. But in this instance Schmidt claimed that he could not handle both jobs satisfactorily and that Brandt's political strength, personal attractiveness, and skill in integrating warring factions made him the ideal chairman. The two leaders arrived at a modus vivendi in apportioning their spheres of operations, but their personal relationship remained cool.

In the 1976 federal election, the SPD and FDP won only a ten-seat majority. This loss of seats was caused by continuing national economic problems (especially high unemployment and mounting welfare costs) and SPD intraparty squabbles and corruption scandals. Although the CDU/CSU reemerged as the party with the highest percentage of votes, its inability to find a coalition partner put it once again in opposition. On December 15, Schmidt was reelected chancellor.

The government's policy statement (December 16) made no promises of major economic and social reforms, given their financial costs. Instead, it focused on the government's need to restore full employment, reduce public borrowing, and put the old-age pension and health systems on a better financial footing. But domestic and foreign pressures forced Schmidt in 1977 to start some pump-priming public works construction programs. Within the SPD, muted criticism of Schmidt's leadership style, his failure to accept enough party recommendations, and his willingness to make too many compromises with the FDP continued.

In 1977 the SPD also suffered a series of damaging reverses, from which it recovered only slowly. Factional disputes in Munich and Frankfurt did not subside, financial scandals erupted, Brandt and Wehner feuded openly, and dissidents in the Bundestag Fraktion voted against or abstained from some government bills. On the other hand, Schmidt and cabinet members won popular support for their cool response to terrorist acts, culminating in the rescue of passengers from a hijacked Lufthansa aircraft in Mogadishu, Somalia. The Chancellor's increased prestige enhanced that of the party. Moreover, the November 1977 Hamburg convention produced less friction between party wings than earlier conclaves. The party could not afford continued feuds, with the rise of environmental groups beginning to sap its strength.

From 1978 to 1980 the party, despite occasional setbacks, did well in state (Land) elections. Schmidt's national stature and that of the Federal Republic had risen dramatically, his foreign policies had broad popular support, the ideological schisms within the party were beginning to subside (although important differences remained on such issues as nuclear power and defense), and the fratricidal feuds in Munich and Frankfurt were diminishing. Hence, the signs for the party, and its FDP coalition ally, to win the 1980 national election were propitious. When the CDU/CSU nominated the Bavarian leader, Franz Josef Strauss, as its candidate—to the chagrin of many in the CDU who were aware of his low popularity ratings in the nation—Schmidt's chance of reelection was enhanced. Although in the election the SPD did not fare as well as it had hoped, a strong vote for the FDP easily led to a majority for the two parties. The result was a renewed SPD/FDP coalition cabinet led by Schmidt. Despite the victory over the CDU/CSU a sense of frustration arose within the SPD over its inability to emerge from the shadow of the Chancellor, who did not want to be too closely identified with a party lacking his own appeal within the nation.

From 1980 to 1982, Schmidt's coalition cabinet faced increasing difficulties. The economy became stagnant; unemployment rose in 1982 to 1.7 million people (7.4 percent), the highest in thirty years. SPD and FDP cabinet ministers disagreed sharply on how to combat the recession. In discussions on the 1982 and 1983 budgets, FDP ministers insisted that cuts be made in social programs and corporate taxes be lowered in order to spur more business investments. SPD ministers, on the defensive, had difficulty preventing cuts in social welfare expenditures, increasing outlays for public works programs, and raising taxes on upper-income groups. Most of the SPD rank and file, including union members, were dissatisfied by SPD concessions to the FDP in the cabinet.

Another source of difficulty was the SPD general membership's inability to agree on two major policies strongly supported by Schmidt: the 1979 NATO decision to deploy medium-range missiles in West Europe and the construction of more nuclear power stations to meet the country's energy needs. The party's schism tarnished its image and hurt it in several Länder elections. Many SPD voters abstained or voted for the Greens, a new party espousing environmental and peace issues. By September 1982, the Greens had won seats in several Länder legislatures, increasingly replacing FDP deputies.

Partly to prevent the extinction of their party and partly because of continuing differences on economic policy, FDP leaders therefore decided (over internal opposition) to withdraw from the Bonn coalition and to cast their lot with the CDU/CSU. On September 17, the thirteen-year-old SPD-FDP coalition, the longest in West German history, collapsed. On October 1, CDU/CSU and FDP deputies ousted the SPD-government in a no-confidence vote. Helmut Kohl (CDU) became chancellor of a CDU/CSU-FDP coalition cabinet, and the SPD moved once again to the opposition benches in the Bundestag. A historic period of the SPD governing the nation in coalition had come to an end.

In summary, the party's evolution from its inception in the 1860s to 1982 is characterized not only by its remarkable continuity or revival (after Bismarck and Hitler) but also by its ideological and factional schisms and its leadership struggles spanning the decades of the Empire, Weimar Republic, and Federal Republic. For the party to have been spared such difficulties would have been unique given the propensity of elites in a mammoth organization to differ on policies, means, and goals and to vie for positions of power. Although the SPD was in political opposition during most of its century-long existence, it governed briefly in the Weimar era and again (as the senior party) from 1969 to 1982. More often, it governed states and municipalities. Assumption of political power gave the SPD much-needed legitimacy, respectability, and stature.

NOTES

1. For accounts of the SPD spanning the period up to 1933 or to the post-1945 era, see Evelyn Anderson, Hammer or Anvil: The Story of the German Working-Class Movement (London: Gollancz, 1945); Helga Grebing, The History of the German Labour Movement (London: Oswald Wolff, 1969); Heinrich Potthoff, Die Sozialdemokratie von den Anfängen bis 1945 (Bonn-Bad Godesberg; Neue Gesellschaft, 1974); Franz Osterroth, Chronik der deutschen Sozialdemokratie, 3 vols. (Berlin, Bonn: Dietz, 1975, 1976, 1978); Wolfgang Abendroth, Aufstieg und Krise der deutschen Sozialdemokratie (Frankfurt: Stimme, 1964); Georg Fülberth and Jürgen Harrer, Die deutsche Sozialdemokratie, 1890-1933, Vol. I, Arbeiterbewegung und SPD (Darmstadt: Luchterhand, 1974); Joseph Rovan, Histoire de la Social-Démocratie Allemande (Paris: Éditions du Seuil, 1978), Richard Breitman, German Socialism and Weimar Democracy (Chapel Hill, N.C.: University of North Carolina Press, 1981); W. L. Guttsman, The German Social Democratic Party, 1875-1933: From Ghetto to Government (Winchester, Mass.: Allen and Unwin, 1981).

2. For accounts of the SPD before and/or during the Empire period, see Franz Mehring, Geschichte der deutschen Sozialdemokratie, 2 vols. (Berlin: Dietz, 1960, reprint of 1897 and 1898 ed.); Richard W. Reichard, Crippled from Birth: German Social Democracy, 1844-1870 (Ames: Iowa State University Press, 1969); Vernon L. Lidtke, The Outlawed Party: Social Democracy in Germany, 1878-1890 (Princeton: Princeton University Press, 1966); Guenther Roth, The Social Democrats in Imperial Germany: A Study in Working-Class Isolation and National Integration (Totowa, N.J.: The Bedminton Press, 1963); Carl E. Schorske, German Social Democracy, 1905-1917: The Developoment of the Great Schism (Cambridge: Harvard University Press, 1955); Hedwig Wachenheim, Die deutsche Arbeiterbewegung, 1844-1914 (Cologne, Opladen: Westdeutscher Verlag, 1967); Hans-Josef Steinberg, Sozialismus und deutsche Sozialdemokratie: Zur Ideologie der Partei vor dem I. Weltkrieg (Hannover: Verlag für Literatur und Zeitgeschichte, 1967; reprint, Bonn: Dietz, 1979).

3. For full text, see Bertrand Russell, German Social Democracy (New York: Simon and Schuster, 1965; reprint of 1896 ed.) pp. 137-141.

4. Ibid. p. 143.

5. Eduard Bernstein, Evolutionary Socialism (New York: Huebsch,

1909). See also Peter Gay, The Dilemma of Democratic Socialism (New York: Columbia University Press, 1952).

6. Richard N. Hunt, German Social Democracy, 1918-1933 (New Haven: Yale University Press, 1964).

7. Susanne Miller, Burgfrieden und Klassenkampf: Die deutsche Sozialdemokratie im ersten Weltkrieg (Duesseldorf: Droste, 1974).

8. For accounts of the SPD during the Weimar era, see Hunt; A. Joseph Berlau, The German Social Democratic Party, 1914-1921 (New York: Columbia University Press, 1949); Hans J. L. Adolph, Otto Wels und die Politik der deutschen Sozialdemokratie, 1894-1933: Eine politische Biographie (Berlin: de Gruyter, 1971).

9. For instance, in 1919 the SPD received 11.5 million votes (37.9 percent of the total) and the USPD slid to 6 million votes (20.5 percent).

10. For the SPD in the Nazi era, see Lewis J. Edinger, German Exile Politics and the Social Democratic Executive Committee in the Nazi Era (Berkeley: University of California Press, 1956); Erich Matthias, Sozialdemokratie und Nation: Ein Beitrag zur Ideengeschichte der sozialdemokratischen Emigration in der Prager Zeit des Parteivorstandes 1933-38 (Stuttgart: Deutsche Verlags-Anstalt, 1952); Peter Grasmann, Sozialdemokraten gegen Hitler, 1933-1945 (Munich: Olzog, 1976).

11. For a biographical study, see Lewis J. Edinger, Kurt Schumacher: A Study in Personality and Political Behavior (Stanford: Stanford University Press, 1965).

12. Theo Pirker, Die SPD nach Hitler: Die Geschichte der Sozialdemokratischen Partei Deutschlands, 1945-1954 (Munich: Rütten and Loening, 1965), p. 127. For the SPD in the post-1945 period, see Susanne Miller, Die SPD vor und nach Godesberg (Bonn-Bad Godesberg, Neue Gesellschaft, 1974); Klaus Schütz, "Die Sozialdemokratie im Nachkriegsdeutschland," Parteien in der Bundesrepublik, ed. Max Gustav Lange, Gerhard Schulz, Klaus Schütz (Stuttgart, Duesseldorf: Ring, 1955), pp. 157-271; Douglas A. Chalmers, The Social Democratic Party of Germany (New Haven: Yale University Press, 1964); David Childs, From Schumacher to Brandt: The Story of German Socialism, 1945-1965 (Oxford: Pergamon Press, 1966).

13. See Arno Scholz, Turmwachter der Demokratie: Ein Lebensbild von Kurt Schumacher, 2 vols. (Berlin: Arani, 1952), Vol. II, Reden und Schriften.

14. Cited by Harold K. Schellenger, Jr., The SPD in the Bonn Republic: A Socialist Party Modernizes (The Hague: Nijhoff, 1968), p. 34.

15. For the role of the SPD in opposition, see Otto Kirchheimer, "Germany: The Vanishing Opposition," pp. 237-259; Klaus Günther, Sozialdemokratie und Demokratie, 1949-1966: Die SPD und das Problem der Verschrankung innerparteilicher und bundesrepublikanischer Demokratie (Bonn-Bad Godesberg: Neue Gesellschaft, 1979); Wolfgang Kralewski and Karlheinz Neunreither, Oppositionelles Verhalten im ersten Deutschen Bundestag, 1949-1953 (Cologne and Opladen: Westdeutscher Verlag, 1963); Michael Hereth, Die parlamentarische Opposition in der Bundesrepublik Deutschland (Munich: Olzog, 1969).

16. For full text, see SPD, Jahrbuch der Sozialdemokratischen Partei Deutschlands 1960-61 (Hannover and Bonn: Neuer Vorwärts Verlag Nau, n.d.), pp. 403-418 (hereafter referred to as SPD, Jahrbuch, year), or SPD, Basic Programme of the Social Democratic Party of Germany (Bonn, n.d. [1959]). See also Schellenger, Jr., pp. 57-110.

17. For details, see Gerhard Lehmbruch, "The Ambiguous Coalition in

West Germany," Government and Opposition, III, No. 2 (Spring 1968), 181-204; Franz Schneider, Die grosse Koalition zum Erfolg verurteilt? (Mainz: von Hase and Koehler, 1968); SPD, Executive, Bestandsaufnahme 1966: Eine Dokumentation (Bonn, 1967).

18. SPD, Bundestagsfraktion, 147 Mal Soll und Haben: Zwischenergebnisse Sozialdemokratischer Politik in der Grossen Koalition (Bad Godesberg, 1968), and Soll und Haben: Bilanz sozialdemokratischer Bundespolitik in Regierung und Parlament von 1966 bis 1969 (Bonn, 1969).

19. For details on the period 1969-1982, see subsequent chapters.

2
The Organization: From Presidium to Local Branch

That party organizations reflect national character is unlikely, but perhaps the SPD is an exception. For there can be little doubt that if Germans are characterized as hard-working, efficient, and prone to plan to the most minute detail, then the party's leaders and top staff—in control of its hierarchical structure, its bureaucracy, and its rules and regulations—fit this mold. To dissect the elaborate organization, one must do more than describe its units from the national through the regional to the local levels, its membership requirements, and its voting and arbitration procedures—all of which are precisely specified in the periodically revised SPD statutes. [1] One must also capture the dynamics of the party (as will be done especially in later chapters) by focusing on the locus of policymaking, the distribution of power among the policymakers, the factional struggles among its diverse groups, the role of the rank and file, and the relationships to parliamentary party and government.

Three related hypotheses bearing on the distribution and maintenance of power within a mass organization must be tested: first, that a party elite will be able to organize the structure so that it can manipulate power, politically socialize the members, and minimize challenges to its rule; second, that a party elite will be reluctant or find it difficult to make a highly rigid and bureacratic organization responsive to the demands of new members; and third, that a party elite will ensure that it controls the subunits of the organization having actual powers, regardless of the statutory powers assigned to such bodies. The numerous units that make up the complex Weberian-type organization (see figure 1) will be discussed with these hypotheses in mind.

THE ORGANIZATION

The Presidium

Nominally, the highest party organ is the convention, but in reality it is the presidium, to which the fifty-four-page statute devotes but one paragraph, buried in the section on the executive. Created in 1958, this "inner cabinet" consists at present of eleven top leaders who are simultaneously members of the party executive (to be described below). [2] Presidium members who automatically receive a seat owing to their party

FIG.1 ORGANIZATION CHART

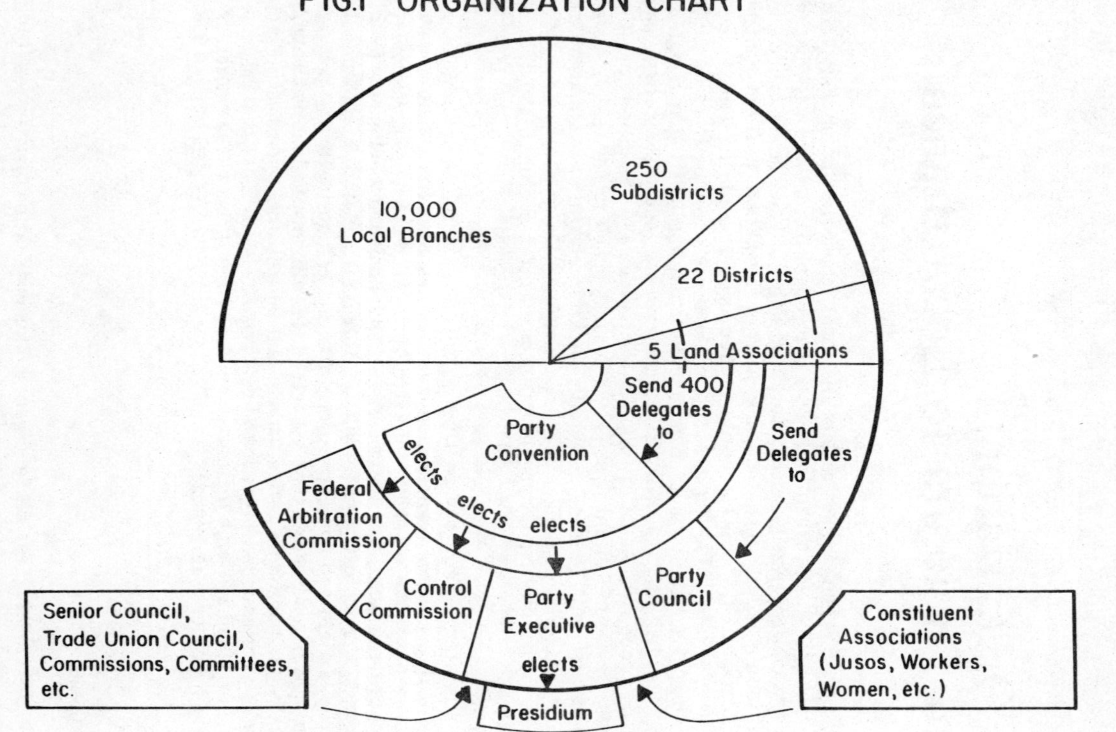

Source: Adapted from SPD executive, Kraft für die 80er Jahre. Machen Sie mit (Bonn, n.d.)

offices are the chairman, the two deputy chairmen, the Fraktion chairman, the secretary, and the treasurer. In addition to this six-person "rump presidium," the executive chooses five members at-large. [3] Since 1966, when the SPD entered the government, a number of members have been ministers and other high officials. One member has always been a woman, primarily, one suspects, to prevent charges that the presidium is an all-male enclave. Yet the practice is nothing but tokenism.

The limited number of the highly-coveted seats means that many top leaders who would like to serve cannot be selected. For the few seats available, there is much competition among the ideological factions. However, for the left, with about one-third of the seats on the executive since 1973, it has been a losing struggle. Center and right wings have been able to place their candidates more easily. A left-wing proposal at the 1971 convention suggesting that from 1973 on, convention delegates rather than executive members elect presidium members in the hope that left representatives would have a chance of winning seats was voted down by the "conservative" majority of delegates. [4]

The presidium, meeting weekly, is charged with carrying out the decisions voted on by the executive and with setting political and organizational guidelines. But in practice the presidium makes the decisions that are then affirmed, normally without much discussion, by the executive. To what extent the political decisions affected government policy depended to some extent on the inclination of the SPD chancellor—Brandt in his time more than Schmidt thereafter—to consult informally with top presidium members in order to minimize any potential government-party conflict. Yet in most instances, the chancellor first made policy and then sought presidium support. [5] As the chancellor and several ministers also held presidium seats, it was easy for them to convince the other members of the correctness of their policies. Soon after Schmidt became chancellor, he made it a practice to meet with Chairman Brandt privately before the presidium meetings, to discuss government and party matters. [6] On numerous occasions, as a result of such coordination, the presidium issued policy statements on national domestic and foreign policy issues that coincided with those of the government.

As to party matters, the presidium determines the general guidelines, the content of crucial resolutions, intraparty and organizational questions, the scheduling and agenda of upcoming party conferences, budgetary matters, and strategies for election campaigns. On occasion, one- or two-day retreat meetings (Klausurtagungen) to discuss a major topic are held, to which nonpresidium SPD cabinet members and Fraktion leaders may have been invited. In addition, the presidium or its individual members hold talks with the executives of SPD associations and with representatives of other organizations.

Before the presidium can try to act as an integrative unit within the party, it must first seek consensus within its own ranks. Despite the absence of a left wing, controversies do erupt in this top policymaking body, because left-center and right-wing members may not concur on a number of issues or because the members, regardless of political views, may not concur on other issues. If a controversy is not settled peacefully, a decision will be postponed rather than forced to a vote. If there is accord among the members—normally the case—then the decision (in the form of a statement or declaration) is either announced or transmitted to the executive for its approval. [7]

The presidium is not omnipotent. Its members know that other party organs can challenge its decisions and that it is constrained by convention guidelines. Nevertheless, it has a prestige unmatched by others within the organization that gives its decisions a symbolic value.

The Executive

Second in importance to the presidium is the executive (Vorstand). This larger body consists of the party chairman, the two deputy chairmen, and the treasurer, as well as thirty-two other members (increased to thirty-six in 1979), all elected by the biennial party convention. Nominees must receive a majority of votes to win on the first round or a plurality on the second round. Until the late 1960s, the top leaders drafted a slate of candidates who could then be expected to win without challenge. To put up a candidate in opposition was viewed as damaging to party unity and discipline, but since then, with the rise of ideological factions, elections have assumed a plebiscitary character in which each faction, seeking maximum representation, drafts a slate of candidates in behind-the-scenes politicking at the conventions.

As an indication of the politicization of executive posts, the 1973 results are revealing. Chancellor Brandt, running again as party chairman, received 404 affirmative and 20 negative votes, with 4 abstentions, from the Hannover convention delegates. This strong support from all factions was not matched by Schmidt, then a cabinet minister, running as deputy chairman, who received 286 affirmative and 129 negative votes, with 16 abstentions. The left delegates, with one-third strength at the convention, had voted against him for ideological reasons. [8]

At the 1975 Mannheim convention, Schmidt received nearly as many votes as Brandt, because of the increased prestige the former had accrued as chancellor and because of a compact made before the convention by left and right wings in which the left pledged to vote for Schmidt and the right for Brandt. In addition, the two wings had agreed to vote for a slate of other candidates acceptable to both. This part of the compact was broken, with the left claiming that the right had not abided by it. As a result, the left put up an unofficial slate excluding five right-wingers while the right excluded nine leftwing and center candidates. [9] In the balloting, the left again succeeded in having one-third representation on the executive, although the well-organized right produced more votes for each right-wing candidate. Erstwhile executive members who could not command full support from left or right wings failed to be reelected. [10]

In 1977 and 1979, the competing wings resumed their feuds, but as a result of mediating efforts by Brandt and party secretary Egon Bahr, they agreed to vote for each other's candidates. Nevertheless, the number of candidates exceeded the number of executive seats available, because contests emerged between various associations and regions as well as among dissident leftists who did not want to abide by the left accord with the right.

In the 1970s, few women served on the executive. At the 1975 convention, when none of the twenty-three candidates who won a majority on the first ballot were women, Brandt appealed to the delegates to vote also for women on the second ballot. His intervention led to the election of two. At the 1979 Berlin convention, the pressure of the Association of Social Democratic Women (ASF) for more representation produced an accord to expand the number of elected seats (excluding the top officers) from thirty-two to thirty-six in order to give women four extra seats. As a result seven were elected, although the ASF indicated that membership expansion was a poor way of ensuring more female representation. [11]

According to party statute, the executive is "responsible for the business of the party and controls the basic position of the party organs."[12] Meeting once a month, it deals with basic party policies, programs, organizational questions, personnel matters, and domestic and foreign policy issues—many of these already having been discussed in the presidium. Until 1958 the executive was the policymaking organ, but since then, as indicated, it has become the passive recipient of information (including cabinet matters from 1966 to 1982) from the presidium. In 1973, left-wing members, calling for an end to such passivity, asserted that too often the executive heard long-winded speeches from party leaders and specialists and that "its sessions cannot be refuse products of cabinet sessions." Instead it should deliberate on government reform policy initiatives. [13]

For the left, such a proposal makes sense, because it has representation in the executive and none in the presidium. The left could influence decisions coming from the executive but not from the presidium. Yet, from the point of view of the more conservative party leaders, such a proposal would mean a diffusion of authority that could lead to conflicting policies. They rejected it, although in 1974 they created a planning group that was to work closely with and submit recommendations to the presidium. The group was expected to deal with current political problems, set priorities for party actions, and draft position papers based on advice from the diverse party groups. [14]

Despite left-wing complaints of the executive's failure to take policy initiatives, the mere presence of left-wing members on the executive ensures their occasionally getting into lively debates with their more conservative colleagues. If the left-wing members can convince left-center members to vote with them on an issue, then right-wing members may even be the losers.

The Convention

According to the Party Law of 1967 and the SPD statute, the party convention (Parteitag), normally meeting biennially, is nominally the highest organ, but, as noted, in practice the presidium is the body formulating policy. Since 1971 the number of convention delegates elected at district or Land conventions has been set at 400 (it had been 300 until then). The quota of delegates allowed each district is based on the total of its enrolled party members. In addition, executive members have voting rights, while other representatives from party institutions may participate in an advisory capacity but without voting rights.

Left critics within the party have assailed, without success, the indirect selection of delegates and the large number of functionaries and deputies who are seated on the basis of the posts they hold. The critics maintain, as did Robert Michels in his study of the SPD in the Empire era, that this system does not maximize intraparty democracy. [15] Instead, power is concentrated in the hands of leaders who want the large number of functionaries seated as delegates to approve the party line. One nonleft SPD observer concurred: "The party conventions have primarily a symbolic character; to determine the party policy, however, is not their task."[16]

Yet, since 1968 the new bloc of left-wing delegates, constituting about one-third of the total, has challenged the leaders on a number of issues—and not always unsuccessfully. The dissidents have sparked heated debates to counteract the earlier image of the convention serving merely as an organ of approbation and integration. Because one primary function of the convention is to vote on resolutions submitted by local and regional branches, the dissidents have effectively used this tool of direct democracy. For instance, at the 1968 Nuremberg convention, party leaders nearly lost a vote on a resolution critical of their joining the coalition government in 1966. At more recent conventions, debates have ranged from education policy to Third World development policy; they have served as a safety valve for delegates to voice their views.

But the status enjoyed by the leaders makes it easier for them to convince delegates to accept their recommendations, made in their keynote speeches and during discussions. They may also seek to keep highly controversial subjects off the agenda by pleading for a postponement of the issue. They will fend off locally and regionally initiated resolutions that are too critical of the party line by ensuring that loyal functionaries sit on the commission on resolutions (Antragskommission), which recommends that certain ones not be acted on if they duplicate others. Delegates normally vote for those resolutions drafted by the party's executive or for the least controversial ones and shunt others to various party organs for disposition—in effect killing most of them. The convention's presiding officer often calls for votes only on all-encompassing resolutions drafted by the executive and declares superseded all others dealing with the same subject. Hence only about 20 percent of the resolutions are accepted, many of these carrying the executive's imprint of approval. [17] If the opposition to the party or government line is strong, the executive may seek to work out a compromise.

Although conventions are hardly the locus for integrating party and government policies, by focusing on major issues facing the Federal Republic they may provide some programmatic direction and stimulus to policymakers at national, state, and local levels. For instance, delegates at the 1979 Berlin convention spent most of the time discussing the two issues of national security and energy but also, more briefly, north-south problems, unemployment, and protection of the environment and then voting on hundreds of resolutions on these topics. Because the harried delegates also must listen to long reports from party leaders and elect members to the executive, the control commission, and the arbitration commission, they have been sympathetic to proposals to streamline convention procedures. In 1980, a reform commission proposed a drastic reduction in the number of themes discussed at future sessions, which normally last from four to five days.

Although the conventions play a limited role in policymaking within the party, in the 1970s they were the foci of important debates between party factions. As a result, proceedings have attracted the attention of the news media and public opinion as well as of the international community. The number of guests from social democratic parties in other countries attests to the symbolic importance the SPD attaches to these well-staged and costly meetings. [18]

Party Council

Another party organ at the national level sharing in the decision-making process is the party council (Parteirat). In order to coordinate the activities of the party at all levels, this large body (114 members in 1977) consists of two-thirds representatives from the districts and one-third from the Länder, the Bundestag, and the federal cabinet. [19]

According to the party statute, the council is to be consulted before the executive arrives at decisions concerning "basic foreign and domestic policy decisions, basic organizational questions, establishment of central party institutions that will recurrently burden the party financially, [and] the preparation of Bundestag elections."[20] But meeting only four times a year, normally, the council cannot be an active participant in policy-making. (On special occasions it also meets with other party units.) Rather it serves as a body receiving information from the executive, coordinating federal and Länder policies, and giving regional spokesmen an opportunity to air their views.

Control and Arbitration Commissions

The nine-member control commission serves in theory as a watchdog over and a recipient of complaints concerning the executive. In practice, it examines mostly the treasurer's financial reports and the secretary's report about party matters entailing expenditures.

A seven-member federal arbitration commission (Bundesschieds-kommission)—others exist at lower levels—deals with disputes over the statute and over the guidelines of constituent groups. It can institute proceedings against a member who has grossly violated party principles or directives. Penalties range from censure, prohibition against holding party office, and suspension of membership rights to expulsion in case of a member who has caused "severe damage" to the party. [21]

In the 1970s, the commission was kept busy adjudicating cases stemming mostly from the influx of left-wing members into the party. In the 1977-1979 period, for instance, it dealt with the cases of fifty-eight members, of whom thirty were subsequently expelled. [22] A typical case was that of the economics professor Gerhard Kade of Darmstadt Technical University, who had been active on the communist-controlled Committee of Peace, Disarmament and Cooperation. He had spoken at a Frankfurt mass rally of the committee at which a German Communist Party presidium member also spoke. A local arbitration commission ruled that Kade could not hold any SPD office for three years; but the federal arbitration commission, following an appeal by the party executive, expelled him for breach of party principles and regulations. [23]

Senior Council

When young people streamed into the party in the late 1960s and early 1970s, they pushed older members onto the sidelines. As a result of a Brandt initiative in 1973, a senior council (Seniorenrat) chaired by former Bundestag Vice President Carlo Schmid was constituted in July 1974. Its purpose was to give its members—retired party chiefs—a chance to advise the younger leaders and to serve as the moral conscience of the party. The majority of members, holding conservative views, wanted to participate in discussions about the SPD programs; Brandt assured them that the executive would occasionally ask for their views and that unsolicited views would be welcomed. [24]

The senior council has had little influence on the party. Only before federal elections would leaders, nervous about the size of the SPD vote, show concern. Thus, in August 1980, Brandt urged the senior party members at a Mannheim meeting to participate in day-to-day politics and the election campaign and to share their experiences with younger members, who were more willing to listen to them and were more receptive about the old traditions than had been the case in the early 1970s. In 1980, SPD leader Elfriede Eilers was appointed head of a section in the executive to deal with the work of older members and to set up sections at lower levels. Whether this attempt at integration will be more successful than in the 1970s remains to be seen. One senior member, on a party-sponsored Rhine ship cruise, had his doubts: "No one is so easily forgotten as a former functionary or a politician without office and dignity." [25]

Trade Union Council

In 1968, party leaders formed a trade union council (Gewerkschaftsrat) to ensure better coordination with the German Trade Union Federation (Deutscher Gewerkschaftsbund, DGB), most of whose leaders and members were Social Democrats. Initially, Brandt chaired the council's meetings, but later Heinz Oskar Vetter, president of the federation, insisted that as a recognition of equality between the two organizations, he be made co-chairman. In the forty-eight-person council sit the seventeen presidents of the DGB constituent unions (in 1968, sixteen unions) and representatives of other union federation, union enterprises, and the consumers' cooperative movement, as well as SPD presidium and executive members. [26]

The council's primary task is to facilitate an exchange of views among the members on union questions. Among these have been the extension of codetermination, workers' capital accumulation, vocational training, and social security reforms. But they also have included less direct issues, such as political extremism in the Federal Republic, peace initiatives, and contacts with the East. SPD cabinet ministers, especially labor, have reported to council members on government legislative plans.

The council serves as only one means of contact between the two movements. As will be noted later, the SPD has also established an association for workers within the party and shop groups in factories and has maintained informal contacts with labor leaders. Conversely, labor is well represented in the Bundestag Fraktion and provides membership and other support to the SPD.

Other Groups

To provide policy advice to its organs, the SPD has created a number of commissions, committees, councils, and ad-hoc working groups. To emphasize their importance but also to ensure that their advice will not stray too far from party principles, most groups are chaired by presidium or executive members. The groups' membership, chosen by the executive, consists of functionaries, specialists, and Bundestag deputies who share an interest in a specific field and who can help to coordinate party and Fraktion actions. The group specialists do extensive research on a topic, consult outside specialists, receive advice from other organs (especially at the local level), and then prepare a position paper to be submitted to the presidium or the executive. Many groups have subgroups that specialize in a more narrow aspect of the topic, such as the commission on media with its subcommissions on radio and television, press, and film.

The range of topics is wide; new commissions or groups are formed when necessary. In the late 1970s, they included international relations, Third World development, Europe, national security, economics and finance, self-employment policy, food and agriculture, social policy, energy, media, political education, party organization, party finance, legal affairs, domestic affairs, sports, expellees, and youth unemployment. [27]

Party Associations

The SPD has attempted to gain maximum support from important but disparate social groups within the party and the general population. It has created associations (Arbeitsgemeinschaften) for workers, women, youth, the self-employed, health workers, teachers, municipal politicians, and lawyers. [28] These associations are not party organs entitled to collect dues or send delegates to the SPD conventions; rather, their membership is in many instances open to anyone sympathetic to their goals, although in practice most association members are also party members. The total membership of the associations consists of only one in five party members, of whom few are active participants, and then primarily in the three largest associations—youth, women, and workers. [29] The associations have been unable so far to convert passive members into active participants.

Most of the associations have a hierarchical structure of organs at the national, regional, and local levels, corresponding somewhat to the party structure. Ever since the Young Socialists (Jusos) became a politically dissident intraparty force in the late 1960s, the question of how much autonomy to grant the associations has arisen. At the 1971 SPD convention, Juso leaders sought to gain more powers for the associations, such as the right to draft their own statutes and to introduce motions at party conventions. Their efforts did not succeed. Rather, the executive received the power to form and dissolve associations and to control their financial accounts. It did not want the associations to form "parties with the party" for fear of weakening the local SPD branches.

In 1973, to preclude a proliferation of new associations and a bigger bureaucracy, a reform commission under Wehner's leadership recommended to the executive that the number of associations be limited to the Big Four—Jusos, women, workers, and self-employed—and that the status of the others, primarily professional groups, be reduced to specialist circles (Fachkreise), without the laboriously created hierarchical organizational structure. When the professional associations protested this potential loss of status the reform commission withdrew its proposal. [30]

In 1974, another conflict between party and association leaders broke out. Party officials in Franconia denounced Juso attempts to establish contacts with Italian and French Communist parties and charged the Jusos with a breach of the party statute. The arbitration commission ruled that association officials had to clear their political declarations and other public statements with the party executive at the appropriate local, regional, or national level. If they failed to do so, the executive could forbid such declarations or remove them from office. Resolutions considered damaging to party unity also could be declared void. [31)

Left-wing party leaders and association officers protested the ruling. They argued that it violated a decision of the 1971 convention denying the executives the right to confirm the election of association officials; that it did not correspond with the principle of the West German party statute requiring all parties to have democratic guidelines; and that it violated the spirit of a 1972 executive decision granting relative autonomy to the associations. [32]

On February 1, 1975, the executive, by a narrow majority, issued new guidelines, which stipulated that executives must explicitly approve any association publications but no longer mentioned the loss of office for a functionary who had not cleared public declarations with them. The Jusos remained bitterly opposed to what they labeled a "muzzle decree" (Maulkorberlass). At their 1975 congress, they passed a resolution declaring that they would not accept any restrictions on their publicity work by the "mills of a party bureaucracy" which would force associations to become "recipients of orders."[33]

After four years of an uneasy truce, the executive in May 1979 liberalized its rigid stance. It decided that in the future it would be up to the secretaries at all party levels whether or not to apply the decree. Party secretary Bahr declared that he did not intend to apply it at the national level unless the associations committed a breach of confidence. The more liberal districts announced that associations would need merely to inform the executives about the content of publications or statements without having to worry about a veto. The Jusos would have preferred a scrapping of the decree but had no choice in the matter. [34]

These constitutional battles between the semiautonomous associations, especially the Jusos, and the party establishment had become inevitable. They were caused by the need of associations to assert themselves and to justify their continued existence and by the party's ideological debates in the late 1960s and early 1970s. Such battles could be construed as a sign of a democratic spirit or of the weakening of party unity and strength. In either case, the party elite realized the need for associations (and other groups) to remain in existence as a means of attracting new members into the SPD or "energizing" present ones.

The Secretariat

Symbolic of the party's climb to power in the Federal Republic was its move in 1975 from a run-down temporary "barracks" in Bonn, in which it had been housed for nearly twenty-five years, to a modern and costly edifice of steel, concrete, and glass that had finally enough space for the 240 professional and nonprofessional staff members working there. Heading the staff is the party secretary (Bundesgeschäftsführer), who provides support for the party chairman and is in charge of operational activities.

The importance of the post sometimes produces a struggle between various wings or leaders over who should fill it when a vacancy occurs. In 1968, the executive chose Hans-Jürgen Wischnewski, former minister for economic cooperation, to be the new secretary. He, and Brandt, viewed the post as political and administrative, in which the secretary would not only supervise publicity, prepare for the coming election, and maintain contact with the Land and regional party organs and various social groups but also take part in long-range political planning. By 1971, Wischnewski, seeking to further raise the status of the post, urged the party convention to change the rules: henceforth the convention, rather than the executive, should choose the secretary, who ought to be on a par with the treasurer, rather than, as had been the practice, having to take orders from the treasurer. Wischnewski resigned when he could not obtain the necessary two-thirds support from convention delegates; many right-wing delegates, miffed that he had not supported them on all occasions, had voted against him. [35]

The search for a successor who could work with all factions, the presidium, and the executive was difficult. In January 1972, party leaders chose Holger Börner, then parliamentary state secretary in the Ministry of Transportation and a former chairman of the once less radical Young Socialists. The politically conservative secretary did a competent job as head of organization but lacked new ideas. In 1976, he took over the suddenly vacated post of minister-president in Hesse, and once again a replacement had to be found.

On occasion, politics and personalities influence the selection. This time, Brandt favored Horst Ehmke, the former Chancellery head, but Chancellor Schmidt and Wehner opposed him for personal reasons and because as a left-center leader he had occasionally allied himself with the left wing. When Schmidt suggested Egon Bahr, the foreign policy advisor to Brandt, former Chancellery head, and minister for economic cooperation, Brandt easily concurred. But Bahr's lack of experience in domestic and party affairs was a liability. He had joined the SPD only in 1956 and thus did not have the experience of the party veterans in the districts, who looked at the appointment with misgivings or skepticism, especially because organizational weaknesses had nearly cost the party the election. [36] Although many viewed him as the wrong man in the wrong place, he had the capacity to adapt quickly to his job. He appealed for solidarity, made a tour of the hinterlands, sought to strengthen the political middle, and instituted limited party reforms. A man of ideas—a rare talent—he also became a crisis manager.

After four years in office, Bahr announced his resignation in late 1980, partly because he was sensitive to criticisms that he remained more interested in foreign than in party affairs but partly because he wanted a change in position. Even though Schmidt would have preferred a Bonn official as successor, Brandt pushed hard for Peter Glotz, a former Bavarian leader and then Berlin Senator for Science and Research, who, as a skilful mediator, had kept the lines open in Berlin to disaffected youth. Schmidt, whom Glotz once reproved for his "rudimentary concept of politics," relented. Glotz, ideologically in the party center, called on the party to integrate factions, to accentuate local activities and to have a broad political spectrum. He viewed his new post as that of a bridge builder between the executive, the Fraktion, and the government. [37]

In 1980, national headquarters had between 80 and 100 professional staff members, with an additional 150 working in the Länder and district headquarters and about 600 in the subdistricts, for a total of about 830 to 850. This total is more than double the estimated staff of 405 in 1969; yet both figures belie the charge that the SPD is a vast bureaucracy. [38] Of course, much of the work is also done by nonprofessionals or by unpaid staff, especially at the local level, where no paid professionals are hired.

The staff at Bonn headquarters is apportioned to the six

divisions—organization, associations, media and publicity, elections, international, and finance and administration; members work closely with the executive and subunits to coordinate organizational and political questions.

Länder Associations

The federal character of the West German state makes it imperative for political parties to avoid centralization in their organization in order to give them more flexibility in the Länder. On the other hand, the SPD has been traditionally averse to excessive decentralization for fear that its political cohesion and the power of its national leaders would be impaired.

The SPD statute calls for the creation of Land associations if all district associations within a Land give their consent. Should a Land association be established, the district associations, considered the key party units, must be able to retain their own power and be in a position to provide it with the necessary financial, and personnel support. [39] Only some of the ten federal states have corresponding SPD Länder associations, while others call themselves Land organizations or associations but perform district functions and are counted as districts. [40]

In 1977, party officials shifted power away from the districts to the Länder associations in order to reduce the status of the district barons. Until then, the Länder associations had little political power and only a small apparatus. Soon they made plans to strengthen their organization, set up conferences, and open new headquarters in areas with weak SPD support. Baden-Wuerttemberg, Bavaria, and Lower Saxony, with relatively few SPD members compared with the total population, requested the Bonn executive to shift some funds from Länder with high membership to them. The executive agreed in principle to such a scheme of greater revenue equalization. [41]

The Länder association structure resembles that of its national counterpart, with individual variations. In North Rhine-Westphalia, for example, the Land convention elects a Land executive (Landesvorstand) of fifteen members. The chief policymakers in the executive are the chairman, two deputy chairmen, and district executive members (all unpaid), as well as Bundestag deputies and mayors. Normally meeting once a month, the executive members discuss Land politics, including any pending election. A Land committee (Landesausschuss), whose thirty members are elected by the district conventions, protects the interests of the districts.

The Land convention, meeting biennially, deals with broad policy matters, including resolutions submitted to it by lower-level units. In election years the Land convention must approve the slate of SPD candidates for the Land lists and a program submitted to it by the Land executive. The Land bureau is headed by three secretaries responsible for day-to-day policies. [42]

District and Subdistrict Organizations

The twenty-two districts (Bezirke) have traditionally held significant power within the party. [43] Policy is made by an executive, headed by a normally strong chairman, often labeled as a boss (Bonze) by journalists and critics. Executive members, aided by district secretaries, must in the course of a year deal with the reports of a host of commissions and groups studying local, regional, and national problems; organize meetings and conventions; advise the Landtag Fraktion on pending legislation; and prepare for elections at all levels. The chairman must frequently go to Bonn to attend party council meetings and to coordinate activities with national headquarters.

There are other organs at the district level: the convention, whose delegates are elected by the subdistricts and which has the power to choose candidates for parliament and delegates to the national convention; an advisory council with limited powers; and an arbitration commission.[44]

Each district is divided into subdistricts (Unterbezirke) or county associations (Kreisverbände), which in turn are divided into local branches. The 250 subdistricts represent another geographic and administrative layer between the base and the top party organs. Normally, the subdistrict encompasses a city or county and corresponds in structure to the districts. It is responsible for local election campaigns and works closely with the local branches. [45]

Local Branches

At the base of the SPD are the more than 10,000 local branches (Ortsvereine) situated in city districts or small communities (Gemeinden). Membership may be as low as 15 or 20 and as high as 200 to over 400. Each branch is headed by a nonpaid executive that must consist, according to federal law, of at least three members. The SPD national headquarters recommends more: a chairman, one or two deputy chairmen, a treasurer and a secretary, and possibly officials in charge of education and publicity.

Meeting at least once a month, the executive decides on the admission of new members, prepares the yearly membership assemblies and carries out its decisions, assists in election campaigns, maintains links with the subdistrict and district, helps the constituent associations and working groups, and discusses local politics. In addition, it must inform members about party activities, recruit new members, prepare meetings and social gatherings, publicize educational activities and seminars organized at the subdistrict and district levels, and contact the media about party activities.

In theory, the membership assembly is the highest organ at the local level. It is empowered to vote on resolutions (although those directed to the national convention would normally need the support of subdistrict or district conventions), vote for the executive and delegates to the subdistrict convention, and help select candidates for town councils (Gemeinderäte).

According to a 1977 survey commissioned by the SPD, while attendance at the yearly assemblies, open to any member, averaged 40 percent of the membership of the local branch, regular attendance at monthly or other scheduled meetings averaged less than one-third of the members, with close to one-third hardly ever attending. [46] For years the party, priding itself as the model of organization, has been concerned about the apathy of many members, the lack of participation in its activities, and the retreat into the private world of the home, the television set, and the automobile. As will be noted in chapter 3, it is trying in various ways to counteract this tendency—one that is not restricted to the Federal

Republic.

PARTY FINANCES

To any political party the state of its finances is crucial to its strength in the nation. Unlike the CDU/CSU, which receives considerable support from the business community, the SPD traditionally has been more dependent on membership dues. When expenditures climbed for all parties, they voted themselves yearly additional revenues from the public treasury; the Constitutional Court ruled, however, that such funds could only be disbursed for campaign expenditures. These generous sums, calculated on the basis of the number of registered voters and distributed on the basis of the number of votes received by each party, amounted in the 1969-1972 period to 100 million DM and in the 1972-1976 period to about 145 million DM. [47]

As table 1 indicates, in 1969 membership dues and public subsidies amounted to about one-third each of the total income of 65 million DM, while more modest amounts came from donations; contributions from SPD deputies, who customarily have been requested to give 20 percent of their salaries to the party; income from SPD properties (such as printing houses and journals) and income from meetings and other miscellaneous sources.

TABLE 1
PARTY INCOME BY CATEGORIES, 1969 AND 1977

Categories	1969[a] (DM)	1977[a] (DM)
Membership dues	20,620,010	56,391,964
Contributions from Fraktion members	5,501,367	11,796,841
Income from SPD properties	2,436,675	1,167,797
Income from meetings sale of pamphlets, etc.	806,053	299,647
Donations	11,675,460	6,167,057
Bank loans	137,805	13,103,572
Public subsidies	22,315,581	14,136,455
Other income	1,624,817	3,167,313
Total	65,117,768	106,230,645

Source: SPD, Jahrbuch 1970-1972, pp. 344-345; SPD, Jahrbuch 1977-1979, pp. 316-317.

[a]All figures have been rounded off to the nearest DM; hence the 1977 total does not correspond to the sum of the subentries.

By 1977, the party's income had risen to over 106 million DM, with a sharp boost in income from membership dues but a drop in donations. Not included in these totals are donations to individual candidates running for office and to closely affiliated but officially autonomous party associations, income from advertisements placed by local publicly owned firms, official funds provided the parliamentary groups at all levels, and indirect electoral assistance by the Press and Information Office and other ministries (restricted by a court ruling in the wake of the 1976 election) as well as by individuals donating their services. [48]

The party has faced increasing difficulties matching income with expenditures. In 1977, for instance, the income of the party's national executive which receives a yearly fixed 15 percent of membership dues (the rest flowing into district and local coffers), amounted to over 20 million DM but expenditures ran over 35 million DM, for a deficit of close to 15 million DM that had to be met through costly bank loans (see table 2). The high personnel and administrative costs erased nearly all of the income; but much more was needed for publicity and for aid to state electoral campaigns, party associations, and working groups as well as unspecified subsidies, the costs of conferences, and debt service. With spiraling costs, stagnating income, and declining donations, the debts piled up each year; by 1980 they totaled 55 million DM. [49]

To cut costs or increase revenues in order to produce a balanced budget was not easy. Party treasurer Friedrich Halstenberg (who had been preceded in that post in the 1970s by Alfred Nau and Wilhelm Dröscher) warned the party not to overextend itself, especially in election campaign and operating expenditures. However, the SPD had little incentive to cut back election outlays below the maximum agreed on in recent campaigns by the treasurers of all major parties, especially because federal subsidies cover most of the campaign costs. None of the parties have been very budget conscious, as any observer of campaigns can testify. For instance, in 1980 the treasurers agreed that the SPD was allowed to spend up to 40 million DM, the FDP 8 million DM, the CDU 36 million DM, and CSU 9 million DM. The parties had no difficulty spending that amount or even exceeding it. [50]

Hence the SPD could eliminate its debts only by either cutting back on operating expenses or increasing its income. It has usually chosen the latter, because it claims that few cuts can be made in operating expenses, such as in the number of staff (where its low ratio of one staff per 1,000 members would be hard to reduce), in the number of conferences, and in outlays for publicity. [51] To increase its income, the party has pleaded for more honesty in paying full dues, whose level is based on the income of the member. But in 1978, nearly 10 percent had not paid any dues and the others had paid, on the average, yearly dues for 10.9 rather than 12 months. [52] According to the already cited 1977 party survey, the net income of members averaged 1,500 DM a month; the dues should, then, have amounted to 15 DM a month, but they only reached 6 DM, proportionately a much lower figure than the 1978 estimate. [53] According to one informant, a number of wealthier members did not pay their full share because, as newcomers to the party, they lacked the commitment of party veterans or because they joined the party as a vehicle for a political career. [54] To gain more commitment from members, the party emphasized that 85 percent of dues remained at the district and local levels, with the district deciding how much would go to the local branches (normally 20 percent), the subdistricts, and itself. [55]

A plea for more honesty was coupled with a decision to raise dues in the hope of increasing income by another 8 million DM per year. At the December 1978 special party convention, dues were increased by 1 DM to 5 DM a month for those with a monthly income of 600 DM to 1,200 DM, and substantially more for those earning above 7,000 DM. In the more typical income group of 2,000 DM to 3,000 DM, members can themselves choose to pay any one of seven levels of dues ranging from 12 DM to 45 DM a month. In addition, members on supervisory boards of private firms or on administrative councils were requested to pay the party 30 percent of their income from these additional lucrative sources. [56]

Although the party has been forced to borrow money to meet its expenses, the total level of income has risen over the decade, permitting it to improve its organization, hire better-qualified staff, and strengthen its educational and research work. It has close links to the Friedrich-Ebert Foundation, which receives public financing as well as private and trade

TABLE 2
PARTY EXECUTIVE BALANCE SHEET, 1977

Income	DM[a]
Membership dues	8,876,429
Donations	1,560,557
Public subsidies	6,321,403
Other income	3,979,433
Total	20,737,821
Expenditures	
Publicity, election campaigns	5,045,875
Meetings, conferences	2,994,738
Subsidies	4,728,040
Associations, working groups	2,012,720
Personnel	11,444,409
Administration	6,720,271
Debt service	2,551,427
Total	35,497,479
Deficit (covered by loans)	14,759,658

Source: SPD, *Jahrbuch 1977-1979*, p. 318.

[a]Rounded off.

union donations. The Foundation engages in research projects on the party as well as on such topics as the Third World. It maintains a number of residential centers where courses on the history and theory of the labor movement, among others, are often scheduled.

To sum up: the positive aspects of the additional state revenue given to the parties and the foundations are partly offset by the negative effects on parties. State revenue strengthens the parties' bureaucracy, especially in the conduct of election campaigns at the expense of the volunteer workers. This development reflects new political, social, and cultural norms that until recently emphasized the role of the state at the expense of citizen participation in public affairs. Only gradually is a balance being restored, but the parties—if they are going to thrive and not wither—will have to come up with creative and imaginative plans to engage their members more fully in political matters.

CONCLUSION

This survey of the party's structure and finances has only partly confirmed the hypothesis that the moderate and conservative elite can manipulate power and minimize challenges to its rule. On a number of occasions, though an articulate and well-organized left bloc was able to wring concessions from the elite, the concessions did not fundamentally change the ability of the latter to perpetuate itself in power. The survey has confirmed the second hypothesis—that an elite controlling a bureaucratic organization is reluctant to meet new members' demands for changes. Any changes made by the elite, such as enlarging the executive, were done at a glacial pace and with fears of the consequences. The survey has confirmed the third hypothesis—that the party elite above all seeks to control the subunits of an organization having actual powers, even when such subunits are not given equivalent statutory powers. For example, the convention, symbolically the highest party organ, has less actual power than the presidium, hardly mentioned in the SPD statute. The SPD, of course, is not the only party that has to grapple with such internal problems, but because it has served for so long as a model for other socialist parties, the way it solves its problems may influence other organizations.

NOTES

1. The statute, *Organisationsstatut, Wahlordnung, Schiedsordnung der SPD*, issued by the executive, was agreed to on December 18, 1971, and revised on April 12, 1973; November 15, 1975; December 10, 1978; and December 7, 1979 (hereafter referred to as SPD, *Organisationsstatut*).

2. Revisionists pushed for the creation of the presidium in order to curb the power of the paid functionaries in the executive.

3. In 1980, for instance, Brandt was chairman; Schmidt and Hans-Jürgen Wischnewski were deputy chairmen; Wehner was Fraktion chairman; Bahr was secretary; and Friedrich Halstenberg, former finance minister of North Rhine-Westphalia, was treasurer. The five members-at-large were Hans Koschnick, Mayor of Bremen; Holger Börner, Minister-President of Hesse; Erhard Eppler, Land chairman of Baden-Wuerttemberg; Antje Huber,

Minister of Youth, Family, and Health; Johannes Rau, Minister-President of North Rhine-Westphalia; and Hans-Jochen Vogel, Minister of Justice. For a list of presidium members see SPD, Jahrbuch, various dates.

4. SPD, Protokoll der Verhandlungen, Ausserordentlicher Parteitag, December 1971, pp. 186-199 (hereafter referred to as SPD, Parteitag, year).

5. Personal interviews with Brandt and Wehner, Bonn, Jan. 19, 1975.

6. Nina Grunenberg, Vier Tage mit dem Bundeskanzler (Hamburg: Hoffman und Campe, 1976), p. 13.

7. For a list of decisions, see SPD, Jahrbuch, various dates. Protocols of presidium (and executive) sessions are kept secret.

8. The vote for the other deputy chairman, Heinz Kühn, then minister-president of North Rhine-Westphalia, was 280 affirmative, 127 negative, and 19 abstentions. Wehner, as Fraktion chairman and, until then, SPD deputy chairman, gained 419 votes, more than any other candidate (SPD, Auslandsbrief, May 17, 1973).

9. Frankfurter Allgemeine Zeitung, Nov. 15, 1975.

10. SPD, Parteitag 1975, p. 789.

11. The ASF at first had demanded ten seats (Sozialdemokratischer Informationsdienst, Frau und Gesellschaft, No. 9, Nov. 1979).

12. Organisationsstatut, Paragraph 24, p. 20.

13. Der Spiegel, July 2, 1973, pp. 25-26: SPD, Parteitag 1973, I, 119. In the typical election year of 1976, the executive discussed such questions as the political crisis in Lower Saxony, the leadership problem of the Young Socialists, the pending campaign, and the results of a United Nations conference on trade and development (SPD, Jahrbuch 1975-1977, pp. 275-281).

14. Frank Grube, Gerhard Richter, Uwe Thaysen, Politische Planung in Parteien und Parlamentsfraktionen (Göttingen: Otto Schwartz, 1976), pp. 177, 178.

15. Robert Michels, Political Parties; Jürgen Dittberner, "Die Bundesparteitage der Christlich Demokratischen Union und der Sozialdemokratischen Partei Deutschlands von 1946 bis 1968: Eine Untersuchung der Funktionen von Parteitagen" (unpublished Ph.D. dissertation, Free University, Berlin, 1969), pp. 144-151; Dittberner, "The Role of the Party Congress in the Inner Party Process of Policy Making," German Political Studies, Vol. I, 1974, ed. Klaus von Beyme (London: Sage Publications, 1974), pp. 187-188.

16. Ulrich Lohmar, Innerparteiliche Demokratie (Stuttgart: Ferdinand Enke, 1963), p. 84.

17. A tally of the fate of resolutions at SPD conventions from 1946 to 1968 shows that 20 percent were accepted, 8 percent rejected, 40 percent incorporated into the accepted resolutions or tabled; 14 percent were assigned to the executive, 11 percent to the Fraktion, 5 percent to other bodies, and 1 percent withdrawn (Dittberner, "The Role of the Party Congress," p. 209). The resolutions handled by the 1977 convention were typical of the wide range of subject matter: about 200 dealt with economic and financial issues, 150 with energy, 100 with party reorganization, 50 with health policy, and 37 with foreign and security issues. Hundreds of resolutions dealt with other issues (SPD, Parteitag 1977, pp. 713-985).

18. The conventions have become mammoth affairs. The 1977 convention, for instance, cost about 1.5 million DM, consumed 1,750,000 sheets of paper; and attracted more than 1,000 correspondents (Nordwest Zeitung, Nov. 14, 1977).

19. For a list of members, see SPD, Jahrbuch, various dates.
20. SPD, Organisationsstatut, Paragraph 30, p. 22.
21. SPD, Organisationsstatut, pp. 24-26.
22. SPD, Jahrbuch 1977-1979, pp. 302-303.
23. Die Welt, Nov. 23, 1977.
24. Süddeutsche Zeitung, July 30, 1974; Der Spiegel, Aug. 5, 1974.
25. Vorwärts, Sept. 25, 1980; see also Aug. 28, 1980.
26. Wehner urged the council's formation as early as 1966 (SPD, presemitteilungen und informationen, No. 193/68, April 23, 1968; No. 419/68, Sept. 15, 1968; No. 211/71, May 17, 1971). For latest list of members, see SPD, Jahrbuch 1977-1979, p. 338.
27. For lists of groups and membership, see SPD, Jahrbuch, various dates.
28. The literal translation of Arbeitsgemeinschaften is "working communities," not an apt term in English for their structure. For a description of the important association, see chs. 5, 6, 7.
29. According to a 1977 SPD-commissioned sample survey of party members and functionaries (Infratest Sozialforschung, Kommunikationsstudie zur SPD-Organisation, Zusammenfassung [hectographed, 1978], p. 17) (hereafter referred to as Infratest survey, 1977).
30. Vorwärts, Dec. 27, 1973. In 1977, the executive advanced a similar plan, but had no success either.
31. For text of ruling, see SPD, intern-dokumente, No. 10, n.d.
32. Among the critics were Peter von Oertzen, Land chairman of Lower Saxony, and Mayor Rudi Arndt of Frankfurt (Vorwärts, Nov. 28, 1974; Dec. 26, 1974; Kölner Stadt-Anzeiger, Dec. 11, 1974).
33. See SPD executive pamphlet, Grundsätze für die Tätigkeit der Arbeitsgemeinschaften in der SPD (Bonn, n.d.); Klaus Heimann, Hans-Peter Altrogge, Jochen Stemplewski, "Arbeitsgemeinschaften benötigen politischen Spielraum," Neue Gesellschaft, XXII, No. 9 (1975), 719-720.
34. Vorwärts, May 17, 1979.
35. Der Spiegel, Dec. 27, 1971.
36. Frankfurter Rundschau, Oct. 25, 1976; Der Spiegel, Nov. 22, 1976; Die Zeit, Nov. 26, 1976.
37. Vorwärts, Dec. 18, 1980.
38. Personal interview with Peter Winkelmann, SPD staff, Bonn, March 21, 1980; Bodo Zeuner, Innerparteiliche Demokratie (Berlin: Colloquium, 1969), p. 86.
39. SPD, Organisationsstatut, p. 10.
40. In the first category are Lower Saxony, North Rhine—Westphalia, Hesse, Bavaria, and Rhineland Palatinate. See SPD, Jahrbuch 1975-1977, pp. 410-412; Jahrbuch 1977-1979, pp. 353-355.
41. Vorwärts, Nov. 17, 1977.
42. Personal interview with Ernst Knäpper, secretary, Dortmund-West district, Jan. 21, 1975.
43. For a listing of the districts, see table 6. Brief district reports appear in SPD, Jahrbuch, various dates.
44. For a typical report, see SPD-Bezirk Hessen-Süd, Berichte, Jahresberichte 1976 der Abteilungen, Ausschüsse und Arbeitsgemeinschaften.
45. See, for instance Unterbezirk Dortmund, Bericht zum Unterbezirksparteitag, various years.
46. At the yearly assemblies, 81 percent of the active and 19 percent of the passive members took part (Infratest survey, 1977, pp. 26-28). See

also Herbert Wehner, Bruno Friedrich, Alfred Nau, Parteiorganisation (Bonn: Neue Gesellschaft, 1969); Heino Kaack, "Die Basis der Parteien: Struktur und Funktion der Ortsvereine," Zeitschrift für Parlamentsfragen, II, No. 1 (1971), 23-38.

47. For the national campaigns, a sum based on 3.50 DM for each registered voter is put aside in the budget. From this sum, the parties that have won at least 0.5 percent of the total popular vote are permitted to draw funds in proportion to their share of Land list votes at the previous election. Advance payments may be made up to 60 percent in the three-year period before the next election (David P. Conradt, The German Polity [New York: Longman, 1978], p. 111).

48. Uwe Schleth, Parteifinanzen (Meisenheim am Glan: Anton Hain, 1973), pp. 109-110, 168-170.

49. Vorwärts, Dec. 18, 1980.

50. FRG, Inter Nationes, "The Election Campaign Agreement of 19 March 1980 between CDU, CSU, FDP and SPD." For actual 1980 outlays and income, see Frankfurter Allgemeine Zeitung, Dec. 5, 1981.

51. SPD Service, Presse, Funk, TV, No. 201/79, May 9, 1979.

52. SPD, Jahrbuch 1977-1979, p. 313. See also SPD, intern-dokumente, No. 1/76 (Feb. 1976); SPD executive, Parteiarbeit, Handbuch für die Arbeit in sozialdemokratischen Ortsvereinen, Finanzen (hereafter referred to as Parteiarbeit, topic).

53. Infratest survey, 1977, p. 5.

54. Personal interview with SPD staff member, Bonn, March 27, 1980.

55. Sozialdemokrat Magazin, Feb. 1979.

56. Ibid., Jan. 1979.

3
Membership: A Social Shift at the Base

Maurice Duverger, in classifying parties by membership, noted three types: the decentralized caucus party, with few members; the party based on cells and militias, with a fanatical mass membership; and the party based on branches, with many members, representing a middle ground in party solidarity between the first two types. The SPD, ever since its inception, has fallen into the third category. Duverger, not content with one typology, also offers another tripartite party classification based on the theme of social groups as posited by Ferdinand Tönnies and Herman Schmalenbach: the community (Gemeinschaft), with close, spiritual bonds and class solidarity; the association (Gesellschaft), with a loose common interest among its adherents; and the order (Bund), with fanaticism among its members, who belong primarily to totalitarian parties. [1] The SPD has gradually moved from the Gemeinschaft model (Empire and Weimar eras) to the Gesellschaft model (Federal Republic), although among its older members the spiritual bond to the party remains.

The evolution toward Gesellschaft occurred primarily because the party was exposed to external, societal changes that affected the composition of its membership. When its core group—the manual workers—began to decline gradually in percentage of the total labor force in the post-1949 era, the party tried to broaden its membership base among other social groups whose commitment to it was less intense and not tradition-bound. Among these groups, students, salaried employees, and civil servants were the most responsive to recruitment. These groups form part of the "new middle class" that has assumed a more important role in the advanced industrial states. As affluence, social mobility, and modernization reduced class conflict in West Germany, the new middle class became more liberal politically and supported the SPD domestic reform policies. When many of its members joined the SPD, the social base of the party changed significantly. The emergent middle-class character, or "embourgeoisement," of the party will now be explored. The resultant effect on party cleavages, ideology, program, and appeals to the electorate will be discussed in later chapters.

In its recruitment strategy, the party appealed to the political instincts of new members by telling them that they could help to shape the destiny of the party and, by implication, the country. According to the SPD statute, each member "has the right and the obligation within the framework of the statutes to participate in the formation of political policy [Willensbildung], elections and votes, and to support the goals of the party." [2] The SPD has also repeatedly emphasized that members can participate in the selection of candidates for public office.

The statute notes that membership is open to any person over sixteen who acknowledges the basic principles of the party. An applicant seeks membership through the local branch, which makes the decision to grant it or not. If admission is denied, an applicant can appeal to two higher organs, but the decision of the district executive is final. Membership ends through death, resignation, or expulsion. A ground for expulsion, which needs an arbitration commission approval, is simultaneous membership in another political party or in an organization that the party's executive and council have deemed incompatible with SPD goals.

MEMBERSHIP PROFILE

Membership in the party has fluctuated considerably over the decades. During the Empire era it reached 1,086,000 in 1914, and in the Weimar era it ranged from a high of 1,261,000 in 1923 to a low of 806,000 in 1926. From 1946 to 1948, when social democracy seemed a possibility on the political horizon, membership rose sharply but thinned precipitously in the 1950s and early 1960s when the party could not break out of its opposition role and when many older members died. When it came into power as the senior coalition party in 1969, new members flooded in. A crest occurred in 1972 when more than 150,000 applied for membership; with more than 40,000 deaths and resignations the same year, total membership rose by nearly 110,000. A peak of over 1 million was reached in 1976 and 1977, but membership has gradually receded since then, because youth, especially, is growing disillusioned with the SPD and because of continuing mortality among older members (see table 3 and figure 2).

Most significant about the membership pattern is that in 1977, according to an SPD-sponsored survey, more than half the members—mostly new middle class—had joined the party during the previous decade (22 percent from 1967 to 1971 and 30 percent from 1972 to 1977)—the period in which the SPD shared in governing the nation. As a result, veteran members who had joined the party before 1949 constituted only 14 percent of the total membership; those between 1950 and 1959, just 10 percent; and those in the shorter time span between 1960 and 1966, a more impressive 15 percent. [3]

Motivations for joining the SPD

What brings new members into the party? In the 1977 infas and Infratest sample of 5,000 members and 450 functionaries, the activist members stated that they wanted to be represented politically by the party most closely attuned to their views (72 percent), to participate in the selection of candidates and in the formulation of policy (61 percent), and to ensure that the SPD gained its political goals (60 percent) and that the CDU/CSU did not attain power again (54 percent). Less often mentioned were interest in running for office (9 percent), in seeking a job through the party (8 percent), and personal reasons (6 percent). [4] The passive members joined because the SPD was most closely attuned to their views (67 percent), they were on good terms with a member who had joined earlier (48 percent), or politics was a part of their life (43 percent). [5]

TABLE 3
SPD MEMBERSHIP, 1946-1981

Year	Membership
1946	701,448
1950	683,896
1955	589,051
1960	649,578
1965	710,448
1966	727,890
1967	733,004
1968	732,446
1969	778,945
1970	820,202
1971	847,456
1972	954,394
1973	973,601
1974	957,253
1975	998,471
1976	1,022,191
1977	1,006,316
1978	997,444
1979	981,805
1980	986,337
1981	954,119

Source: SPD, Jahrbuch, various years, except for 1981, in Frankfurter Allgemeine Zeitung, April 22, 1982. All figures are for December 31.

The political socialization process provides clues to how interest in politics can be aroused among potential SPD members. To one question (in the 1968 infas survey of SPD members) about the beginning of their interest in politics, 31 percent replied that it occurred while they were living at home; 8 percent, after joining a youth group; 18 percent, during their school years away from home; 24 percent, after founding a family; and 18 percent, after securing a position. [6] Queried about the political interest of their parents, of whom 45 percent were SPD members, 35 percent recalled high interest; 30 percent, mild interest; and 27 percent, no interest. [7] Nearly one-third of the respondents also noted frequent discussion of politics at home, especially if the parents were members of a political party. Indeed, the more interested the parents were in politics, the earlier they awakened an interest in politics among the respondents.[8]

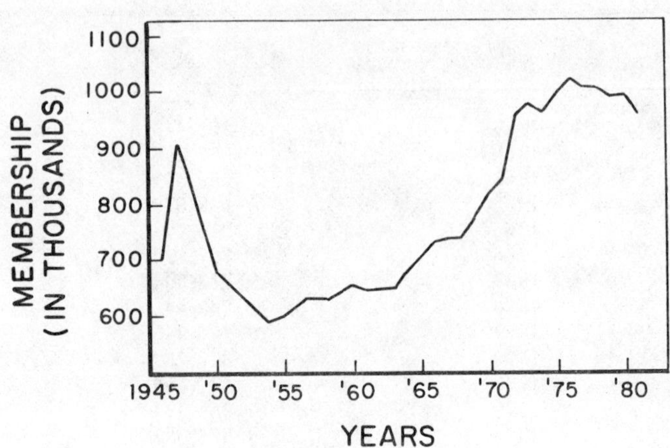

Source: See Table 3.

Sex, Age, and Religious Distribution

The male-female ratio among the party's more than 1 million members in 1976 did not correspond to the 48-52 percent ratio in the West German population. Rather, as in other parties, most SPD members were men. In 1976, there were about 807,000 male members (79 percent) and 215,000 female members (21 percent). [9] The Association of Social Democratic Women was partly successful in reducing this imbalance through strenuous recruiting efforts. In the mid-1960s, only 13 out of every 100 new members were women, mostly housewives; by the 1970s, the proportion had risen to 30 out of 100, primarily because of an influx of the new middle class: female professionals, white-collar employees, and civil servants. [10]

As to age distribution, the massive entry of young people into the party increased the proportion of new members under 35 from 49 percent in 1963 to 66 percent in 1971. In some city organizations, such as in Munich, close to 40 percent of the total membership was under 35, mostly students and teachers. [11] As table 4 indicates, in 1973 and 1976 about 30 percent of members throughout West Germany were under 35, but in 1980 there was a decline to 26.5 percent, primarily because of a strong drop in members under 30. Although there was a trend toward an increase in the young age cohorts, members over 50 still outnumbered those under 25—a distribution not markedly different in the Weimar period. The proportion of members over 60, however, dropped from 22 percent in 1973 to 17 percent in 1976 and rose to over 19 percent in 1980. (In 1930, for which comparable data is available, it was only 8.5 percent.) The largest age group was that from 41 to 60. This group's 36 percent of SPD membership in 1976 and nearly 42 percent in 1980 (46.9 percent in 1930) was higher than its percentage in the total population. [12]

Shifts in age distribution affect party cohesion and ideology. Members born before 1920 are a homogeneous group who shared experiences in the

TABLE 4
AGE DISTRIBUTION OF SPD MEMBERS, 1973, 1976, AND 1980

Age	1973		1976		1980	
	Number	Percent[a]	Number	Percent[a]	Number	Percent[a]
To 21	42,745	4.5	39,800	3.9	24,816	2.5
22-25	57,429	6.0	63,011	6.2	43,893	4.5
26-30	78,929	8.3	101,261	9.9	87,797	8.9
31-35	98,607	10.3	105,871	10.4	104,626	10.6
36-40	94,154	9.9	122,422	12.0	120,259	12.2
41-50	180,114	18.8	211,157	20.7	221,427	22.4
51-60	138,389	14.5	160,987	15.7	190,443	19.3
61-70	119,924	12.5	121,653	11.9	101,954	10.3
70 and over	91,830	9.6	53,149	5.2	89,423	9.1
No answer	53,626	5.6	42,880	4.2	2,234	0.2
Total	955,747	100.0	1,022,191	10.0	986,872	100.0

Source: Organization division, SPD headquarters, Bonn. For 1973 (June 15), Mitglieder-Statistik; for 1976 (Dec. 31), EDV-Mitgliederkartei; for 1980, Mitgliederstand per 31. Dezember 1980 (unpublished).

[a] All percentages have been rounded off; hence the total does not necessarily correspond to the subentry percentages.

Weimar SPD and who have difficulty adapting to its post-1959 pragmatism. Members born between 1920 and 1940 are a less homogeneous social grouping. They lost their collective identity during the Nazi period and were apolitical after the war. They are oriented toward pragmatism more than ideology and welcome the SPD's becoming a people's party. Many of them entered the party as a step toward getting a government position. Members born after 1940, not exposed to the SPD subculture of earlier decades, are less prone to accept decisions of the top party bosses. As Young Socialists, they have challenged the pragmatism of the older generation. [13]

SPD surveys indicated the religious affiliation of members in 1968 to be 68 percent Protestant, 18 percent Catholic, and 14 percent other denominations or unaffiliated. By 1977, 53 percent of members were Protestant, 28 percent Catholic, 17 percent unaffiliated, and 2 percent unknown. [14] The increase in the number of Catholics in the party, of whom 61 percent do not attend church regularly, and the decrease in the number of Protestants can be traced to secularization within the Federal Republic, especially marked among the Catholic population. (In contrast, the 1977 survey showed that among CDU/CSU members 68 percent were Catholic, 30 percent Protestant, 1 percent unaffiliated and 1 percent unknown.) [15]

Occupational Distribution

The high percentage of blue-collar workers within the SPD during the Empire and Weimar eras (in 1930, workers constituted close to 60 percent of members) greatly declined during the Federal Republic era. In 1952 workers were still 45 percent of members but by 1980 had declined to 28 percent (see table 5). Conversely, the number of salaried employees, who made up 10 percent of the SPD total in 1930, increased to 17 percent in 1952 and 25 percent in 1980. The percentage of civil servants climbed from 4 percent in 1930 to 10 percent in 1980. [16] This shift in the occupational composition of the party reflects a parallel shift in the German labor force, although in the SPD the percentage decline of workers since 1952 is higher than in the total population. [17] The membership is no longer primarily "proletarian," but its social background remains largely working class. For instance, in 1977 a majority of members (56 percent) came from working-class families. Of the others, 28 percent had fathers who were salaried employees and civil servants and 15 percent had fathers who were self-employed and professionals. [18]

A 1973 occupational survey of members showed that a high percentage of blue-collar workers was in skilled trades, such as metal, construction, carpentry, electrical, and mining. Among white-collar workers, office employees predominated, followed by salesclerks. Among the professionals, architects, engineers, technicians, and technical personnel made up the strongest component, followed by teachers and professors. Skilled workers and civil servants (primarily teachers) were overrepresented, while farmers, unskilled workers, housewives, and the self-employed were underrepresented in the SPD compared with their numbers in the total population. [19]

The 1973 survey also revealed that nearly 25 percent of the SPD members were simultaneously trade union members. Of this group, 89 percent were men and 11 percent, women. The latter percentage is only

TABLE 5
OCCUPATIONS OF SPD MEMBERS, 1973, 1976, AND 1980

Occupations	1973 Number	1973 Percent[a]	1976 Number	1976 Percent[a]	1980 Number	1980 Percent[a]	1980 Total Population Percent
Salaried employees[b]	209,639	21.9	244,447	23.9	245,657	24.9	15.3
Manual workers	252,639	26.4	284,174	27.8	277,113	28.1	17.2
Civil servants	85,603	9.0	97,564	9.5	99,630	10.1	3.7
Soldiers (professional)	7,291	0.8	5,510	0.5	5,895	0.6	-[c]
Housewives	94,823	9.9	104,961	10.3	113,728	11.5	15.2[d]
Farmers	3,305	0.4	2,377	0.2	2,150	0.2	1.0
Pensioners	127,639	13.4	106,343	10.4	86,587	8.8	19.0
Students	54,239	5.7	72,881	7.1	66,759	6.8	1.5
Professionals and self-employed	46,148	4.8	46,167	4.5	43,577	4.4	3.8
Apprentices	11,205	1.2	15,415	1.5	16,372	1.7	2.2
No answer	63,272	6.6	42,352	4.1	29,404	3.0	-
Total	955,747	100.0	1,022,191	100.0	86,872	100.0	-[e]

Source: See table 4. Last column based on microcensus, April 1980, Statistisches Bundesamt.
[a] All percentages have been rounded off; hence the total does not correspond to the subentry percentages.
[b] Includes government employees at all levels.
[c] Soldiers included in civil servants category.
[d] Based on category "married nonsalaried women," subsumed under category "nonsalaried women" totaling 35.8 percent.
[e] Total is less than 100 percent because the categories do not always correspond to SPD categories.

half the total number of women in the party; the low figure seems to indicate that most female members either are housewives or work in professions that are less prone to unionization. Nearly two-thirds of all union members were in the Public Service, Transport and Communications Workers Union (76,867 members) or the Metal Workers Union (72,531). [20]

Two surveys (CDU and infas) in 1977 showed a much higher percentage—from 50 to 58 percent—of SPD members who were concurrently union members. Regardless of the accuracy of the total when compared with the 25 percent in the 1973 survey, the SPD was stronger within the unions than was the CDU (19 percent in 1977), and its percentage of union members exceeded the unions' percentage of the total population (20 percent). [21] Its strength in the unions was important to the SPD but also of constant concern, because it needs the support of union members at election time and for its government policies (see chapter 6).

As party officials survey the relative strength of the members' occupations and union affiliation, they also keep close watch on the occupations of new members, to determine the SPD's standing among the socioeconomic groups in the Federal Republic. Until the mid-sixties, manual workers were about 50 percent of all new members admitted into the party, but by 1970 the percentage had dropped to 38.6 and by 1978, to 29.7. The proportion of salaried employees and civil servants remained at about 25 percent from the 1960s to the 1970s. But if the 9.9 percent of newly admitted students, most of whom will move into the white-collar ranks, are added to the 1978 total for salaried employees and civil servants, then the resulting 39.6 percent in the nonmanual category is relatively high. [22] In short, the SPD, once a workers' party, has become increasingly bourgeoisified.

Membership Distribution

The party constantly attempted to increase its membership. New members were sought as energetically in areas with above-average membership density, such as in Hesse, Saar, and Lower Saxony, as in small and medium-sized cities (from 20,000 to 500,000 population). Efforts in smaller communities were less successful, especially in the southern areas of Bavaria and Baden-Wuerttemberg, where the membership density was below the national average. [23]

Table 6 lists the 1977 membership totals for the various districts, including the distribution of male and female members. It indicates the continuing strength of the party in West Westphalia (more than 140,000 members) and Hesse-South (close to 100,000 members) and its weakness in the primarily rural districts of Rhine Hesse and North Lower Saxony (about 10,000 members each). It also indicates that the ratio of female to male members varies considerably from one district to another, with a relatively high proportion of women in the city-states of Berlin, Hamburg, and Bremen, and a low proportion in more sparsely settled districts.

The party, knowing that its members are much more aware politically than the electorate in general, attempts to tap this interest as a base for recruitment. [24] Members were urged, through their branches, to set up political booths at fairs and open neighborhood citizens' centers to provide information and handle complaints. The party also asked them to leaflet factories and to recruit new members at their workplaces, in local bars, or in nonpolitical organizations. One poll showed that in the latter the task might not be difficult, because 87 percent of SPD members belonged, on the average, to two organizations (58 percent were in trade unions, 33 percent in sports clubs, and 23 percent in workers' welfare, charity groups, cooperatives, and parent and other associations). With 20 percent of the SPD members also on the executive boards of these organizations, opportunities for proselytizing were further enhanced. [25]

Another poll showed a high potential for such attempts at conversion. In the nonparty associations, only 16 percent of members were sympathetic to the party's goals; the ratio was somewhat better, however, among colleagues at the workplace (27 percent), neighbors (30 percent), and

TABLE 6
SPD MEMBERSHIP BY DISTRICTS AND BY MALE/FEMALE TOTALS, 1977

Districts	Men	Women	Total
1. Schleswig-Holstein	29,452	10,211	39,663
2. Hamburg	22,499	9,810	32,309
3. Bremen	12,574	3,860	16,434
4. North Lower Saxony	8,034	1,909	9,943
5. Weser-Ems	21,305	4,717	26,022
6. Hannover	54,301	13,821	68,122
7. Braunschweig	16,601	4,065	20,666
8. East Westphalia-Lippe	23,646	5,396	29,042
9. West Westphalia	106,578	34,645	141,223
10. Lower Rhine	55,648	17,000	72,648
11. Middle Rhine	35,057	11,619	46,676
12. Hesse-North	37,573	6,767	44,340
13. Hesse-South	80,243	15,831	96,074
14. Baden-Wuerttemberg	56,883	13,924	70,807
15. Franconia	47,324	9,696	57,020
16. Lower Bavaria-Upper Palatinate	19,085	3,468	22,553
17. South Bavaria	34,626	10,554	45,180
18. Rhineland-Hesse-Nassau	25,535	5,029	30,564
19. Rhine Hesse	8,521	2,385	10,906
20. Palatinate	24,872	5,359	30,231
21. Saar	22,674	5,657	28,331
22. Berlin	27,070	11,210	38,280
Total	770,101	206,933	977,034
Percent	78.8	21.2	100.0

Source: Organization division, SPD headquarters, Bonn, "Mitgliederbestände der Bezirke—aufgeteilt nach Männern und Frauen, I./1977" (mimeographed, unpublished). The SPD Jahrbuch, 1975-1977 (p. 287) has a similar breakdown by districts but lists a total of 1,022,191 members for December 31, 1976. According to party staff, the unpublished figures in table 6 may be more accurate, because they do not contain unavoidable duplications in the published figures.

friends and acquaintances (41 percent). Not surprisingly, it was highest (83 percent) among the families of SPD members. [26] But not every SPD member took the opportunity to spread the gospel. Leaders and activists at the party base talked much more about politics with non-SPD people than did the more passive SPD members, who—often because of lack of time or energy—only paid their dues and wanted no further responsibilities (and were therefore whimsically known as party cadavers).

The recruitment challenge was greatest in small communities with no local branch organization. In an experiment, the party sent mobile teams of SPD organizers to contact the few members living in such communities. They tried to enlist new members through a saturation campaign of personal letters, home visits, media publicity, public meetings to discuss local problems, and weekend seminars for new members. How successful the varied recruitment efforts were depended not only on the activism of members but also on the degree of popular support of government policies within the communities.

Other Characteristics

The influx of youth into the party in the late 1960s and early 1970s intensified its middle-class character and at the same time led to a higher average educational level. Between 1968 and 1977, those members who had continued their education beyond public school increased from 23 to 37 percent (see table 7). The earlier total corresponded to the level of

TABLE 7
EDUCATIONAL LEVEL OF SPD MEMBERS, 1968 AND 1977

	1968 SPD Members (In percent)	1968 Population (In percent)	1977 SPD Members (In percent)
Public School			
Without apprenticeship	4	34	13
With apprenticeship	61	44	49
High school and university	23	22	37
No answer	7	-	1
Number of cases	(554)	(5943)	(2534)

Source: 1968 infas survey figures in Nils Diederich, "Zur Mitgliederstruktur von CDU and SPD," p. 39; 1977 figures in Infratest survey, 1977, p. 7. For 1977, data is lacking for a sample of the population comparable to 1968. However, for 1978, microcensus figures show that in the typical 30-to-40-year-old age group, 70.2 percent had finished public school (no breakdown on the number with or without apprenticeship), 17.4 percent had finished a commercial school (Realschule), and 11.6 percent had finished academic high schools and universities (FRG, Presse- und Informationsamt, Gesellschaftliche Daten 1979, p. 59).

education reached by the population at large, but the later total did not match the 59 percent average of the more highly educated CDU members. [27] Not surprisingly, SPD functionaries spent more years in school than members; both functionaries and members had a higher educational level than SPD voters and the electorate at large. [28]

The party's middle-class character is also demonstrated by the income figures of the members. A 1968 sample survey showed that 31 percent had monthly incomes of under 800 DM, compared with 36 percent of the population; 34 percent, between 800 DM and 1,200 DM (30 percent for the population); and 28 percent, over 1,200 DM (20 percent for the population). [29] The 1977 survey indicated that members' average personal monthly net income had risen to 1,500 DM and household net income to 2,250 DM, a figure somewhat higher than that of the average of the total population. Moreover, about half the members lived in their own apartments or houses and 57 percent owned property. [30]

These statistics confirm the image of the SPD as a middle-class party, many of whose members are upwardly mobile. Indeed, a high proportion of members (in a self-evaluation question in the 1977 survey) ranked themselves in the middle class (48 percent) and upper-middle or upper class (5 percent)—a far cry from the nineteenth century party representing primarily the lower-income class. In 1977, nevertheless, 43 percent still ranked themselves in the lower or working class. Among CDU/CSU members surveyed, the corresponding rankings were 5 percent working class, 74 percent middle class, and 18 percent upper-middle and upper class. For the population as a whole, the rankings in 1977 were 40 percent working class, 53 percent middle class, and 4 percent upper-middle class. [31]

In a related profile of SPD members, Peter Glotz (now party secretary) put them into three major groups. The first, the "lower middle class," consisted of members of the old social democracy. After World War II, they were able to climb slowly up the social ladder. Labeled "petty bourgeois" by intellectuals, they held traditional values in religious, sexual, social, cultural, and ideological questions and challenged the new mores adopted by other groups. In this group were primarily older members with no higher education. The second group, the "left-liberal establishment," consisted of high-income members of the upper-middle and upper class with a higher education. Although dedicated to social justice and ready to help weaker groups, they neither saw all-encompassing solutions to the ills of society nor believed in a "new man." Repelled by authoritarian tendencies, they preferred instead liberal solutions to moral, sexual, and religious questions and a better quality of life. The third group, the "counterculture" or the "humanist left," consisted of younger members, primarily Jusos and those in the women's movement, who did not share the lifestyle of the older generation. Seeking to make politics more relevant, they protested against technical civilization, blind consumerism, and economic growth. In rejecting the middle-class values of their parents and wanting instead a moral turnaround in society, they clashed with the more traditional workers' values. [32] Friction between these three groups resulted at times in fratricidal feuds that weakened the party.

In 1977, the Infratest pollsters set up a classification scheme (see table 8) somewhat at variance with that of Glotz. On the basis of a set of attitudinal questions posed to members, Infratest found that one-quarter of the respondents were "left intellectuals" who rejected authoritarian positions as well as antisocialist and orthodox free-enterprise views. Instead, they espoused basic socialist views, were relatively free of fear

TABLE 8
POLITICAL PROFILE OF SPD MEMBERS, SPD VOTERS, AND ALL VOTERS, 1977

	SPD Members	SPD Voters (In percent)[a]	All Voters
Left intellectual	25	14	8
Traditional left	26	21	14
Apolitical or embittered	11	18	20
Authoritarian	15	29	29
Individualist	6	4	8
Antisocialist	17	14	20
Total	100	100	100

Source: Adapted from Infratest survey, 1977, p. 30.

[a]All percentages have been rounded off; hence the total does not necessarily correspond to the subentry percentages.

and insecurity, and looked at the future optimistically. Typical members of this group were students under 25 with high school or college educations or teachers and salaried employees over 25. There were few unskilled workers and self-employed in this category. [33] The second group, the "traditional left," also made up one-quarter of SPD respondents. They too supported a socialist order, rejected the free enterprise system, and were optimistic about the future but held some authoritarian views. Four out of ten members 60 or older and three out of ten between 45 and 60 were in this group. Most of them had a minimum of education, were unskilled or skilled workers, and were less active in the party than the left intellectuals. [34]

These two left groups totaled 51 percent. The remaining 49 percent were divided among conservative categories, including those espousing authoritarian, individualistic, and antisocialist viewpoints. In the latter two groups, encompassing 23 percent of respondents, were those who feared socialist egalitarianism and preferred the free enterprise system. The typical adherent was a young member of the upper-middle class whose ties to the party were not firm. (In contrast, 85 percent of active CDU/CSU members were committed antisocialists.) [35]

If the profile of SPD members in this poll is compared with those of SPD voters, the latter cluster more in the political middle. Voters in general also cluster in the middle as well as on the right (see figure 3). Such findings indicate that a committed socialist will join the SPD rather than just vote for it and that voters for the SPD and other parties are more authoritarian or apolitical than SPD members. [36]

The 1977 Infratest poll provides an interesting insight into how members classified themselves in a political left-to-right spectrum within

FIG. 3
POLITICAL SELF-IDENTIFICATION OF SPD MEMBERS, 1977 (1)

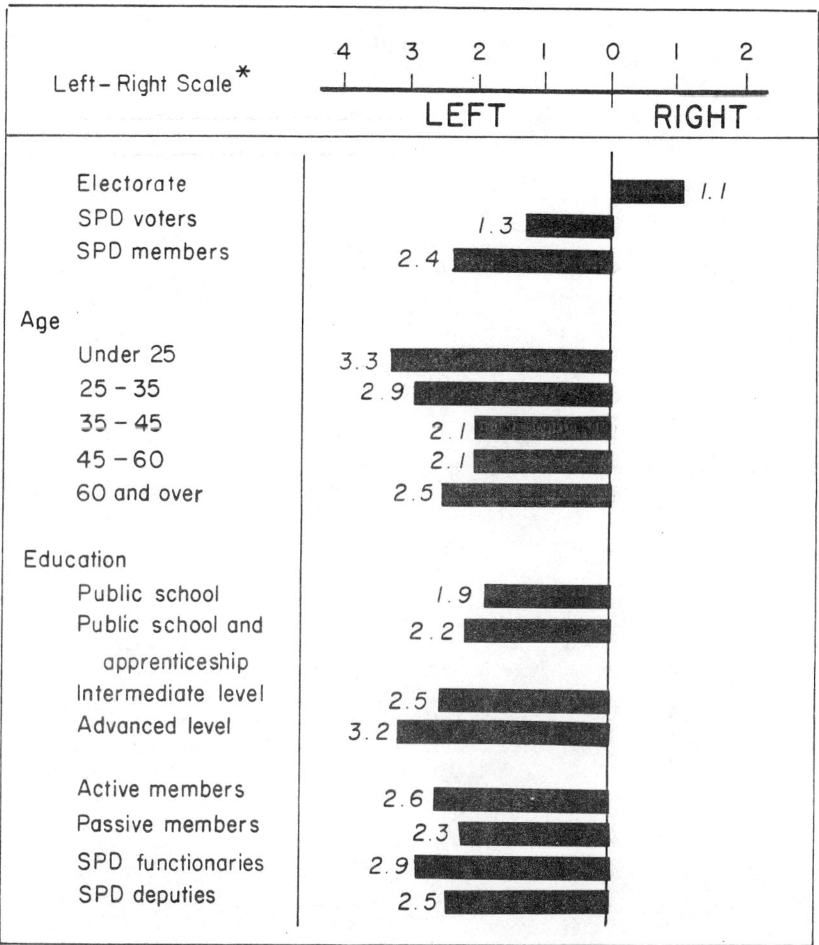

Source: Infratest survey, 1977, p.34, based on interviews with 2508 members and 208 functionaries.
*The scale is based on a maximum score of 10 on the left to 10 on the right. Each score number (1.1 on right, 1.3 on left, etc.) is based on a composite of answers given by respondents.

the party. The great majority (especially the middle-aged) ranged themselves in the left-middle or middle group, with only 2 percent of the members (young, well-educated, plus some Old Left) on the extreme left of the scale and even fewer on the extreme right (see figure 4). Of the active members, including functionaries, more ranked themselves on the left than did passive members and the party's public office holders. [37] Despite this range of views, on the average the members were politically more to the left than SPD voters and, unsurprisingly, than the electorate. [38] Among the latter, in a 1978 survey, 2 percent categorized themselves as being on the extreme left; 19 percent, on the moderate left; 35 percent, middle of the road; 15 percent, conservative; and 3 percent, strongly conservative. [39]

The Active and Passive Members

Surveys have indicated that although the activists and the passive members undergo the same political socialization and belong to the same social groups, the activists, many of them students and teachers, are more often on the political left within the SPD than are their passive colleagues. As a result, the activists, who shape policy at the base, were not necessarily representative of all members and clashed with more conservative senior leaders on many issues. [40]

SPD leaders at all levels tried to decrease the passivity of the membership—estimated to characterize as many as 75 percent of all members. The 1977 survey indicated that this total consisted of 50 percent who only paid dues; 15 percent who could be mobilized, especially during election campaigns; and 10 percent who were on the margin of being active, because on occasion they attended branch meetings. The other 25 percent of the members were the activists, including functionaries, who were the most loyal in attending these meetings. [41] Needless to say, 25 percent was an estimated average, which means that in many branches even fewer members showed an interest in party affairs, while in others, such as the Ruhr with a strong party tradition, the percentage was higher. [42] The degree of passivity and activism also fluctuated over time in many branches. When in the early 1970s the Jusos tried to take over as many local branches as possible, spirited discussions and counter campaigns by conservative blocs produced an activism that normally could not be sustained over a long period. Factionalism was especially prevalent in one-fourth to one-third of the large branches. Younger members viewed the existence of factions as a healthy sign of intraparty democracy, but the leaders and SPD public office holders saw them as damaging to the party. [43]

The local struggles for power often temporarily mobilized inactive older, conservative members, including many workers, who had stopped attending meetings when the radical academic youth increasingly discussed theoretical issues (using sociological jargon incomprehensible to them) and passed radical resolutions at night after their elders had left. In the late 1970s when the power of the Jusos waned, the disaffected older members, becoming active, tilted the political balance in many branches toward a more conservative position. Nevertheless, the older members felt less comfortable in the SPD of the 1970s. They missed the rapidly vanishing subculture, the red flag and other party symbols, and the traditional solidarity.

FIG. 4
POLITICAL SELF-IDENTIFICATION
OF SPD MEMBERS, 1977 (II)

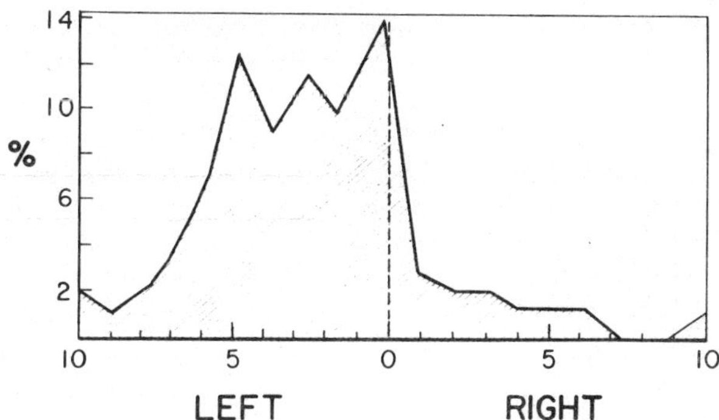

Source: Infratest survey, 1977, p. 35; appendix, n.p.

Leaders realized that branch meetings, viewed for decades as the focus of party activity, had become a nonspontaneous ritual to perpetuate the organization. They knew that something was wrong when only a minority of members volunteered to distribute handbills and put up posters and when sometimes not enough members could be found to run for local and regional party offices.

After his resignation as chancellor, Brandt made a nationwide tour to speak with thousands of local executive members about these and other problems and to hear their suggestions. Among the solutions he and colleagues heard and subsequently recommended were the following: integrate new members into the organization; schedule special social events for older members and youngsters; stage festivals, outings, dances, and exhibits; organize panel discussions and debates at meetings; have closer links to the press and to the city council SPD Fraktionen; have better communication between Bonn and the branches; and ensure that executive members not use the branch as a vehicle for their own advancement. [44] Many branches have adopted these suggestions; a few have tried the Swedish Social Democratic model to increase the members' political involvement. In a Swedish local branch, two resource persons with contrasting viewpoints prepare controversial topics for discussion. Then, at a meeting, members, divided into small groups, discuss the themes and produce majority and minority reports for the entire group.

In June 1979, two left-leaning SPD leaders, Heinrich Junker and Henning Scherf, submitted to top party organs a widely publicized and controversial report dealing primarily with membership problems. The report stated that the member must not feel that he or she is solely a statistical digit, whose complaints and views do not merit consideration. Personal involvement is stymied by excessive routine and bureaucracy, an increasing gap between members and leaders and deputies, and the government's failure to accept a number of party resolutions. Resignation and passivity result when members are viewed only as a support group for individuals seeking political power and when decisions are made without encouraging their participation. When too many branches become uninteresting to members, then citizens' initiative groups will form as an alternative for political action.

The report decried the party's costly administrative structure, which formulated an exaggerated set of legal safeguards and rules of conduct. Where once unpaid executive members wrote their own speeches, prepared position papers, and worked on details of meetings and conventions, now paid functionaries at intermediate and national levels increasingly perform such functions. The result is the destruction of individual initiatives, spontaneity, and improvisation—accelerated by the government's bureaucratic requirement that all party organs fill out multiple forms in the quest for perfection.

The report noted that during the Empire and Weimar eras the party was in close touch with members but that contact has been lost, especially in the large anonymous cities. As one remedy, the report called for a membership dialogue in the branches to be followed by larger regional assemblies where experiences and results can be exchanged. Such dialogues could range from ways to recruit new members to how to activate present members. [45]

The list of recommendations for changes made in this report and by party leaders was long. How many will be accepted by all echelons, leaders included, remains to be seen. The need for action will increase as passivity increases or more members leave the party—a matter of some concern to leaders confronted with a potential loss, according to one party study, of 5 percent of members (or even more, as in Hamburg where membership dropped from 47,000 to 29,000 in the 1970s). [46] Among the many reasons for a loss in membership throughout the Federal Republic were frustrations with party and government policy, a perceived decline of the party's moral credibility, and the difficulty for younger members to rise in the party if older members cling to their positions. A less typical reason for leaving was that given by an elderly saleswoman in a Munich bakery to a party volunteer who sought to collect dues from her: She had no money, could not get satisfaction from the SPD when she needed something, and feared that remaining in the party might again become dangerous some day "the way conditions are." [47]

Intraparty Communication

National party headquarters is interested not only in the substance of members' views but also in maintaining an effective communication network to help shape their views and inform them of current problems. The Land and district secretaries serve as one link in this network, but some of them fail to transmit information to the lower party levels. [48] There are other channels of communication, none completely satisfactory. Each year the party schedules a host of weekly seminars and weekend conferences on many specialized topics, but these can be attended by only a small number of members. It also isues pamphlets and newsletters, such as *Politik* and *SPD-intern*, on party matters, which are read by numerous lower-level functionaries but few members. The party's constituent associations publish their own journals, adding to the quantity of reading material received by members. In addition, the party has maintained financial support for the weekly Vorwärts, a nominally independent newspaper that seeks not to be a house organ but one able to criticize the party if necessary and to ward off occasional party pressures on the presidium-appointed editor. Since 1976, Vorwärts has been issued in a streamlined format but with a circulation of less than 60,000 (1978). [49] The party also issues Die Neue Gesellschaft, a theoretical monthly journal containing occasional critical articles. The Jusos publish the more radical Sozialistische Tribüne: Zeitschrift für sozialistische Theorie and forum ds.

The party, resolving to close the communication gap, decided to publish a free monthly magazine to be sent to all members. The first journal, Einblick, issued in 1973, soon folded because it failed to be lively and informative. Its more appealing successor, Sozialdemokrat Magazin, was designed to be read by the average member, characterized as a thirty-year-old skilled worker who has finished public school and an apprenticeship program. The journal contains news about the party (including its history), the Fraktion, and the government, a contra page about the CDU/CSU or employers unfriendly to labor, and other features. Financed from dues, Sozialdemokrat Magazin is read by an estimated four out of five members. [50]

THE MEDIA

The party media can hardly overcome the disadvantage of not being as up to date as the mass media in providing members with a modicum of SPD news. Two-thirds of members relied on the daily press for local SPD events, and the same number relied on television and the press for news about the national SPD. [51] This dependence on the mass media produced uneasiness among party leaders who considered much of it, especially the press, as biased against the SPD.

The Press

During the Weimar era, when parties owned most newspapers, the SPD (in 1929) controlled about 200, but with a circulation of only 1.3 million. In the wake of the Hitler era, the public was surfeited by twelve years of Nazi press propaganda. American occupation authorities also looked askance at a partisan press. But when British and French occupation authorities gave newspaper licenses to party officials with clean political records, there appeared by late 1949 twenty-two newspapers, with a circulation of 1.6 million copies, which stood close to the SPD, plus six official SPD organs with a weekly circulation of 100,000. These papers accounted for about 10 percent of the 15 million total circulation.

As ownership of newspapers concentrated, their number shrank. The mortality rate among the papers supporting the SPD was especially high, partly because of mismanagement or poor quality, and partly because some publishers were too beholden to party officials through trusteeship agreements, which stamped such papers as SPD organs in the public eye. By the mid-1970s, only eight of nearly 400 papers remained that could be counted on to be sympathetic to SPD goals. [52] The party attempted to combat this unfavorable development, but without success.

Earlier, at the behest of the left wing, the SPD tried to break the power of conservative newspaper czars as a means of enhancing its image among readers of their press empire. At the 1969 SPD convention, Hesse South introduced a resolution seeking a separation of editors from publishers. It hoped thereby to give liberal editors more freedom to express their views, even when working for conservative publishers. It also proposed that papers with large circulations intending to merge must receive government permission. These proposals were tabled but, along with others, became the focus of discussion of an SPD media commission. At the insistence once again of the party left, a special convention to discuss media policy (and other subjects) was convened in late 1971. Delegates approved the commission's proposal to create press committees on newspapers, designed to give editors and reporters more freedom, but rejected a left proposal to decartelize the press. [53]

In January 1973, the party executive issued a ten-point program calling for the formation of a federal communications commission and for legal protection for journalists to express their convictions. In 1974, it agreed to a left proposal demanding a restriction on the right of publishers to shape their papers' policies. In addition, the SPD media commission met occasionally with publishers and editors to discuss with them questions of cartels, concentration of the press, competition, and structural problems. In most instances, SPD proposals had little effect on them, as they sought maximum independence from government restrictions.

But, as in other countries, since they were also dependent on advertising and on big business support, they could not afford to alienate their financial angels too often. The result was that 85 to 90 percent of SPD members had no choice but to read conservative or mildly liberal newspapers (especially in cities with only one newspaper) or if they did have a choice, frequently read the Springer mass-circulation, conservative tabloid Bild-Zeitung. [54]

Specialists in the party's public relations and media section contend that because the press has been generally hostile to the SPD and a party press was no longer fashionable, ways had to be found to get the SPD message not only to its own members but to the general public. Numerous shop newspapers have been distributed to the workers, and low-cost city district newspapers, often not identified as having been launched by the SPD, have been printed to inform readers of local problems from a social democratic perspective. SPD headquarters has provided short news items and cartoons and has suggested headlines to the papers. In addition, copies of a four-page flyer inserted into the Sozialdemokrat have been distributed to the general public. Finally, the party has held numerous press conferences, issued releases in profusion, and sent out fillers to newspapers to be included in their news sections. [55] The party also relied until 1982 on materials issued by the government's Press and Information Office to inform the public of the accomplishments of the SPD-FDP coalition. This was especially important during election years, when many leading newspapers portrayed the CDU/CSU more favorably than the SPD. [56]

The intellectual community has been another, but more limited, target for the SPD. In 1976, Johano Strasser, the Juso theoretician, and Heinrich Vormweg, author and literary critic, launched the political-literary journal L'76. After several years of publication, it was succeeded by L'80, founded by the writers Heinrich Böll, Günter Grass, Tomas Kosta, and Carola Stern. According to the editors, the journal's purpose is to serve as a forum for discussion and to reactivate the democratic-socialist potential in German society in order to solve the problems of the 1980s. Even though the editors are SPD sympathizers, they also view themselves as its critics.

Their first pungent editorial set the tone: "The social-liberal coalition lives more from the obvious incompetence of its opponent than from the conviction of its deeds." [57]

Television and Radio

Of all the mass media, television has been the most important in politically influencing the voters. According to one public opinion institute, persons who normally have no or little interest in politics were influenced more than were politically interested persons by the political coverage of television networks. This was especially true for apolitical women in the 1972 election, more of whom became SPD than CDU/CSU voters. [58] Another 1972 survey sought to measure how individual political opinions were shaped. Fifty-six percent of a sample of SPD voters cited television; 19 percent, newspapers; 13 percent, personal conversations; and 2 percent, radio (11 percent had no political interest). [59] Most striking is the greater effect of the television image compared with the radio voice on the respondents, who in nearly all households (96 percent) owned both a television set and a radio.

Not only the SPD but all parties attempted to influence public television programming, emanating from two national networks which include nine and eleven regional stations. (There is no private network.) The attempts were made through each station's legally required broadcasting council, whose members must be primarily representatives from social groups, including parties. The council elects a supervisory board, which in turn chooses (with the council's approval) the station manager and top staff. The station manager supervises the day-to-day programming. This institutional machinery is independent of the government but assumes political coloration depending on the location of the station. Five stations (North German, Berlin, Bremen, Hesse, West) have been labeled as SPD "red" or as neutral, and four (Bavaria, Southwest, South, Saar) have been labeled as CDU/CSU "black." [60] In many instances, however, the staff is appointed on a party proportional basis.

Although no staff member will ever admit to producing biased programs, each party has complained of such practices and has accused the other of dominating the airwaves. The SPD has been especially concerned about the content of nationwide news shows, which it claimed often do not adequately present its (or the union) point of view. [61] In the late 1970s, the party also became concerned about the attempt of industry and CDU/CSU to establish rival private commercial stations and satellite and cable networks. It insisted that television and radio remain in public hands, independent of economic interests and the government. It denounced the CDU/CSU plea for a plurality of systems as a subterfuge to gain more control of the media. [62]

Despite the partisan struggle over control of the airwaves, the mixture of competing centralized and decentralized programming has guaranteed a degree of freedom to the television viewers and radio listeners. The SPD knew that it was but one organization seeking maximum exposure and favorable reporting of its activities through these media. Hence it could not rely primarily on them but had to make use of the press as well as encouraging its members to do outreach work in their shops, clubs, and cafés—especially during election years.

CONCLUSION

The milieu in which the SPD operates has a bearing on its membership. In contrast to the Empire and Weimar eras when the stratified class system made it primarily a worker's party, the post-1949 period, but especially the years since 1966, made it increasingly a people's party. The country witnessed more secularization, social mobility, and economic prosperity; less class consciousness; and a shift from the manufacturing to the service sector. These changes in turn produced a new "postmaterialist" middle class which was ready to become politically engaged. [63] Much of it streamed into the SPD after 1969, thereby changing the social base of the party. The membership became younger, less Protestant, occupationally more diversified, wealthier, more educated, and politically more leftist. This shift, characteristic of modernization and "embourgeoisement," was not restricted to the SPD but was common to other social democratic parties in advanced industrial states. As the following chapter demonstrates, the consequence for the SPD was an increase in leadership struggles and factional cleavages but also a greater degree of intraparty democracy.

NOTES

1. Maurice Duverger, Political Parties (2d ed. rev.; New York: Wiley, 1959), pp. 62, 124-132.

2. Organisationsstatut, paragraph 5, p. 8. See also paragraphs 2-4, 6, pp. 6-8. Paragraph 7 stipulates that an ousted member can seek readmission through the district executive.

3. Infas-Report, Parteisoziologische Untersuchungen 1977—Zusammenfassung der Ergebnisse (hectographed, Bonn-Bad Godesberg, 1978), pp. 8-9 (hereafter referred to as infas survey, 1977). Holger Börner and Hans Koschnick had commissioned the Institut für angewandte Sozialwissenschaft (infas) and Infratest, Munich, to each obtain sociological and attitudinal data from about 2,500 members and 225 leaders and to identify weaknesses in communication between Bonn and the base. For a summary, see Börner-Koschnick "Kommunikationsstudie zur SPD-Organisation," Vorwärts, March 9, 1978; Sozialdemokrat Magazin, Apr. 1978, pp. 8-13.

An infas study in 1968, based on North Rhine-Westphalia, Hesse, and Lower Saxony, noted that one-third of members joined the SPD during their period of schooling or apprenticeship, one-third after founding a family, and one-third after having obtained a secure job (Nils Diederich, "Zur Mitgliederstruktur von CDU and SPD," Parteiensystem in der Legitimationskrise: Studien und Materialen zur Soziologie der Parteien in der Bundesrepublik Deutschland, eds. Jürgen Dittberner and Rolf Ebbighausen [Cologne and Opladen: Westdeutscher Verlag, 1973], p. 48).

4. Infratest survey, 1977, pp. 23-24. See also infas survey, 1977, p. 11. In a 1975 survey of 417 respondents in the subdistrict Oldenburg, 15.6 percent said they joined the party primarily as a way to advance in their career, 53.5 percent cited this as a partial cause, and only 27.3 percent said it was not a factor (3.6 percent gave no answer) (Rüdiger Meyenberg, SPD in der Provinz [Frankfurt/Main: R.G. Fischer, 1978], p. 60).

5. Infratest survey, 1977, p. 23. The party does not publicize the

fact that it admitted ex-Nazi members into its midst after 1946, many of whom had been coerced into joining the NSDAP or one of its organizations. Cf. Hans See, "Strukturwandel und Ideologieprobleme der SPD—eine empirische Studie," *Auf dem Weg zum Einparteienstaat*, ed. Wolf-Dieter Narr (Cologne and Opladen: Westdeutscher Verlag, 1977), pp. 101-103.

6. Twelve percent cited other reasons. Because multiple answers were allowed, the total exceeds 100 percent (Diederich, pp. 49-50).

7. Other affiliations of parents: 5 percent CDU/CSU, 5 percent NSDAP, 5 percent liberal, 5 percent other parties; the remainder gave no answer (ibid., pp. 51-52).

8. Twenty-nine percent of members discuss politics regularly at home, 35 percent occasionally, 19 percent seldom, and 15 percent never (2 percent gave no answer) (ibid., pp. 54-55).

9. SPD, *Jahrbuch, 1958/59*, p. 268; SPD organization division, Bonn headquarters, "Mitgliederbestände der Bezirke—aufgeteilt nach Männern und Frauen, I./1977" (mimeographed, unpublished). See my table 6 for male-female breakdown by district.

10. SPD, *Jahrbuch, 1964/65*, p. 176. See also ch. 6 below.

11. Peter Glotz, "Anatomie einer politischer Partei in einer Millionenstadt," *Aus Politik und Zeitgeschichte*, Supplement to *Das Parlament*, No. 41, Oct. 11, 1975.

12. Figures for 1930 in Hunt, pp. 106-107.

13. Bernd Rabe, *Der Sozialdemokratische Charakter: Drei Generationen aktiver Parteimitglieder in einem Arbeiterviertel* (Frankfurt/Main and New York: Campus, 1978), pp. 127 ff, 152 ff.

14. Infas poll for 1968, cited by Diederich, p. 45; infas survey, 1975, p. 7.

15. Data based on 483 CDU/CSU members who were polled in the same survey as SPD members (ibid.).

16. Horst W. Schmollinger and Richard Stöss, "Sozialstruktur und Parteiensystem," *Das Parteiensystem der Bundesrepublik*, ed. Dietrich Staritz (Opladen: Leske and Budrich, 1976), p. 220.

17. Schmollinger, "Abhängig Beschäftigte in Parteien der Bundesrepublik: Einflussmöglichkeiten von Arbeitern, Angestellten und Beamten," *Zeitschrift für Parlamentsfragen*, V, No. 1 (Mar. 1974), 63.

18. Infratest survey, 1977, p. 4.

19. SPD, organization division, Bonn headquarters, "Mitglieder-Statistik, June 15, 1973" (mimeographed, unpublished), pp. 3-4. There were 71,293 metal workers (7.8 percent) in the SPD; 29,496 construction workers (3.2 percent); 14,034 carpenters (1.5 percent); 13,060 electricians (1.4 percent); 12,245 miners (1.3 percent); and fewer members in a host of other trades. There were 78,239 office employees (8.6 percent); 50,502 salesclerks (5.5 percent); 35,617 architects, engineers, etc. (3.9 percent); and 20,058 teachers and professors (2.2 percent). These figures exclude Schleswig-Holstein as well as 319,209 members (34.9 percent), such as housewives and pensioners, who did not provide information about their occupation or had none. For the 1977 occupational breakdown of the population, see Peter Gluchowski and Hans-Joachim Veen, "Nivellierungstendenz in den Wählern und Mitgliedschaften von CDU/CSU und SPD 1959 bis 1979," *Zeitschrift für Parlamentsfragen*, X, No. 3 (Sept. 1979), 328.

20. Many others were in the mining (23,478) and construction (19,482) unions, but few (141) in the Garden, Agricultural and Forestry Workers Union. Most union members who also held SPD membership belonged to one

of the DGB constituent unions while only 3,819 members of the German Salaried Employees Union (DAG) held SPD membership. (The DAG is a powerful rival federation to the DGB for salaried employee support.) SPD, organization division, Bonn headquarters, "Mitglieder-Statistik, 15. Juni 1973," p. 5.

21. Infas survey, 1977, p. 7; Konrad-Adenauer-Stiftung, Presse Information, No. 11, Oct. 22, 1979.

22. SPD, Jahrbuch, 1970-1972, p. 307; 1977-1977, p. 264. (Comparisons between 1960s and 1970s figures are difficult to make because the occupational classification changed. Students, for instance, were not separately listed in the 1960s.) Munich may serve as an illustration of the great shift in the party's social composition. In 1906, about 77 percent of the members were wageearners; by 1974, the total was down to 41 percent. On the other hand, those belonging to the petty and high bourgeoisie (Robert Michels' term) and the academic group rose from 13 to 59 percent during the same years (Manfred Güllner, "Daten zur Mitgliederstruktur der SPD: Von der Arbeiterelite zu den Bourgeoissöhnchen," Transfer 2: Wahlforschung Sonden im politischen Markt, eds. Carl Böhret, et al. [Cologne and Opladen: Westdeutscher Verlag, 1976], pp. 98-99).

23. Infratest survey, 1977, p. 6; Schwäbische Zeitung (Friedrichshafen), Oct. 16, 1978. Baden-Württemberg ranks high in number of members because they are concentrated in urban areas.

24. Sixty-eight percent of members, 87 percent of leaders, but only 36 percent of the electorate were strongly interested in political affairs; 28 percent of members, 11 percent of leaders, and 41 percent of the electorate were only mildly interested; while no members, 3 percent of leaders, and 22 percent of the electorate were hardly or not at all interested (Infratest survey, 1977, p. 8).

25. Infratest survey, 1977, pp. 20-21.

26. Armin Meyer, "Parteiaktivitäten und Einstellungen von CDU- und SPD-Mitgliedern," Parteiensystem in der Legitimationskrise, eds. Dittberner and Ebbighausen, p. 59.

27. Infas survey, 1977, p. 7; Gluchowski and Veen, p. 326.

28. Infratest survey, 1977, pp. 4-5.

29. Diederich, p. 40.

30. Infratest survey, 1977, pp. 4-5.

31. In both SPD and CDU/CSU surveys, 3 percent gave no answer. The CDU/CSU respondents numbered 483 (infas survey, 1977, p. 8). The total population rankings are from a 1976 infas random probability survey (2,000 respondents) (Ursula Feist, Manfred Güllner, Klaus Liepelt, "Structural Assimilation Versus Ideological Polarisation: On Changing Profiles of Political Parties in West Germany," Elections and Parties, eds. Max Kaase and Klaus von Beyme [London; Beverly Hills, Calif.: Sage, 1978], p. 179), and for 1977, from a similar 1977 infas survey (communicated to author by Horst W. Schmollinger, letter, June 25, 1982).

32. Glotz, Der Weg der Sozialdemokratie: Der historische Auftrag des Reformismus (Vienna, Munich and Zurich: Fritz Molden, 1975), pp. 221-223.

33. Infratest survey, 1977, pp. 31-32.

34. Ibid.

35. Ibid., p. 33.

36. The infas survey results are slightly different: 39 percent of SPD members hold authoritarian and 61 percent liberal views, confirming the ideological schism within the party (infas survey, 1977, pp. 49-50).

37. Infratest survey, 1977, p. 35. In a survey of Oldenburg SPD members, a question on political self-assessment showed that 3.6 percent saw themselves as radical; 38.1 percent, as progressive (they included students, high civil servants, some self-employed and workers); 40.5 percent, as liberal; 11 percent, as conservative (middle-level managers and civil servants, self-employed); and 6.7 percent gave no answer (Meyenberg, p. 143).

38. The 1977 infas poll categories vary from those of Infratest and hence are not quite comparable. The infas poll indicates that one-third of the respondents categorize themselves as being on the left, one-third on the middle-left, and one-third in the middle or on the right (infas survey 1977, p. 2).

39. The 1978 survey of the electorate by the Institut für Demoskopie (Study No. 3061), as well as a 1980 survey (Getas Institut, Bremen) with almost comparable results, are cited in David P. Conradt, The German Polity (2d ed.: New York: Longman, 1982), pp. 128-129.

40. Infratest survey, 1977, p. 22.

41. Ibid., pp. 14, 16. Of those who attended meetings, 30 percent did so regularly, 26 percent on occasion, 13 percent seldom, and 31 percent practically never (ibid., p. 26).

42. A 1970 infas poll of Dortmund (Ruhr) indicated that one-third of the members were leaders and active members who attended practically every meeting, one-half were moderately interested and attended meetings occasionally, and 15 percent were passive members who never attended (Manfred Güllner and Dwaine Marvick, "Aktivisten in einer Parteihochburg: Zum Beispiel Dortmund," Transfer 2, ed. Böhret, p. 123). On the other hand, in Oldenburg, a city with less SPD strength, a survey showed that 53.8 percent of the members were hardly engaged in party affairs, 34.5 percent were moderately engaged, and 11.3 percent strongly engaged (Meyenberg, p. 69).

43. SPD executive, Parteiarbeit, Ortsverein (Bonn, 1979); Infratest survey, 1977, p. 29.

44. SPD executive, Parteiarbeit, Ortsverein.

45. Report in "Vorlage für die gemeinsame Sitzung von Parteirat, Parteivorstand und Kontrollkommission am 22./23. Juni 1979 in Bonn, Bundeshaus" (hectographed); see also Henning Scherf, "Notwendige Fragen," Die Neue Gesellschaft, XXVI (No. 8), Aug. 1979, 659-662.

46. Infratest study, 1977, p. 24. In Hamburg, the party initiated a pilot project to find out why so many members left and to seek ways of regaining members (Vorwärts, Sept. 6, 1979).

47. Ibid., Jan. 4, 1979.

48. Infratest survey, 1977, pp. 36-38; personal interview with SPD staff member, Bonn, Apr. 1, 1980.

49. Personal interview with Gerhard Gründler, Vorwärts editor, Bonn, Jan. 13, 1975; Süddeutsche Zeitung, Jan. 13, 1972; Frankfurter Rundschau May 4, 1976.

50. Personal interview with Friedhelm Merz, Bonn, Jan. 20, 1975.

51. Infratest survey, 1977, p. 8.

52. Karl H. Pruys and Volker Schulze, Macht und Meinung: Aspekte der SPD-Medienpolitik (Cologne: Wissenschaft und Politik, 1975), pp. 17-18. Figures vary: Vorwärts (Nov. 6, 1975) cites seventeen SPD papers with a circulation of 2.5 million in 1948, with a shrinkage to three papers having a circulation of 250,000 in 1975. See also Horst Schmollinger and Richard Stoss, Die Parteien und die Presse der Parteien und Gewerkschaften in der

Bundesrepublik Deutschland, 1945-1974 (Munich: Dokumentation, 1975).

53. SPD, executive, Ausserordentlicher Parteitag '71, Massen-Medien (Bonn, 1971); Pruys and Schulze, pp. 40-60. See also Horst Holzer, "Medienpolitik der SPD," Der SPD-Staat, eds. Frank Grube and Gerhard Richter (Munich: Piper, 1977), pp. 171-188.

54. Infratest survey, 1977, pp. 10-11; personal interview with an SPD editor, Bonn, Jan. 20, 1975.

55. Ibid.

56. Vorwärts, Oct. 9, 1980.

57. L'80, I, No. 1 (1980), p. 2.

58. Elisabeth Noelle-Neumann, "Wahlentscheidung in der Fernsehdemokratie," Auf der Suche nach dem mündigen Wähler, eds. Dieter Just and Lothar Romain (Bonn: Kollen, 1974), pp. 193-194.

59. Forschungsgruppe Wahlen, "Politik in der Bundesrepublik," p. 105.

60. Personal interview with Gert Kopper, SPD media staff member, Bonn, July 20, 1977. See also Dyson, pp. 50-55.

61. Vorwärts, Jan. 20, 1977; Frankfurter Rundschau, Oct. 28, 1977.

62. SPD, executive, Dokumente, Forum Zunkunft SPD, Medienpolitischen Fachtagung der SPD am 22./23. Nov. 1979 in Bonn; "SPD Aktion 80, Sicherheit für Deutschland, Medien" (flyer).

63. On the growing literature of the new middle class, see Ronald Inglehart, The Silent Revolution: Changing Values and Political Styles among Western Publics (Princeton: Princeton University Press, 1977); "Post-Materialism in an Environment of Insecurity," American Political Science Review, LXXV, No. 4 (Dec. 1981), 880-900. For a critique, see James D. Wright, "The Political Consciousness of Post-Industrialism," Contemporary Sociology, VII, No. 3 (May 1978), 270-273.

4 Leaders, Factions, and Intraparty Democracy

In a democratic polity, no large organization can do without leadership to provide guidance and, conjointly with the members or their delegates, set goals and seek to achieve them. As French political scientist Jean Blondel points out: "A good or effective party leader is not merely concerned with the activities of his own party. He must relate to the country at large, both guiding the party and providing a link between it and the nation." [1]

But questions arise as to the degree of power such a leader should have. According to Robert Michels, observing the German Social Democrats around the turn of the century, the "German people [especially] exhibits to an extreme degree the need for someone to point out the way and to issue orders. This peculiarity, common to all classes not excepting the proletariat, furnishes a psychological soil upon which a powerful directive hegemony can flourish luxuriantly." He writes of the Germans' predisposition to subordination, discipline, a "Prussian drill-sergeant mentality," and "a trust in authority which verges on the complete absence of a critical faculty." [2] He quotes the advice written by Karl Marx to the German Socialist leader Jean Baptiste von Schweitzer in 1868 that the bureaucratically controlled workers must be taught to walk by themselves in order to lose their faith in constituted authority. [3]

From his observation of the SPD and the trade unions, Michels concludes that any large social organization operates under the "iron law of oligarchy," in which a few leaders at the top, "practically irremovable," have a near monopoly of power. The result is that such an organization denies its followers democratic participation in decision making. [4]

Michels' theory raised a storm of controversy that has not yet settled. Joseph Schumpeter argues that political elites compete for votes among the electorate, thereby strengthening the democratic system. Samuel Eldersveld contends that power, granted to the proliferating ruling groups, is diffused or "balkanized" at the national, state, and local levels. Under such a "stratarchy" of power, there are pluralized sets of leaders whose tenure is unstable, whose personal relationships are uncertain, and whose power begins to vanish. [5]

We must examine in this chapter whether the SPD of the 1970s was a near replica of its 1911 vintage. Were the leaders still unchallenged by a docile membership, or did ideologically oriented factions challenge one another for leadership supremacy and did dissidents force the party leaders to grant a measure of intraparty democracy? Before we attempt to answer these questions, it is necessary to draw a profile of the SPD leaders and functionaries, nearly all of whom fell into Max Weber's "bureaucratic" leadership category (rising through a hierarchical institution) and perhaps two (Brandt and Schmidt) into the "charismatic" category (being recognized by the population as a whole and having a strong personal following). [6] Such a profile will serve as a background for explication of intraelite cohesion, links to the members, recruitment and selection patterns, and policy directions.

LEADERS

Their Profile

The SPD elite at the national, Länder, and local levels ranges from the thousands of unpaid low- and middle-level functionaries holding posts in local branch executives to the prestigious members of the national presidium. There are no precise figures for their total number. In a 1968 small sample survey, an impressive 21 percent of members (150,000 on a national scale) were either executive members of their local branches (15 percent) or held posts in higher party organs, advisory councils, and auxiliary organizations (6 percent). [7] A 1973 survey counts members who also held elected political posts as less than 5 percent. Table 9 indicates that most of those in political posts were town councillors and the rest were city and district councillors and mayors. A 1980 calculation puts the number of SPD officials in the national and state governments and parliaments and top party posts at 212. [8]

TABLE 9
SPD MEMBERS HOLDING PUBLIC OFFICE, 1973

	Number[a]	Percent
Town councillors	22,643	2.47
City councillors	8,915	0.97
County and district councillors	4,046	0.44
Lord mayors and mayors	2,389	0.26
Land councillors	124	0.01
Members of Landtag	635	0.07
Members of Bundestag	230	0.03
No public office	876,488	95.75
Total	915,470	100.00

Source: Corrected version from Schmollinger, "Abhängig Beschäftigte in Parteien der Bundesrepublik," p. 80, based on SPD, organization division, Bonn headquarters, "membership statistics," June 15, 1973, p. 6.

[a] Excludes Schleswig-Holstein.

The socioeconomic background of the party functionaries shows that the SPD's shift from a workers' to a people's party took place more swiftly among them than among the members. As a result, salaried employees and civil servants, who, as a group, have more education, expertise, and articulateness than other SPD groups, are overrepresented among the leaders. According to the party's 1977 membership data, salaried employees constituted 25 percent of the members but 33 percent of the branch officers, 47 percent of the subdistrict officers, and 41 percent of the district officers. Civil servants constituted about 10 percent of the members but close to 20 percent of the branch officers and more than one-third of the subdistrict and district officers. [9] In 1968 manual workers were still slightly overrepresented in party offices and underrepresented in political offices; by 1977 they were underrepresented in party offices as well (see table 10). They then constituted 29 percent of members and 27 percent of branch officers, yet only 8 percent of subdistrict and 7 percent of district officers. Among the self-employed and students, membership strength and leadership strength was about even. Housewives and pensioners were underrepresented among functionaries (see table 11). [10]

There is a close relationship between the leaders' occupations and their membership in trade unions. Because more leaders were white-collar than blue-collar workers, more of them were in the public service and transport (ÖTV) and teachers (GEW) unions, especially at the subdistrict and district levels, than, for instance, in the metal or mining unions. [11]

TABLE 10
SPD MEMBERS HOLDING PUBLIC AND PARTY OFFICES, BY OCCUPATION, 1977

	Public Offices	Party Offices	Proportion Among Members[a]
		(in percent)	
Manual workers	29	23	31
Salaried employees	30	33	30
Civil servants	22	22	15
Self-employed	8	7	7
Housewives	2	2	3
Students	5	4	3
No answer	4	9	11
Total	100	100	100
Number	(181)	(407)	(2534)

Source: Infas survey 1977 (Tabellenband, table 9.21).

[a]The figures do not correspond to those in the first column, table 11, primarily because of a variance in occupational categories.

TABLE 11
SPD MEMBERS HOLDING PARTY OFFICE, BY OCCUPATION, 1977

	SPD Members	SPD Leaders in Local Branches	Subdistricts	Districts
	(In percent)			
Manual workers	29.0	27.4	7.5	6.8
Salaried employees	25.0	32.6	47.1	40.6
Civil servants	10.0	18.9	34.8	34.6
Farmers	0.2	0.5	0.3	0.0
Self-employed	4.7	4.8	5.6	1.5
Soldiers (professional)	0.6	0.5	0.4	0.0
Housewives	10.9	5.2	5.4	4.5
Pensioners	10.5	5.5	2.4	6.8
Students	7.4	4.1	6.2	5.3
Apprentices	1.6	0.4	0.3	0.0
Total[a]	100.0	100.0	100.0	100.0
Number	(981,300)	(47,500)	(1,531)	(133)

Source: SPD, organization division, Mitgliederkartei, June 30, 1977; cited by Holger Thielemann, "Neuere Daten zur Sozialstruktur von CDU und SPD," Gegenwartskunde SH '79, p. 83, who based it on Schmollinger data (see table 9).

[a]Rounded off to nearest decimal.

The embourgeoisement of the leaders was not a phenomenon restricted to the SPD but was characteristic of socialist parties throughout Western Europe. Michels noted the "bourgeois elements" in socialist leadership around the turn of the century, yet at that time workers or former workers held more leadership positions than in the post-1945 period. During the latter period, an increasing number of leaders with higher educational levels and professional achievements, whose parents were working class, took over the reins of power. As socialist parties became legitimized and controlled governments, the chances for promotion for such individuals were strong, especially because they competed less with an entrenched elite than did their counterparts in more conservative parties. According to one observer, the socialist parties' policies were not affected by this embourgeoisement of their leaders. [12] This was also true within the SPD, where there was no direct correlation between the leaders' class background and their policy preferences. They could be found in both the party's mainstream and its left dissident factions.

In 1977, female membership in the party was 21 percent, but only 3 percent of the chairpersons or deputy chairpersons and 12 percent of the executive members-at-large in the branches were women. [13] If just chairpersons are counted, the ratio for women is even lower. For instance, in a 1974 study, women chaired only about thirty (less than 0.5 percent) out of 8,800 branches, two subdistricts out of 233, and none of the districts. [14] As will be discussed in chapter 7, the low number of women in leadership positions has been a perennial problem to the women members; a satisfactory solution does not seem to be in the offing.

In 1977, about two-thirds of all functionaries and holders of public office were age 35 to 59, with only 4 percent over 60 but about 30 percent under 35. [15] Before the great influx of youth into the party a decade earlier, the proportion of young leaders was considerably lower. In 1977, most of the leaders had joined the party between 1960 and 1969; only one in ten had been a member in 1950. [16] Yet this average hides the fact that elections to posts above the branch level, especially, normally are not won by those who have been in the party for a short time. Thus, in 1977 most branch officials had been party members from seven to fourteen years; in the subdistricts, from ten to twenty-eight years; and in the districts, from fifteen to thirty-three years. [17] According to these officials, they had joined the party because it was the best vehicle for political participation, expression of views, and achievement of political goals. Although they had been in the party for a number of years, few were veteran old-timers to whom the party was a political home with a valued family tradition. [18] In 1977 the average household net income of all leaders was estimated at 3,000 DM a month, compared with 2,250 DM for the members. The middle-class status of the leaders is further attested to by the fact that two-thirds of them owned property. [19]

Statistical surveys of SPD leaders provide a profile that needs to be supplemented by information on individual careers. Interviews of a few local and regional leaders reveal how some party members managed to rise above the ranks and occupy policymaking posts. The story of a former deputy mayor in a small North Rhine-Westphalia city is typical of the older generation of leaders who grew up in the Social Democratic subculture. Born in 1902 of a working-class father who had become an SPD member in protest against the oppressive factory system, the son joined the workers' youth organization at 17 and the party at 18. Until 1933 he was a local branch chairman and liaison person to the youth organization. Persecuted by the Nazis, he found private employment. In 1945 SPD leaders asked him to rebuild the branch once Allied permission was granted. From 1948 to 1969 he was the local party leader and for ten years a member of the city council and deputy mayor. [20]

A former teacher in Baden-Wuerttemberg who had been a trade union member since 1947 joined the SPD in 1953 and became branch deputy chairman six months later, because of the paucity of qualified leaders in his city. Soon he rose to chairman and four years later to chairman of the subdistrict, at the same time becoming city councillor. By 1965 he had become a Bundestag deputy. He credited his swift rise in the party to diligently recruiting an untold number of members and making many friends who then supported him. [21]

In another instance, typical of those whose parents were never in the SPD, the respondent was a former university student whose father was a CSU member and mother an FDP member. A generational and ideological gap caused him to gravitate toward the SPD in the late 1960s. His rise in the party also was swift. He became a local Juso chairman after only five months in the party and retained that post for two years, after which he became deputy chairman and then chairman of the local branch, followed by election to the subdistrict executive. He, too, noted the importance of friends backing his repeated candidacies for party offices. [22]

One case illustrates the close linkage between party activism and political office. A member became active in the local Jusos and after a two-year battle successfully ousted a corrupt executive. She became inactive for two years after having a child, then joined a citizens' initiative to lobby for a kindergarten in her community. When she became active in the SPD again, she competed with many candidates for a few city council posts. She won primarily because of her commitment to civic affairs, rather than length of party membership. [23]

Party activism can lead not only to a political career but also to a paid position in the SPD. A former blue-collar worker, born in 1932, had a father who had been unemployed during the Depression and then had joined the Nazi party and a mother who had died when he was 15. In 1950, school friends asked him to join the SPD-allied Falcon youth organization. Because of his organizational talent, he was soon elected local chairman of the Falcons and reelected for six years. As a result of knowing someone at SPD headquarters, he worked there from 1953 to 1955, then at the _Vorwärts_ office, followed by a public relations job with a SPD journal specializing in local politics. In 1961 he became a city councillor; one year later he was appointed secretary in an SPD subdistrict. [24]

This small sample of elites is hardly typical of the broad spectrum of policymakers within the party. Of the thousands of leaders each one will have had a different life experience, with the majority climbing the party ladder more slowly than most of those interviewed. Leadership characteristics vary: some leaders are unimaginative and lack distinction; others are articulate, intellectually alert, talented in organizational matters, able to make compromises and retain friendships, tactically cautious, and quietly ambitious. One city chairman aptly put it: "I must be careful not to appear too strong or to implement my plans too readily, for there are always those who are outside the door and wish . . . me away." [25]

THE TROIKA

Willy Brandt

Although the thousands of leaders at all levels of the party affect the direction it takes, the elite elected to the presidium and executive in Bonn provides the greatest impetus and initiatives. Among those leaders, let us focus on the top three policymakers of the 1970s: Willy Brandt, Helmut Schmidt, and Herbert Wehner.

Brandt, born in 1913 in Lübeck, was exposed to socialism by his grandfather and by his mentor Julius Leber, a right-wing SPD editor and Reichstag deputy who gave him his first journalistic experience. In 1930, at the age of 16, he entered the SPD but soon quit to join the more radical Socialist Workers Party (SAP). After Hitler's assumption of power in 1933, Brandt fled to Oslo to resume his dual careers of journalism and politics. He remained in exile in Norway and Sweden until 1945. Upon his return to Germany, he first became correspondent for Scandinavian newspapers and then press attaché with the Norwegian military mission in Berlin.

Brandt's new career in the SPD began in 1948 when Chairman Schumacher appointed him director of the West Berlin liaison office. From 1947 to 1957 and again from 1969 on, he was a Bundestag deputy. He was also elected to the Berlin Chamber of Deputies in 1950, becoming its president five years later. Against heavy odds—being an outsider, young, reform-oriented, and not a disciple of Schumacher—Brandt was elected lord mayor of West Berlin in 1957, serving in that post through the cold war years until 1966, and was also elected chairman of the Berlin SPD from 1958 to 1964. As mayor of the beleaguered city, he soon became internationally famous. Consequently, he was chosen as the party's candidate for the chancellorship in 1961 and 1965 and ascended the party's political hierarchy: member of the executive in 1958, vice chairman in 1962, and chairman in 1964 upon Ollenhauer's death.

As noted earlier, Brandt's initiation at the national government level occurred in 1966 when he served as vice chancellor and foreign minister in the Grand Coalition, followed in 1969 by his five-year stint as chancellor. In 1976 he was elected president of the Socialist International, and one year later he accepted the chairmanship of the prestigious Independent Commission on International Development Issues (known informally as the North-South Commission). [26]

Brandt's rise to the top was facilitated by the image he projected, reflecting reality, of being fair, generous, and compassionate—a man with personal integrity, charm, and sympathy for the underclass. He did not favor authoritarian or coercive rule, used power sparingly, refused to manipulate people, was tolerant of dissent, sought consensus among colleagues, and carefully weighed alternatives before making important decisions. His skill at integrating the warring factions was important on many occasions when the party was rent with strife. Party members responded positively to his speeches, in which he emphasized the values of freedom, justice, and peace and provided a humanitarian and idealistic vision of the future.

Yet there were negative aspects to Brandt's leadership qualities that contributed to his downfall as chancellor. His reluctance to make enemies meant that he let problems ripen and then made unsatisfactory compromises. He was not a strong leader who was ready to make necessary personnel changes or capable of dealing effectively with mounting political and economic crises. He was unable to settle all intraparty disputes or rally the party behind him at crucial times. He could not shake off periods of emotional withdrawal and stress when he suffered setbacks to his career. After his resignation as chancellor, he had difficulty finding a role for himself, although he remained party chairman. He was never enthusiastic about being party administrator, even giving the impression that he was more interested in Eurosocialism than in his own party. [27] Many members became disillusioned with his role as a jet-set elder statesman, the left wing noted his increasing difficulty in relating to youth, and the workers viewed him as being too aloof from them. By 1979, fewer delegates at the Berlin convention voted for his reelection as chairman than ever before. Nevertheless, he still commanded enough respect as party leader among all factions that his party chairmanship was not endangered.

Helmut Schmidt

The political career of Helmut Schmidt illustrates another way to reach elite status in the party. Born in 1918, the son of a high school teacher, Schmidt finished high school in 1937, was drafted into the armed forces, served eventually as an officer until the end of World War II, and later studied social sciences at the University of Hamburg, receiving a degree in economics in 1949. He joined the SPD in 1946 and only one year later became national chairman of the German Socialist Student Federation (SDS), a post that he held for a year. In 1949 he began his professional career in the Hamburg city administration, soon heading the economics and transportation division. From 1953 to 1961 he served in the Bundestag, where he became an articulate spokesman on transportation and subsequently defense questions. In 1957 he was elected member of the Fraktion executive and one year later, member of the SPD executive.

From 1961 to 1965 Schmidt returned to Hamburg to become senator of the interior, a post that thrust him into the national limelight in 1962 when he commanded a flood-fighting operation in the city. In 1965 he was reelected to the Bundestag, serving as Fraktion chairman from 1967 to 1969. In the meantime, he rose within the party to become member of the presidium in 1967 and deputy chairman in 1968, posts that he still holds. After achieving such high party status, it was but one step further to be appointed member of the Bonn cabinet. From 1969 to July 1972, he served as minister of defense; from July to December 1972, as minister of economics and finance; and upon the formation of the new Brandt government at the end of 1972, as minister of finance. When Brandt resigned, Schmidt became chancellor on May 16, 1974.

Like Brandt, he too has positive and negative leadership qualities. A skilled and pragmatic leader with high intelligence, technical expertise, imagination, authority, and vigor, his ranking as a chancellor was high. Known as a "Macher" (doer), who, without much consultation with colleagues, tackles complex governmental problems, he enjoyed great popularity with the electorate. He tried to play down his reputation as "Schmidt-the-lip," the "big mouth who knows it all," the "knife thrower," but negative features remain: an abrasive manner, frequent irritability, arrogance, and lack of warmth—he was convinced that "most of the time . . . he's the only real leader in the world." [28]

Schmidt's relations with the SPD since 1974 have been complex, never very close and at times strained. As a right-winger in the party who is sympathetic to the unions and industry—not to mention the free enterprise system—he tags the left-wingers as utopians who have no sense of reality and whose economic security was won for them by a self-sacrificing older generation. At a Hamburg Land convention in 1974, he lashed out at them: "You busy yourself with the crisis of your own brains instead of the economic conditions that we have to face." [29] In turn, the left-wingers were embittered by his abandonment of reformism and his policies' lack of social democratic content. Before elections, knowing that he could strengthen his position vis-à-vis the voters by maintaining an independent stance, he gave the appearance of not wanting the support of the left-wingers in his party, who are still tainted as "Red" in many voters' minds. The SPD conservative members were sympathetic to his tactical position and always fully backed him, but the left and middle-left members were less supportive, for ideological and personal reasons, except at election time. Schmidt was aware of factional strife within the party but left to Brandt the attempts to unify it. As chancellor, Schmidt characterized his relations with the SPD most aptly: "I am not completely satisfied with my party, and it not with me. Bu I do not find a better party, and it has no substitute for me. . . . Thus we must get along with one another." [30]

Herbert Wehner

As chief party strategist and boss of the Fraktion, Wehner has made a strong imprint on the party. Born in 1906 in Dresden, the son of a shoemaker, he studied business administration and in the 1920s was in a radical socialist youth organization. In 1927, he joined the German Communist Party (KPD). Swiftly rising in party ranks, he was elected in 1932 to the central committee. From 1933 to 1935 he worked underground in Germany but then had to go into exile in Czechoslovakia. After imprisonment there, he lived in the Soviet Union, where he held a number of jobs, including one working for the political secretary of the party's executive committee.

In 1941, Wehner left the Soviet Union for Sweden. One year later the Swedish government imprisoned him for alleged spying for the Soviet Union and the KPD ousted him for having turned against communism. In 1946 he returned to Germany. Shedding his communist past, he joined the SPD, soon becoming an editor and member of the Hamburg Land executive. From 1949 to the present he has been a Bundestag deputy. As a result of his interest in a reunited Germany, he chaired the Bundestag committee for all-German affairs from 1949 to 1966. One of the authors of the Germany Plan for reunification, Wehner also was a leader of the party's foreign affairs committee.

From 1958 to 1973 he was deputy chairman of the party but decided in 1973 not to stand for reelection partly because he did not want to identify himself with Brandt's weak leadership. For three years he was minister for all-German affairs in the Grand Coalition cabinet, but then preferred to devote full time to the party. As head of the Fraktion since 1969 he has remained the master technician of the party, and has been one of the principal architects of German politics. There have been few politicians who have served the SPD for so long, who have not sought power for power's sake, and who have been willing to make any sacrifice to enhance the party's fortune. [31]

His personality traits are well known. He is often bitter, gruff, tough, brusque, and unpredictable; has fits of rage; or remains mysteriously silent for long periods at Fraktion meetings. Known as a taskmaster in the Fraktion, he is more feared than loved by the deputies. According to one left-wing deputy: "Wehner, who is known as Uncle Herbert, is inimitable, commands respect but can be disrespectful, is sometimes endearing and sometimes crushing. In short, there is nothing avuncular about him." [32] He has angered many within and outside the party and has not hesitated to tell colleagues in the SPD that they were not capable or to denounce those who disagreed with him. His tight hold on the Fraktion has been slipping since 1977, when he began to have difficulty integrating the warring factions. Often the deputies or other leaders did not know which course of action he was going to choose. [33] As will be seen below, his public criticisms of party matters or foreign policy developments have rankled others in the party. Yet Wehner has also shown solidarity with the critics in the party and has offered them help if needed. In 1982, for personal and health reasons he did not stand for reelection to the party's executive.

The Feuding Troika

When three senior leaders with different personalities work together for a long time in shaping party policy, they are bound to sometimes clash and sometimes be irritable toward one another. These three have had difficulty working as a team, even though their ideological differences have not been great, Schmidt standing to the right of Brandt and Wehner. Their strained relationship has not helped the image of the party or added to its cohesion.

The feuds go back to the SPD's years in opposition but became sharper and more serious when the party was in power. On several occasions when Brandt was vice chancellor and chancellor, Schmidt and Wehner publicly accused him of weak leadership. In 1968 Schmidt intimated to friends that unless he received a top post in the party he would resign and take a top management post in industry. Brandt counseled Schmidt to be patient. But the ambitious Schmidt had difficulty holding himself back. In the spring of 1969, he is alleged to have sharply and vulgarly criticized Brandt's indecisiveness as foreign minister at an international conference in Denmark. [34]

Once Brandt became chancellor, new conflicts emerged among the troika. One of the most spectacular was a public statement made by Wehner in Moscow in September 1973 that the West German government had pushed too hard for concessions from the East. This statement, undercutting Brandt's Ostpolitik, caused a sensation in Bonn. Brandt, on a visit to Washington, rushed back to Bonn to meet with Wehner and try to undo the political damage. While professing publicly that all was well, Brandt never forgave Wehner. The Chancellor viewed Wehner's remark also as a breach of party practice: criticism of policy should be made only behind closed doors. Wehner, on the other hand, felt that only a dramatic statement would change foreign policy, make Brandt a more forceful leader, and restrain the coalition Free Democrats from making too many demands on the SPD in the government program. As a result of this spat and an earlier public remark by Wehner that "what is missing in the government is a head," Brandt and Wehner have hardly been on speaking terms. [35]

In a television broadcast in early 1974, as the government faced a number of crises, Schmidt also assailed Brandt for his "weak" leadership. By then, Brandt was incensed that his two chief lieutenants were not maintaining party loyalty and were openly challenging his incumbency. In the case of Schmidt, the public looked at the challenge as a bid for power that soon became successful when Brandt resigned. Thereafter the ex-chancellor repeatedly declared his loyalty, and also requested that of party members, to the new Chancellor. Despite public expressions of the need for a team effort, relations between Brandt and Schmidt remained as cool as ever. As Brandt once remarked: "It is not true that I don't get along with Helmut Schmidt. The fact is that I get along with him splendidly as long as we don't talk politics." [36] At the 1975 Mannheim conference, the troika leaders reaffirmed their vow to work together, but behind the scenes the old rivalries remained, fueled by a new political biography of Brandt in which the author (David Binder) described Wehner's verbal assaults against Brandt, including Wehner's reluctance to persuade Brandt to stay in office in 1974. [37]

Before the 1976 and 1980 elections, official harmony prevailed among the three chiefs, who each had an interest in maintaining the status quo. Schmidt needed Brandt, still a relatively popular party chairman, and Wehner, whose Fraktion support for government policies was essential; Brandt and Wehner needed Schmidt, whose popularity among the voters remained strong. One functionary linked the three somewhat differently: "Brandt is the best salesman of the policy that Wehner designs and Schmidt enacts." [38] But this trilateral need did not diminish the tension and diversity of outlook between them, well expressed with a twinge of sarcasm by the deputy Ulrich Lohmar: "Helmut Schmidt knows everything and most of it better. Herbert Wehner does everything, and the most important alone. Willy Brandt sees all, and looks straight at the future." [39]

Between the national elections, the fragile truce among the three chiefs was frequently broken. In June 1977 Wehner renewed his attack against Brandt. The Fraktion chairman, furious that not all SPD deputies had supported a government tax bill, blamed Brandt for not having sufficiently informed the party of the government's tax needs. In effect, Wehner implied that Brandt was not supporting Schmidt sufficiently. Brandt thereupon assailed Wehner's "unbridled" public statements and reaffirmed his loyalty to Schmidt. The presidium was convened to restore peace, but too late to undo the new damage that had been created. [40]

The press tried to guess why Wehner kept assailing Brandt. Did he want Brandt to stop being a sluggish party leader who vainly sought to integrate the "counterproductive" left into the mainstream of the party? Did he want Brandt to resign and have Schmidt become party leader also? Was he angry about Brandt's alleged damaging dual strategy of supporting the government position but at the same time protecting the party from some "corrupting" government positions? Psychological factors may also have contributed to his critical attitude. Wehner saw that talented Brandt, with lucky breaks in his career, did not have to work hard to achieve, while he, Wehner, remained perpetually in second position, not least because he was an ex-Communist. Wehner also must have felt that he had not received enough recognition for the tough job of keeping the Fraktion nearly always together. [41] No matter what the motivations—most likely a combination of them—may have been, Wehner maintained his critical stance toward Brandt in the late 1970s. In the summer of 1979, he complained that the SPD was only partly the model of organizational unity that it once had been and that it had developed instead into a "confused" group of party associations. [42] Not long after this implicit criticism of Brandt and party secretary Bahr, he is reported to have said of Brandt: "This gentleman is only busy with his afterlife." [43) At the 1979 Berlin convention, Wehner, intent on maintaining party unity as the primary goal, tried to step into the void left by Brandt, who, according to Wehner's private assessment, neglected his responsibility to lead the party firmly and to integrate its factions.

The Fraktion chief did not spare Schmidt from criticism either—in this instance, not of the leadership style but, rather, of the direction of some foreign policies, such as arms control and East-West relations (see chapter 14). Yet except for occasional policy differences, Wehner's loyalty to Schmidt remained firm. Schmidt, in turn, was grateful for Wehner's support and his clear strategic thinking. On the other hand, he viewed Wehner as often unpredictable in his statements and in his ability to keep the

Fraktion united. To gain the support of the Fraktion, Schmidt spoke to it on many occasions.

By 1979, Schmidt's stature in the party had risen as that of Brandt and Wehner declined. The press began to write increasingly of the SPD as a chancellor's party, whose chairman had lost interest in the day-to-day politics, was taking less advice from his friends, and no longer provided new long-range perspectives to counter Schmidt's policy of crisis management. The party's right wing hinted that Brandt had lost control and must stop wasteful discussions in the organization; the left wing wanted Brandt to be firmer against Schmidt's influence within the party. Symptomatic of the shift in power among the three leaders was Schmidt's insistence in 1979 that his trusted Minister of State, Hans-Jürgen Wischnewski, replace Hans Koschnick as SPD deputy chairman. The party's left wing was critical; it viewed the nomination as proof that Schmidt tried to plant a government spokesman in the top party organs. [44] Brandt, less critical, knew that Schmidt must be supported if the party was to repeat its electoral successes. To placate his left opposition, Schmidt in December 1979 appointed a young left-leaning taxation expert in the Fraktion, Gunter Huonker, to replace Wischnewski in the Chancellery.

The troika feuds have repeatedly made the headlines and given the impression of a party rent by continuous schisms among its elite. Much can be said about the personality clashes, policy differences, and the loss of élan visible among the three leaders, who by 1982 knew that they would sooner or later be retiring from their posts (in late 1982, Brandt was 69, Schmidt 64, and Wehner 76). Yet much should also be said about the remarkable continuity in office of these top leaders. Each had a role to play in the party, and each had to cooperate with the other two to ensure maximum cooperation between the triad of party, government, and Fraktion. Nevertheless, the SPD had to begin thinking about possible successors to the party chairman, deputy chairman, and Fraktion chairman. Although a number of names have been advanced for the various positions, the party will not find it easy to replace the incumbents with talented persons who have accrued similar status and prestige.

Not only must the SPD pay attention to the leadership succession at the top but it must also recruit new able leaders at other levels. Too often, men and women are coopted into leadership posts on the basis of political criteria rather than ability. The party press has noted on more than one occasion that some leaders fear being succeeded by persons more qualified than they and will not promote their candidacy. If ability, initiative, and integrity are not rewarded, the consequence is a mediocre, gray leadership that is servile to its superiors and arrogant to its inferiors.

FACTIONS

Few political parties are without factions. Whether in a cadre or mass party, leaders and followers are normally bound to differ on a host of issues and organize into rival units. According to Giovanni Sartori, subparty units can develop along four dimensions: (a) the organizational dimension—factions develop a minimal to maximal structure; (b) the motivational dimension—factions organize for power for its own sake or for spoils; (c) the ideological dimension—factions range from pragmatism to ideological fanaticism; (d) the left-right dimension—factions range over a political spectrum that could lead, Sartori contends, to a "grand oversimplification resulting from a compound of fuzzy criteria." [45] As we shall see, the SPD factions often combined these dimensions but primarily reflected the left-right political spectrum. It goes without saying that the terms "left" and "right" are relative, for in the SPD they would not encompass the views of extremist groups within the Federal Republic.

As noted earlier, the SPD historically has been split into warring factions that at times seemed to have little more in common than a commitment to a socialist utopia—even then, with disparate visions of the future. Ideological and pragmatic differences were at the root of the schisms among the three wings during the Empire era and between the left dissidents and the majority wing during the Weimar era. In the post-1945 era, a left wing emerged again, whose strength increased considerably after the tumultuous late sixties. [46] Right-wing groups responded by trying to stem its activities during the seventies. A loose middle bloc, left center in orientation, tried to maintain a fragile peace between the left and the right but, as we shall see, had little luck nationally; while in some of the party's most important strongholds, such as Berlin, Munich, and Frankfurt, open warfare erupted.

The Left Wing

Not only has the SPD suffered from left-right factionalism but in each faction there have been subfactions differing on tactics and goals within a more limited ideological framework. In the SPD left wing, an Old Left and a New Left maintained a fraternal link from the late 1960s on, despite a generational gap. Circulation in and out of leadership posts has been frequent. Some leaders, especially those of the New Left, have moved to the left-center wing after being graduated from the Jusos; other "burned-out," battle-scarred veterans have left the party; still others have remained true to their earlier commitment.

The Old Left is a loosely organized group of Marxists, many with a proletarian background, who formed a small opposition group throughout the post-1945 period. With strength in Hesse-South, Schleswig-Holstein, and Berlin, they led the fight against remilitarization and atomic armaments and for a rapprochement with the East during the 1950s. They were critical of the Godesberg program for its opening to the right but succeeded in including some neo-Marxist planks in it. [47]

A typical leader of the group has been Harry Ristock of Berlin. He joined the SPD in 1950, was elected to the party executive in 1973, became Berlin senator of building and housing in 1975, and deputy chairman of the Berlin SPD in 1976. Another leader was "Red Jochen" Steffen, Land chairman of Schleswig-Holstein (1965-1975) and chairman of the SPD basic values commission (1973-1976), who quit the party in 1979 because it had become too conservative. Ristock, Steffen, and others attempted to steer the SPD in an anticapitalist, socialist direction. They have been critical of the SPD for pursuing a technocratic course and for trying in its electoral platforms to satisfy all organized groups. They concur with more moderate SPD leaders that the socialist movement must develop within the existing framework and avoid a confrontation with the economic power structure, but they emphasize the need for a step-by-step democratization and capture of key political and economic units that control society.

Their views of the Juso elite have been mixed. On one hand, they have criticized its dogmatism, elitist jargon, impatience, and failure to integrate fully into the SPD, and on the other, they have welcomed the influx of youth into the party, hoping that as the left thereby became stronger within the party, their own position within the left would be strengthened. This occurred to only a limited extent, partly because some of the left leaders, such as Peter von Oertzen (Lower Saxony), Klaus Matthiesen (Schleswig-Holstein), Günther Jansen (Schleswig-Holstein), and Hans Matthöfer (Hesse), moved into the more moderate left stream of the SPD and partly because the New Left leaders, by their sheer numbers, soon occupied many leadership positions of the party's left wing. [48] As will be noted in chapter 5, the Juso leaders, heading different factions, had major difficulties in maintaining cohesion. Yet despite their ideological differences, they presented a common front against many SPD policies.

To produce even more cohesion between the Old and New Left, in spring 1967 their leaders formed the Frankfurt Circle (Frankfurter Kreis). Meeting informally several times a year to discuss national problems and to prepare for a joint position on convention issues, the group, headed by former Juso chairman Karsten Voigt, includes left Bundestag deputies, Juso leaders, Land chairmen, and party functionaries. It has had considerable strength at party conventions, but its effect on policy has been more modest, primarily because it serves only as a coordinating unit. [49]

In Baden-Wuerttemberg, the Tübingen Circle (Tübinger Kreis) performed the same functions as its Frankfurt counterpart at the national level. The group was formed in May 1968, when distress within the SPD about its participation in the Grand Coalition was high, by a number of moderate-left regional leaders, including Horst Ehmke, Erhard Eppler, and Peter Conradi. They wanted to introduce internal democracy into the Land party, discuss important issues, and eventually capture a number of leading positions in the regional or national party. [50] In early 1974, having achieved their objectives, they disbanded the circle.

Despite these attempts at institutionalizing the left wing and despite the existence of a left minority in the Bundestag (see chapter 11), no united major left force under one leader has emerged to seriously challenge the SPD establishment. In 1979, Voigt claimed that the left does not exist anymore; rather, individuals formulate policy alternatives and regional organs criticize the party executive. In response, Juso chairman Schröder said that the Jusos wanted to take the initiative to reform and strengthen the left. He suggested that in preparation for the 1979 convention, where important domestic and foreign policy problems would be discussed, the Frankfurt Circle and sympathetic district and Land organs should prepare positions under the guidance of coordinators for each major problem. [51]

After the convention, at which the left could not gain majority support for its alternative policies on energy and defense, it was still seeking a charismatic leader. Erhard Eppler, Land chairman of Baden-Wuerttemberg, who had played a major role at the convention, was shaken by the poor electoral showing of the SPD in his Land, although he continued to be one of the left-wing leaders in the early 1980s. Harry Ristock's reputation as left leader had been damaged when he veered toward Schmidt's position on energy and defense but could not secure enough left executive posts. By the end of the 1970s, however, other leaders were emerging or consolidating their power in the left or moderate-left camp. Among them were Oskar Lafontaine, Mayor of Saarbrücken, who had won a Saarland election; Karsten Voigt, Bundestag deputy and foreign policy expert; Peter Conradi,

Bundestag deputy from Baden-Wuerttemberg; and Henning Scherf, Bremen finance senator. [52]

But leadership was not the left's only problem. Many of its supporters were leaving the party to join the ecology and peace movements or abandoning politics altogether. Others despaired of ever getting a majority in the party, of producing significant changes in German society, or of reestablishing the close links with the trade unions enjoyed in the 1960s. Although the left had lost some of its punch, it still held majorities or strong pluralities in Hamburg, Bremen, Schleswig-Holstein, Hesse-South, South Bavaria, Lower Rhine, and Baden-Wuerttemberg. The establishment had reason to worry if it attempted to ram through crucial policy decisions that the left strongly opposed. Such a possibility seemed unlikely as long as Chairman Brandt, somewhat sympathetic to the left, remained in his post.

The Right Wing

Reacting to the activities of the left, right-wing officials began to organize groups and take positions on issues. Like the left, they formed an amorphous force within the party. The right wing's leaders and followers, such as Helmut Schmidt, Hans Apel (defense minister), Holger Börner, and Hans-Jürgen Wischnewski, were (and are) powerful within the party. They often claimed to represent the middle of the political spectrum, but their ideological views—strong anticommunism, rapprochement with business, opposition to any further nationalization, and hostility toward the Jusos—put them in the right-center. Strong in the SPD-led cabinets, the Bundestag (where their faction has been the largest in the SPD), the Länder parliaments, the trade unions, and top party organs, this group, especially after 1974, set much of the tone and determined policy. [53]

Some of its leaders helped to form moderate rightist groups; others, who have moved from right center to right, formed extreme rightist groups. In 1968, a number of West Berlin conservative leaders who were former political prisoners from the German Democratic Republic organized a local Kurt Schumacher-Kreis. When enough groups organized in other Länder, a national organization was founded in November 1971. Its constituent assembly in Bonn party headquarters gave it legitimacy. It was organized to fight the increasing influence of the Jusos in the party and Brandt's failure to take tough measures against them. Among its leaders were Annemarie Renger (Bundestag president and vice president) and Hermann Kreutzer (Berlin administrator). In 1980 it had only about 300 members. [54]

Before the 1972 election, a number of right-wing leaders, seeking support from conservative SPD members who were not wooed by the Kurt Schumacher-Kreis, founded the Fritz Erler-Kreis. Among them were cabinet members Helmut Schmidt (Economics and Finance), Georg Leber (Defense), and Egon Franke (Intra-German Affairs); Hamburg Senator of the Interior Heinz Ruhnau; Parliamentary State Secretary Karl Herold; deputies Kurt Mattick (Berlin) and Werner Buchstaller (Koblenz); and Munich Mayor Hans-Jochen Vogel. Chancellor Brandt, displeased about the proliferation of party factions, was even angrier when several of his cabinet ministers were among the founding members. The inspiration for the group, named in honor of the deceased Fraktion head and defense expert, came from the leaders of the right-wing Bundestag faction, who attempted to draw intellectual partisans into the battle against the left wing by providing theoretical analyses and energizing the party's base. [55]

In March 1976, a number of Fritz Erler-Kreis leaders and others founded the more formal Fritz Erler Association (Gesellschaft), whose membership ranged from 2,000 to 2,500. It claimed to be moderate and "freedom-oriented," but its statements were rabidly anticommunist. It asserted that because the SPD had fallen under the spell of the left, conservative SPD members must stop being a silent majority and start a counteroffensive. Brandt accused the association's members of "party-damaging" behavior but refrained from publicly denouncing Hans Erler, the son of Fritz Erler, who had written a book, "Fritz Erler Against Willy Brandt—Democracy or People's Front in Europe," in which he blasted Brandt (who had been close to Fritz Erler) for having sold out the SPD to the communists. [56]

In the meantime, other groups had formed using the names of deceased leaders—an Ernst Reuter group in Berlin and Julius Leber association in Lübeck. In March 1976, the SPD presidium stated that the memory of all leaders should be a political legacy for the entire party. One newspaper claimed that with this proliferation of groups, the party had become a playground for extremist views. [57]

The Fritz Erler Association began to lose its appeal for SPD conservatives when two of its officials, Hans-Günther Weber, a Braunschweig municipal official, and Winfried Döbertin, a teaching fellow at Hamburg University, sympathized with the CDU/CSU slogan of "freedom instead of socialism" during the 1976 election. In October 1979, a court ruled that the association no longer could carry the name "Fritz Erler," because it had endorsed the CDU in a Schleswig-Holstein election. [58]

The party has had to confront rightist groups and splinter parties that emerged outside its periphery. One of the earliest, the League for a Free Germany (Bund Freies Deutschland), with headquarters in West Berlin, was founded by several prominent ex-SPD officials who assailed the SPD for its dogmatic socialism. The SPD executive ruled that SPD members could not simultaneously be League members; it made a similar ruling for members who joined the Social Democratic Union (Soziale Demokratische Union), founded in June 1977 by Hans-Günther Weber. The new short-lived party, with a nucleus of 3,500 members of whom about one-third were formerly in the SPD, failed in its goal of becoming a magnet for dissatisfied voters from both established parties. As soon as Weber dissolved it in June 1979, he and a number of former SPD members and others founded the Citizens' Party. Avowedly antisocialist and opposed to the social-liberal Bonn coalition, it, too, failed.

The Effects of Factionalism

The left-right confrontation in the party was unavoidable in the aftermath of the youth rebellion of the late 1960s. Although the factions were at times vituperative against each other, most members remained in the party knowing that they would have little political influence on the outside. But the atmosphere of tension and hate that pervaded the SPD damaged its reputation and standing in the nation. Party leaders, who constantly warned members about the formation of factions and cliques, feared a major secession or a split leading to new political parties. In November 1974, Chancellor Schmidt told top party leaders that the feuds, labeled "Berlin sickness" for the long left-right struggle in that city, were fodder for media publicity. In again assailing the left for its theoretical discussions and saying that people wanted to know how the governing party would solve national problems, he was voicing the concerns of the right.

A year later, at the Mannheim convention, he moved more to the middle, admonishing both left and right to behave responsibly. Quoting Chinese sayings, he told all members, "Don't fear walking slowly, only fear standing still"; to the left he said, "A 100,000-foot-high tower rests also on the ground;" and to the right, "Who does not climb high mountains does not know the plains." [59]

Brandt, especially, tried to keep the party intact. As a leader of a loosely knit left-center bloc, whose spokesmen included a number of former left-wing leaders and more moderate politicians (such as Horst Ehmke, Peter von Oertzen, Hans Matthöfer, Klaus Matthiesen, Peter Glotz, Volker Hauff, and Egon Bahr, with an occasional visit from the peripatetic Wehner), the party chairman played a skillful integrationist game. He reiterated the need for the SPD to absorb the restless youth on the left and to allow the pragmatic right a chance to be heard. At the Mannheim conference, he pleaded for peace: "I can't order you to be brotherly with each other, but I have to insist that tolerance, consideration, and helpfulness be the rule in this party." [60]

Peter Glotz cautioned the right that the left also has a role to play: "Whoever in politics unthinkingly pushes 'theory' aside, confronts the danger that he might receive power and not know what to do with it." [61] To him, theoretical discussions and seeking power were complementary, not contradictory. However, he warned that the spectrum of the party was too broad and had to be narrowed, because the groups at its edge were paralyzing the party.

In most cities, such as West Berlin, Bremen, Erlangen, Frankfurt, Hamburg, Hannover, and Munich, SPD factions were battling one another, leading if not to paralysis, at least to major confrontation. Although some confrontations—in West Berlin, for example—date back to the postwar period, in most the struggle began at the end of the sixties when youth confronted their elders. [62] Once the Jusos captured the local party organization, they clashed with conservative SPD municipal officials and legislators. Bonn leaders were wary of intervening in local matters; when they did mediate a dispute, it was often too late. In some cities or towns, factionalism was minimal and the party could present a united front to the electorate.

The proliferation of factions in the 1970s had positive and negative consequences. Positively, it allowed the articulation of views by those with a common ideology, and it injected more internal democracy into the party when mainstream leaders were challenged by dissident factions. Negatively, it weakened the party through membership losses, growing apolitical feelings among the followers, weakening of fraternal bonds, and electoral losses. The majority of the SPD governing elite would have concurred with R. T. McKenzie's observation, in writing about the British political parties, that "there are clearly defined limits beyond which organized minorities cannot be permitted to go if the parent party is to function as a coherent contender for office."[63] The SPD leaders would have argued that the same provision would apply to maintenance of the party in office.

INTRAPARTY DEMOCRACY

Elite competition among factions may limit the power of national leaders to govern a party monolithically and may enhance internal democracy. McKenzie, although agreeing with Michels that a small group of leaders can easily have "enormous" powers (in this instance, in the British Conservative and Labour parties), also contends that Michels' "iron law of oligarchy" is not an iron law, primarily because the leadership groups cannot "ignore with impunity the moods and aspirations of their followers; they must carry their followers . . . with them." [64]

What about the degree of intraparty democracy in the SPD of the 1970s? Before answering, we must return once more to Michels' 1911 observations about oligarchy and the SPD: "It is organization which gives birth to the dominion of the elected over the electors, of the mandatories over the mandators, of the delegates over the delegators. Who says organization, says oligarchy." [65] He argued that every party organization consists of an oligarchical power grounded on a democratic base. If the leaders are reproached for having an antidemocratic attitude,they will say: "Since the masses have elected us and reelected us as leaders, we are the legitimate expression of their will and act only as their representatives." [66] He denied the claim that once socialists have gained control of the government, the leaders' interests will coincide perfectly with the interests of the led. [67] On the contrary, the gap between leaders and followers will produce sluggishness, "not in respect of action alone, but also in the sphere of thought." [68]

Michels' observations hold true to a limited extent for the present SPD, but there are powers countervailing the elite. First, let us look at the evidence supporting Michels' theory. In a 1968 survey 26 percent of members stated that they had no influence on the leaders; in the 1977 survey more than half the members considered their influence in the branches minimal, although a passive two-thirds of those did not mind. In the 1968 survey, 35 percent of respondents also claimed that leading functionaries worry little about the views of average party members. [69] A letter by a branch chairwoman in the _Vorwärts_ is symptomatic of the frustration felt by many low-level functionaries and members. She wrote that in many subdistricts the chairpersons or the Bundestag deputies representing the districts did not want the rank and file to discuss or criticize policies they advocated and made attempts to stifle initiatives by members who no longer wanted to be mere "applauding spectators." When quiet is restored, "we must ask whether it is not a quiet of a cemetery." She argued for more lively discussions—and not just by those few comrades who seek higher ofice. [70]

In a study of the SPD from 1946 to 1966, Klaus Günther concluded that only a minimum of intraparty democracy existed. Leaders constantly tried to prevent schisms and to present a united front to the electorate. [71] Such attempts at unity have often been made since then—not always successfully. Other specialists have noted that as the importance of party associations increases, that of the local branches decreases. The oligarchical tendency becomes stronger when the views of the rank and file are no longer adequately represented in higher party organs, primarily because members have little opportunity to become delegates to policymaking conventions. Instead, unpaid or paid party officials are elected delegates and thereupon make up one policymaking group. [72] In turn, this group supports the top leaders, whom it considers indispensible to make quick decisions and to oversee the smooth functioning of the organization. These leaders rarely need to use a heavy hand to keep the party in line, because the functionaries at lower levels have internalized the direction the leaders want them to take.

The top leaders pay lip service to the theory of maximum intraparty democracy but in practice pay less attention to it. They cannot restrict intraparty elections that legitimize the organization, but they can determine in many instances who the candidates will be. They ensure that their own views will be transmitted from the top, through conventions and conferences, to the base for the members' support and that contrary views from the base will be stymied. [73] Typical of such maneuverings was the leaders' attempt to postpone consideration of party reforms advocated by two districts at the 1977 convention. Wehner, presiding over the organization commission, reluctantly formed a subcommission to deal with the districts' demand. The subcommission issued the already cited Junker-Scherf report calling on the party to make some necessary reforms. The report was ready for submission to the party council at its February 1979 meeting, but presidium leaders, afraid of its impact on impending state elections and disagreeing with some of its conclusions, urged council members to be absent from the meeting so that a quorum would be lacking. Thus the report was not discussed by the council and other top organs until June. [74]

Although a good case can be made that intraparty democracy was limited in the SPD of the 1970s , a more compelling case can be made that intraparty democracy flourished more than in earlier decades. The legal framework for making German political parties democratic was established by the Basic Law (Article 21, Paragraph 1) and the Party Law of 1967. The parties are required to have statutes and programs, regional subdivisions and periodic elections, membership assemblies, and an executive committee elected every two years. The rank and file is to participate in determining party policy.

In the SPD, enough members have used these provisions to challenge oligarchical rule. The influx of young members into the party in the late 1960s precipitated lively challenges, controversies, factionalism, and policy debates at all levels. On the defensive, the establishment could not hold down the new energizing force; it had to allow more intraparty democracy, especially to dissident groups, to preclude massive resistance or resignations. As will be seen, the Jusos challenged, sometimes successfully, decisions made at the top. As a result, the leaders had to be more cautious in policy formulation and execution. No longer could they expect the rank and file to automatically approve their decisions without extensive discussions. They had to seek support from the base because members were needed for election campaigns and for their own reelection. [75] Hence they could not formulate policy drastically opposing members' views.

In the 1970s there was a stalemate on some policy initiatives because the leadership had suffered a number of reversals or was itself split. For instance, at the special 1971 convention, the failure of an economic commission to agree on the concept of wealth formation led to no action; on the other hand, convention delegates supported the high wage demands of the Metal Workers Union in its negotiations with industry over the objections of Chancellor Brandt and other top party leaders who feared the wages' inflationary impact. The number of reversals or stalemates has never been great, but several isolated instances indicate that determined activists building subcoalitions can occasionally win against the top elite, particularly if the latter lacks unity or cannot muster the support of lower-level elites. The left activists, especially, have been determined to challenge the elite's oligarchical tendencies and to broaden intraparty democracy, notably when they were a minority at the branch level. Once they controlled a branch, their enthusiasm for maximum democracy waned when challenges from the right threatened their own newly gained power.

In summary: a vocal left minority in the party has on occasion successfully challenged the establishment, especially when issues commanded wide support. When the minority has been weak, however, chances for success were dim. The extent of intraparty democracy depends not only on the strength of the internal opposition but also on the degree of cohesion among leaders, accord on issues at different party levels, and the calendar of upcoming election campaigns (when pleas for party unity will outweigh those for internal democracy). Michels' theory of oligarchy cannot be shrugged off, even for the SPD of the 1970s. But there have been enough countervailing tendencies to indicate that intraparty democracy flourished to a limited extent during this turbulent period.

As Hans Daalder remarks in surveying the party scene:

> Most European parties would seem to be comparatively open agencies that allow for a great deal of intra-elite conflict as well as for the rise of new elite groups in competition to older ones. Parties work, moreover, generally in a democratic environment that permits publicity and criticism by competitors and outsiders and that forces actual accountability to independent electoral groups; this cannot but blunt oligarchical proclivities. [76]

NOTES

1. Blondel, p. 162.
2. Michels, pp. 88-89.
3. Ibid., pp. 89.
4. Ibid., p. 121. See also Seymour Lipset introduction in ibid.
5. Joseph Schumpeter, Capitalism, Socialism and Democracy (New York: Harper, 1947), p. 269; Eldersveld, pp. 9, 11.
6. Max Weber also has a third category: "traditional" leadership, based on status in a nonmodern social group (Max Weber, Max Weber on Charisma and Institution-building, ed. S. N. Eisenstadt [Chicago: University of Chicago Press, 1968], p. 46). See also Blondel, pp. 170-183.
7. Armin Meyer, p. 63, citing a 1968 poll of 567 members. Ulrich Lohmar deals with a Wuerttemberg study of 36,000 members, of whom an estimated 5,000 held leadership positions. He considered the latter figure too high and estimated a ratio of one leader to ten members (Innerparteiliche Demokratie, p. 48).
8. Heino Kaack, "Zur Struktur der politischen Führungselite in Parteien, Parlamenten und Regierung," Handbuch des deutschen Parteiensystems, Vol. I, Parteienstrukturen und Legitimation des Parteiensystems, eds. Kaack and Reinhold Roth (Opladen: Leske, 1980), p. 197.
9. Michael Bretschneider, "Mitgliederzahlen der Parteien und ihre räumliche Verteilung 1977," issued by Deutsches Institut für Urbanistik, n.d.

(c. 1978), (hectographed). In a 1974 survey of North Rhine-Westphalia functionaries, 44 percent of the members were workers but only 23 percent of the branch chairmen and 30 percent of the other executive members (including 44 percent among the treasurers). Forty-nine percent of the members were salaried employees and civil servants, but 69 percent of the branch chairmen and 83 percent of the subdistrict chairmen (Güllner, pp. 99-100).

10. The 1977 infas survey (p. 8) classifies the leaders as 15 percent upper class, 60 percent middle class, and 22 percent working class (3 percent gave no answer).

11. In 1977, of the SPD members who belonged to a union, 27 percent were in the Public Service and Transport Workers Union (ÖTV) but more than 40 percent of SPD subdistrict and district functionaries who were union members were in the ÖTV. The 27 percent of branch executives in the ÖTV corresponded closely to the SPD membership percentage in the ÖTV. On the other hand, while 27 percent of SPD members and 24 percent of the SPD branch executives who were in a union were in the Metal Workers Union, only 14 percent of SPD subdistrict leaders and 13 percent of district leaders fell into this category (Bretschneider, p. 46).

12. M. A. Marsh, "European Social Democratic Party Leaders and the Working Class: Some Linkage Implications of Trends in Recruitment," Political Parties and Linkage: A Comparative Perspective, ed. Kay Lawson (New Haven: Yale University Press, 1980), pp. 47-74.

13. Holger Thielmann, "Neuere Daten zur Sozialstruktur von CDU und SPD," Gegenwartskunde SH '79, p. 85.

14. Anke Riedel-Martiny, "Genosse Hinderlich und die Frauen—Die Situation weiblicher Mitglieder der SPD," Neue Gesellschaft, XXII, No. 9 (1975), 731. See also Susanne Miller, "Frauenfrage und Sexismus in der deutschen Sozialdemokratie," Sozialismus in Theorie und Praxis: Festschrift für Richard Löwenthal zum 70. Geburtstag am 15. April 1978, eds. Hannelore Horn, Alexander Schwan, and Thomas Weingartner (Berlin: Walter de Gruyter, 1978), p. 547.

15. Infratest survey, 1977, p. 7. The infas survey, 1977 (p. 7) notes that 56 percent were in the 35-to-59 age category.

16. Infratest survey, 1977, p. 7. The infas survey, 1977 (pp. 8-9) notes that 58 percent of leaders joined the party since 1966, but only 7 percent before 1949.

17. Bretschneider, p. 41.

18. Infas survey, 1977, p. 11.

19. Infratest survey, 1977, p. 7.

20. Personal interview, July 26, 1977.

21. Personal interview, July 22, 1977.

22. Personal interview, July 17, 1977.

23. Personal interview, July 17, 1977.

24. Personal interview, July 26, 1977.

25. Hans Gert Peter Wallach, "Leadership Styles in West German Political Parties" (Paper read at the American Political Science Association meeting, New Orleans, Sept. 4-8, 1973), p. 14.

26. For political biographies, see David Binder, The Other German: Willy Brandt's Life and Times (Washington, D.C.: New Republic Book Co., 1975); Terence Prittie, Willy Brandt: Portrait of a Statesman (New York: Schocken Books, 1974); Klaus Harpprecht, Willy Brandt: Portrait and Self-Protrait (Los Angeles: Nash, 1974); Barbara L. Kellerman, "Willy Brandt: Portrait of the Leader as Young Politician" (Unpublished Ph.D.

dissertation, Yale University, 1975); Gerard Braunthal, "Willy Brandt: Politician and Statesman," Governments and Leaders: An Approach to Comparative Politics, ed. Edward Feit (Boston: Houghton Mifflin, 1978), pp. 212-226. For an autobiography, see Willy Brandt, My Road to Berlin (Garden City, N.Y.: Doubleday, 1960); People and Politics: The Years 1960-1975 (Boston: Little, Brown, 1978).

27. Braunthal, "Willy Brandt," p. 264.

28. For accounts of Schmidt, see Helmut Wolfgang Kahn, Helmut Schmidt: Fallstudie über einen Populären (Hamburg: Holsten, 1974); Grunenberg; Wolfram F. Hanrieder, ed., Helmut Schmidt: Perspectives on Politics (Boulder, Colo.: Westview Press, 1982).

29. Der Spiegel, Sept. 30, 1974.

30. Grunenberg, p. 67.

31. For political biographies, see A. Freudenhammer and K. Vater, Herbert Wehner: Ein Leben mit der Deutschen Frage (München: Bertelsmann, 1978); Gerhard Jahn, ed., Herbert Wehner: Beiträge zu einer Biographie (Cologne: Kiepenheuer and Witsch, 1976). For a critical account, see Peter Kohnen, Deutschland, deine SPD: Die Frustrierten und die Manipulierten (Munich: Politisches Archiv, 1972).

32. Hannoversche Allgemeine Zeitung, June, 7, 1978.

33. Die Zeit, July 9, 1976.

34. Kahn, pp. 54, 62-63.

35. See Arnulf Baring, Machtwechsel: Die Ära Brandt-Scheel (Stuttgart: Deutsche Verlags-Anstalt, 1982), pp. 571-573, 601-607.

36. Hamburger Abendblatt, Dec. 31, 1981.

37. Der Spiegel, Nov. 17, 1975. For Binder's biography, see fn. 26 above.

38. Viola Herms Drath, Willy Brandt: Prisoner of his Past (Radnor, Pa.: Chilton Book Co.), p. 349.

39. Der Spiegel, Oct. 6, 1975.

40. Süddeutsche Zeitung, June 22, 1977.

41. Die Welt, June 22, 1977; Welt der Arbeit, July 1, 1977.

42. Süddeutsche Zeitung, June 22, 1979.

43. Die Welt, Sept. 13, 1979.

44. Süddeutsche Zeitung, June 22, 1979.

45. Sartori, p. 79; see also pp. 75-80. For a useful analysis, see Frank P. Belloni and Dennis C. Beller, eds., Faction Politics: Political Parties and Factionalism in Comparative Politics (Santa Barbara, Calif.: ABC-Clio, 1978), including Peter Merkl, "Factionalism: The Limits of the West German Party-State," pp. 245-264.

46. For a documentation of intraparty disputes to 1968, see Ossip K. Flechtheim, Innerparteiliche Auseinandersetzungen, Vol. VII, Part II, Dokumente zur parteipolitischen Entwicklung in Deutschland seit 1945 (Berlin: Dokumenten-Verlag Wendler, 1969).

47. Best known was Professor Wolfgang Abendroth (Marburg) who was expelled from the party. For details of the Old Left, see Graf, pp. 160-186; Claudio Pozzoli, ed., Die Linke in der Sozialdemokratie, Jahrbuch 3, Arbeiterbewegung, Theorie und Geschichte (Frankfurt/Main: Fischer, 1975), p. 174.

48. For details, see Jochen Steffen, Strukturelle Revolution (Hamburg: Reinbek, 1974); Kremendahl, Nur die Volkspartei, p. 55.

49. Among those active in the group, not necessarily continuously, have been Steffen, von Oertzen, Dröscher, Ristock, Matthöfer, Ehmke, Rudi Arndt (Frankfurt mayor), Fred Zander (Frankfurt party head) and

Roth. See Peter Arend, Die innerparteiliche Entwicklung der SPD, 1966-1975 (Bonn: Eichholz, 1975), pp. 56-57; Konkret, Jan. 11, 1973; Feb. 8, 1973. Personal interview with Karsten Voigt, Frankfurt, Jan. 7, 1975.

50. Eppler was chairman of SPD Land Baden-Wuerrtemberg; Conradi, an architect, became Bundestag deputy. See Stuttgarter Zeitung, Jan. 29, 1973; Mannheimer Morgen, Feb. 20, 1973; Die Welt, May 30, 1973. Personal interview with Peter Conradi, Bonn, March 20, 1980.

51. Vorwärts, July 14, 1979; Mittelstandsmagazin, Oct. 1979.

52. Others who have been in the limelight: Heidi Wieczorek-Zeul, Gunter Huonker, Wolfgang Roth, Hugo Brandt and Herta Däubler-Gmelin. See Die Zeit, Dec. 7, 1979; Der Spiegel, May 12, 1980; Frankfurter Allgemeine Zeitung, Aug. 20, 1980.

53. Other rightists have been cabinet members Helmut Rohde, Kurt Gscheidle, Karl Ravens; state secretaries Marie Schlei, Hermann Buschfort, Heinz Ruhnau; party executive members Herbert Ehrenberg, Bruno Friedrich, Antje Huber, Diether Posser. See Der Spiegel, June 24, 1974; Heinz-Gerd Hofschen, Erich Ott, Hans Karl Rupp, SPD im Widerspruch: Zur Entwicklung und Perspektive der Sozialdemokratie im System der BRD (Cologne: Pahl-Rugenstein, 1975), p. 161.

54. Süddeutsche Zeitung, Jan. 27, 1972; Vorwärts, Mar. 22, 1979; Arend, p. 57; Ferdinand Müller-Rommel, Innerparteiliche Gruppierungen in der SPD: Eine empirische Studie über informell-organisierte Gruppierungen von 1969-1980 (Opladen: Westdeutscher Verlag, 1982), pp. 118-121; letter from Wilhelm van Ackern, Kurt Schumacher-Kreis, Jan. 28, 1981.

55. Der Spiegel, Dec. 18, 1972; Kieler Nachrichten, Feb. 13, 1973.

56. Title in translation (there is no English ed.): Hans Erler, Fritz Erler contra Willy Brandt—Demokratie oder Volksfront in Europa (Stuttgart: Seewald, 1976).

57. Süddeutsche Zeitung, Mar. 31, 1976; SPD, pressemitteilungen und informationen, 172/76, Mar. 30, 1976.

58. Frankfurter Allgemeine Zeitung, Oct. 6, 1979.

59. Welt der Arbeit, Nov. 21, 1975.

60. New York Times, Nov. 15, 1975.

61. Glotz, Der Weg der Sozialdemokratie p. 232. See also his Die Innenausstattung der Macht: Politisches Tagebuch, 1976-1978 (Munich: Steinhausen, 1979).

62. See Sylvia Streeck and Wolfgang Streeck, Parteiensystem und Status quo: Drei Studien zum innerparteilichen Konflikt (Frankfurt/Main: Suhrkamp, 1972).

63. R. T. McKenzie, British Political Parties: The Distribution of Power within the Conservative and Labour Parties (2d ed.; New York: Praeger, 1963), p. 643.

64. Ibid., p. 644.

65. Michels, p. 365.

66. Ibid., p. 216.

67. Ibid., p. 367.

68. Ibid., p. 337.

69. Survey of 1968 cited by Armin Meyer, pp. 70-71; Infratest survey, 1977, p. 29.

70. Vorwärts, July 26, 1979.

71. Günter, pp. 255-263.

72. Lohmar, p. 45, personal interview, Heino Kaack, Bonn, Feb. 1, 1980.

73. These views were expressed by Michael Th. Greven in Vorwärts,

Jan. 27, 1977; Ute Müller, Die demokratische Willensbildung in den politischen Parteien (Mainz: von Hase and Koehler, 1967); Joachim Raschke, Innerparteiliche Opposition: Die Linke in der Berliner SPD (Hamburg: Hoffmann und Campe, 1974); Christoph Butterwegge, Parteiordnungsverfahren in der SPD (Berlin: Demokratische Verlags-Kooperative, 1975).

74. Der Spiegel, Feb. 12, 1979; Weser-Kurier (Bremen), Aug. 30, 1979.

75. Critical of the Michels theory is Emil Hübner, Partizipation im Parteienstaat (Munich, Ehrenwirth, 1976); Zeuner, Innerparteiliche Demokratie; Werner Siebeck, "Demokratisierung oder Machtkampf? Studien zur innerparteilichen Demokratie am Beispiel der jüngeren Entwicklung der Münchner SPD" (Unpublished M.A. thesis, University of Munich, 1977).

76. Hans Daalder, "Parties, Elites and Political Developments in Western Europe," Political Parties and Political Development, eds. Joseph LaPalombara and Myron Weiner (Princeton, N.J.: Princeton University Press, 1966), p. 71.

5
The Young Socialists

The constituent associations are important in the structure of the SPD. They were designed to give the diverse groups—youth, workers, women, the self-employed, and others—an organizational home, a base for mobilization of new members and voters, and a platform for making programmatic demands. When the associations were created, SPD leaders did not realize the Pandora's box they were opening. No other units in the SPD organization were able to generate the ferment stemming from the associations--especially the Young Socialists (Jusos). If the Jusos had not mounted an offensive, seeking power within policymaking councils and challenging government policies, the SPD would have remained more quiescent and nonideological. Its unity of action would have been less impaired, but it would have lacked the dynamics of intraparty democracy that the Young Socialists and other dissidents provided.

In this chapter, we examine the Jusos' structure, history, ideology, factionalism, and links to the parent organization, in order to underscore the central theme of the book--how the SPD, on the pinnacle of success as a governing party, was beset by a host of insurmountable externally-generated problems, including the Juso rebellion against society and the party's system-sustaining policies. In the two chapters to follow we examine the other SPD constituent associations.

THE JUSO ORGANIZATION

If political parties are not to die, they must organize youth to become the potential cadres and architects of new ideas and policies. All SPD members from 16 to 35 years old are automatically non-dues-paying Juso members, but in 1977, of the estimated 300,000 SPD members in that age category, only 80,000 thought of themselves as Juso members—the rest just as SPD members. Of the 80,000 aware of their Juso membership, 35,000 at the most were active in the organization. The others often had no time or lived in areas without a local branch. Juso membership is also open to those not in the SPD, but without a vote or the right to office. Nonparty members were estimated at less than 8 percent. [1]

The average age of Jusos in the mid-1970s was 24; only one in six was female, a percentage varying little from the proportion of women in the SPD. Among the activists, about half had jobs and the other half were high school and university students and apprentices in training. [2] Among the passive members, manual workers predominated. Although the students formed a high percentage of the activists, their overall strength in the Juso membership in 1972, according to one survey, was only 7 percent; 31 percent were salaried employees; 24 percent, manual workers; and 22 percent, civil servants. [3]

The degree of activism varied over time. In the early 1970s when enthusiasm for Brandt's reform policy was still high, Juso activity was correspondingly high; in the late 1970s passivity had increased in the face of few new government reform programs, a mounting apolitical attitude among youth, and SPD disciplinary measures against rebel Jusos. Right-wing SPD members' blocking of their attempts to capture party organizations in some districts caused frustration among the Jusos; a minority left the party, while moderate Jusos devoted more of their time to working in SPD local branches, especially when their own branches became inactive. [4] Reflecting the mood of the times was one Juso automobile sticker: "The SPD is not good. But it is better than all the others."

The organization of the Jusos corresponds to that of the party. At the base are the branches, whose number varied over time, with an estimated 3,000 in 1977. (But of these nearly half were inactive or barely active.) [5] The branches coalesce into subdistricts and district or Land organizations. At the national level, an annual congress determines policy and elects the federal executive (Bundesvorstand). In addition a federal board (Bundesausschuss) consisting of district representatives serves as the political advisory board to the executive. [6]

The Young Socialists, attempting to abide by internal democracy, emphasized the theory of the "imperative mandate," under which leaders were to be responsible to their constituents. The leaders tried to make members more aware of their responsibility to control the work done at the top and to supply them with sufficient information. But the Jusos also were beset by oligarchical problems, especially because the leaders had more information about party matters than the members. Becoming a Juso leader had payoffs: many moved into SPD leadership positions at all levels and/or ran for political office. Conversely, it was possible to climb the SPD ladder without having been active in the Jusos. Even among the younger SPD deputies in the Bundestag only a minority had held a Juso office. The Juso members' perceptions of their chances to move up in the SPD differed: in a 1970 survey, 24 percent viewed them as good; 38 percent, as not very good; and 24 percent, as poor. While a majority of respondents felt comfortable in their local branch, many said that there was not enough contact with the party, that SPD officials should speak to the Jusos more often, that the younger generation must be taken more earnestly, and that the Jusos should be given more projects. [7]

Student Groups

The Jusos, backed by the party, attempted to recruit new members among high school and university students. The potential was there: in 1977, among the youth up to 24 years old, 6 percent were members of a political party. Of these, 46 percent were in the SPD, 31 percent in the CDU/CSU, 1 percent in the FDP, and 11 percent in other parties, especially those of the left (another 11 percent gave no answer). [8] Despite an SPD lead among the committed youth, the Jusos in the early

1970s sought to capitalize on the increasing student interest in politics and educational reform among nonparty students. The task was facilitated when the minimum voting age was lowered to 18 and when an antiauthoritarian student movement emerged.

In high schools, the Jusos formed school project groups, with the blessing of the party executive in September 1974. They organized seminars and regional conferences for group members, who in 1976 numbered between 42,000 and 50,000 in about 500 groups. By 1980 enrollment had shrunk and about 300 groups remained, primarily in the Gymnasien. [9] One of the groups' chief activities was to issue student newspapers as a way of politicizing more students and making them aware of Juso demands: integrated rather than separate-track high schools, improvements in vocational training, an end to admission quotas for university studies in a number of fields, democratization of course content, more student representation in school government, easing of pupil stress, and opposition to newspaper censorship by school authorities. [10]

While these demands may have seemed reasonable from the students' point of view, they contained political dynamite for educational authorities in the SPD-governed Länder whose policies were being criticized by the project groups. Some groups, not wanting to be identified too closely with the SPD, demanded more autonomy within the Jusos or even independence from them, as happened in West Berlin in 1979. In turn, the party cut off funds to the "renegade" groups. [11]

At the university level, the SPD, in the immediate postwar years, sponsored the creation of the German Socialist Student Federation (Sozialistische Deutsche Studentenbund, SDS), with Helmut Schmidt, among others, as chairman. By 1958, the left wing had gained strength as the anti-nuclear-arms debate intensified; two years later the right wing seceded from the SDS and constituted itself as the Social Democratic University League (Sozialdemokratischer Hochschulbund [SHB]), upon which the SPD broke off connections with the SDS and endorsed the SHB. However, as the SHB also became more radical, the SPD in March 1969 canceled financial support for it, in March 1971 broke off relations with it, and in June 1972 forbade it to use the term "Social Democratic." [12]

During its difficulties with the SHB, the party also had to contend with the "Extraparliamentary Opposition" (APO), emerging in the wake of the 1966 Grand Coalition. The APO was a loose spontaneous amalgamation of pacifist-neutralist, radical democratic, Marxist socialist, and New Left (SDS) groups. The SPD and the Jusos urged university students favoring social democracy to organize to compete with SHB and APO groups. Between 1969 and 1971 the first Juso university groups (Juso-Hochschulgruppen) formed and in 1973 met to coordinate their activities. Their potential membership was large: in 1971, a survey showed that 62 percent of students sympathized with the SPD, although by the end of 1973 that support had shrunk to 45 percent. [13] After 1973, the number of new Juso groups rose swiftly, reaching nearly 100 by the end of 1975. Since then the number has stabilized at between 85 and 90, with a total membership of about 2,500. That figure represents a shrinkage from the mid-1970s, when some chapters had up to 100 active members. [14]

The cyclical interest in the groups among students reflected their degree of sympathy with government policies. In the late 1970s many students, disillusioned with state cuts in education, fewer job prospects, and SPD support of a university framework law that eliminated earlier democratizing reforms, quit the Jusos and joined other organizations or became apolitical. However, the Juso groups maintained their existence, demanding more student self-government, more admission of students from low-income families, study reforms such as "repression-free" and collective learning, and less emphasis on technocratic perspectives. [15] Their goals did not increase membership, but brought them support in student government elections. Competing with Marxist, Christian, and liberal student groups, the Jusos were able to capture about 30 percent of the vote, more than any of the others. If all students who agreed with the Juso positions had supported them, their total would have been even higher. A 1979 survey showed that 38 percent of all students were sympathetic to the SPD; 14 percent, to the CDU; and 14 percent, to the environmentalists. [16] The Jusos had strength in the peak organization of student governments (Vereinigten Deutschen Studentenschaften [VDS]), representing about 800,000 students. In order to maximize their VDS strength, most Juso groups allied themselves with liberal and leftist "spontaneous" groups, a few with communist groups, but none with their "arch-enemy" Christian groups.

The Juso university groups had a good deal of political autonomy; relations to local Juso branches or national heaquarters were not very close. The central office sponsored a working group on universities, issued a socialist theoretical journal, and organized seminars, but usually the same persons participated. Some Juso group leaders found their experience useful as a stepping stone to top Juso leadership. [17] Despite problems, the university groups were useful recruiting agents for the party, which needed the infusion of young articulate people with new ideas and energy.

For a fuller understanding of one of the largest political youth organizations in Western Europe, this brief survey of the Juso organization and its student affiliates must be supplemented by a more detailed examination of its historical development and ideological schisms. Later chapters will provide additional details on Jusos' activities within the party and their effect on the government's domestic and foreign policies.

HISTORICAL DEVELOPMENT

Soon after the war, SPD leaders, as part of reconstructing the party, recruited many young members. In May 1946, the convention authorized the formation of young socialist working groups, which then formed a peak organization, "Young Socialists in the SPD." To prevent a clash between the youth groups and the party, as occurred in the Weimar era, the convention adopted a resolution calling on the groups to remain an integral part of the party. The Jusos served as a base for talented youth to rise within the party and to seek public office. They also helped in electoral campaigns; organized seminars; and scheduled vacation camps, international trips, and political cabarets to convert apolitical youth.

Until the mid-1960s, the Jusos and their elders had common interests. The Jusos endorsed the Bad Godesberg program; they were not overconcerned with theoretical issues but, rather, with educational and vocational issues facing youth. The Jusos of the 1970s viewed them as having been "meek as a lamb," serving the party primarily as "a biological feeder service of Social Democracy." [18] The first rumbling of dissent occurred at the 1963 Juso congress when delegates of the traditional left stronghold of Hesse-South tried in vain to spark discussion of the controversial emergency legislation and the antinuclear campaign. At the

1965 congress, left delegates demanded that the Jusos exert more influence on the party and be allowed more freedom to dissent from it. They unsuccessfully challenged the candidacy of the incumbent Juso chairman (Peter Corterier), who was seen as being too conformist with the SPD establishment. [19]

The Juso left wing gained strength with its opposition to the SPD decision in 1966 to join a CDU/CSU government, its denunciation of the Vietnam war, its recruitment of New Left students from the APO, and its interest in the writings of neo-Marxist theoreticians. At the 1967 Juso congress it was strong enough to elect from its ranks half the executive members but not yet strong enough to beat the conservative candidate for chairman. One year later, the congress endorsed a resolution calling on the SPD to engage in a dialogue with the APO as a means of recruiting New Left students. [20] Brandt gave it his blessing as one way to defuse a potentially destabilizing situation and integrate a restless youth generation into the political mainstream.

The left made a breakthrough at the Munich Juso congress in December 1969—ironically, just at the time that Brandt became chancellor. A majority of delegates elected the 28-year-old Karsten Voigt as chairman. He was head of political education for the Frankfurt People's High School and had been in the SPD only since 1962. The delegates also elected an all left slate to the executive and adopted a program calling for more intraparty democracy and the right to form a faction within the party and asserting the necessity of discussing socialist theory and working for system-changing reforms. The program was sharply critical of the SPD:

> The SPD at the national level has increasingly adapted itself to the existing social conditions and the prevalent consciousness of the West German population. Thereby it has given up its socialist conception in favor of a false pragmatism and in favor of a widespread sterility of party life and party discussion. It has given up its character of a class party in order to allow bourgeois groups to enter and to be elected by them. The ideology of the "people's party" forces all groups represented in the SPD to make compromises already in the preparliamentary sphere. Thus the SPD presently does not represent sharply enough the real interests of the wage-earning segment of the population. [21]

The Old Left in the party was buoyed by the vigorous critique of the SPD; one left liberal writer characterized the "feared and feted" Jusos as "the only relevant socialist force in the Federal Republic." [22] Symbolic of their socialist orientation, the Jusos changed the name of their publication from "Journal of the Young Social Democrats" to "Journal of the Young Socialists in the SPD." Optimistically, they predicted that "we are the SPD of the eighties."

The SPD top officials attempted to block the Juso radical offensive. As early as November 1968 the party council wanted to lower the Juso maximum age from 35 to 30, or even 25, as a way of weeding out the radical militant leaders and members, most of whom were in the 25-to-35 age category. But the Jusos, supported by the SPD centrists who disliked this tactic, were able to defeat the attempt to limit their power within the party.

In April 1970, the SPD went on the offensive to curb the Young Socialists. On the basis of a secret strategy paper written by a former

Juso secretary, it stated:

> The dispute over people's party on the one side and class party on the other is false. Here fronts are built that have long been overcome within the SPD. It is expected of each SPD member to be conscious of the responsibility for solidarity and loyalty. A party which successfully has taken over the leadership of German politics cannot return to the isolation of a class party. This would be tantamount to the abandonment of the political transformation of our society. [23]

In tough language, the SPD executive warned "revolutionaries" that the party stands for reform and evolution and therefore is not a home for them. It reminded Jusos that the party convention determines policy and only its resolutions are binding on all members. If the Jusos do not want to accept this procedure, they must become an independent youth organization free of party ties. The executive admitted that the consequences would be damaging to the party and to the Jusos but said that the Jusos cannot have it both ways. [24]

To underscore the tough policy, on November 14, 1970, the top party organs issued a resolution threatening expulsion of any SPD member who encouraged joint activities by Social Democratic and Communist party members. Typical of the problem facing the party was the decision of the Hamburg Jusos to participate with other left organizations in an action aimed at preventing a city transit fare increase. Because Hamburg was in SPD hands, the action was aimed at party policy. The SPD arbitration commission tried to expel from the party Juso leaders collaborating with Communists, but a higher commission ruled that the leaders would merely lose office for a limited time.

In the wake of the Bremen Juso congress of December 1970, at which the Young Socialists passed radical resolutions on capitalism, defense policy, codetermination, and other issues, the SPD executive again issued a position paper. It defended the party's domestic and foreign policies, answered each Juso resolution, averred the need to make compromises in a democracy, and reminded the Jusos that all party members were to maintain solidarity and refrain from polemics. [25]

The party executive expressed its willingness to enter into serious discussions with the Juso executive during this time. Both sides shunned a total confrontation—the Jusos because they wanted to avoid a break with the party, and the party because it needed youth. Moreover, the party would have lost credibility if it had kept emphasizing the need for reforms and more democratic content in society and then had tried to oust the Jusos. Yet Juso strategy produced a new cold war between them. The Jusos urged their members to begin a "long march through the institutions" and seek to capture them. Many SPD officials, knowing that the institutions included not only those of the government but also those of the party, were not too displeased when SPD right-wingers counter-mobilized to recapture some local branches fallen to the Jusos. SPD officials also feared a confrontation with the Jusos should the latter be successful in their parallel concept of the "double strategy": Mobilize the population for radical "system-changing" rather than "system-maintenance" reforms and at the same time try to gain a majority within the party. [26] The Jusos spent much time discussing the double-strategy concept that became controversial in the party and elsewhere. Their executive formulated the concept as follows:

> In view of a realistic assessment of both the prevailing power relationships and the narrow range of government policies due to the hegemonic position of capital, the Jusos pursue a double strategy, which aims at the transformation of society through a combination of work in the political institutions and mobilization of the population for their own interests. In many cases this means conflict with one's own party; but this is not a policy against the SPD. On the contrary: only the massive pressure of an enlightened and mobilized population can realize democratic socialism and the new social and economic order, as demanded in the Godesberg program. [27]

More specifically, the strategy meant intensive work at all SPD levels to set the political preconditions for a better social order. It meant reforming the party—seeking democratic majority decisions—in order to organize and politicize the population as a way of strengthening the democratic anticapitalist sector. Within the SPD, the Jusos tried to reach this goal through Marxist theoretical analyses, anticapitalist critiques, and provocation of individual situations to make visible the oligarchical decision-making structure, especially at the party base.

The difficulty with the double strategy was that many SPD members did not understand it, and that even within the Juso organization rival factions interpreted it differently, with one deciding that the emphasis must be not on party work but on work done at the community "base."

The anticapitalist critique embodied in the double strategy made it difficult for the Jusos to make significant inroads into many SPD branches where members were more conservative. Hence by the time of the 1970 Saarbrücken SPD convention, the Jusos could claim no more than one-fourth of the delegates. But at least they had a chance in a party forum to articulate their domestic policy demands: increased taxation of the wealthy, increased property taxes and a tax on capital, an end to the system of graded hospital care and private doctors, and an end to private property speculation. Internationally, the Jusos supported Brandt's Ostpolitik but not his acquiescence to United States involvement in Southeast Asia. SPD leaders were not unsympathetic to most of the demands in the domestic sphere but feared that if the party were to adopt them, the middle-class voters would be frightened away and tensions would develop with the FDP coalition partner. Yet the Jusos achieved two limited successes at the national level. The convention agreed to the summoning of a special congress in late 1971 to deal with taxation reforms and to the formation of a commission to work out a long-range party program. [28]

As expected, the Juso offensive did not find enthusiastic public support. In one 1971 survey, two-thirds of the respondents stated that the more the left wins influence within the party the less will be the party's electoral chances. Those surveyed also expressed more sympathy for the conservative SPD leader, then Lord Mayor of Munich, Hans-Jochen Vogel (70 percent), than for the Jusos (13 percent). Not surprisingly, these respondents were more hostile to the Jusos than were SPD voters. The Jusos' goals were considered too radical by 63 percent of the population sample and 52 percent of SPD voters, while 22 percent of the population and 35 percent of SPD voters said the goals were just. [29]

Although the Jusos' hope of creating a socialist consciousness among the public failed, when their demands were concrete and not too radical and the connection between political and economic factors was made clear, they scored a number of successes, especially at the municipal level. In the early 1970s, they demanded more kindergartens, playgrounds, and schools; better transit systems; improved housing; less pollution; and improved vocational education—goals that people could easily identify with and support. Focusing on these goals, the Jusos used a wide array of methods: they gathered signatures, set up information booths, sent out questionnaires, issued press releases, and scheduled meetings and demonstrations. They also organized citizens' initiatives, project and base groups, tenant unions, and action committees. [30] The Juso municipal planks were accepted in principle by party leaders. Many communities and cities put a number of the planks into practice, although budgetary limitations were often a constraint.

How did Jusos envisage creating a social democratic state beyond reforms at the municipal level? Their double strategy and march through the institutions provided some answers. The Jusos tried to convince the lower and middle classes about the true nature of their condition and to activate them politically in an anticapitalist direction. As a next step—so went the dream—the ruling business elite would be forced to make concessions to those demanding more social democracy, including workers who would take over plants closed by management during periods of economic crisis. As part of the grand design, the Jusos nominated left candidates to run on SPD tickets for local, state, and national parliamentary seats. This was a way of ensuring more progressive SPD policies when the candidates were successful against more conservative SPD candidates put up by other party groups.

Factionalism

The Jusos' offensive was weakened when ideological fissures developed within their ranks. From 1971 on, three chief factions battled for supremacy. One major group was the "Reformists" or "Federal Executive Line" (Bundesvorstandslinie), which governed the Jusos for the entire period, excepting 1977 to 1980. Led in the initial years by Karsten Voigt, Wolfgang Roth, and Heidemarie Wieczorek-Zeul, with the support of the theoreticians Johano Strasser and Hermann Scheer, the reformist wing had its strength in Hesse-South, North Rhine-Westphalia, Bavaria, and Baden-Wuerttemberg. It was influenced by the writings of André Gorz, Lelio Basso, Ernst Mandel, and Herbert Marcuse, who had publicized the need for system-changing reforms. It contended that to achieve such reforms, the political consciousness of the people must first be raised by dealing with their daily concerns as tenants, apprentices, or workers. The people must be mobilized, politicized, and organized to ensure their active participation in the long process of transforming the system. This process can be facilitated if democracy is instilled, especially on a decentralized basis, in most societal spheres, ranging from family and party, schools and universities, shops and factories to administration and justice.

The reformists criticized the existing power relationships, the restrictions on democracy, and the government's subservience to powerful minorities. To change these negative features, a majority of the population must be won over to support measures, such as nationalization, designed to transform the capitalist system into a socialist system within the framework of parliamentary democracy. [31] The reformists claimed that the Brandt government's domestic reforms could be incorporated into the forefront of anticapitalist politics.

A second Juso faction vying for political power was the "Stamokaps" (state monopoly capitalism). This group, which surfaced at the 1971 Juso congress, stood farthest left within the SPD. Led by its theoretician, Detlev Albers (Bremen University vice rector in 1977), Berlin lawyer Kurt Neumann, Kurt Wand, and Klaus-Uwe Benneter, the group had strength in Hamburg, Berlin, and North Lower Saxony. Its members—about 20 percent of the Juso membership—split into two subfactions: the "hard" Stamokaps, who agreed to action pacts with communists, and the "soft" Stamokaps, who opposed such pacts and favored a more flexible policy within the Juso movement.

The group's theoretical position, akin to that of the communists, was set forth in the 1971 "Hamburg strategy paper." As capital becomes increasingly concentrated, the state encourages monopolies to exploit natural resources. Because the state aids the monopolies, it becomes an instrument of monopoly capital. As a result, an alliance develops between state functionaries and the owners of production on one side and manual workers and salaried employees on the other. To change the system, the latter groups, aided by the SPD and unions and by citizens' initiatives and youth groups, must assume the offensive. But before the SPD participates, its establishment leaders would need to be replaced by more progressive leaders. [32]

SPD critics of the Stamokaps argued that neither were the links between government and big business so interwoven as charged nor was parliament an instrument of bourgeois monopolists. They said that although, admittedly, the business elite had much power and company profits were excessive, many political decisions were made against this elite. They also argued that for the SPD to become Marxist would mean a loss of members and voters. Partly as an answer to the critics, the Stamokaps issued in 1978 the "Herford theses," modifying the 1971 paper. They viewed the state no longer as the instrument of monopoly bourgeoisie but as one that stood in "contradictory interlock" with the monopolies and that could be moved to represent the interests of the workers in their parliamentary and extraparliamentary struggles. [33]

The third Juso faction, the "Antirevisionists," led by Gerhard Schröder, also constituted about 20 percent of the Juso membership. Its strength, primarily among New Left students, was concentrated in Hannover and Göttingen. The faction criticized SPD social welfare reform policy on the grounds that it is an illusion to believe that the policy will lead to socialism; rather it will perpetuate the workers' link to a strengthened capitalist system. In the process, the SPD, as a government party, will maintain the existing cozy relationship with business and be unable to break its power.

The antirevisionists advocated instead mobilizing and politicizing the working population at the "base," from where it can put pressure on the state. They emphasized the extraparliamentary but nonrevolutionary struggle to weaken the capitalist system, expecting this struggle to be the chief guarantee of a successful transition to socialism. [34]

All factions injected Marxist or neo-Marxist theory into their discussions and were often able to agree on strategy. But the discord over theory did not end, despite repeated pleas for unity. Intense ideological debates took place at congresses and in position papers, especially in the middle 1970s. Reformists and antirevisionists favored an antiauthoritarian, emancipatory movement based on the critical theory of the New Left and the Frankfurt school. The reformists accused the Stamokaps of overestimating the rationality of the capitalist system and not emphasizing enough its crises, of advocating an authoritarian and bureaucratic socialism, of judging the SPD from a false class analysis of society, and of accepting uncritically the theoretical arguments of the German Communist Party. In reply, the Stamokap theorists accused the reformists of being anticommunists who wanted to stifle dissenting views without presenting a viable alternative. They reaffirmed the need to maintain a united front with other leftist organizations. [35]

Renewed Juso-SPD Feud

In 1973, party officials did not try to exploit the rift within the Juso organization but, rather, assailed the Young Socialists publicly for their radical proposals, while at the same time making some concessions (e.g., on land speculation, control of multinational corporations, and the decree banning extremists from public service) in their program. At the 1973 Hannover party convention, Brandt was critical of the Jusos' double strategy, their speaking in sociological and political jargon, and their lack of human solidarity with older party members who had helped rebuild the country and the party since 1945. [36]

After the party convention, the Jusos renewed their discussion about what path to follow. Wolfgang Roth, Juso chairman from 1972 to 1974, a leader of the reformists and town planner by profession, defended his readiness to work within the SPD and to make compromises, but the Juso left assailed him. All factions worked out new anticapitalist models but had difficulty putting them into practice or receiving acknowledgment from party leaders for the positive work they had done in recent years, especially at the municipal level. As a result, there was much frustration among Juso members; their hope of being a radical avant-garde and the SPD of the eighties was fading. Many would have felt ambivalent about an editorial comment concerning their Munich congress in January 1974: "In Munich the Jusos were clearly no longer on the march through the party institutions but on the road toward an existence as an insignificant debating club of disputing theoreticians hopelessly exaggerating their own importance." [37] They would have taken exception to their organization being labeled "insignificant," because they still had enough punch to frequently shake up the SPD. They were able to capture a number of posts in policymaking bodies and to raise issues that the party had sought to keep off its agenda—on investment controls, a ceiling on personal income, free medical services, and nationalization of banks and key industries.

At the Munich Juso congress, the Stamokaps and antirevisionists continued to try to transform the SPD into a socialist party. They opposed a proposal to let the government become involved in investment guidance, for fear this would lead to stabilization of the capitalist system. But they were not strong enough to block the election of 31-year-old Heidemarie Wieczorek-Zeul as the new chairwoman. Known as "Red Heidi," more for the color of her hair than for her politics (she headed the reformist faction), she had joined the SPD in 1965 and was a schoolteacher in Hesse-South.

Once again, in the wake of the 1974 Juso congress and SPD losses in state elections, blamed partly on the Jusos, some SPD leaders mounted a campaign against the Juso radicals. They assailed the Stamokaps who equated an SPD-led government with "agents of monopoly capitalism" and dreamed of smashing the existing state. Conservative SPD officials wanted to expel Juso radicals en masse from the party but were stopped by moderate SPD leaders. All senior leaders, however, supported a ten-point program entitled "The Condition of the Party and its Future Tasks," issued by Brandt on April 2, 1974. The program endorsed an SPD-FDP political new center (moderate liberal) and assailed those who had veered away from democratic socialist tenets. Point 2 noted: "The theoretical foundation of politics is important, but the party is not a debating club; rather, it is responsible for the destiny of a major industrial state. Intraparty discussions must not paralyze the political capacity to act." Point 3 warned that those who maliciously criticize the party and its leaders must leave. [38] The embittered Jusos viewed the declaration and the blame heaped on them for losses in state elections as unfair. They emphasized their solidarity with the party and claimed that wrong government policies were primarily responsible for the election results.

When Schmidt became chancellor, further clashes were inevitable. Juso Chairwoman Wieczorek-Zeul asserted that the new government program containing few reforms "can be accepted with pleasure only by conservatives of all shades." [39] She also criticized continuing SPD calls for unity, moves to discipline or expel dissident Juso members, and attempts by Bavarian SPD leader Bruno Friedrich to dissolve some branches in his district. Party Chairman Brandt emerged as a mediator between conservative SPD leaders, including the new chancellor, and the Jusos. He was instrumental in quashing the Friedrich plan but again warned the Jusos not to become a party within the party.

The Jusos soon realized the futility of pushing for a socialist program, especially with mounting national economic difficulties, and avoided direct attacks on Schmidt. They knew that they could influence the SPD only if they supported Schmidt, whose ability to regain voters for the party was being demonstrated. They agreed to defer theoretical discussions; in one 1974 state election campaign they refrained from calling for immediate reforms and voiced full support of the SPD, but urged it to think more of long-range goals. In brief, the Jusos made a tactical withdrawal in order not to jeopardize their position altogether. In July 1974 they met with older SPD left-wingers, who offered to help them integrate into the party's left wing. Juso theoretician Strasser knew that confronting and winning over conservative forces in society can succeed only with the full support of the SPD. He urged the Jusos to exercise self-restraint.

Not all Juso leaders were as restrained as Strasser. Wieczorek-Zeul, who insisted that the Jusos had not changed their tactics, said: "We do not take back any of the demands we have made." [40] She also accused Schmidt of governing by plebiscite, as if the SPD did not exist, and wondered what social democratic content his policies had. Other Juso leaders accused Schmidt of merely administering capitalism instead of initiating reforms. In turn, Schmidt sharply assailed the Juso position at the September 1974 Hamburg state party convention. He accused the Jusos of "preaching the people right out of the church," and of "philosophizing about socialization or nonsocialization [of industry]," while the world is in danger of an economic crisis. He also asked sarcastically, who is this Heidi (Wieczorek-Zeul) and in what ministries does she sit? [41]

Henning Scherf, chairman of the Bremen Land organization, countering

Schmidt's statements, accused the Chancellor of demagoguery and a desire to isolate the intellectuals in the party. At their 1975 Wiesbaden congress, the Jusos resumed their verbal assault against Schmidt and the SPD. They accused party leaders of transforming the organization into a mere machine for electing the Chancellor. They attacked the party for not producing a democratic socialist alternative in a period of capitalist crisis. They said that in order to capture the youth vote, the party must develop new initiatives, emphasize democratic planning, accept a double strategy, and explain to the voters the sources of crises in the capitalist system.

Despite these critical comments, unity did not prevail at the Wiesbaden Juso congress. The Stamokap and antirevisionist factions tried to push through a resolution accusing the SPD of serving the capitalist cause by attempting to make reforms within the system—an impossible task given its inflexibility. Wieczorek-Zeul, up for reelection as chairwoman, threatened to quit unless delegates accepted a substitute resolution calling on the party to work for reforms leading to democratic socialism. She won reelection, but with 40 percent of the delegates voting against her or abstaining. [42]

As the 1976 national election neared, the Juso factional disputes declined and their leaders were willing to support the party fully during the campaign, even though numerous policy differences remained. [43] The Jusos decided to deal with youth problems, especially unemployment, and to show their social concern in order to attract more young voters to the SPD.

After the election, the Jusos resumed their critical stance. They accused the party of lacking a political perspective and the government of being only a better technocratic alternative to the CDU/CSU. In January 1977 they assailed sections of the government declaration as being contradictory and not concrete enough. They urged more citizen participation in politics and democratization of the economy so that "tomorrow we will not live in an authoritarian police state which will solve crises only through suppression." [44]

SPD leaders retorted that the democratic system remained strong and that given the difficult economic circumstances since 1973, it was remarkable that Schmidt was the only Western leader who had survived parliamentary elections and who could still make some domestic policy reforms. They also reminded the Jusos that the German economic difficulties were caused by worldwide and European crises and that the government declaration represented a necessary compromise with the FDP. [45]

Despite the continuing Juso-party divergences, the SPD leaders were beginning to be less concerned about the Jusos' threat to further stain the party's public image. The new, but reduced, influx of 18-to-20-year-olds into the Juso organization consisted of apolitical or "emotionally liberal-conservative" persons with no interest in the theoretical disputes and even a mild liking for Schmidt. (Juso leaders viewed them as subjects for intensive political indoctrination.) The SPD leaders also knew that the euphoria of the Brandt government era had dissipated and that the Jusos admitted not having a solution for every social problem. The Jusos' resultant concentration on youth problems (a partial return to the pre-1966 period) contributed to a decline in the number of militant members and active local branches, furthered by continuing SPD intimidation or disciplinary actions against some dissidents. The antirevisionists and Stamokaps criticized the reformists for not defying the disciplinary actions. But the three factions maintained their unstable truce and dampened their theoretical debates. They resented the continuing political restrictions imposed on them by the SPD leadership, the conservative trend in the nation, and the failure of SPD resolutions to be enacted into government policy.

The Benneter Affair

When Chairwoman Wieczorek-Zeul, three years in office, approached the Juso age limit of 35, she could no longer be a candidate for reelection. At the March 1977 Hamburg congress, the three factions fought hard for their candidates. In the first round of balloting no one had a majority; in the second round, Klaus-Uwe Benneter, a 30-year-old Berlin lawyer who had been active in the APO in the 1960s and was head of the "hard" faction of the Stamokaps, with the support of the antirevisionists, won by a narrow margin over the candidate of the revisionists. As a result, the executive had four Stamokap and antirevisionist and three revisionist members.

Even though Benneter's victory came as a bombshell to the party, the opposition to the Juso reformists had built up in the previous three years among the Stamokap and antirevisionist factions. They were frustrated over Wieczorek-Zeul's "all-or-nothing" tactics. In 1976 she had threatened not to stand for reelection as chairwoman (knowing that at the time they did not have enough votes to elect their own candidate) unless they voted for less radical resolutions. At the Hamburg congress, one such resolution became the center of a new debate among the three factions—and the SPD. It concerned the advisability of forming political alliances with Communist action groups. This time another intra-Juso compromise was worked out: under certain circumstances, if the Jusos had contributed to the organizational preparation and formulation of slogans for contemplated actions, they would be permitted to work with action committees in which Communists participated. [46] The compromise resolution intensified the strain between Jusos and SPD. The party had always been opposed to demonstrations and direct actions with Communists. It feared their possible radical nature and their reinforcing the conservatives' argument that the SPD was soft on communism. The Jusos, on the other hand, knowing that they were not strong enough to initiate direct actions themselves, did not consider alliances with Communists as damaging if both held the same view on an issue. [47]

The new Juso chairman favored joint actions with Communists as a way of preventing their taking over the social action field. Challenging the SPD, Benneter asserted that on May 21, 1977 he would be at the head of one of several scheduled demonstrations sponsored by the Committee for Peace, Disarmament and Cooperation. [48] Party Secretary Bahr, who labeled the committee as Communist-dominated, issued an ultimatum to the Juso executive: unless it abandoned the plan to join the demonstrations, it would have to face the inevitable consequences. The Juso executive yielded and decided to organize its own demonstrations with other noncommunist groups. [49]

Despite this tactical retreat, Benneter seemed bent on a collision course with the SPD. He blamed it for a "foundering of illusionary reform politics in view of the capitalist economic crisis," for abandoning social democratic content in government policy, and for favoring national and international monopolies. [50] In an interview in the left journal Konkret (May 1977), Benneter stated that SPD membership was not a necessity for the Young Socialists to which they would hold fast in every instance and that from a class perspective the Christian Democrats were class enemies, while Communists were political adversaries. The SPD reaction was swift and unprecedented. On April 26, its executive first made a futile request to Benneter to rescind the interview or resign. Then it suspended him from office for three months and ordered that party expulsion proceedings be initiated. In justification, Brandt claimed that Benneter's interview statements were incompatible with SPD principles and had done great harm to the party and to the Jusos, most of whom wanted "to fight for more freedom, justice, and solidarity within the party." [51]

National press and radio commentary supported the SPD action. The Hannoversche Allgemeine Zeitung praised the uncommonly fast and hard move: "The party desperately needs this liberating action to give itself greater leeway for internal reform and reorganization." [52] The radio station Westdeutscher Rundfunk noted: "The tough action of the SPD committee against . . . Benneter shows that things are by no means as bad as they often might seem to be in regard to the defensive strength of social democracy and its will to assert itself." [53] Bavarian Radio queried why a part of the middle-class youth showed such a propensity for socialism and Marxism. It stated that every democracy has to develop forces that work toward the integration of its youth into the system. [54]

The Juso executive, however, contended that Benneter's suspension from office had been a flagrant SPD administrative interference in internal Juso afairs, especially when the chairman had been democratically voted into office, and that Juso activities would be hampered considerably by this move. It also noted that the real problems lay with the party or with the government which had broken its promise to pensioners after the 1976 election, had been unable to solve unemployment, had conducted unconstitutional wiretapping actions, and whose leaders in Hesse were involved in financial scandals. [55] The Juso executive position was not shared by the Juso board, on which the reformists were still a majority. In an April 30 declaration, the board members reaffirmed Juso ties to the party. [56]

Many Juso branches initiated solidarity actions for Benneter, gathering signatures to protest the SPD action. But when Bahr threatened Juso executive members with a disciplinary move if they decided on a central solidarity action and when a left SPD group of deputies counseled them to avoid a personal conflict with the party, they refrained from exacerbating the already tense situation. However, the SPD took punitive action against Baden-Wuerttemberg executive members who had refused to cancel an invitation to Benneter to speak at a political rally in Stuttgart. Similarly, when sixty-two Juso members in Hamburg signed a statement supporting Benneter in May, the SPD Land executive gave them the ultimatum of withdrawing their signatures by June 21 or leaving the party. If they refused, the party would begin expulsion proceedings.

No doubt, SPD leaders had decided on stringent action against uncooperative Jusos as a way to get rid of them. For the few expelled, the party would gain many more voters who had rejected its "radicalism." But the leaders did not endorse the proposal of one conservative SPD mayor to expel the entire Stamokap wing from the SPD. Such a step, they reasoned, would make it even more difficult to attract youth into the party. Some moderate critics of the SPD, however, argued that the party had overreacted and created a near-panic situation. In any case, the Benneter affair came opportunely for the problem-ridden party because it could use him as a convenient scapegoat. [57]

While the confrontation between the Jusos and their parent organization continued, Benneter took his case to a Berlin Land civil court. He claimed that the SPD executive action against him should be voided because Bahr had violated the party statute by not convening executive members into session on April 26. Instead, to save time, Bahr had telephoned the members for their views. On May 13, the court sustained Benneter's claim. The Jusos thereupon insisted that their chairman had been reinstated, but the SPD executive, angry that Benneter had used the state judicial machinery to settle an intraparty matter, met immediately in formal session to again remove him from his post and to demand his expulsion from the party. On June 2, the SPD Berlin Land arbitration commission expelled him from the party; he appealed the decision, lost it, and was finally expelled in the fall.

A New Beginning

The Jusos could not meet in congress session until February 1978 to choose a new chairman—after having governed without one from April 1977. For weeks before the congress, much behind-the-scenes maneuvering took place to find acceptable candidates. As in 1977, the revisionists had a plurality of delegates but were unable to get support for their candidate from either of the other two factions in order to have a majority. Hence the "negative coalition" of Stamokaps and antirevisionists was formed again. It was strong enough to elect as chairman Gerhard Schröder, a 33-year-old Hannover lawyer and head of the antirevisionist faction, and to pass a number of resolutions critical of government and SPD policy. Nevertheless, party chiefs were relieved that Schröder had become chairman, because he was seen as a moderate, whose faction was not interested in cooperating with communist groups. Bahr promised the Jusos that the party would be tolerant of them and urged their tolerance of the SPD. [58]

Despite an auspicious new beginning in relations with the SPD, the Jusos' problems continued. An internal report of a Juso district executive (Lower Rhine) for 1978/1979 pinpointed some of their difficulties. It noted that there were not enough qualified Jusos to provide new blood for the party. There was danger that the Juso organization was drying up; in many branches and university groups only functionaries were active. Juso influence in the cities was weak, as shown by the few Jusos who were elected delegates to the subdistrict party conventions. They had more chances in rural areas, where the party lacked enough personnel. But, in general, their influence on the party had declined in recent years.

According to the district executive, the Jusos' theoretical views had no consequences for their practical work. They had insufficiently discussed alternative lifestyles, the environment, ecology, energy, and growth. They had become mere supernumeraries whose links to the unions and the party left were weak. A surprising number who were members of a DGB union had been inactive in the organization, because few subdistricts had active shop and union groups. Although membership in university groups was increasing, the number of activists was "dismayingly" low. Thus the activists who were forced to work primarily on university problems had developed narrow horizons, which gave nonuniversity SPD members the impression that the Jusos were a "bunch of university exotics." The executive concluded its pessimistic report with a plea for more work at the local level, where the interests of the citizens were directly affected. The importance of Juso work done already at that level had never been sufficiently publicized to the public and the SPD. [59]

Nationally, Juso chiefs faced additional problems. New members, who in the past had become the activists, were less interested in politics. The links between Jusos and young SPD members, including manual workers, who were not active in the Juso organization, were still tenuous. In addition, the stream of resolutions passed at numerous Juso congresses and meetings had little impact on the party or the public, including youth. As increasingly fewer young people showed an interest in politics, the Jusos found it more difficult than ever to reach this crucial segment of the voters. They wanted instead to continue providing initiatives and alternative policies to the party left in its battle with the SPD establishment. But they kept demanding fundamental changes in the capitalist system that were too utopian even for the party left under existing conditions. As a result of this all-or-nothing strategy, fatigue and frustration set in among many Juso members, compounded by a growing conservative movement in the Federal Republic that labeled the left as sympathetic to terrorism.

In spite of these problems, the Juso leadership did not drop its challenges to the party establishment. Chairman Schröder, who was easily reelected for another term in 1979, maintained that conflicts with the party were necessary if they were based on honest differences. To increase Juso strength, he attempted to minimize the differences within his organization and to produce a pragmatically oriented agenda: eradication of youth unemployment, maintenance and extension of democratic rights, and no further nuclear reactor construction. [60] He criticized the Chancellor's crisis management: "Objectively, the danger exists that the social base of the party slips away because a very technocratic policy is being pursued." [61] Emphasis on such a policy means that the Jusos and the SPD will be relegated to the background and lose much of their raison d'être. The Juso chairman maintained that thereby Schmidt "saws off the branch on which in the future the Social Democrats should sit." [62] Schmidt did not make any attempt to forestall such public criticisms by meeting privately with Juso leaders to explain his policies. Rather, he alienated them further at the 1979 SPD convention when he said that it would be useful if the Young Socialists were to set up bird protection areas and engage in other such activities.

Yet during Schröder's term of office (1978-1980), relations with SPD leaders other than Schmidt improved considerably. The party gave more support to the Jusos and restricted their political activities less. In this period of consolidation and renewal the Jusos strengthened their links to high school students, apprentices, and women. They became increasingly active in the unions and were able to attract more workers, as well as young employees and public servants, into their ranks. The new members, primarily in the 16-to-25 age category, came from urban areas. Most had not been active politically before, but now became the new activists, little interested in theoretical discussions still conducted by a small core of older Jusos.

For the Jusos, the late 1970s produced a new mood of pragmatism and an end to theoretical bickering. Symbolically, a reformist-wing leader, Willi

Piecyk, was elected Juso chairman at the May 1980 Hannover congress. Piecyk, head of an adult education school in Schleswig-Holstein, defeated, in this instance with antirevisionist support, the Stamokap candidate. The party's continued backing of the Jusos was demonstrated by the appearance of Brandt, who addressed the delegates for the first time in five years. The party's attention to the Jusos was, of course, motivated by the national election scheduled later that year, but also by the desperate need to hold young people in the party and recruit new ones.

A BALANCE SHEET

In 1973, the Economist provided a dramatic commentary on the Young Socialists:

> The Jusos, although probably now past their peak, provide the most fascinating political phenomenon in modern Germany—the picture of an epic ideological wrangle in full spate inside the party which dominates government. Such fights for the soul of a major political party in modern times have invariably taken place in opposition, not during the years of power. [63]

During the 1970s the wrangles were not always so intensive; yet even in comparatively calm times the basic policy differences remained, glossed over for such practical reasons as the need to maintain unity for the sake of elections.

Juso influence on the party also has varied over time. On the credit side, as part of an SPD-sanctioned strategy, the Jusos were able to attract and integrate into the party—and thereby into German society—tens of thousands of APO students, some of whom otherwise might have become a permanent revolutionary faction trying to drastically change societal institutions through extraparliamentary confrontations. Instead, as Juso members they helped to produce electoral victories for the SPD while at the same time democratizing the party's practices and putting theoretical discussions back on its agenda. In the early 1970s, as part of their broad criticism of society, the Jusos convinced the party to initiate municipal and educational reforms. They were able to make deputies more accountable and, in the late 1970s, raised important defense and energy policy issues.

On the debit side, the Jusos were unable to produce a proper mix of theory and practice. They often lacked an adequate strategy for dealing with social problems or became isolated from the party mainstream when they discussed Marxist theory, which in turn led to damaging factionalism. Before 1972, their expectations for a radical change of the system were at a peak; thereafter their disappointments and frustrations were great, leading to an exodus of members who were unable to convince most SPD adherents and the bulk of the population that their goals for a more just and humane society under a socialist system should not be postponed forever. In the SPD, the Jusos had some sympathy among students and the 18-to-29-year-old group but less among manual workers, who filled few Juso leadership positions. Moreover, when able Juso officials were coopted into the party leadership, those remaining were overworked. Juso officials prepared position papers on a host of issues but often failed to discuss them with the membership or to implement them vigorously, or they ran into insurmountable opposition. [64]

Whether the Jusos can solve their own problems and help to solve those facing the nation in the years to come, even when the SPD is in opposition, remains to be seen. Their task is difficult, but their case for necessary changes in the public sphere is compelling to many in the Federal Republic.

NOTES

1. Infratest survey, 1977, p. 17. Dieter Stephan calculated that there were only 16,250 activists in 1977, a drop from 27,080 in 1972. As activists, he included those who attend a Juso meeting at least once a month (Jungsozialisten: Stabilisierung nach langer Krise? Theorie und Politik 1969-1979—Eine Bilanz [Bonn: Neue Gesellschaft, 1979], pp. 98-100, 104). In an earlier 1970 SPD poll, 29 percent of the Jusos said they were active members; of the inactive ones, 28 percent said no branch existed in their area and 18 percent said they had no time (SPD, executive, Rundschreiben No. 754-3001, cited by "Strategie und Taktik der Jungsozialisten, August 1971," Berichte des DI [Deutschen Industrie-instituts] zur Politik, V (P), No. 2, 1971, pp. 4-5).

2. Infas survey, 1977, p. 55; Stephan, p. 109.

3. Frankfurter Rundschau, Feb. 26, 1972. A 1970 SPD poll, however, shows twice as high a percentage (14) were pupils and students, while 5 percent were apprentices; 19 percent, workers and employees in private industry; 12 percent, employees in public service; 22 percent, civil servants ("Strategie und Taktik der Jungsozialisten, August 1971," pp. 4-5).

4. Stephan, pp. 101, 103.

5. Stephan estimates that 1,720 groups were not active (ibid., p. 100).

6. For details, see Juso executive, Handbuch für die Jungsozia-listenarbeit (Bonn, 1971); Bundeskongressbeschlüsse: Jungsozialisten in der SPD, 1969-1976 (Bonn-Bad Godesberg, 1978); Organisations-Leitfaden (n.d.); Richtlinien der Jungsozialisten, (June 1975).

7. Fourteen percent gave no answer. Jusos, "Befragung Junger Sozialdemokraten: Ergebnisse einer Erhebung bei SPD-Mitgliedern unter 35 Jahren, Juni 1970" (hectographed). See also Paul Ackermann, "Die Jugendorganisationen der politischen Parteien," Demokratisches System und politische Praxis der Bundesrepublik, eds. Gerhard Lehmbruch, Klaus von Beyme, Iring Fetscher (Munich: Piper, 1971), p. 310.

8. Jusos, Informationsdienst, No. 10, Oct. 1977, p. 3. The age category was from 14 to 24, but the younger ones could not join a political party.

9. Ibid., No. 12, Dec. 1976; Schröder letter to SPD executive and council, Apr. 21, 1980.

10. Vorwärts, May 27, 1976.

11. Joachim Hofmann, Die Schülerabeit der Jungsozialisten (Bonn-Bad Godesberg: Neue Gesellschaft, 1976), pp. 48-49. For a discussion of the Berlin situation, see Berliner Stimme, Nov. 3, 1979.

12. William D. Graf, German Left since 1945 (Cambridge: Oleander Press, 1976), pp. 229-231; SHB, press release, July 17, 1973. The SHB opposed emergency legislation because it feared that the executive branch

would become too powerful in a national crisis situation.

13. Infratest cited by Die Zeit, Mar. 1974.

14. Richard Meng, Juso-Hochschulgruppen: Geschichte, Praxis, Perspektiven (Giessen: Focus, 1979), pp. 21, 73, 89; Der Spiegel, Feb. 7, 1977; personal interviews with Juso leaders, Bonn, various dates.

15. Juso Hochschulgruppe Frankfurt, "Wer ist und was will die Hochschulgruppe der Jungsozialisten in der SPD," June 1977.

16. Unidentified survey cited by Meng, pp. 95-96.

17. Ibid., pp. 108-109, 112.

18. Rudolf Schöfberger, "Die Jungsozialisten sind die SPD der achtziger Jahre," Quo vadis SPD? Aktuelle Beiträge zur Mobilisierung der Sozialdemokratie, ed. Rolf Seeliger (Munich: Seeliger, 1971), p. 109. For a history of the Jusos, see Gert Börnsen, Innerparteiliche Opposition (Jungsozialisten und SPD) (Hamburg: Runge, 1969); Christoph Butterwegge, Juso und SPD (Hamburg: Runge, 1975); Stephan, passim.

19. Butterwegge, Juso und SPD, pp. 26-27, 32.

20. Helmut Bilstein, et al., Organisierter Kommunismus in der Bundesrepublik Deutschland (Opladen: Leske and Budrich, 1975), pp. 28 ff.

21. SPD, executive, j 1, Reihe Jugend, Heft 1 (Bonn 1970), p. 9.

22. Walter Jens, quoted in Welt der Arbeit, Mar. 4, 1977.

23. SPD, executive, j 1, Reihe Jugend, Heft 1, p. 5. The secretary was Ernst Eichengrün.

24. Ibid., pp. 6 ff.

25. SPD, executive, j 2, Reihe Jugend, Heft 2 (Bonn 1971). For a conservative critique of Jusos, see Emil-Peter Müller, Juso-Sozialismus: Programm und Strategie der Jungsozialisten in der SPD (Cologne: Deutsche Industrieverlags-GmbH, 1972).

26. Hermann Scheer, Johano Strasser, Heidemarie Wieczorek-Zeul, "Zehn Jahre Juso-Doppelstrategie," Forum d s, No. 8 (1979), pp. 33-46; Stephan, pp. 28-29; Butterwege, Juso und SPD, p. 81; Horst Heimann, Theoriediskussion in der SPD (Frankfurt/Main and Cologne: Europäische Verlagsanstalt, 1975), pp. 169 ff.

27. Der Spiegel, Apr. 10, 1972, p. 88.

28. SPD, Parteitag 1970, passim.

29. Fifteen percent of the population sample and 13 percent of the SPD voters gave no answer (Emnid-Institut survey commissioned by Der Spiegel [Mar. 1, 1971]).

30. Häse and Müller, pp. 283-288.

31. Ibid., pp. 280-281; Hans Kremendahl, Nur die Volkspartei ist mehrheitsfähig: Zur Lage der SPD nach der Bundestagswahl 1976 (Bonn-Bad Godesberg: Neue Gesellschaft, 1977), pp. 56-59.

32. Stamokap und Godesberg: Auseinandersetzung und sozialdemokratische Praxis und Theorie (Bonn-Bad Godesberg: Neuer Vorwärts, 1977); David P. Conradt and Ferdinand F. Mueller, "West Germany's Social Democrats since 1969: Factions, Policies, and Electoral Development" (Paper read at the annual meeting of the American Political Science Association, Chicago, 1976), pp. 9-10.

33. Lothar Kramm, Stamokap—eine kritische Abgrenzung (Bonn-Bad Godesberg: Neue Gesellschaft, 1974), pp. 50-52; Stephan, p. 95.

34. Conrad and Mueller, pp. 10-11; Kremendahl, pp. 65-68; "SPD und Doppelstrategie, Diskussionsthesen der Jungsozialisten Göttingen-Stadt" (n.d., hectographed).

35. Reformist accusation against Stamokaps appeared in Strasser position paper "Zur Theorie und Praxis des Juso-Bundesvorstandes," issued

by Juso executive, January 1973. Stamokap reply submitted to Juso congress in "Anmerkungen zur Theorie und Praxis des Juso-Bundesvorstandes" (hectographed). Cf. Butterwege, Juso und SPD, pp. 107-108.

36. SPD, Parteitag 1973, p. 105.

37. Süddeutsche Zeitung, Jan. 28, 1974.

38. Full text in SPD, intern-dokumente, No. 6, Beilage zu "intern," No. 6/74, Apr. 4, 1974.

39. Süddeutsche Zeitung, May 22, 1974.

40. Ibid., Aug. 9, 1974.

41. Neue Zürcher Zeitung, Sept. 23, 1974; New York Times, Oct. 4, 1974.

42. SPD, presse und information, 120/75, Feb. 28, 1975; Stuttgarter Zeitung, Mar. 1, 1975; Süddeutsche Zeitung, Mar. 3, 1975; Der Spiegel, Mar. 10, 1975.

43. Juso 2/76; "Jungsozialisten, Bundeskongress, 26.-28. März 1976, Dortmund, Presse-Dokumentation" (hectographed); Berliner Extradienst, No. 26, Mar. 30, 1976; Juso, Informationsdienst, No. 4/76; Vorwärts, June 17, 1976.

44. Süddeutsche Zeitung, Jan. 22, 1977.

45. Ibid.

46. Ibid., Mar. 21, 1977; Stephan, 83-86; SPD informiert, Bezirk Hannover, No. 43, Mar. 30, 1977.

47. Vorwärts, Apr. 14, 1977.

48. Frankfurter Rundschau, Feb. 5, 1977.

49. Süddeutsche Zeitung, March 29, 1977.

50. Frankfurter Allgemeine Zeitung, March 22, 1977.

51. Brandt letter to SPD district and subdistrict officials, Apr. 28, 1977. See SPD, Pressemitteilung, 189/77, 190/77, Apr. 27, 1977; 192/77, Apr. 28, 1977; Süddeutsche Zeitung, Apr. 28, 1977.

52. Hannoversche Allgemeine Zeitung, Apr. 28, 1977.

53. Westdeutscher Rundfunk, Apr. 27, 1977.

54. Radio Bayern, Apr. 26, 1977.

55. Jusos, Pressemitteilung, Apr. 28, 1977.

56. The board's vote was fourteen to six (ibid., Apr. 30, 1977).

57. Der Spiegel, May 23, 1977.

58. Jusos, executive, Beschlüsse--Bundeskongress der Jungsozialisten Hofheim 1978; Bundeskongress '78, Hofheim: Aktionsprogramm; Süddeutsche Zeitung, Feb. 13, 1978.

59. Jusos, "Rechenschaftsbericht des Bezirksvorstandes der Jungsozialisten in der SPD, Bezirk Niederrhein, Zeitraum: April 1978 bis Mai 1979" (hectographed).

60. Jusos, "Beschlüsse--Bundeskongress der Jungsozialisten, Aschaffenburg 1979, 30.3—1.4. '79"; Süddeutsche Zeitung, Mar. 31-Apr. 1, 1979; Apr. 2, 1979.

61. Der Spiegel, Mar. 26, 1979, p. 74.

62. Stern, Mar. 29, 1979.

63. The Economist, Dec. 1, 1973.

64. The Jusos often had the support of the left-oriented Socialist Youth of Germany—the Falcons, a semi-autonomous organization of 150,000 mostly working-class youths ranging in age from 13 to 20. The Falcons have only a loose association with the SPD, although they receive some financial support and the Falcon chairman attends SPD executive meetings (personal interviews with four Falken leaders, Bonn, Apr. 1, 1980).

65. Wolf-Dieter Narr, Hermann Scheer, Dieter Spöri, SPD—Staatspartei oder Reformpartei? (Munich:Piper, 1976), pp. 129-146. See also speech by Scheer to Land Baden-Wuerttemberg Juso conference, Dec. 20, 1975, reprinted in Frankfurter Rundschau, Jan. 8, 1976.

6
Social Democratic Workers and Trade Unions

Individuals and groups compete for power in all major organizations and at all levels of society. When the Young Socialists began their march through the SPD institutions in the late 1960s, the SPD workers knew that they in turn would have to organize their own interest group within the party to counter the Juso offensive and put pressure on the party to establish closer links with the trade unions. This chapter concerns itself with the constituent Association of Workers and the party's symbiotic ties to the major union organization—the German Trade Union Federation (DGB).

In this study we assume that as the party becomes increasingly bourgeoisified and loses its historic character as a worker's party closely linked to its fraternal union partner, intraparty group tensions are bound to mount, even though the party seeks to aggregate the various interests. Therefore the Social Democratic blue-collar workers, on the defensive, will compete for power with the new middle-class groups, including youth, that make up a considerable segment of a more heterogenous and less class-conscious SPD.

We also assume that when the SPD is in political opposition, its links to the DGB are bound to be relatively harmonious, but when it is in the government, its links to the DGB are bound to weaken. Then the government, under multiple domestic and international constraints and claiming to represent a national interest, will sometimes initiate policies inimical to DGB interests. In addition, the SPD, intent on maintaining itself in power, will need to appeal for support from nonunion groups whose interests may clash with those of the DGB.

Finally, we assume that as the role of the government increases in economic affairs, the DGB and the business community become key actors in the emergent neocorporatist network, in which the three institutions make joint decisions on incomes and social policies. The network consists of an informal and formal consultation and advisory system on the periphery of the parliamentary system. As a result, the governing parties—in this instance SPD and FDP—become less important in shaping the nation's domestic affairs, creating another set of difficulties between the parties and the government. [1]

THE ASSOCIATION OF WORKERS

The blue- and white-collar workers have constituted the largest group within the party. Because officials viewed workers' interests as being more than adequately represented in the party's programs and policies, they were most reluctant to agree to the formation in 1967 of two regional associations of Social Democratic unionists. It took another four years for an SPD reform commission to urge the party to establish a nationwide coordinating unit for the existing SPD shop groups (Betriebsgruppen) in factories. Thereafter, at two party-sponsored conferences, workers' representatives demanded a more formal association.

On June 24, 1972, the party executive finally approved the creation of an Association of Workers (Arbeitsgemeinschaft für Arbeitnehmerfragen [AfA]). Its formation was proof of the extent to which the party had moved from its proletarian origins; ironically, the former "workers' party" had to organize a special constituent group for workers' questions. The guidelines stipulated that the AfA was to bring into the party more workers in the shops and employees in administrative units, support Social Democrats in the unions and the shop councils, establish more shop groups, receive information about party policies, and convey information about workers' interests to the party leaders. [2]

Party chiefs had other reasons for creating the AfA than those publicly proclaimed. They wanted it to serve as a counterweight to the increasing Juso influence within the party. In May 1973, Helmut Schmidt, worried about the "silent majority" being manipulated by the Jusos, stated at a Dortmund conference that workers could not leave theory discussion within the party only to academicians. Friedhelm Farthmann, SPD deputy and union functionary, said that the AfA should be the "last bastion against the intellectual undermining of the party." [3] More colorfully, a union steel worker (who was a Juso executive member) told his Juso colleagues: "Comrades, no worker will understand the nonsense that you have decided on here." [4] AfA leaders, however, publicly denied a bias against Jusos. One stated: "We are not a cheap bastion for pragmatists and 'sewer workers' [the nickname for the conservative bloc in the SPD Fraktion] against progressive forces." AfA Chairman Helmut Rohde, then parliamentary state secretary in the Ministry of Labor, also rejected the Juso claim of a bias. In concluding a nonaggression pact with Juso Chairman Roth, he pleaded for an end to the division between Jusos and workers: "It is not right that some deliver the theory and others do the dirty work." [5]

The AfA was also created to keep alienated workers within the party, especially in SPD strongholds and university cities where the Jusos were capturing the local branches, and where the workers, still voting for the SPD, had transferred their activity to the unions.

The SPD attempt to let the silent majority speak up in the AfA backfired at the Duisburg AfA convention in October 1973. Most delegates, whose average was 40, were not leftists who wanted to change the system but were more radical than the leadership had assumed. Many came from the Ruhr coal and steel region; others from the public service, especially Hamburg and Berlin. They adopted motions calling for active government intervention in companies' investment policies, a price freeze on gasoline and transportation, the nationalization of banks and market-dominating industries (as demanded earlier by the DGB), and full codetermination. On the last issue, they were critical of SPD concessions to the FDP, but

Brandt argued that compromises had to be made in order to achieve some gains.

The AfA demands should not have shocked the SPD high command. Since 1967 new and young union cadres, who had also become active in the SPD, were replacing some of the Old Guard members, who, incidentally, had not always been so conservative. These cadres reflected an unrest among rank and file about SPD policies that could not be bottled up for very long. [6]

The Organization

As with the other constituent associations, the hierarchical structure of the AfA parallels that of the SPD. There were in the mid-1970s perhaps 1,800 to 2,800 liaison persons in shops and firms and 1,200 shop groups of which only 300 were active. Thus about 10 percent of the total number of firms, mostly the larger ones, had some AfA representation. Many of the groups were in public sector firms and only a minority in private industry. [7]

As a result, the AfA membership has been modest. Although in 1977 about 600,000 SPD members were workers and employees, just 50,000 (8.3 percent) viewed themselves as AfA members. Of these 25,000 claimed to have been active in the groups or as liaison persons. AfA leaders were concerned because this was less than one in twenty SPD workers or employees and because most of the active members were salaried employees and civil servants. [8]

The SPD has not been very successful with its work in the plants. The shop groups date back to the late 1940s but were moribund in the 1960s because the party emphasized residence rather than workplace as the center of activity. Thereafter, some groups served more as social than as political clubs, with few meetings scheduled in a year. They had difficulty recruiting young workers, who were often apolitical or dissatisfied with government policies. For instance, in the Ford company plant near Cologne, the SPD group in 1977 had 468 members out of a total of more than 31,000 employees. According to one group member, it was hard to mobilize passive workers whose attitude was that "the little man keeps losing." [9]

But there have been other problems. Because no partisan activity is allowed inside plants, the groups have to meet on the outside, although their members could informally try to identify SPD members and recruit new members within the plants. If there is no group, then the SPD seeks to have a presence in the plant through its liaison people or its members elected on union slates in the shop councils (which serve as workers' advisory bodies to management). To form a new group, the AfA schedules well-advertised meetings immediately at the end of a workshift, at which a speaker discusses work problems. Its groups publish up to eighty shop newspapers, with a circulation of 250,000 to 300,000 in the larger firms. These contain information for workers about SPD and government policies. The AfA also prints several issues of Debatte, with a circulation of 2.5 million, to be distributed at plant gates. It organizes trips to Bonn for shop councillors, liaison persons, and youth representatives. In addition, each year it organizes 300 to 400 day, weekend, and week-long seminars, at which economic and social issues are mainly discussed. [10]

For the AfA, the shop work has been the most important activity, but it also has organized about 300 working groups in local areas and subdistricts, as well as committees and conventions at the Land, district, and national levels. The link to the DGB unions has been strong. At the 1979 AfA convention, for instance, 225 of the 315 delegates were DGB functionaries, most of them either shop or personnel councillors, including many chairmen. Other delegates were members of local, state, and national parliaments. [11] But the AfA has had to be cautious in its relations with the unions, where self-consciousness is high and where other political parties also vie for the workers' allegiance. It knows that many union members who vote for the SPD sympathize with its aspirations but have no time to work for it. The AfA has maintained contacts not only with the DBG and its constituent unions but also with a small rival Catholic labor federation, with the Salaried Employees Union (DAG) social democratic working group, and with the executive of the Protestant Association for Workers to discuss workers' problems.

The AfA has also tried to maintain close contacts with other SPD associations and the party itself. After initial difficulties, talks with the Jusos became more productive; for example, in 1977, on such issues as youth unemployment, vocational education, and elections of delegates to national youth organizations. The AfA talked with the Association of Social Democratic Women about vocational education, especially for women, and about the need for more women to work in the AfA. [12] One test of AfA effectiveness has been its linkage with the SPD. As noted earlier, few workers were elected to party offices and parliaments in comparison with their strength in the party. For instance, in Rhineland-Palatinate, only three AfA representatives sat on the eighteen-member Land executive and even fewer in the Land's districts. [13] The AfA has repeatedly appealed to its members to become more politically active in the party, but relatively few have responded, except at national election time in 1976 and 1980, when membership mobilization was at its highest and when AfA told its members that the social gains must be safeguarded by an SPD-led government. [14]

Relations with the SPD-FDP government were poor at times, primarily because of AfA claims that the SPD cabinet members made too many concessions to the probusiness FDP. Ironically, this happened to Rohde who, as a cabinet member (Minister of Education from 1974 to 1978), tried to represent AfA interests in the cabinet but at the same time had to bow to its discipline and accept policies not always palatable to him. The AfA has also had problems with SPD cabinet members, such as Labor Minister Herbert Ehrenberg who it expected would uphold the workers' interests. There was, for example, a 1979 government ruling, supported by Ehrenberg's ministry, that after a certain period, an unemployed worker would have to accept a lower-level job or be ready to relocate. As a result of considerable union, AfA, and SPD pressure, the cabinet modified the proposal. The conflict produced much bitterness, which was only partly lifted when Ehrenberg appointed a new section chief who sympathized with Rohde and the unions. [15]

The AfA's demands on the government have centered primarily on economic and social issues. In 1978 and 1979, because of persistent high unemployment, it suggested a workweek limited to forty hours with minimum overtime, improved vocational training in conjunction with adding a tenth obligatory school year, a more balanced economic policy, a federal development plan that would protect existing jobs and create new ones in the 1980s, and regular submission of labor market reports to the public.

The AfA warned the government that subsidies to the private sector must be tied to controls and to job security guarantees and must allow workers' shop representatives a voice in management decisions. On energy, it cautiously agreed to a nuclear option, partly because of the pressure of workers in the nuclear industry. [16]

The tension between AfA and government bubbling under the surface spilled over at the 1979 AfA convention. The AfA had invited the left-leaning Hamburg Mayor, Hans-Ulrich Klose (SPD), to give the keynote address. Schmidt viewed the invitation to Klose as an affront, because they had clashed on several previous occasions, most notably over Klose's characterization of the West German state, with its close links to the monopolies, as a "repair shop" for capitalism. Schmidt, who had not been pleased by Klose's partial and temporary endorsement of the Stamokap theory, declined AfA's invitation to speak at the convention, where he had always appeared in order to drum up workers' electoral support for the party. He did not want to precipitate another clash with Klose—and Rohde—who were going to introduce an economic proposal that he could not accept. The proposal, as endorsed by convention delegates, called on the government to create federal and Länder structural councils that would set up development plans for each sector, within which private but government-controlled investment plans would operate. Representatives of the government, business, and the unions would sit on the councils. Klose and Rohde saw this proposal as a step toward more democracy in the economy, but Schmidt disliked the components dealing with planning and control of private investment decisions. However, Brandt and other SPD leaders who were present at the convention implicitly supported the AfA. [17]

The AfA's assertiveness in the late 1970s was a replay of its 1973 beginning. It made bold economic and structural proposals that reminded government chiefs of earlier unacceptable Juso proposals. By the end of the decade, the AfA had partly replaced the Jusos as the SPD organization putting pressure on the government to change its policies. Ironically, the pragmatically oriented AfA, still not interested in theoretical discussions, was turning against the pragmatic Schmidt, who was putting a brake on proposals to help the embattled workers. Rohde, attempting to push the SPD into the battle against the government, said: "Now politics must come again to the fore in the SPD." [18]

The AfA claimed to have scored some achievements in the passage of laws on social welfare, a shop constitution, codetermination, humanization of the workplace, vocational education, and protection for workers. The gains could not have been made if the unions and the SPD had not put simultaneous pressure on the government. The remark of a delegate at the 1979 AfA convention that "in the SPD, nothing runs anymore without the AfA" is exaggerated—but not the comment of the Metal Workers Union journal: "The weight of AfA within the SPD has without a doubt risen. SPD workers are no longer the voiceless crew of hangers of posters and distributors of flyers. They vigorously represent their demands and think of the future." [19]

THE TRADE UNIONS

A people's party must rely on major groups for membership and electoral support. The SPD and AfA look to the trade unions as a prime target for conversion of their apolitical members or those members loosely committed to another party. For the SPD, such union support is crucial. Until 1933, the major labor federation was socialist and institutionally linked to the party; hence less effort was needed to get organized workers to join the SPD or to vote for it. [20] But after 1945 erstwhile Social Democratic union leaders resolved that the fratricidal division during the Empire and Weimar eras between their federation and competing nonsocialist federations must not recur. Thus, joined by former Christian and liberal union leaders, they decided on a centralized and united federation, independent of any political party or church. In October 1949, they founded the DGB, under the presidency of Hans Boeckler, a Social Democrat. The DGB became one of the most important federations in West Germany, soon attaining a membership of 6 million, rising to nearly 8 million by 1980. That year, the total of 9.5 million organized workers (of whom 1.5 million were in smaller competing federations) accounted for 40 percent of the labor force. The DGB is the central federation of seventeen national industrial unions, ranging from the powerful Metal Workers Union, with nearly 2.7 million members (the largest in the world), to the small Gardening, Farming, and Forestry Workers Union, with about 41,000 members. [21]

In theory, the DGB top governing body is the triennially held federal congress. It determines general guidelines and elects members to the executive board, which includes the president, two vice presidents, and the presidents of the national unions. Meeting monthly, the board controls personnel and financial matters. In addition, a 100-member executive committee meets occasionally to fulfil its broad supervisory functions between congresses. Within this centralized structure, power is shared between the DGB and the constituent union officials. The DGB president has some prestige but acts more as a coordinator of the constituent unions than as chief policymaker. The incumbent can ill afford to pursue a policy contrary to the wishes of the most powerful affiliated unions (Metal, Public Services and Transport, Chemical, and Building Workers).

During the Weimar era, the three important social groups—manual workers, salaried employees, and civil servants—had their separate union federations within the socialist, Christian, and liberal union movements. All attempts at the time to bring the two status-conscious groups of salaried employees and civil servants under the cover of one umbrella organization failed. Since 1949, the DGB has tried, with some success, to bring the two groups into its industrial union framework. But a sizable number of employees and civil servants, unwilling to be overshadowed by the large bloc of manual workers in the DGB, formed their own federations: the German Salaried Employees Union (Deutsche Angestelltengewerkschaft [DAG]), with a membership in the 1970s of less than 500,000 (the DGB, though, has more than 1.5 million salaried employees), and the German Federation of Civil Servants (Deutscher Beamtenbund [DBB]), with an average of 800,000 members in the 1970s (the DGB claims over 800,000 members in this category). [22]

Even though the dream of a unified labor movement was dashed by the founding of the DAG and DBB as rivals to the DGB, the DGB viewed the failure of competing ideological federations (with the exception of a small Christian federation) to arise after 1945 as a giant step forward. As noted, DGB leaders insisted that their new federation would have to be politically neutral toward all political parties in order not to endanger a unity never achieved in the turbulent Weimar years. They did not eschew, however, lobbying activities in the executive and legislative branches, and encouraged unionists to run for public office on any party ticket in order to advance the union cause.

The official nonpartisan (or multipartisan) DGB stance produced internal strain between the majority of SPD-oriented and the minority of CDU/CSU-oriented union members and officials. In the 1972 national election, for instance, according to one estimate, 66 percent of manual workers voted for the SPD and 27 percent for the CDU/CSU. (In the Weimar era also, two-thirds of socialist union members voted for the SPD.) One DGB staff official contended that the Social Democrats were not sufficiently wooing the CDU/CSU or uncommitted blue-collar workers to cast their vote for the SPD but were more concerned with other social groups. [23] A Printers Union official noted that the SPD seemed to worry more about floating voters than about workers, whom it takes too much for granted. Although the SPD had become a people's party, the majority of blue-collar workers and salaried employees still expected the party to support their goals. He contended that it was a contradiction for the party to also safeguard the interests of employers. Society remained class-stratified; therefore the SPD must remain the party of the nonprivileged. [24]

But the SPD chiefs argued that the party's task was to mobilize all groups if it expected to win elections. Brandt told the 1968 SPD convention that "one cannot on one hand affirm the development of the SPD unto a people's party and on the other hand expect it, in its activities and internal structure, right up to the sociological composition of its leadership circles, to be an old-fashioned workers' party." [25] At the 1972 DGB congress, he said that the "trade unions are not the instrument of the party, but the party is also not the instrument of the trade unions." [26]

Yet the SPD, aware that its chief clientele, the workers, could not be slighted, and dissatisfied with the low percentage of DGB members who were simultaneously SPD members, sought to recruit more of them. At first glance, the figures of dual membership do not seem low. According to one 1977 survey, 58 percent of SPD members belonged to a union. Of this number, 47 percent were with the DGB, 3 percent with the DAG, and 8 percent with another federation. [27] Although a 47 percent membership in a DGB union totals an impressive 470,000 unionists out of about 1 million SPD members, these 470,000 who were simultaneously SPD members constitute only about 6.3 percent of the 7.5 million DGB membership that year. (During the Weimar era, it was about 12 to 14 percent.) [28]

The SPD leaders wanted to increase that percentage, primarily through the efforts of the AfA and its shop groups. But the task was difficult because, according to one skilled auto worker interviewed, many manual workers lack interest in the party even though they vote for it. To them, the union comes first and the party, with its different groups, second. [29] They find it hard to adjust to a party in which their own numbers are steadily declining and public servants and salaried employees are increasing. The result is a shift in perception among SPD members as to which groups should receive primary consideration. According to the 1975 Oldenburg SPD survey, nearly three-fourths of respondents wanted the party to represent all groups and about one-fourth said it must represent workers exclusively. [30]

Despite this shift in membership and perception, the SPD did not have much difficulty making its presence known within the DGB, because most union officials are Social Democrats. They do not hide their party loyalty, as illustrated by the fraternal greetings of DGB presidents to delegates at

SPD conventions. [31] Ever since its founding, all presidents of the DGB and its constituent unions have been SPD members. In 1969, twenty-one of the twenty-five-member DGB executive board were in the SPD, two in the CDU, and two without a party or party affiliation unknown. According to a 1969 sample survey of eighty-six top union officials at state and local levels, nearly 92 percent were in the SPD. [32] There was similar strong SPD representation in the constituent unions. For instance, in the Metal Workers Union, twenty-eight of thirty executive board members belonged to the SPD (two to the CDU), and ten of eleven executive committee members. In plant works councils, SPD members were strongly represented on the DGB union lists, but they have had to keep a low partisan profile in the plants, where political activities are prohibited.

The SPD penetration of the DGB is a two-way process. Sixty percent of the officials surveyed in 1969, although occupying few top positions in the SPD, held seats on town or county councils as SPD members, served on party or government advisory committees, held seats in state legislatures or were judges on labor and social courts. [33] A few union leaders were members of the SPD executive or council and in their capacity as cabinet members, sat in the presidium. In the already described trade union council of the party, labor leaders of all unions sometimes met with top party leaders to discuss common problems.

The SPD leadership's relations with DAG (the salaried employees federation) are fairly close because most of its officials are Social Democrats (although a lower percentage than in the DGB), but less close with the DBB (the civil service federation), because the DBB represents mostly upper-level civil servants who usually are politically more conservative than lower-level civil servants.

DGB in Politics

The interlinkage between the SPD and the labor federations has advantages for both sides. The SPD can expect to gain members and voters, and the federations can expect to gain SPD support for their legislative objectives. As will be noted, the DGB leaders indirectly supported the SPD at election time, although also giving a nod to the CDU/CSU labor wing, which has been a perennial minority in that party. The SPD has received some credits from the DGB-owned Bank für Gemeinwirtschaft; its candidates who have been sympathetic to unions have received financial support from DGB-affiliated union locals for campaign costs. Normally, help is in the form of services, volunteer aid, and advertisements in the SPD press and yearbooks, rather than cash transfers. [34] The DGB officials sympathetic to the SPD at the national level could not officially proffer financial aid, because they must remain officially nonpartisan; the few CDU/CSU officials would raise an outcry if such help were given openly.

To keep the DGB on its side, the SPD chancellors appointed a number of labor leaders to the cabinets. Walter Arendt, former president of the Mine Workers Union, was minister of labor from 1969 to 1976; Georg Leber, former president of the Construction Workers Union, was defense minister from 1972 to 1978; Kurt Gscheidle, former vice president of the Postal Workers Union, became minister of transport and post in 1974; Hans Matthöfer, erstwhile staff official in the Metal Workers Union, was minister for research and technology from 1974 to 1978 and then became minister of finance; and Helmut Rohde, AfA chairman since 1973, was minister of education and science from 1974 to 1978. [35] Brandt had appointed only two former labor officials, but Schmidt, seeking maximum support from the unions, boosted the total to five (out of fifteen ministries) from 1974 to 1978. Thereafter their representation was reduced again. The other SPD ministers were usually nominal members of a DGB union, but party work was their priority. The former labor leaders, when they served in the cabinet, were also expected to give priority to the party, although they could be expected to still represent union interests in cabinet sessions.

Schmidt not only appointed a record number of union officials to his cabinets but often held informal talks with other union presidents to maintain a close rapport. Brandt is alleged to have remarked sarcastically that "Helmut Schmidt has three coalition partners, the DGB, the FDP, and SPD—in that order." [36] But despite his close links with the unions, Schmidt cautioned them not to expect the government to always agree with them, any more than he expected them to always agree with the government. [37]

The SPD elite had another opportunity to court the labor federations by promising some of them safe seats in parliaments. Although nearly all SPD Bundestag deputies have been nominal union members, there were relatively few union officials among them. During the 1972-1976 Bundestag term, for instance, the 242-member SPD Fraktion had only twenty-two officials, of whom two were union presidents. [38] The SPD expected union deputies to vote according to SPD rather than DGB requests on the rare occasions when the two organizations clashed. This happened, for instance, during the Bundestag debate on legislation to cope with a national emergency. The bill was supported by the SPD leaders but opposed for some time by the DGB presidents who feared the bill's possible restriction on strikes during a national emergency. When the bill came up for a final vote in 1968, most SPD deputies supported it, even though 188 out of 217 Fraktion members were also nominal union members. However, fifty-three deputies, primarily unionists, broke party discipline and voted against it. [39]

The limited representation of DGB leaders in the SPD Fraktion (with even less in other parties) does not preclude DGB officials' trying to influence the parties to sympathize with the DGB legislative program. The DGB maintains a liaison office in Bonn, which receives its directives from DGB headquarters in Düsseldorf. Its staff has close links with the Bundestag deputies, civil servants, top government officials, and party leaders. When the DGB appointed a new head to the office in 1977, Brandt assured him of full SPD support and hoped that the office would serve as a communication link between the SPD (especially the workers' division) and the DGB executive officers. [40]

At the beginning of a legislative session, the DGB and its unions invite their Bundestag deputies from all parties to official receptions, but these have been formal affairs. More important, when bills make their way through the Bundestag, the DGB high command writes to the deputies about its position and in some cases sees them personally. [41] The DGB has had strong representation on the Bundestag labor and social affairs committee, which handles legislation of concern to it. As a result, the committee has endorsed its position on most legislative issues.

Despite DGB efforts in the executive and legislative arenas, not all its members agree on the need for such action. In a 1979 "Trade Union Barometer" survey commissioned by it, only half the members were supportive while the other half, favoring political abstinence, wanted the unions to restrict their activities to collective bargaining. Only 40 percent of unionized and nonunionized workers agreed with the statement, "The living conditions of the workers depend more and more on decisions by parliaments and government administrations. This is why the trade unions must exert corresponding pressure in these fields." [42]

The informal linkage between SPD and DGB at their organizational level as well as at the executive and legislative levels can be productive or discord-laden for both sides. When the SPD was in political opposition to the CDU/CSU governments from 1949 until 1966, the areas of agreement with the DGB were seldom punctured by discords. As the political scientist Richard Willey notes, "the more accurate picture is not so much one of party views and union views separately formulated and then accommodated, but of continual mutual shaping of views into similar positions." [43] This process continued after 1969 but produced dilemmas for the SPD. No longer could it listen only to DGB demands but had also to take those of other groups and the FDP into consideration. When it did so, the DGB officers realized that their identity of interests with the SPD was eroding; at times, as we shall see, the two fraternal organizations became sharp adversaries, even though the SPD-led government members knew that in the long run they could not govern against the unions and even though the DGB officers knew that the SPD would support their goals more than would any other party.

The Godesberg program called for strong support of the unions and their role in society and stated that neither the SPD nor the unions ranked above the other. The long-range SPD program, adopted in 1975 (see chapter 8), noted the common historical struggle of the two movements and also called for close rapport with the unions while maintaining institutional independence. It admitted that the party cannot achieve democratic socialism alone; it must work jointly with the unions for economic and social reforms. Shades of Weimar discord between the two giants appeared in the statement: "The trade unions cannot relieve the party of the tasks of political leadership, nor of the activation and mobilization of members, supporters, or the population as a whole." [44] This clause reflects the tenacity of the SPD in holding on to its prerogative of setting the political course.

The change in relationship between the SPD and DGB after 1969 can be explained in part by the view of SPD government leaders that they must represent the general rather than the DGB special interests. SPD leader Heinz Kühn, writing in the DGB theoretical journal, bluntly argued that the DGB should of course make demands on the government, but not those that would produce a loss of votes for the party at the next election or a loss of the coalition. The state needed a strong labor movement, but the unions must know that without a strong SPD they could not realize their goals. [45] Labor chieftains did not fully accept Kühn's views. Too often, they felt, the SPD was using the DGB as a transmission belt for membership and voting support. The union leaders knew that they had to depend more on their own resources and even, at times, on support from other parties.

Concerted Action

The government-sponsored "Concerted Action," begun in 1967 by then SPD Minister of Economics Karl Schiller, was one of the first tests of the extent of cooperation between the SPD and DGB. As part of the law to promote stability and growth, Schiller sought, by setting up a neocorporate machinery, to create more consensus between labor and management. In an effort to mitigate the effects of the typical expansion-recession cycles, he and his staff met periodically with labor and business leaders to voluntarily fix wage, price, investment, productivity, and profit guidelines. Using macroeconomic data and projections, the minister and his successors intended to set a moderate economic policy by warning both sides against excessive wage demands or steep price hikes. [46]

The DGB officers cooperated fully in the talks and the implementation of policy, although many of them were mistrustful of attempts to limit wage hikes, which would injure workers' interests. In 1977, the DGB withdrew from the Concerted Action in protest against the employers' decision to challenge the constitutionality of the codetermination law before the Constitutional Court. Since then, Concerted Action has been dead and neocorporatism has been weakened. Radical workers were pleased; they had denounced Concerted Action as a plan to perpetuate the gross inequities of the capitalist system and to maintain the DGB in a system-sustaining position. Other workers, who had participated in wildcat strikes against wage restraints, also were pleased, although they knew that even without Concerted Action their leaders were still under government pressure to exercise moderation in collective bargaining with employers.

Codetermination

Codetermination, the plan for labor and capital to share in economic decision-making at all levels, was another test of SPD-DGB cohesion. The SPD had always been sympathetic to the DGB plan to make the worker less dependent economically on the employer and to enlarge the sphere of economic democracy. The ambitious plan called for the establishment of works councils in the shops, equal labor and management representation on the boards of directors of enterprises, and the creation of economic and social councils in regions, Länder, and the Federal Republic.

Works councils were created, but management resisted codetermination in enterprises. The CDU/CSU government backed a 1951 bill calling for full parity for workers on the boards of directors of the coal and steel industries only after intensive DGB pressure. Since then the DGB has tried to extend the parity principle to the boards of other industries. The 1952 law gave workers only one-third representation on such boards. Not until 1968, when the SPD shared power with the CDU/CSU, could the DGB hope for a change in the law that would give workers parity with management. It requested the SPD to introduce legislation directly in the Bundestag. The SPD was reluctant, however, to break its informal accord with the CDU/CSU to refrain from any legislative initiative until a study by a government commission had been completed. It feared that precipitous action would identify it too closely with the unions and cost it votes at the next election. But it stopped its delaying actions when the CDU labor wing reaffirmed support for the parity principle and planned to introduce its own bill in the Bundestag, and when a survey showed that 71 percent of the population supported codetermination. [47] The SPD drafted five bills, dealing with various aspects of codetermination and changes in a plant organization law that coincided closely with DGB objectives. In January 1969, the bills received their first reading in the Bundestag, but the impending end of the parliamentary session precluded their passage. They would have to be reintroduced in a new session.

After the 1969 election, SPD and FDP leaders met to discuss the government program. FDP leaders, dependent on middle-class and employer support, adamantly opposed the parity principle in a new codetermination bill. They told SPD negotiators that they would join a cabinet only if the SPD agreed to shelve legislation on this subject. The SPD, eager finally to be the senior governing party, assented reluctantly. During the 1969-1972 parliamentary session, however, both parties supported a revision of the plant organization law, strengthening the powers of the works councils.

More confident following its 1972 electoral triumph, the SPD convinced the FDP that this time both would have to concur on a new codetermination bill. In early 1973, Minister of Labor Arendt requested his staff to prepare a bill to reflect the SPD and DGB views by the end of the year, but the FDP insisted that the bill must contain a provision that senior salaried employees in a company have to be included on the worker's side of the board of directors. The DGB and the union bloc in the SPD Fraktion rejected the FDP proposal as a dilution of the parity principle and urged Arendt and other SPD ministers to abide by the pledges made at several SPD conventions to support parity.

Arendt faced a dilemma. As a former union president, he favored parity; as a cabinet member he had received instructions to work out a compromise with the FDP. He had to take the path of compromise; his bill called for the inclusion of at least one senior employee on the workers' side. The DGB viewed the bill as a surrender to the FDP but muted its criticism in order not to embarrass the SPD too greatly, especially with elections nearing. SPD spokesmen, trying to convince the DGB to support the bill, argued that labor fears of the senior employee tilting the board to the management side were unwarranted, because such an employee must receive the electoral support of the workforce delegates. The spokesman also reminded the DGB that the party's lack of a Bundestag majority made a compromise essential if any bill with gains for labor is to be passed. A perfect bill could be enacted only if the SPD were to govern alone.

In 1974, the bill made its way through the cabinet, the Bundesrat, and the Bundestag. Other disputed sections of the bill produced a stalemate. At the 1975 DGB congress, Schmidt urged the delegates to support a new revision drafted by SPD and FDP. He warned the delegates that if no bill passed during the legislative session, prospects for new legislation were bleak. DGB leaders maintained their opposition to some provisions, and a number of unionists voted against the bill in the Fraktion.

After drawn-out negotiations, all parties agreed to support a new revised bill that gave management an edge in policymaking. The SPD accepted the revisions with misgivings, maintaining that it had no realistic alternative. On July 1, 1976, the bill became law. [48] At an SPD conference, Arendt summed up the SPD position. He said that party leaders had repeatedly asked themselves whether they should accept a compromise-laden codetermination or wait until all their goals were achieved. But how long were they going to wait? The correct alternative was to achieve the maximum possible now—a "giant stride forward"—rather than wait for an uncertain tomorrow. [49]

In 1980, DGB and SPD were involved in a struggle to maintain the full codetermination principle in the steel industry as set forth in the 1951 law. The mammoth Mannesmann Company planned to merge its steel-making with its pipe-making operations to save money. Such a reorganization, according to the company, would make it no longer subject to the 1951 law but rather to the 1976 law that applies to all companies other than coal and steel having more than 2,000 employees. The DGB charged that labor would then lose its parity with management on the board and that, according to another provision of the 1976 law, the board chairman, who must be a shareholder appointee, would receive a tie-breaking vote in case of a deadlock.

The Metal Workers Union, backed by DGB and SPD, contended that any company reorganization must not affect codetermination. When union-management talks failed to resolve the dispute, there was mention of a political strike. A sizable number of SPD deputies backed a draft bill that would have blocked a reorganization unless there was a codetermination guarantee. Cabinet members Ehrenberg and Matthöfer supported it. But Schmidt, worried about the coming national election and the FDP support of Mannesmann that could trigger a coalition crisis, refused to sign the SPD draft bill. Wehner, angry that the cabinet took no action, said that Schmidt and other SPD government leaders were looking at codetermination through FDP glasses.

In December 1980, the Mannesmann board of directors, in an eleven-to-ten vote (in which management was pitted against labor) agreed to a reorganization in July 1981. But in a January 1981 special session, the cabinet decided not to allow the reorganization until 1987. This was a compromise between the SPD members, who did not want codetermination weakened when companies changed their operations, and the FDP members, who were fully backing Mannesmann management. The Metal Workers Union was unhappy about the cabinet decision because it meant that the SPD had yielded on the principle of not watering down codetermination. The employers were unhappy because they wanted an immediate change and viewed the long postponement as a cabinet sellout to union pressure. [50]

The saga of the protracted postwar union struggle for codetermination shows that victory cannot be achieved automatically when the SPD becomes the major governing party in the nation. It took seven years for legislation to be enacted, and then it was diluted as a result of coalition bargaining with the FDP. The flareup over the Mannesmann reorganization plan proved to the unions once again that the SPD, even though sympathetic in principle, cannot be counted on to fully support their objectives.

SPD-DGB Relations, 1969-1974

During the Brandt administration, DGB-SPD ties began quite harmoniously but deteriorated over time. When SPD and FDP formed a government in 1969, the DGB leadership submitted to it a statement of aims, containing demands for the improvement of workers' conditions (codetermination, capital accumulation, an increase in the workers' share of the wealth, safety at work, industrial hygiene, family allowances, and health insurance for white-collar workers) and for improvements in the international arena (European unity, harmonization of social policy within the Common Market, closer ties with the Soviet Union and Eastern Europe, and disarmament). The statement bluntly said: "The DGB expects that the new federal government will pay greater attention than has been the case in the past to the needs of the workers who with their families represent more than 80 percent of the Federal Republic's population." [51]

The DGB leadership knew that the SPD, dependent on FDP support, would not be able to include all union demands in the government declaration of policy. Yet DGB President Heinz Oskar Vetter, a Social Democrat and former vice president of the Mine Workers Union, hailed the formation of an SPD-led government and welcomed Chancellor Brandt as a man devoted to the cause of the workers. Vetter said:

> Workers look forward with special confidence to the new government, in the hope that it will succeed in solving the many urgent problems of our days in a progressive manner. . . . The DGB notes with satisfaction that, for the first time, and in contrast to all governmental statements of policy since 1949, the justified demands of the workers and their unions have met with a high degree of consideration. Nevertheless, the DGB will judge the new federal government by the degree to which it translates its promises and plans into actual deeds. [52]

During the honeymoon period, labor leaders cooperated with the new government to prevent inflationary wage increases. They explained to a restless rank and file why wage moderation was essential in the government's attempt to maintain a stable economy. This view was not accepted by many steelworkers, miners, and public service employees who, with wildcat strikes in September and October 1969, warned their leaders not to cooperate too much with the government and employers, as for instance in Concerted Action. As the economic situation improved, real incomes rose and growth seemed assured. The majority of DGB and SPD leaders worked well together, primarily because they looked at the world from the same perspective. Politically moderate and pragmatic, they supported the neocapitalist system, provided important reforms could be made. They both rejected the visionary Juso initiatives (backed by a number of young DGB professional staff persons).

In 1970, a DGB vice president told an SPD workers' conference how impressed the DGB was with the SPD's intent to seriously tackle the problems of domestic reforms and with its progress on most of them. He praised the minister of labor for significant improvements in legislation affecting the workers. [53] Yet at the 1972 DGB Congress, Vetter called for additional reforms (e.g., guaranteed full employment, more paid holidays, an annual bonus, flexible-age retirement). Chancellor Brandt thanked the DGB for its solidarity with the government and noted the wide area of accord between them on important union demands. But he also underlined that because of the government's need to represent the entire population, not all union demands could be met. He said, "I cannot expect the trade unions to agree with everything that the government which I head holds to be correct or possible." [54]

Before the 1972 election, the DGB leadership requested all parties to take a position on its eight-point labor reform demands. Testing their readiness to respond positively, the DGB leadership said that only parties supporting the demands would receive full backing. The SPD officials responded that they agreed with most demands and that their vision of future social policy coincided closely with that of the DGB. Other parties also gave their approval. [55]

Even though the DGB could not officially endorse the SPD for reelection, its sympathies were obviously with Brandt and were manifested especially during the spontaneous workers' demonstrations after the April 1972 unsuccessful vote of no-confidence against him in the Bundestag. Big business support of the CDU/CSU further pushed the DGB toward the SPD. After the November election, the DGB hailed the SPD-FDP electoral victory as a "decisive consolidation of democracy in Germany" and expected Parliament to continue on its reform journey. [56] At the 1973 SPD convention, Vetter reminded the delegates that millions of workers had voted for the party in the expectation that it would solve the most pressing problems of society. He hoped the SPD would proceed to change the existing one-sided power and dependency relationships in economic affairs and society. [57]

But the government could not swiftly solve deep-rooted problems. In 1973, it initiated an anti-inflationary program, yet prices rose nearly 7 percent. As wages did not rise proportionately, worker dissatisfaction was high. In the summer, steelworkers, angry at the slow pace of management-labor negotiations, started wildcat strikes. The Jusos supported the strikes as part of a class struggle against the capitalists. In turn, Chairman Brandt and other top SPD chiefs, in sympathy with the DGB leaders who had condemned the wildcat strikes, denounced the Jusos for attempting to divide the workers from their officials (and embarrassing the latter), for needlessly endangering the union position, and for trying to break the solidarity between SPD and DGB. Vetter assailed the Jusos too: "We will not permit a group consisting primarily of professors, students, and pupils to regulate the political activity of the trade unions. We are not going to be led around by the nose." [58]

One underlying reason for DGB resentment of the Jusos was the labor chiefs' and workers' middle-class values, which clashed with the Jusos' lifestyle, "post-bourgeois" values, and demand for radical social changes. [59] Most Juso members were not workers, hence their rapport with unionists was weak. Many of their attempts to support the workers in union-backed strikes backfired, even when they had first cleared their actions with union leaders. Juso calls for more of its members to join and be active in unions or to exchange views with young unionists often did not have the desired result. One Munich May Day rally symbolized shifts in traditions among Jusos and workers. Before the speeches by labor leaders, the officially sponsored German Dixieland band named "Hot Dogs" played jazz music to the primarily working-class audience, while a loudspeaker truck manned by leftist counterdemonstrators played workers' socialist songs. Were the unionists conforming to the present and the leftists nostalgically recalling the past?

The DGB had differences not only with the Jusos but also with the government over wages and projected reforms that had not materialized by 1974. For instance, the unions had hoped that educational opportunities for workers' children would open up, but for various reasons little came of school reforms. In February 1974, leaders of the DGB-affiliated Public Service Employees Union, unable to stem the pressures of their members for a 15-percent wage hike, authorized a three-day strike of many municipal services, which paradoxically affected cities controlled by the SPD. The motto of the strikers was, "With all love for the party, our first concern is cold, hard cash!" They rejected a plea from Chancellor Brandt that a raise be kept under 10 percent to maintain economic stability and promote national interest. The strike was ended when the union settled for an 11 percent boost. [60] This painful schism with a powerful DGB union contributed to Brandt's resignation several months later.

SPD-DGB Relations, 1974-1982

As noted, Chancellor Schmidt appointed a number of top union officials to his cabinet in 1974 in order to improve relations with the DGB. Until the 1976 election the hope was fulfilled except for his decision upon assuming office to postpone further consideration of a proposal on workers' capital accumulation, pushed by a majority of the SPD and DGB executive bodies. The proposal called for companies to put aside a certain amount of dividends each year in a central fund, to be disbursed to workers in the form of share certificates. The party and union left wings opposed it because workers should not become small capitalists; more important was to reform the tax structure and society. Schmidt did not table the proposal because of the leftist arguments but, rather, because the FDP and employers had serious reservations about the administration of the central fund and because in 1974 the government needed to increase its revenues. [61]

Before the 1976 election, the DGB again issued a catalog of demands (ten this time) to test the parties' willingness to fulfill them. They included full employment, more social security, improvement of vocational education, equal opportunities for women, control of economic concentration, improved codetermination, capital accumulation, and disarmament. Once again, the SPD responded positively, citing the government's achievements and its programs for the future. [62]

But when Schmidt formed a new cabinet, government-DGB relations deteriorated. In appointing new labor minister Herbert Ehrenberg, the Chancellor failed to consult the DGB, as had been the custom. Vetter also questioned Ehrenberg's abilities and his primarily nonunion background. Moreover, Vetter, Eugen Loderer (president of the Metal Workers Union), and other labor leaders accused the SPD of not sufficiently considering the workers' interests in coalition negotiations with the FDP. They sharply criticized the government program's failure to make full employment one of its priorities. Because employer profits were not plowed back into new investments and because of automation, unemployment remained a central problem that only government intervention could solve. The DGB leaders also criticized the government's failure to improve the pension and health insurance systems and its agreement to an unsatisfactory codetermination bill. They told the SPD that it must not be blackmailed by conservative forces and that the time had arrived for it to tell the FDP of the Social Democrats' need to fulfill responsibilities. The DGB leaders said that their honeymoon with the government was over. [63]

What caused this unprecedented attack on the SPD government leaders—despite a statement in the government program lauding the unions for their restraint in making demands? The labor chiefs had no intention of bringing down the government but, rather, sought to ventilate pent-up grievances over the SPD's unpalatable compromises with the FDP. They were also trying to promote unity within the DGB—where there was none—on how to combat unemployment and to meet the government's pleas for wage moderation. In short, they were passing the buck, holding the SPD responsible for programmatic compromises that they themselves had (reluctantly) agreed to.

The government attempted to deflect the onslaught. One of its spokespersons said that the DGB leaders had oversimplified solutions to the serious social and economic problems, some of which were structural. The government could not easily advance solutions, especially because it did not control the market economy. Schmidt warned the DGB that in difficult economic times, groups cannot keep making demands on the government. He admitted that during coalition negotiations the SPD had had to make some concessions to the FDP in the government program. But even if the SPD were to govern alone, much in the program could not be changed. For instance, Vetter's proposal to increase current 10-to-12 billion DM public investments to 20 billion DM would cause interest rates to shoot up to meet high credits. Moreover, full employment can be achieved only in a healthy economy. [64]

On December 7, 1976, the DGB executive board and government representatives met. Ehrenberg promised to improve relations with the DGB and other social groups. Two months later, the SPD trade union council convened to make peace between the DGB and the SPD. Yet the DGB mini-warfare with SPD ministers continued in the following years as economic growth nearly halted and unemployment remained high. DGB leaders, for instance, wanted the government to introduce a more flexible age limit in the pension scheme, and index higher pensions to gross earnings. Not only did Schmidt and Ehrenberg disagree, but they intended to boost the value added tax, which the DGB strenuously opposed as socially wrong. They also did not sustain the imposition of a special tax to finance more vocational training, because the time was not propitious—to which the DGB retorted, when will it ever be? [65] They endorsed strikes in principle yet tried to avoid sharp confrontations between employers and unions.

By then, relations between Vetter and Schmidt had cooled considerably, even though the DGB chief had once remarked that "there is no better chancellor." At the May 1978 DGB congress, Schmidt received a low-key welcome, not helped by his criticism of the workers' unwillingness to move to other geographic areas or into different jobs (in response, a delegate accused the Chancellor of advocating a trailer society). Schmidt also warned the delegates that if the state were to become a "self-service store" in which all groups could satisfy their demands, it would shortly be ruined financially. The unions, having a duty to uphold the general welfare, must restrain their demands. [66] Schmidt's remarks caused the unions to remain distrustful of the government.

In late 1978 a strike in the metal industry erupted—the first official one in fifty years—when the employers refused to grant the workers a thirty-five-hour week as a way of reducing unemployment in the industry. The SPD supported the strike and chastised the employers for using retaliatory lockouts. The government did not intervene but expressed concern over the slow course of negotiations. When the strike was settled (not to the satisfaction of the union), it increased the gap between the SPD, fully supporting the workers, and SPD ministers, who had remained neutral. It also increased a gap within DGB unions, where a Communist minority opposed the SPD and the government, another group was critical of the SPD-led government, and still another backed the government. [67] A strike in the printing industry over the use of new technology produced similar rifts.

SPD leaders worried about the recurring tensions between the DGB and the government, caused primarily by the Chancellor's tough stance on limiting wage increases. As a result, union workers became more alienated not only from the government but from their own leaders who reluctantly accepted the wage restraints. Discontent among workers also led to fewer joining the party or voting for it. Those workers who were dependent on nuclear industry jobs had the additional complaint that the growing antinuclear movement within the SPD threatened their livelihood (see chapter 13). Moreover, the manual workers in local SPD branches continued to feel isolated, as other groups dominated meetings to discuss issues not germane to them and captured leadership positions. The workers wondered why intellectual brilliance, such as that of many Jusos, should count within the party more than practical life experience.

As the 1980 election approached, Schmidt needed to mend fences again. At the 1979 SPD convention, he emphasized his solidarity with the unions, and declared that economic growth and full employment must have the highest priority. In March 1980, the SPD Fraktion executive met with Vetter and top DGB leaders to discuss social, economic, and foreign policy isues. As in previous elections, the DGB issued a catalog of demands to see how the parties would respond. The SPD concurred with most of the demands. [69]

However, Vetter wanted to keep lines of communication open to the CDU/CSU and not alienate it altogether, should it come back to power. He told the CDU presidium: "If we want to prevent left dogmatists and system transformers from gaining the upper hand in our organization, we also need your help." DGB Vice Chairwoman Maria Weber (CDU) asserted that "the DGB is not the electoral assistance troop of the SPD." The CDU, too, wanted to improve its relations with the DGB, partly to make up for the party's hostility against the union federation in the 1976 election campaign. Helmut Kohl, the CDU chairman, told the DGB that "we are right now on your side." [70] Yet, once Kohl became chancellor in 1982, he was confronted by DGB-sponsored demonstrations protesting the new government's proposed wage restraints and cuts in social welfare.

CONCLUSION

The SPD and DGB mutual support system had many ups and downs during the Brandt and Schmidt administrations. When the SPD moved into a position of power in Bonn, its relations with the DGB were bound to become more strained. A parallel development occurred in Great Britain whenever Labour formed a government. It invariably enacted some measures that the Trades Union Congress, organically linked to the party, could not fully support; relations between the government and the TUC then became less intimate.

In the Federal Republic, the SPD as the major governing party had to make decisions transcending the narrower interests of the DGB. Clashes were the inevitable result, especially in the post-1973 period when the economic situation became gloomier. Although the SPD had to maintain an independent stance vis-à-vis the DGB, it could never afford to move too far away from the DGB demands, for fear of alienating a most powerful federation with millions of votes. But a massive shift of worker support to the CDU/CSU is most unlikely because of the historical link between the twin pillars of the labor movement.

The DGB had to depend on SPD and FDP support for its legislative program, which it often equates with the national interest. As the largest organized group in the Federal Republic, its officials and members view themselves as the bulwark of democracy, intent on battling the rise of extremism on left and right, and as the agent for promoting social justice. But as the issues have narrowed increasingly to bread-and-butter ones since 1973, the DGB leaders clashed repeatedly with SPD government leaders. Some of the clashes were exaggerated by DGB leaders, who wanted to divert to government leaders the anger of members about moderate wage increases or to impress the members with their courage in standing up to government leaders.

Despite genuine and less genuine clashes, agreement between the two organizations was wide. They concurred on domestic economic, social, and political objectives and on détente in foreign policy. The DGB leaders' acceptance of the existing neocapitalist system—not endangered by small left and communist minorities in lower ranks—paralleled that of the SPD leaders. Consequently, they rarely jeopardized the continuation of the government by making unreasonable wage demands, exceeding wage guidelines, or calling frequent strikes. [71] Such an attitude supports the thesis of Herbert Marcuse, who in One-Dimensional Man (written before the New Left challenge) noted that unions and labor parties have become an integral part of the capitalist system. [72] DGB and SPD left wings opposed such integrationist moves and called—unsuccessfully—for more nationalization of industry.

However, the natural alliance between DGB and SPD, as well as the neocorporatist network of DGB, employers, and the government, began to show strains when the government was unable to solve a number of economic problems (mild as they may have been from the perspective of other, more crisis-ridden nations). The German unions were worried about cyclical and structural unemployment, price hikes, government pressure to restrain wage boosts, and the growing protectionism among nations. Should such problems worsen in the future, radicalization among the workers would be a natural consequence. Then the workers might possibly develop, in Anthony Giddens' term, a "revolutionary consciousness" to replace their present "conflict consciousness." [73]

NOTES

1. There is a burgeoning literature on neocorporatism. See, for instance, Suzanne Berger, ed., Organizing Interests in Western Europe: Pluralism, Corporatism, and the Transformation of Politics (Cambridge, England: Cambridge University Press, 1981); Leo Panitch, "Trade Unions and the Capitalist State," New Left Review, No. 125 (Jan.-Feb. 1981), pp. 21-43.

2. Horst W. Schmollinger, "Gewerkschafter in der SPD—eine Fallstudie," Parteiensystem in der Legitimationskrise, eds. Dittberner and Ebbinghausen, pp. 233 ff.; SPD executive, Richtlinien der Arbeitsgemeinschaft für Arbeitnehmerfragen, Beschlossen vom Parteivorstand am 24.6.1972 (Bonn, 1972). AfA literally means Working Community of Workers' Problems.

3. Süddeutsche Zeitung, June 29, 1973.

4. Vorwärts, Jan. 31, 1974.

5. Süddeutsche Zeitung, June 29, 1973; Die Zeit, Oct. 19, 1973.

6. Ibid., Nov. 2, 1973; Süddeutsche Zeitung, Oct. 17, 1973.

7. Berlin 1976 survey, cited by Hella Kastendiek, Arbeitnehmer in der SPD: Herausbildung und Funktion der Arbeitsgemeinschaft für Arbeitnehmerfragen (AfA (Berlin: Die Arbeitswelt, 1978), pp. 115-116; personal interview with Walter Edenhofer, AfA secretary, Bonn, July 6, 1977.

8. Infas survey, 1977, p. 55; Infratest survey, 1977, p. 17.

9. Interview with Wilfred Kuckelhorn, Cologne-North, July 18, 1981.

10. SPD, executive, AfA-Materialen 1, Sozialdemokratische Betriebsarbeit, Praktische Hinweise (Bonn, 1976); AfA, "Tätigkeitsbericht des Bundesvorstands der AfA in der SPD zur 3. Bundeskonferenz, Saarbrücken, 17-19. Juni, 1977" (hectographed); Handelsblatt, Sept. 3, 1970; personal interview with Heinz Dollny, AfA staff, SPD subdistrict, Dortmund, Jan. 21, 1975.

11. Vorwärts, June 23, 1977; Handelsblatt, Sept. 5, 1979.

12. AfA, "Tätigkeitsbericht, 1977"; AfA, "Rechenschaftsbericht Helmut Rohde, Bundeskonferenz der AfA, Saarbrücken, 17-19. Juni, 1977" (hectographed); Betriebspolitik, Aug. 21, 1979.

13. Ibid., Kastendiek, p. 152.

14. "Rechenschaftsbericht Helmut Rohde, AfA, 1977."

15. Der Spiegel, Apr. 23, 1979.

16. ppp (Bonn), No. 12, Jan. 17, 1978; Vorwärts, Aug. 30, 1979; Kölner Stadtanzeiger, Sept. 7, 1979.

17. Hannoversche Allgemeine, Aug. 30, 1979; Der Spiegel, Sept. 3 1979; Frankfurter Allgemeine Zeitung, Sept. 10, 1979. In March 1980, Schmidt, making up for his 1979 nonappearance, spoke before 4,000 workers at an AfA-sponsored conference in Bochum. Rohde repeated some of the AfA demands on the government (Betriebspolitik, Mar. 19, 1980).

18. Deutsche Zeitung, Sept. 14, 1979.

19. Metall, No. 19 (n.d.), cited by Betriebspolitik, No. 17, Oct. 9, 1979.

20. See Gerard Braunthal, Socialist Labor and Politics in Weimar Germany: The General Federation of German Trade Unions (Hamden, Conn.: Archon books, 1978).

21. German Information Center (New York), Relay from Bonn: The Week in Germany, Vo. XI/25, July 2, 1981.

22. In 1978, the DAG had 479,000 and the DGB 1,548,000 employee members; the DBB had 731,000 and the DGB 832,000 civil servant members (Press and Information Office [Bonn], Gesellschaftliche Daten, 1979, p. 294).

23. Hans-Hermann Hartwich, "Gewerkschaften und Parteien—Die aktuellen Probleme im Licht politikwissenschaftlicher Untersuchungen und Konzeptionen," Gewerkschaftliche Monatshefte, XXV (Apr. 1974), 228-229; personal interview with Heinz Markmann, head, DGB economic institute, May 4, 1971; Braunthal, Socialist Labor and Politics, p. 137.

24. Vorwärts, May 4, 1978.

25. SPD, Parteitag, 1968, p. 106.

26. Press and Information Office, Bulletin (German ed.), No. 95, June 27, 1972, pp. 1271-1272.

27. Infratest survey, 1977, pp. 20-21.

28. Braunthal, Socialist Labor and Politics, p. 117.

29. Personal interview, Cologne-North, July 18, 1981.

30. Mayenberg, p. 116. In the same survey, 72 percent of the SPD respondents agreed with the statement that strong unions are a prerequisite for a democratic system, but 23 percent said that the unions could endanger it. In the latter group were primarily nonunionized members (self-employed, middle-management persons, and soldiers) (ibid., pp. 90-91).

31. See, for instance DGB President Walter Freitag speech, SPD, Parteitag, 1954, p. 21, cited by Richard J. Willey, "Trade Unions and Political Parties in the Federal Republic of Germany," Industrial and Labor Relations Review, XXVIII, No. 1 (Oct. 1974), 42.

32. Ibid., p. 44.

33. Ibid., pp. 44-45.

34. Ibid., pp. 47-48; Klaus von Beyme, "The Changing Relations between Trade Unions and the Social Democratic Party in West Germany," Government and Opposition, XIII, No. 4 (1978), p. 406.

35. For a list of cabinet members, see Deutscher Bundestag, 30 Jahre Deutscher Bundestag: Dokumentation, Statistik, Daten (Bonn, 1979), pp. 159-182.

36. Die Zeit, Mar. 31, 1978.

37. Press and Information Office, Bulletin (German ed.), No. 109, Sept. 5, 1975, pp. 1071-1072.

38. Walter Böhm, "Gewerkschafter im Deutschen Bundestag," Zeitschrift für Parlamentsfragen, V, No. 1 (Mar. 1974), 22. In the 1969-1972 Bundestag, 265 out of 518 deputies held union cards. Of the 265, twenty-five were union officials, of whom twenty-one were in the SPD (Kurt Hirche, "Gewerkschafter im VI. Deutschen Bundestag," Gewerkschaftliche Monatshefte, XX, No. 12 [Dec. 1969], 721). Among the union card-carrying deputies, the public service and teachers' unions were overrepresented and the blue-collar unions underrepresented in terms of their total membership (Emil-Peter Müller, "Vertreter von Arbeitnehmerorganisationen im 8. Deutschen Bundestag," Zeitschrift für Parlamentsfragen, VIII, No. 2 [Aug. 1977], 187). During the Weimar period, the percentage of union officials in the Reichstag SPD Fraktionen was higher, ranging from 16.7 to 21.1 percent (Braunthal, Socialist Labor and Politics, p. 137).

39. For details, see Braunthal, "Emergency Legislation in the Federal Republic of Germany," Festschrift für Karl Loewenstein, ed. Henry Steele Commager et al. (Tübingen: J.C.B. Mohr, 1971), pp. 71-86.

40. Letter, Brandt to Klaus Richter, June 29, 1977.

41. Friedhelm Farthmann, "Gewerkschafter und Parlamentarier: Loyalitätskonflikt unvermeidbar?" Gewerkschaftliche Monatshefte, XXV, No. 4 (Apr. 1974), 248-249.

42. Marplab-Forschungsgesellschaft made the survey (DGB Report, No. 18, 1/1980 E, pp. 4-5).

43. Friedrich-Ebert-Foundation, Framework of Economic and Political Orientation, p. 103.

44. Heinz Kühn, "Zum Verhältnis zwischen der Sozialdemokratischen Partei und den Gewerkschaften," Gewerkschaftliche Monatshefte, XXV, No. 10 (Oct. 1974), 614-620. See also Peter von Oertzen, "Die Gewerkschaften in der Sicht der SPD," ibid., XXVII, No. 4 (Apr. 1976), 210-216.

46. For details, see reports of ministers of economics in Press and Information Office, Jahresbericht der Bundesregierung, various years.

47. DGB, Informationsdienst, Nov. 7, 1968.

48. For details, see Braunthal, "Codetermination in West Germany," Cases in Comparative Politics, eds. James B. Christoph and Bernard E. Brown (Boston: Little, Brown, 1976), pp. 215-247; Helmut Schauer, "Critique of Co-Determination," Workers' Control: A Reader on Labor and Social Change, eds. Gerry Hunnius, G. David Garson, and John Case (New York: Vintage Books, 1973), pp. 210-224.

49. SPD, executive, Mitbestimmung, Sozialdemokratische Fachkonferenz, June 3, 1976, Bonn, pp. 9-13.

50. Hannoversche Allgemeine, June 27, 1980; Vorwärts, Nov. 20 and 27, 1980; German Information Center (New York), Relay from Bonn: The Week in Germany, Feb. 6, 1981.

51. DGB Report, III, No. 7/8 (1969), 67-68. See also IV, No. 1 (1970), 6.

52. Ibid., III, No. 7/8 (1969), 62-63.

53. Speech by Gerd Muhr (DGB Report, IV, No. 10 [1970], p. 91).

54. Press and Information Office, Bulletin (German ed.), No. 95, June 27, 1972, pp. 1271-1272.

55. SPD, Auslandsbrief, No. 22, Sept. 7, 1972.

56. DGB Report, VI, No. 11/12 (1972).

57. Welt der Arbeit, Apr. 13, 1973.

58. Frankfurter Allgemeine Zeitung, Sept. 10, 1973. See also Rainer Deppe, Richard Herding, and Dietrich Hoss, Sozialdemokratie und Klassenkonflikte (Frankfurt/Main: Campus, 1978), pp. 118-122.

59. Hans-O. Hemmer, "Jungsozialisten und Gewerkschaften," Gewerkschaftliche Monatshefte, XXV, No. 4 (Apr. 1974), 256-257; Ronald Inglehart, "The Silent Revolution in Europe: Intergenerational Change in Post-Industrial Societies," American Political Science Review, LXV, No. 4 (Dec. 1971), 991-992.

60. Die Zeit, June 1, 1971; Baring, pp. 694-699.

61. SPD, Parteitag, 1973, Beschlüsse zur Vermögensbildung (Bonn, 1973).

62. DGB Report, 3/1976 E, pp. 13-15; SPD, "Stellungnahme des SPD-Partei-Vorstandes zu den Prüfsteinen des DGB" (mimeo.); Politik, July 1976. See also Herbert Wehner, Politik für Arbeitnehmer: Reden und Beiträge, 1973-1979 (issued by AfA, Bonn, n.d.).

63. Süddeutsche Zeitung, Dec. 28 and 30, 1976; Jan. 10, 1977; Vorwärts, Jan. 6, 1977; Die Zeit, Jan. 7 and 21, 1977.

64. Süddeutsche Zeitung, Dec. 28, 1976; Frankfurter Rundschau, Jan. 29, 1977.

65. Die Zeit, Mar. 31, 1978.

66. Frankfurter Rundschau, May 24, 1978.

67. According to Henning Scherf, 20 percent of delegates at printers and metal union conventions were sympathetic to the Communist Party, 40 percent were critical of the government, and 40 percent were supportive (Juso-Zeitschrift, Sozialist, Oct. 1978; cited by Der Spiegel, Mar. 5, 1979).

68. Frankfurter Rundschau, July 10, 1979.

69. Politik, Aug. 1980.

70. Der Stern, Sept. 27, 1979.

71. Bodo Zeuner, "'Solidarität' mit der SPD oder Solidarität der Klasse? Zur SPD-Bindung der DGB-Gewerkschaften," Prokla, VII, No. 1 (1977), 3-32.

72. Herbert Marcuse, One-Dimensional Man: Studies in the Ideology of Advanced Industrial Society (Boston: Beacon Press, 1966), pp. 19-20, 29-30, 35-38.

73. Giddens, p. 202.

7
Social Democratic Women and the Self-Employed

The Young Socialists and the Association of Workers were not the only groups to demand a voice in SPD policies. In this chapter we turn to the women and the self-employed making similar claims. They set up their own constituent associations to rally and organize their members, recruit new adherents and voters, and make demands on the leadership. Thus, their objectives resembled closely those of private interest groups that attempt to influence public policy. In both instances, the groups try to maximize their political power—in the case of women and the self-employed, primarily through the internal machinery of the SPD, and in the case of interest groups, through pressures on the parties, the executive, and the legislature.

We must now examine the profile of those SPD associations not yet studied, in order to gauge their standing within the party and to evaluate their record in meeting stated objectives. We must ask whether the proliferation of associations within the party had some payoffs for the leaders and whether any advantages were lost as a result of a mushrooming bureaucracy and more frequent intraparty feuds. In terms of the central theme we must also ask what impact the social and cultural forces gaining momentum in the Federal Republic in the late 1960s had on the associations.

THE ASSOCIATION OF SOCIAL DEMOCRATIC WOMEN

Ever since the founding of the SPD, women have demanded more political, economic, and social equality. In the nineteenth century, in most German states they were not allowed to participate in politics. SPD leaders Clara Zetkin and August Bebel did not support the bourgeois-led feminist movement but tried instead to arouse class consciousness among women. They argued that because women could not be emancipated under the capitalist system, only socialism could produce full equality of the sexes.

In 1908 the government lifted the legal ban on women participating in politics, but that made little difference to women who still did not have the right to vote and to many who had to work twelve to fourteen hours a day in factories and then take care of their families. Within the SPD, the female minority reluctantly integrated into the male-dominated organization. Although losing maneuverability, the women were willing to subordinate the feminist cause to the broader goal of socialism. During the Weimar period, the government introduced female suffrage, lifted legal discrimination against women, and undertook major social reforms. Yet men continued to dominate the party, and the number of SPD female deputies in the Reichstag Fraktion averaged only 7.2 percent, after peaking at 9.6 percent in 1919 (in other parties their percentage was even less). [1]

After World War II, the SPD executive again created a central women's bureau and women formed local groups within the party. They also succeeded in including in the 1959 Godesberg program a section "Woman-Family-Youth," which called for legal, social, and economic equality for women and the right to have the same opportunities as men in education and choice of profession. But the emphasis was on protecting women as housewives and mothers rather than as workers and on identifying women in their relationship to their family (no such identification was made for men). There was no mention of women's emancipation. [2]

It took another decade for women's consciousness within the SPD to be raised as a result of ferment outside. Activist SPD women, incorporating some of the women's movement demands into their own program, insisted, at a party convention in December 1971, that there should not be a minimum number of seats on the party's executive and council reserved for women, because they should be judged on their own qualifications. As a result, the party's statute was changed and (in boomerang fashion) only two women were elected to the executive at the following party convention—rather than the five who had served until then. [3] The activist women also pressed for establishment of a constituent association for SPD women, while more conservative women opposed the plan for creating separateness (one admitted later that she had changed her mind after hearing the oratory of her male colleagues).

On June 24, 1972, the executive accepted the guidelines drafted by a commission of women for the new Association of Social Democratic Women (Arbeitsgemeinschaft für Sozialdemokratische Frauen [ASF]). The ASF structure resembles that of the other constituent associations. At the base are women's groups, formed in nearly all the 10,000 SPD branches. The active groups participate in political actions, draft position papers, issue press releases, talk with politicians, and meet with other SPD associations to increase their visibility and to make programmatic gains.

The hierarchical structure ranges from the local groups up to the biennial conferences attended by delegates chosen by district conferences. The national conference votes for an executive consisting of a chairwoman, two deputy chairwomen, and ten members. At the ASF founding convention in March 1973, Elfriede Eilers (SPD member since 1945, Bundestag deputy since 1957, and an SPD executive member since 1966) was chosen chairwoman, defeating a left candidate by 60 to 40 percent. However, the left was strong enough to elect one of the two deputy chairwomen. Eilers called on women to become more engaged politically but cautioned them to base their actions on the Godesberg principles. [4]

On January 18, 1974, the party executive approved the ASF goal of integrating women into the party and society by acquainting them with the party's policies, by making them conscious of needed changes in society, and by ensuring that in the party's formulation of views their demands would receive maximum consideration. [5]

The ASF could not escape the left-right political schism bedeviling the

Jusos and the party. At the 1975 ASF convention, the right defeated a left-drafted position paper by a narrow margin. Its introductory political-economic section included a provision which stated that only through a job could a woman be freed from dependence on and subjugation by man. Convention delegates reelected Eilers as chairwoman and a majority of rightists to the executive. The minority of leftists elected chose not to serve on the executive but, rather, to work in local branches. [6]

At the 1977 convention, Elfriede Hoffmann was elected to succeed Eilers, not running for reelection. The 53-year-old Hoffmann, a former deputy chairwoman who had made her career in the union movement, won by a slim margin over Karin Junker, a 38-year-old journalist who had been active in the student movement of the 1960s and who was not averse to waging a sharp ASF offensive against the party and the government for their inadequate record on meeting ASF goals. Hoffmann, to avoid conflicts, promised the delegates to crusade for a shorter workweek for men and women and for greater partnership between them in the household in order to reduce women's double duty in the home and at work. [7]

ASF leaders occasionally complained to party officials that some projects planned for election campaigns had to be dropped because of insufficient organizational and financial support. In early 1980, they requested funds for a major conference; party officials denied the request on the ground that another convention could not be financed in an election year when the party had already scheduled a major one. They were willing to finance a smaller conference, but the ASF was not willing to change its plans.

Like any other organization, the ASF sought additional members. Although in 1977, for example, it could draw from a pool of more than 200,000 female party members, only about 40,000 belonged to the ASF, of whom about 16,000 were active. Most of the activists (few of whom were working women) had functions in the ASF. [8] The ratio of female members to total members rose from 17 to 25 percent in the decade from 1969 to 1978—higher than in any other party, but to ASF leaders, still too low, especially when one party study noted that many politically interested women would join the party if it were to shed its male chauvinism. [9]

The profile of the average female SPD member changed in the course of time. In the 1950s and early 1960s many women were interested in doing social welfare; from the mid-1960s on, younger, emancipated women streamed into the party. Many had university training, grew up in middle-class families, or married middle-class men. Rejecting the earlier narrow concentration on social welfare activities, they focused on the same politics and policies as men. The new, politically left members found it hard to recruit into the party or the ASF not only conservative nonparty women but also feminist group members who wanted to achieve their aims from outside rather than inside the party system. [10] The feminists, who had collaborated with the ASF on joint activities (such as abortion law reform) were at times critical of the ASF, noting its difficulty in making gains within the party and its inability to focus on the central question of how women can realize their full potential within a patriarchical society. In 1980, the feminists and the ASF temporarily cut the loose ties between them, because the feminists were toying with a women's boycott of the national election while the ASF insisted that many gains could be achieved only through party and legislative actions. [11]

Relations with the SPD

The ASF has waged an uphill struggle to gain some of its objectives within the party, a chief goal being to secure adequate representation in the policymaking bodies. The record has been poor, although it improved slightly over the decade at national party conventions, where the number of female delegates rose from 19 out of 337 in 1971 to 56 out of 436 in 1979. At district party conventions 10 to 12 percent of the delegates were women. As noted earlier, there were few or no women in leadership positions in subdistrict and district executives and only somewhat more (about 10 percent) in the national executive. In 1979, party bosses tried to pacify the ASF by enlarging the national executive from thirty-two to thirty-six members (excluding the top officers), reserving the four added seats for women (as a result seven won seats). [12]

The main reason women find it so difficult to move up in the party is the male "proletarian antifeminist" prejudice against their participation in politics, either because women are unqualified or because their place should be at home. If a woman does get a post in a branch or a subdistrict, she is usually relegated to the office of secretary or treasurer; to become a branch chairwoman is difficult, given women's lower prestige and status in the community. As one ASF delegate noted bitterly at a conference: "There is unusual tolerance in this party; it would like best to have one woman in each executive, only she should not interfere." [13]

The ASF and party have discussed introducing quotas for women in policymaking posts, but the question has never been settled satisfactorily. The quota system was abolished in 1971 as a result of the power of new feminists in the ASF. At the 1977 ASF convention however, a minority of delegates voted for its reintroduction, because men were giving only token votes to women. They were defeated by a majority who argued that quotas would endanger the emancipatory movement, that women must become a political factor within the party in their own right to effectuate change, and that it would be insulting to women if they gained party positions on the basis of a quota system rather than their qualifications.

Prior to the 1979 ASF convention, a working group recommended the temporary reintroduction of a quota system, calling for women to receive 25 percent of all party offices and places on legislative lists until party members see the participation of women in party and political affairs as natural. But again, a convention majority did not accept the proposal, because a quota system violated the principle of intraparty democracy and was not in women's interest. It would put a psychological burden on women seeking public office, who if elected would be labeled as belonging to a "percentage" category. [14]

Although the ASF did not accept the quota system, it called on the party to elect more women to party posts. In 1979 it urged the party to support the candidacy of Anke Fuchs, state secretary in the Ministry of Labor, for one of the two SPD vice-chairmanship slots, to be vacated by Hans Koschnick, mayor of Bremen. When Fuchs did not become a candidate, the ASF proposed, in vain, that the party create a third vice-chairman position with the understanding that it would be reserved for a woman.

Brandt has been most sympathetic to the ASF demand for more representation. In his writings, he notes that he has asked himself often why there was inequality between men and women in the party, why the percentage of women in the party was hardly higher than fifty years earlier, why there were not more women in party and parliamentary offices, why politically interested women let themselves be pushed aside, why women felt that politics was a man's job, and why education may have an effect on women's aversion to conflict and their hesitancy in speaking up at meetings. In a comment on the quota system, he proposed that even though young women were opposed to it, women should occupy 25 percent of all posts in the party. [15] Brandt's repeated pleas for more representation of women in leadership posts failed, except in 1979 when he said that he would become a candidate for election to the European Parliament only if at least eight women (or about 20 percent of the SPD candidates) received positions on the list high enough to be assured of election. This time the party heeded his call.

One ASF executive member, Karin Hempel-Soos, offered a simple—but least likely to be followed—solution to how women can increasingly win party offices. She argued that some men should simply withdraw from politics and make room for women: "In their consequently expanded free time the men could cultivate partnership in the family and also find necessary relaxation in the happiness of educating the children." [16] Her proposal would solve the problem of one participant at a woman's conference in Berlin who said: "As a mother, I cannot participate in party meetings three times a week. Male colleagues show no interest in taking care of children, household, and all that." [17] More likely, according to ASF leaders, the male majority will continue to meet in bar-restaurants and to give the impression that women are unwelcome and that they would prefer to make decisions among themselves. In turn, many women, especially workers' wives, associate politics with such a male atmosphere and prefer to stay home, thereby remaining apolitical. [18]

A high-level ASF working group recommended in 1979 that, to increase the number of active female members, the ASF hold seminars to school women in political affairs, role conflicts, and SPD history and that questions relevant to women be increasingly discussed at all party levels. One such question, relevant not only to women, has been family policy. For years, the ASF urged party chiefs to accept its proposals on equality and burden-sharing between parents as a base for discussion and to set up a commission to deal with the issue. In 1974 the ASF sponsored a conference on the family. Brandt spoke out against the double burden of household duties and jobs many women had to carry, and said that slogans for equality did not suffice; better education, vocational training, and housing were needed. Katharina Focke, Minister for Youth, Family, and Health, in order to defuse the CDU/CSU emphasis on the family, said that it is as important as ever. This conference helped the ASF to publicize its views within the party, in the hope that the party executive would incorporate most of them in a position paper on family policy. [19] Following another conference in 1976, party headquarters did draft such a policy paper, but without ASF participation. The ASF was not pleased.

Its officials were equally displeased when by 1979 the party's district offices still had not yet established the promised working groups on women's issues, on which women would have parity. [20] They also resented that SPD drafts for the long-range 1985 party program and for the 1980 election program mentioned few problems of concern to women. The party made more satisfactory revisions only when they objected. ASF officials told their male colleagues that enough women voted for the party for it to respond with more emphasis on women's issues and with more publicity and financial support. [21]

ASF and Politics

The scarcity of women in party positions was matched by their poor representation in legislative and executive bodies. Most frustrating to the ASF was the fact that the percentage of women in the 1919 Reichstag SPD Fraktion was higher (9.6 percent) than in, for instance, the 1972-1976 Bundestag Fraktion (6.8 percent). At the Länder level, the record was slightly better. In 1979, of 595 SPD members of Land parliaments, sixty (10.1 percent) were women. [22] The ASF tried to maximize its representation in the Bundestag—as well as in legislative bodies at lower levels—in order to facilitate enactment of legislation favorable to its interests. But often it could not gain enough seats when its nominees were placed too low on the SPD lists. In Bavaria, for instance, the SPD list for the 1976 Bundestag contained the names of only two women among the top thirty-three candidates with a chance of winning, based on SPD strength in the previous election. Male officials argued that all interests must be equitably represented on the list. Therefore the ASF sent letters to all district chairmen (who had always been males) to insist that at their conventions more women be put on the list. Only half the chairmen even responded; although they agreed, the letters had no immediate impact. Neither did the ASF printing of a pamphlet "More Women into Parliament," which listed questions of interest to women to be asked candidates for public office. Neither did ASF meetings with a sympathetic party executive and with Brandt to work out ways of improving the situation.

ASF members discussed other possibilities. One was to establish quotas for lists of candidates to public office, but nothing came of it except for the cited European Parliament slate. [23] In Schleswig-Holstein, after the names of only three women were put on a list of thirty safe slots for a Landtag election, ASF members demanded the sole right to nominate a minimum number of female candidates for Landtag and Bundestag elections. In a carrot-and-stick approach, national ASF officials informed their male colleagues that a potentially large number of women then active in the feminist movement might be willing to join the SPD if it became less male chauvinist but that if the party did not budge, some women were talking of forming a new women's party. [24]

The national ASF also attempted to improve its relations with the chancellor. Thus ASF Chairwoman Eilers explained ASF proposals to Schmidt before the drafting of the 1976 SPD election platform and the subsequent government statement. Schmidt had experts incorporate the proposals, with only one major change, into the statement. [25]

Another ASF target is the cabinet, especially ministers who deal with economic and social affairs. As in other countries, one token woman has served in the cabinet, heading the "female portfolio" of Ministry for Youth, Family, and Health. The ASF has no special rapport with Antje Huber, who has headed the ministry since 1976 (Katharina Focke preceded her), considering her little interested in the theme of emancipation. When it requested Schmidt in 1978 to create the post of ombudsperson for women, he wanted to give the title to Huber or to set up a civil service post within the ministry. But the ASF, not wanting to identify women's issues only with the ministry, suggested that a new post be created within the chancellery. Upon Schmidt's negative reaction, the ASF proposed the formation of an equal rights commission at the chancellery, which would review all drafts of bills dealing with women's issues. Schmidt pointed out that such a proposal would need legislative approval, not to be expected for several years, and that the ministry's section on women's questions could handle the task. The ASF reluctantly agreed, but it remained critical of his lukewarm support of its struggle for equality. [26] In 1974, years before this dispute, Schmidt had appointed a woman, Marie Schlei, as parliamentary state secretary in the chancellery, and in 1976, as minister for economic cooperation. Before her resignation in 1978, she once said that "no quarter was given to a woman" in Bonn politics. [27]

As part of its lobbying efforts, the ASF contacts civil servants in various ministries. Schmidt urged the ASF to submit drafts of legislation to the ministries rather than merely requesting the government to do something about problems. [28] The ASF had submitted drafts on earlier occasions, but such a step does not lead automatically to their acceptance. For instance, it demanded a tough antidiscrimination law because women were still earning up to one-third less than men for the same jobs; unemployment was higher among women than men; women constituted a high proportion of unskilled workers; men still held most top positions in the economy; and some educational barriers, including apprenticeship programs, against women remained. A broad antidiscrimination law would not solve most of these problems, but it would put the government's prestige behind calls for a change.

The ASF made specific proposals (such as reducing the workday to six hours at the same pay in order to decrease female unemployment) to combat economic problems. It scored some successes. The federal and SPD-led Länder governments instituted vocational training programs for women to increase their job opportunities and supported women who started legal proceedings against employers for failing to pay them the same wages as men. As a result of ASF and other pressures, the maternity protection act was revised in 1979 to extend job guarantees in maternity cases by several months.

In the social field, the ASF record was mixed too. As will be detailed in chapter 14, the ASF was fully involved in the dramatic debate on abortion. It also took a stand on reform of the marriage and divorce law, welcoming equal rights in marriage and the end of role allocation (man equals job, woman equals household), and more fairness in divorce proceedings (no finding of guilt in the breakup of marriage; pension accumulation to be divided in half). It also proposed other reforms in the law that were not enacted. [29]

Overview

The ASF valiantly fought discrimination against women in the party and in the economic, social, and political spheres. This fight goes back a century, with a mixed record of successes, defeats, and no gains. Obviously the ASF is not strong enough to battle discrimination everywhere, but it could have a chance within the SPD. Its record of achievement has been slim, not for want of trying but because the party, with its more subtle discrimination against women, mirrors the ethos of the general society. Too often, male SPD leaders have looked on women in party offices and the Fraktionen as hangers-on who serve only as tokens for the female membership and vote. As a consequence, the ASF has felt isolated and without decisive influence within the party. Many of its most perceptive members became apathetic or quit the party altogether. The party can ill afford their loss.

THE ASSOCIATION OF SELF-EMPLOYED

The SPD historically has considered itself as the party of the workers. It did not identify as strongly with other classes, even though it always has a large minority of members who were not workers. The 1921 Görlitz program still contained references to the class struggle, but as part of an ongoing revisionism it cited the "producing masses" rather than the proletariat as the party's membership base. While big businessmen especially found the party antagonistic, liberal-oriented small businessmen found less hostility. After World War II, Chairman Schumacher blamed the antidemocratic attitude of big and small business for contributing to the rise of Nazism. But he saw the importance of wooing small and medium-size business as a way of broadening the base of the party and making it into a people's party. To justify his action in terms of socialist theory, he contended that small business, having arisen in the precapitalist era, had not been a participant in the capitalist exploitation of the workers and could exist within a socialist economy. No matter whether the economy was capitalist or socialist, he said, small business should be strengthened, especially as a way of checking big business.

Since Schumacher's time, small and medium-size enterprises in the Federal Republic have played an important role in the economy. In the 1970s, 95 percent of firms, or about 1,855,000 had fewer than 100 employees. Their 13 million workers constituted about two-thirds of the 22 million labor force. [30] But as concentration proceeded relentlessly in the private sector, big business bought out small businesses, including many "Aunt Emma" ("ma-and-pa") stores. In the 1960s, more than 200,000 small businesses perished; in the 1970s the process slowed down; from 1977 to 1978 there was even a modest rise in the number of small businesses. [31]

The SPD knew that most small business people and professionals supported the FDP or the CDU/CSU; nevertheless, it sought to tap those who were sympathetic to its goals. As early as 1954 it founded the Association of Self-Employed (Arbeitsgemeinschaft Selbständige [AGS]), the first of several constituent associations. The AGS goals are to spread the tenets of social democracy among small businesspeople and professionals, to increase their political activity within the party, to draw the attention of party leaders and members to their special economic and social problems, and to gain new members for the party. [32]

Policy in the AGS is made by a biennial conference and an executive body. Until 1975-1977, the organization did not reach below the district level, but then subdistricts and local branches were established. According to the AGS, it had about 60,000 of the 1 million SPD members in 1976—92 percent men and 8 percent women. Of the self-employed, 23 percent were merchants, 22 percent professionals, 19 percent craftsmen, 14 percent hotel and restaurant owners, and 22 percent in miscellaneous categories. However, because the self-employed active in the AGS are relatively few, proportionately many active members fill functionary positions. [33]

For most of the 1970s the AGS was headed by Horst Auschill, who had come from the German Democratic Republic where he had been imprisoned for "illegal activity for the SPD." After arriving in the Federal Republic in the 1950s, he became head of a small business firm. In the SPD, he was selected treasurer of district Hesse-South and member of the economic affairs committee. Upon retirement from his AGS office in 1978, Auschill was succeeded by Hilmar Selle, head of an insurance agency, mayor of a small city, SPD member since 1953, and economic spokesman of the SPD

Fraktion in the North Rhine-Westphalia Landtag.

The AGS has had difficulty recruiting more self-employed into the SPD, although the potential is there. One reason is the conservativeness of most of the 3.5 to 4 million independents and their families, who comprise about 26 percent of the total electorate. But the AGS and the SPD are counting on political liberalization as innovative and achievement-oriented members of the service sector become more important within the self-employed group. [34] Some employers, however, may have joined not for the reasons the SPD wanted them but for selfish reasons: they expected to get government orders if they were loyal members.

Another cause of difficulty in recruitment has been the historic animosity of many SPD members toward all employers, including the AGS "small capitalists." Too often, SPD leaders still asserted that the party was a worker's party, momentarily forgetting that it was supposed to be a people's party. Conversely, many small employers still tagged the SPD as a bastion of socialism with no interest in their problems. To them, the AGS was on the periphery of the party, tolerated primarily as an organ to help the party at election time. To them, government policy favored big business or labor, but not small business. The SPD repeatedly denied this, claiming that it was interested in strengthening the small business sector as a third force between big business and big labor.

AGS Chairman Auschill attempted to ease the animosity among many SPD members toward the employers. He argued that small and middle-size businesses employed a large workforce, much of it nonunionized. If employers identified politically with the SPD, then the workers, who were close to their employers, also might support the party. He also argued that those employers who joined the party wanted justice and a better social order and looked upon the workers in their shops as coparticipants. Finally, he pointed out that if the party wanted to continue winning elections, it must increasingly turn to the middle class for additional votes. [35]

With these clashing and sometimes outdated perceptions, the AGS had difficulty making its mark on the party. It was hardly active until 1973, but then members plunged into political activity, partly to counteract the growing influence of the Jusos and partly to receive government help for the self-employed.

By 1973 the Brandt government had fulfilled a number of demands made by AGS and the small business sector. It had set up a structural program to assure the survival of most small businesses, improved the pension system for the self-employed, and tightened the cartel policy. But the AGS, not entirely satisfied, wanted more credit assistance for new small businesses and better coordination of existing aid programs. [36] In 1976, the party executive, at the request of the AGS, formed a commission for small-business policy whose chief purpose was to ensure that AGS goals would be incorporated into the party program.

In a postmortem unpublished analysis of the 1976 election, the AGS pointed out to the party executive that workers in small businesses had not been convinced to vote for the SPD, because mention of employer exploitation had not been a credible argument to them in view of the longer hours put in by the employers. Too much talk of class conflicts and the party's failure to push the government to carry out an effective policy to aid the self-employed were other reasons that the SPD did not succeed in capturing the votes of more self-employed than in 1972. Conversely, it did not emphasize enough how the upwardly mobile have been helped by government policies. The AGS urged the party to include AGS propaganda themes in its electoral propaganda. It also reminded the SPD of the importance of having an AGS member on its executive committees and in the powerful chambers of industry and employer associations. Finally it urged Schmidt to include AGS employers in business delegations that accompany him abroad. [37]

This analysis shows once again how much on the defensive the AGS was vis-à-vis the SPD and the government, even though it had just helped to deliver one bloc of votes to the party. But it could not expect, in the brief time of its existence, to erase the deep-seated prejudices within the party against most of its members. As one way of getting around this barrier, it cultivated closer relations with Schmidt and the Ministry of Economics in order to have a more sympathetic hearing for its demands. In turn, this caused disquiet among SPD union chiefs who viewed the ministry (headed by an FDP leader) as a hostile fortress against union interests.

Despite difficulties with the SPD, the AGS needed it as a vehicle for continuing pressure on the government. Through the SPD commission for small-business policy, the AGS prepared a position paper for submission to party organs. It called on the government to aid new small firms, help develop new technologies, prevent big business from absorbing small and medium-size businesses, and eliminate tax disadvantages for them. It welcomed the increasing number of apprentices being trained, and the inclusion of the self-employed in a revised retirement scheme. [38] At the 1979 SPD convention, Wolfgang Roth, deputy chairman of the SPD economics and finance commission, urged the delegates not only to vote for the position paper but also to push for legislative enactment of its provisions, to support the AGS local branches, and to back employers for city council lists. The delegates backed the paper unanimously. [39]

As the decade drew to a close, more self-assured AGS leaders were pleased with progress made in the executive and legislative spheres (cartel office strengthened, subsidies to small business made where necessary, etc.) They still complained, however, that the party, not caring enough about the AGS, did not show sufficient solidarity. They hoped that the party would draw more first-class economists into its ranks who would act as a counterweight to government specialists tuned to the big-business community. They also hoped that party leaders would occasionally take the initiative and contact them, especially if a party position was to be adopted that would oppose the interests of their clientele, for instance, the call for a thirty-five-hour week included in the European Parliament manifesto.

CONCLUSION

This review of many (but not all) SPD constituent associations—the Big Three (Jusos, workers, women) and a smaller one (self-employed)—provides an additional explanation for the party's complex organizational and bureaucratic structure. [40] SPD leaders consciously created such a mammoth structure in order to win over the loyalty of its adherents and provide them with a milieu—a communal setting. Each constituent association was expected to appeal to the specific interests of individuals who in many cases might not have joined a political party or have voted for the SPD.

But as the associations multiplied, or became more active politically as a result of changes in the sociocultural environment in the late 1960s, SPD leaders were faced with the challenge of integrating them into the organization. Many of the associations became mini-parties subject to internal political cleavages, leadership struggles, status rivalries, and membership apathy. The associations made claims on the parent organization that were often difficult for it to accept, for political or "overload" reasons. David Easton's comments about one characteristic of a political system apply to the SPD: "Because of the way in which the political structure of a system has emerged historically, it may prove difficult for the volume of demands with which the system has to deal to move along in a clear and orderly fashion to the points of consideration, decision, and action." [41] In vain, the SPD leaders tried to stem the proliferation of constituent associations, which they had authorized earlier and which through constitutional processes made a host of demands on the top party organs. When these demands were not accepted, association leaders became bitter or frustrated.

SPD leaders were faced with another problem. As the associations developed a political dynamism of their own, that of the local SPD branches atrophied correspondingly. Newspaper headlines featured political intra- or inter-associational feuds, making it that much more difficult for the branches to activate old members, recruit new ones, or win elections. When the SPD was simply a worker's party, it did not have to face some of these problems. Thus it had to pay for widening its membership net as a people's party to encompass more groups than ever before—groups which, in the spirit of the times, insisted on maximum self-assertiveness and had divergent ideological views. We now turn to these views.

NOTES

1. August Bebel wrote Die Frau und der Sozialismus (Zurich: Volksbuchhandlung, 1879), a best seller with fifty reprints (e.g., Berlin: Dietz, 1954) and translations into fifteen languages. See Jean Quataert, Reluctant Feminists in German Social Democracy, 1885-1917 (Princeton: Princeton University Press, 1979); Richard J. Evans, "Liberalism and Society: The Feminist Movement and Social Change," Society and Politics in Wilhelmine Germany, ed. Richard J. Evans (London: Croom Helm, 1978); Werner Thönnessen, The Emancipation of Women: The Rise and Decline of the Women's Movement in German Social Democracy, 1863-1933, trans. Joris de Bres (London: Pluto Press, 1973); Susanne Miller, "Frauenrecht ist Menschenrecht," Frauen heute—Jahrhundertthema Gleichberechtigung, ed. Willy Brandt (Cologne, Frankfurt/Main: Europäische Verlagsanstalt, 1978), pp. 52-68; Renate Pore, A Conflict of Interest: Women in German Social Democracy, 1919-1933 (Westport, Conn.: Greenwood Press, 1981).
2. Vorwärts, Oct. 19, 1978.
3. Miller, "Frauenfrage und Sexismus," p. 561; SPD, Jahrbuch 1970-1972, p. 384; Jahrbuch 1973-1975, p. 354.
4. SPD-Pressedienst, Mar. 28, 1973; Konkret, Mar. 29, 1973.
5. SPD executive, Richtlinien der ASF, Beschlossen vom Parteivorstand am 18.1.1974 (Bonn, 1974).
6. Vorwärts, May 29, 1975.
7. Neue Ruhr Zeitung, May 17, 1977.
8. Figures from various sources do not tally: SPD, organization division, Bonn headquarters, "Mitgliederstände der Bezirke, 1977" lists

206,933 female members (see my table 6, ch. 3), but the SPD computer (EDV) tally lists 217,881 for 1977 (see EDV, Nov. 5, 1979, unpublished), and Infratest survey, 1977, lists "about 250,000."

9. ASF, "Frauen und SPD-Mitgliedschaft" (n.d., mimeo.); Vorwärts, Apr. 27, 1978.

10. Gerhard Noller, Die Veränderung der SPD (Reutlingen: Siegfried Noller, 1977), p. 27.

11. Vorwärts, Apr. 27, 1978; Emma, Apr. 1980, pp. 44-51; Frankfurter Rundschau, Sept. 20, 1980.

12. ASF, "Frauen und SPD-Mitgliedschaft;" Riedel-Martiny, p. 731; ASF, "Bundeskonferenz der ASF, Siegen, 3. - 5. Juni 1977, Arbeitsbericht 1975-1977," pp. 3-7.

13. Vorwärts, May 29, 1975; personal interview with Frau Anni Jansen, ASF staff member, Bonn, July 13, 1977; Riedel-Martiny, p. 734. For a sharp critique of the position of women in the party, see Luc Jochimsen, Sozialismus als Männersache oder Kennen Sie "Bebels Frau"?: Seit 100 Jahren ohne Konsequenz (Reinbek bei Hamburg: Rowohlt, 1978).

14. ASF, "Protokoll, Bundeskonferenz der ASF, Siegen, 3. - 5. Juni, 1977" (Bonn, 1977), pp. 64, 71; Vorwärts, Jan. 4, 1979; Irm Scheer-Pontenagel, "Gegenargumente zur 'Frauenquote'," Die Neue Gesellschaft, XXVI, No. 2 (Feb. 1979), 151-153; Emma, Mar. 1979.

15. Ibid., Sept. 21, 1978; Introduction to Frauen heute: Jahrhundertthema Gleichberechtigung, ed. Brandt.

16. Sozialdemokratischer Pressedienst, Vol. 34, No. 148, Aug. 6, 1979. See also Karin Hempel-Soos, "Die ASF zwischen SPD und Frauenbewegung," Die Neue Gesellschaft, XXVII, No. 2 (Feb. 1980), 111-114.

17. Vorwärts, Oct. 6, 1977.

18. Riedel-Martiny, p. 732; Cordula Koepcke, Sozialismus in Deutschland (Munich, Vienna: Olzog, 1970), p. 151.

19. ASF, "Bundeskonferenz, 1977; Arbeitsbericht 1975-1977," pp. 8-9; "Familienpolitische Konferenz der ASF in Bremen," Familie und Gesellschaft, Dokumente, No. 3, Dec. 1974; Vorwärts, Dec. 5, 1974.

20. Ibid., Jan. 4, 1979.

21. Ibid., June 5, 1980.

22. Riedel-Martiny, p. 731; ASF, ASF—das sind wir Frauen in der SPD (Bonn, n.d.), p. 6.

23. ASF, Mehr Frauen in die Parlamente (Cologne: Deutz, 1974); ASF, "Bundeskonferenz, 1977; Arbeitsbericht 1975-1977," p. 11; ASF, "Frauen und SPD-Mitgliedschaft."

24. Die Zeit, Mar. 9, 1979; Emma, No. 3, Mar. 1979. See interview with Eva Rath of Kiel, who left the ASF to help lay the groundwork for a new woman's party in 1984 (Brigitte, 15/79, July 11, 1979).

25. For financial reasons he dropped the emphasis on full-time jobs for women. Personal interview with Frau Jansen, ASF staff member, Bonn, July 13, 1977.

26. Süddeutsche Zeitung, Apr. 29, 1978; Der Spiegel, June 26, 1978; Vorwärts, Jan. 29, 1981.

27. Bremer Nachrichten, June 16, 1975.

28. ASF, Protokoll, Bundeskonferenz, 1977, pp. 64, 71.

29. ASF, ASF—das sind wir Frauen in der SPD; SPD, Jahrbuch 1970-1972, pp. 323-324; Ute Canaris, "Orientierungsrahmen und Frauenfrage," Die Neue Gesellschaft, XXII, No. 11 (Nov. 1975), 888-891.

30. Horst Ehmke, "Perspektiven der 80er Jahre," Was sind der SPD die Selbständigen wert?, ed. Wolfgang Roth (Bonn: Neuer Vorwärts, 1979), p.

25; Klaus von Dohnanyi, "Beispiele aus der Bundespolitik," Was sind der SPD die Selbständigen wert?, p. 77. The Federal Statistical Agency (Wiesbaden) cites a higher figure (2,437,000) for the number of small and medium-sized businesses in 1979 (The Week in Germany, [German Information Center, New York], XI, No. 28, July 10, 1980).

31. Heinz Rapp, "Gründen und Überleben," Was sind der SPD die Selbständigen wert?, p. 179.

32. See SPD, executive, Richtlinien für die Arbeitsgemeinschaft Selbständige in der SPD (AGS), Beschlossen vom Parteivorstand am 13. November 1972 mit Änderung vom 7. Oktober 1974 (Bonn, 1974).

33. Selbständige in der SPD, Geschäftsbericht für die Jahre 1978-1980 (Bonn, n.d.), p. 64. For occupational categories, see SPD, Jahrbuch 1975-1977, p. 325, and "Bundeskonferenz der AGS, 19. - 20. Aug. 1976, Wiesbaden, Rechenschaftsbericht" (hectographed), p. 1. The latter two entries cite a higher membership figure, but this was inaccurate. Personal interview with Herr Wolfgang Flechman, AGS staff member, Bonn, July 8, 1977; letter, Gerd Fröhlich, AGS staff member, to author, July 8, 1981.

34. Was sind der SPD die Selbständigen wert?, passim.

35. Frankfurter Allgemeine Zeitung, Nov. 13, 1973.

36. SPD, presse und informationen, No. 229/75, Apr. 22, 1975.

37. AGS, internal memorandum (n.d., c. 1977).

38. Bilanz, May-June 1979, pp. 8-9; Frankfurter Rundschau, Nov. 8, 1979; Politik für Selbständige, Sept. 1979.

39. SPD, executive, Dokumente: Sozialdemokratische Politik für Selbständige; SPD, Parteitag, 1979, pp. 1179-1180.

40. In addition to the major constituent associations, there are associations for members working in education, health, municipal construction and hospitals, municipal politics, and law.

41. David Easton, A Systems Analysis of Political Life (Phoenix ed.; Chicago: The University of Chicago Press, 1979), p. 120.

8
The Quest for an Ideology

Most political observers in the 1950s and 1960s did not predict an ideological renaissance in advanced industrial countries in the near future. They wrote about "the end of ideology" in societies where class differences were vanishing, consumers were more affluent, educational opportunities were greater, and social and geographical mobility was widespread. They also wrote about differences between political parties narrowing as each one accentuated pragmatic rather than doctrinal solutions to problems, and about the increased openness of parties to compromises and conflict resolution. A small band of primarily left academicians, rejecting the "end of ideology" thesis, argued that the thesis itself was an expression of an ideological framework which accepted the capitalist system, and that increased affluence was neither universal nor prone to produce system satisfaction. [1]

The Godesberg program of 1959—with its emphasis on doctrinal revisionism, an end to the class struggle, a mixed economic system, internal pluralism, and making the SPD a people's party—had defused the Marxist programmatic orientation of earlier decades. In the decade after Godesberg, the new generation of reformist SPD leaders pursued a pragmatic course that rejected ideology as the basis for action. In the 1961 and 1965 elections, the leaders minimized their differences with the CDU/CSU. In the campaigns, they claimed to have a better governing team than the opposition and also the ability to better administer the existing system. They did not meet the yearning among younger intellectuals to link politics to basic ethical and theoretical questions.

In the late 1960s, as discussed earlier, the Jusos tried to raise the consciousness of the pragmatists about the injustices and weaknesses of the capitalist system. They asked their elders why the words "socialism" or even "democratic socialism" had been dropped from the SPD vocabulary and from the 1968 programmatic statement on "social democratic" perspectives, which extolled individual freedoms but was silent on long-range goals. They were not satisfied with the explanation that the concept of "socialism" had been misused by communist bloc nations and would frighten voters away from the SPD. Accusing the SPD leaders of "philosophical primitive pragmatism" and "theory deficit," the Jusos demanded that the party come to grips with socioeconomic and political issues and changes in the value system. [2] Many rank-and-filers welcomed their demand for a dialogue on doctrinal issues. In the 1975 Oldenburg survey, 85 percent of the SPD members considered a discussion on theory necessary and only 12 percent, as unnecessary. However, the survey also indicated that the members' views hardly changed once the discussions had started. [3] Whether in other regions the percentage of members eager for such discussions was as high is doubtful given the antipathy among workers toward "interminable" Juso speeches about Marxism and socialism.

Nevertheless, the leaders knew that they could no longer pursue only a pragmatic course if they wanted left-oriented youth to join the party. Left-center spokesmen in particular began to spark an ideological discourse. They spoke not only of social democracy (with an emphasis on the social welfare aspects of democracy) but dared once again to speak of democratic socialism (with the same emphasis but linking immediate reforms to the utopian socialist goal).

A high proportion of youth was receptive to their message, but the leaders had to use the word "socialism" carefully, primarily for electoral reasons. They knew that most voters would respond negatively to a pure socialist program. For example, in one 1972 public opinion survey (by a public opinion institute friendly to the CDU), to the query "would you vote for a government that asserts it will introduce socialism"?, 53 percent said no, 17 percent said yes, and 30 percent were undecided or had no opinion. One year later, the responses were even more antisocialist: 64 percent, no; 15 percent, yes; and 21 percent, undecided or with no opinion. Although the antisocialist sentiment was strong, more respondents concurred than disagreed with the statement that "we are slowly moving toward socialism." [4]

THE CAMPAIGN AGAINST MARXISM

Reformist-oriented SPD leaders and publicists tried to defuse the bias against socialism, which implicitly included democratic socialism, by launching a well-orchestrated campaign against Juso-supported Marxist theory. They argued that major system-changing reforms demanded by the Jusos were impractical given the socioeconomic situation in the Federal Republic and that it was an illusion to think such reforms could lead peacefully to socialism. The ruling economic elite would put up stiff resistance, deliberately create shortages of goods, and worsen the workers' conditions. They rejected a revolutionary approach; as one wrote: "Whoever wants to overcome or blow up the system cannot hope that he will thereby remain gentle, democratic, and parliamentary." [5] They also noted that in a party such as the SPD, which was becoming more middle class than working class, it was not possible to push through an anticapitalist, system-changing stragegy. Such a strategy would succeed only if the population were to live under the most miserable circumstances without hope of improvement. [6]

The reformists stated that the Juso interest in classical Marxism would lead to dogmatism and inability to critically discuss non-Marxist authors. They acknowledged that most Jusos did not want the SPD to become a revolutionary cadre party but said that their phraseology gave that impression. [7] They argued that the Jusos were looking at socialism as a well-set historical stage that cannot brook small steps toward it. To think that socialism could be achieved at once was a delusion, because capitalist crises were less extreme and the organized workers had already made gains under the system. They warned that there was no guarantee that sweeping nationalization of industries would lead to maintenance of productivity or more democracy and justice. There were too many negative examples to be optimistic and to claim that nationalization was the sole means of controlling the concentration of economic power. [8]

Right-wing SPD politicians were the most outspoken critics of the Juso positions. Helmut Schmidt denounced the Jusos for being ideologues who were blind to reality and hostile to pragmatists. While the latter were "men of action" and capable of solving problems, the Jusos, in their theoretical discussions, were frightening voters away from the SPD. At the 1973 convention, he said that the SPD would serve people "not with ivory tower models of sociology or futurology but with tangible gains in net wages, with tangible progress in accumulating funds of their own. . . ." [9]

Others spoke up against those Juso Stamokaps who had not seen the incompatibility between their radical program and the reformist Godesberg program. [10] The right-wingers also assailed the Jusos for making a fetish of ideologies, which leads to political defeats. Too many Jusos are unrealistic, prone to making basic errors, and willing to go into an opposition ghetto in order to maintain ideological purity, rather than making political compromises. [11] The right-wingers maintained that the party's attempted bridge-building to the Catholic community would be undermined by its Juso-inspired reideologization. [12]

AN IDEOLOGICAL OFFENSIVE

These anti-Marxist statements, some couched in pragmatic and others in theoretical terms, formed the negative segment of an ideological counteroffensive. On the positive side, SPD leaders and writers, especially those in the left-center camp, attempted to work out a theory of democratic socialism that would fill the ideological void existent since 1959 and break the monopoly on theoretical discussion in Juso hands since 1969. The proponents of a Godesberg reevaluation concurred that too often the Jusos' views had little value for practical action and that the pragmatists did not reflect on how their actions would match basic party principles. Needed was a discussion on theory that would not merely be the game of a few intellectuals at the fringe of the party but that would draw the mainstream activists to help integrate the party. [13] To spur an accord on theory, reformist leaders agreed at the 1970 Saarbrücken SPD convention with the proposal of the leftist Frankfurt Circle to develop a long-range party program. As we shall see, it took five years for the task to be accomplished.

Right-Wing Ideology

To understand the flow of ideas that merged into the program, and into the SPD ideological perspectives thereafter, requires first a brief survey of the views of right-wing, center, and left-wing leaders and authors. Not until the winter of 1973-1974, years after the Jusos had made their spectacular entrance on the SPD stage, did the right wing belatedly enter. By then, its leaders had asked some intellectuals to assume the lead in countering the arguments of Juso theoreticians, or the leaders themselves had joined the fray.

In early 1974, Bruno Friedrich, chairman of the Franconia district, submitted a report entitled "Godesberg Renewal" to the party executive in

Bonn, as the beginning of the right offensive. He called on the party to remember the Godesberg principles, to maintain solidarity, and to oppose those who wanted to improve the world in one surgical strike, because their views would alienate potential voters. He saw no guarantee that a continuing historical process would lead to democratic socialism but said that the best way to move forward was to strengthen the Brandt reformist government. [14]

In 1974, Hans-Jochen Vogel, in a theoretical contribution, emphasized the need for a higher quality of life, freedom from fear, a chance for self-realization, the fulfillment of life beyond material consumption, and an end to unrestrained growth. He assailed full nationalization as an invitation to more bureaucratization and an end to trade union freedom and autonomy but approved regional planning. [15] Early in 1975, Vogel and other nonleft Social Democrats issued the "Würzburg Paper," in which they maintained that left and right were too far apart in the party for them to agree on one theoretical framework. (Their thesis was proved wrong with the passage of the long-range program later that year.)

In spring 1975, Vogel and colleagues published Godesberg und die Gegenwart (Godesberg and the Present) as another attempt to mobilize the right against the left and to contribute theoretical insights from the nonleft point of view, one that the "silent majority" was not verbally expressing. They supported the existing political system, the theory of pluralism, and the state that could generate reforms; and they seemed willing to give up the goal of socialism if the voters failed to support it. The authors' emphasis on the Godesberg program was an implicit criticism of the left, which allegedly had strayed from it. [16]

Political science professor Richard Löwenthal (Berlin) contended that in the long run, western democracies could survive only if social democrats exerted increasing controls over the economy and expanded political democracy in order to gain more social justice and security. But, he added, they must maintain a middle course between a free and a guided economy. [17] His political theory colleagues, Alexander and Gesine Schwan (Berlin), on the extreme right, claimed that the SPD had become a "left people's party." They noted the dangers of a theory discussion based on Marxism. To try, like the Jusos, to harmonize Godesberg and Marxism, was dangerous, because Marxism cannot be divorced from Leninist dictatorship. The alternative was to endorse the Godesberg program as the basis for constructing a "social democratic" rather than "democratic socialist" order. [18]

The relative moderation of most right-wing exponents and the similarities of their views to those of the left-center exponents were remarkable. They saw themselves as heirs of the Bernstein revisionist tradition but were more strongly anti-Juso and anticommunist, more reluctant to speak of democratic socialism, and more supportive of the neocapitalist system than were left-center leaders. In this respect, their position was closely akin to that of the newly formed (1981) British Social Democratic Party, whose founders seceded from a Labour Party moving further left.

Left-Center Ideology

A brief survey of the views of left-center leaders and authors also shows their acceptance of Bernstein revisionism, but modernized and updated to deal with the problems of the 1970s. Their views corresponded to those of the Scandinavian and Austrian Social Democrats and the moderate wing of the British Labour Party. The German left-center leaders, who were more sympathetic to some of the Juso positions and had better rapport with Juso leaders than did the right, attempted to bridge the gap between left and right by developing theoretical guidelines that might be acceptable to both sides.

Peter von Oertzen gave a major address entitled "Theses for a Strategy and Tactics of Democratic Socialism in the Federal Republic of Germany" to the strife-torn Frankfurt convention in November 1973, which was reprinted in a widely publicized pamphlet and submitted to the party executive. It became the starting point for a new discussion on theory and had an effect on the final draft of the long-range program. In his speech, Oertzen pleaded for a reformist approach in which the party would serve as both a stabilizer and an agent of change of the capitalist system. Whenever the system fails, structural changes must be made. This can be done if the masses identify socialism as a better alternative to capitalism. The socialist movement must unfold within the existing order and not be bent on a confrontation. It must democratize piecemeal the political and economic power centers and not attack them frontally, in order to preclude the destruction of a democratic socialist alternative. It must change the social structure through local self-administration as well as by legislative and administrative means. Only if the SPD remains united and powerful and maintains its roots in the society, can it achieve its ends. Oertzen emphasized that because of a dialectical relationship between goal and movement, purpose and means, socialism cannot be realized through authoritarian methods and forms of organization. [19]

Willy Brandt on several occasions tried to bridge the gap between the left's emphasis on socialism and the right's emphasis on social democracy. He maintained that the two concepts are synonymous and concurred with Olof Palme, Swedish Social Democratic Workers Party chairman, who once said: "If we do not dare talk any more about socialism, the foe has won half the battle." [20] To Brandt, socialism was a constant fight for more freedom and justice, equality of opportunity, and the elimination of gross inequalities of income and property.

Erhard Eppler wrote that the old recipes were no longer attractive and new ones were still being tried. He stressed improving the quality of life and safeguarding the environment—these would receive the approval of the public. [21] Horst Ehmke dealt with the SPD support of a constitutional state that has democratic legitimation and of a government that has the ability to solve the problems of an industrial society. He assailed bureaucrats and politicians who stymied the government's long range planning and called for a mixed centralized and decentralized state. [22]

Peter Glotz favored a "controlled system change" that would meet the needs of the millions of people who had hoped that reforms would satisfy their rising expectations. He acknowledged that the Jusos had provided a new creative dimension in raising issues that the SPD had failed to raise when it was too busy securing the material existence of the people. The party must tackle two goals simultaneously: to be receptive to new ideas and translate them into policy, but also to remain the political force that a majority of voters will trust to be capable of governing. Reformists must walk a tightrope: they must not unduly put fear into those who defend the status quo, but at the same time they must satisfy those who suffer under the existing system. To Glotz, creative reforms were possible under liberal capitalism, although he wanted to move beyond it. He feared that the party, stuck in a pragmatic approach, would lose its identity and become a repair troop rushing from one damaged site to another or an organization dispensing patronage to one group or other. It must set new goals wrapped in the mantle of a "relative utopia" (in Mannheim's terminology) rather than an absolute utopia. In short, Glotz argued for a synthesis of reality and utopia in which the party chooses a path that will bring society closer to socialism. [23]

Other writers urged a discussion of theory as a way to promote the integration of the party. Juso and non-Juso theories were not always contradictory but overlapped in such realms as improving the quality of life, lowering income differentials, and controlling big business. Both sides were in accord on basic values, a humanist orientation, and evolution rather than revolution, but they eschewed a theoretical discussion on the question of whether the party's goal was to maintain or change the system. These writers saw the SPD as moving in a system-changing direction because it wanted to change the relationship between the political and economic sectors by making the democratic state dominant over the undemocratic business community. [24]

The writers also argued that where sharp differences persisted between left and right wings, as on nationalization of industry, both sides should be able to agree on a statement such as that nationalization forms but one element in a democratization strategy. They urged the party not only to theorize more but to make abstract concepts more real to the people, most of whom were not convinced that socialism is the best goal. Finally, they said that credit should be given to the Jusos for mobilizing the younger generation and to the right for mobilizing the older generation. [25]

Left-Wing Ideology

The doctrinal views of the Jusos and Old Socialists have already been surveyed but not those of writers sympathetic to the left wing whose ideas were greatly shaped by the critical social theory of the Frankfurt School (led by Max Horkheimer and Theodor Adorno) and, more indirectly, by the interwar Austro-Marxist movement, which had emphasized the continuing class struggle. Their views also corresponded closely to those of the left-wing and center of the French Socialist Party and the left wing of the British Labour Party.

These writers' responses to the SPD's right-wing and left-center arguments had an effect on the theoretical intraparty debates. In a critical book on the SPD, Wolf-Dieter Narr, Hermann Scheer, and Dieter Spöri maintained that the party, in order to sell its "people's party" concept, deemphasizes class divisions and speaks instead of differences in social strata and of ways in which the economic pie could be cut up. Because the pie is not getting larger, structural differences remain and stresses within the party, especially among workers, increase. The party covers up these problems, which are endemic to the capitalist system. At the same time it seeks to depoliticize and demobilize interests which may challenge its views, and makes the maintenance of its organization one of its main goals. As a result, the party's character changes from the old SPD "milieu" to a mixture of organizational bustle and modern career advancement.

The authors acknowledged that the main goal of the party is to govern the nation. But when still in opposition, the SPD copied the faulty CDU/CSU domestic and foreign policy programs rather than developing alternative policies. Once in power, the SPD did introduce planning, but not of the type demanded in the 1950s to control capitalism. Instead, planning was modeled on the United States planning-programming-budgeting scheme, as a way of stabilizing the crises of the West German capitalist economy. Although from 1969 on, the social-liberal coalition was headed by sympathetic and energetic leaders, their operational rules remained the same as those of their predecessors. If the SPD had undertaken a real reform policy, there would have been electoral dividends. Instead it became a "state" party showing little interest in making fundamental systemic changes. [26]

Other authors contended that the party's emphasis, for instance, on a better quality of life and a workers' capital accumulation scheme, was still an endorsement of the capitalist system. To help socially weak groups was important, but some of these groups were not too keen on government help even from the hands of the Social Democrats. [27]

This sample of views from the right wing, center, and left wing of the party shows some fundamental discords between them but also a measure of accord on issues that all could accept, even if without enthusiasm. To enhance the measure of accord and to revive theoretical discussions, Brandt in 1973 wanted to create an institute for democratic socialism. The idea was soon aborted when disputes arose as to who should head the institute and under whose control it should be. The right, fearful that a Marxist institute would emerge, suggested that Richard Löwenthal become head. Juso theorist Strasser rejected the nomination because of the conservative views of Löwenthal; he suggested instead Jürgen Habermas of the Frankfurt School. His name in turn was unacceptable to the right. The left wanted the institute to be independent, but the right insisted that it be a part of the Ebert Foundation. No consensus emerged between the two wings; the institute was never created.

THE LONG-RANGE PROGRAM

Party leaders and writers of all persuasions presented their views partly to have an effect on the deliberations of a commission, authorized at the 1970 Saarbrücken convention, to work out the draft of an "Economic-Political Framework for Orientation for the Years 1973-1985" (labeled "long-range program"). The convention's decision rested on the 1968 document "Perspectives—Social Democratic Policy in Transition to the Seventies," characterized by one writer as "a kind of preliminary futurology of the party's major policies. . . ." [28] The commission, headed by Helmut Schmidt with the assistance of Hans Apel and Jochen Steffen, began its deliberations in 1970. On June 2, 1972, it submitted a preliminary draft of its "Long-Range Program" to the party. The lengthy document called for step-by-step reforms based on quantifiable economic growth rates between 4 and 6 percent of the gross social product and attempted to link the party's programmatic commitments to limited government planning. [29] Apel, in defense of the technocratically oriented document, argued that since Godesberg "we have given up the belief in a previously exactly defined socialist society," and that in the future, too, the "general march route of the Godesberg program could not be replaced by ideological light beacons." [30] Schmidt bluntly said: "To program totally and plan to perfection the things that must be achieved would, technically speaking, be a crazy adventure, for politically minded people a nightmare, and above all . . . an absurdity." [31] To defuse potential opposition to the draft proposal, he admitted that it lacked a theoretical basis. The gap was not unintentional, because Apel and Schmidt had no desire to go beyond the Godesberg principles and steer the party in a more socialist direction.

The Jusos, dissatisfied with the document and the apologia for it, issued a position paper criticizing the draft as one-sided and lacking social analysis and commitment. To propose a series of expensive reforms dependent on constant economic growth is to emphasize economic fetishism at the expense of qualitative changes. The document is "merely a government program for three legislative periods," in which "long-range and short-range goals of social democratic politics are nowhere defined beyond the degree of generalization of the Godesberg program," the Jusos maintained. [32]

In reply, Apel stated that without a doubt the long-range document was based on maintenance of the existing order but that its goal was to achieve qualitative changes in the spirit of democratic socialism. Schmidt asserted that the quality of life could not be improved without increased productivity and economic growth and that the present system was capable of moving toward democratic socialism. But when both leaders realized that the document, even when amended, had aroused widespread opposition within the party, which felt uncomfortable about the emphasis on technocratic changes, they knew that the party at its Hannover 1973 convention would demand a complete overhaul of the draft. [33]

As expected, the convention authorized a new thirty-member commission, to be headed by Oertzen and assisted by Ehmke (both left-center) and Klaus Dieter Arndt (right wing; when he died, Herbert Ehrenberg replaced him). The executive deliberately coopted a more leftist leadership in order to absorb its intellectual energies and to defuse the renewed opposition from the Jusos. It nominated only eight members and requested the districts to choose the other twenty-two members. As a result, eight Jusos were on the commission, but only one woman. The commission was charged with drafting a new long-range program and taking the criticisms of the first draft into consideration. The new program was to be based on Godesberg, but with a more precise formulation of democratic socialism; an analysis of social developments; and ways in which reforms could produce more freedom, justice, and solidarity in the Federal Republic.

The new commission's task was made easier because the first draft had already been thoroughly discussed; on the other hand, the commission had to meet a two-year deadline. It appointed ad hoc groups and a planning staff and commissioned specialists to submit advisory reports. On January 24, 1975, it submitted its 245-page draft report, again entitled "Economic-Political Orientation Framework for the Years 1973-1985" (but this time referred to as "OR '85") to the executive. Even though the second draft was more theoretical than its predecessor, omitted the quantitative components (by then, to talk of unlimited growth was no longer _de rigueur_), and was based on compromises among the party's ideological factions, it nevertheless occasioned much debate at all party levels thereafter. [34]

OR '85 was submitted for approval to the Mannheim convention, meeting in November 1975. Before that date, the commission convened several times to deal with more than 1,000 resolutions for changes and additions that had poured in from party organs. Many of these were incorporated into the draft in order to preclude a lengthy debate at the convention. The delegates approved the draft nearly unanimously, after defeating two controversial left-wing minority reports calling for more nationalization and direct government controls of private investments.

The contents of OR '85 must be examined in detail because it represents a consensus within the SPD on the latest doctrine of social democracy and because this was the first time that a party had developed a long-term political perspective on the basis of its fundamental program. OR '85 consists of four main sections; a separate section dealing with individual reforms (e.g., transportation, environment, agriculture) was not discussed at the convention but was referred to specialized committees for further deliberation and action.

In the first section, "Goals of Democratic Socialism," the program reads: "The doctrine of socialism encompasses the goal of a new, better order of society and the way to achieve it. The concrete shape of goal and means must constantly be refined given the ever-changing social conditions. Socialism is a never-ending task [of renewal]." The program then defines the three basic values of socialism—freedom, justice, and solidarity. Freedom means being free from degrading dependencies and providing for the possibility of self-realization. In the social realm it must apply to all and not be the privilege of a few. Justice means providing all with equal rights and opportunities. Solidarity means cohesive groups, especially labor, fighting together for a more humane world at the national and international levels.

In the second section, "Conditions and Frame of Reference," OR '85 shows the interrelationship of politics and economics on the international level. To solve the problems of raw materials and to combat the power of multinational corporations, European socialist parties will need to work out common policies. Traversing a middle path, the program notes that neither unfettered free enterprise nor centrally controlled economies have produced socially desirable conditions. New economic structures based on parity between management and workers should be created that can improve the workers' social and cultural life, provide them with capital accumulation, ensure their full employment, and add to their influence in economic policymaking.

The role of the state is important as an organ to steer economic and social policies in a politically desirable direction, especially because 40 percent of the social product is distributed through public institutions. The program thus rejects the liberal bourgeois theory, which contends that the state is an autonomous unit perched high over clashing social forces, and the Stamokap theory, which contends that the bourgeois state is dominated by monopoly capital.

On economic policy, OR '85 takes a middle path between growth and nongrowth policies. It favors both a mixed economy, in which the market forces and planning complement one another rather than being at opposite ends, and public ownership under democratic controls.

One of the most controversial sections of the program deals with the government's role in private investments. The left minority in the commission had demanded that the government be vested with strict, direct investment controls and prohibitions to prevent industry from weakening the economy, environment, and social conditions. The majority rejected the proposal because it would endanger free market competition. OR '85 urged the government to appropriate for itself limited and indirect steering instruments to prevent wrong private investment decisions and to produce balanced structural and regional policies. The instruments would be in the form of taxes, incentives, granting or withholding public services, quality norms, environmental restraints, and controls (including prohibition) on location of plants. The government should create a center to register major investment intentions and a federal development plan, through which it would develop public investments and influence private investments. There should also be stronger controls over banks and their drive for more big business mergers.

In the third section, "Implementation of Social Democratic Policies," OR '85 reflects the left dual strategy of mobilizing local party groups and other democratic groups. It calls on the party to inquire about voters' problems and wishes; to inform voters of SPD policies; to develop a long-term political orientation that would identify social democracy beyond the everyday problems; to cooperate with other democratic forces and rebut the views of opponents of social democratic reform politics; to further citizens' activities in fields directly affecting them; and to enter into a dialogue with churches, unions, and other associations.

In the fourth section, "Fields of Particular Importance," OR '85 lists those which should be initiated by 1985: modernization of the economy—to secure jobs and create new ones in economically deprived areas; reform of vocational training; humanization of work; reform of the health service; city planning and development; and equality of women on a de facto and not a de jure basis.

In summing up OR '85, Brandt wrote: "The Orientation Framework is no substitute for the Godesberg Basic Program. It not only confirms the fundamental positions of Godesberg, but supplements them in important fields, and formulates solutions for problems we are likely to face in the time span to 1985." [35]

The orientation framework was a herculean task; five years in the making, its final draft was the outcome of protracted intraparty discussions that reinvigorated the SPD at all levels. Yet despite the impressive record, criticisms of OR '85 continued to be voiced after its passage. Leftist critics, viewing it as a reaffirmation of the capitalist system and a victory for the right wing, asked rhetorically, how do you achieve freedom, justice, and solidarity in a capitalist system? How do you maintain free competition among monopolies? They complained that the main sections were not bound together in a grand creative design; that the formulations were too abstract and tentative, enabling each party faction to pick out those it likes best; and that OR '85 failed to deal with the state bureaucracy, interest articulation, the imperative mandate, relations to trade unions, and solidarity with the Third World.

The left critics noted how difficult it was for the party to bring the diverse wings under one roof and formulate a program satisfactory to all, and how the party only discussed the main sections at Mannheim, while shunting the separate section dealing with individual reforms back to party committees. But these reforms were precisely the ones the party should have linked together as part of a long-range government program.

The critics admitted that the reforms were costly and would have put the government in a bind. On the other hand, the critics had cause to rejoice, because the Jusos on the commission had scored some victories in comparison with the first draft: OR '85 did not fully support the free enterprise system, it called for controls on multinational corporations, it included a section on investment steering and sectoral and regional planning that the right had originally opposed, it dropped the notion of economic growth as a precondition for reforms, and it included the demand for codetermination reform. [36] One foreign scholar also pointed to some omissions in OR '85: there is little mention of the problem of income redistribution and equalization, the problems of foreign workers, the burden of armaments on domestic policy, and foreign policy. [37]

Defenders of OR '85 soon came to its rescue. They contended that it bridged the gap between the Godesberg program and actual politics, served to integrate the party after too many years of sloganeering, narrowed the differences between ideologues and pragmatists, made the theoretical discussion more concrete, moderated the slogans and demands of the left, broadened the limited pragmatic perspectives of the right, acted as a guide for the government's and the Fraktion's social democratic initiatives, and clarified to outsiders the nature of the party. They noted that as a result of the SPD's pathbreaking venture into long-range programming, it can claim to be the party looking toward the future and to be a model for its brethren parties in Sweden, Belgium, and Switzerland, which were also going to draw up long-range programs. To rightist critics who viewed OR '85 as being more Marxist than the Godesberg program, they retorted that the occasional Marxist terminology used in the discussions had no bearing on the final document. [38]

But the defenders were chagrined that once OR '85 was accepted, it did not have the effect they had hoped for on the party and the government. Within the party, discussion centered only on the section dealing with ways to mobilize other democratic groups to support the party's goals. At Mannheim, Schmidt warned the delegates that OR '85 could not be used as the "transport medium for love doctrines" and as the basis for the daily tasks of the government. The party, he claimed, would lose power to govern if it were to be too distant with its demands and decisions from the realities of the government's legislative program. Oertzen himself pointed to the difficulties involved in putting OR '85 into practice, given the need to make compromises with the FDP. [39] There was little mention of the program in the 1976 election campaign. According to political scientist John Herz, "In this respect it had died a peaceful death (if not undergone formal burial) at hardly age one." [40] The claim of death seems a bit premature. OR '85 will most likely serve as one theoretical guideline for future actions, although forecasts for one decade ahead are fraught with possibilities of error in the face of new situations and crises unpredictable during its gestation period between 1973 and 1975.

BASIC VALUES

In the meantime, theory-building was moving on another front. In 1971 Brandt appointed Willi Eichler, one of the architects of the Godesberg program, as head of the basic values commission (Grundwerte-Kommission) to study how the Godesberg section on basic values (freedom, justice, and solidarity) could be expanded. [41] When Eichler died in late 1971 and the party executive did not appoint a successor, the commission remained moribund. In 1973 the Hannover convention urged that the task be resumed. In 1974 a new commission, with Steffen as chairman and Eppler as deputy chairman (changed two years later to Eppler as chairman, with Löwenthal and Heinz Rapp as deputy chairmen), began its deliberations. The commission, whose members represented the different party factions, was charged with applying the basic values to the new problems, conflicts, power structures, modes of behavior, and values that have arisen since 1959.

In 1977 the group members were able to concur on its findings, published in a brief report entitled "Basic Values in an Endangered World." In an attempt to define who is a socialist, they said it is someone who always tries to apply the basic values to the solution of any problem. These values were of equal importance and none could be sacrificed for the sake of another. The report acknowledged that the values antedate the socialist movement (as, for instance, the French Revolution's liberty, equality, fraternity); hence the SPD cannot claim a monopoly on them.

With new political, technological, economic, and social developments in the previous two decades, the concept of "progress" has to be redefined. It must preclude those developments that hinder rather than further the three values. The report assails those social policies, such as rent rebates, children's allowances, educational grants, and unemployment benefits, that are becoming "more expensive, more bureaucratic, and more ineffective all the time," and that are incapable of eliminating the serious injustices in society. As a way out, it suggests, for instance, increasing the wage levels of lower income groups and of women, establishing a state income adjustment scheme based on the partner's income and the number of children, and aiming for higher productivity to increase real income. The report acknowledges the difficulty of maintaining justice and solidarity when the economic pie shrinks in a no- or minimum-growth situation and sharp conflicts erupt over its distribution. But freedom can be enhanced if decentralization and democratization are supported fully. [42]

In 1979 the commission submitted another report to the party executive. It welcomed both the party's discussion about basic values with nonparty groups and the interest other political parties had developed in the subject. The discussions should continue, but clarity in concepts was necessary because all parties were using the same words with different meanings. To the credit of the SPD, it historically struggled for the realization of the values. The report concluded with the definitions of the three values formulated earlier in OR '85. [43]

IN SEARCH OF ROOTS

While some party theoreticians were busy debating the basic values on which economic and social programs should rest, a few neo-Kantian adherents turned to the philosophies of Immanuel Kant and Karl Popper for added ammunition against the party's left wing. In two volumes edited by Georg Lührs and colleagues, blessed by Chancellor Schmidt's foreword, the authors praised Kant's rationalism, in which human progress is possible through critical rational discussions of competing ideas. [44] The authors also acknowledged the importance of ethical realism (emphasized by Leonard Nelson, and propagated by Gerhard Weisser and Willi Eichler in the Godesberg program) but maintained that because Godesberg did not have enough of a theoretical and philosophical base, its defenders in the party had difficulties in the 1970s in debating with neo-Marxists, and countering their offensive.

The authors thus endorsed the critical rationalist views of Popper, as expressed in <u>The Open Society and Its Enemies</u>, [45] where he argued that there is at present no one proven scientific theory. In his antidogmatic stance, he opposed any theories (namely, Marxism) that seek to delegitimize competing theories. The goal of politics is not utopia, which harbors force rather than compromise, but the elimination of mistakes and human suffering. A multifaceted open society should not be looked at from one perspective, but should tolerate gradual changes and eliminate injustices, he noted. Lührs and colleagues claimed that Popper's views paralleled the SPD views of free party competition and piecemeal reforms. [46]

By writing a foreword to the Lührs volumes, Schmidt attempted to correct the prevalent view that he was a pragmatist or opportunist who was not interested in theory. He endorsed Popper's "piecemeal social engineering" (taking small steps through compromises and consensus) to achieve reforms, and also his belief that a democratic society can be perverted into a totalitarian state if those who back totalitarian utopias win the ideological struggle. Schmidt reminded his readers that democratic socialism flows not only out of theory but also out of the experiences of its adherents. Although a critical spirit was the necessary precondition to achieving a better society, it was folly "to flee into the world of ideas" in reaction to a disappointing reality. [47]

Not unexpectedly, the "Popper boom," as it became known (with little justification), produced ripples of open support from conservatives and waves of dissent from left critics. Those who supported Popper's views pointed to the recognition by Lührs and others of the lack of a scientific base for Marxism; the theory dealt with prophecies that could not be substantiated. [48] Leftist critics labeled Popper as "the secret chief-ideologue" of the SPD, who was needed to provide a useful theory to the party's antileft. The critics claimed that the surprised Popper was happy to play this role, although he did not expect the SPD to take his criticism of Marx seriously. They contended that his social engineering proposal was not suitable for solving the problems of an industrial society and that it reinforced the party's shying away from reforms in less prosperous times. [49]

No sooner did the interest in Popper pass than Eduard Bernstein became the source of a revival. The theories of the architect of revisionism within the SPD were easier to accentuate and more acceptable to a wider spectrum of party adherents than those of Popper, who was viewed by many as a conservative outsider. Moreover, an ancient leader with a "human face" was sought as a hero who would bestow a "historical perspective to routine perspective." [50] In the mid-1970s, a number of revisionist theoreticians were responsible for and capitalized on a new interest in Bernstein. The renaissance was marked by an outpouring of new editions of his works and commentaries on his theory. [51]

Horst Heimann, one of the chief revivalists, admitted that the purpose of moving Bernstein into the focus of discussion was to serve the nonleft in the SPD as an additional weapon to counterattack the Old and New Left but said it was also to integrate contending party factions, to recruit university youth, to fill an ideological vacuum, and to build the base for a reform policy. To get a well-founded historical overview of the Social Democratic movement, Heimann contended, one must not ignore a leading theorist who had contributed so much to the party's development; it was also important to correct a distorted picture of him. Only then could the party, in a theoretical paradigm, link Bernstein's revisionist-reformist course to the current left democratic-socialist reform course. Such a linkage would prevent the wings from being too far apart and remove the inferiority complex too many SPD members have when confronted by leftist theorists. [52]

Responding to the Bernstein revival, one leftist writer pointed to the difficulty the nonleft had in theoretically justifying current socioeconomic developments that had little bearing on revisionism. He recalled that Bernstein, who had wanted the SPD to be a workers' party, had favored nationalization of industry, antimilitarism, and political mass strikes. But times have changed; to use Bernstein currently presents difficulties. [53] American scholar Henry Pachter noted that present economic and social welfare programs administered by social democrats were much more comprehensive and complex than during Bernstein's time. He contended that Bernstein's "kind of reformism is as obsolete as Marx's model of revolution," and that it was ironical for Bernstein, who was averse to all ideologies and "was everything but a prophet," to be used as the model for a theory revival. [54]

A NEW THINK TANK

While the nostalgia wave for Bernstein was going on, more than 200 academicians, politicians, and publicists from the left, non-Marxist wing of the party formed the "University Initiative of Democratic Socialism" (Hochschulinitiative Demokratischer Sozialismus) in October 1975. Their purpose was to end their isolation and defensiveness at universities, to meet with one another to analyze contemporary conditions, and to develop theories that would move the existing neocapitalist system in a socialist direction. They wanted their group, on the theoretical left of the SPD, to be critical of the party if necessary and to overcome the social democratic lack of perspective as well as Marxist dogmatism. They assailed the technocratic managers and the counter-reformers on the right and the Marxist orthodox followers and "pseudo-left" antireformists on the left for turning their backs on a reformist, state-affirming socialism based on full-fledged democracy. They attempted to fill the theoretical vacuum, which had made many university youth reluctant to join the party, by organizing a number of conferences (e.g., one on educational reform, another on theory of reforms); setting up a communications network; and issuing several volumes, each written by a team of scholars. [55]

In the first volume (1977), Christian Fenner and colleagues maintained that at present there is no consistent theory encompassing goals, means, and consequences; indeed, there is no global theory of human and social development. Although there have been some useful programs, theory is still fragmentary and in its infancy. This theory deficit has been caused by recourse to pragmatism, by programs designed to appeal to voters, and by a failed Marxist analysis. Analytical and instrumental goals of democratic socialism must be developed through multidisciplinary and pluralist methodological approaches. Short-, middle- and long-range goals must be emphasized as well as the relationship between the means and ends of socialism.

The authors dealt with a number of themes that should underlie SPD strategy. All spheres of life, especially the economic, must be democratized and humanized, class privileges dismantled, equality given a chance, and conflicts between states ended. As democratic socialism, with its emphases on democratic rights and freedoms, does not lie historically at the end of capitalism, it is an alternative that must be striven for continuously. Within the parliamentary system, thought should be given to plebiscitary and council ideas, the imperative mandate, and more rotation in office, collegial leadership, and direct democracy.

The authors opposed revolution as a tool to achieve socialism. The social costs are too high, and the consequences are uncontrollable and incalculable; besides, a revolutionary romanticism strengthens the nonsocialists' fear of socialism. Instead, they opt for system-changing reforms that do not fit into the mold of a single, inevitable end but are a part of broader utopian goals. [56] In another volume, Fenner makes a distinction between these democratic socialist goals ("a 'concrete utopia' that projects into the present") and the middle-range goals of social democracy, which consist of quantitative steps for the emancipation of the individual and for societal progress (such as those pledged by the social-liberal coalition). [57]

NEW PERSPECTIVES

As the quest for an ideology continued into the late 1970, it remained diffuse, sporadic, and shapeless. Once again, a number of theorists advanced ideas to cope with new problems; once again, their prescriptions varied or coincided. But many of these ideas were soon forgotten or were not understood by the members, who were more concerned with their own daily tasks. To close this communication gap, the party in 1979 scheduled a number of forums dealing with questions about the future. Among them were "Work and Technique," "Environmental Policy Between Ecology and Economics," and "Power of the Bureaucracy—Powerlessness of the Citizens?" The forums were designed for specialists to do some preparatory work, ask the right kinds of questions, and gain theoretical perspectives for the 1980s—but keeping in mind that their work had to relate to the concerns of the members. While in Berlin, Glotz opened a series of dialogues between people who had not talked with one another for years because of political differences. To him the dialogues served the party as an "early warning system" to resolve pressing problems.

Most theorists concurred on the need for the party to broaden its appeal, explain problems to the members and the electorate, and gain consensus for its program. Some warned the party to make a more intensive and systematic effort to diffuse theory findings into its "soul," and to clarify socialist goals and means. But these tasks were not easy to accomplish, especially when the motivations of members and their identification with goals were unknown. The theorists lamented the party's failure to initiate post-OR '85 debates about economic policy, disarmament initiatives, and dangers to civil liberties—these should go on the agenda again at all party levels. [58] They wanted the party to remain one step ahead of the government in its formulation of goals. The party should set priorities and propose solutions to pressing problems. This would give it an ideological framework; without ideology, it would lose its raison d'être and become merely a chancellor's party ready to approve his policies. The theorists would have agreed with Italian political scientist Giovanni Sartori's comment about parties and ideology: "Granted that in an affluent society the intensity of ideology will decrease, a lessening of its intensity should not be confused with a withering away of ideology itself." [59]

The intriguing question is how many SPD adherents still believe socialism will ever materialize. In the early 1970s when a reform euphoria pervaded the scene, more of them were optimistic about the future than in the late 1970s when few major reforms were visible. In any case, the party attempted to maintain an ideological profile. It remained in the mainstream of the moderate reformist parties (e.g., the British Labour party in the 1970s; the British Social Democratic party in the early 1980s; the Scandinavian, Swiss, and Austrian parties), operating within a liberal-democratic political framework. Hence, as will be seen in chapter 14, its relations with more left-oriented socialist parties were strained at times for ideological and pragmatic reasons.

The official SPD doctrinal position represented the triumph of the party's nonleft factions. As we have seen, throughout the 1970s there were rival streams of thought about how to achieve social democracy or democratic socialism. The ideological cleavages were not clear-cut; in some instances, two factions took the same position; in other instances, as with the Jusos, internal cleavages made cohesion more difficult. Yet the SPD was to maintain its organizational unity, unlike Italy and Great Britain where rival socialist and social democratic parties emerged in different postwar decades.

Although left-wing theorists relied strongly on the writings of Marx, Engels, Gramsci, Gorz, Bauer, and others for their inspiration, they were also commited to the few socialist planks in the Godesberg program. They sympathized with the views of left wing leaders in the French, Belgian, Italian, British Labour, and other socialist parties who took a radical position on economic policies.

The left-center theorists in the SPD leaned heavily on Bernstein's revisionist doctrine and on the entire Godesberg program into which flowed socialist, humanist, Christian social, and neo-Kantian views. They backed leftist proposals to democratize all spheres of life, but with reservations. The right-wing theorists differed little from their left-center colleagues, except that they underscored more strongly the neo-Kantian tradition espoused by Nelson and Popper, were more anticommunist, and did not support socialist economic proposals. Their views at times corresponded to the neoconservative movements in France and the United States.

The greatest discord among all SPD factions was in their attitude toward system-changing reforms (which the left favored, the left-center was ambivalent about, and the right rejected). The greatest measure of accord concerned the need to proceed on an evolutionary, parliamentary path toward social democracy or (in more hushed tones) socialism. While the goal of reformism was clearly delineated, the utopian view of socialism remained dim.

Kurt Tucholsky relates the story of an old, slightly tipsy gentleman who felt no ambiguity about SPD goals. When asked in the 1920s whether he would vote for the SPD, he replied (in inimitable Berlin slang) in the affirmative: "It is such a reassuring feeling. One does something for the Revolution, but one knows exactly: with this party it will not come. And that is very important for a family-owned vegetable store." [60]

NOTES

1. See Daniel Bell, The End of Ideology (New York: Free Press, 1960); M. Rejai, ed., Decline of Ideology (Chicago, New York: Aldine-Atherton, 1971); Chaim I. Waxman, ed., The End of Ideology Debate

(New York: Funk and Wagnalls, 1968).

2. Klaus Lompe and Lothar F. Neumann, eds., Willi Eichlers Beiträge zum demokratischen Sozialismus: Eine Auswahl aus dem Werk (Berlin, Bonn: Dietz, 1979), pp. 24-25; Kremendahl, Nur die Volkspartei; SPD, executive, Sozialdemokratische Perspektiven im Übergang zu den siebzieger Jahren (Bonn, 1968); Kurt Klotzbach, "Die Programmdiskussion in der deutschen Sozialdemokratie 1945-1959," Archiv für Sozialgeschichte, XVI (1976), 469-483.

3. Meyenberg, pp. 119, 150.

4. Elisabeth Noelle-Neumann, "Zum Einfluss des Meinungsklimas auf das Wahlverhalten," Union alternativ, eds. Gerd Mayer-Vorfelder and Hubertus Zuber (Stuttgart: Seewald, 1976), pp. 513-514.

5. Peter Glotz, "Systemüberwindende Reformen?" Beiträge zur Theoriediskussion, ed. Georg Lührs, Vol. I (Berlin, Bonn-Bad Godesberg: Dietz, 1973), pp. 205-244.

6. See Glotz, Der Weg der Sozialdemokratie, p. 149.

7. For instance, Peter von Oertzen, "Die Zunkunft des Godesberger Programms: Zur innerparteilichen Diskussion der SPD," Freiheitlicher Sozialismus, eds. Heiner Flohr et al. (Bonn-Bad Godesberg: Neue Gesellschaft, 1973), p. 98.

8. See Kremendahl, Nur die Volkspartei, pp. 50-51, 73-75.

9. SPD, Parteitag, 1973, pp. 22-30.

10. Hans-Jochen Vogel in Vorwärts, Aug. 25, 1977. See also SPD, executive, p 1, Reihe Parteien, Heft 1, Zum Verhältnis von Sozialdemokratie und Kommunismus (Bonn, 1971).

11. Heinz Kühn in Süddeutsche Zeitung, July 30, 1973.

12. Hermann Schmitt-Vockenhausen in ibid., May 23, 1973.

13. Kremendahl, Nur die Volkspartei, pp. 69-70.

14. Bruno Friedrich, "Godesberger Erneuerung: Überlegungen zum Standort der SPD" (hectographed, c. 1974).

15. Hans-Jochen Vogel, Grundfragen des demokratischen Sozialismus (SPD, executive, Theorie und Grundwerte series, Bonn, 1974; reprint from Beiträge zur Theoriediskussion, ed. Lührs, Vol. II, 1974).

16. Hermann Buschfort, Heinz Ruhnau, Hans-Jochen Vogel, eds., Godesberg und die Gegenwart: Ein Beitrag zur innerparteilichen Diskussion über Inhalte und Methoden sozialdemokratischer Politik (Bonn: Neue Gesellschaft, 1975).

17. Richard Löwenthal, Sozialismus und aktive Demokratie: Essays zu ihren Voraussetzungen in Deutschland (Frankfurt/Main: S. Fischer, 1974).

18. Alexander Schwan and Gesine Schwan, Sozialdemokratie und Marxismus: Zum Spannungsverhältnis von Godesberger Programm und Marxistischer Theorie (Hamburg: Hoffmann and Campe, 1974).

19. Peter von Oertzen, Thesen zur Strategie und Taktik des demokratischen Sozialismus in der Bundesrepublik Deutschland: Diskussionsthesen zur Arbeit der Partei (SPD, executive, Theorie und Grundwerte series, Bonn, 1974; reprinted in Beitrage zur Theoriediskussion, ed. Lührs, Vol. II, pp. 13-50). See also Oertzen, Die Aufgabe der Partei, (Bonn-Bad Godesberg: Neue Gesellschaft, 1974).

20. Willy Brandt, Godesberg nicht verspielen (SPD, executive, Theorie und Grundwerte series, Bonn, 1979), p. 5; Brandt, People and Politics, p. 439. See also Albert Lauterbach, "Socialism and Social Democracy: An Exercise in Concepts and Semantics," Association for Comparative Economic Studies Bulletin, XX, No. 1 (Spring 1978), 1-36.

21. Erhard Eppler, "Politik nach der Zäsur," Mitte-Links: Energie,

Umwelt, ed. Harry Ristock (Bonn-Bad Godesberg: Neue Gesellschaft, 1977), pp. 11-24. See also Eppler, Ende oder Wende: Von der Machbarkeit des Notwendigen (Stuttgart: Kohlhammer, 1975).

22. Horst Ehmke, "Demokratischer Sozialismus und demokratischer Staat," Beiträge zur Theoriediskussion, ed. Lührs, Vol. II, pp. 87-103.

23. Glotz, "Systemüberwindende Reformen?" pp. 243-244; Der Weg der Sozialdemokratie, pp. 14 ff.

24. Heimann, Theoriediskussion in der SPD, pp. 94-152.

25. See Lührs, ed., Beiträge zur Theoriediskussion, Vols. I, II; Fritz Vilmar, Strategien der Demokratisierung (Darmstadt: Neuwied, 1973); Imanuel Geis in Vorwärts, June 6, 1974.

26. Naar, Scheer, Spöri, pp. 80-95.

27. Christian Fenner, Demokratischer Sozialismus und Sozialdemokratie: Realität und Rhetorik der Sozialismusdiskussion in Deutschland (Frankfurt/Main, New York: Campus, 1977), pp. 171-178; Hofschen, Ott, Rupp, pp. 153-155.

28. John H. Herz, "Social Democracy Versus Democratic Socialism: An Analysis of SPD Attempts to Develop a Party Doctrine," Eurocommunism & Eurosocialism, ed. Bernard E. Brown (New York: Cyrco Press, 1979), p. 254; see Horst Ehmke, ed., Perspektiven—Sozialdemokratische Politik im Übergang zu den siebziger Jahren, erläutert von 21 Sozialdemokraten (Reinbek: rororo, 1969).

29. See SPD, executive, Ausserordentlicher Parteitag, 18.-20. Nov., 1971, Bonn, Zwischenbericht über die Arbeit der Kommission Langzeitprogramm (Bonn, 1971). See also Langzeitprogramm 1, Texte; Horst Heidermann, ed., Langzeitprogramm 2, Kritik; 4, Kommentare (Bonn-Bad Godesberg: Neue Gesellschaft, 1972).

30. Süddeutsche Zeitung, Feb. 19/20, 1972.

31. Hannoversche Allgemeine Zeitung, Feb. 28, 1973.

32. Süddeutsche Zeitung, Dec. 21, 1972. See also Horst Heidermann, Langzeitprogramm 3, Jungsozialisten: Kritische Stellungnahmen zum Problem einer gesellschaftspolitischen Langzeitplanung (Bonn-Bad Godesberg, 1973); Rudolf Scharping and Friedhelm Wollner, eds., Demokratischer Sozialismus und Langzeitprogramm (Reinbek: Rowohlt, 1973).

33. SPD, executive, Orientierungsrahmen '85, Die Anträge zum Parteitag 1973—Synoptischer Überlick (Bonn, n.d.).

34. SPD, executive, Dokumente, Ökonomisch-politischer Orientierungsrahmen für die Jahre 1975-1985 (Bonn, 1975); Friedrich-Ebert-Foundation, Framework of Economic and Political Orientation of the Social Democratic Party of Germany for the Years 1975-1985 (English transl., Bonn-Bad Godesberg, 1976). For a history of OR '85, see Jost Küpper, Die SPD und der Orientierungsrahmen '85 (Bonn-Bad Godesberg: Neue Gesellschaft, 1977).

35. In foreword to OR '85, Framework, p. 3.

36. Institut für Marxistische Studien und Forschungen, Der SPD Orientierungsrahmen '85 (Frankfurt: Verlag Marxistische Blätter, 1975); Narr, Scheer, Spöri, pp. 45-56.

37. Herz, p. 259.

38. Rightist criticism in Wilhelm Hennis, Organisierter Sozialismus: Zum 'strategischen' Staats- und Politikverständnis der Sozialdemokratie (Stuttgart: Klett, 1977); for discussion or OR '85, see Peter von Oertzen, Horst Ehmke, Herbert Ehrenberg, eds., Orientierungsrahmen '85—Text und Diskussion (Bonn-Bad Godesberg; Neue Gesellschaft, 1976); Oertzen, "Die

innerparteiliche Diskussion zum Orientierungsrahmen '85," Neue Gesellschaft, XXII, No. 11 (1975), 882-884.

39. SPD, Parteitag, 1975, p. 184; Frankfurter Rundschau, Dec. 2, 1975.

40. Herz, p. 269.

41. See Willi Eichler, Zur Einführung in den demokratischen Sozialismus (Bonn-Bad Godesberg: Neue Gesellschaft, 1972).

42. SPD, Grundwerte-Kommision, Grundwerte in einer gefährdeten Welt (Theorie und Grundwerte series, Bonn, 1977).

43. SPD, Grundwerte-Kommission, Grundwerte und Grundrechte (Theorie und Grundwerte series, Bonn, 1979). In 1980, the commission submitted a third report on political culture in a democracy. It called for greater participation of the people in the cultural life of the nation (Heinz Rapp, "Zwischen Tagespolitik und Grundsatzprogramm—Die Arbeit der Grundwertekommission der SPD," Neue Gesellschaft, XXVIII, No. 2 [Feb. 1981], 138-144). See also Marie Schlei and Joachim Wagner, Freiheit—Gerechtigkeit—Solidarität: Grundwerte und praktische Politik (Bonn: Neue Gesellschaft, 1976); Ulrich Sarcinelli, Das Staatsverständnis der SPD (Meisenheim am Glan: Anton Hain, 1979), pp. 48-62; Thomas Meyer, Grundwerte und Wissenschaft im Demokratischen Sozialismus (Berlin-Bonn: Dietz, 1978), pp. 150-215.

44. Georg Lührs, Thilo Sarrazin, Frithjof Spreer, Manfred Tietzel, eds., Kritischer Rationalismus und Sozialdemokratie (Berlin-Bonn: Dietz, 1978).

45. Karl Popper, The Open Society and Its Enemies (London: G. Routledge, 1945).

46. Lührs et al., Kritischer Rationalismus, p. 3.

47. Ibid., p. xv.

48. Felix von Cube review of Lührs et al. book, in Die Zeit, Nov. 14, 1975.

49. Wieczorek-Zeul review of Lührs et al. book, ibid.; Kurt Bayertz, "Der Popper-Boom in der SPD oder die theoretische Offensive des Reformismus," Blätter für deutsche und internationale Politik, No. 3 (1976), pp. 278-289; Lompe and Neumann, pp. 31-33.

50. Henry Pachter, "The Ambiguous Legacy of Eduard Bernstein," Dissent, Spring 1981, p. 203.

51. See Helmut Hirsch, ed., Eduard Bernstein, Ein revisionistisches Sozialismusbild: Drei Vorträge (Berlin, Bonn-Bad Godesberg: Dietz, 1976); Horst Heimann and Thomas Meyer, eds., Bernstein und der demokratische Sozialismus: Bericht über den Wissenschaftlichen Kongress; Die Historische Leistung und Aktuelle Bedeutung Eduard Bernsteins (Berlin, Bonn-Bad Godesberg; Dietz, 1978).

52. Vorwärts, Oct. 13, 1977.

53. Christoph Butterwegge, "Der Bernstein Boom in der SPD," Blätter für deutsche und internationale Politik, No. 5 (May 1978), pp. 579-592.

54. Pachter, p. 216.

55. Vorwärts, June 9, 1977.

56. Christian Fenner et al. (Arbeitsteam der HDS), Zur Einführung in die Theorie des demokratischen Sozialismus (Frankfurt/Main, Cologne: Europäische Verlagsanstalt, 1977).

57. Fenner, Demokratischer Sozialismus und Sozialdemokratie, pp. 177-178.

58. Scherf, "Notwendige Fragen," p. 659; Johano Strasser, Die Zukunft der Demokratie: Grenzen des Wachstums—Grenzen der Freiheit? (Reinbek:

Rowohlt, 1977); "Grenzen des Sozialstaats oder Grenzen kompensatorischer Sozialpolitik?" Unfähig zur Reform? Eine Bilanz der inneren Reformen seit 1969, eds. Christian Fenner, Ulrich Heyder, and Johano Strasser (Cologne: Europäische Verlagsanstalt, 1978), pp. 110-146.

59. Giovanni Sartori, "European Political Parties: The Case of Polarized Pluralism," Political Parties and Political Development, eds. Joseph LaPalombara and Myron Weiner (Princeton: Princeton University Press, 1966), p. 159.

60. Cited by Stephen Russ-Mohl in review of Fenner, Heyder, Strasser book, Süddeutsche Zeitung, June 22, 1979.

9
The Quest for Voters

Anthony Downs wrote that "the main goal of every party is the winning of elections. Thus all its actions are aimed at maximizing votes, and it treats policies merely as means towards this end." [1] The SPD has been no exception, although its leaders would claim that its policies are based on principle and not mere opportunism. This claim will be examined later; suffice it to say now that the preceding survey of the party indicates that despite internal cleavages and strains, one of its central concerns from 1969 to 1980 was to maximize its votes at every election in order to remain in power at the national level and to be able to execute its policies, regardless of how they may have differed from those of the CDU/CSU.

This quest for votes thus became a matter of ensuring that the party's traditional voters, the blue-collar workers, would remain loyal and that other major groups in society would be mobilized for additional support. In this chapter, we will examine first the profile of the average SPD voter and then the efforts to gain more support among three of several key voter segments—youth, citizens' groups, and church communities. Such a survey should provide us with clues as to whether the party, in the search for politically moderate voters in the center of the political spectrum, ran the danger of alienating both its politically left activist membership and its worker core by pursuing governmental policies devoid of ideological content or not conciliatory enough to the workers. A similar dilemma had faced the British Labour governments of Prime Ministers Wilson and Callaghan, who successfully steered a moderate course in the face of radical rank-and-file opposition (which included many workers) within their party.

A brief glance back into German history shows that most SPD leaders had not been averse to participating in elections as the chief means of improving the conditions of the workers and eventually achieving socialism. Engels optimistically wrote in 1895:

> We can count even today on two and a quarter million voters. If it continues in this fashion, by the end of the century we shall conquer the greater part of the middle strata of society, petty bourgeois and small peasants, and grow into the decisive power in the land, before which all other powers will have to bow, whether they like it or not. [2]

After Engels' death in 1895, the SPD became a mass organization whose chief purpose was to enter the periodic electoral battles. Although the party continued to strongly emphasize elections, it did not hesitate to engage in demonstrations, marches, strikes and other forms of political activity. But the SPD also began to weaken its emphasis on Marxist ideology—and then abandon it entirely in 1959—in order to attract the "bourgeois" voters, despite the Marxist prediction that "all but a handful of exploiters" (the big business and "haute bourgeoisie" fraternity) would become proletarian and flock to the party. [3]

PROFILE OF SPD VOTERS

The SPD of the 1970s, considering itself to be a people's, or catch-all, party, pursued the same policy. [4] It attempted to capture a potentially high percentage of the electorate by seeking the votes, first, of workers and then of most other societal groups. Consequently, as Adam Przeworski points out (in writing about social democratic movements in general), social democrats "cannot remain a party of workers alone and yet they can never cease to be a workers party." [5] In the 1970s, the traditional core of the SPD remained the unionized blue-collar workers (see table 12). In addition, a high percentage of unionized members in other occupations backed the SPD rather than the CDU/CSU or the FDP, although the correlation between union and nonunion members and their vote for the SPD was becoming less important. [6]

Among members of other occupations shifting their support to the SPD by 1969 because of issue competence, attractive candidates, and party performance were those in the rapidly expanding new and heterogeneous middle class of salaried employees (doing routine and nonmanual work), civil servants, and salaried professionals, who had become more educated, politicized, and receptive to SPD reform proposals for the nation. But because many in this new middle class of the tertiary service sector did

TABLE 12
OCCUPATION AND SPD VOTE, 1953, 1969-1980

	Vote for the SPD (%)				
	1953	1969	1972	1976	1980
Workers	48	58	66	52	57
Civil servants and employees	27	46	50	41	41
Self-employed	11	17	23	31	27
Farmers	4	16	10	11	5

Source: Franz U. Pappi, "Parteiensystem und Sozialstruktur in der Bundesrepublik," Politische Vierteljahresschrift, XIV, No. 2 (1973), 199, adapted by Horst W. Schmollinger, "Abhängig Beschäftigte," p. 65. For 1976 and 1980 postelection surveys, Forschungsgruppe Wahlen, Mannheim.

not identify strongly with the SPD or had weak ideological convictions—partly because of conservative partisan cues from their parents—the party in its programmatic position emphasized doctrinal issues less and pragmatic issues more. [7] Voting support for the SPD also came from some nonunionized Catholic workers, farmers, the old middle class (self-employed tradesmen and tradition-bound dependent employees), and the upper-middle class, although most of them still voted for the other parties. [8] Similar trends of increasing middle class support for socialist parties occurred in other Western European countries in the 1970s.

Income among occupational groups had lost some of its validity as an explanatory variable for voting behavior. The SPD, with exceptions, received the support of low-income groups; upper-income groups gravitated more to the FDP and CDU/CSU. Middle-income groups voted for all parties, but the more affluent workers remained loyal in most cases to the SPD. Although social class status in terms of occupational group remained an important variable and colored an initial attitude and political disposition, it was not as important in the seventies as it had been earlier. New young, middle-class supporters of the SPD who came from conservative socioeconomic families were no longer voting along class lines. Rather, they cast their ballots for the SPD as the party most supportive of their lifestyle and their interest in such "New Politics" issues as quality of life, environment, détente, and aid to Third World countries, in contrast to such "Old Politics" issues as the economy, price stability, old age pensions, and reduced taxes. [9]

Educational level and party preference appeared not to be closely linked any longer. Although education was correlated with occupation, within each occupational category there was little difference in party preference between those with a minimum and those with an advanced education. [10] As indicated, the SPD profited from support of the new middle class, which was more highly educated than manual workers.

Age made a difference in voting preference, especially in the 1972 and 1980 elections when the 18-to-24-year-old voters supported the SPD—and the FDP—to a greater extent than the CDU/CSU. However, the SPD was aware that such voters had weak party identification and were ready to switch parties, especially if they lived in a CDU/CSU environment. [11] Politically, the young SPD voters were slightly more left of center than all SPD voters. For instance, in a 1975 sample survey, 30 percent of the former put themselves into the left category, but only 22 percent of the latter. On the other hand, 55 percent of the young SPD voters and 64 percent of all SPD voters categorized themselves as middle of the road and 2 percent of the young voters and 3 percent of all voters as on the political right. [12] If such a shift to the left among young SPD voters continues, the party will have to make changes in its electoral and programmatic strategy.

The female/male variable in votes for the party was less important in the 1970s. Until 1972, fewer women than men voted for the SPD, but after that the gender difference began to disappear in several age categories. For instance, in 1972 more 18-to-24-year-old women than men cast their ballots for the SPD, although in 1976 the total male vote still exceeded the female vote by 1 percent. By 1980 the female vote exceeded the male vote for the first time. The SPD position on questions important to women and the tendency of women to support the ruling party and the chancellor were factors influencing their vote for the SPD. [13]

A persistent and traditional determinant of voting behavior has been the degree of religious devoutness of voters. As detailed below, the CDU/CSU has received the bulk of votes from Catholics and Protestants who attend church frequently, while the SPD has received primary support from the nonpracticing Catholics and Protestants. [14] Catholics who have supported the SPD come primarily from the lower socioeconomic classes, except for churchgoing manual workers, who have continued to support the CDU/CSU. The SPD has been unable to make inroads into this latter group—about 11 percent of the population. The party has received more of its support from Protestants, including a rapidly rising percentage of salaried employees. [15]

In terms of urban-rural divisions, the SPD has never had any strength in farming constituencies, except in those rural and semirural areas whose inhabitants increasingly commute to work in industrial areas. With exceptions in the late 1970s, the larger the urban community, the greater was the voters' support for the SPD. [16] The SPD has also had to face a north-south barrier. Its social structural strength traditionally has been in the northern industrial areas and its weakness in the more sparsely settled southern rural areas.

To summarize the profile of SPD voters: tables 13 and 14 indicate that the educational level, age, and gender of the citizens influenced their voting behavior, but even more important were their degree of religious conviction, trade union membership, and social class. Socioeconomic cleavages among voters of different parties, less sharp in the seventies than in the past, persisted even with a shift in their occupational profile. The system remained nonconsensual, partly for historical reasons: today's less exploited working class could not easily forget its subordination in an authoritarian industrial caste system. As the number of blue-collar workers continues to decline and that of salaried employees and public servants increases, the system may still remain nonconsensual, with the emergence of new political subcultures and cleavages on new noneconomic issues.

Thus, Otto Kirchheimer's prediction that there will be a complete transformation from class to catch-all parties in Western democracies has not been borne out entirely in the Federal Republic. [17] Because the continued class conflicts, lines of cleavage, and capitalist crises have not disappeared, the SPD and CDU/CSU continue to attract different sets of voters whose social milieu is fixed in the hierarchical class order and whose intensity of party identity is strong. On the other hand, among a minority of voters, including those in the middle class whose class-determined social milieu has withered away, party identification is not very strong. This minority often shifts its vote from one election to another, casting ballots for the party it thinks has had a good legislative track record, raised the most salient issues and shown competence to solve them, and fielded the most attractive candidates.

Hence, voting is based on a mixture of immediate considerations and fairly fixed socioeconomic characteristics. The SPD has to ask itself whether, despite a continuation of class voting (among workers especially), it has made a permanent breakthrough in holding on to the new middle-class voters whose values do not coincide with those of most workers. It is too early to give a definite answer; some of its new voters in 1969 and 1972 strayed away in 1976 and 1980, but most maintained their new loyalty. The party must continue to integrate its various supporters if it expects to win future elections. Otherwise, Jürgen Habermas's observation about German parties, SPD included, as mass parties "of superficial integration," restricting themselves "to mobilize the voters . . .

TABLE 13
SOCIOECONOMIC PROFILE OF VOTERS BY PARTIES, 1972

Group Identification of Voters	All Respondents	SPD	CDU/CSU	FDP
		(In percentage)		
Women	53	54	53	43
Men	47	46	47	57
Age				
18-29	22	27	20	27
30-49	38	40	36	46
50 and over	40	34	45	27
Education				
Public school	74	77	72	45
Intermediate school	19	17	21	41
High school and university	6	5	7	13
Monthly household net income				
Under 1,000 DM	24	23	22	17
1,000-2,500 DM	65	68	64	59
Over 2,500 DM	8	6	10	22
Occupation of head of household				
Workers	40	50	31	22
Civil servants and employees	35	35	37	39
Self-employed	16	8	24	27
Trade Union Membership				
Member [a]	35	44	26	25
Nonmember [b]	65	56	74	75
Religion				
Catholic	48	38	64	31
Protestant	46	55	35	58
Other or none	5	6	1	9
Church attendance of Catholics				
Regular	20	8	27	9
Seldom or never	28	30	17	22

[a] Respondent or member of household is a union member.
[b] No union member in the family.
Source: Jürgen W. Falter, "Die Bundestagswahl vom 19. November 1972," Zeitschrift für Parlamentsfragen, IV (Mar. 1973), 126, based on survey data of Forschungsgruppe Wahlen, University Mannheim (Mannheimer Befragung, 2. Welle, except for union membership based on first wave). Rounded to the nearest percentage; hence the subtotals of each column are not necessarily 100 percent. Table is slightly rearranged.

TABLE 14
OCCUPATIONS OF VOTERS BY PARTIES, 1976

Occupation	SPD	CDU/CSU	FDP
Workers			
skilled	62	36	2
unskilled	49	44	6
Salaried employees, civil servants			
low and middle-level	44	45	10
upper level	28	58	14
Self-employed			
small and medium-size firms	32	63	5
large firms	28	62	10
Farmers	11	87	2

Source: Manfred Berger et al., "Bundestagswahl 1976: Politik und Sozialstruktur," Zeitschrift für Parlamentsfragen, VIII, No. 2 (Aug. 1977), 215.

temporarily for acts of collective acclamation," will become a stark reality. [18]

The party's perpetual need to mobilize maximum support among the voters meant that it had to target potential recruits from the major groups in the Federal Republic. As noted, its links to the trade union movement were close enough to facilitate such a recruitment effort. But its links to other groups or organizations were less intimate; hence it could not expect to reap similar electoral dividends from them. Let us examine what success the SPD had with three such key groups—youth, citizens' initiatives, and the churches—whose members had widely divergent political views. Many (especially in the Protestant Church) were already SPD members and/or voters, but a substantial number were less inclined to support the party.

YOUTH

No political party can do without the young people who form the future political cadres of the nation. But if the young are more radical than their elders, intraparty clashes are inevitable. In the SPD the Jusos provided the organizational base for attracting young people, but found recruitment difficult in the mid- and late-1970s when a sizable segment of youth was either apolitical or hostile to the "establishment" parties. Yet, of a target of 8 million 15-to-25-year-old youths in 1974, of whom about half were studying and half working, 6 percent had joined a party, a higher percentage than those over 25. Nearly half (46 percent) of the young people had entered the SPD; 31 percent, the CDU/CSU; 1 percent, the FDP; and 11 percent, other, primarily left, parties. [19]

The SPD, as the party most open to societal reforms, had won substantial support from young voters in the 1972 election, but in 1976 their enthusiasm for the party had waned, even though more of them voted for it—many on a "lesser evil" basis—than for other parties. A 1978 poll showed a conservative trend among the 15-to-19-year-olds: 34 percent rejected socialism decisively, while only 5 percent approved it fully and 16 percent with major reservations. A 1980 poll indicated a new mood: a growing number of youth wanted to be left alone and/or were bent on material security and professional success. [20]

Other youth, like their counterparts in other advanced industrial states, joined alternative and countercultural groups, which offered them emotional identification and a collective identity. Many youth were critical of the lack of systemic changes and of authoritarian tendencies in the SPD-led government. They had little interest in supporting one of the established parties, which were blamed for the perpetuation of a bureaucratized society incapable of solving major problems facing the nation. They viewed politicians, who were not concerned with their problems, as tied too much to interest groups and lacking compassion, humanity, and solidarity. [21]

In 1979, Peter Glotz wrote about the SPD's difficulty in holding its youth. Among the many reasons were the party's inability to counter an ideological counteroffensive of the political right, uncertainty about the party's program among a majority of its functionaries, and the awakening of false hope among youth that through the political process one can make fundamental changes in human relations and achieve unattainable goals. He blamed the Jusos for promising to manipulate the economic system to produce socialism. Such a promise led to resignation when little happened. [22]

Brandt acknowledged that the SPD was encountering increasing difficulties in recruiting young people. Many did not join because politics seemed boring. They saw little in party work to engage their attention and were not aware enough of the many governmental reforms since 1969. [23] He contended that youth must know that it does not live in the worst of worlds and that the SPD is not as bad as some had pictured it. He sympathized with youth's mistrust of bureaucracy, but said the party must counter youth's tendencies towards indifference and denial and its stepping out of society and fleeing into sects and drugs. It must convince the young to work politically for a policy of peace, an end to world hunger, protection of the environment and more humane economic growth—problems affecting not only youth but all age groups. [24] On the other hand, he noted that in 1976 the SPD received 51 percent of the votes from young first-time voters, a record no other party could match.

Left-leaning SPD leaders argued that to regain youth's confidence the party must be in the vanguard of democratic development in the nation. If it sought merely to gain the vote of young people in order to obtain a majority, their skeptical mood would only be confirmed and democracy would not be believable to them. The Jusos, opening a dialogue with youth, warned the party not to let the opportunity to capture their loyalty slip by. The party must support those who desire a simpler life and satisfactions that the modern world does not provide. The party should make an inventory of ways to open a dialogue with the alternative movement. Only then will young people see that the SPD is the party most likely to solve important problems facing German society. [25]

These appeals for action had no immediate effect. The generational gap between the party's young and senior elite was still too wide. Some party and government policies still ran counter to youth's aspirations. Many problems, ranging from unemployment to educational barriers, facing youth still had not been solved. Bureaucracy and consumerism still had not been tamed. The result: by 1980 many youths were apolitical; joined the alternative and ecology movements; or led squatters' protests, leading to violence, in a number of cities.

CITIZENS' INITIATIVES

The young protest movement was partly responsible for the mushrooming of citizens' initiative groups in the 1970s which absorbed the political energy of millions of predominantly young (18-to-35), new middle-class, white-collar people. They showed political consciousness and political behavior atypical for West Germany. Concerned about the parties' inability to solve a multitude of problems dealing with energy, the environment, industrialization, economic growth, centralization, and other issues pertaining to the quality of life in an advanced industrial state, citizens formed ad hoc single-issue groups, whose grass roots participatory democracy often limited them to a short existence. Although a number of SPD adherents were among the groups, most of the members were disaffected from the established parties. [26]

In an attempt to win converts, SPD officials contended in the late 1970s that the programmatic demands of the groups coincided with the party program. For instance, on environmental issues, as early as 1961 the SPD had been the first party to raise the issue of "a blue sky over the Ruhr" in an electoral campaign. Brandt's government declaration of 1969 emphasizing environmental protection had led later to legislation, e.g., on water purification and pollution control. Party officials admitted, however, that not all goals, such as controls of injurious chemicals, had been reached. On nonenvironmental matters, they noted the party's support of humanization of the workplace, greater citizen participation in local affairs, and extension of codetermination. [27] The officials tried to convince group members that their goals would be achieved more easily if they worked through the system rather than on its periphery, because single-issue goals would have to be integrated into a broader political and economic framework encompassing research and technology, regional infrastructural development, and a balance between ecological concerns and jobs for workers.

SPD attempts to win converts from the citizens' initiatives met with little success, especially when a number of them—usually known as the Greens or the Alternatives—began to organize in 1977 as ecological and antinuclear parties and run slates of candidates in local and state elections. The traditional parties, especially the SPD and FDP, looked with trepidation on their new competition. The FDP feared a loss of votes and legislative representation should it fall below the 5 percent electoral barrier. SPD and FDP fears were not exaggerated: in some Länder elections, youth flocked to the Greens. In the 1978 Hamburg Land election, for instance, the Greens received 9.5 percent of the total vote, mostly at the expense of the SPD and FDP. The SPD lost 7 percent of its vote compared with the 1974 Land election—not all caused by defections to the Greens, but enough to cause concern among its leaders. The Greens also scored successes in Baden-Wuerttemberg, Bremen, Hesse, and Lower Saxony.

In 1979 the fluidity of the party system increased when the Greens decided to become a national party and formed the Federal Association of Citizens' Initiatives for Environmental Protection (Bundesverband Bürgerinitiativen Umweltschutz [BBU]). [28] Its electoral platform emphasized environmental protection, opposition to nuclear energy, nonviolence in public policy, and democratic rights. Before the 1980 national election, SPD leaders feared that most votes for the BBU would come from those voters who in 1976 had supported the government coalition. Worried that the consequence might be a CDU/CSU victory, some leaders warned Green adherents that to vote for the BBU meant voting for Franz Josef Strauss, a prospect unalluring to most of them. But the BBU, partly because of internal left-right schisms, captured only 1.5 percent of the national vote, insufficient to gain Bundestag representation.

During this electoral struggle, left-wing SPD leaders advised their more conservative party colleagues not to alienate the Greens, because they were needed as allies in the 1980s. The left leaders formed an ecology group, "The Greens in the SPD," to win the Greens over to the SPD banner. The new group insisted that the SPD support a moratorium on new nuclear plants, develop a new alternative energy policy, and become more sensitive to environmental concerns. It should also encourage SPD members active in the citizens' initiatives to bring their experiences and interests into SPD decision making. [29]

The Jusos, sympathetic to the Green movement, contended however that it was not technology that threatened mankind but capitalist property relations, which use technology for profits. They urged the Green adherents to join the SPD in order to strengthen the humanist wing battling the "insufferable incrusting" in the party. At the 1979 SPD convention, Brandt welcomed the idealism of the young who had joined the Greens to create a better society but pointed out that the Greens' concentration on a single issue rather than on many issues facing the nation was illusionary. Convention delegates approved a position paper calling for an ecologically responsible policy. It included sectoral planning to take into account the interrelationship between natural and technical-industrial systems, and priority of ecological over economic factors whenever people's health or lives were at stake. [30]

On the other hand, the convention majority did not adopt a sharp anti-nuclear energy program acceptable to the Greens. As a result, the Greens maintained their distance from the SPD and even from the Jusos, who were in accord with an antinuclear policy but were part of the SPD machine. A 1980 Juso delegation visiting Gorleben, the site of repeated antinuclear demonstrations, to show solidarity with the protesters received a cool reception. The protesters held aloft signs with the symbolic inscription, "Who betrayed us? Social Democrats" (in German, more poetically, "Wer hat uns verraten? Sozial Demokraten"). Even should the Social Democrats change their policy on nuclear energy, they would continue to have difficulties with the Greens and the alternative movement, whose adherents are presently reluctant to support the established parties. As a result, the SPD may face serious electoral reverses, especially in local and Länder elections, which in turn may affect the party's political fortunes at the national level. With the breakup of the SPD-FDP coalition cabinet in 1982 and the possibility that the Greens may gain Bundestag representation in future national elections the SPD may need to turn to the Greens as a potential coalition partner (thereby making concessions to them) if it expects to return to power in Bonn—unless the Greens are ready to support an SPD minority government or the SPD is willing to form a Grand Coalition with the CDU/CSU once again. The building of future coalitions has become more uncertain than ever.

RELIGIOUS INSTITUTIONS

SPD relations with the Protestant and Catholic hierarchies have seldom been close, especially given the party's secular heritage. In the nineteenth century, Marx declared religion to be the opium of the people. Liebknecht viewed socialism as the new religion for the masses and could not conceive of two religions paralleling one another. Bebel saw socialism and Christianity as different as "fire and water." Such views led to a confrontation course between the party and the churches, especially between 1890 and 1914. But during the Hitler period the antagonism abated when both SPD and church leaders were persecuted. In the postwar era, the emergence of the CDU/CSU as the party trying to gain the support of Catholics and Protestants produced new tensions between the SPD and the churches.

Conservative Protestant bishops such as Hanns Lilje or Martin Dibelius of Hannover tacitly supported the CDU, and liberal Protestants such as Martin Niemoeller formed first a neutralist and pacifist movement and then the All-German People's Party. Lacking enough support, the party soon folded, and many of its adherents, including Gustav Heinemann, later West German president, joined the SPD. Left Catholics also wanted a rapprochement with the SPD in the immediate postwar years, but the Church hierarchy ostracized the party. In 1958, fifty Social Democrats and fifty Catholic priests, theologians, and laypersons met publicly to discuss a possible rapprochement. In 1959 the party adopted a new positive stance toward religion and the churches in the Godesberg program, noting that "socialism is no substitute for religion." [31]

Protestant Church

The Godesberg program, fully acknowledging the roots of Christian socialism, made it easier for the party to gain support from both churches, but obstacles remained. The SPD had to confront the Protestant Church's principle of unwavering neutrality toward parties. The bishops encouraged laypersons to be active in all parties, especially given the doctrinal differences among the autonomous regional federations loosely federated in the Evangelical Church in Germany (EKD). Hence the EKD's 120-member synod, functioning also as a pressure group, has discussed political and social matters and transmitted its views to the government and the Bundestag.

Despite the EKD's nonpartisan position, the SPD, most of whose members and voters are Protestants, sought a rapprochement with it as a way of gathering additional support. On several occasions since 1959, meetings took place between officials of both organizations, facilitated in the 1970s by Helmut Schmidt's earlier membership on the synod of the Lutheran Church in Hamburg. In 1973, SPD headquarters set up a Protestant Church section to serve as liaison to church officials. During the 1976 election campaign, 180 engaged Protestants in the SPD issued an appeal to Protestants to vote for a party that stood for reforms. At the same time, Schmidt published a book Als Christ in der politischen Entscheidung (A Christian in Political Decision-Making) in which he called on churches to take a stand on political and social issues without making such issues the central focus. The implicit plea was for an endorsement of the government's policies. [32] Typical of the meetings between the SPD and Church authorities was one held in January 1980 in Bonn at which Brandt and other SPD presidium members met with top EKD leaders headed by Bishop Eduard Lohse. The topics discussed ranged from domestic policies such as education and the role of churches in the Federal Republic to foreign policies such as détente and the Middle East. (33] The SPD was interested in these meetings to gain support for its policies and increase Protestant membership in the SPD; its task was made easier by the fact that two well-known SPD left-wingers, Erhard Eppler and Henning Scherf, were leading Protestant laymen who could be expected to receive a favorable hearing from Protestant youth. Moreover, a new group "Christians within the SPD" was formed to work closely with the churches. It intended to criticize unpalatable SPD policies and to reconcile the social aspects of socialism with the responsibility of being a Christian.

Catholic Church

The SPD courting of the Catholic Church after Godesberg was more complicated given the historical antagonism between them. In March 1964, Pope Paul VI received an SPD delegation led by Fritz Erler—the first such meeting in the party's history. The SPD officials emphasized their desire to establish close relations with the Church, and the Pope praised the party's contribution to German economic and social life. [34] Despite the Pope's statement and the signing in spring 1965 of a concordat between the Lower Saxony SPD government and the Vatican providing for continued state aid to parochial elementary schools, most of the German Catholic hierarchy remained antagonistic toward the SPD. In pastoral letters and sermons, the clergy urged parishioners to vote on grounds of conscience, an implicit endorsement of the CDU/CSU.

But a thaw developed when the SPD joined the CDU/CSU in the Grand Coalition (1966-1969). A Catholic Office representative in charge of liaison with parties met often with leading Social Democrats to discuss policy questions. He promised that the German Conference of Bishops would remain neutral in the 1969 national election if the SPD did not change the church tax system as it had intended. In the election, the party made its first significant inroads into Catholic constituencies, especially in urban middle-class areas.

Brandt's government declaration of October 1969 accentuated partnership with the churches and cooperation with their social programs in Germany and the Third World. In November, Wehner and Leber (the only Catholic SPD cabinet member) met with the Pope in Rome to assure him of the government's desire for friendly relations with the Church and to receive Vatican backing for the Oder-Neisse border between Germany and

Poland. In July 1970, Chancellor Brandt saw the Pope on a similar mission, broadening the topic to other Ostpolitik issues. As a result of these talks and a more progressive mood within the Federal Republic, the party hoped to reach accommodation with the Church. In 1968, Leber had been elected to the Central Committee of German Catholics, which in the past had supported the Christian Democrats. He established a bureau in his ministry to monitor the government's relation with the Church and often spoke to Catholic groups on the theme that a good Catholic could be a Social Democrat and vice versa. After a three-year stint on the central committee, Leber was succeeded by Hermann Schmidt-Vockenhausen, Bundestag vice president. But because both of them were in the party's right wing, they did not serve as a magnet for liberal Catholics who were potential party recruits. Brandt, in the meantime, instructed his ministers to discuss any matter touching upon ecclesiastical interests with the Bonn representatives of the churches. [35]

Yet the rapprochement did not last long, because the bonds between the Catholic Church and the CDU/CSU remained firm, because many CDU/CSU political appointees in Bonn ministries were replaced by SPD and FDP appointees (some Catholic journals labeled the move an "anti-Christian bloodbath"), and because the new government planned to change the penal code (to abolish penalties for adultery, blasphemy, and homosexual offenses and to liberalize divorce, abortion, and pornography provisions). [36] When the Church opposed key provisions of the divorce bill, Minister of Justice Gerhard Jahn (SPD) deleted some sections, not wanting to be responsible for the collapse of the earlier détente with the Church. The government parties' plan to permit abortions during the first three months of pregnancy renewed the strain between the SPD and the Church (see chapter 13). [37]

By 1972, an election year, the politically conservative majority of bishops saw in the government's social program the beginning of socialism, the secularization of society, and violations of Christian principles. They were determined to challenge the government's alleged intention to set society's values. In turn, some Social Democrats blamed an "inflexible doctrinaire group" within the Church for blocking reforms designed to create a more humane, tolerant, and progressive society. [38] Although the Church refrained from openly endorsing the CDU/CSU during the election campaign, its feelings were not hidden. To preclude direct Catholic press support, SPD officials met with twenty-five of its editors. The officials expressed their concern about the CDU/CSU's attempt to mobilize the Church against the SPD and about the statement made by a CDU spokesman labeling Catholics in the SPD as "renegades." [39]

Despite deteriorating SPD-Catholic relations, 35 percent of the Catholic vote went to the SPD in 1972, more than ever before or in the subsequent 1976 and 1980 elections, when it declined to 31 percent, while from 60 to 62 percent voted for the CDU/CSU in all elections. [40] Most Catholics who voted for the SPD were in the liberal wing of the Church or no longer practicing Catholics. In a 1972 poll (which included Protestants), only 11 percent of SPD voters compared with 41 percent of CDU/CSU voters said that they attended church regularly. Questioned whether they were personally interested in the church and its positions on contemporary issues, only 18 percent of the SPD voters compared with 38 percent of the CDU/CSU voters said that they were. [41] The determining factor for many Catholics who voted for the SPD was rather the party's position on détente and social justice.

After the 1972 election, SPD-Catholic relations improved again. In 1973, the German Conference of Bishops, not wanting to alienate Catholics who had voted for the SPD, ordered the clergy to be neutral toward political parties. Justice Minister Vogel, a Catholic, noted that the Second Vatican Council had helped to ease the strains between the German Church and its SPD parishioners. In Bonn, the Catholic Club, which serves as a center for deputies and civil servants, for the first time opened its doors to SPD members. In Hesse, the SPD minister-president increased subsidies to Catholic private schools. In January 1974, SPD headquarters set up a Catholic Church section to serve as liaison to the bishops. Wehner insisted that the Catholic section chief be a person not allied with the progressive or conservative wings of the Church, but neutral in the intra-Catholic schism. In effect, he did not want the SPD to side openly with the Catholic left for fear that such a move would arouse the ire of the conservative bishops. [42]

But once again, as in earlier intervals between elections, the armistice between party and Church did not last and new verbal battles erupted. Before the 1976 national election, Cardinal Julius Döpfner, chairman of the Conference of Bishops, appealed to the government to safeguard the basic moral values. He was concerned about legislation on marriage, divorce, abortion, and education that ran counter to the position of the Church. The Cardinal admitted that the vast majority of the people were no longer following the Church on a number of social issues, but he remained especially critical of abortion legislation, which was "destroying all moral consciousness" and making society "less humane." [43] Chancellor Schmidt, in reply, said that "our state cannot amend and pass laws that suit only transcendentalists, religious organizations or their basic moral values. By favoring one social sector the state would no longer remain ideologically neutral." [44] Schmidt reminded his listeners at the Catholic Academy that the government had put no obstacles in the path of the Church's efforts to convince the people of its values.

After the 1976 election, relations remained strained. In November 1978, Brandt, Schmidt, and other presidium members met with Cardinal Höffner of Cologne and members of the Conference of Bishops to discuss the smoldering controversies between them. As in previous encounters, both sides presented their views but no rapprochement resulted. How far apart they were was evident in 1980—another election year. In September, a number of bishops issued a pastoral letter implicitly endorsing the CDU/CSU. They decried (just as the CDU/CSU did in its campaign) the state's expanding role in daily life and the resultant growth of bureaucracy, mounting state debts, the new marriage law that was destroying marriages, the revised law on abortions, and the threat to family life. Predictably, top SPD chiefs denounced the bishops' action; Schmidt reminded them that there was "nothing in either the Old or the New Testament about how to manage state finances," and that "pulpits should be used for pastoral work and not for politics." [45] The pastoral letter—not read in all parishes—had little effect on the voting of Catholics. It symbolized a rear-guard action on the part of the conservative bishops who were worried about secularization among their parishioners. An increasing number of Catholics attended church less often and were less involved with Catholic associations. For instance, between 1963 and 1980 the proportion of Catholics reporting regular church attendance (one to four times a month) dropped from 55 to 31 percent. [46]

It is not surprising that relations between the SPD and the Catholic

Church did not improve significantly after the 1959 Godesberg program, despite the new image of a moderate left-center SPD no longer taking a strong anticlerical position or espousing Marxist doctrines. When the party clashed with the Church over a number of important social issues, compromises were hard to achieve. In addition, the existence of a neo-Marxist wing in the SPD reinforced many bishops' views that the party was still imbued with atheism and Marxism, ready to seize property and precipitate moral decay in a secularized society. As a result, SPD attempts to improve links with the Church made little progress. This was true especially during election years, when the bishops implicitly gave their blessing to the CDU/CSU, which was ideologically more in tune with their own views than the SPD. They remained skeptical about SPD assertions that the party was interested in long-range cooperation with the Church, believing that this was a subterfuge to increase the Catholic vote for the SPD. On the SPD side there was mistrust too. Many Protestant members still identified Catholics as old-fashioned, uncritically obedient to the pronouncements of the bishops, and not ready to move into the twentieth century. They viewed a dialogue with Catholics as unproductive. [47] SPD leaders, however, were eager to woo progressive Catholics away from the CDU/CSU and to talk with conservative Church leaders in order to erase prejudices and increase trust between them. [48]

Although the task has been difficult, time may be on the side of the SPD. In 1980, one signal of an improvement in relations was the invitation extended to leading SPD politicians to participate in podium discussions at the Church-sponsored Catholic Day. At meetings in previous years, fewer invitations to SPD chiefs had been made and audience hostility had been more evident. In future years, once the conservative bishops retire, the Vatican may appoint more progressive ones. In addition, progressive lay associations may become more powerful. Thereupon, SPD-Church relations are bound to improve, and the SPD claim to be a catch-all party will become more valid when a higher percentage of Catholics vote for it.

NOTES

1. Anthony Downs, An Economic Theory of Democracy (New York: Harper, 1957), p. 35.

2. Introduction to Marx, The Class Struggles in France, 1848 to 1850, in Karl Marx and Friedrich Engels, Selected Works (New York: International Publishers, 1968), p. 665.

3. Ralph Miliband, Marxism and Politics (London: Oxford University Press, 1977), p. 161; Adam Przeworski, "Social Democracy as a Historical Phenomenon," New Left Review, No. 122 (July-Aug. 1980), p. 34.

4. For a perceptive analysis, see Otto Kirchheimer, "The Transformation of the Western European Party Systems," Political Parties and Political Development, eds. LaPalombara and Weiner, pp. 184, 186.

5. Przeworski, p. 44.

6. Kendall L. Baker, Russell J. Dalton, and Kai Hildebrandt, Germany Transformed: Political Culture and the New Politics (Cambridge: Harvard University Press, 1981), p. 347, note 21. According to another survey, "52 percent of the Catholic trade unionists prefer the SPD, while 33 percent support the CDU" (Derek W. Urwin, "Germany: Continuity and Change in Electoral Politics," Electoral Behavior: A Comparative Handbook,

ed. Richard Rose [New York: The Free Press, 1974], p. 131).

7. Helmut Norpoth, "Party Identification in West Germany," Comparative Political Studies, XI, No. 1 (Apr. 1978), 37; Ursula Feist and Klaus Liepelt, "Vom Mehrparteien- zum Zweiblocksystem: Veränderungen in der Wähler- und Sozialstruktur der Bundesrepublik Deutschland," Revue d'Allemagne, IX, No. 2 (Apr.-June 1977), 214; Schmollinger and Stöss, "Sozialstruktur und Parteiensystem," pp. 220-221; Franz Urban Pappi, "Parteiensystem und Sozialstruktur in der Bundesrepublik," Politische Vierteljahresschrift, XIV, No. 2 (May 1973), 191-213; Hans D. Klingemann and Charles L. Taylor, "Partisanship, Candidates and Issues: Attitudinal Components of the Vote in West German Federal Elections," Elections and Parties, eds. Kaase and von Beyme, pp. 97, 126.

8. See Klaus Liepelt and Alexander Mitscherlich, Thesen zur Wählerfluktuation (Frankfurt/Main: Europäische Verlagsanstalt, 1968), p. 74; Rainer-Olaf Schultze, "Nur Parteiverdrossenheit und Diffuser Protest? Systemfunktionale Fehlinterpretationen der grünen Wahlerfolge," Zeitschrift für Parlamentsfragen, XI, No. 2 (July 1980), 299-306. A 1980 infas survey showed that of every 100 SPD voters, 41 came from the traditional left sphere (unionized workers or those with a social conscience); 20 from the unionized middle class; 17 from the new middle class; 16 from the traditional conservative sphere (dependent employees, tradesmen, farmers); and 6 from the traditional Catholic sphere (workers, middle class) (Infas--Report Wahlen: Baden-Wuerttemberg 1980: Analysen und Dokumente zum Landtagswahl am 16. März 1980 [Bonn-Bad Godesberg, 1980], pp. 44-45).

9. Baker, Dalton, and Hildebrandt, pp. 142-147, 192-193; Conradt and Mueller, pp. 25-27.

10. Urwin, p. 151.

11. Liepelt and Mitscherlich, p. 105.

12. Infas study, 1975, cited by Ursula Feist, "Unterwegs zur politischen Identität: die Jungwähler," Transfer 2, ed. Bohret et al., p. 181.

13. Urwin, p. 156; Jesse Eckhard, "Die Bundestagwahlen von 1953 bis 1972: Im Spiegel der repräsentativen Wahlstatistik. Zur Bedeutung eines Schlüsselinstruments der Wahlforschung," Zeitschrift für Parlamentsfragen, VI, No. 3 (1975), 317; Conradt, The German Polity, 2d ed., pp. 130-132.

14. Feist and Liepelt, p. 214; Gluchowski and Veen, pp. 322-323.

15. Urwin, pp. 147-150.

16. Ibid., pp. 133, 153-154.

17. See note 5 above.

18. "Über den Begriff der politischen Beteiligung," Student und Politik, eds. Jürgen Habermas et al. (Berlin: Luchterhand, 1969), p. 31.

19. In addition, 11 percent gave no answer (Infas-Jungwählerstudie 1974, cited by Juso Informationsdienst, No. 10 [Oct. 1977], pp. 2, 3).

20. Munich Institute of Youth Research and McCann poll, cited by Kölner Stadt-Anzeiger, Mar. 11, 1978; New York Times, Sept. 25, 1980.

21. Some of these youth joined religious cult, drug, alcohol, or terrorist groups (Scherf, p. 660; Vorwärts, Nov. 29, 1979).

22. Ibid., Nov. 1, 1979.

23. Ibid.

24. Ibid., Nov. 29, 1979; Stuttgarter Zeitung, Dec. 4, 1979.

25. Vorwärts, Mar. 29, 1979; Scherf, pp. 660-662.

26. According to the Federal Environmental Agency 1980 directory, more than 5 million people belonged to 1,138 regional and 130 national environmental protection groups in the Federal Republic (Frankfurter

Rundschau, Jan. 30, 1980). For details of the citizens' initiative movement in West Germany and Europe respectively, see Bernd Guggenberger, Bürgerinitiativen in der Parteiendemokratie: Von der Ökologiebewegung zur Umweltpartei (Stuttgart: Kohlhammer, 1980); Jörg R. Mettke, ed., Die Grünen: Regierungspartner von morgen? (Reinbek: Rowohlt, 1982); Suzanne Berger, "Politics and Antipolitics in Western Europe in the Seventies," Daedalus, Vol. 108, No. 1 (Winter 1979), 27-50.

27. SPD, Intern-dokumente, No. 4 (Aug. 1978).

28. For details, see Klaus G. Troitzsch, "Die Herausforderung der 'etablierten' Parteien durch die 'Grünen'," Handbuch des deutschen Parteiensystems, eds. Heino Kaack and Reinhold Roth, Vol. II, pp. 260-294.

29. Vorwärts, Nov. 8, 1979; Informationen der Sozialdemokratischen Bundestagsfraktion, No. 1170, Nov. 19, 1979.

30. Frankfurter Rundschau, Dec. 4, 1979; Politik, No. 2 (Feb. 1980); Juso Schüler-Express, VI, 2/80.

31. SPD, Basic Programme of the Social Democratic Party of Germany, p. 17.

32. Schmidt, Als Christ in der politischen Entscheidung (Gütersloh: Gütersloher Verlagshaus, 1976). See also Frederic Spotts, The Churches and Politics in Germany (Middleton, Conn.: Wesleyan University Press, 1973), pp. 144 ff.; Richard Sorg, Marxismus und Protestantismus in Deutschland (Cologne: Pahl-Rugenstein, 1974), pp, 156 ff.; SPD, executive, "Sozialdemokratie und Protestantismus: Christen in der Tradition der Arbeiterbewegung—Christen in der SPD (1930-1979)" (hectographed, 1979); Johannes Rau and Franz Böckle, Sozialdemokratie und Kirchen (Bonn: Neue Gesellschaft, 1979).

33. SPD, Service, Presse, Funk, TV, 29/80, Jan. 17, 1980.

34. Spotts, pp. 341-342.

35. Ibid., pp. ix, 179-180; 345-346.

36. Ibid., p. 347.

37. Ibid., p. 348.

38. Ibid., p. 349.

39. Süddeutsche Zeitung, Feb. 24, 1972. See also Demosthenes Savramis, Das Christliche in der SPD (Munich: List, 1976).

40. Frankfurter Allgemeine Zeitung, Oct. 11, 1980; Vorwärts, Oct. 16, 1980.

41. Forschungsgruppe Wahlen (Mannheim), "Politik in der Bundesrepublik vor und nach der Bundestagswahl 1972; Tabellenband" (n.d.), pp. 117-119.

42. Frankfurter Rundschau, Feb. 14, 1973; Dec. 11, 1973; Frankfurter Allgemeine Zeitung, Mar. 6, 1973; General-Anzeiger (Bonn), June 22, 1974. See also Anton Rauscher, Kirche-Partei-Politik (Cologne: J.P. Bachem, 1974); especially chapter by Gerhart Schmidtchen (pp. 57-103).

43. Deutsches Allgemeines Sonntagsblatt, May 30, 1976; Kölner Stadt-Anzeiger, June 5, 1976. See also Frédéric Hartweg, "Les églises, les partis et les élections de 1976," Revue d'Allemagne, XI, No. 2 (April-June 1977), 231-254.

44. Kölner Stadt-Anzeiger, June 5, 1976.

45. New York Times, Sept. 15, 1980. See also Vorwärts, July 31, 1980; Oct. 16, 1980; Vogel open letter to bishops, "Einige Fragen an die deutschen Bischöfe zum jetzt bekannt gewordenen Hirtenbrief zur Bundestagswahl 1980" (hectographed, n.d.).

46. Elisabeth Noelle-Neumann, ed., The Germans (Westport, Conn.: Greenwood, 1981), p. 235.

47. Heinrich B. Streithofen, SPD und Katholische Kirche (Stuttgart: Seewald, 1974), p. 25.

48. ppp (SPD news service), No. 52, Mar. 14, 1980. See Hans Buchheim, "Kritische Anfragen an das Menschen- und Gesellschaftsbild der SPD," Kirche-Partei-Politik, ed. Rauscher, pp. 131-154.

10
National, State, and Local Elections

In democratic systems citizens formally influence the policymaking process when casting their votes for competing parties at election time. As one specialist noted: "Modern mass parties were created to contest elections and electoral systems exist to structure competition among parties." [1] In the Federal Republic, the SPD could not expect to gain and maintain power without maximum efforts to mobilize its own members and the centrist voters in national, state, and local elections. Its efforts were made within a moderate pluralist party system in which it competed with only one other major dominant party and a host of smaller parties in a political environment free of the polarization found in such states as France and Italy.

The SPD knew that it had only a slim chance of winning more than 50 percent of the vote in a national election. Hence it had to keep the interests of the FDP—its expected coalition partner—and the centrist bloc of voters constantly in mind during the campaigns. Such cautiousness alienated the SPD's left activists, who insisted that they be given adequate representation in the nomination of candidates. This precipitated internal struggles but also compromises during the nomination and election stages that formed key ingredients in the party's raison d'être as a political organization.

NOMINATION OF BUNDESTAG CANDIDATES

The West German parties select nominees for the 496-member Bundestag on the basis of a complex electoral system that combines proportional representation at the Land level and plurality at the district level. A citizen casts two votes: the first for a candidate in a single-member district and the second for the Land party slate, with half the Bundestag seats allocated to the districts and half to the the Länder. The second vote is more crucial, because the final number of seats for each party depends on the proportion of votes it receives on the Land lists. [2] To reduce the number of splinter parties, the electoral law stipulates that a party must either obtain a minimum of 5 percent of the total vote on the second ballot or win at least three seats in the districts in order to gain seats in the Bundestag. The SPD did not have to worry about the latter provision, but the FDP did. Since 1957 the FDP has not been able to win a direct district mandate. Hence it was in the interest of the SPD—unlikely to get 50 percent of the vote—to ensure the survival of the FDP so that both parties could gain and maintain political power by outpolling the CDU/CSU. One method of enhancing this probability was ticket splitting. Among the maximum of 10 percent of voters who engaged in this tactic were many SPD and FDP voters who cast their first ballot for the SPD (to increase the chance of victory for the SPD rather than the CDU/CSU district candidate) and their second for the FDP (to ensure a minimum FDP representation in the Bundestag).

This electoral system enables both the local branches and the regional organizations of all parties to participate in the nomination process. According to law, district candidates must be chosen by membership assemblies or delegate conferences. The SPD chose the latter alternative because of its large membership. The branches elect delegates to the local conference, their number based on the branch's number of dues-paying members. Nomination to the Bundestag slate is by secret ballot, with the winner needing at least a plurality to become the party's candidate.

According to the SPD guidelines, district candidates must be selected on the basis of competence and ability to represent the party in public, rather than as reward for prior service. Women and persons with special expertise needed in the Fraktion should be especially considered, while few employees of the party and allied organizations should be nominated. [3]

As for candidates for the Land slate, a Land delegate conference (Landesdelegiertenkonferenz) or a Land party convention (Landesparteitag) makes the final choice by secret ballot, including their ranking on the list. Because the number of successful nominees on each SPD Land list is determined by the number of votes the party receives, its top candidates are placed high on the list to ensure election and less important candidates receive a lower place. The SPD tries to present a balanced list of candidates in terms of sex, age, interest groups, and religious denomination. The party guidelines insist that only those who are indispensable to the Fraktion or who by being well known could attract voter support should be nominated and also urge that women and specialists (especially those who have little chance of being elected in the district) be put high on the list. [4] But important candidates who are unsure of district election may also receive a place on a Land list.

The formal nomination process gives no clues to who makes the initial selection of candidates. One deputy elected in a district recalled that in his county (Kreis) an informal group of sixty elite members, consisting of the chairmen of the branches, city councillors, mayors, and deputies, met to discuss various possible candidates. Their suggestions were then transmitted to the executives of the branches, county, and subdistrict for further deliberation. His name was selected from the contenders and placed in nomination at the local conference of delegates, where he easily won nomination. [5]

In 1965, contests between rival nominees occurred in only 23 out of 248 districts. But when the Jusos became more activist, they challenged either incumbent deputies who sought reelection or new "conservative" nominees. By 1969, the number of contests had risen to 74 and three years later to half the districts. In nominating left candidates, the Jusos challenged the party ideologically and attempted to introduce more intraparty and participatory democracy into the nomination process. They made it clear in a congress resolution that "only those Social Democrats will be nominated who can be expected to give unlimited support to a consequential reform politics in the democratic socialist sense." [6] In some instances, they nominated persons who had no chance of winning approval at the local conference, but the occasion gave them an opportunity to challenge the nominee put up by the "establishment." The Jusos sometimes distributed questionnaires to candidates or questioned them orally about their stand on issues and their views on the imperative mandate (in which deputies are bound to support party decisions even if they conflict with an SPD-led government decision). If the Jusos were satisfied with the responses, they would agree to support the candidate.

One conservative newspaper labeled the Juso action an "inquisition" against all potential party candidates, but a liberal newspaper contended that most of the Juso questions were harmless and that the Jusos had done a service to the party by enhancing intraparty democracy. [7] The party executive had misgivings about some Juso actions, such as their threat to prevent the renomination in 1969 of any deputy who had voted for the bitterly contested emergency legislation. The executive contended that this constituted an unacceptable pressure on deputies, who were supposed to vote according to their consciences.

In the 1970s the number of prominent right-wing incumbent candidates challenged for renomination rose swiftly. For instance, in 1976, in Frankfurt, the left accused Georg Leber of not doing enough for the local organization. Knowing that he would not be renominated, he decided not to seek the constituency seat. Brandt and Schmidt thereupon intervened with state leaders to ensure that Leber was placed at the top of the Land list. Other right-wing candidates who in the past had easily won renomination by acclamation were also under pressure not to run again, but about three-fourths of all deputies did win renomination. The others decided to retire or lost a contest for renomination even though the party executive had recommended them. [8]

Ideological differences were not always the chief cause of the battle for constituency seats. In many districts, contests took place between candidates from two SPD county associations (Kreisverbände) which together formed one election district. In such instances, the stronger association normally won. In other districts, a contender challenged an incumbent who had neglected his or her constituency or who was too authoritarian. [9]

At the Land level, much of the intraparty schism was eliminated, because the left had less strength on the district or county executives, which recommend the list nominees to the Länder executives. (In cases where the Länder are not subdivided into districts, the Länder executives suggest the names of candidates directly to the Land delegate conference or party convention.) The Länder executives attempted to give fair representation to the districts and to satisfy different party factions; conversely, they did not normally recommend persons who had been too controversial in the Land. Yet in some districts or Länder, such as Hesse-South, South Bavaria, and Schleswig-Holstein, the left had enough strength to ensure the nomination of some of its candidates, or it tried at the nominating convention to push a conservative nominee into a lower slot on the list. Needless to say, it did not attempt to use such a tactic on the party's top-drawer candidates, such as Schmidt and Wehner who had received the number one and two places on the Hamburg list. [10]

Before the 1969 election, the left-wing Tübingen Circle in Baden-Wuerttemberg set up a "candidate mirror" scoreboard, in which it compared all aspirants for the Land list on the basis of eleven criteria—openness to new ideas, independent political thought, expected

Bundestag activity, expertise, visibility among party and public, skill in publicity, rhetorical ability, relationship with the younger generation, involvement in intraparty democracy, general political impression, and humor. This scoreboard was to be helpful to delegates in choosing nominees, but no other Land adopted it.

In all Länder, most nominees who subsequently were elected deputies had been active in the party for some time. According to one 1976 Land survey, 49 percent had been members or chairmen of the branch or county executives; 14 percent, of the Land executive; and 2 percent, of the national executive. On the other hand, 35 percent had had no position in the party (many of them were minor union officials or specialists whose expertise was needed in the Bundestag). [11]

NATIONAL ELECTIONS

A brief survey of the national elections of 1969, 1972, 1976, and 1980 provides us with a kaleidoscopic overview of the SPD's style of politics, its shifting voter base, the salience of issues, and campaign strategies. It sheds further light on the nature of German politics during the 1970s, when the SPD-FDP coalition took power full of zest, ideas, and promises at the beginning of the decade and ended the decade with less of each.

Let us look at the characteristics common to the SPD's campaigns in all these election years before assessing each election separately to capture its distinguishing features. The SPD had to know during election intervals what shifts in the profile of voters had taken place: who were its core supporters, who were its sympathizers, and who were its potential voters from the bloc of floaters and nonvoters. One author estimated that the SPD (and the CDU/CSU) must address itself to the same voter potential of more than 70 percent in order to obtain 40 to 50 percent of the vote, knowing that the rest will never support it. To reach such a wide audience, most of which was accustomed to political participation, the SPD had to create campaign strategies containing the proper mixture of appealing candidates, forceful slogans, and key nonideological issues—reinforcing Richard Rose's observation that a "general election is about a choice between organizations, not ideas." [12]

Yet such strategies could not absolve the SPD leaders and managers from taking stock and looking at the party's legislative record. They knew that the CDU/CSU would assail this record and point to promises not kept. Hence they were also forced to devise an effective counterstrategy to rebut the CDU/CSU charges. In addition, they had to combat political boredom and disillusionment among the public about the lack of significant choices between parties at elections—a phenomenon not restricted to the Federal Republic but characteristic of the United States, the Netherlands, Scandinavia, etc., where consensual rather than adversarial politics is the rule.

In the intensive preparations for each national campaign, the SPD made long-range plans soon after elections. One year before a campaign started, Brandt and other top party leaders, supported by an electoral campaign commission, worked out the strategy, while national headquarters and an advertising agency worked out the technical details, including the contents of pamphlets—a difficult task, given the long interval before the election. The party deemed it crucial to mobilize as many as possible of the 1 million SPD members and the additional 3 million family members and sympathizers (out of about 14 to 16 million SPD voters in each election from 1969 to 1980). This was not easy, as only a minority was normally willing to be active in each campaign. Party headquarters needed to know who the nonactive members were and what problems they encountered; hence what central issues to accentuate in order to arouse their interest in the election. To provide answers, it commissioned public opinion institutes to conduct surveys and to schedule group discussions—expensive but necessary methods, according to an SPD election research specialist. [13]

The party leaders in small local branches found it easier than those in large branches to mobilize members for the campaign, although, according to one 1977 survey, 75 percent of members queried noted their participation in the campaign in some manner. For most of them, however, activity was limited to participating in SPD-sponsored rallies or drumming up support for the party among their closer acquaintances. About 25 percent of members did the grass-roots campaigning: distributing party propaganda in towns and outside factories, visiting non-SPD families, putting up billboards, raising money, organizing rallies, and taking voters to the polls. [14]

The party had to mobilize not only its own members but the voters as well. One public opinion institute, commissioned to prepare a list of target groups, came up with seven: traditional SPD voters (constituting 10 percent of the electorate); older voters, 60 and up (28 percent); women, 21 to 40 (17 percent); young people, 18 to 25 (12 percent); middle-class voters (23 percent); nonunionized workers (30 percent); and Catholic workers (17 percent). Members of these groups (in many cases, of more than one group) were to be won over by distinctive appeals to their interests and by reminders of what the government had done for them. [15]

Each campaign was marked by a time sequence, beginning with leaders and specialists preparing an election platform that was then accepted, normally with modifications, by the top party organs and by a special election convention. The platform extolled government or SPD achievements in the previous term and emphasized party objectives for the coming term. After the convention (usually in early summer if the election was to be held in mid-fall) the first phase of the campaign consisted of mobilizing the SPD members, who in turn were to help mobilize the uncommitted voters. In the second phase, the slower summer period, the party undertook low-key efforts to raise and paint the opposition in stereotyped negative images. In the third phase, the four-week "hot phase" just before election, the party again mobilized its members and launched a nationwide propaganda blitz. In this saturation phase, each household received a flyer giving many reasons why one should vote for the SPD, millions of posters of the party's leaders were put up, and top officials spoke at rallies throughout the nation and made television and radio appearances. [16] While these professionally run campaigns had some similarities to those in the United States, each campaign and election had distinctive features that must now be assessed.

The 1969 Election

In early 1969, most SPD leaders, except for Wehner and Schmidt, did not want to continue governing with the CDU/CSU after the election. They knew that among SPD members less than half had supported the coalition in the first place. They hoped instead to govern with the FDP. Polls had shown that the public viewed the SPD, based on its government performance from 1966 to 1969, as more competent than the CDU/CSU to handle economic and social policy as well as relations with the East bloc. [17]

In its electoral strategy, the SPD stressed its differences with the CDU/CSU, although choosing such bland slogans as "The best future you can choose" and "We create the modern Germany." Because the then CDU/CSU chancellor, Kurt Georg Kiesinger, had high voter appeal, SPD strategists emphasized the powerful and united SPD leadership team, rather than singling out Brandt as a future chancellor. At the same time, they assailed the divided CDU/CSU leadership that would not be able to match the SPD's reformist record and its ability to promote economic growth, enhance educational opportunities, expand industrial democracy, achieve arms control, and improve relations with the East. [18]

For the SPD, this was the first professional and costly campaign matching that of the other parties. The party also received support for its campaign from Günter Grass and other artists and intellectuals who founded the "Social Democratic Voters' Initiative." These multiple efforts paid off in electoral dividends. Continuing its steady gains, labeled "Comrade Trend," of previous elections, the SPD broke through the 40 percent barrier and got 42.7 percent of the vote. When the FDP received 5.8 percent, the combined total of 48.5 percent exceeded that of the CDU/CSU's 46.1 percent (see figure 5 for election results from 1949 through 1980). The SPD gain in votes in 1969 meant that it obtained 227 Bundestag seats (25 more than in 1965). The FDP received only 30 seats (down from 49). Because the two parties had a combined total of 257 seats, 15 more than the CDU/CSU total of 242 (245 in 1965), they decided to form a coalition government. The CDU/CSU, as the largest party, attempted to do the same, but could not find the coalition partner necessary to give it a Bundestag working majority. [19]

In the meantime, SPD specialists met to analyze the election results. They noted with satisfaction that most of the former voters for the party again cast their ballots for it; that a sizable fraction of first-time 21-to-25-year-old voters supported it; and that of those who switched parties, 40 percent were former CDU/CSU voters who crossed over to the SPD. The CDU loss in Catholic urban (but not rural) areas was pronounced. [20] Those who switched to the SPD voted on a socioeconomic rather than a religious basis; they were hopeful that an SPD-led government would solve social and economic problems more satisfactorily than the CDU/CSU. They made the shift because the SPD had assumed respectability as a coalition governing party. The SPD outpolled the CDU in Protestant urban constituencies, especially in large cities. In Protestant rural constituencies, the SPD for the first time gained as many votes as the CDU.

Although the SPD's gains among workers in the manufacturing and extractive industries were low, it made spectacular advances among those employed in the tertiary, or service, sector of the economy. Salaried employees increased their support from 22 percent in 1961 to 45 percent, civil servants, from 28 percent in 1961 to 38 percent. [21] Seen as the more progressive party and one that addressed itself to salient issues facing the nation, the SPD received backing from highly educated middle-class voters as well as a sizable proportion of housewives and youth. In short, it had become a party with a broad geographical and social base. [22]

FIG. 5
SPD, CDU/CSU, AND FDP VOTE IN BUNDESTAG ELECTIONS, 1949 to 1980. (%)

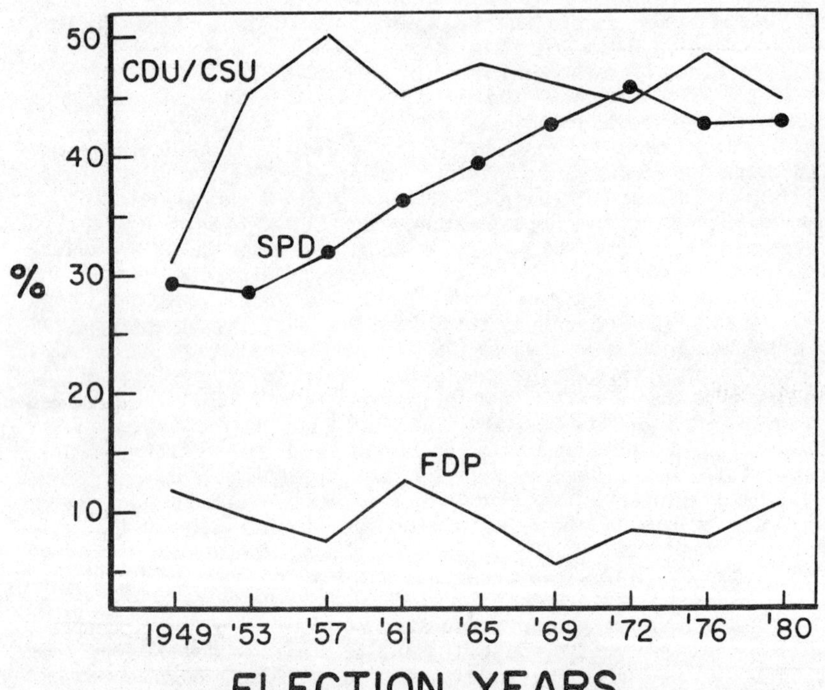

Source: Adapted from Inter Nationes, The Federal Republic of Germany elects the German Bundestag on 5 October 1980: Procedures, Programmes, Profiles (Bonn, 1980), p. 23: for 1980, Statistisches Jahrbuch 1981 für die Bundesrepublik Deutschland (Stuttgart, 1981), p. 84.

The 1972 Election

Three years later, the SPD had to face another election. Brandt's record in domestic reforms had been relatively good; in foreign policy it had been impressive—he earned a Nobel peace prize as a result of it. Therefore, the party counted on the "chancellor bonus" (the advantage of incumbency) to boost its vote. [23] It also expected to reap dividends from the lowering of the voting age to 18 and the CDU/CSU attempt to topple Brandt in April 1972 in a no-confidence vote. On the other hand, the party was worried about reactions to Minister of Economics Schiller's resignation in the summer, price increases, and people's insecurity about terrorist activities.

Yet optimism pervaded national headquarters because surveys showed Brandt to be the clear favorite over his challenger, Rainer Barzel (CDU/CSU). By capitalizing on the Chancellor's popularity and his success in Ostpolitik, the campaign became personalistic. Brandt toured the country and attracted large crowds at meetings, where banners proclaimed "Willy must stay!" and "Vote for Willy—who else is there?" He spoke in defense of the government record and assailed the CSU and Franz Josef Strauss ("the last Prussian from Bavaria") for dominating the CDU—a tactic to stir up the existing distrust of many CDU voters toward their Bavarian brethren. Most voters for the SPD were not swayed by campaign arguments, but many identified themselves more openly with the party than in earlier elections. They wore lapel buttons and put bumper stickers on their automobiles. [24] On the other hand, CDU/CSU voters maintained a "spiral of silence," as one pollster put it. [25]

The November 19 election results were not entirely unexpected. For the first time since the war, the SPD became the largest party in the Bundestag, gaining 230 seats to 225 for the CDU/CSU and 41 for the FDP. Electorally, the SPD received 45.8 percent of the vote, the CDU/CSU 44.9 percent, and the FDP 8.4 percent. [26] One explanation for the SPD victory was the number of voters who switched parties on election day. Of more than 17 million SPD votes, an estimated 1.7 million came from those who had supported the CDU/CSU in 1969 and 330,000 from those who had supported smaller parties, 800,000 votes from those who had previously abstained, and 2.3 million votes (55 percent) from new young voters. On the other hand, the SPD lost 1.1 million votes to the CDU/CSU, nearly half a million to the FDP, and 35,000 to minor parties. Furthermore, 188,000 previous SPD voters had decided to stay home on election day and 561,000 had died since the last election. The pluses outweighed the minuses by a few million votes. The SPD also benefited from considerable vote splitting: more than 50 percent of FDP voters cast their first vote for the SPD and their second for the FDP. [27]

There were socioeconomic explanations for the SPD victory. The party maintained strength (except for some losses to the FDP) among the new middle class who continued to expect the SPD to support their aspirations, including a high standard of living and an improved quality of life.

The party fared better than in 1969 in Protestant rural communities and Catholic rural areas. It made inroads among the increasingly secularized Catholic industrial unionized workers in the Ruhr and the Saar. It also gained votes among women, who had become more emancipated and who backed government reforms in domestic and foreign policy. [28] Many SPD voters characterized the CDU/CSU as having narrow, old-fashioned interests, a privileged elite, and an ideological gap between its business and labor wings.

The 1972 campaign and election showed majority support among SPD and FDP adherents for continuation of the government coalition. In one preelection poll, 54 percent of SPD respondents were so inclined, while 33 percent would have preferred an SPD-only government. [29] The election results, of course, made the latter impossible. With little difficulty, Chancellor Brandt formed a new SPD-FDP cabinet.

The 1976 Election

By the next scheduled election, Schmidt had replaced Brandt, a worldwide oil crisis had produced unemployment and inflation in the Federal Republic, the SPD had lost Land elections, and intra-SPD feuds had erupted. If the party expected to retain power, it had to emphasize positive developments since 1972 and mute its own factionalism. At the November 1975 SPD convention, Juso and right wings refrained from feuding, not wanting to give the CDU/CSU an opportunity to exploit intraparty rifts. But the SPD had difficulty in its mobilization effort because members had less enthusiasm for Chancellor Schmidt than they had had for Brandt in 1972. In turn, Schmidt's staff was disappointed about the lethargy of the party organization and tried to establish better coordination between the Chancellor's Office, the government's Press and Information Office, and party headquarters. As a result of the members' reservations about Schmidt, much of the campaign assumed a more official and professional character than the 1972 campaign. For instance, in the 1976 campaign, the Social Democratic citizens' group "Social Democratic Voters' Initiative," founded in 1969 by Günter Grass, was nearly dormant, as intellectuals and artists had difficulty warming up to a technocratically inclined chancellor. [30]

During the summer, while the SPD did little campaigning, the government took the initiative. In a series of press advertisements, the Chancellor informed readers of central problems and themes, and the ministries extolled their reform initiatives. The CDU took the government to court for using tax money for so costly an implicit endorsement of the coalition parties. In its postelection decision, the court upheld the CDU, ruling that such money cannot be used for partisan purposes. (From 1949 to 1969, the CDU/CSU-led governments had engaged in similar propaganda.)

Even though Schmidt's popularity in the SPD was limited, he was very popular with the electorate. Once again, the "chancellor bonus" was effective. Polls showed that he outranked CDU/CSU candidate Helmut Kohl (minister-president of Rhineland-Palatinate since 1969) by 13 percent (48 to 35) because voters saw him as more competent than Kohl, a better speaker, and more a "man of the people." [31] Thus the Chancellor appealed for support to groups that stood at a critical distance from the party, without neglecting visits to factories and shops. At the same time, party chief Brandt mobilized SPD members.

The campaign had no issues, except for the CDU's controversial slogan "Freedom Instead of Socialism" (CSU: "Freedom or Socialism"), which angered SPD officials just as the Christian Democrats had hoped. SPD officials stressed the advances in welfare policies and détente that would be endangered by an opposition victory and emphasized its greater understanding of "liberty" in such matters as environment and abortion reform. [32]

The SPD and FDP won the election more because of the popularity of their chancellor candidate than that of the issues. The wave of sympathy for the two parties in 1972 had subsided four years later. The SPD lost more than 1 million votes from its 1972 peak as a result of the already cited government and party difficulties, receiving 42.6 percent of the votes (45.8 percent in 1972) and 214 seats in the Bundestag (225 in 1972). The FDP obtained 7.9 percent (down 0.5 percent) and 39 seats (down 2); hence the two parties again had a majority over the CDU/CSU, but slimmer than in 1972. The latter received 48.6 percent (44.9 in 1972) and 243 seats (225 in 1972) but could not convince the FDP to join it in a new coalition. Thus the CDU/CSU remained in opposition. [33]

Postmortem analyses showed that the SPD had lost votes among all groups. Unionized workers remained faithful to the party, but many Catholic workers returned to the Christian Democrats probably because of the abortion issue and the neo-Marxist discussion within the SPD. [34] The female vote for the SPD dropped from 45.7 percent in 1972 to 40 percent in 1976. The CDU/CSU captured 50 percent, including many in the 35-to-44 age category who had strayed to the SPD in 1972. (The FDP and minor parties received the rest.) For the SPD this was a bitter blow, because of its legal and social efforts to improve the position of women. One observer saw the high 1972 female vote for the SPD as an aberration and the 1976 vote as more typical. [35] Brandt's greater popularity compared with Schmidt's may also have been a factor.

The SPD lost 4.8 percent of the vote among the 18-to-24-year-old youths (1972, 54.6 percent; 1976, 49.8 percent), primarily because those 18 through 21 supported the party less than youths of the same age four years earlier. [36] An analysis of the age factor among all SPD voters showed that the older the voter the less likely to switch parties. Of those who had voted for the SPD in 1972, among voters aged 60 or over only 0.2 percent abandoned the SPD in 1976, contrasted to 6.8 percent of the 35-to-44-year-old voters. While the SPD retained 86 percent of its 1972 voters, the other parties fared better. [37]

The north-south line remained, with the SPD again capturing (with reduced votes) the northern Länder and the CDU/CSU the southern Länder. The SPD suffered losses in rural areas and in urban areas with a high number of salaried employees, but not in other urban areas. Again, a substantial minority (nearly 30 percent) of FDP voters split their tickets. [38]

For the SPD the 1976 results were disappointing, especially because it no longer could claim to be the strongest party in the Federal Republic. Schmidt, admitting that he and others in the party had made mistakes, called for a show of solidarity. Koschnick stated that in the next round the party must put more emphasis on the future rather than on past achievements. It must end intraparty feuds and financial scandals, maintain the workers' confidence, and get closer to the citizens. [39]

The 1980 Election

For the SPD 1976 to 1980 was a period of consolidation. Intraparty feuds ebbed, although cleavages over nuclear power and defense policies remained. Schmidt's stature as chancellor rose as he grappled successfully with foreign policies and internal terrorism. The CDU/CSU nominated Franz-Josef Strauss as its chancellor candidate, to the chagrin of many CDU members. As a result, SPD chiefs were optimistic that in 1980 they would repeat their previous successes. Indeed, some of them feared that the party's margin of victory would be so big that it alone could gain more than 50 percent of the vote or that the FDP would not reach 5 percent, ending its Bundestag representation. In either case, the SPD might be forced to govern alone—which would pose problems for Schmidt. First, he would be faced by an SPD left wing demanding that the government turn more to the left instead of pursuing a conservative course on the grounds of having to make compromises with the FDP. Second, in 1984 only his party would be blamed for any economic crises and suffer possible defeat. But most observers, not expecting an SPD sweep, predicted an SPD-FDP joint victory.

Another reason for SPD optimism about the prospect for a CDU/CSU defeat was the big business community's decreased hostility to the SPD compared with previous elections. From 1972 on, the Friedrich Ebert Foundation had organized a series of round-table conferences on "Economics and Politics" to bring together business, government, and SPD leaders. The purpose of the meetings was to wean industry away from its automatic support of the CDU/CSU—and less so, of the FDP. Led by Ruhr manager Ernst Wolf Mommsen, a friend of Schmidt, and Alfred Nau (SPD), groups of invited industrialists (corporation chiefs and managers) met privately several times a year with leading government and SPD officials. The meetings, to each of which a different group of fifty to sixty business executives was invited, focused on current economic themes. Some of the executives came not out of sympathy with the SPD but because their firms were interested in getting federal research money or government contracts, especially for the lucrative trade with the East.

In 1980, most big businesses favored Schmidt for chancellor rather than Strauss whom they considered less competent to deal with future economic crises, too unpredictable, too hostile to the trade unions (which could lead to tough wage disputes and an end to the existing social harmony), and too extremist—liabilities that could weaken Germany's image abroad. [40] Yet they did not plan to openly support the coalition, especially because their sympathies lay more with Schmidt than with the SPD. They knew that as long as Schmidt remained chancellor, the party's left wing would not gain the upper hand.

Despite good omens the SPD did not expect an easy victory, knowing Strauss to be a formidable opponent. It meticulously planned a campaign strategy, again based on an electoral platform, this time entitled "Security for Germany." The platform, drafted by Schmidt and Wischnewski, emphasized the government's financial constraints, but catalogued needed domestic reforms ranging from more codetermination to improved vocational education. [41] There was unhappiness within SPD circles, especially among the Young Socialists, about the omission of some party planks in a document originating in the executive branch and about the party turning into a machine to raise votes for the Chancellor. At the party's election convention in June 1980, delegates introduced changes in the draft of the platform, but few were accepted. [42]

The 1980 campaign had striking parallels to that of 1976. Issues and new programs receded as personality clashes moved into the foreground. The confrontation between SPD and CDU/CSU leaders reached an unprecedented emotional and vituperative level. Brandt stated that Strauss was "incredibly uncontrolled . . . and therefore not qualified to govern this country." Koschnick remarked that the CDU/CSU candidate was a man "without scruples," and another SPD spokesman called Strauss an "arsonist who was ready to set democracy ablaze." In turn, Strauss accused Schmidt of "intellectual neutralism," of not supporting the Atlantic Alliance sufficiently, and of being a "peacenik" and a "prophet of panic." The CDU/CSU candidate also labeled the SPD as "the party of capitulation" in domestic and foreign policies. In his electoral strategy, he linked the SPD left—the "Moscow faction"—with sympathy for the Soviet Union and alleged that the Soviet Union was understandably interested in a Social Democratic victory over the CDU/CSU. Kohl contended that "important segments of the SPD speak the language of system transformers." [43] An official Board of Campaign Practice Overseers reprimanded both sides, but with little effect.

The campaign was marked not only by name calling and warnings of impending doom if the other party were to gain victory but by the mobilization of members. A rally of 200,000 SPD faithful in a carnival atmosphere of beer tents and sausage stands offered some political speeches as well. As in previous elections, party chiefs emphasized the need for détente and disarmament as well as full employment and social security. The party also published four weekly issues of an election newspaper, Zeitung am Sonntag, designed to appeal to the masses. It had a circulation of 15 million, the "biggest in the world," according to party publicists.

In the meantime, the CDU/CSU, in its electoral themes, played up conflicts between the SPD and FDP, contended that the government had not solved some major domestic problems, and said that the SPD was suffering from an identity crisis. [44] Despite this campaign hoopla and attempts to discuss issues, one foreign newspaper characterized the campaign as "dull and stupid." The correspondent wrote that "if candidates were marketing soap instead of politics they would surely be looking for new advertising agencies." [45]

As predicted, on October 5 the SPD and FDP easily won reelection. Again, the SPD could not match its 1972 performance but had to be satisfied with 42.9 percent of the vote, close to its 1976 total (42.6 percent), and with 218 Bundestag seats (214 in 1976). The FDP received 10.6 percent (7.9 percent in 1976) and 53 seats (39 in 1976), a dramatic gain for a minor party that was thought to be close to extinction in the Bundestag. Although the CDU/CSU remained the largest party, its vote skidded to 44.5 percent (48.6 percent in 1976) and its Bundestag representation to 226 seats (243 in 1976). The SPD lost votes to the FDP and the Greens, but gained votes from the CDU/CSU and from those who had turned 18 since the 1976 election. The chief cause for defection from the SPD to the FDP was the moderate voters' fear that the SPD might gain an absolute majority, which was thought to have unfavorable policy consequences if no other party acted as a brake on it in the cabinet. [46] The CDU/CSU lost votes because of the controversial Strauss candidacy.

Compared with 1976, the SPD made its largest inroads among Catholic voters (the secularization process was continuing), in agricultural districts, and in regions where the educational level of voters was low or there were many service employees. Yet the gains were limited because the New Politics-oriented SPD members found it difficult to convince marginal CDU voters to switch to the SPD. The party did not pick up strength in industrial areas (where the CDU/CSU made gains) or in Protestant areas with highly educated voters (where the FDP made gains). The pattern of north-south Land voting did not change appreciably from previous elections; once again, the SPD did well in the north and poorly in the south. In Bremen and Hamburg, the party picked up more than 50 percent of the total vote; in the Saar, Lower Saxony, North Rhine-Westphalia, Schleswig-Holstein, Hesse, and Rhineland Palatinate, it received (in descending order) between 50 and 40 percent, but in Baden-Wuerttemberg and Bavaria less than 40 percent. [47] One poll revealed the reason for the coalition parties' gain: 41 percent spoke favorably of Schmidt's ability and experience and 34 percent of his character; 18 percent had an aversion to Strauss. [48]

Despite the CDU/CSU defeat, there was much gloom at SPD headquarters. Staff members decried the party's inability to surmount the 43 percent voting barrier—except for 1972—and to close the gap between the Chancellor's popularity and its own, its failure to pick up 1 percent more and become the largest party, and its defensive posture and tactical campaign mistakes (such as not courting anti-Strauss CDU voters). They said that the party should not have avoided its own campaign themes and that it relied too much on the Chancellor, who did not want to be closely identified with it—indeed, who wanted to appear as a "better CDU chancellor."

Top party leaders of course did not publicly support these views, but dissatisfaction among them was also discernible. They contended that during the campaign the party had not sufficiently differentiated its policy positions in the coalition government from those of the FDP, insisted that the party must not only back the government and the Fraktion but also indicate its basic and long-range orientation, and maintained that the campaign had been too academic and not close enough to the middle class and the workers. [49] Juso Chairman Willi Pieczyk said that the party should have neither allowed the CDU/CSU to determine the electoral issues nor tailored the SPD campaign to Schmidt's personality as chancellor, because it did not result in more votes. [50]

Behind these statements lay frustration with Schmidt and his entourage, who had encouraged the cult of personality—resulting in the Chancellor putting himself at the center of the campaign and the SPD on the periphery. This development reflected a subtle partial shift of power from Brandt to Schmidt within the party—a shift that created friction between Brandt and Schmidt loyalists and contributed to the party's fall from power in 1982.

LAND ELECTIONS

The SPD machinery has to gear up not only for national elections, which must take place at a maximum of four-year intervals, but also for Länder parliament elections. [51] Although attention focuses more on the national contests, from the party point of view the staggered Land elections every four years are important too. They are a barometer of trends among the voting public in the interval between national elections. They affect party strength in the Bundesrat (the upper house), and they may have a psychological and policy effect on the national government—an SPD victory in a Land election will increase the confidence of the Bonn administration; an SPD loss may shake it and produce some policy changes. They determine who the powerholders in a Land will be and what policy direction they will take in such fields as education, health, and internal security.

The Land elections generally favor the opposition party in Bonn. Many voters, dissatisfied with the government for a variety of reasons, will vote symbolically against it at the next opportunity—in their own Land election. [52] They are less reluctant to vote for the opposition because the formation of a new central government, with all the uncertainty that it would bring, is not at issue.

Despite the parties' interest in Land elections, according to one poll the public rated them low (4 percent) compared with the national election (37 percent) and the local election (18 percent). [53] Yet if national policies, such as social security or job protection, affect a Land election, as they often do, the voters' interest will pick up. Conversely, a Land issue, such as education, may produce an avalanche of votes. Indeed, a mix of national and regional issues makes it difficult to speak of a trend for or against the Bonn government. To add to the difficulty, observers query whether parties should compare their election results with the result of the Landtag election held four years earlier or with the national election held more recently. The parties base that decision on how they fared in each election.

When the SPD was in opposition in Bonn from 1949 until 1966, its record in Land elections was impressive: it received 5.5 percent more votes than in national elections (see figure 6 for an overview of election results). At the end of 1966, it had more seats in Land parliaments than the CDU/CSU and FDP together. [54] But the tide turned once the SPD joined the government in 1966. During the Grand Coalition period, the party lost votes from those who were dissatisfied with its decision to govern with the CDU/CSU and its support of emergency legislation.

1970-1974 Elections

In the first two years of the Brandt administration, the SPD lost 0.2 percent of votes in Landtag elections, compared with the 1969 national election. The party was pleased that its losses were moderate; it remembered greater ones suffered by the CDU/CSU in Länder elections when the CDU/CSU held power in Bonn. Voting analyses showed that lowering the voting age to 18 in 1970 helped the SPD, although only modestly, in the June elections in Lower Saxony, North Rhine-Westphalia, and the Saar. On the other hand, according to one poll, the SPD lost votes in city areas, in Catholic rural areas, and among 30-to-60-year-old men because voters desired price stability more than job security and wanted the national government to deal more with domestic than with foreign affairs. [55]

The Brandt government, heeding the warning signal, decided to explain its economic policies more clearly. The SPD in Bonn concluded that in working with the SPD in Länder where elections took place it had been overconfident, had not differentiated enough among various target groups, had not planned the campaigns sufficiently, and had reacted to CDU actions rather than initiating its own strategy. The SPD warned its Land officials that the CDU did well in Land elections wherever it put up young, reform-oriented candidates. [56]

The Baden-Wuerttemberg election of April 1972 was held just when the Brandt government sought ratification of the Ostpolitik treaties in Bonn. The CDU emphasized its opposition to the treaties and its support for a domestic law-and-order policy. The SPD and FDP had at first planned to speak out on Land political issues, but when polls showed Brandt's

FIG. 6

VOTE IN BUNDESTAG AND LANDTAG ELECTIONS, 1949 TO 1980. (IN ABSOLUTE NUMBERS)

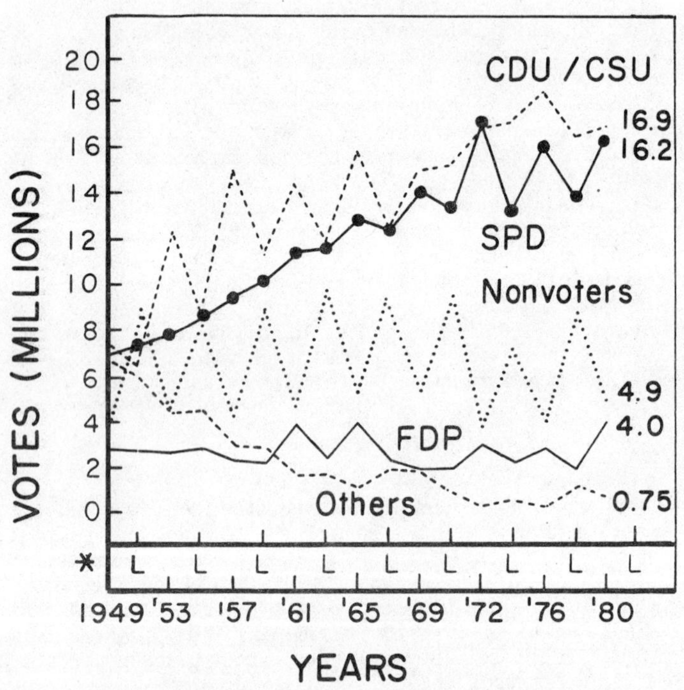

* L = Sum of all Landtag elections between Bundestag elections.

Source: Infas calculations based on official election statistics; 1980 figures based on preliminary statistics, cited by Feist and Liepelt, " Stärkung und Gefährdung der sozialliberalen Koalion: Das Ergebnis der Bundestagswahl vom 5. Oktober 1980," Zeitschrift für Parlamentsfragen, XII, No I (April 1981), 36.

popularity as chancellor and unexpectedly large support for his Ostpolitik, they switched their attention to the national scene—in vain, however; the CDU won an absolute majority because of voter dissatisfaction with economic policies, hardly mentioned during the campaign. [57]

The first land election to follow the 1972 national election was slated for Hamburg in March 1974. There the SPD lost its absolute majority held since 1957. The causes were not local but rather the general malaise sweeping the country, dissatisfaction with Brandt's leadership style, the failure of the SPD to again explain its program clearly, inflation, and the energy crisis.

1974-1980 Elections

After Schmidt assumed the chancellorship, the SPD lost fewer votes in 1974 in Lower Saxony, Bavaria, and Hesse than during Brandt's last years in office. Schmidt's resolute posture, energetic actions, and criticism of the CDU/CSU for blocking popular domestic reforms in the Bundesrat influenced many voters to stay with the governing parties. On the other hand, the CDU/CSU recaptured voters who had switched to the SPD or FDP in 1972 and gained votes from youths who resented radical slogans.

In 1975, SPD losses in several Land elections again were minimal as Schmidt's popularity increased and the economy recovered. For instance, in North Rhine-Westphalia, the most populous state, and in the Saar, the party lost only 1 percent of the vote, compared with the previous Land elections. In 1976, the SPD did poorly in Baden-Wuerttemberg, long a CDU stronghold, because of the state's numerous farmers and skilled workers. It could not exploit the theme of economic recovery because the Land had had no slump. It lost votes in the large cities, partly owing to intraparty factionalism. The reaction of Schmidt to the SPD loss was typical of any chancellor's when his party suffers a strong rebuttal by voters in a Land. He claimed that the Baden-Wuerttemberg election was not fought on matters of national policy, thus shifting the burden to the Land SPD. Moreover, whenever Schmidt knew that his party would fare poorly in a Landtag election, he would campaign less than if the forecasts were favorable. That way, his image could be preserved no matter what the election outcome.

In June 1978, in the first Länder elections after the 1976 national election, the SPD did well in Hamburg but suffered a slight loss in Lower Saxony, where it continued in opposition. In October 1978 the CDU remained the strongest party in Hesse, but the SPD and FDP were able to renew their coalition. In March 1979 a similar development took place in West Berlin. In both instances the public saw the coalition parties as more effective than the CDU in safeguarding old-age pensions and ensuring a continued economic upswing. CDU and FDP occasionally coalesced to form a government at the Land level, contrary to practice in Bonn. In the Saar, the April 1980 election produced a renewal of such a coalition, even though the SPD for the first time received a plurality of votes. But the FDP's unwillingness to ally itself with the SPD in that Land ruled out an SPD-FDP coalition.

The rise of the Greens and alternative parties posed a new challenge to the SPD in some Land elections, such as the ones in West Berlin, Bremen, and Baden-Wuerttemberg. In Baden-Wuerttemberg (March 1980), the Greens took votes from the SPD and surmounted the 5 percent barrier to gain representation in the Landtag. As a result, Eppler, insisting that the loss of votes was directed against him, resigned as Land chairman. Paradoxically, his antinuclear stance paralleled that of the Greens.

In May 1980 the SPD faced a test in North Rhine-Westphalia, where national rather than state issues were the focus of attention. To gain more support for the SPD-FDP coalition in that state, the Bonn government, before the election, authorized an economic program to aid the Ruhr. In a hard-fought campaign in which national leaders from all parties took part, the SPD gained 48.1 percent of the votes, while the FDP fell under the 5 percent barrier and the CDU received 43.2 percent, a loss of about 4 percent. As a result, the SPD formed a minority government. Its victory buoyed the spirit of party comrades who were busy planning for the national election later that year.

In 1979 and 1980, the SPD fared well in Land elections, not following the norm that a party in power in Bonn will suffer reverses at the Land level between national elections. The reasons for the SPD strength differed from Land to Land, although obviously the prestige of Schmidt as a national (and international) leader reflected on the SPD Land parties. Moreover, even though the gnawing fear of a future economic disaster was in the minds of many voters, Germany's relative economic strength could only add to SPD performance in the Länder.

1981-1982 Elections

In 1981 and 1982, SPD strength in most Länder elections began to slip for a variety of reasons. In West Berlin, the coalition government resigned in May 1981 as a result of a scandal involving SPD and FDP public officials. In a special election, the CDU received a plurality of votes, ending the SPD's monopoly of the mayor's post. Another victor in Berlin election was the Alternative List, a movement of primarily young environmentalists, which was able to capture enough votes from the SPD and FDP to gain seats in the legislature.

In March 1982, the CDU retained power in Lower Saxony, gaining votes in urban working-class areas, normally SPD strongholds. National economic problems and dissension within the SPD contributed to the SPD slippage. The Greens gained enough votes to give them representation in the Land parliament. In June, the SPD and the FDP suffered heavy losses to the CDU and the Greens in Hamburg, long the redoubt of the SPD. Although the SPD was able to retain power as a minority government, it could only do so with the parliamentary support of the Greens—the first informal but tenuous alliance between two parties that until then had remained cool toward each other. Given the unstable political situation, a special election was held in December in which the SPD regained an absolute majority and thus no longer had to depend on the backing of the Greens.

In the meantime, in September, an expected majority vote for the CDU did not materialize in the SPD stronghold of Hesse, although it received a plurality. The sudden surge of votes for the SPD and loss of votes for the FDP was caused by the dramatic end of the SPD-FDP governing coalition in Bonn just ten days before the Hesse election. Many voters had little sympathy for the FDP decision to break up the Bonn coalition and join forces with the conservative CDU/CSU. As a result, the FDP lost all seats—mostly to the Greens—presaging a possible realignment in the Bundestag in coming national elections. In Hesse the SPD remained in power with the tacit support of the Greens, but at the national level the latter could replace the FDP as the third national party and enter into an alliance with an SPD that will need their support to obtain a majority in the Bundestag. A leftist SPD-Green alliance, hardly dreamed of in the 1980 national election, may thus become a reality in the years to come. While Brandt seems favorably inclined, Schmidt and other conservative SPD leaders are opposed.

In summation, many Länder elections from 1969 to 1982 assumed a plebiscitary character when national issues became more important than Land issues. When national issues were lacking, the SPD had to contend not only with Land issues but with the CDU/CSU profiting from SPD internal schisms, machine politics, and financial scandals. A survey of Land elections from 1978 to 1980, for instance, shows the difficulty the SPD had in obtaining a relative majority of the votes in most states. Only in Hamburg, Bremen, the Saar, and North Rhine-Westphalia did it receive more votes than the CDU. In seven other states (Lower Saxony, Hesse, Bavaria, West Berlin, Rhineland-Palatinate, Schleswig-Holstein, Baden-Wuerttemberg) the CDU or CSU maintained its lead, even though in some of these states the SPD was able to form a coalition government with the FDP. [58]

LOCAL ELECTIONS AND MUNICIPAL POLITICS

The mass media give less prominence to local than to national or state elections, but for the average citizen they are important. Local decisionmakers are the ones who must deal with street construction, the number of health clinics, the building of new schools, and other problems directly affecting them.

The political parties vie for power at the communal, small-town level, but often they must compete with local notables who run on nonpartisan slates. To compete successfully, the parties will coopt notables for their own slates. But in 1969, according to one study, the SPD put up slates in fewer than one-fourth of local elections and the other parties in even fewer. Where it did run, the SPD received 29.4 percent of the total vote, compared with 26 percent for the CDU, 4 percent for the FDP, and nearly 40 percent for local nonpartisan groups. The weakness of parties in small town elections arises from the tradition of self-government, the importance of personal relationships, and the feeling that parties disrupt local harmony and intrude on local autonomy. [59]

In cities, the parties are more active in electing the lord mayor, mayors, and city councillors. The SPD interest in municipal politics goes back into history. In urban areas, where most organized workers live, it hoped to achieve municipal socialism. But before World War I, the cities were in the hands of nonsocialist parties; during the Weimar era, the party gained strength in urban areas but still could not reach its objective; after 1945, all-party or grand coalition governments were formed to rebuild the cities. Finally, in the 1950s and 1960s, the SPD captured power in many of them. Often, it continued coalitions with the CDU/CSU in the collaborative spirit of the postwar period, even though it had majorities in most city councils. [60]

According to one 1970 study, the party had a relative majority on city councils in 49 of the 57 largest cities (in 31 of these cases it had held the majority since 1946). The CDU had a relative majority in the others. [61]

But then the tide began to turn. A 1978 SPD study based on 143 cities with more than 50,000 population showed the SPD to have a relative majority in only 57 councils, while the CDU/CSU had one in 79 and there were ties in 7 others. [62] Even though the surveys were based on different-size cities, there was no doubt that the SPD had suffered drastic losses. The CDU or CSU had gained power in Munich, Frankfurt, Stuttgart, Duesseldorf, Karlsruhe, and a host of smaller cities (as well as West Berlin in 1981). On the other hand, the SPD retained power in its strongholds of Hamburg, Bremen, Hannover, Nuremberg, Cologne, and a host of Ruhr cities. [63]

Local branches, worried about SPD losses, blamed the decline in part on national headquarters. They felt that the Bonn SPD paid too much attention to national elections and not enough to mobilization for local elections. A mobilization strategy, they insisted, must include solutions to problems in the less affluent city districts, and ways to regain the party's traditional voters. But there were other reasons for the decline of party strength: the SPD-municipal bureaucratization, scandals, and patronage—often the result of the party's long term in office—as well as financial crises and intraparty factional disputes. In the latter, Jusos were pitted against more conservative SPD councillors, mayors, and municipal functionaries. In the ensuing power struggles, the Jusos alienated many SPD voters who remained loyal to these popular SPD politicians. In addition, the Jusos juggled lists of candidates for city councils in order to put on them young candidates lacking seniority in the party.

The power struggles continued in city council SPD Fraktion sessions, which, according to the party's standing orders, must be open to city administrators and leading local party officials. [64] The Jusos attempted to make use of the imperative mandate, which meant that local councillors were expected to vote according to party decisions and that they could be subject to recall if they disobeyed. At a local government conference in Nuremberg in 1974, Brandt unequivocally rejected the imperative mandate because it ran counter to the Basic Law giving the people's representatives the right to vote freely according to their conscience. Most conference delegates concurred; they also argued that representatives must think of the common good and that policies reflecting a narrow grass-roots party sentiment would come to grief. [65] By the middle of the 1970s, the Juso demand for an imperative mandate policy had lost most of its impetus, as representatives at the local, Länder, and national levels vigorously rejected it. On the other hand, the representatives also knew that they were beholden to their party and could not operate in a political vacuum. A spirit of cooperation between party and Fraktion was the ideal. Too often, practice fell short of ideal at the municipal level.

CONCLUSION

One of the primary tasks of the SPD at the national, state, and local levels was to prepare for the numerous public elections held to give voters a choice of who the powerholders should be. Each election campaign had to be carefully planned and organized. Electoral themes and propaganda slogans had to be chosen to appeal to the various target groups. Campaigns became increasingly centralized, although the SPD allowed a degree of initiative to the districts and local branches and their candidates.

During the national campaigns, SPD circles criticized their government leaders' disregard of the carefully drafted party programs and their greater concern with the pending compromise-laden government program. In other words, ideology was shunted aside to make way for a pragmatic course. But regardless of internal criticism, the SPD strategy was to build up a coalition of voters who were satisfied with government achievements (at the Land level too if it was in power), while the CDU/CSU sought to rally a coalition of the dissatisfied.

The outcome of the campaigns was determined not only by their management and strategy but by the record of the SPD-FDP governments and legislatures at all levels, the cohesion of the SPD, the quality of its leadership, and the strength of competing parties. From 1969 to 1980 the SPD, despite many problems, scored one success after another at the national level, but the margin of victory often narrowed, as floating voters shuttled back and forth between the parties (18 percent between 1976 and 1980). [66] The SPD's ability to hold on to its blue-collar workers and white-collar employees during this period was one of its strengths, but its inability, for political, economic, and social-structural reasons, to capitalize on its role as senior governing party prevented electoral gains equivalent to those made by the CDU/CSU in the 1950s. The difficulties contributed to the demise of the coalition with the FDP in 1982.

The SPD kept some of its bastions of power in the Länder and cities, but in many cities its loss of power (for many reasons) was dramatic. In the long run, the party's strategy will have to be to keep its present voters and win over voters from other parties, because the number of new voters, hitherto a power bloc that it successfully mobilized, is expected to decrease with the declining birthrate. Whether it can attract voters both on its left and right flanks remains to be seen.

NOTES

1. Richard S. Katz, A Theory of Parties and Electoral Systems (Baltimore: Johns Hopkins University Press, 1980), p. xi.

2. The number of seats won by each party under the Länder list system is determined by a modified proportional representation system: A party's total number of district seats is subtracted from the number of seats it is entitled to on the basis of its total second votes (calculated proportionately for all 496 Bundestag seats, but with the votes of minor parties unable to gain 5 percent distribututed to the other parties). Thus in the 1980 election the SPD, receiving 42.9 percent of the second ballots, was entitled to 217 out of 496 seats under the proportional representation system. As it had won 127 out of 248 district seats, it was entitled to 90 list seats (217-127 = 90). The SPD received an extra list seat when it won an additional district contest (Conradt, The German Polity, 2d. ed., pp. 117-119).

3. For details, see Stephen F. Szabo, "Party Permeability: The SPD and the Young Socialists" (paper read at the American Political Science Association convention, Washington, D.C., Aug. 31-Sept. 3, 1979), p. 8; Bodo Zeuner, "Wahlen ohne Auswahl: Die Kandidatenaufstellung zum Parlament," Parlamentarismus ohne Transparenz, ed. Winfried Steffani (Opladen: Westdeutscher Verlag, 1971), pp. 165-190; "Grundsätze für die Kandidatenaufstellung zum Bundestag 1969," adopted by executive, Aug.

27, 1968. See SPD, Jahrbuch 1968/69, pp. 482-484.

4. Ibid. Cf. SPD, executive, Parteiarbeit, Handbuch für die Arbeit in sozialdemokratischen Ortsvereinen, Kandidatenaufstellung (Bonn, 1975).

5. Personal interview, Bonn, Mar. 20, 1980.

6. Jusos, Bundeskongressbeschlüsse: Jungsozialisten in der SPD 1969-1976 (Hannover, 1978), pp. 77-78, cited by Szabo, p. 9. See also Arend, p. 162.

7. Die Welt (n.d.), cited by Die Zeit, July 21, 1972.

8. Harry Nowka, Das Machtverhältnis zwischen Partei und Fraktion in der SPD (Cologne, Berlin: Carl Heymanns, 1973), pp. 123-127; Kaltefleiter, Im Wechselbild, p. 89.

9. Ibid., p. 88.

10. Ibid., 89-90; James H. Cohen, "Political Candidate Nominations: A Comparative Study of the Law of Primaries and German Party Candidate Nominating Procedures," Jahrbuch des öffentlichen Rechts der Gegenwart, XVIII (1969), 524; Günter Pumm, Kandidatenauswahl und innerparteiliche Demokratie in der Hamburger SPD (Frankfurt/Main: Lang, 1977), p. 136 ff.

11. Dietrich Herzog, "Partei und Parlamentskarrieren im Spiegel der Zahlen für die Bundesrepublik Deutschland," Zeitschrift für Parlamentswahlen, VII, No. 1 (Apr. 1976), 29, 114-115.

12. Werner Wolf, Der Wahlkampf: Theorie und Praxis (Cologne: Wissenschaft und Politik, 1980), pp. 158-159; Richard Rose, Do Parties Make a Diference? (Chatham, N.J.: Chatham House Publishers, 1980), p. 44.

13. Personal interview, Henning von Borstell, SPD election research section, Bonn, July 20, 1977.

14. Infratest survey, 1977, pp. 18-19; Werner Wolf, pp. 103-118.

15. SPD, executive, Budestagswahlkampf 1972: Ein Bericht der SPD (Bonn-Bad Godesberg: Vorwärts-Druck, 1973), pp. 9-10.

16. For details, see SPD, Jahrbuch, various years.

17. Hans D. Klingemann and Franz Urban Pappi, "Die Wählerbewegungen bei der Bundestagswahl am 28. September 1969," Politische Vierteljahresschrift, XI, No. 1 (Mar. 1970), 135-136; Peter Pulzer, "The German Party System in the Sixties," Political Studies, XIX, No. 1 (Mar. 1971), 13; Institut für politische Planung und Kybernetik (Bonn-Bad Godesberg), "P/A/P, Politische Analyse und Prognose, Folgen 1 bis 9" (Unpublished ms., n.d.), p. 12.

18. For details of the election, see Lewis J. Edinger, "Political Change in Germany: The Federal Republic after the 1969 Election," European Political Processes: Essays and Readings, eds. Henry S. Albinski and Lawrence K. Pettit (Boston: Allyn and Bacon, 1974), pp. 139-140; Werner Kaltefleiter et al., Im Wechselspiel der Koalitionen: Eine Analyse der Bundestagswahl 1969 (Cologne: Carl Heymanns, 1970); David P. Conradt, The West German Party System: An Ecological Analysis of Social Structure and Voting Behavior, 1961-1969 (Beverly Hills, Calif.: Sage, 1972); SPD, executive, Bundestagswahlkampf 1969: Ein Bericht der SPD (Bonn: Neuer Vorwärts, 1970).

19. Among SPD voters, according to one poll taken before the election, only 10 percent desired a coalition with the FDP; 40 percent would have preferred the SPD to govern alone; and 41 percent would have preferred another grand coalition, with the SPD as either the leading or the junior party. The remaining respondents opted for the CDU/CSU governing alone (3 percent), for a CDU/CSU-FDP coalition (1 percent), or gave no answer (5 percent). Because the SPD could not govern alone, the leaders calculated that a coalition with the FDP would be approved by a

majority of their voters. They also knew that more FDP voters desired a coalition with the SPD than with the CDU/CSU (Max Kaase, "Informationen zur Bundestagswahl 1969" [hectographed], pp. xi, xii).

20. Institut für politische Planung, pp. 1, 5; infas, "Wähler 1969: Woher—Wohin?" (hectographed, Dec. 1969), p. 20; Klingemann and Pappi, pp. 116-117.

21. Ibid., p. 123. See also Max Kaase, "Determinanten des Wahlverhaltens bei der Bundestagswahl 1969," Politische Vierteljahresschrift, XI, No. 1 (Mar. 1970), 46-110. Because of different samples, the percentages do not tally with table 12.

22. Pulzer, "The German Party System," pp. 14-17; Lewis J. Edinger and Paul Luebke, Jr., "Grass-Roots Electoral Politics in the German Federal Republic: Five Constituencies in the 1969 Election," Comparative Politics, III (July 1971), 496-497.

23. For strategy suggestions by SPD leaders and publicists, see Rolf Seeliger, ed., SPD 72: Neue Beiträge zur Mobilisierung der Sozialdemokratie (Munich: Seeliger, 1972).

24. Braunthal, "Willy Brandt," p. 252.

25. Noelle-Neumann, "Zum Einfluss des Meinungsklimas auf das Wahlverhalten," Union alternative, pp. 503-530.

26. For the SPD, this was the highest percentage in its history. In 1912, it received 34.8 percent; in 1919, it received 37.9 percent and the USPD 7.6 percent.

27. Süddeutsche Zeitung, Nov. 25/26, 1972; Klaus Liepelt and Hela Riemenschnitter, "Die Wähler-Wanderungsbilanz," Auf der Suche nach dem mündigen Wähler, eds. Just and Romain, p. 154.

28. Voters cast their ballots for the SPD for a variety of reasons: its foreign policy (22 percent), nonpolitical reasons (18 percent), government performance (15 percent), preference for party candidates (11 percent), membership in group supporting the SPD (8 percent), SPD program (6 percent), economic and financial policies (4 percent), other domestic programs (4 percent), and other factors (4 percent). Eight percent did not know or gave no answer (Forschungsgruppe Wahlen, Mannheim, "Politik in der Bundesrepublik," hectographed, Dec. 1972, p. 78). See also David P. Conradt and Dwight Lambert, "Party System, Social Structure, and Competitive Politics in West Germany," Comparative Politics, VII, No. 1 (Oct. 1974), 66-69; William E. Laux, "West German Political Parties and the 1972 Bundestag Election," Western Political Quarterly, XXIII, No. 3 (Sept. 1973), 517.

29. Forschungsgruppe Wahlen, "Politik in der Bundesrepublik," p. 62.

30. For details, see Braunthal, "The 1976 West German Election Campaign," Polity, X, No. 2 (Winter 1977), 152-153; Heino Kaack and Reinhold Roth, eds., Parteien-Jahrbuch 1976 (Meisenhaim am Glan: Anton Hain, 1979); SPD, Ausserordentlicher Parteitag, 1976; SPD, executive, Weiter arbeiten am Modell Deutschland, Regierungsprogramm 1976-1980: Beschluss des ausserordentlichen Parteitages in Dortmund, 18./19. Juni 1976; Kurt Sontheimer, "The Campaign of the Social Democratic Party," Germany at the Polls: The Bundestag Election of 1976, ed. Karl H. Cerny (Washington, D.C.: American Enterprise Institute for Public Policy Research, 1978), pp. 62, 66-67; Conradt, "The 1976 Campaign and Election: An Overview," Germany at the Polls, ed. Cerny, p. 42; Baker, Dalton, Hildebrandt, pp. 261-286.

31. Ibid., p. 43.

32. Kaltefleiter, Vorspiel zum Wechsel: Eine Analyse der Bundes-

tagswahl 1976 (Berlin: Duncker and Humblot, 1977), pp. 160-161; Braunthal, "The 1976 West German Election Campaign," pp. 157-163; Revue d'Allemagne, April-June 1977 (entire issue devoted to 1976 election).

33. Electoral statistics in Deutscher Bundestag, 30 Jahre Deutscher Bundestag, p. 22 ff. The SPD calculated that 6.1 percent of SPD voters were also party members (SPD, executive, Parteiarbeit, Handbuch für die Arbeit in sozialdemokratischen Ortsvereinen, p. 13).

34. SPD, executive, "Sozialdemokraten: Sicherheit für die 80er Jahre, SPD" (flyer, n.d., c. 1976). The SPD estimated that of every 100 SPD voters, 23 percent were workers (compared with 18 percent in the general population), 18 percent salaried employees (16 percent in population), 5 percent civil servants (5 percent), 5 percent students and apprentices (5 percent), 1 percent self-employed (4 percent), 1 percent farmers (2 percent), 31 percent housewives (35 percent), 16 percent pensioners (15 percent) (SPD, executive, "Sozialdemokraten: Sicherheit für die 80er Jahre, [SPD flyer, n.d., c. 1976]).

35. Kremendahl, Nur die Volkspartei, p. 14.

36. Among the 18-to-21-year-old voters, the SPD received 44 percent, the CDU/CSU 45 percent, the FDP 11 percent, and minor parties 1 percent. Among the 22-to-25-year-old voters, the SPD received 50 percent, the CDU/CSU 37 percent, the FDP 10 percent, and minor parties 3 percent (ibid., p. 15). According to another study, nonvoting among the 18-to-24-year-old cohort was 15.9 percent, compared with 9.6 percent of the total eligible population (Federal Statistical Office, Wirtschaft und Statistik, No. 1 [1977], pp. 4, 14-19).

37. Party switches among other age groups: 18-to-24 years, 4.8 percent; 25-to-34 years, 2.9 percent; 45-to-59 years, 1.8 percent. The CDU/CSU retained 90 percent of its voters; the FDP, 96 percent (Kaltefleiter, Vorspiel zum Wechsel, pp. 207, 210).

38. Ibid., pp. 214-217; Wirtschaft und Statistik, No. 1 (1977), p. 19.

39. SPD, Dokumente, Godesberger Parteirat '77 am 27. und 28. Januar 1977 in Bad Godesberg. Protokoll (Bonn, 1977), p. 48.

40. Manager magazin, Nov. 1976, pp. 111-113; Der Spiegel, Jan. 28, 1980, Mar. 17, 1980; New York Times, Oct. 2, 1980.

41. SPD, executive, Sicherheit für Deutschland: Wahlprogramm 1980 (Bonn, 1980).

42. Vorwärts, May 22, 1980; SPD, Wahlparteitag der SPD, 1980, Protokoll. For Juso position, see Jusos, "Leitfaden zur Bundestagswahl 1980" (hectographed, Feb. 1980).

43. The Week in Germany, XI/21, May 23, 1980; New York Times, Sept. 16, 1980.

44. CDU, Unsere Argumente: Handbuch für die politische Argumentation (Bonn, 1980); CDU: Argumente 80, Machterhalt statt Politik: Die Konfliktlinien in der SPD/FDP Koalition (Bonn, 1980).

45. New York Times, Sept. 15, 1980.

46. Infas, "Infas-Wahlanalyse für dpa" (hectographed, n.d.).

47. The totals in percent were: Bremen, 52.5; Hamburg, 51.7; Saar, 48.3; Lower Saxony, 46.9; North Rhine-Westphalia, 46.8; Schleswig-Holstein, 46.7; Hesse, 46.4; Rhineland-Palatinate, 42.8; Baden-Wuerttemberg, 37.2; Bavaria, 32.7 (The Week in Germany, XI/42, Nov. 7, 1980). See also Ursula Feist and Klaus Liepelt, "Stärkung und Gefährdung der sozialliberalen Koalition: Das Ergebnis der Bundestagswahl vom 5. Oktober 1980," Zeitschrift für Parlamentsfragen, XII, No. 1 (Apr. 1981), 34-58; Geoffrey Pridham, "The 1980 Bundestag Election: A Case of

'Normality'," West European Politics, IV, No. 2 (May 1981), 118.

48. In a Sept. 1980 infas poll, cited by Feist and Liepelt (see note 47 above), 58 percent of respondents preferred Schmidt as the candidate for chancellor, 29 percent Strauss, and 13 percent neither or did not answer.

49. Süddeutsche Zeitung, Oct. 7, 1980; Vorwärts, Dec. 11, 1980.

50. Frankfurter Rundschau, Oct. 7, 1980.

51. Voting is by proportional representation, with a minimum vote of 5 percent needed to obtain a Landtag seat in most Länder.

52. Lowell W. Culver, "Land Elections in West German Politics," Western Political Quarterly, XIX, No. 2 (June 1966), 304: Geoffrey Pridham, "A 'Nationalization' Process? Federal Politics and State Elections in West Germany," Government and Opposition, 8 (Autumn 1973), p. 455. See also R.J.C. Preece, 'Land' Elections in the German Federal Republic (London: Longmans, 1968).

53. Georg Fabritius, "Sind Landtagswahlen Bundesteilwahlen?" Aus Politik und Zeitgeschichte, Beilage zu Das Parlament B 21/79, May 26, 1979, p. 24.

54. Ibid., p. 34; Werner Wolf, p. 69.

55. SPD, "Die Landtagswahlen 1970 und 1971" (mimeo.); for a complete listing of electoral results, see Suzanne S. Schüttemeyer, "Ergebnisse der Landtagswahlen in den Bundesländern 1946-1979," Zeitschrift für Parlamentsfragen, XI, No. 2 (July 1980), 250-255.

56. SPD, "Die Landtagswahlen 1970 und 1971."

57. Pridham, pp. 459, 465-466.

58. Inter Nationes, The Federal Republic of Germany elects the German Bundestag on 5 October 1980: Procedures, Programmes, Profiles (Bonn, 1980), p. 33.

59. Linda Dolive, Electoral Politics at the Local Level in the German Federal Republic (Gainesville: The University Presses of Florida, 1976), pp. 35-36; Werner Wolf, pp. 72-75; Heino Kaack, "Parteien und Wählergemeinschaften auf kommunaler Ebene," Aspekte und Probleme der Kommunalpolitik, eds. Heinz Rausch and Theo Stammen (Munich: Ernst Vogel, 1974), pp. 135-150.

60. Karl-Heinz Nassmacher, "Einleitung," Kommunalpolitik und Sozialdemokratie, ed. Nassmacher (Bonn-Bad Godesberg: Neue Gesellschaft, 1977), pp. 9-14.

61. Robert C. Fried, "Party and Policy in West German Cities," American Political Science Review, LXX, No. 1 (Mar. 1976), 15.

62. SPD, executive, Referat Kommunalpolitik, "Sozialdemokratische Oberbürgermeister, Oberstadtdirektoren, Landräte und Oberkreisdirektoren, Stand 10. Juni 1978" (hectographed); personal interview with CDU official, Bonn, Mar. 31, 1980. By 1982, the SPD had lost the majority in 12 out of the 26 largest cities (Der Spiegel, Dec. 13, 1982).

63. Frankfurter Rundschau, Jan. 2, 1975.

64. Fliedner, "Probleme der Organisation und Arbeitsweise von Fraktionen, III," VOP, 5/1979, p. 295.

65. Dyson, Party, State and Bureaucracy, p. 11 ff. See also Werner Kaltefleiter and Hans-Joachim Veen, "Zwischen freiem und imperativem Mandat," Zeitschrift für Parlamentsfragen, II, No. 2 (July 1974), 246-267.

66. Conradt, The German Polity, 2d ed., pp. 129-130.

11
Party and Parliament

One crucial function of political parties in Western democracies is to share in policy formulation in the legislative and executive branches. This chapter examines the SPD's role in Parliament and the next chapter its role in the executive branch. In Parliament, the SPD has been involved in lawmaking since the founding of the Federal Republic, not to speak of its participation during earlier periods of German history. With representation in both legislative houses, it also communicates vertically between its members and voters on one hand and the policymakers in the executive branch on the other. Since 1969, when the chancellor and most cabinet members have represented the SPD, the SPD deputies have been expected to support government policy, but not automatically. Edmund Burke and the West German Basic Law mention the deputies' right to represent all their constituents and freely vote according to their consciences, yet German parties have limited this freedom considerably and expect their deputies to vote en bloc for or against a legislative measure.

This chapter focuses on the parliamentary group (Fraktion) in the Bundestag as one part of the West German Social Democratic triad, and its links to the other two parts—the SPD (in its role, as the British put it, of extraparliamentary party) and the SPD-led government. The Fraktion is examined to see how it balanced multiple interests, how it developed an operational mode to enhance internal cohesion, and why the cohesion could not be maintained once the New Left increased its representation in the Fraktion. Thus one of the central themes reemerges: how the SPD—in this instance in its parliamentary role—could not escape the sociopolitical winds buffeting the nation in the 1970s.

Briefly examined is the party's involvement in a federalist institution—the Bundesrat (upper chamber), in which the SPD was indirectly involved through the Länder which it governed or shared in governing. The Fraktionen in the Land and city legislatures, which mirror to some extent the characteristics of the Bundestag Fraktion, are excluded from this survey.

THE BUNDESTAG FRAKTION

In its representational function, the SPD must be careful to have a balance of interests and occupations in its Fraktion. It did not fully succeed. As tables 15 and 16 indicate, blue-collar workers and the

TABLE 15
OCCUPATIONS OF BUNDESTAG DEPUTIES BY PARTIES

Occupation	Electoral Period	SPD	CDU/CSU (In numbers)	FDP	Total
Present or former members of government	1972	35	15	9	59
	1976	31	13	9	53
Civil servants	1972	76	76	7	159
	1976	74	78	6	158
Public service employees	1972	13	9	0	22
	1976	13	12	1	26
Employees of parties and social groups	1972	57	23	2	82
	1976	47	22	2	71
Employees in the private sector	1972	20	27	5	52
	1976	17	32	4	53
Self-employed	1972	7	48	14	69
	1976	6	49	12	67
Professionals and clergymen	1972	23	29	4	56
	1976	27	37	5	69
Housewives	1972	6	5	0	11
	1976	2	4	0	6
Blue-collar workers	1972	3	2	0	5
	1976	5	3	0	8
No occupation or none given	1972	2	0	1	3
	1976	2	4	1	7
Total	1972	242	234	42	518
	1976	224	254	40	518

Source: Adapted from Emil-Peter Müller, "Vertreter der gewerblichen Wirtschaft im VIII. Deutschen Bundestag," Zeitschrift für Parlamensfragen, VIII, No. 4 (Dec. 1977), 423-424; Deutscher Bundestag, 30 Jahre Deutscher Bundestag, pp. 69-71. For the 1969 election period, see Heino Kaack, Geschichte und Struktur des deutschen Parteiensystems (Opladen: Westdeutscher Verlag, 1971), pp. 659-660. His occupational categories differ from those above; hence comparisons for the three periods cannot be made.

TABLE 16
OCCUPATIONS OF BUNDESTAG DEPUTIES
BY PARTIES AND PERCENTAGES

Occupation	Electoral Period	SPD	CDU/CSU	FDP	Total
Present or former members of government	1972	14.5	6.4	21.4	11.3
	1976	13.9	5.1	22.5	10.3
Civil servants	1972	31.4	32.5	16.8	30.7
	1976	33.0	30.7	15.0	30.5
Public service employees	1972	5.4	3.8	0.0	4.2
	1976	5.8	4.7	2.5	5.0
Employees of parties and social groups	1972	23.6	9.8	4.8	15.8
	1976	21.0	8.7	5.0	13.7
Employees in the private sector	1972	8.3	11.5	11.9	10.0
	1976	7.6	12.6	10.0	10.2
Self-employed	1972	2.9	20.5	33.3	13.4
	1976	2.6	19.3	30.0	12.9
Professionals and clergymen	1972	9.5	12.4	9.5	10.8
	1976	12.0	14.5	12.5	13.3
Housewives	1972	2.5	2.1	0.0	2.1
	1976	0.9	1.6	0.0	1.2
Blue-collar workers	1972	1.2	0.9	0.0	1.0
	1976	2.2	1.1	0.0	1.5
No occupation or none given	1972	0.8	0.0	2.4	0.6
	1976	0.9	1.6	2.5	1.4
Total[a]	1972	100.0	100.0	100.0	100.0
	1976	100.0	100.0	100.0	100.0

[a]Rounded off to the nearest percent.
Source: see table 15.

self-employed had few representatives compared with several other groups. AfA spokesmen contended that the workers did most of the petty election tasks but that their nominees did not get safe seats on the lists. Rather, ambitious, well-educated, articulate members of the new middle class, who had more leisure time, became deputies. Such a development could be dangerous to the party if many SPD voters felt inadequately represented. [1] However, although the well-educated middle class was more than adequately represented in the Fraktion, there were still enough minor union functionaries and others without advanced education in its ranks to give it a lower educational profile than that of the bourgeois FDP and the CDU/CSU. [2]

The proportion of women in the Fraktion from 1969 to 1980 ranged from 5.4 to 7.6 percent. Only during the first Brandt administration was the percentage slightly higher than that of all female deputies in the Bundestag; thereafter it did not even match that of the CDU/CSU or FDP. [3] To women and workers in the SPD, the makeup of the Fraktion was obviously unsatisfactory. For the workers the situation was less grim, because most Fraktion members belonged to a union and supported the labor movement. Indeed, to both groups, their representation in the Fraktion, while symbolically important, was normally less an issue than legislative policy decisions made by the Fraktion on matters affecting them. If the Fraktion supported the women on the abortion issue, say, then the fact that few women sat in the parliamentary party was less significant.

The Fraktion is not a constituent part of the SPD, yet its chief task is to represent the party in the legislative arena. Since 1969, it has also served as a conduit for policy emanating from the executive branch. But, as we shall see, it did not automatically vote for the chancellor and the cabinet; tensions arose at times as the Fraktion insisted on maximum participation in policymaking. Within the Fraktion, policy initiatives flowed from top to bottom (sometimes the reverse on individual or specialized issues). The key policymaking organ in the Fraktion is the twenty-nine-member executive, consisting of the "inner executive" (Geschäftsführenden Vorstand) and eighteen additional members, whose conservative majority normally sets the tone for the Fraktion. [4] In 1979, the "inner executive" was made up of the Fraktion chairman, the five deputy chairmen and the five parliamentary whips (Parlamentarische Geschäftsführer). This body has close links to government and party. It meets weekly to discuss policy matters and prepare caucus sessions. Wehner has headed the Fraktion since 1969, succeeding Schmidt, who held the office for two years. [5] Wehner has been a powerful leader, whose "liberal-authoritarian" style has not endeared him to all SPD deputies. His staying power in a demanding role and his ability to integrate warring wings have been impressive. Yet his sallies against Brandt angered a minority of deputies who several times voted against his reelection as Fraktion chairman and floor leader. [6] His inability to repress anger caused him to insult or offend backbenchers who dared question his policies. As a result, many deputies were hardly on speaking terms with him, yet they appreciated his ability to build party unity within the Fraktion.

In the early 1970s, Wehner's right-hand man was Karl Wienand, the chief parliamentary whip and the second most influential person in the Fraktion leadership. Wienand was skillful in running the Fraktion machinery smoothly, but in 1973 he became embroiled in a corruption scandal. He was suspected of having lied to investigators about receiving money in 1971 from a charter airline and was accused of bribing CDU deputy Julius Steiner to vote with the SPD in the crucial vote in April 1972, when Brandt's survival as chancellor was at stake. Wienand denied the allegations, and senior SPD officials claimed to have had no knowledge of any wrongdoing. But when in 1974 Wienand became too compromised in the unfolding mini-Watergate scandal and the party's moral posture sank rapidly, the Fraktion executive requested Wienand to swiftly resign his post—which he did. [7] As a result of this scandal, Wehner, who had stubbornly backed Wienand throughout the investigation, suffered a decline in authority within the Fraktion.

Deputies participate in the work of the Fraktion not only by attending the weekly caucus sessions but by being members of one of six working groups (Arbeitskreise) handling various aspects of foreign and domestic policies. [8] Each group is headed by a chairman, one or two deputy chairmen, and a foreman (Obmann). The foreman acts as liaison to other groups, to the whips, to the chairmen of Bundestag committees, to the Bundestag Council of Elders (in charge of the agenda), and to the Fraktion's inner executive. Each group, divided into specialized subgroups, deals with the work of its corresponding Bundestag committees. It discusses details of a bill, who will be in charge of the bill in committee or in the plenum, and who will speak. This coordinating function is facilitated by the duality of membership—deputies in the group are also members of the corresponding committees. [9] The ministry also makes sure that its bill will be handled properly by the group and subgroup. It may send its minister, parliamentary state secretary, and civil servants to explain the bill and work out possible compromises. (Such personal appearances are not restricted to the Fraktion level but also take place in the caucus, the Bundestag committees, and the plenum.) When the group finishes its deliberations on a bill, it reports to the Fraktion executive, which may have to reconcile conflicting views from another group that has scrutinized the bill.

The Fraktion leaders have much oligarchical power because of their functions, their length of service, and their multiple posts within the party. Most deputies accept their own role as an acclamation machine for the decisions made by a few, but a minority of deputies chafe at the restrictions imposed on them. One deputy said to this writer: "I must be careful not to appear too much as a rebel within the Fraktion, otherwise I will be tagged as a rebel. I become an outsider if I get too pushy and introduce too many bills drafted by me or my staff." [10] Another wrote that individual deputies cannot just speak up in the plenum when bills of interest to them are being discussed; they must first receive permission from the Fraktion majority (other than in exceptional cases) in order to preserve the myth of a Fraktion collective opinion. This deputy tried within one eighteen-month period to introduce thirty oral or written questions in the plenum addressed to the SPD-led government, but thirteen were disallowed by the "inner executive." Of those disallowed, four dealt with the sensitive issue of whether the government was ready to prohibit the neo-fascist National Democratic Party as an enemy of the Constitution. He claims that he could ask only less controversial questions or those which would put the government in a favorable light, unlike the opposition which used the question hour to embarrass the government. [11]

The average SPD member has little influence in the Fraktion unless he or she has a link with a powerful association, expertise, or enough seniority as a backbencher and loyalty to the leaders to be rewarded eventually with a minor post in the Fraktion. But for the left deputies especially, who did not relish being mere backbenchers, there were opportunities, such as in the weekly caucus sessions, to speak up and criticize the Fraktion leaders' policy recommendations. From 1974 to 1982 Schmidt often reported in these sessions on cabinet meetings and domestic and foreign policy developments; Brandt on developments from the party point of view; and Wehner on the Fraktion executive session and the tactical measures to be used to steer the coming bills—most initiated by the government, a few by the Fraktion—through the Bundestag. The Fraktion chief also informed the members of prior negotiations with government and FDP leaders to ensure accord on the bills' legislative odyssey; officials of the working groups provided additional details. Thereafter the backbenchers had an opportunity to discuss bills and suggest changes. One staff member, who sat through 100 Fraktion meetings, claims that the leaders did not win all points in discussions; on occasion they were convinced by the counterarguments and relented in their perpetual drive to put the Fraktion under pressure. Moreover, they had minimal influence in the renewed candidacy of maverick deputies and had to be reelected to Fraktion executive membership several times within one Bundestag four-year term. [12]

Those dissident party leaders and deputies who favored curbing the power of the party establishment, including the Fraktion bosses, tried to prevent an accumulation of offices (Ämterhäufung) among the functionaries. Brandt, equally concerned with the excessive burdens carried by many leaders, requested the party convention in 1977 to set up a working group to study the matter and make recommendations. Party council members, meeting in June 1979, discussed the recommendations and accepted Rudi Arndt's proposal that no member hold more than one parliamentary office and more than two party posts simultaneously. They rejected a Juso proposal to limit the number of posts to one and rejected warnings by conservatives that if the responsibility for holding office was distributed too widely, no one would carry the load. The party executive introduced a motion at the 1979 convention coinciding with Arndt's proposal except for its recommendation that the parliamentary office include not only the federal but also the European and Länder levels (the local level was excluded). The motion was accepted, but details still have to be worked out. [13]

Right Factionalism

The reideologization of the party stemming from external factors did not spare the Fraktion. From 1969 on, bitter policy schisms and struggles for power erupted among the left and right factions. These reflected the factionalism within the party but also began to have a dynamic of their own. The right faction was organized as a social club in the mid-1950s by Egon Franke, a Bundestag member since 1951, one of the Fraktion deputy chairmen since 1966, and minister for intra-German relations since 1969. He was assisted by Karl Herold, a parliamentary state secretary. Their faction has had an impressive strength of about 100 to 120 members, constituting about 50 percent of the Fraktion total. [14] Many of these members are former blue-collar workers and craftsmen with a petit bourgeois outlook. The right-faction members, dubbed the "Kanalarbeiter" (sewer workers) for their concern with clean, orderly conditions, have hardly been interested in the intraparty ideological debates but in the 1950s and 1960s were eager to get the party into power. Since then, they have been loyal supporters of the SPD-led governments, although they have felt doctrinally more comfortable with Schmidt than with Brandt. In 1972, when right-wing intellectuals wanted to provide an ideological base for the group, the pragmatic Kanalarbeiter rebuffed them.

Critics have characterized the Kanalarbeiter as "mouse-grey" backbenchers who after their parliamentary work prefer to drink beer, gorge themselves, and play skat in a smoke-filled restaurant than to engage in political discussions. (In turn, some Kanalarbeiter call those in the left bloc "idiots" and "screwballs" for their ideological obsession and unawareness of reality.) While the Kanalarbeiter eschew ideological confrontations, they do not avoid political confrontations with the left faction. Before every election of the Fraktion executive, they caucus to nominate conservative candidates and keep the left candidates out. In 1972, for instance, when the left gained nearly forty Bundestag seats, the Kanalarbeiter easily won all executive seats. In 1976, a sharp contest took place for one of the deputy chairman posts. Former Chancellor Office head, Horst Ehmke, was supported for the post by Brandt, Wehner, and Schmidt, who wanted to integrate the left-middle bloc of deputies into the Fraktion leadership. But Franke and the Kanalarbeiter balked and put up a countercandidate, Karl Liedtke, a former educator and chairman of the party coucil. In a runoff ballot, Liedtke beat Ehmke by 108 to 104 votes. While the Kanalarbeiter celebrated their victory, the bitter left contended that the right, eager for a confrontation, did not want to cooperate with it. [15]

After this crisis, Wehner decided that the backbenchers, especially the young left members, had to be given parliamentary tasks to make them feel wanted and useful and to prevent their leaving the party. Hence 72 deputies out of 224 (including the 10 deputies from West Berlin) received posts on Bundestag committees or in working groups. To accomplish this, Wehner enlarged the number of posts and requested the executive members to give up their other offices. Thus, for instance, Ehmke became foreman of the foreign affairs committee; Karsten Voigt (former Juso chairman), deputy foreman; and Wolfgang Roth (also former Juso chairman), deputy foreman in the economic affairs committee. [16]

In November 1980, following the national election, Wehner attempted once again to dampen the hostility between left and right. Not only did he request Schmidt to have Fraktion representatives including those from its left bloc participate actively in coalition talks with the FDP but he urged the Kanalarbeiter to vote for some left members to the Fraktion executive in order to have a broader representation. They refused and once again the executive was pitched politically to the right. Former Juso chairman Gerhard Schröder, newly elected deputy, summed up the left view: "A majority which shows how little it is ready to compromise will produce a minority that it deserves; the majority will thereby produce conflicts which will also be hard for this majority to bear—not the least because these are conflicts between the Fraktion majority and a party that is changing much more rapidly." [17]

Left Factionalism

Only after 1969, when for the first time in the postwar era left-wing SPD deputies won seats to the Bundestag, did a left group form in the Fraktion. About 12 deputies (out of 227) organized the "Group of the Sixteenth Floor," so named for the location of their offices in the parliamentary office building. They took positions on bills and tried to convince the Fraktion majority to support their views. After the 1972 election, the nucleus of the group, led by Dietrich Sperling (Hesse) and Karl-Heinz Hansen (North Rhine-Westphalia), increased to 30 to 40 deputies, with occasional backing from 20 others.

In November 1972, the deputies met in Leverkusen with members of the left-wing Frankfurt and Tübingen circles to discuss strategy. As a result of this meeting, the deputies formed a coordinating group known as the Leverkusen Circle (although many still called it the Group of the Sixteenth Floor). At the meeting the question was raised whether an official left-wing Bundestag faction with a secretariat should be established, but the idea was dropped, especially when Brandt warned against the creation of official factions within the Fraktion. [18]

The left group met weekly in advance of the Fraktion sessions but after the Fraktion executive meetings. It planned what themes to bring up at the Fraktion meetings, who would speak, and who would provide additional support. The group also met monthly to hear from specialists about a major pending bill and to discuss it fully. In the course of the 1970s the group members had to sacrifice much theory in favor of daily work. A number of its members, becoming more technocratically oriented and politically more moderate, were awarded government posts as parliamentary secretaries and ministers. Others remained rebels, most with a political base and support in their districts. They did not hesitate to challenge the establishment in the Bundestag or the party. [19] Typical of this group is Norbert Gansel of Schleswig-Holstein. Born in 1940, he studied history, politics, and law at Kiel University and in 1973 passed the bar examination. In the meantime, he joined the SPD in 1965 and rose swiftly through the rank. Three years later he was already a member of the party council and in 1969 became press spokesman for the SPD in Schleswig-Holstein as well as Juso national deputy chairman. From 1971 to 1973, he was a member of the SPD Land executive in Schleswig-Holstein. Elected to the Bundestag in 1972, he was one of the maverick deputies who dared vote in the Bundestag against some important government legislation.

The Leverkusen group has viewed itself as ghettoized within the Fraktion and as a repressed minority that has had difficulty achieving compromises with the Kanalarbeiter. Its early optimism that the Fraktion would support socialist legislation soon evaporated in the light of stubborn resistance by more conservative colleagues. Instead, the deputies have become resigned to working with the left-center deputies on less ambitious policy changes. As will be seen, the group has scored some successes both within the Fraktion and, in alliance with the party's left wing, within the SPD. One of the most dramatic examples was its ability to corral enough votes at the 1973 convention to prevent the reelection of Kanalarbeiter boss Franke to the party executive. Even though in the 1976 election its strength was maintained and in 1980 slightly enhanced (one-fourth of the 50 new SPD deputies belonged to the left), it decided after the 1980 election to reorganize. It dropped the name "Leverkusen" and became the

Parliamentary Left, with an estimated core of 25 and a total of 60 members, including two cabinet ministers (Jürgen Schmude, Justice; Björn Engholm, Education and Science). It resolved to work even more closely with the left-center group of deputies. [20]

This left-center group was part of a loosely-knit middle bloc that included the right center. In the middle bloc Fraktion deputy chairmen Günther Metzger and Herberg Ehrenberg organized a group (the Metzger Circle) in 1972 that was ideologically conservative but tried to moderate the confrontation between the left and right wings. Most of the 60 to 90 deputies who could be counted on to support the group were young and pragmatic. [21]

Although the Fraktion was plagued by intrafactional schisms, its work in the Bundestag committees and in plenary sessions normally demonstrated a united front against the CDU/CSU opposition on major foreign and domestic policy bills. There were exceptions: a small dissident bloc of SPD deputies on a few occasions broke discipline and voted against their party in the Bundestag plenary sessions, as we shall see below. However all parties voted in the affirmative on most technical or nonpolitical bills going through the Bundestag or made changes in them on a nonpartisan basis.

Relation to Party

Whether a party should give direction to its parliamentary group has been a matter of dispute in Western democracies. For instance, in Britain until 1981, the parliamentary wing of the Labour Party (PLP) had autonomous powers, including the sole right to choose the party leader. But then the left-dominated extraparliamentary party decided that the PLP's powers should be trimmed. Most important, the party leader, who becomes a potential prime minister, should be chosen by an expanded electoral college in which the members of Parliament would be in a minority as compared to the representatives from the local party organizations and the affiliated trade unions. [22]

In West Germany, the Fraktionen of the governing parties had to have close ties to their party organizations and to the government if policy coordination was to be established. But when coalition cabinet policy differed from the parties' policy recommendations, the Fraktionen were expected to sustain the former. In the SPD the Fraktion's degree of independence from the party has varied over time. During the Empire era the Reichstag Fraktion was independent, partly because Bismarck's antisocialist law had a devastating effect on the party organization. In 1911, according to Robert Michels:

> The influence of parliamentarism is particularly great in the German social democracy. This is clearly shown by the attitude toward the party commonly assumed by the socialists in parliament. There is no other socialist party in the world in which the conduct of its representatives in parliament is subject to so little criticism. The socialist members of the Reichstag frequently make speeches in that body which might be expected to give rise to the liveliest recriminations, and yet neither in the party press nor at the congresses is to be heard a word of criticism or of disapproval. [23]

During the Weimar and initial post-1949 years, the balance changed as the party determined the Fraktion policy. From 1957 on, when the reformists became more powerful, a reverse process took place. Increasingly, Fraktion leaders moved into top party positions. In 1965, Brandt characterized the Fraktion as "the most important instrument of the party to push through social democratic politics and to make it comprehensible to the public." [24] Yet, according to observers, the Fraktion was more than an instrument of the party; it provided policy direction to the party.

There were a number of reasons for the Fraktion's strength within the SPD. Fraktion officials insisted at party conventions that the Fraktion as a body officially independent of the SPD would not accept binding resolutions. It was willing to pursue basic SPD policies but wanted freedom to translate them into legislation as it saw fit. At the conventions, Fraktion members have had some power. One-tenth of the entire SPD Fraktion can participate without a vote, but many more (20 percent) have been delegates. Most have been articulate and experts in their fields, especially in foreign policy, and have held leading positions at conventions. Fraktion members or their staff have also helped to shape party executive resolutions that conventions subsequently have adopted. [25]

Other reasons for Fraktion influence have been its more frequent meetings to handle day-to-day political, economic, and social affairs, compared with the less frequent meetings of the top party organs, and the party's liberal use of the expertise, political talent, and high educational level of deputies in its numerous specialized committees (especially those dealing with foreign affairs, security, constitutional questions, and labor affairs). The committees, often headed by Fraktion executive members, have maintained links with their corresponding Fraktion working groups, facilitated by the overlap of members. Moreover, Fraktion executive members have been elected to the party's presidium and to other policymaking posts, again because of their qualifications. [26]

Although the Fraktion's influence on the party has been strong, it has not been absolute. The Jusos and the party left have challenged the Fraktion-party relationship, demanding a greater say in the direction of policy and seeking to make the Fraktion an auxiliary of the SPD. They have been unhappy when the Fraktion took actions contravening convention decisions, which then received the blessings of the party executive. They have known that the Fraktion's request for approval from the executive to stray from the convention line was a hollow formality. In line with their theory of the imperative mandate, they have not been convinced by the Fraktion's argument that it needed freedom of action in its parliamentary work.

While the Fraktion most likely will not become an auxiliary of the party, the party has some influence in Fraktion and Bundestag. From 1970 on, about one-fifth of the party executive members held seats in the Fraktion executive, which amounted to about one-fourth of the Fraktion's membership. The total had been higher in earlier years, but dropped when party executive members were recruited instead into ministerial posts. [27] Many other party executive members became chairmen or deputy chairmen of Bundestag committees such as budget, foreign affaris, social policy, and all-German affairs.

Relation to Government

An SPD-FDP coalition government needs the support of its parliamentary parties to carry out its program. To ensure the least friction between them, executive and legislative leaders developed an informal and formal network of consultations. Periodically, the SPD chancellor and Fraktion chairman Wehner met informally to discuss legislative matters before official meetings with FDP leaders. When a new government was formed, the SPD and FDP Fraktion leaders were involved in the coalition negotiations. Soon thereafter they normally were apprised of the contents of the government declaration which the chancellor delivered at the beginning of a legislative session, and they may have been requested to make suggestions for changes. When the cabinet discussed the political agenda and the contents of an important bill, they (as well as deputies with expertise in the field) were consulted to ensure legislative support. Thereupon the civil servants who drafted the bill may have invited SPD and FDP deputies and their assistants to review the draft point by point with them. Once the cabinet had agreed on the bill and it shuttled to and from the Bundesrat, the chancellor or one of his ministers met with the SPD and FDP Fraktion chairmen and their whips to plan Bundestag strategy. Legislative leaders also met on their own to discuss other legislative matters, including the question hour and the introduction of initiative bills and motions.

In this relationship between the executive and legislative high commands, the latter's role in policymaking, with exceptions, remained limited. True, the legislative chiefs warned the executive chiefs that the Fraktionen must share in policymaking to make the deputies feel they are not just ordinary backbenchers and to prevent a negative vote on a bill that may be anathema to the deputies. However, these warnings did not carry much weight. Within the SPD Fraktion, many deputies felt frustrated about their ministers making unpalatable legislative compromises with FDP ministers and accused them of using the FDP as an excuse to ward off far-reaching domestic reforms agreed on at SPD conventions. The ministers replied that legislative compromises with the FDP are part of the imperatives of coalition politics.

To assuage the deputies' criticisms the chancellor and other executive officials appeared at most weekly Fraktion sessions. After the SPD assumed government power, the Fraktion standing orders were changed to allow SPD ministers and parliamentary state secretaries to be present at Fraktion executive and plenary sessions to explain and defend government policies, answer questions, and hear criticism. Such interchanges usually removed most deputies' doubts about a bill and also ensured that some Fraktion views flowed into government policy. [28] Because nearly all SPD ministers had come from the Bundestag ranks, they were attuned to the Fraktion's political dynamics and atmosphere. As an added insurance to minimize friction between the two branches, in 1974 Schmidt appointed Marie Schlei, parliamentary state secretary in the Chancellor's Office, as liaison person to the Fraktion. Schlei, whose relations with Wehner were cordial, attended Fraktion executive and caucus meetings and kept Schmidt informed about Fraktion views.

Nevertheless, as will be seen, sessions were not free of tension and discord between dissident deputies and government representatives. The deputies posed highly critical questions, which most of them would not dare do openly in the official Bundestag question hour or in plenum debates, although in the Bundestag committees they often made, with little publicity, minor changes in bills emanating from the government.

There were cases in which the entire Fraktion disagreed with a projected government policy or bill. For instance, in early 1970, Minister Schiller wanted to increase the tax on wages and other income. The Fraktion contended that he did not have the backing of the cabinet, but Schiller kept publicizing the proposal and defended it at a party presidium meeting. Wehner, in a letter to Brandt, rejected the plan. When Schiller was asked to appear at a special meeting of the Fraktion, he finally yielded and withdrew his proposal. The Fraktion also criticized portions of Minister of Justice Jahn's bills on reforming divorce and sexual offense statutes. Deputies were worried that such progressive legislation would alienate too many Catholic voters. Accordingly, Jahn made changes in the bills. [29]

In 1976, a crisis erupted over the plan by Schmidt and Labor Minister Arendt to postpone by six months a promised pension increase of 10 percent. The SPD deputies were barraged with protests from party members against the plan. Schmidt, after talking with Wehner and the SPD budget expert, defended the plan at a special session of the Fraktion, but when he realized that the Fraktion would not give its support because of the popular outcry within the party, he withdrew the plan. [30]

The 1976 crisis showed that the Fraktion had residual power to change the course of government policy. Equally dramatic were the well-publicized instances in which dissident SPD deputies, most of them on the political left, voted against government bills that they considered unacceptable. Their actions violated the historic, unwritten party rule of maintaining strict voting discipline in plenary sessions (but not in Fraktion sessions, where pro and con votes were permissible). A breach of party discipline was especially dangerous when the government coalition parties had only a slim majority in the Bundestag. Yet the leaders had to contend with Article 38 of the Basic Law which stipulates that a deputy is not bound by any instructions but only by his or her conscience. Hence the leaders could not force deputies to vote one way or another on a bill. The only telling course they had was to threaten a deputy with expulsion from the Fraktion, which would mean that the party would not support his or her reelection.

A parenthetical note: while party leaders demanded voting discipline from dissidents in the Bundestag, they objected strenuously to the left-inspired imperative-mandate principle which demanded that deputies maintain voting discipline for party-approved resolutions. The leaders had a rational explanation for their seemingly inconsistent stand: government policy takes priority over party policy—but this was not always convincing to those advocating policies at variance with the government line.

The first confrontation between dissident deputies on one hand, and their colleagues and ministers on the other occurred in June 1977 over the government's projected 1 percent rise in the value-added tax in exchange for selected tax reductions. The original group of forty-four dissidents (politically both left and right) argued that the tax reductions would benefit 25,000 high-income and corporate taxpayers while the increased value-added tax would adversely affect low-income families in particular. At a five-hour Fraktion session, government spokesmen and Wehner, rejecting the arguments, contended that no changes could be made in the bill because FDP support was essential. They warned dissident deputies not to vote against it; otherwise the coalition, having only a ten-vote majority, would be endangered. Brandt said that the voters had given the SPD and FDP a mandate to govern for an entire legislative period (four years) and not just for a few months. [31] Most deputies reluctantly supported the bill in its final reading on the Bundestag floor, but two left-wing deputies—Karl-Heinz Hansen (a school teacher from Duesseldorf) and Manfred Coppik (a lawyer from Offenbach) voted against it and three deputies (Rudolf Schöfberger, Erich Meinike, Ernst Waltemathe) abstained. [32]

Perhaps for the first time in Bundestag history, SPD deputies voted—but for different reasons—on the same side as the CDU/CSU and against their own government. They took this action because to them party loyalty increasingly stood for conformity and parliamentary impotence. They viewed the tax package as a violation of party principles and could not in good conscience vote for it. They had reached the limit of compromise. The Social Democratic leaders, angry at the breach of discipline, were relieved that other dissidents had not joined the rebellion and that the bill passed the Bundestag with a three-vote majority. Wehner, on the other hand, was irritated because the government and the party had put the Fraktion into an exposed position; future controversial legislation would make it difficult for him to keep the Fraktion together. [33]

The second confrontation occurred a few months later. Following a series of spectacular domestic terrorist acts against high public and private officials, the government introduced tough antiterrorist bills. On September 29, four deputies (Hansen and Coppik, joined by Dieter Lattmann, a writer, and Klaus Thüsing, a university lecturer) voted against one of them, the contact ban bill, which prohibits suspected terrorists from having access to lawyers for a limited time. (Twelve other SPD and four FDP deputies abstained.) The four SPD deputies said on the Bundestag floor that they could not in good conscience vote for a bill that would limit the civil liberties of any individual; hence in their dissenting vote they were upholding the free, social, and legal base of the state. The angry Wehner, who characterized their dissenting vote as a grave breach of Fraktion discipline, retorted that the great majority of the Fraktion had supported the Federal Republic. Fifteen of the sixteen dissidents, in a written reply to Wehner, noted that they too were acting in the best interests of the country. Thereupon, nearly two hundred deputies signed a letter of support for Wehner, whom they praised for having upheld the principles of social democracy in the Bundestag. The Fraktion executive also backed Wehner. [34]

Dissident leader Coppik stated that he did not want to bring down the government but merely wanted a different coalition politics. The problem, he complained, was the unwillingness of the Fraktion majority to listen to the dissident group. The Juso chairman supported his views and saw nothing wrong in the dissidents occasionally attempting to force the SPD to shift course. To clear the poisoned atmosphere and produce a token spirit of harmony, Wehner, Brandt, and Schmidt met with the sixteen mavericks. The three chiefs argued that in principle all deputies must support the decisions arrived at in the Fraktion by majority vote if the 1976 mandate to govern for four years is to be carried out. The deputies said that in the future they would back the coalition but could not give a blank check for support on all occasions. [35] Despite this political uproar, the contact ban bill became law.

Not many months elapsed before the next occasion of dissidence. Once again, the controversy concerned a government sponsored antiterrorist bill, which granted the police the right to search an entire apartment building for terrorists believed to be in hiding and barred defense lawyers suspected of having secretly helped terrorists from serving in terrorist trials. On February 16, 1978, the bill came up for a final reading in the Bundestag. This time, the parties agreed to let deputies vote on it according to their consciences. Thereupon, four SPD deputies (Coppik, Hansen, Lattmann, Meinike) voted against the bill, asserting that it was too stringent and likely to violate civil liberties. The CDU/CSU also voted against it, but for the opposite reason—the bill was not harsh enough. It passed 245 to 244; the four deputies had nearly prevented its passage.

As anticipated, the CDU/CSU-dominated Bundesrat rejected the bill. To override the veto, the Bundestag would have to assent to the bill by an absolute majority. Therefore the four dissidents reluctantly voted for it. They stated that the CDU/CSU opposition was trying to introduce an even more drastic antiterror bill, which had to be prevented at all costs. But in reality, they did not want to see their government fall, to be replaced by a more conservative CDU/CSU government. [36]

These crises may seem like a tempest in a teapot—but not for those involved in the controversy. In a parliamentary system where party discipline has been a historic practice, many SPD leaders considered the actions of the maverick deputies to be close to treason. The leaders contended each time that if discipline was broken, the end of the coalition was at hand. After the February 1978 vote, the majority of SPD deputies also were bitter against the infidels in their midst; some deputies wanted the party to start ouster proceedings against them. Other deputies accused the dissidents of harboring a "profile neurosis" in taking a negative position to enhance their own political reputation. There was talk at party conventions that the SPD could not allow its image to be tarnished by those who did not support majority decisions. The presidium said that the party was not elected in fall 1976 in order to ensure that the Federal Republic would be governed from the right in 1978.

The dissidents felt that the party leaders were readying a "stab in the back" legend against them. Instead, they contended, the Fraktion should evaluate the minority proposals fairly rather than automatically voting against them. It should be thankful to the dissidents for making clear when compromises with the FDP had to be rejected. Too often, the dissidents stated, the SPD leadership announced in the Fraktion that a bill had to be passed because the FDP refused to make any more concession. Such an argument was not convincing; it was time for the Fraktion to stop being beholden to the coalition and to develop its own political line. [37]

The dissident deputy Hansen, in a long 1977 position paper, wrote that the government had to be pushed toward fulfilling social democratic policies. He defended his negative votes by referring to the Basic Law, which should not be merely a decorative document whose use by dissident SPD deputies is answered with threats of expulsion and by tagging them as "unprincipled trash" (gesinnungslose Lumpen). SPD deputies, he wrote, did not receive with their mandate the task of maintaining the government until the end of the legislative period; rather, deputies should, through constant pressure, ensure that an SPD-led government promotes social democracy. Hansen assailed Wehner for putting pressure on all deputies to sustain government bills in order not to narrow Schmidt's authority. He denounced Schmidt for putting the dissident vote in a global context by saying: "Carter, Brezhnev, and Giscard would not understand this." [38] He also took issue with Brandt for drawing an analogy with the crisis of 1930. Then SPD Chancellor Hermann Müller and his cabinet resigned over the failure of the Fraktion to support his proposed change in unemployment insurance. Finally, Hansen urged the Fraktion to develop a sense of "critical solidarity" with the government. The Fraktion must become a trustee of the party's local base, the party programs, and convention resolutions vis-à-vis the government. Only then could it have more influence on the government's willingness to renew the SPD reform policy. [39]

The views of Hansen and colleagues would not merit so much attention if they were merely the diatribes of a handful of embittered or eccentric individuals. Rather, they represented the views of a broad minority spectrum of the party, including the Jusos and several Land organizations. Their potential opposition to any controversial conservative legislation stemming from an SPD-FDP government had the effect of putting the establishment on guard. As one deputy put it in an interview:

> We, on the left, deliberately challenge the government policy in the Bundestag. It is a healthy sign for a democratic political system . . . . Obviously we cannot do it too often. The CDU/CSU opposition cannot gain political dividends from this because it was supporting the government on many measures. . . . My position also helps me in my district because voters see that I am not a tool of the party establishment. The government is wary of too much criticism; our challenges serve as a brake on their unpopular policies. [40]

He noted that Wehner viewed his occasional negative votes in the Bundestag plenum less apocalyptically than the Fraktion leader's public statements indicated. Wehner told him privately that he had no objections to the negative votes as long as they would not lead to the government's downfall. Incidentally, the deputy had no hesitation in running for the Bundestag again in 1980—and winning. But Lattmann, another dissident, decided not to run again for office, even though he was sure of a place on the party list. Identifying himself as a committed social reformist rather than a typical left-wing politician, he saw only an "all-embracing conservatism" in the SPD and the Federal Republic. Yet he had come to realize that an individual deputy who is determined and persistent enough can initiate and shape legislation. [41]

Not all deputies were as confident as he. One left-wing deputy who had supported the government bills said in an interview: "The decision-making process is very impenetrable. Even though I have been in the Bundestag for two years, I still do not know how to avoid all the wrong paths. There are ever fewer alternatives and no rationality. One is forced to deal with political realities. . . . My colleagues and I have to battle hard for every minor gain." [42]

In the last weeks of the legislative term in 1980, the governing coalition itself lost hold of political realities. For the first time in the eleven-year coalition period, it did not receive a majority of votes on two bills—dealing with conscientious objectors and noise abatement—because it had elevated the votes for or against to a matter of individual conscience. As a result, ten deputies, not all on the political left, voted against the conscientious objector bill. They contended that to maintain a test on conscience for military service was neither compatible with their own consciences nor with party convention resolutions.

The party organ Vorwärts commented that whoever elevates a Bundestag vote to a matter of conscience runs the danger of precipitating an inflation of votes based on that criterion. There will always be bills that do not coincide with party convention resolutions. In such cases, Fraktion leaders should prepare for votes with utmost caution. This certainly was not done in the present instance. Similar mishaps must be avoided in the future, it concluded. [43] After the 1980 election, Vorwärts urged the Fraktion not to be an automatic voting machine for government bills but to participate creatively in policymaking. [44]

The impression, however, should not be gained that party discipline has become a dead letter. On the contrary, on nearly all bills, SPD deputies have unanimously followed the party line in Bundestag plenary sessions. Perhaps more disquieting to parliamentary observers has been the degeneration of "so-called major debates" in the Bundestag into "nothing but ritual struggles between government and opposition," as one newspaper put it. [45] In the interval between debates, Bundestag members became bogged down in committees and plenum in changing the details of bills rather than in concentrating on broad political principles. The CDU/CSU at times put parliamentary tactics before political content. Whenever it sensed that the coalition was having difficulties getting a majority, it voted against bills that it basically agreed with, hoping to lure the coalition into the trap of a parliamentary defeat. Some bills in the late 1970s had to be shelved because SPD and FDP in turn found it increasingly difficult to agree on a lowest common denominator. Others fell by the wayside because of financial and other constraints. [46] By 1982, the SPD and its Fraktion, including especially the left wing, became increasingly disenchanted with Schmidt's conciliatory policies toward the FDP. The resultant tension contributed to the end of the governing coalition.

BUNDESRAT

Although the SPD had to concentrate attention on its work in the Bundestag, it could not neglect the Bundesrat, the country's federalist symbol. This forty-one member legislative chamber does not have coequal powers with the lower house but represents the Länder in legislation directly affecting them, where it has a direct veto, or in other legislation, where it has a suspensive veto. [47] Each Land is represented by three to five members, depending on its population. The members, who must vote in a bloc, receive voting instructions from their Länder governments. Hence it is in the political parties' interest to gain control of the Länder governments. From 1969 to 1982 the SPD was not able to break the CDU/CSU Bundesrat majority, which ranged from one to eleven votes. In 1979, for instance, the CDU controlled Baden-Wuerttemberg, Lower Saxony, Rhineland-Palatinate, and Schleswig-Holstein; a CDU-FDP coalition governed the Saar; and the CSU held Bavaria—for a total of twenty-six seats. The SPD controlled Bremen and Hamburg, and a SPD-FDP coalition held Hesse and North Rhine-Westphalia—for a total of fifteen seats.

Once the SPD-FDP coalition came into power in Bonn in 1969, the CDU/CSU, adopting a polarization strategy, did not hesitate to use its Bundesrat majority to force the governing coalition to make compromises on bills affecting the Länder. The SPD and FDP were irritated and frustrated by the resulting delays. On Ostpolitik, the CDU/CSU pursued a tough "competitive opposition" policy, but on domestic issues it pursued a "cooperative opposition" policy, supporting most government bills, especially noncontroversial ones. [48] Occasionally, the SPD and FDP accepted CDU/CSU initiatives and suggestions for changes or shaped bills to make them palatable to it (e.g., tax reform, university "framework" bill). Consequently, mutual accommodation developed as the antagonism between coalition and opposition blurred. No party dared to publicize this rapprochement for fear of alienating its activists. But the net effect was to lower interparty competition and increase bargaining, diluting even further the coalition government's policymaking function. [49]

The Bundesrat became more important politically than in the period when the CDU/CSU held governmental power. As a result, domestic policy changes became even more incremental than they already had been. The Christian Democrats were eager to make the Bundesrat an effective second chamber, which had not been the goal of the Basic Law architects. Rather than creating a democratically elected body, the latter wanted a chamber proffering advice on federal issues and protecting the Länder interests in legislation, but not becoming a structural constraint in the political system. [50]

SPD government leaders had to contend not only with the limited CDU/CSU opposition but also with occasional policy discord from their own Länder ministers or from FDP ministers in SPD-FDP-governed Länder. Such discords had to be resolved between the parties first at the Land level and then, if necessary, at the Bonn level. In the rare cases where the FDP allied itself with the CDU in a Land—as for a time in Lower Saxony and the Saar—the FDP had the opportunity to curb excessive CDU opposition to bills emanating from the SPD-FDP coalition in Bonn. For instance, the FDP threatened to resign from its coalition with the CDU in Lower Saxony unless the CDU in that Land supported the Bonn government's health insurance and old-age pension reforms. The CDU minister-president concurred reluctantly in order to prevent a political crisis in his government. [51]

The need for all parties to make continuous compromises (in the Bundestag too) led often to de facto all-party cooperation or a grand coalition. It was facilitated by the lack of profound ideological differences on many economic and social issues—although obviously not on all, as we shall see.

The SPD instituted a variety of practices to minimize differences between its national and Länder leadership on specific bills and to act as a transmission belt between the chancellor and the SPD Länder ministers in the Bundesrat. At the informal level, talks were scheduled between national and Länder leaders at Bonn party headquarters or in government offices before the drafting of a bill. Many national leaders who had come through the Länder hierarchy were conditioned to Länder needs and could often be expected to be sympathetic. From March 1970 on the party executive established closer links between the municipalities, the Bundestag Fraktion, and the Bundesrat. It requested party officials to organize several meetings each year at which chairmen of the Landtag Fraktionen and officials from SPD-controlled Länder governments and municipalities would meet with Bundestag Fraktion specialists. Representatives from the Chancellery and Bonn ministries were also to be present. Moreover, the SPD Länder plenipotentiaries in Bonn were to inform the Landtag Fraktionen about Bundesrat sessions. [52]

In 1972 the SPD established a Federation-Länder coordination office in its Bundestag Fraktion, not only to facilitate an exchange of views between the Bundestag Fraktion and the Länder Fraktionen and horizontal coordination between the Länder Fraktionen but also to coordinate all legislative proposals that were to be routed through the Bundesrat and Bundestag. One hoped-for result was to get early feedback from SPD Länder governments and Landtag Fraktionen on bills being drafted in the Bonn ministries. The coordination office also scheduled a number of Bonn-Länder meetings, at which ministers and ministry experts participated, to deal with current economic, financial, and legal problems. In addition, Länder Fraktion chairmen met periodically to exchange views about the parliamentary activities of their Fraktionen in the Land legislatures. Bonn ministry officials and Bundestag Fraktion whips and other deputies were often present to coordinate policy and strategy. [53]

While the SPD and other parties set up coordinating mechanisms between their national and Länder organizations, they also made frequent use of an interparty unit in the Bonn parliament, the mediation committee (Vermittlungsausschuss), established to resolve differences on bills between the Bundesrat and the Bundestag. In most cases the committee, composed of eleven members from each chamber, succeeded in producing accord on the conflicting Bundesrat version of a bill, reflecting CDU/CSU views, and the Bundestag version, reflecting SPD-FDP views. For a number of years after 1969, the SPD and FDP had a majority of votes on the committee and thus could shape bills to their objectives, including bills affecting the Länder, where the Bundesrat had to give its assent. When the CDU captured control of the Lower Saxony government in 1976, its Bundesrat majority increased; hence it was able to dominate the committee. The degree of cooperation between parties, despite shifting majorities on the committee and mutual public denunciations, was relatively high. For instance, in the 1972-1976 legislative period, the committee handled but 96 out of 516 bills approved by the Bundestag. Of the 96, it assented to 89 with or without changes; only 7 fell by the wayside. [54]

The CDU/CSU occasionally used another institution to block the government program. When the party knew it had a chance to kill an important bill on constitutional grounds, it requested the Federal Constitutional Court in Karlsruhe to give a ruling, as in the case of abortion and codetermination legislation, because it gambled that the politicized Court might find in its favor. The Court is divided into two Senates, whose judges are chosen indirectly by the parties. If a CDU-contested bill is handled by the First Senate, a majority of whose members have been politically progressive, the bill has less chance of being declared unconstitutional than in the politically more conservative Second Senate. [55] Needless to say, the SPD was not pleased by the CDU/CSU recourse to judicial review for political purposes, although it too had made use of it during its years in opposition.

CONCLUSION

This survey of the party's parliamentary bodies shows once again the intricate organizational pattern it has developed over the decades. Formal line and staff functions of its parliamentary organizations were augmented by links to the party's own organization at all levels and to the government. Policy flowed from top to bottom,, but also horizontally, to connect the Länder with one another. Yet despite this impressive bureaucratic model, the human and political factors could not be disregarded. Once again, the intraparty ideological schism had a widespread effect: in this instance on Fraktion cohesion. The young, rising left elite challenged the old elite; dissident Fraktion members challenged some government policies. In addition, coalition and Länder politics produced tensions. Party members wanted their deputies to make fewer concessions to the FDP, and Länder bosses demanded input on issues affecting the Länder. In the light of these challenges and tensions, the elaborately constructed machinery had its operating troubles.

Yet the SPD Fraktion, despite being hemmed in by the institutional constraints of the Bundesrat and the Constitutional Court, demonstrated that it had enough autonomous powers vis-à-vis the party and the government to sometimes make policy. Normally, it could be expected to support government bills, enthusiastically or not, but there were occasions when it made significant changes in government bills or warned the government beforehand not to expect support for a bill (see chapter 13). Its links to the SPD were close on a structural and personal level. Thus its relative superiority in power over the party organization did not create excessive friction between the two segments of the triad.

NOTES

1. Peter Glotz, Die Innenausstattung der Macht, p. 138. See also Noller, p. 28; Westdeutsche Allgemeine, Sept. 8, 1979.

2. For instance, in the 1976-1980 legislative period, 81 percent of CDU/CSU and 83 percent of FDP deputies had an advanced education, but only 57 percent of SPD deputies. For details, see Deutscher Bundestag, 30 Jahre Deutscher Bundestag, pp. 73-74.

3. Emil-Peter Müller, Die sozio-ökonomische und verbandliche Struktur des VIII. Deutschen Bundestages (Cologne: Deutscher Instituts-Verlag, 1977), p. 11.

4. For a list of members, see SPD, Jahrbuch, various dates; SPD, Dokumente, Die Sozialdemokraten in der Verantwortung im Bund, Bericht der SPD-Bundestagsfraktion 1973-1975, p. 9.

5. Kurt Schumacher held the post from 1949 to 1952, Erich Ollenhauer from 1952 to 1963, and Fritz Erler from 1964 to 1967.

6. In December 1973, 47 out of 219 SPD deputies present voted against him; in June 1979, 29 out of 182 voted negatively and 11 abstained (Süddeutsche Zeitung, Dec. 5, 1973; Vorwärts, June 7, 1979).

7. Der Spiegel, June 11, 1973; New York Times, July 14, 1973; Aug. 24, 1974. See also Deutscher Bundestag, Verhandlungen des Deutschen Bundestages, 7th election period, 90th session, Mar. 27, 1974, p. 5966 ff.

8. Working group 1 deals with foreign and security policy, intra-German relations, Europe, development policy; group 2 with interior, education, sports; group 3 with economic policy; group 4 with social policy; group 5 with public finance; group 6 with legal matters. For details, see "Organisations- und Geschäftsverteilungsplan der Fraktion der SPD im Deutschen Bundestag (Stand: Okt. 1974)" (hectographed); SPD, Informationsdienst, intern (Feb. 1979); Hans Apel, "Die Willensbildung in den Bundestagsfraktionen—Die Rolle der Arbeitsgruppen und Arbeitskreise," Zeitschrift für Parlamentsfragen, I, No. 2 (1969-1970), 223-229.

9. For details, see Ortlieb Fliedner, "Probleme der Organisation und Arbeitsweise von Fraktionen (II)," VOP (Verwaltungsführung Organisation Personalwesen), 4/1979, pp. 228-229; Tony Burkett, "Developments in the West German Bundestag in the 1970s," Parliamentary Affairs, XXXIV, No.

3 (Summer 1981), 291-307.

10. Personal interview, Bonn, Jan. 16, 1975.

11. Karl-Heinz Walkhoff, "Parlamentarismus kritisch betrachtet," Quo vadis SPD?, ed. Seeliger, pp. 87-88.

12. Hartmut Soell, "Fraktion und Parteiorganisation: Zur Willensbildung der SPD in den sechziger Jahren," Politische Vierteljahresschrift, X, No. 4 (Dec. 1969), 625.

13. The motion also prohibited deputies or government officials from accepting money from institutions that they supervise or from other donors who expect financial advantage or policy change. A party commission may be set up to get information from officials about their functions, income, and time commitment (Vorwärts, Feb. 22, 1979; June 28, 1979; Nov. 29, 1979).

14. Müller-Rommel, pp. 161-182; Conradt and Mueller, p. 8; Der Spiegel, Nov. 14, 1977; personal interviews with deputies, Bonn, various dates.

15. Süddeutsche Zeitung, Dec. 18/19, 1976; Vorwärts, Dec. 23, 1976.

16. Süddeutsche Zeitung, Jan. 21, 1977.

17. Vorwärts, Nov. 20, 1980.

18. Frankfurter Rundschau, Dec. 12, 1972; Müller-Rommel, pp. 132-161.

19. See recollections of fourteen left deputies in Hugo Brandt, ed., Hoffen, zweifeln, abstimmen. Seit 1969 im Bundestag: 14 Abgeordnete berichten (Reinbek: rororo, 1980).

20. Letter, Manfred Hiltner (SPD Fraktion staff member) to author, Sept. 16, 1982.

21. The Metzger Circle called itself "left middle," but was really a right-middle group (Arend, p. 56; Frankfurter Allgemeine Zeitung, Dec. 21, 1972; Feb. 28, 1973; Der Spiegel, Nov. 14, 1977).

22. The decision precipitated the resignation of right-wing leaders, who then formed the Social Democratic Party (Michael Rustin, "Different Conceptions of Party: Labour's Constitutional Debates," New Left Review, No. 126, pp. 18, 19, 27).

23. Michels, p. 154.

24. SPD, Fraktion, Pressemitteilung, No. 293, Oct. 19, 1965, cited by Soell, p. 611.

25. Ibid., pp. 623-624; Nowka, pp. 59-60, 135.

26. Ibid., pp. 56-57.

27. Ibid., pp. 52-53.

28. Ibid., pp. 117-118.

29. Ibid., p. 121.

30. Süddeutsche Zeitung, Dec. 11/12, 1976.

31. Ibid., June 15, 1977.

32. Schöfberger was a lawyer and former head of the Munich SPD (1972-1976); Meineke and Waltemathe were city administrators in Oberhausen and Bremen respectively. For roll call, see Deutscher Bundestag, Verhandlungen, 8th el. pd., 32d session, June 16, 1977, pp. 2378-2380.

33. Die Zeit, June 24, 1977. In 1968, fifty-three SPD deputies had voted against a government bill, but then the CDU/CSU deputies voted with the majority of SPD deputies.

34. Deutscher Bundestag, Verhandlungen, 8th el. pd., 44th session, Sept. 29, 1977, p. 3383. For roll call, ibid., pp. 3384-3385.

35. Süddeutsche Zeitung, Oct. 13, 14, 1977.

36. Relay from Bonn, Feb. 21, 1978; Hannoversche Allgemeine, Apr. 14, 1978.

37. Norbert Gansel and Erich Meineke in Vorwärts, Feb. 23, 1976; Mar. 29, 1979.

38. Der Spiegel, June 20, 1977. In 1981, deputy Hansen was expelled from the party and the Fraktion for having made derogatory attacks on Schmidt. In 1982, deputy Coppick resigned from the SPD. In November 1982, they founded a new left party, the Democratic Socialists. Observers expected the party to remain small.

39. Ibid., Nov. 7, 1977.

40. Private interview, Bonn, Mar. 20, 1980.

41. Kieler Nachrichten, June 26, 1980.

42. Private interview, Bonn, Jan. 20, 1975.

43. Vorwärts, July 10, 1980.

44. Ibid., Oct. 16, 1980.

45. Süddeutsche Zeitung, July 12, 1980.

46. Ibid.

47. Legislation affecting the Länder which the Bundesrat can veto pertains to state and local finance, education, police, land use, and transportation. The Bundesrat can also veto federal laws administered by the Länder. On other legislation, the Bundestag can by absolute majority override the Bundesrat's suspensive veto. Normally the Bundesrat has recommended changes to bills, which the administration and the Bundestag may or may not accept.

48. From 1969 to 1976, the CDU/CSU supported about 93 percent of all bills in both chambers, and voted against or abstained on the others (Deutscher Bundestag, 30 Jahre Deutscher Bundestag, p. 271). See also Hans-Joachim Veen, Die CDU/CSU-Opposition im Parlamentarischen Entscheidungsprozess (Munich: Ernst Vögel, 1973), p. 106 ff; CDU, Die Leistungen der CDU während ihrer Regierungszeit von 1949-1969 im Vergleich zur Linkskoalition (1969-April 1972) (Bonn, n.d.), p. 44; Friedrich Karl Fromme, Gesetzgebung im Widerstreit: Wer beherrscht den Bundesrat? Die Kontroverse seit 1969 (2d ed.; Stuttgart: Bonn Aktuell, 1980), pp. 21-33.

49. Lehmbruch, "Party and Federation in Germany: A Developmental Dilemma," Government and Opposition, XIII, No. 2 (Spring 1978), 166.

50. See Heinz Laufer, "Der Bundesrat als Instrument der Opposition," Zeitschrift für Parlamentsfragen, I, No. 3 (Oct. 1970), 318-341.

51. Relay from Bonn, June 27, 1977.

52. SPD, press release, 70/70, March 20, 1970.

53. SPD Dokumente, Die Sozialdemokraten in der Verantwortung im Bund, Bericht der SPD-Bundestagsfraktion 1973-1975 (Bonn-Bad Godesberg, 1976), pp. 155-156.

54. Deutscher Bundestag, 30 Jahre Deutscher Bundestag, p. 274. For the 1976-1979 period, the committee voted against eight bills, made compromises on five, rejected two, and had not yet acted on one (Bulletin, No. 103, Sept. 11, 1979, pp. 960, 962). See also Lehmbruch, "Party and Federation in Germany," pp. 161-162.

55. For details, see D. P. Kommers, Judicial Politics in West Germany (Beverly Hills, Calif.: Sage, 1976); William E. Paterson, "Problems of Party Government in West Germany—a British Perspective" (unpublished paper, 1980); "Political Parties and the Making of Foreign Policy—the case of the Federal Republic," Review of International Studies, No. 7 (1981), pp. 227-235.

12
Party and Government

British political scientist Richard Rose aptly noted: "Every party is dualist when in government, for there is inevitably a gulf between the party in office and the party outside the gates." [1] Whether the gulf is narrow or wide depends in part on whether the government consists of one or more than one party. In theory a single-party government should be able to carry out the party's program or manifesto, but in practice the party leader, once in office as chief executive, may disagree with aspects of the program or feel that it is too narrowly conceived and does not represent the general interest. A two-party or multiparty coalition will find the gulf widened by the policy distances between the governing parties. [2] But even if the distance is short, other institutional and political constraints will make it difficult for the major party program to be carried out without significant changes. On the other hand, regardless of whether the government consists of one or more parties, programmatic innovations reflecting party goals will have more chance of adoption when a new government comes in than when one succeeds itself after a general election. [3]

As noted in later chapters, in West Germany, SPD participation in governments after 1966 gave it an opportunity to influence domestic and foreign policies. This chapter deals with the nature of the relationship between the party and the government from 1969 to 1982. The main focus is on the party's strategy for ensuring that its inputs (policy recommendations) into the nerve centers of executive power—the chancellorship, the cabinet, and the civil service—will have a maximum effect on the policy outputs (laws and decrees). [4] But this strategy had its limitations, as noted below.

This chapter also deals with other aspects of SPD involvement in the executive realm: its role in one chief executive succession period (Brandt to Schmidt), coalition bargaining for ministerial posts and the contents of the government program when new cabinets were formed, the nature of ministerial appointments reflecting the diverse party interests, and the finale of the coalition government.

THE FEDERAL PRESIDENT

In the relationship between the SPD and the government, the party's interest in the federal presidency was only sporadic, rising whenever a candidate had to be chosen and ebbing once he was in office. The explanation is that as chief of state, the president has primarily ceremonial functions, although through the force of his personality, he has an opportunity to emphasize some political themes for the national agenda. When Gustav Heinemann became president in March 1969 (in the last year of the Grand Coalition), the SPD was pleased that one of its members had finally assumed the highest office in the country. His election gave the party further respectability among the voters who went to the polls in the Bundestag election later that year. [5] Heinemann, who remained in office until 1974, set a tone as a "citizen president" who sought to integrate minority and socially deprived groups into the maelstrom of society. He was succeeded by Walter Scheel, until then FDP foreign minister, who remained in office until 1979. That year, the Christian Democrats had enough votes in the electoral college, consisting of all Bundestag deputies and an equal number of Länder parliament deputies, to elect one of their leaders, Karl Carstens. SPD and FDP fought over whether one of their leaders should run in a hopeless race. The SPD Fraktion backbenchers urged the party to put up a candidate to give electors a choice, but Brandt was reluctant if the FDP was not willing to support such a candidate. At the last minute the SPD chose Annemarie Renger, but Carstens was easily elected. [6]

THE CHANCELLOR AND THE CABINET

Unlike its only occasional hold on the presidency, the SPD held the chancellorship and the majority of cabinet posts throughout the period 1969-1982. Because the chancellorship is the top policymaking post in the Federal Republic, the party's prestige rose considerably within the country and abroad. In chapter 4, the qualities of Brandt and Schmidt as political leaders were sketched. Suffice it to say that their styles of governing differed considerably and that the relationship of chancellor to party before 1974 was conditioned by Brandt heading the government and the party, while after 1974 Schmidt as chancellor and Brandt as party leader had to carefully work out a satisfactory cooperative arrangement. As chancellors, their appeal to the public was also important. Both enjoyed great popularity during most of their incumbency—although Schmidt's declined somewhat after 1980. Brandt had an emotional rapport with the population that Schmidt lacked. On the other hand, Schmidt was more popular as a "man on horseback," who is firm-willed, ambitious, skillful, brilliant as an orator, and tough toward his opponents. [7]

A Successorship Case Study

Brandt's resignation in 1974 and Schmidt's assumption of power provide clues to how the SPD gets involved in a successorship situation. Although such an event is exceptional in the German political system, where normally a chancellor does not resign before the legislative period ends, it does illustrate the party's role in an executive branch upheaval. It must be recalled that Brandt's resignation was triggered by the Guillaume spy scandal and other factors. On Saturday, May 4, soon after Guillaume's arrest, Brandt consulted Wehner and two other party leaders about his decision to resign. Wehner was noncommittal, but the others urged Brandt to remain in office. The following day, the Chancellor met again with several SPD leaders, told them of his decision, and suggested that Schmidt be his successor. That evening, Brandt composed a letter of resignation addressed to President Heinemann, in which he requested the president to accept the resignation immediately and to appoint Vice Chancellor Scheel as acting chancellor. Brandt showed the letter to a few party friends and to Scheel, who asked him to remain in office, even though by then Brandt had made up his mind. On Monday evening, May 6, he informed government and opposition leaders about his decision.

At midnight, the letter of resignation had reached Heinemann. When radio listeners heard the news, several hundred SPD sympathizers appeared before Brandt's private residence, and later on Tuesday tens of thousands demonstrated in major cities as an expression of sympathy and support. In the meantime, Brandt made a farewell address to the Fraktion, and Scheel, becoming acting chancellor, requested the cabinet ministers to remain in their posts until a new chancellor had been chosen. On May 16, the SPD and FDP Fraktionen voted for Schmidt to succeed Brandt. [8]

Coalition Formations

While succession crises are rare in West German history, coalition-building of cabinets after national elections has become almost routinized. William Riker's theoretical observations about political coalitions apply to the West German scene. In discussing the size of coalitions, he maintains that "participants create coalitions just as large as they believe will ensure winning and no larger." [9] From 1969 to 1982, the SPD followed this concept, although with only three parties represented in the Bundestag, the size of the coalitions was limited from the outset. A coalition with the CDU/CSU was ruled out by most SPD leaders because of policy differences and lack of ideological affinity; the FDP therefore became the preferred coalition partner—until 1982.

A description of how the SPD was involved in the formation of cabinets provides clues to the nature of coalition bargaining in West Germany. At stake in each bargaining period was the distribution of cabinet portfolios, in which the coalition partners had to agree on the number of posts to be allotted to each one, which party should receive which ministry post, and who should receive the post. Also at stake was accord on policy goals, in which the FDP made minimum demands as the price for its participation, producing in turn discontent within the SPD about the extent of concessions made to the minor party. Despite these structural and political problems, reflecting systemic constraints on SPD strategy, the SPD-FDP coalitions throughout the period of study showed remarkable stability. [10]

The First SPD-FDP Cabinet (1969-1972)

The 1969 national election gave the SPD and FDP enough Bundestag seats to form a government. Brandt and Scheel had secretly decided months earlier to enter into a coalition if the election results made it possible, although Wehner and Schmidt, for a variety of reasons, would have preferred a renewed SPD coalition with the CDU/CSU. [11] But an SPD alliance with the FDP had become more logical by 1969. At the time, the FDP liberal wing had triumphed over the conservative wing as the party attracted its share of the new middle class, especially highly paid salaried employees and civil servants. Consequently, the FDP had become more reform-oriented than during its earlier coalition pacts with the CDU/CSU.

When the election results were in on that memorable Sunday night, September 28, 1969, party chief Brandt declared that he was ready for coalition talks with the FDP. A few leading SPD and FDP politicians met immediately to prepare for the talks to be held two days later. On Monday, Brandt visited President Heinemann to announce his candidacy for the chancellorship; SPD and Fraktion executives convened the same day to pledge their support of Brandt's initiative and to choose a seven-member negotiating team to meet with its FDP counterpart. On Tuesday, the SPD executive, council, and control committee unanimously agreed that negotiations with the FDP should begin that evening. The SPD team, headed by Brandt, was carefully chosen to represent different geographic areas; religions; groups (Leber was included because of his close ties to the Catholic church and the unions); specialized fields (Schiller for economic affairs, Möller for finance, Schmidt for defense); the Fraktion (Wehner); and the Länder (Kühn). Its task was to come to an agreement with the FDP negotiating team on the distribution of cabinet seats and on the content of the government program for the ensuing four-year legislative session.

After the teams met twice, the SPD presidium, behind the scenes during the negotiations, was informed of developments and gave the signal to continue. On October 3, the Fraktion executive and members, including the newly elected deputies, heard reports from Brandt concerning the progress of the talks and also approved further negotiations. From then until October 15, the teams met often to pursue their objectives. The SPD members had wide latitude in the negotiations, being bound only by the proposed government program approved at the Godesberg SPD election convention of summer 1969. That program rested on an SPD executive draft, written by some of the same members who were on the negotiating team. Hence, there was little chance of a collision between party and Fraktion on one hand and the team on the other.

When the talks were concluded, top SPD organs and Fraktion, meeting separately, approved the proposed cabinet slate and coalition government program. On October 21, Brandt was sworn in as chancellor, and on the following day, the cabinet, consisting of twelve SPD and three FDP ministers and one without a party, was sworn in. The interval from national election to government formation was twenty-four days, a record of brevity. [12]

The socioeconomic profile of the SPD ministers varied considerably. In their youths, they had been politically socialized by family members who had been active in the party or the union movement. Their fathers' occupations ranged from mineworker (Arendt), mason (Leber), and artisan (Lauritzen, Strobel) to doctor (Ehmke, Jahn), educator (Schmidt), civil servant (Möller), and engineer (Schiller). In a tabulation of SPD ministers, including those in the 1966-1969 cabinet, seven had upper-middle-class backgrounds; two, lower-middle-class; two, upper-lower-class; and one, lower-lower-class. [13] This preponderance of middle-class backgrounds (a higher ratio than in the total population) was not usually matched by advanced educations. There was danger that having distanced themselves from their original careers, some ministers would find it difficult to relate to members of the class from which they had come.

Often, career advancement had begun for the ministers in their youths, when most of them had been politically active (unlike ministers in other parties). Jahn (Minister of Justice), Schmidt (Defense), and Ehmke (Special Affairs) had held leading positions in the SDS; Franke (Intra-German Affairs) in the socialist workers' youth movement; and Lauritzen (City Construction and Housing) in another socialist student group. Others (Arendt, Minister of Labor; Leber, Transportation; Möller, Finance) had become union officials. [14]

The ministers, on the average, had been SPD members for twenty-four years and had served in the Bundestag for ten. The majority had moved up the party ladder from branch to Land to national executives. Of those who had not been in top party positions before entering the cabinet, some sought such positions soon thereafter to gain legitimacy. [15] As in previous cabinets, only one woman, Käte Strobel, received a post, heading (as usual) the Ministry for Youth, Family and Health. Her career, however, was typical of ministers who came up through party ranks. Born in 1907, she went to a business school and from 1923 to 1938 worked in Bavarian businesses. From 1921 to 1933 she was active in the SPD youth and education movement. After World War II, she became chairwoman of the SPD women's groups in Franconia and eventually a member of the party executive and presidium. In the Bundestag, she held high posts in the Fraktion; in 1966 she became minister for health (the ministry was reorganized in 1969 to include youth and family). [16]

The Second SPD-FDP Cabinet (1972-1974)

The cabinet formed in 1969 did not remain in power for the full four years. As a result of the already cited stalemate between the government and opposition parties, an election was called for November 19, 1972. The result was a victory for SPD and FDP, after which Brandt and Scheel met to work out details of the negotiating teams. Thereupon, the SPD executive approved Brandt's choice of the seven team members: Wehner, Möller, and Wienand to represent the Fraktion; Brandt, Schmidt, and Leber, the cabinet; and Kühn, the Länder. While both teams convened to discuss the future government program, Schmidt and Wehner met informally with some FDP team members to discuss the distribution of cabinet posts.

There was discontent in SPD circles that not only party organs but even the full negotiating team had too little influence on the selection of cabinet members. The Bremen organization successfully requested the party council to meet one week earlier to participate more in shaping the government program. Despite these problems, the SPD and FDP teams reached accord after just three weeks of negotiations. [17] On December 14, Brandt was sworn in as chancellor for a second term.

Among the thirteen SPD ministers, only three new ones joined the cabinet, although there was some reshuffling of ministerial posts. The linkage between party and government remained strong. Five ministers (Brandt, Schmidt, Leber, Franke, Vogel) were party presidium and executive members, and two others (Arendt and Eppler) were executive members. Ehmke was elected into the executive in 1973, but Schmidt was not reelected. All members except Brandt also held seats on the party council. [18]

The Third SPD-FDP Cabinet (1974-1976)

Chancellor Brandt's sudden resignation in May 1974 and Schmidt's succession produced a cabinet reshuffle. The background of the new SPD ministers reflected Schmidt's penchant for a more pragmatic policy. He named Hans Apel, who had been parliamentary state secretary in the Foreign Office, as minister of finance. Kurt Gscheidle, deputy chairman of the Postal Workers Union, became minister of transportation, post and telecommunications. Karl Ravens, a parliamentary state secretary, headed the Ministry for Town Planning, Housing and City Construction. Hans Matthöfer, a former staff member of the Metal Workers Union and thereafter of the Organization for European Economic Cooperation in Washington, became minister for research and technology. Helmut Rohde, parliamentary state secretary in the Ministry of Labor and Social Welfare, was appointed minister for education and science. Most of these new ministers were in the party's right wing. Schmidt did not reappoint three left-center ministers—Ehmke, Bahr, and Klaus von Dohnanyi (Education and Science).

After seven weeks in office, Eppler, another left-center leader, resigned as minister for economic cooperation because the cabinet intended to cut his budget outlays for Third World aid. The Jusos criticized Schmidt's belt-tightening policy and feared that Eppler's departure represented a turn toward a more conservative policy. Schmidt informed the SPD presidium about the government's budget plan but cautioned it not to make any public statement, in order to maintain unity. The Schmidt-Eppler fracas was exacerbated by personality differences and Schmidt's feeling that Eppler was too much of a missionary. [19] The Chancellor was more comfortable having no exponent of the party's left wing in the cabinet, but he did appoint the moderate Bahr, whom he had let go in the initial cabinet shuffle, to succeed Eppler. Although not too much should be made of one cabinet resignation, the move portended a shift in policy, as was already evident in the pragmatic government program declaration. One critical parliamentary state secretary labeled the new coalition program as "sheer CDU." [20]

The Fourth SPD-FDP Cabinet, 1976-1980

The October 3 national election produced another round of coalition negotiations paralleling those of 1969 and 1972. Once again each party appointed a negotiating team, which did not begin serious negotiations on a government program until October 25. [21] The teams eventually reached accord on several key points—reduction of unemployment, codetermination, emphasis on health and social policy, and budget review—but the FDP team did not accept SPD demands for pension reform and an investment policy. Schmidt insisted that the two teams must settle all the differences then and there to preclude their surfacing later in the cabinet. But the teams decided to shelve those issues on which they could not agree. In the meantime, Schmidt worked on the outline of the government declaration, with only a minimum of consultation with Social Democratic leaders. However, on December 13 and 14 the members of the outgoing cabinet participated in the team discussions concerning the declaration.

On December 14, Brandt and Genscher in their capacity as SPD and FDP chairmen formally requested Federal President Scheel to suggest to the Bundestag that Schmidt be voted on for chancellor. On the following day, Schmidt won election, but with only a one-vote plurality. The formation of the cabinet produced a last-minute hitch. Arendt was slated to again become minister of labor but withdrew his name after the crisis resulting from Schmidt's attempt to postpone pension benefit increases. Arendt also knew that the SPD would have to make a painful compromise with the FDP on codetermination legislation. Schmidt and Brandt tried to keep Arendt in the cabinet, but he demurred. Herbert Ehrenberg, who had been on the staff of the Construction Workers Union and a secretary of state in the Ministry of Labor, was appointed instead. In addition, Antje Huber became minister for youth, family and health; and Marie Schlei became minister for economic cooperation. Schmidt reappointed eight other SPD ministers who, according to the pro-SPD Frankfurter Rundschau, were "brave middle-class" members. The newspaper contended that Schmidt was afraid of nominating top party officials to the cabinet because he feared strong personalities. "Hence the SPD ministerial team is less a mirror of the qualitative level of the German Social Democracy than a group of aides that especially orients itself toward the characteristics of the boss." [22] The newspaper was particularly critical of Schmidt's retention of Gscheidle, who had not been an effective minister of transportation, and of Vogel, who had not given the Ministry of Justice new impulses. But regardless of such criticisms, the new cabinet was sworn in on December 16, and on the same day Schmidt issued the government declaration.

Major cabinet reshuffles during the term of an administration are rare in the Federal Republic. Although one was expected in spring 1978, it came as early as February when Defense Minister Leber resigned following an intelligence bugging scandal in his ministry. Schmidt, after consulting top SPD and FDP leaders, took the occasion not to reappoint Ravens (Town Planning), Rohde (Education and Science), and Schlei (Economic Cooperation), all of whom he felt had performed inadequately in their posts. Schmidt also shifted the conservative Apel from Finance to Defense and the liberal Matthöfer from Research to Finance. Partly to appease the party's left wing, which had been critical of many of his earlier appointments, he appointed four young, university-educated secretaries of state as ministers, not all of whom, however, were on the left. Their careers provide an illuminating profile of the new generation of SPD leaders.

Jürgen Schmude (Education and Science) was born in 1936, received a law degree, and practiced law from 1964 to 1971. He had joined the SPD at age 21 but never held more than local party offices. He was elected to the Bundestag in 1969 at age 33. From 1974 to 1976 he also held a top post in the Ministry of the Interior. Volker Hauff (Research and Technology) was born in 1940, received a doctorate in economics, and managed a data processing institute from 1966 to 1970. He joined the SPD at age 19, was active in the antinuclear campaign in Berlin, and returned to Swabia to oppose the local SPD establishment. In 1969, he was elected to the Bundestag; three years later, he was appointed parliamentary state secretary in the Ministry of Research and Technology, and then in Post and Telecommunications. At age 37, he was the youngest minister in the cabinet.

Rainer Offergeld (Economic Cooperation) and Dieter Haack (Town Planning, Housing and City Construction) had backgrounds similar to those of Schmude and Hauff. Both were born in the 1930s, received law degrees, held posts in the party, were elected in 1969 to the Bundestag, and received top political appointments in ministries. The four new ministers represented the third generation of postwar politicians who rose rapidly to the top because the war had decimated an earlier generation and because they were bright and able. Schmidt's reappointment of them to the new cabinet in 1980 indicated his satisfaction with their performance in office. [23]

The Fifth SPD-FDP Cabinet, 1980-1982

SPD and FDP negotiators meeting after the October 5, 1980, election had little difficulty agreeing on the composition of the new cabinet, which consisted again of thirteen SPD and four FDP members (but with some changes in posts), but they had difficulty agreeing on a coalition program. Schmidt first requested SPD officials in the Chancellor's Office to negotiate for the SPD side but abandoned the idea when SPD and Bundestag Fraktion leaders, seeking a share in policymaking, vigorously objected. Thus top SPD leaders became the chief negotiators and informed a sixteen-member "feedback" commission, consisting of other SPD leaders and deputies, about their daily talks with FDP negotiators on a coalition program. When labor leaders heard that the program would contain no new social reforms but rather, among other planks, subsidies to employers and higher gasoline taxes, they demanded that SPD negotiators stop making concessions to the FDP. They remained bitter even after Schmidt's explanation that given the poor fiscal situation, costly reforms had to stay off the agenda. Many SPD leaders also complained that there were no social democratic accents in the coalition program.

The SPD-FDP Coalition's Finale

The painful eight days of negotiations manifested the increasingly strained atmosphere between the two parties, especially in the cabinet. At issue was the deteriorating economic and financial situation in the Federal Republic caused primarily by an international recession—another external factor that affected the SPD, in this instance negatively. In 1981 and 1982, SPD and FDP cabinet members clashed repeatedly on ways to overcome the national recession—a reflection of ideological differences. FDP ministers favored a probusiness solution based on the Reagan and Thatcher supply side economics model, while SPD ministers favored an orthodox Keynesian pump-priming approach. Although both sides achieved a compromise in 1981, one year later it became evident that many FDP leaders, but by no means all, wanted to break up the coalition and join the CDU/CSU (their erstwhile coalition partner) in a new government. Led by Foreign Minister Genscher, the FDP ministers, viewing a coalition with the strife-torn SPD as a liability, decided that an alliance with the CDU/CSU was a better instrument for achieving their economic objectives.

While cabinet members feuded, what did the SPD do in the final weeks of the coalition? SPD leaders, prodded by the left wing and the unions, repeatedly told Schmidt that he and other SPD cabinet members must stop making concessions to the FDP, especially when the Hesse FDP had announced that after the Land election it would no longer remain in a coalition cabinet with the SPD but would switch to a CDU-led cabinet. Incidentally, the SPD left wing was not averse to seeing the SPD end its government role and move into opposition where no further concessions would be made and where the party could assume a more socialist profile.

On August 30, Schmidt assured SPD presidium members that his Bonn cabinet members would make no further concessions to FDP economic demands. As a result, a coalition crisis could not be avoided because Minister of Economics Otto Lambsdorff (FDP) insisted that the cabinet accept his probusiness solution to the economic crisis (drastic cuts in social programs and tax concessions for industry to stimulate investment). Labor leaders, SPD officials (Brandt, Wehner, and Glotz), and party executive members told Schmidt on separate occasions in early September that he must not accept Lambsdorff's proposals. Schmidt, knowing that he had the backing of his party and the Fraktion for a possible break with the FDP, met on September 15 with SPD cabinet members to inform them of the party's views and to discuss Genscher's intention to force an end to the coalition with the SPD. While the cabinet gathered that day for its last session, Brandt and three top SPD officials met to pledge their support for Schmidt's actions, including his proposal to dissolve the Bundestag and call for new elections. They informed Schmidt that the party would be ready to immediately schedule a special convention to agree on an electoral platform and to support his nomination as the chancellor candidate. Schmidt accepted their support with gratitude; the feuds of the past were momentarily forgotten.

On September 17, the four FDP cabinet ministers resigned from their posts after Schmidt insisted that they either adhere to the coalition program or leave. Angry that they had not abided by the 1980 electoral mandate to govern jointly for four years, he lambasted them for their departure and announced the end of the coalition in an address to the Bundestag. Yet the FDP must not be blamed entirely for the coalition's demise. The SPD's internal feuds—salutary as they may have been in creating intraparty democracy—had weakened the governing authority of Schmidt who had not been able to rely on the full support of the party for his domestic and foreign policies for many years.

Once the coalition fell apart, his plan was to remain head of a temporary SPD minority government and then, like Brandt in 1972, request and deliberately lose a vote of confidence in the Bundestag in order to call for an early election. Schmidt's plan, however, was not acceptable to CDU leader Helmut Kohl, who preferred to hold a "constructive" no-confidence vote, in which the Bundestag must have a majority for a new chancellor before ousting the incumbent. Thereupon Kohl expected to become the chancellor and form a CDU/CSU-FDP coalition cabinet. Kohl's plan prevailed—on October 1, 1982, he narrowly won the constructive vote of no confidence, the first successful one in West German history. He became chancellor, ending the SPD's sixteen-year participation in governments since 1966—the first three years, ironically, in coalition with the CDU/CSU. Kohl promised an election for March 1983, when Schmidt's popularity might have waned and the stature of the FDP might have increased or, as Franz Josef Strauss hoped, when the CDU/CSU might gain an absolute majority.

In late October, Schmidt withdrew his name as candidate for chancellor, citing his health as the primary reason. But political factors also played a role, because he did not want to become a losing candidate and could not expect to enter into possible coalition negotiations with the Greens, whose views were so antithetical to his. SPD leaders swiftly chose Hans-Jochen Vogel as the party's candidate for chancellor. The 56-year-old former housing and justice minister and former mayor of Munich and Berlin, who had become head of the SPD Fraktion in Berlin, was an admired politician within the SPD. A pragmatist with a streak of idealism, he was expected to follow the Brandt line: try for reconciliation of the warring SPD factions and work for rapprochement with the Greens without abandoning the pro-NATO line. Originally a right-winger in the party, he had gradually moved toward the center, showing since 1981 a tolerance of the left-wing protest movements in West Berlin (where he had been sent to rescue the local SPD). With his nomination, he was expected to become one of the top leaders in the party.

The 1982 finale of SPD governance indicates that Schmidt coordinated his tactical moves closely with SPD and Fraktion leaders who knew that in a politically exposed position the Chancellor needed maximum assistance. Such a harmonious relationship had not existed while Schmidt and the FDP were making joint policy decisions. The 1982 finale also indicates that the 1980 coalition building and bargaining between SPD and FDP had been tenuous; in a political system where the parties do have some ideological differences, one coalition does not necessarily last the length of its term, not to speak of remaining in power for decades, when external conditions put strains on the government or when party factions become dissatisfied with government policies. On the other hand, because of limited interparty ideological differences, different coalition combinations are possible—as seen by the SPD shift from its coalition with the CDU/CSU to the FDP in 1969 and the FDP shift from SPD to CDU/CSU in 1982. In nearly all coalitions since 1949, the minor parties have assumed an importance in sharing government power far above their small representation in the Bundestag. But from 1983 on this pattern may change. As the formation of party coalitions becomes more difficult, they may be replaced occasionally by minority governments, which are bound to be unstable.

The SPD loss of power in 1982 serves as a case study of how coalitions can break up under certain circumstances; whether in another West German crisis situation a replication can be expected is extremely doubtful given a different set of political actors and actions. Nevertheless, the 1982 case study provides one useful model to assess the end of coalitions—and not just for West Germany.

MINISTRIES AND CIVIL SERVICE

Any party in power needs the support of cabinet members, top ministerial officials, and civil servants to enact its program into legislation. As in other countries, the German ministries' top officials—state secretaries and heads of divisions—are political appointees whose incumbency may last only as long as their party is in power. Thus the Christian Democrats' loss of power in 1969 gave the SPD and FDP an opportunity to put their people into the upper ministerial echelons (the SPD had begun the task in 1966 at the time of the Grand Coalition). Not all Christian Democratic appointees were forced into retirement; a number were shifted to less desirable posts to make room for appointees from the new coalition. In all ministries, eleven state secretaries and eight heads of divisions were replaced, not always by SPD or FDP members but by nonpartisan experts as well. In some instances, the purge was generational, rather than partisan.

Whether political appointees within a ministry were replaced wholesale or selectively depended partly on the views of the new minister. In 1969, Ehmke, as head of the Chancellor's Office, brought in many SPD members, yet could not make a clean sweep of all division heads. Minister Eppler formed a group of left-oriented specialists to advise him outside the hierarchical structure. Minister Schmidt preferred to appoint a number of nonpartisan experts. [24]

Some FDP-controlled ministries, such as Foreign and Interior, had little political coloration, and Economics was populated by conservative appointees. Because of the importance of the three ministries, this was a handicap for the SPD, but the arithmetic of coalition politics, in which the other party must have a share of power, allowed little choice. The SPD also had difficulties in the government's Press and Information Office where the CDU/CSU was strongly entrenched.

By 1972, the number of high ministry officials who openly identified themselves as SPD or FDP members had grown considerably. In one poll, of thirteen state secretaries six belonged to the SPD, three to the FDP, four to no party, and none to the CDU/CSU. Of seventy-two division heads, twenty-two belonged to the SPD, eleven to the CDU/CSU, five to the FDP, and thirty-four to no party. [25] The SPD leadership was especially interested in getting SPD members into the ministries' planning sections, which had important responsibilities to set priorities and goals. It succeeded in most of its top staffing efforts, normally appointing center and right-wing rather than left-wing adherents, but retained some CDU/CSU department heads. [26] This was because there were not enough qualified SPD personnel and because the CDU/CSU officials might more easily gain the support of conservative interest groups and Bundesrat members for controversial government bills.

At the ministries' lower levels, tenured civil servants cannot be ousted when a new administration comes into office. Moreover, they are permitted by law to be active politically and to be candidates for the Bundestag. Hence, the parties seek their support and try to enroll them as members. The SPD has been relatively succesful, gaining members especially among the lower-rank civil servants and having a high percentage of them in its Bundestag Fraktion. Party permeation of the civil service (labeled pejoratively Verfilzung) may lead to promotions for loyal party members within the ministries, and not for others. The SPD denounced this patronage system when it was in opposition but then made use of when it was in power. Conversely, the CDU/CSU decried the system when it was in opposition.

To facilitate patronage, the SPD after 1969 attempted to gain control over ministry sections handling personnel and budgetary questions. It usually had to wait, however, for normal attrition before appointing pro-SPD young career servants. [27] In some ministries, SPD ministers created new units to bypass divisions or bureaus populated by conservative civil servants who wanted to delay or sabotage aspects of the government program not conforming with their views. But mostly the civil servants loyally performed their functions. Needless to say, this politicizing of the administrative hierarchy, not begun by the SPD, caused tensions and conflicts between those conservative, nonpartisan civil servants ensconced comfortably in their posts and the fresh-minted young liberal entrants into the public service, some of whom had joined the SPD to further their careers rather than because of ideological conviction.

PARTY-EXECUTIVE RELATIONS

It would be illusory to expect the SPD's policy recommendations to be accepted by an SPD-led government in coalition with the FDP or for the SPD to concur with all government decisions. The economically conservative FDP had no intention of supporting legislation that would have strongly impinged on the capitalist system. Hence a number of SPD resolutions were repeatedly postponed for consideration or torpedoed by the government, whose SPD ministers might have been sympathetic but could not convince their FDP colleagues to support them.

Yet more than FDP opposition lay at the root of party-executive tensions. At the 1971 convention, Chancellor Brandt rejected the argument of one left delegate who contended that convention decisions must be binding on SPD ministers. Brandt argued, as prime ministers have elsewhere, that an SPD-led coalition government or even a solely SPD-led government cannot be merely an executing organ of party conventions. He acknowledged that convention decisions can set important signposts for the government, but no more than that. A Social Democratic chancellor has certain duties and national responsibilities under the Basic Law that stand above party resolutions. His program is based on the government declaration, which in turn is supported by a parliamentary majority. [28]

In December 1972, Brandt told the party executive that he was the one who bore responsibility for the government policy guidelines to the voter. He urged the party to remain loyal to the cabinet. [29] When Schmidt became chancellor, Brandt repeatedly requested SPD members to give their support to the new government. The SPD chief noted that party recommendations could not always correspond to the cabinet's views on what is realizable. He insisted, as did Schmidt on other occasions, that "the goernment is not a recipient of orders from the party." [30] On the other hand, Brandt did acknowledge the necessity of government and parliamentary leaders who had been recruited by the party hewing to a party line which would be recognizable. In 1974, he said: "It is the party's task to point in the direction of goals and then to depend on friends in the government to fulfill as many of them as possible within the given situation and constellation." [31]

In a 1975 Spiegel interview, Brandt was more specific. To the question what was the point of the party passing convention resolutions that the SPD chancellor, faced with empty coffers, was bound to ignore, Brandt replied optimistically that the resolutions would eventually be fulfilled. To the question whether he would plead for tax increases at the convention, he stated that as party chairman it was not correct for him to be a government spokesman. Rather the government would tell the party what was possible and necessary in light of budgetary projections. Thereupon the party would give counsel, and the Fraktion would decide. [32] At the 1975 convention, he called for a mesh of government policy with long-range party goals and warned the delegates to close the wide gap between Chancellor Schmidt's high prestige and the party's low prestige. Other party and government leaders backed Brandt, partly to mollify the left wing, which had become increasingly restive under Schmidt's policies and which had not hesitated in election off years to openly criticize them. Although the leaders warned about unrealizable utopian goals, they supported limited goals ranging beyond one legislative period. [33]

At the 1977 convention and earlier, Schmidt underlined his constitutional power to set political guidelines. On occasion, he said, he would have to make decisions which the entire party would not support, but that was partly due to lack of intraparty unity. He reaffirmed his willingness to receive ideas and criticism from the party. [34]

Yet despite these pleas for party-government cooperation, party discontent about government policies kept rising. Eppler gave one reason: "Tried and experienced politicians like Helmut Schmidt cannot be told what policy they are to follow. At most they can be persuaded and convinced through public and party debate." Eppler also charged that Schmidt had excluded many important national issues from the 1976 election campaign but immediately afterwards had presented a government declaration including all those topics. [35]

Other politicians thought that Schmidt should have let the party feel—however mistakenly—that it, too, had a say in government policy. The Lower Rhine SPD district issued a position paper to the 1977 party convention in which it complained that the government style diffused coolness and made party and public into mere spectators. Such a development corresponded to the government's technocratic understanding of politics. As a result, party members and voters did not see the causes and consequences of the present structural crisis. The party, in turn, through delegate selection, nomination of candidates for legislatures, and waging of electoral campaigns, became a bureaucratic appendage to the government and the legislative process. According to the position paper, the government viewed party criticism of its policies as a hindrance to the smooth execution of its four-year mandate, a loss of time, and an indication of intraparty or party-government conflict. The government gave the impression that it was primarily interested in "doing" things and solving problems without concern for values. It allowed the FDP to have too much weight within the coalition. Consequently, many members and voters became politically apathetic and lost interest, leading to party "listlessness" and failure to present policy alternatives. [36] The position paper's anti-Schmidt stance was political dynamite. Therefore the convention shunted it to the party council for further deliberation, and its inclusion on the agenda was repeatedly delayed.

Political apathy did not vanish in the following years. The Juso district executive of Lower Rhine in its 1978-1979 annual report reiterated the arguments of the 1977 position paper, also noting that the government was constantly "blackmailing" the party to urgently support its short- and medium-range policies and not to criticize Schmidt. The party is damaged when government leaders use the imperative mandate from the top to seek its constant support. An incapacitated party, the report concluded, is not in a position to solve present and future problems. [37] The left-wing finance senator of Bremen, Henning Scherf, also assailed the party for becoming a "propaganda troop" for the government. Party members must articulate their views even if they diverge from government views, and the party itself must end its "loyalty at all costs" policy vis-à-vis the government. In addition, the government must once again institute reform policies. [38] Not only was the left upset about government policies, but on occasion the party as well. As will be detailed in the following chapters, major domestic and foreign crises produced tensions between party and government. But time and again, the underlying problem was Schmidt's political style and personality. His attempt to present himself to the electorate as a chancellor above parties, his pragmatic crisis management policy and his infrequent consultations with top party leaders (unlike Brandt) were not welcomed by the more idealistic party, even though it profited from his popularity among the electorate. According to some party leaders, Schmidt's policies left an "emotional deficit" and a "demotivation process" among SPD members, who saw their party as being relegated to a "chancellor electoral association" (Kanzlerwahlverein). Even Minister Hauff spoke up: "If we don't succeed in motivating the party by showing goals and values that go beyond the economic ones, then we will witness a fast downfall." (39] Scherf warned that when Schmidt is no longer chancellor, the party's political structure must not fall apart. Arndt told Bonn party leaders that their narrow concern with national politics was detrimental to crucial state and local issues. [40]

Such expressions of discontent surface during any administration, but Brandt as chancellor was able to work more harmoniously with the party than was Schmidt. The latter's remarks to the 1979 SPD convention showed once again that the gap between him and the party was not narrowing. Faced by resolutions inimical to his program, Schmidt said that as chancellor, "I cannot represent a position that, after testing my own conscience, I find wrong. . . ." [41] He also could not refrain from attacking his young opponents within the party: "With almost an entire life in the SPD, I find it difficult to be told by much younger ones how a Social Democrat should be defined." [42] He complained to visitors bitterly that he had to justify his policies more to the party than to the public. This was a burden to him because his governing style was to work with the least amount of friction. To minimize the friction, Schmidt and Brandt were in constant touch to coordinate government and party policies. They often met alone before the SPD presidium sessions; in addition, a minister informed Brandt of the cabinet deliberations and Brandt participated in the weekly coalition talks attended by the chancellor, the FDP party chairman, the SPD and FDP deputy chairmen, and Fraktion chairmen.

The frequent SPD-government schisms had other causes. Even if Schmidt had been more receptive to the SPD proposals, his FDP ministers often blocked them in the cabinet. Moreover the cabinet had to worry about a Bundesrat veto on important legislation. It had to worry about monetary decisions made by the autonomous Federal Bank (Bundesbank) that might not correspond to its own design. It had to worry after 1974 about financial constraints, resulting in the scuttling of some promised reforms.

SPD decision-makers in the executive branch also were exposed to pressures from the Länder, regardless of which party governed them, and from a multitude of interest groups, public opinion, and mass media. When they had to respond to sudden domestic and international crises, SPD policy recommendations were often shunted aside or had not yet been formulated. During such crises, the ministries tapped the technical expertise available to them, while the party, whose top organs (except for the presidium) do not meet as frequently as government agencies and who do not command comparable resources, found it difficult to come up with instant solutions. Aside from crises, the ministries were also busy issuing a host of technical and nonpolitical decrees and orders without first consulting with the coalition parties.

As one SPD minister in the government wrote:

> The overwhelming number of bills submitted by me can be traced to me and to my ministry's conceptions and preparatory work. In one or another case the suggestion to prepare a specific bill came from the coalition Fraktionen, but was limited to their suggestion for a

(ministerial) initiative. The way in which such initiatives were then considered and formulated was left up to me. [43]

The constraints on SPD government policymakers, on one hand, and the initiatives they take, on the other, seem to suggest that the SPD had hardly any input into government policy. That would not be correct. The overall direction the government took could not range too far from the policy recommendations of the two coalition parties. The SPD chancellor expected policy direction from his party on some basic issues. For instance, in 1973 Chancellor Brandt requested his party to agree swiftly on an incomes policy for which preparatory work had been done by a party commission. Then serious discussions could begin with the FDP in order to implement the government declaration on the subject. [44] Similarly, preparatory work had been done in party organs on, among other topics, property reform, which the government promised to consider as a legislative issue. This conversion or transfer from the SPD to the executive branch was facilitated by its often taking place between individuals who held party and government offices simultaneously. When they wore two complementary hats, they themselves may have found it difficult to distinguish one from the other.

The degree of policy transfer between SPD and government obviously varied with each piece of legislation. As another SPD minister wrote:

> The source of bills nearly always goes back to multiple impulses and demands, thus making "monocausal" explanations rare. Parliamentary decisions, resolutions, and electoral programs of parties; discussions among the public about long-range development trends or suddenly emerging problems; preparatory work in the ministries; the chancellor's decision about the government program; and, last but not least, the personal interest of a minister produce the most diverse combinations, which often make it impossible subsequently to sort out the decisive factors for the origin of a law. [45]

NOTES

1. Rose, p. 11.
2. Eric C. Browne, "Introduction," Government Coalitions in Western Democracies, eds. Browne and John Dreijmanis (New York: Longman, 1982), pp. 2-3.
3. Valerie Bunce, Do New Leaders Make a Difference? Executive Succession and Public Policy under Capitalism and Socialism (Princeton: Princeton University Press, 1981), pp. 89-90.
4. For details on theory, see Easton, passim.
5. In 1949, Heinemann had been president of the All-Germany Synod of the Protestant Church. A pacifist, he resigned as CDU minister of the interior in 1950 when the new German army was created. In 1952, he founded the All-German People's Party but dissolved it in 1957 when he joined the SPD. In 1966 he became minister of justice.
6. Süddeutsche Zeitung, May 16, 1979.
7. Institut für Demoskopie, The Allensbach Report 1979/E 05. For a general appraisal, see Renate Mayntz, "Executive Leadership in Germany: Dispersion of Power or 'Kanzlerdemokratie'?," Presidents and Prime

Ministers, eds. Richard Rose and Ezra N. Suleiman (Washington, D.C.: American Enterprise Institute, 1980), pp. 138-170.

8. Braunthal, "Willy Brandt," pp. 256-258.

9. Riker, p. 47.

10. Helmut Norpoth, "The German Federal Republic: Coalition Government at the Brink of Majority Rule," Government Coalitions in Western Democracies, eds. Browne and Dreijmanis, pp. 7-32.

11. Baring, pp. 125-133.

12. Wolfgang F. Dexheimer, Koalitionsverhandlungen in Bonn, 1961-1965-1969: Zur Willensbildung in Parteien und Fraktionen (Bonn: Eichholz, 1973), pp. 102-120; Udo Bermbach, "Stationen der Regierungsbildung 1969," Zeitschrift für Parlamentsfragen, I, No. 1 (June 1970), 5-23; Manfred Nemitz, ed., Machtwechsel in Bonn (Gütersloh: Bertelsmann-Sachbuchverlag, 1970); Baring, pp. 165-182.

13. See Rolf-Peter Lange, "Auslesestrukturen bei der Besetzung von Regierungsämtern," Parteiensystem in der Legitimitätskrise, eds. Dittberner and Ebbighausen, p. 146; Klaus von Beyme, "Regierungswechsel 1969: Zum Wandel der Karrieremuster der politischen Führung," Demokratisches System und politische Praxis der Bundesrepublik, eds. Lehmbruch, von Beyme, Fetscher, p. 263. For a list of cabinet members for this and other legislative periods, see Deutscher Bundestag, 30 Jahre Deutscher Bundestag, pp. 154-159.

14. Ibid., pp. 263-264; von Beyme, Die politische Elite in der Bundesrepublik Deutschland (Munich: Piper, 1971), pp. 48-49.

15. In 1969, of twelve SPD ministers, seven were in the party presidium and executive and one other was only in the executive. The average length of service is based on ministers who also served in the 1966-1969 cabinet.

16. For biographical data on ministers (and deputies), see Kürschners Volkshandbuch, Deutscher Bundestag, 6. Wahlperiode, 1969 (Darmstadt: Neue Darmstädter Verlagsanstalt, 1970).

17. Baring, 511-539; SPD, Auslandsbrief, No. 30, Nov. 27, 1972; Süddeutsche Zeitung, Dec. 7, 1972.

18. The new cabinet members were Bahr, Focke, Vogel. Two members (Lauritz Lauritzen and Klaus von Dohnanyi) were appointed in March 1972 and were reappointed to the new cabinet.

19. Die Zeit, July 12, 1974.

20. Gerard Braunthal, "The Policy Function of the German Social Democratic Party," Comparative Politics, XIX, No. 2 (Jan. 1977), 140.

21. The SPD team consisted of Brandt, Koschnick, Wehner, Schmidt, Apel, Arendt; the FDP team, of Ministers Genscher (Foreign Office), Hans Friderichs (Economics), Werner Maihofer (Interior), Josef Ertl (Agriculture), Fraktion chairman Wolfgang Mischnick (Süddeutsche Zeitung, Nov. 25, 1976).

22. Frankfurter Rundschau, Dec. 16, 1976, cited by Udo Bermbach, "Stationen der Regierungs- und Oppositionsbildung 1976," Zeitschrift für Parlamentsfragen, VIII, No. 2 (Aug. 1977), 181.

23. For list of 1980 cabinet members, see The Week in Germany, XI/42, Nov. 7, 1980.

24. When Brandt was foreign minister (1966-1969), he had difficulty getting the cooperation of some top staff who were not in accord with his Ostpolitik. For details on 1969 staffing, see Dyson, Party, State and Bureaucracy, pp. 20-25.

25. Bärbel Steinkemper, Klassische und politische Bürokraten in der

Ministerialverwaltung der Bundesrepublik Deutschland (Cologne: Carl Heymanns, 1974), 47-48. In another poll, 21 percent of the top civil servant respondents said they were SPD members; 6 percent, SPD sympathizers; 16 percent, CDU members; and 27 percent, CDU sympathizers (Robert D. Putnam, "The Political Attitudes of Senior Civil Servants in Britain, Germany, and Italy," The Mandarins of Western Europe: The Political Role of Top Civil Servants, ed. Mattei Dogan (New York: John Wiley, 1975), p. 114.

26. Müller-Rommel, pp. 228-229.

27. Dyson, Party, State and Bureaucracy, pp. 22-24; Rolf Seeliger, ed., Bonns Graue Eminenzen: Aktuelle Beiträge zum Thema Ministerialbürokratie und sozialdemokratische Reformpolitik (Munich: Rolf Seeliger, 1970).

28. SPD, Parteitag, November 1971, pp. 35-36, 67-69. 73-75. For a discussion of transfer of party policy to government policy, see Anthony King, "Political Parties in Western Democracies," Polity, II (Winter 1969), 111-141; Howard A. Scarrow, "The Function of Political Parties: A Critique of the Literature and the Approach," Journal of Politics, XXIX (Nov. 1967), 770-790.

29. Relay from Bonn, Dec. 11, 1972.

30. Süddeutsche Zeitung, Aug. 8, 1974.

31. Ibid.

32. Der Spiegel, May 12, 1975.

33. Vorwärts, Nov. 6, 1975; Die Zeit, Nov. 7, 1975; Süddeutsche Zeitung, Jan. 22/23, 1977; SPD Service, Presse, funk, TV, 215/77, May 10, 1977.

34. Süddeutsche Zeitung, Nov. 9, 1977; Vorwärts, Nov. 24, 1977.

35. Die Zeit, Jan. 7, 1977.

36. Süddeutsche Zeitung, Sept. 13, 1977.

37. Jusos, Rechenschaftsbericht des Bezirksvorstandes der Jungsozialisten in der SPD, Bezirk Niederrhein; Zeitraum: April 1978 bis Mai 1979.

38. Der Spiegel, Oct. 23, 1978.

39. Ibid., Mar. 5, 1979; Frankfurter Allgemeine Zeitung, Dec. 3, 1979.

40. Der Spiegel, Mar. 5, 1979.

41. SPD, "SPD-Parteitag, 3.-7. Dez. 1979," Politik, No. 14, Dec. 1979, p. 38.

42. Süddeutsche Zeitung, Dec. 5, 1979.

43. Letter, Minister of Justice, Gerhard Jahn, to author, June 25, 1974, quoted by Braunthal, "The Policy Function," p. 143.

44. SPD, Parteitag 1973, pp. 95, 119, 121.

45. Letter, Minister of Youth, Family and Health, Katherina Focke, to author, July 30, 1974, quoted by Braunthal, "The Policy Function," p. 143.

13
Domestic Policy Issues

Whether political parties that have won control of the executive branch can have a significant effect on governmental policy output, especially on domestic issues, has become controversial among scholars. A number of social scientists, both conservative and neo-Marxist, contend for different reasons that it does not matter whether social democratic or conservative parties control a government. Conservatives argue, for instance, that the hypothesis that social democratic governments are responsible for greater outlays on social welfare cannot be proved. Economist Harold Wilensky states that because the parties' ideological convictions are weak, welfare development hinges rather on the wealth of a country (rich countries, regardless of which party is in power, will spend more than poor countries). [1] Some social scientists insist that as parties become "catch-all" and attempt to win over the middle-of-the-road voters, they will pursue noncontroversial policies near the middle of the political scale. [2] Richard Rose writes that because party politics is consensual, there will be continuity of policy regardless of which party gains power. He notes that there are too many forces outside the control of any government which impinge on policy decisions and that interparty ideological differences have abated, even though party activists will continue to take adversarial positions. [3]

Still other observers, such as Frank Parkin and Richard Scase, maintain that social democratic governments do favor a more egalitarian society and seek to distribute the wealth created under a capitalist society according to criteria of justice and equality, though in practice they have failed to achieve their objective. They have been able neither to equalize the distribution of income, earnings, and wealth nor to change the reward structure under capitalism. The reasons vary from country to country, but often social democratic ministers must contend with structural and institutional constraints—a conservative civil service, powerful industrial lobbies, recalcitrant banking firms and multinational corporations, a worldwide economic recession, and hostile foreign governments. If a coalition governs, concessions must be made to the other party or parties in power, and if the country has a federal system, concessions must be made to the states. [4]

Neo-Marxists assert that if social democrats gain political power, the capitalist elite will not tolerate any loss of its economic power (Allende's Chile is cited as an illustration). Consequently, social democrats have made no progress toward their goal of socialism; indeed they have abandoned the goal and have instead strengthened capitalism. Because they are committed to maintaining the private sector, they have ceased to be a reformist movement. Adam Przeworski writes that "the current policy of social democrats by its very logic no longer permits the cumulation of reforms," and concludes that "social democrats will not lead European societies into socialism." [5]

While these sets of arguments that parties have little impact on policies seem quite convincing, those who contend that parties do have influence have an equally convincing, if not a stronger, case. Many writers note that in Scandinavia, social democratic governments, backed by strong union movements, have introduced new socialist concepts and expanded the welfare state. In power for decades, they have made gradual but extensive changes in social welfare and improved educational mobility for the less privileged children and economic opportunities for the laboring class. As a result, the workers' standard of living has risen and the disparities in social status and in economic opportunities have declined. [6] Proof that socialist ideas are not dead is the plan advanced in 1976 by Swedish union federation economist Rudolf Meidner, which calls for the transfer of a portion of company profits to a workers' fund. This would gradually lead to most firms becoming employee-controlled, thereby strengthening the public sector and eventually producing a socialist economy. With Palme's election as prime minister in 1982, the plan has a chance of receiving legislative approval. It points the way toward a road to socialism alternative to the traditional one of nationalization.

The case that parties do matter is reinforced by the argument that bourgeois parties are less eager to push welfare reforms because the result would be more state interventionism, higher budgetary outlays, and social egalitarianism. In periods of economic crisis, such parties prefer low inflation and high unemployment to leftist governments' preference for the opposite. [7] Bourgeois parties are also less interested in funding the public sector, as can be seen in Britain whenever the Conservatives replace Labour in power. One scholar, Edward Tufte, insists that in the short run parties in power can manipulate the course of the national economy. As there are differences between them in economic ideologies, platforms, and policy statements, they can steer the economy in different directions. Anthony Downs maintains that parties "tend to carry out as many of their promises as they can whenever they are elected." [8]

Although some of the scholarly debate has centered on Sweden and Britain, the Federal Republic has also been subject to scrutiny. Again, there is no unanimity among observers on whether or not the SPD-FDP rule since 1969 has made a difference in domestic programs. Stephen Leibfried, contrasting the United States and West Germany, claims that the German Social Democrats have left an imprint on the pattern of reform and the instruments of welfare policy. [9] David Cameron, in a comparative study of eighteen countries, contends that Social Democrats in the Federal Republic have had a clear partisan effect on the economy—for instance, being responsible for a cumulative increase in the scope of the public sector. [10] Valerie Bunce writes that leftist (or left-center) parties are more innovative when they first win power; after 1969 the SPD-FDP government moderately increased the budgets for health, education, and welfare. [11] Manfred Schmidt notes that SPD-controlled Länder governments are more active in the social sphere and transfer more funds to education, public employment, and even internal security than CDU/CSU-controlled Länder. But he warns that interparty differences are relatively small (a change of 5 percent in course direction is estimated), especially in economic policy and in crisis periods. [12] Finally, Klaus von Beyme emphasizes the difficulties of making comparisons, because the FDP shared in policymaking, Länder claims confronted Bonn, and international economic crises caused repercussions in the Federal Republic. He maintains that SPD coalition governance—contrary to commonly held hypotheses about policy effects stemming from social democratic-led governments—did not produce an immediate expansion of funds for the public sector (unlike Sweden, Norway, and Denmark), a significant increase in the national debt, a decline in unemployment (on the contrary, unemployment increased for various reasons), or a steep rise in inflation. Yet he concludes that ideological commitments of parties do matter in policy output; the SPD interest in more social and income equality and in the distribution of public funds cannot be measured by a few indicators and budget figures. [13]

It is difficult to measure changes during a comparatively brief period of SPD-FDP governance, especially when SPD ministers do not make policy alone; nevertheless it is important to provide a tentative answer to the question whether the SPD's assumption of power produced policy changes. Hence this chapter focuses on the SPD's effect on the government's domestic policies from 1969 to 1982, with attention to the intraparty decision-making process on given issues. It examines first the reform package in general and then five important (but not all-inclusive or related) national and state issues in detail—fiscal policy, the decree barring political radicals from public service, abortion, education, and energy—as well as municipal programs.

REFORM POLICY

Like many other social democratic and socialist parties, the SPD has been committed to incremental reform within the existing neocapitalist economic system. [14] The thrust of the program has been to maintain political and economic stability while embarking on programs, especially in taxation and social welfare, to aid the party's chief target groups—trade union members, low- to middle-income salaried employees and civil servants, and youth.

Before the SPD entered the government in 1966, the CDU/CSU-led government had already embarked on a reindustrialization policy designed to promote full employment. The "economic miracle" had produced growth and prosperity for most classes, but by the 1960s a recession facilitated the SPD's entrance into the Grand Coalition. The government pursued Keynesian fiscal policies through deficit spending and enacted a Stability and Growth Act designed to stabilize wages and prices and improve fiscal coordination between federal and state ministries and the Bundesbank. Even after 1969, the accent remained on free market competition, economic and monetary stability, the promotion of exports, and subsidies to the business sector. After the oil crisis of 1973 and a further recession, the government tried to improve the economy by allowing business to increase profits in order to stimulate investment, moderating union demands for higher wages, producing a tight money policy, introducing an austerity program in social welfare, and limiting inflation by reducing government spending. [15] Despite economic difficulties, the government in the mid-1970s still boasted of having created the "Model Germany."

Compared with other countries facing deep economic crises, West Germany was an oasis enjoying economic prosperity with relatively low inflation and unemployment.

But critics within the SPD wondered throughout the 1970s where the social democratic component lay in the government's economic program, which seemed to reflect more strongly the FDP's probusiness neoliberalism. In response, SPD leaders contended that there were a number of progressive features built into the government program. When Brandt became chancellor, he had ambitious plans to make reforms in all domestic spheres. Such reforms were implemented a step at a time, rather than through sweeping radical and swift changes and were coordinated through an elaborate finance and sectoral planning system in each ministry. Overall planning was assigned to the Chancellor's Office, which devised short- and medium-range reform goals, especially in the fields of finance, education, and land use and regional development. But after 1972, the Chancellor's Office planning machinery was cut back because of political opposition from a number of cabinet members. The Jusos especially assailed this retreat and demanded even more state centralized planning.

The Jusos also called on the government to steer and control investments for ideological reasons and to combat the recession, unemployment, and structural problems. Government spokesmen said, however, that the state was already using cyclical measures, tax relief, subsidies, and other privileges to help sectors ranging from agriculture to shipbuilding. Finance Minister Apel, supported by his FDP colleague Economics Minister Friderichs, also pointed out that consumer choice must remain free in any pluralistic and democratic system. At the 1975 Mannheim party convention and in the long-range 1985 plan, the Juso proposals were rejected, although the party leaders did accept the principle of indirect investment guidance. [16]

The government's emphasis on economic stability made the introduction of costly welfare reform programs difficult. Yet it was committed to a reform policy and had the backing of the coalition parties. SPD leaders, pushing for reforms, based their views on the 1968 party document, "Perspectives of Social Democratic Politics in Transition to the 1970s." The Bundestag, without significant dissent, passed a host of laws designed to improve the social welfare system. For instance, the Ministry of Labor sponsored a pension reform package incorporating a flexible retirement age, controlled increases of veterans pensions, an additional year of insurance for mothers, and other pension changes. It also called for a fairer property distribution and maintenance arrangement in divorces, sickness and accident insurance reform, doubling of the savings allowance deducted from the income tax to encourage private capital accumulation, and revision of the company law. The Ministry also wanted to expand vocational training, reduce the number of accidents at work, and improve the rehabilitation of the handicapped. Many of these programs were based on party convention resolutions.

In other fields, the government made reforms such as liberalizing the penal code or poured funds into transportation, housing, schools, and research. But the reform euphoria evaporated by 1971 when funds began to get tight. After the 1972 election, critics contended that the listless government lacked a coherent, imaginative program and was needlessly postponing reforms. In the January 1973 government declaration, Brandt promised to speed up reforms and simultaneously ensure stable economic development. Yet when the oil crisis erupted in late 1973, the government, in an attempt to maintain economic growth and full employment, had to again abandon many of its ambitious reform programs. Schmidt's ascent to power was marked by the beginning of an austerity program that, among other cutbacks, scuttled the recommendations made at the 1973 party convention calling for a greater percentage of state revenues to be plowed into social reforms and public investments.

A number of party officials were disillusioned by the insufficient past reforms and the pessimistic prospect for future major reforms. In retrospect, they felt that Brandt had oversold his reform campaign and that the mass media had nurtured high expectations of miracles among the public. They cited a June 1974 infas survey which indicated that respondents who supported basic reforms had dropped from 42 percent in 1968 to 23 percent in 1974 and reform opponents had increased from 34 to 54 percent. [17] At the root of the difficulty facing the SPD was not only a change in psychological attitude among the public but also its own internal conflicts, the economic crisis, the CDU/CSU strategy of moving to the political center, and Schmidt's preoccupation with crisis management.

According to Ehmke, von Oertzen, and Steffen, the new Chancellor's accent on stability at the expense of reforms produced an impression that "there can no longer be talk of continuity of Social Democratic reform policies." [18] Major reforms, such as in codetermination, the apprenticeship program, capital accumulation schemes for workers, cartel legislation, and the judicial and constitutional spheres, were delayed or abandoned.

Yet the period from 1974 to 1982 was not devoid of major reforms. As Schmidt noted, the reform policy continued, but it had shrunk to those reforms not costing too much money. There were, for example, further reforms in pensions, the marriage and divorce laws, penal laws concerning homosexuals, and social security, as well as new legislation on environmental protection. The Chancellor noted that "consolidating what has been achieved takes priority. The precondition for costly reforms is more economic growth." [19] He admitted that disappointment about reform cutbacks was inevitable in light of earlier expectations, but political realities, including making compromises with the FDP and the Bundesrat, made it impossible to pursue them all. An FDP spokesman retorted that the SPD's failure to credit the FDP with reform willingness was unfair, because on a number of occasions the FDP had been as liberal or more on such issues as maintenance of individual rights, wider educational opportunities, secure pensions, environmental planning, and increased capital accumulation and shop democracy for workers. Rather, he contended, the SPD was using the FDP as an excuse to put the brakes on a major reform policy. [20]

Be that as it may, the two parties had to cooperate if legislation was to be passed. In economic policy, programs were designed to balance the demands of SPD and FDP. For example, the SPD plank for more aid to low-income groups was countered by the FDP plank for more aid to employers. In some instances, government legislation reflected directly the preparatory work done by the parties. To illustrate, as a result of pressure by the Jusos and other SPD groups, party chiefs established a property reform commission, which discussed at length what position the party should take and what compromises it was willing to make with the FDP. In 1977, the government enacted about one-third of the SPD proposal. [21]

Even if the government had suddenly embarked on another major reform drive, it would have needed more support from a public reluctant to back costly programs or those that would significantly change the existing economic system. According to one 1979 poll, 37 percent were in favor of more reforms, 37 percent were opposed, and 26 percent were undecided. [22] SPD left-wingers contended that, even though the percentage of proponents for reforms had increased from 1974 (see above), if the government were serious about reforms it could also gain the support of the undecided. They asked what had happened to the Brandt slogans of 1969 to "risk more democracy" and "improve the quality of life." These had been nearly forgotten as the reforms proposed in their spirit were so diluted as to be unrecognizable. They argued that low-cost reforms in society, in the university system, in the humanizing of work, and in codetermination should be pushed energetically and that government leaders had an obligation not to lose sight of the party's long-range goals. Otherwise the SPD would lose its character as a reform party and be tagged as a party interested only in maintaining itself in power.

Along the same lines, Wolf-Dieter Narr, Hermann Scheer, and Dieter Spöri indicate in their volume criticizing the party: "In the SPD, one works, but thinks less, and ventures even less." [23] They note that electoral majorities for the party will not just materialize but will be possible only if reform concepts are pushed hard, even if the reforms will hurt some interests (such as in health). They are bitter about the postponement of reforms that would have aided the poor or socially weak groups and critical of government policies that did not seriously tackle the inherent weaknesses of the capitalist system or provide for greater social justice and redistribution of wealth. They indict the party for becoming "structurally conservative" and restricting itself to quelling crises. [24]

FISCAL REFORMS

The left critique against SPD and government policies was well illustrated in the protracted debates about fiscal policy. The left's emphasis on redistributive justice was not shared for tactical reasons by the more conservative wing of the party or by SPD ministers. The discord began in 1970 when a majority of delegates at the party convention backed a left resolution demanding that an expert commission's report on tax reform be debated within a year and discussed at a special 1971 convention. The party leaders wanted to stall any reform proposal until the 1972 convention, when delegates might change their minds about supporting drastic tax reforms if the consequence would be to scare off middle-of-the-roaders who normally might vote for the SPD in the coming national election. But the leaders lost the first round in the fight to delay discussion of tax reform.

At the special 1971 convention, a large majority of delegates endorsed a scheme prepared by a commission of experts headed by Eppler, then minister for economic cooperation, to raise the tax rate from 53 to 60 percent on incomes of 20,000 DM and above. By voting for this scheme, the delegates rejected the government's tax plan, presented by Finance Minister Schiller, which called for a more modest tax hike from 53 to 56 percent. [25] They were not persuaded by Schiller's argument that this was not the time to announce a steep tax increase just when the recession was beginning and the economy needed a stimulus. Eppler retorted that the increase was not meant to be enacted immediately. In any case, only 500,000 out of 23 million taxpayers would be affected. In the wake of this dispute, SPD businessman Philip Rosenthal resigned as parliamentary state secretary in the Ministry of Economics, assailing his boss, Schiller, for his conservative economic philosophy. [26]

Even though convention delegates had supported the Eppler proposal, the government took no action on it. Chancellor Brandt's view was that the convention could articulate long-range goals and desires but had no power to force him and his cabinet colleagues to follow a definite course. Most delegates criticized Brandt's stance, which reduced their resolutions to a farce, because it disqualified their work a priori. One delegate noted that the leaders wanted to pursue a course of their own choosing and accepted only convention resolutions that coincided with their own policy. He requested that resolutions be binding on ministers, but Brandt, as on other occasions, rejected the proposal. [27]

No major tax reform bill went into effect until January 1, 1975. The government stuck to the Schiller plan to boost the tax from 53 to 56 percent. However, it made tax cuts of about 14.1 billion DM to benefit primarily low- and middle-income families and those with many children. On the other hand, the cabinet eliminated the SPD ministers' proposals for other reforms, such as a provision to tax special expense accounts, as a concession to the Christian Democrats who were ready to block the bill in the Bundesrat. Thus the final bill was only a shadow of the original, even though it reflected the SPD's aspirations to help the economically deprived class. The degree of redistribution was modest, affecting individuals within groups rather than producing interclass changes. Moreover, lower taxes had only a short-lived effect as inflation and higher wages put many taxpayers into higher tax brackets, which in turn meant that they lost out on some social welfare payments. [28]

In 1977, SPD dissidents in the Bundestag criticized the government's new tax package boosting the value-added tax. In 1978, they urged SPD ministers to stop providing benefits to the FDP's wealthy clientele in the latest tax bill. Only after strenuous efforts by SPD Fraktion chiefs did the dissidents promise to support the tax bill (two deputies abstained in the plenum vote).

Earlier, in 1975, the Jusos had presented to the SPD a catalog of fiscal proposals, which included one that no German citizen could earn more than 5,000 DM monthly (at the time, the average net monthly income was 1,336 DM). The Jusos demanded that on the basis of democracy and equality the wide disparity in incomes be reduced. They asked rhetorically why a top doctor should earn twenty to thirty times the salary of a nurse who had as much responsibility for a life or why an automobile executive, accomplishing little more than the worker in the plant, should earn ten to twelve times as much and not be subject to dismissal during an economic slump. The Jusos noted that their plan would affect only 200,000 persons under the existing tax rate and even fewer (50,000) if the tax rate were boosted to 80 percent rather than 56 percent. Moreover, they noted, other European socialist parties had advanced similar proposals. But the SPD establishment reacted negatively to the Juso proposal; some leaders argued that the Jusos wanted to stifle individual initiatives and others said that the plan was completely impractical under existing circumstances. [29]

In 1979 and 1980, a fiscal reform of the pension scheme became the center of controversy. In this instance, Wehner and a commission of party specialists, rather than the Jusos, were unable to convince Schmidt and Finance Minister Matthöfer to accept their recommendations, which were first submitted to the 1979 party convention. Among other proposals, the report called for pensions to be pegged for a time to an increase in nominal wages and for a surviving spouse, widow or widower, to have an equal pension claim. In February 1980, the party executive supported most Wehner commission proposals. However, the government ministers refused to give their backing, not wanting to promise expensive reforms in an election year. [30]

RADICAL DECREE

Political issues divided the party and caused friction between its left wing and the government. One of the most hotly contested issues was the promulgation on January 28, 1972, of a decree signed by Chancellor Brandt and the ten minister-presidents to prohibit left- and right-wing political extremists from entering or staying in the civil service. The officials were worried about radicals infiltrating the service in order to subvert the democratic system. The decree would have been less controversial if it had been restricted to sensitive civil service posts, but it included all 3.5 million public servants, from the municipal to the federal levels, ranging from school teachers and railroad conductors to judges and top ministerial employees. It resulted in a massive security check and a ban on employment for a number of applicants.

In 1972, most SPD leaders, eager for electoral purposes to draw a line between their party and the Communists, accepted the decree. They noted that in Hamburg, for instance, before the decree 2,000 Communists, many of them teachers, had been able to get civil service jobs. The first sign of dissent came in June 1973 when Schleswig-Holstein SPD leaders urged the SPD-governed Länder to suspend its application. Top SPD officials retorted that at the April 1973 party convention they had supported a resolution calling on SPD-led Länder governments to ensure that all applicants receive maximum legal protection (such as rejection of testimony from anonymous witnesses as a basis for keeping an applicant out of the civil service). [31]

Although the SPD position was more liberal than that of the CDU/CSU-governed Länder, where rigid standards governed the screening, SPD officers took an equally rigid position toward SPD members who worked with radical-led committees seeking revocation of the decree. But that did not deter the Jusos who from 1973 on continued to criticize the decree, contending that they saw no reason why Communists could not be employed in the public service.

In May 1975, the Constitutional Court ruled that membership in a party with unconstitutional objectives may be considered sufficient reason not to grant someone civil servant status. The following month, the top SPD organs expressed their concern with the administrative practices of some Länder and the resultant climate of suspicion. At the 1975 party convention, delegates passed a resolution requesting authorities to administer the decree in a legal manner but did not cite SPD authorities specifically, as the Jusos had requested. [32]

Late that year, the federal government attempted to enact a bill that would have harmonized the different systems of recruitment. It acted after most conservative Länder interpreted the decree and the court decision more stringently than the SPD-FDP-governed Länder. The Christian Democratic opposition in the Bundesrat, arguing that nominal membership in a radical organization should be enough to cast doubt on an applicant's suitability for a post, successfully blocked the bill.

Only in early 1976, when some SPD members applying for jobs in CDU/CSU-governed Länder also became victims of the decree, did SPD officials become concerned about administrative excesses. In a typical case, a young SPD law student in Bavaria was barred from the bench because she had once been a member of an organization to which Communists also belonged. The SPD was in a bind: it did not want to be accused by the CDU/CSU of being soft on Communists and unable to guarantee internal security, but it was upset when its own members were adversely affected. The party also could not remain immune from criticism pouring in from socialist parties in other European countries, including France, where Socialist chief Francois Mitterrand formed a civil rights defense committee.

As a result of these developments, on May 19, 1976, the federal cabinet in conjunction with the SPD-FDP governed Länder adopted new guidelines for appointments to the civil service. The assumption of the guidelines was that applicants were loyal to the Constitution unless proven otherwise. The burden of proof was shifted to the national or state governments, which had to prove their cases with evidence that would stand up in court. An investigation into a candidate's loyalty could be initiated only if the appointing agency was already aware of facts that "severely" questioned an individual's allegiance to the democratic order. The new guidelines were not accepted by the CDU/CSU-governed Länder, which still contended that membership in a party with unconstitutional goals was sufficient ground for barring an applicant. [33]

By summer 1976, Brandt admitted that he had erred in approving the 1972 decree and Schmidt asserted that in individual cases in which a threat to the democratic order was indicated, the Basic Law and civil service codes were sufficient to take appropriate action. Ehmke said that with typical German perfectionism "we were hurting ourselves and doing more harm than good." Yet in 1977 SPD leaders denounced Juso support for the establishment of a Bertrand Russell international tribunal to investigate the charges, among others, that German citizens holding unorthodox political views were deprived of their right to practice some profession.

In 1978, SPD chiefs and Minister Gscheidle (SPD) were at odds over the decree. Brandt and Bahr had suggested that automatic security checks should be restricted to civil servants working for security agencies; in other sectors only individuals whose conduct was suspicious should be kept under surveillance. Gscheidle, in charge of the postal and railroad systems employing workers on civil service status, contended that he could not differentiate between one civil servant and another. As a result of this dispute and continuing unease among the SPD rank and file, Klose and Koschnick took new initiatives. Klose, with the approval of SPD leaders, proposed to the Hamburg Senate a new model for screening applicants. Hamburg officials would presume that an applicant would uphold the constitution; a screening or investigative process would be initiated only if there was evidence to the contrary. Neither membership nor activities in a radical organization or party should in the future constitute grounds for investigating an applicant. [34]

In October 1978, Koschnick submitted to the party executive a report suggesting that authorities no longer consult the Constitutional Protection Office (the German counterpart of the U.S. Federal Bureau of Investigation) for routine checks. Instead, the employing authority would make the decision to hire or not only on the basis of facts already available to it. [35] The SPD executive approved the report, but intraparty differences continued.

An SPD Bundestag Fraktion working group prepared a position paper critical of the decree. Vogel accused the group of having been swayed by the views of left deputies who contended that members of extremist parties did not constitute any danger to the Federal Republic—only 330 (0.07 percent) of 500,000 applicants investigated had been rejected. At the November Hamburg Land convention, Schmidt cautioned against changing the administration of the decree if that meant a clash with the 1975 Constitutional Court decision. But Klose called for changes in order to clear the venomous atmosphere surrounding the decree. [36] Finally, in December, Koschnick, after consulting with SPD, FDP, and union leaders, submitted a revised report to the top SPD organs, which accepted it.

In the meantime, the cabinet had requested Minister of Interior Baum (FDP) and Minister of Justice Vogel (SPD) to prepare a position paper. But when Baum wanted to wait to see what position the FDP would take at its convention, Schmidt responded that an FDP or SPD convention should not prevent the government from acting. In November, the cabinet deferred a decision until a position paper was ready. On January 17, 1979, after a marathon nine-hour session, it decided on changes in the administration of the decree for the federal civil service. In its statement the cabinet admitted that the investigations had weakened rather than strengthened the democratic order in the nation and had alienated parts of the young generation from the Basic Law. The government would abandon routine loyalty investigations into the background of all federal job seekers. Instead, national security officials were to initiate investigations only when there were tangible indications that a candidate did not fulfill the requirements for the public service.

The cabinet decision fell short of SPD and FDP recommendations adopted at their conventions. But cabinet members could not eschew all recommendations, because they feared that young voters would no longer support the two parties. The SPD and FDP had recommended that the grounds for rejection of an applicant be limited to demonstrated activity against the Basic Law's "free democratic fundamentals." The cabinet insisted that it could not set such a limit, because the Constitutional Court had upheld the constitutionality of the decree, which speaks of civil servants' duty to involve themselves actively in the maintenance of democratic life. [37]

In the Bundestag, CDU chief Kohl attacked the cabinet decision as a capitulation to the enemies of democracy. Hence, the cabinet's hope that all Länder would make changes in the administration of the decree corresponding to its decision proved in vain. The CDU/CSU-governed Länder maintained their policy, but some SPD-governed Länder did not liberalize their practice either and continued their automatic security checks. As Koschnick noted: "Given the practices of some federal states . . . the young Willy Brandt would have no chance of being accepted into the civil service." On another occasion, Klose made an equally telling observation: "Better 20 Communists in public service than 200,000 insecure and doubting young people in our country." [38] But such criticisms were not accepted by conservative Social Democrats who were afraid to call for an end to all loyalty checks, especially given the CDU/CSU electoral campaign charges that the SPD was soft on communism. Yet in 1979 the criticisms had an effect on Minister Gscheidle; worried about not being reappointed to the cabinet in case the party won the 1980 election, he changed his mind and tried to stop ouster proceedings initiated by the federal disciplinary attorney against several alleged Communist members of the postal and railroad services.

The protracted feud about the 1972 ministerial decree proved that the factionalism within the SPD made accord on its position difficult but that its pressure forced the government to finally make some concessions. The feud also highlighted the SPD-FDP government's inability to order the CDU/CSU-governed Länder to change course on a matter that was clearly within their jurisdiction. Finally, the feud demonstrated the difficulty the SPD and its government had in drawing a line between the protection of the democratic state and the creation of a dangerous witch hunt, McCarthyism, and the suppression of minority rights.

ABORTION

The national controversies over social policies which pitted the social-liberal coalition against the CDU/CSU did not mean that within the SPD a common front existed. One such issue, abortion reform, left deep wounds on all sides. Before we turn to the recent dispute, a brief historic survey is necessary to show that a schism within the party was eclipsed by government attempts to make reforms in the face of stiff resistance from the Catholic Church. The 1851 Prussian penal code and the 1871 Reich penal code provided penalties of up to five years in the penitentiary for women having illegal abortions. During the Weimar period, the Ministry of Justice on four occasions submitted to the Reichstag a penal reform bill lessening the penalty for abortions, but in each instance it could not gain a majority of votes for passage. However, by a 1926 decree the ministry reduced abortion from a crime to a misdemeanor. In 1927, the Supreme Court ruled that abortion was not punishable if there was direct danger to the life of the mother. In 1935, a government decree supporting the court decision stipulated that certifying agencies must in each case determine whether a "medical indication" (danger to life or health of a pregnant woman) existed.

In 1960, the Ministry of Justice drafted a major penal code reform. The draft included the elimination of penalties for abortion in the case of medical indication, rape, and other sexual offenses ("ethical" or "criminological" indications). But the Ministry, primarily because of Catholic Church opposition, could not gain legislative support. In 1970 also, the SPD-FDP government tried to make major changes in the penal code, but the Church remained adamantly opposed and lobbied strenuously against such changes. In the meantime, the feminist movement became active and staged street demonstrations for abortion reform.

In 1971 a major controversy erupted within the SPD over the stand the party should take. Minister of Justice Jahn had his staff prepare a draft, revised several times, which paralleled the 1960 draft favoring the legalization of abortions primarily for medical reasons. In October the SPD council debated it, but the leaders did not hold a vote for fear the majority of members would not give their support. At the November SPD convention, Jahn, supported by Brandt, Wehner, and Minister for Youth, Family and Health Käte Strobel, defended the draft bill and urged the delegates to vote for it. The position of the SPD leaders was determined partly by their worry about losing too many Catholic votes if the government chose the more liberal alternative option put forth by many party groups—among them, the Association of Social Democratic Women (ASF), whose rank and file was strongly influenced by the feminist movement. The liberal option, preferred by 75 percent of women in a national poll, called for abortion on demand or request within the first three months of conception (Fristenlösung) and on medical grounds thereafter. The women delegates were able to gain the support of all but thirty-one delegates (who voted against or abstained), but the leaders made it clear that the victorious resolution was not binding on the government. [39]

The spotlight then shifted to the government. In February 3, 1972, Jahn, disregarding the overwhelming proabortion sentiment within the SPD and FDP, submitted to the cabinet his latest version of a bill, which stipulated only four certifiable cases—medical, ethical (rape), eugenic, and emergency—in which abortion was not punishable. It also included an exemption for "social components" (which meant that authorities would consider the woman's standard of living and other socioeconomic aspects in granting permission) and a provision obligating health insurance funds to pay the bills of women seeking medical advice and receiving abortions in hospitals. Ministers Ehmke, Lauritzen (SPD), Genscher (FDP), and others still favored abortion on demand contending that it conformed to the Basic Law, but the cabinet, by a bare majority, sustained Jahn's proposal. [40]

When the government bill reached the Bundestag, the SPD Fraktion met several times to discuss it and decided to allow deputies to have a free vote without party discipline. At the same time, the SPD deputies favoring abortion on demand, in close touch with their FDP colleagues, readied an alternative bill in the Fraktion. [41] The Association of Social Democratic Jurists endorsed it. This bill was then introduced in the Bundestag under joint SPD-FDP deputies' sponsorship. In April 1972, the Bundestag scheduled three days of hearings on the rival government and deputy bills. But when it had to adjourn before the national election, all bills not yet acted on were dead.

Chancellor Brandt thereupon announced that the new government, stalemated on the abortion issue, would allow the Fraktionen to take the initiative and would not reintroduce its own bill. As a result, the Bundestag, for the first time in its history, was confronted by four rival bills: the already cited SPD-FDP bill calling for abortion on demand; an SPD bill, signed by a minority (twenty-seven) of deputies, based on the government's bill (medical indication); a CDU/CSU bill permitting abortions only for medical and ethical reasons; and a CDU/CSU bill permitting them only for medical reasons. Between September 1973 and March 1974 a special Bundestag committee handled all bills, receiving further data for its deliberations from the Ministry of Justice, by then remaining neutral in the burgeoning controversy.

On April 26, 1974, the Bundestag sustained the SPD-FDP bill by 247 (including 2 CDU/CSU votes) to 233 (including 8 SPD and 2 FDP votes), with 10 SPD members abstaining. Thereupon the CDU/CSU-dominated Bundesrat vetoed the bill, but the Bundestag overrode it by a 260 to 218 vote. On June 18, the president signed the bill into law, with the promulgation following three days later. Immediately, 193 CDU/CSU members, joined by five CDU/CSU-governed Länder, filed a petition in the Constitutional Court. They argued that making abortions within the first three months of conception not punishable violated the constitution, although they wanted to permit abortions for medical, eugenic, and ethical reasons. On February 25, 1975, the Court found for the petitioners. The judges, of whom a majority were conservative, declared the law unconstitutional because it violated the principle of the guarantee of life. They agreed, however, that abortions should be authorized when there was a danger to the mother's health, when there was likelihood that the child would be deformed or would cause grave hardship, or when pregnancy resulted from rape.

The Court's decision caused deep disappointment among ASF and Juso members, who were also bitter that the SPD had not mobilized the public for abortion on demand. In the Fraktion, a working group was formed to draft a new bill to meet the Court's objections. Cosponsored by the FDP, the bill abandoned abortion on demand and resembled Jahn's 1972 government bill. It permitted abortions for medical, ethical, eugenic, emergency, and social reasons. On February 12, the Bundestag passed the bill; soon thereafter it became law. [42] While the bill was not as restrictive as those proposed initially by the CDU/CSU, it still did not satisfy the SPD and FDP majority, which would have preferred abortion on demand. But this majority could not prevail against the power of the CDU/CSU, the Catholic Church, and the Court.

EDUCATIONAL REFORM

The SPD has been greatly concerned about another social field—education. During the Weimar era, it made major efforts to overhaul the system in order to provide more opportunities for the economically and socially weaker groups, but had only limited success. In the post-1945 era, the Western Allies attempted to democratize the system, but also could not achieve most of their goals. The Basic Law stipulated that education would remain a prerogative of the Länder. The SPD therefore had to face the opposition of CDU/CSU-governed Länder to reform demands at all school levels. But even in SPD-governed Länder the interests that wanted to maintain the status quo were powerful.

In the 1960s, the impetus for reforms came from leftist student organizations demanding democratization of the universities. They wanted hierarchical privileges for professors to be ended and decision-making powers to be shared with students and staff. This external pressure, as in many other fields, had an effect on the SPD (and the FDP). In 1969, the Jusos and the Young Free Democrats put pressure on their parties to propose university reforms, including the admission of more youths from working-class families into universities. Chancellor Brandt, concurring with their views and eager to have students join the SPD, was receptive to their demand to make educational reform one of the cornerstones of his domestic policy.

Partly as a result of their pressures, the SPD and FDP programs and the 1969 government declaration put high priority on such a reform. But Minister for Education and Science Leussink (nonparty) found himself in a quandary. If his ministry had drafted a bill corresponding to the Juso demand for democratization of the universities, the CDU/CSU would have vetoed it in the Bundesrat. To prevent a veto, Leussink framed a compromise bill that left neither side satisfied. The bill contained hardly any sharing of powers (codetermination) as demanded by the Jusos; instead, it sought to expand the number of students admitted to the universities and cut the years of study to between three and five. The Jusos, denouncing the minister as a "technocrat," criticized the bill because it would educate students for industrial needs rather than for the critical analysis of society. The CDU/CSU conditioned its acceptance of the bill on more concessions to its viewpoint—a return to the status quo ante. [43]

Discussions dragged on for two years, but few reforms materialized as long as the bill did not pass. In February 1972, Leussink resigned his cabinet post when the Ministry of Finance did not provide him with enough financial support for the expanding university system. SPD-FDP-governed Länder introduced the codetermination model, but in May 1973 the Constitutional Court struck it down.

In August, Leussink's successor, von Dohnanyi (SPD), introduced a new draft of a university frame law (Hochschulrahmengesetz). The Jusos strongly criticized the draft for being worse than the earlier aborted one. They contended that the time limit on university study was too rigid, that the possibility for students and staff to govern jointly was reduced drastically, and that universities were not given the opportunity to make curricular reforms. [44] In November, at their first congress on educational policy, the Jusos again assailed the government bill. They asserted that the bill was shaped to maintain the capitalist system, and that the government was making unnecessary concessions to the CDU/CSU and the conservative League for Freedom of Science (Bund Freiheit der Wissenschaft). Instead, it should listen more to the League of Democratic Scientists (Bund demokratischer Wissenschaftler), founded by SPD and liberal professors as a counterorganization. [45]

Their criticism had little effect on cabinet members or on older SPD leaders who were not close to the educational scene. Minister Dohnanyi, sympathetic to Juso arguments for reform, had only limited political influence in the cabinet. By the time the Bundestag passed the bill (December 12, 1974), its provisions were close in spirit to those of the CDU/CSU. The bill gave the Länder powers to restrict the autonomy of universities, started the amalgamation of teachers' colleges with universities, and made admission to universities more restrictive. [46]

The SPD was also interested in reforms at the high school level. In tune with its philosophy of equal opportunity for disadvantaged youth, it proposed to gradually supplant the existing system of separate low-prestige main schools (Hauptschulen), business-preparatory intermediate schools (Realschulen), and elite academic secondary schools (Gymnasien) with integrated comprehensive schools (Gesamtschulen). Such schools, according to the SPD, would provide youth with a high-quality education. (Most students end their schooling at the age of 15 and then receive part-time vocational education and on-the-job-training.)

Brandt's government declaration of 1969 incorporated the party's proposal. In June 1970, a federal-Länder joint commission was formed to develop an educational master plan. Three years later the plan was completed, but not all Länder backed it. The five governed by the CDU/CSU (Baden-Wuerttemberg, Bavaria, Rhineland-Palatinate, Saar, Schleswig-Holstein) opposed the comprehensive school proposal because they considered the existing system the best method to educate students with different levels of ability. The six governed by the SPD alone or with the FDP (Berlin, Bremen, Hamburg, Hesse, Lower Saxony, North Rhine-Westphalia) opted for the gradual establishment of comprehensive schools. Prior to 1973, the SPD had already gone ahead in some of its Länder, especially Hesse and Berlin, with opening such schools and giving parents a choice of sending their children to the new or to the existing schools. [47]

After the 1976 election, the SPD knew that its vaunted educational reform program had not been as successful as it had hoped. In 1977, to gain more popular support for reforms, it restructured its own education division, incorporating the Association of Social Democratic Teachers (Arbeitsgemeinschaft sozialdemokratischer Lehrer) into the new Association for Social Democrats in the Educational Sector (Arbeitsgemeinschaft für Sozialdemokraten im Bildungsbereich [AfB]).

The impetus for the creation of the AfB came from SPD teachers in Hesse who for two years had tried to meet on an organized basis with Social Democratic parents, students, social workers, and politicians interested in education. The teachers were alarmed about the reduction in funds for schools as a result of the economic crisis, about the hostile attitude toward education on the part of many SPD families, and about the shrinking number of deputies interested in the educational sector. They were also worried about diverse groups within the SPD pushing for narrow educational reforms but not agreeing on an overall concept. Hence they wanted the AfB to analyze why the reform euphoria had turned into resignation; how to implement equality of opportunity; how to further a dialogue between parents, teachers, and students; and how to convince the citizenry about the necessity for educational reforms. [48]

In May 1977, the AfB founders organized a three-day conference at Freiburg to discuss the tasks of the new organization, including action plans for schools, apprenticeship schemes, and the preparation of a general education program for the SPD convention (to be coordinated with the work of a party executive commission). The difficulty of meshing party and government policy was epitomized in the appearance of only four out of eight SPD Federal and Länder ministers of education at the conference, and then briefly. Minister Rohde, making an appearance, admitted that the government had done too much from above, under the motto that it knew what was best for the children. He assailed the Länder, including those governed by the SPD, for putting brakes on his reform plans. The Länder had reached an accord on broad principles, but when these were translated into concrete measures, the parliamentary majorities crumbled. He also complained about Social Democrats who approved comprehensive schools but sent their children to the elite Gymnasien.

Johano Strasser, formerly Juso theoretician and at the time a member of the party's basic values commission, catalogued the major mistakes made in carrying out government reforms in education. First, it was a mistake to let state agencies go ahead with reforms without mobilizing the "reform lobby" of parents, students, teachers, and educational planners. Second, it was a mistake not to contest more energetically elections to parent advisory councils dominated by Christian Democrats, who then waged an effective campaign against comprehensive schools. Third, it was a mistake for Social Democrats at the federal level not to coordinate their policies with those at the state level. Strasser complained about the contradictions in policy: while the party stood for more equality of opportunity, its politicians canceled teaching positions or failed to fill them; and while the party wanted to eliminate unfair status differences among teachers, its politicians supported salary schedules that reinforced the privileged position of a minority of teachers. [49]

Although the 1977 AfB convention was but one of innumerable conferences organized over the decades by educational organizations, teachers' unions, and government agencies, the issues raised typify the problems of coordination between party and Länder governments and between the national and the Länder governments, including those led by the SPD and FDP. During the following years, the AfB called on SPD-FDP-governed Länder to officially back integrated schools. It took issue with Peter Glotz, then chairman of the party's commission for educational policy, who maintained that it was up to the parents whether they wanted to send their children to comprehensive schools. The AfB insisted that if parents were the key factor, the SPD had an obligation to speak to them directly—especially working-class parents, whose children would profit most from such schools. [50]

Yet, the CDU/CSU posed the major obstacle to the establishment of more comprehensive schools. Since 1974, the party had become more vocal in its opposition, partly because it feared—without saying so publicly—that these schools would raise the educational qualifications of underprivileged youth, who then would become more competitive with privileged youth in a tight job market. In North Rhine-Westphalia especially, the CDU fought the social-liberal government's plan to introduce cooperative schools as a preliminary to the establishment of comprehensive schools. Because the cooperative schools were designed as consolidated centers for the existing three nonintegrated schools, the SPD-FDP-led government hoped that they would meet less opposition than comprehensive schools. In October 1977, the Landtag, in which its parties had a majority, approved a bill to create cooperative schools. But the CDU and other opponents decided on a citizens' initiative to petition for repeal of the law. They succeeded, with 30 percent of the state's 12.2 million registered voters signing the petitions. The government acknowledged defeat; in April 1978, its parties in the Landtag supported an amendment to the law to replicate the citizens' initiative, which meant that cooperative schools would be established only if in each instance a majority of local citizens was in favor. [51]

The SPD had learned a lesson; in the 1980 federal election campaign it promised to build comprehensive schools only if parents so desired, noting, however, that where such schools already existed, the number of available places fell short of demand. In some SPD-governed Länder where the population backed the schools, the party planned to increase their number, but in other Länder it faced resistance, even among SPD supporters whose children would benefit most from restructuring of the high schools.

In addition to seeking university and high school reforms, the SPD, prodded by the trade unions, also attempted to make changes in vocational education. After 1969, a shortage of places in vocational schools developed, which meant that many youth had difficulty gaining apprenticeship training. In 1973, Minister Dohnanyi finally readied a bill, but it reflected more the probusiness views of FDP ministers than union wishes. The latter wanted the state to control the industry-run apprenticeship programs to provide for more equal opportunities, to end injustices for the underprivileged, and to integrate vocational and general education. [52] As a result of union pressure, the bill was withdrawn.

In May 1974, Helmut Rohde (SPD) succeeded Dohnanyi as minister, but difficulties with the FDP in the new cabinet did not ease. Minister of Economics Friderichs (FDP) informed him that the employer associations were willing to expand the apprenticeship program by 10 percent, but only if the government gave up its plan to impose a compulsory levy on industry. The levy was to finance the expansion of the program and to increase state supervision of training schemes. Chancellor Schmidt, to the irritation of the SPD and the unions, sided with Friderichs because he feared an adverse effect on the investment climate and because he wanted the FDP to make concessions on industrial codetermination legislation. Consequently, Rohde, like his predecessor, had to accept a much watered-down bill. [53]

In sum, the SPD could not fulfill its ambitious educational reforms. In a number of instances the Länder and the CDU/CSU blocked reforms, or financial constraints made their postponement necessary. The SPD had underestimated the barriers to reform, even within its own ranks, although the federal government and the Länder it controlled were able in the early 1970s to make some reforms. To meet the increased demand for education, all Länder started costly expansion programs, but these reforms did not satisfy the high hopes for fundamental changes which SPD youth had expected.

ENERGY POLICY

As the major governing party of a leading industrial state, the SPD has not been spared the difficult choices policymakers have faced in meeting the demand for energy since the 1973 oil crisis. Once again, as in other policy fields, intraparty schisms resulting from external factors impaired the SPD's ability to act forcefully. In the wake of the momentary Arab embargo on oil shipments to the Federal Republic, the Brandt government imposed a ban on Sunday driving and a reduction of speed on highways. The SPD left wing demanded that the government take more radical actions, such as converting the giant oil firms into public corporations in which representatives of the state, the unions, and the consumers would sit on the boards of directors. The Jusos rejected the alternative of nationalization because the firms' "profit bureaucracy" would merely be replaced by a new ministerial bureaucracy. The Frankfurt Circle maintained that the energy crisis showed the urgent need for the government to steer investments. The circle created an ad hoc group to study the problem and urged the party executive to form a working group for the same purpose. [54]

In the meantime, at a Fraktion session SPD deputies criticized the government's moves as being insufficient to save gasoline and urged it to regulate supply more firmly. The government acceded to their proposal and incorporated it into a comprehensive energy program, which, however, did not include the left-wing proposals. The program envisaged the scaling down of national oil consumption from 55 percent to 44 percent, a commitment by private firms to ensuring sufficient energy at reasonable prices, and the intensification of efforts to diversify energy sources, including exploitation of indigenous ones. [55]

Nuclear power was one prime candidate for an additional energy source. In the early 1970s the government had developed ambitious plans to build thirty-five to forty generating plants to supply 25 percent of electricity by the mid-1980s. By 1975, eleven plants were in operation (supplying 4 percent of electricity), eight were under construction, and fourteen were in the planning stage. When energy consumption began to decline, economic growth slowed, and more efficient methods of using coal and oil were developed, the government cut back its projected number of plants to twenty-five. [56] But in the mid-1970s even this target was too high for citizens' initiatives, which made their opposition to the construction of new plants known through demonstrations and sit-ins.

Within the SPD and FDP, serious discussions about the nuclear option started late. In November 1976, following demonstrations by environmental groups, the SPD Land executive of Schleswig-Holstein demanded a moratorium on the construction of new nuclear plants until adequate safeguards for waste disposal had been met. A Land court made a ruling to this effect for the Brokdorf plant, thereby overturning permission for construction made by the CDU-led Land government.

In November 1976, Brandt created a working group within the presidium to prepare a party position on nuclear energy. The executive issued a declaration reaffirming the 1975 guidelines, which had approved the construction of plants if the population's safety was assured and which urged opponents and proponents of nuclear energy to end their confrontations. Yet a compromise was not in the offing. In December, the Juso federal board demanded a moratorium on plant construction and a halt to existing nuclear production of electricity. It requested that less environment-damaging alternatives be developed. [57] Schmidt, however, in the 1977 government declaration, said that the Federal Republic could not do without nuclear energy. But he acknowledged that the nuclear waste problem must be solved, energy conserved, and new coal plants built. He also admitted that his party had neglected to take sufficient account of the population's fears about nuclear energy.

In the SPD Länder organizations, discussion about nuclear energy intensified that year. Especially in Hamburg, a number of party leaders who had been pronuclear in the past began to change their minds when pressure from local branches mounted. In addition, nuclear opponents in Bremen, Schleswig-Holstein, and Baden-Wuerttemberg assailed SPD ministers for their pronuclear position. They urged that talks be held with citizens' initiative groups. As a result of the protests, as well as court injunctions, the recession, and the government's requirement that disposal centers for spent fuel must first be built, the construction of sixteen new nuclear plants was halted. [58]

The party made extensive preparations for an energy conference to be held in April 1977. Minister Matthöfer sent a lengthy discussion guideline to 2,000 functionaries, in which he tried to calm the emotion-laden atmosphere and produce a consensus based on cautious expansion of nuclear energy rather than its outright rejection. Before the conference, 100 left-wing and center leaders met to work out a common position. They did not accept the Juso call for a permanent moratorium but favored a temporary moratorium. On the pronuclear side, the Fraktion's right wing and the unions, fearful of job losses, stood behind the cabinet ministers. Bahr, worried about the polarization within the party, requested both sides to compromise.

At the conference, Schmidt urged the delegates to keep all energy options open. He opposed any moratorium, because of the already huge investments made and the danger of large-scale unemployment. He could not mollify the left delegates who were angered by his announcement one day before the conference that the government would make massive outlays for atomic technology in its research program. The delegates also heard from Adolf Schmidt, president of the DGB Construction and Energy Workers Union, who pleaded for more economic growth and energy as means of achieving full employment, environmental protection, and aid for the Third World. Eppler, however, warned that growth alone would not produce full employment. More important was to discuss political goals and qualitative criteria. [59] Despite these disparate views, the proponents and opponents were not far apart. The former knew about nuclear risks and the latter knew about the employment question.

While the party anguished over the energy problem, the DGB adopted a cautious position. It urged the completion of plants under construction but a moratorium on new ones until the waste problem was settled. Even thereafter, expansion should be restricted, it concluded. In the wake of this multiple opposition, the cabinet froze nuclear research and development funds until it could convince skeptical Bundestag deputies that the program was safe and not too costly. But when a few left-wing SPD deputies from Schleswig-Holstein, a center of antinuclear resistance, threatened to break party discipline and vote against the projected plutonium-based breeder-reactor program, thereby possibly bringing down the government, the temporary freeze on research funds was maintained (even though the Ministry of Research and Technology denied any connection with the threatened revolt). [60]

The intra-SPD debate continued at a high pitch for months preceding the Hamburg convention in November 1977. The SPD organizations throughout the country adopted various positions encapsuled in 142 motions ranging from complete rejection to cautious acceptance of nuclear energy. In September, Schmidt publicly announced that he would not be bound by any convention resolution supporting a moratorium. He was upset that the executive had decided, in an eleven to ten vote, to ask the convention to stop construction of nuclear plants for a minimum of three years until a permit for a planned waste plant had been issued. [61] But when the DGB, in a volte-face, rejected the moratorium—after considerable pressure from Schmidt and Matthöffer—and when nuclear opponents lost a battle in the FDP, the SPD executive changed its mind shortly before the convention. Its new motion called for finishing plants under construction and resuming construction on others once a preliminary permit for the construction of a waste reprocessing plant at Gorleben had been granted.

Party leaders were desperate to prevent a major clash at the convention. Hence on its eve the executive set up a commission to work out a compromise. Eppler urged other members to reject the latest DGB and FDP positions and hew to the first executive motion, but Matthöffer argued that the party could not approve a motion contrary to that of the DGB. Schmidt supported the latest executive motion. Finally, both sides in the commission reached a compromise: new plants could be built only if expanded coal production could not meet the demand for energy and if the nuclear waste problem was solved through swift construction of a reprocessing plant at Gorleben. Although Schmidt and Eppler were satisfied with the compromise, Schleswig-Holstein, South Bavaria and Juso members remained adamant in their opposition. They insisted that the SPD position was a sellout to the nuclear and electrical industries and still preferred a three-year moratorium. [62]

At the convention, Eppler pleaded for unity on an energy policy. He reminded the delegates that the executive motion called for priority of German coal over nuclear energy and oil and for the government to steer investments into various energy sources. Eighty percent of the delegates approved the motion. The compromise formula satisfied most opponents because it called for a de facto moratorium; it satisfied most proponents because the nuclear option was retained. [63]

In March 1979, the Three Mile Island accident in Pennsylvania reinforced the opponents' argument that nuclear plant safety was questionable. Brandt, who had not been on their side, said that the situation warranted a renewed discussion of nuclear energy. The Jusos demanded that the existing fourteen reactors be shut down. A public opinion poll at the time showed that 61 percent of respondents of all parties favored a ban on new plant construction or total abandonment of nuclear power. But Schmidt told the SPD Bundestag Fraktion that the power stations would not be shut down, because such action would do nothing to solve the problem of waste disposal and would only lead to an economic catastrophe. On another occassion, he did acknowledge that the government, responsible for nuclear safety, would look at the scientific and technical safety lessons to be learned from the Pennsylvania accident. [64]

After this reactor incident, the Lower Saxony SPD revolt against Schmidt's pronuclear policy made the CDU-controlled Land government decide to postpone building the Gorleben reprocessing plant. Minister-President Albrecht (CDU), whose party had been pronuclear all along, reasoned that he was not going to support Schmidt against the rebels in the SPD who happened to be strong within the Land. Albrecht noted that even if the health risks for the population were removed, "the double question remains—if construction of such a facility is indispensable and if it can be carried out politically." [65] Despite this new obstacle, Schmidt told an SPD meeting in May that he still supported plans for an integrated disposal site, including a reprocessing plant.

The Jusos resumed their offensive against nuclear power. At their 1978 congress, they rejected the export of nuclear plants—a profitable venture for the German nuclear industry for years—as creating additional hazards in other countries. They also noted that in West German plants, 266 accidents had occurred between 1965 and 1977, that police surveillance had increased to protect nuclear plants (which led to unnecessary confrontations), and that other energy sources provided more jobs than the nuclear industry. Once again they rejected the continued construction of a fast breeder facility at Kalkar and the possible construction of a reprocessing plant at Gorleben. [66]

At their March 1979 congress, the Jusos approved a resolution calling on the government to close existing plants. Chairman Schröder assailed the government: "What right do the government leaders have to force on us a technology that will threaten our and an untold number of future generations, when those who make decisions now will by then not be responsible any more?" [67] Soon thereafter Reinhard Schultz, Juso deputy chairman, bluntly asserted: "We do not want the SPD to be the party going down in history, with 'atomic Chancellor' Schmidt, as having guaranteed future generations a life in civil defense bunkers." [68]

From July 1979 to the Berlin party convention in December, the intraparty schism deepened once again. The Baden-Wuerttemberg SPD passed a resolution recommending a ban on nuclear plants in its Land until 1984. The Jusos announced that they would introduce a motion at the convention calling for public ownership of energy companies and a moratorium on nuclear plants. The party executive formed a fifteen-member energy commission, headed by Ehmke, with Eppler and Hauff as deputy chairmen, to prepare a resolution for the convention. After heated discussions the commission submitted its report to the party executive, which accepted it overwhelmingly. The report, reflecting the majority view, stated that existing plants should continue operating, plants under construction should be finished, and some new plants should be constructed if the requirements for waste disposal and safety have been met. The minority on the commission were opposed to any new construction. [69]

In the meantime, Schmidt made the rounds of district conventions pleading for support of the government program. A majority backed him, but a minority vigorously dissented. [70] The latter formed an ecological working group "Greens in the SPD" and, supported by the Frankfurt Circle, drafted an alternative proposal to be presented at the convention. But as expected, the majority of convention delegates upheld the commission's report. [71]

The Jusos viewed the convention vote as only an interim one; for them the party's abandonment of nuclear technology remained on the agenda. In 1980, they—and the Hesse SPD—bitterly opposed the plan by Hesse's Minister-President Holger Börner (SPD) to construct still another nuclear plant in that state. In June, the Bundestag-appointed Investigative Commission on the Future of Nuclear Energy Policy issued its report. The majority of members, including SPD and FDP members as well as scientists, recommended postponing further development of nuclear energy for a decade to see what the effects of energy conservation measures and the development of new alternative sources would be. The CDU/CSU members, in a minority, wanted further expansion of the nuclear energy program to shore up the economy. [72]

In 1981, a new controversy on nuclear energy erupted within the party. Mayor Klose of Hamburg resigned when a majority of party chiefs in his city did not back him in his opposition to the further construction of a nuclear power plant in nearby Brokdorf. (Klaus von Dohnanyi replaced him; the party feud cost the party many votes at the next Land election.) Chancellor Schmidt maintained his commitment to nuclear energy. Within the party, he could count on a majority, reaffirmed at the 1982 party convention, albeit not very enthusiastically, for his program. Nevertheless, he could not forget the power of the party opposition and the citizens' initiatives which threatened him with damaging political consequences if he were to remain unyielding. Ironically, the CDU/CSU, and more haltingly the DGB, provided the Chancellor with additional support.

MUNICIPAL POLITICS

The SPD has had to take positions not only on crucial national and Länder issues but also on local issues. SPD policies at the local level have not changed drastically over the decades. The party programs have repeatedly called for popular participation and local autonomy. During the Weimar period, the party demanded less state supervision, the use of popular initiatives and referendums, a uniform municipal code, and the nationalization of private enterprises. After World War II, the SPD gained some good will by its vigorous reconstruction of the damaged cities that were under its political control. At its 1954 convention, it again emphasized the need for administrations to be democratic, to be given financial support, and to retain enterprises in the public sector.

As in other fields, the Jusos engendered a new dynamism and ideas into municipal politics. From 1970 on, as part of their double strategy, the Jusos attempted to mobilize the population in cities to support reform actions that might raise their anticapitalist consciousness. The Jusos demanded the democratization of municipal politics, such as the direct election of city councillors in major cities, public access to municipal committee meetings and documents, parents' election of school committee members, and the support of citizens' initiatives. Despite the hesitancy of more conservative SPD politicians to accept such demands, many cities enacted laws providing for greater citizen participation in planning bodies and advisory councils. [73]

The Jusos also urged city officials to speed up slum clearance, improve health services, fight privatization of municipal services, aid city finances, clear up traffic problems and build traffic-free zones, buy more private lands, limit the power of real estate interests, establish rent controls, expand planning, establish environmental safeguards, and reform education. These demands were approved in principle at the 1971 Nuremberg SPD conference on municipal politics. Party leaders gave credit to the Jusos for their initiatives, although for pragmatic reasons they were unwilling to accept all demands. [74]

The convention proposals were submitted to party organs; a commission of specialists; and working groups on villages, towns, and cities, which spent several years discussing and reformulating them. Then they were submitted as the party's municipal program to the 1974 conference on municipal politics and to the 1975 Mannheim convention, which gave their approval. The program called for public enterprises to have priority over private enterprises and for citizens to have the right to jobs, education, adequate housing, and full social and cultural opportunities. The convention also adopted the long-range program (OR '85), whose planks included help for disadvantaged groups in cities, reform in land use, environmental safeguards, and freedom for cities to draw up their own development plans. [75]

After 1975, the party attempted to carry out many proposals in the cities, but fiscal problems often caused their postponement or produced new problems. For instance, at the 1977 conference on municipal problems, discussion centered on the shrinking population of inner cities as residents moved into suburbs. Delegates called for a mix of social groups in the inner cities to stem the tax losses. One year later, SPD municipal officials created the Social Democratic Association of Municipal Politics (SGK), whose chief goal was to make national SPD and government leaders more aware of municipal problems.

The politically "conservative" municipal officials also had to cooperate closely with the local party organizations, often dominated by the left wing. This was not easy, as seen in the bitter factional struggles in Munich, Frankfurt, and other cities. In some instances, the officials or municipal staff employees were able to gain the majority of seats on subdistrict executives, thus gaining a new power base in the SPD.

When the party in the 1970s developed a municipal program, the question arose whether it could implement its program in the cities it still controlled. In one study, Robert Fried noted that whether the SPD or another party was in power in a city had little impact on the scope of governmental activity, such as per capita spending, although SPD-controlled cities were more interested in public ownership of enterprises, multifamily housing, and public hospitals. Surprisingly, in cities such as Hannover, Munich and Frankfurt, dominated by commercial and service activities, there were more public enterprises than in the traditional workers' stronghold cities in the Ruhr. Less surprisingly, cities that were financially independent, hence more autonomous, were able to pursue socialist policies more easily than less independent cities. Moreover, a city's pursuit of socialist policies depended also on how strongly other parties were represented in the council or in municipal posts, the extent of Juso activism, and the receptivity of the population. In a number of smaller municipalities, the implementation of an ideological program negatively affected the party's electoral record. [76]

CONCLUSION

The intriguing question whether parties matter in policymaking and effectuating policy changes can now be answered. In the context of the Federal Republic, we conclude, as one of the themes of this volume, that the SPD had an effect, but a limited one on the government's domestic policies at the national and municipal levels. The effect was spotty because of intraparty—and interparty—dissension on specific policies, the coalition government's fiscal difficulties, and its insistence on maximum freedom to shape its course of action. The SPD, having to adjust to these constraints, still provided long-range guidelines and made reform proposals on current issues, hoping that the proposals would not be too emasculated in the legislative process. The Jusos, characteristically taking the offensive, demanded reforms in many domestic fields, but their radical proposals were usually filtered out during the intraparty decisionmaking process; the more moderate system-maintaining ones were transmitted to the government.

The SPD reform package sought to improve the welfare system already firmly established over the decades. It also gingerly attempted to redistribute the national wealth to increase the income of the economically disadvantaged groups, but did not press hard for major shifts in income. Proposals for a radical income redistribution were rejected by SPD leaders who were philosophically opposed or who knew that given the power of the entrenched business community and of the FDP in the cabinet, such proposals had no chance of enactment.

The Brandt and Schmidt administrations had a mixed record in making significant domestic reforms. Their claims of having left a strong Social Democratic imprint on the decade must be examined with care. [77] According to SPD leaders, the Brandt and Schmidt administrations made more reforms than their conservative predecessors in social welfare, pensions, codetermination, education, and environmental protection. They also claim to have improved the quality of life in the cities and to have been more responsive to citizens' demands than previous administrations. They assert that even though the reforms were often minor, the cumulative effect was considerable.

There is some validity to these claims, although SPD leaders do not give enough credit to CDU/CSU-FDP reforms before 1966 or to the FDP support for those reforms after 1969 with which it was in accord. Instead, they criticized FDP leaders for blocking reforms that would have adversely affected the business community but failed to point out that the SPD ministers had frequently failed to stand up to their FDP colleagues, the business community, and the CDU/CSU in the Bundesrat. As a result, dissatisfaction surfaced time and again among SPD groups; for instance, about the government's failure to reduce social inequities at the workplace and in the schools and to obtain more equality for women. The groups acknowledged that perhaps half the reform bills involved some form of mild redistribution. But they noted that the reforms had little impact on the SPD and FDP target groups when compared with the earlier CDU/CSU distributive policies that had more effectively favored the old middle class, especially the industrial bourgeoisie and the self-employed. [78]

The SPD left wing often accused the party's ministers of abandoning social democratic positions (more equality, democracy, and planning) step by step, and merely modernizing the capitalist system. It claimed that the government paid greater attention to the welfare of business executives than of workers, that after 1974 it became too interested in crisis management and political stability rather than domestic reforms, that during the fiscal crisis it abandoned reforms which would not have been too costly, and that it lacked the will and imagination to embark on an alternative economic policy.

SPD leaders were, of course, aware of the shortcomings in the official reform policy, especially when they initially had raised high expectations among the public. After many reforms in the mid-1970s were shelved or cut back, a sizable bloc of potential voters for the party, especially youth, turned away from it, viewing it as just another segment of the establishment. For the SPD, riding on a reform "high" during its initial years in power, such an alienation of its former or potential supporters was a bitter blow and could have serious electoral consequences in the 1980s.

NOTES

1. Harold Wilensky, The Welfare State and Equality: Structural and Ideological Roots of Public Expenditures (Berkeley: University of California Press, 1975); "Leftism, Catholicism, and Democratic Corporatism: The Role of Political Parties in Recent Welfare State Development," The Development of Welfare States in Europe and America, eds. Peter Flora and Arnold J. Heidenheimer (New Brunswick, N.J.: Transaction Books, 1981), pp. 345-382.

2. Kirchheimer, "The Transformation of the Western European Party Systems," p. 200; Downs, p. 141.

3. Rose, pp. 17 ff.

4. Frank Parkin, Class Inequality and Political Order (New York: Praeger, 1971), pp. 109, 119, 124-125; Richard Scase, Social Democracy in Capitalist Society: Working-Class Politics in Britain and Sweden (London: Croom Helm, 1977), p. 165. See also David Coates, Labour in Power? A Study of the Labour Government, 1974-1979 (London: Longman, 1980), p. 155.

5. See, for instance, Francis G. Castles, The Social Democratic Image of Society: A Study of the Achievements and Origins of Scandinavian Social Democracy in Comparative Perspective (London: Routledge and Kegan Paul, 1978), pp. 48-51; M. Donald Hancock and Gideon Sjoberg, eds., Politics in the Post-Welfare State: Responses to the New Individualism (New York: Columbia University Press, 1972), pp. 117-145, 223 ff.

7. John D. Stephens, The Transition from Capitalism to Socialism (Atlantic Highlands, N.J.: Humanities Press, 1981), pp. 129 ff.; Douglas A. Hibbs, Jr., "Political Parties and Macroeconomic Policy," American Political Science Review, LXXI, No. 4 (Dec. 1977), p. 1468.

8. Edward R. Tufte, Political Control of the Economy (Princeton: Princeton University Press, 1978), pp. 4, 89; Downs, p. 300.

9. Stephen Leibfried, "Public Assistance in the United States and Federal Republic of Germany: Does Social Democracy Make a Difference?," Comparative Politics, XI, No. 1 (Oct. 1978), pp. 59-76.

10. David R. Cameron, "The Expansion of the Public Economy: A Comparative Analysis," American Political Science Review, LXXII, No. 4 (Dec. 1978), pp. 1251-1254.

11. Bunce, pp. 63, 74, 82, 84.

12. Manfred Schmidt, CDU and SPD an der Regierung: Ein Vergleich ihrer Politik in den Ländern (Frankfurt: Campus, 1980), passim.

13. Klaus von Beyme, "Do parties matter? Der Einfluss der Parteien auf politische Entscheidungen," Politische Vierteljahresschrift, XXII, No. 4 (1981), 343-358.

14. A 1970 European Community survey indicated that in the Federal Republic only 2 percent of working- and middle-class respondents wanted revolutionary changes, 80 percent of the middle class and 76 percent of the working class desired gradual reforms, and 17 percent of the middle class and 22 percent of the working class were satisfied with the status quo (cited by Ronald Inglehart, The Silent Revolution: Changing Values and Political Styles among Western Publics [Princeton, N.J.: Princeton University Press, 1977], p. 213).

15. For an overview, see Jeremiah M. Riemer, "Alterations in the Design of Model Germany: Critical Innovations in the Policy Machinery for Economic Steering," The Political Economy of West Germany, ed. Andrei S. Markovits (New York: Praeger, 1982), pp. 53-89; Kenneth H.F. Dyson, "The Politics of Economic Management in West Germany," West European Politics, IV, No. 2 (May 1981), 35-55.

16. Die Zeit, Sept. 26, 1975; Sozialdemokrat Magazin, 11/75; Der Spiegel, Oct. 6, 1975; SPD, Parteitag 1973, p. 95 ff.; Thilo Sarrazin, ed., Investitionslenkung: "Spielwiese" oder "vorausschauende Industriepolitik" (Bonn-Bad Godesberg: Neue Gesellschaft, 1976).

17. Christian Fenner, "Das Parteiensystem seit 1969—Normalisierung und Polarisierung," Das Parteiensystem der Bundesrepublik, ed. Staritz, p. 210.

18. Der Stern, Oct. 17, 1974.

19. Nordwest Zeitung, Dec. 22, 1978. See also Politik, No. 12, Nov. 1979; Rovan, Histoire de la Social-Démocratie Allemande, pp. 447-449; Schmollinger, Zwischenbilanz: 10 Jahre Sozialliberale Politik, 1969-1979 (Hannover: Fackelträger, 1980), passim.

20. Personal interview with FDP official, Bonn, April 3, 1980.

21. See, for instance, SPD executive, Bodenreform: Vorlage "Bodenrechtsreform" zum Parteitag Hamburg, 1977 (Bonn, n.d.).

22. Vorwärts, Nov. 22, 1979.

23. Narr, Scheer, Spöri, SPD—Staatspartei oder Reformpartei?, p. 22.

24. Ibid., passim.

25. Socialist Affairs, Dec. 1971, p. 244.

26. Westdeutsche Zeitung, Nov. 19, 1971; Süddeutsche Zeitung, Nov. 20, 1971; SPD, Informationsdienst, intern, No. 21/71, Nov. 24, 1971.

27. SPD, Parteitag, Nov. 1971, pp. 43, 63, 68, 71, 157 ff.

28. Manfred G. Schmidt, "Die 'Politik der inneren Reformen' in der Bundesrepublik seit 1969," Unfähig zur Reform?, eds. Fenner et al., pp. 53-65.

29. Frankfurter Rundschau, Nov. 3, 1975; Der Stern, Nov. 13, 1975; Konkret, Nov. 27, 1975; Juso Rundschreiben, A 16/ 1975, Dec. 8, 1975.

30. SPD, executive, "Materialen, Alterssicherung: Zunkunftsgerechte

Weiterentwicklung der Alterssicherung" (hectographed, 1979); SPD, executive, *intern-dokumente*, No. 2, Mar. 1980; *Der Spiegel*, May 12, 1980.

31. SPD, "Dokumentation über die Beschäftigung von Extremisten im öffentlichen Dienst der Bundesrepublik Deutschland" (hectographed), pp. 11-12.

32. Jusos, *Informationsdienst*, No. 15/1975 (Dec. 1975), pp. 8-9, 23, 25.

33. *Relay from Bonn*, May 20, 1976; *The Bulletin*, May 25, 1976.

34. *Süddeutsche Zeitung*, June 22, 1978; *Vorwärts*, June 29, 1978; SPD, *Intern, Intern-dokumente*, No. 2 (July 1978); *Relay from Bonn*, Oct. 6, 1978.

35. For text, see SPD, *Dokumentation, Grundsätze zur Feststellung der Verfassungstreue im öffentlichen Dienst; Bonn, 16. Oktober 1978* (Bonn, 1978).

36. *Süddeutsche Zeitung*, Nov. 17, 1978; Nov. 27, 1978.

37. Text of Koschnick's revised proposal in *Politik*, No. 7, Dec. 1978; cabinet statement in *New York Times*, Jan. 19, 1979. See also *Info: West Germany* (New York), I, No. 3, Oct. 1978.

38. *Der Spiegel*, May 22, 1978, p. 46; *New York Times*, Nov. 7, 1978.

39. SPD, *Parteitag, Nov. 1971*, pp. 638-659.

40. *Der Spiegel*, Oct. 25, 1971; Nov. 29, 1971.

41. SPD, *Information der Fraktion*, No. 84, Feb. 2, 1972; *Frau und Gesellschaft*, No. 10, March 10, 1972; No. 11, March 17, 1972.

42. *ppp dispatch*, Feb. 28, 1975; Jusos, *Informationsdienst*, No. 9, Sept. 1976; *Bulletin*, No. 6, May 27, 1980.

43. Guntram von Schenck, *Das Hochschulrahmengesetz* (Bonn-Bad Godesberg: Neue Gesellschaft, 1976), pp. 17-37.

44. *Süddeutsche Zeitung*, June 29, 1973.

45. Ibid., Nov. 5, 1973.

46. von Schenck, passim.

47. SPD, executive, Reihe Bildungspolitik, Heft 2, b 2, *Warum Gesamtschule?* (Bonn, 1970).

48. Angela Brauer, "Zu den Bedingungen von Reformpolitik am Beispiel Berufsbildungsreform," *Unfähig zur Reform?*, eds. Fenner et al., pp. 172-184; Hans Jochen Brauns et al., *Die SPD in der Krise: Die deutsche Sozialdemokratie seit 1945* (Frankfurt/Main: Fischer, 1976), p. 245; *Frankfurter Rundschau*, May 16, 1977; *SPD-Pressedienst*, May 16, 1977.

49. *Süddeutsche Zeitung*, May 14/15, 1977, May 16, 1977; SPD, *Sicherheit für Deutschland, No. 8, Schule, SPD Aktion 80* (flyer).

50. Klaus-Peter Wolf, "Die SPD-Bildungspolitik am Beispiel der Gesamtschule," *Sozialistische Tribüne*, 2/1980, pp. 101-102.

51. Hans-Georg Lehmann, "Schulreform und Politik," *Aus Politik und Zeitgeschichte*, Beilage, *Das Parlament*, B 36/78, Sept. 9, 1978, pp. 3-23.

52. *Der Spiegel*, Oct. 29, 1973; Brauer, pp. 151-158; SPD, executive, Reihe Bildungspolitik, Heft 1, b 1, *Berufsbildung: Ziele und Massnahmen* (Bonn, 1973).

53. See SPD, Dokumente, *Wege zur menschlichen Schule—Die Reform muss weitergehen, Beschluss der AfB auf der Bundeskonferenz vom 23. bis 25. März 1979 in Osnabrück* (Bonn, 1979).

54. *Süddeutsche Zeitung*, Nov. 27, 1973.

55. Ibid., Nov. 28, 1973; Nov. 29, 1973; *Die Zeit*, Oct. 25, 1974.

56. *Relay from Bonn*, Feb. 13, 1975.

57. SPD, *Service Presse, Funk, TV*, 657/76, Nov. 23, 1976; *Frankfurter Rundschau*, Dec. 6, 1976; Jusos, *Informationsdienst*, No. 2/Jan. 1977. See

also Jusos, Problem 26: Energiepolitik 1, Atomkraft ist totsicher; Für ein menschliches Leben (Bonn, n.d. [c. 1977]).

58. New York Times, Feb 7, 1977; Mar. 30, 1977; Der Spiegel, Feb. 7, 1977; Feb. 21, 1977.

59. Der Spiegel, Apr. 11, 1977; Stuttgarter Nachrichten, Apr. 19, 1977; Süddeutsche Zeitung, Apr. 20, 1977. For details, see SPD, Dokumente, Forum SPD, Fachtagung "Energie, Beschäftigung, Lebensqualität" am 28. und 29. April 1977, Köln (1977). For text of Matthöfer's guideline, SPD, Forum SPD, Energie, Ein Diskussionsleitfaden (1977).

60. Dissident SPD deputies denied planning any putsch against the government or wanting to see its downfall (Süddeutsche Zeitung, May 3, 1977, May 4, 1977, June 18/19, 1977; Der Spiegel, May 2, 1977; New York Times, May 12, 1977). The United States government also opposed the projected breeder-reactor program.

61. Süddeutsche Zeitung, Sept. 24/25, 1977.

62. Ibid., Nov. 9, 1977; Nov. 10, 1977; Nov. 14, 1977; Nov. 15, 1977.

63. SPD, Dokumente, Energie, Parteitag Hamburg, 15.-19. Nov. 1977, Beschlüsse zur Energiepolitik (1977); SPD, Intern, Dokumente, No. 3, May 1979.

64. Relay from Bonn, Apr. 26, 1979; New York Times, May 4, 1979.

65. Ibid., May 17, 1979.

66. Jusos, Bürgerinitiativen: Maschinenstürmer oder politischer Rettungsanker? (Bonn, 1977); Aktionsprogramm, Bundeskongress '78 (Bonn, n.d.) pp. 30-34; Gegen ein atomares Europa; für eine humane Umwelt—und Energiepolitik (Bonn, n.d. [c. 1979]).

67. Süddeutsche Zeitung, Mar. 31/Apr. 1, 1979.

68. Ibid., May 9, 1979.

69. SPD, Materialen, Energiepolitik, Erster Zwischenbericht der Kommission Energiepolitik beim Parteivorstand der SPD (Bonn, 1979). The vote was 24 to 4, with 1 abstention (Frankfurter Allgemeine Zeitung, Oct. 5, 1979).

70. Among Länder or districts in support were Franconia, Berlin, North Lower Saxony, Rhineland-Palatinate, Westphalia; among those in opposition were South Hesse, Schleswig-Holstein, Hamburg, Hannover, Bavaria; the Saar was undecided (Die Zeit, Oct. 12, 1979).

71. Der Spiegel, May 12, 1980.

72. Relay from Bonn, July 2, 1980; "Energie: Sicherheit für Deutschland," Sozialdemokrat Magazin (special issue, n.d., c. 1980).

73. Scheer, Strasser, Wieczorek-Zeul, pp. 37-41; Jusos, Forderungskatalog der Jungsozialisten zur Kommunalpolitik, beschlossen auf der Arbeitskonferenz am 24./25. April 1971 in Mannheim (Bonn, 1971).

74. For details, see Wolfgang Roth, ed., Kommunalpolitik—für wen? Arbeitsprogramme der Jungsozialisten (Frankfurt/Main: Fischer, 1971); Lutz-Rainer Reuter, "Kommunalpolitik im Parteienvergleich," Aus Politik und Zeitgeschichte, Beilage, Das Parlament, B 34/76, Aug. 21, 1976; SPD, executive, Reihe Gesellschaftspolitik, g 4, Die Zukunft unserer Städte (Bonn, 1971).

75. The texts of the basic municipal programs can be found in SPD, Leitfaden für die kommunale Praxis (Hannover-Bonn, 1960); Jusos, Kommunalpolitisches Aktionsprogramm (Mannheim, 1971); SPD, Materialen, Entwurf Kommunalpolitisches Grundsatzprogramm, beschlossen von der XII. Kommunalpolitischen Bundeskonferenz vom 11.-13. Oktober 1974 in Nürnberg (Bonn, 1974); SPD, Dokumente, Kommunalpolitisches

Grundsatzprogramm der SPD (Bonn, c. 1975).

76. Robert C. Fried, "Party and Policy in West German Cities," American Political Science Review, LXX, No. 1 (Mar. 1976), 18-23. See also Rainer Frey, Kommunale Demokratie (Bonn-Bad Godesberg: Neue Gesellschaft, 1976); Nassmacher, passim.

77. See Klaus Lompe, "Bilanz der Politik, Innerer Reformen," Die Mitarbeit, No. 2/3, 1979; Strasser, Grenzen des Sozialstaates, p. 120 ff.; Brandt interview in Der Spiegel, Sept. 17, 1979; Manfred G. Schmidt, "Die 'Politik der inneren Reformen' seit 1969," passim; Horst W. Schmollinger and Peter Müller, Zwischenbilanz: 10 Jahre sozialliberale Politik, Anspruch und Wirklichkeit (Hannover: Fackelträger, 1980).

78. Manfred G. Schmidt, "The Politics of Domestic Reform in the Federal Republic of Germany," Politics and Society, VIII, No. 2 (1978), 174-175.

14 Foreign Policy Issues

To the average SPD member the salience of foreign policy varied from issue to issue but at times was less controversial or of less concern than domestic questions. Hence from 1969 on, the SPD leaders had to cope with little intraparty opposition on such issues as Ostpolitik and the European Community—topics that engendered few ideological differences—but more on such discord-laden issues as defense, the party's relations with foreign socialist parties, and government relations with the Third World. In assessing these key foreign policy issues, we will not deal with their substance, explored fully in the scholarly literature, but only with the discussion within the party and, where relevant, between it and the government. Such an approach can serve as a way of gauging the SPD position on foreign policy issues or its effect on public policymakers and tell us once again whether parties matter in policy formulation. [1]

Although foreign policy discussions were not important at most SPD conventions, the coalition government's policy rested on a bipartisan SPD-FDP accord on basic principles as well as on support from the CDU/CSU on most questions. Within the SPD, policy was formulated at various levels. The commission for international relations, headed by Wischnewski, included members from the different party wings. Its preparatory work on issues was done primarily by the Fraktion's foreign affairs specialists. The commission's recommendations were given to the top party organs, which, after discussion and approval, sent them to the Foreign Ministry and other government agencies. On occasion the recommendations were sent to the Fraktion to be introduced in the Bundestag as SPD initiatives or as questions to the government. According to one Fraktion staff specialist, he formulated the questions, sent them to the government in advance of the formal question hour, and received a draft of the answer to ensure that it would be satisfactory to the Fraktion and not lead to embarrassing additional questions. Thus, the Fraktion staff and leadership had to maintain close links with the FDP, whose leaders Scheel and Genscher successively headed the Foreign Ministry. [2]

When the Ministry took policy initiatives that needed legislative approval, it informally cleared bills with the SPD and FDP Fraktionen prior to final cabinet approval and introduction into Parliament. The SPD Fraktion staff also drafted the party's version of the foreign policy section of the government declarations, taking into consideration the views of the FDP to preclude possible discord with it. [3] Finally, the staff prepared resolutions by top SPD organs to be submitted to the conventions, primarily because the party did not have its own staff of experts. (The SPD has a section on international relations, but its primary function has been to maintain fraternal relations with foreign socialist parties.)

The SPD occasionally sponsored foreign affairs conferences to generate ideas on major issues and to discuss them with government leaders. At one typical meeting, in January 1975, the participants—party specialists, deputies, and government officials as well as experts from the East, West, and Third World—heard reports by SPD leaders on the Atlantic Community, the Common Market, Ostpolitik, and the Third World. The speakers praised government accomplishments since 1969 but did not expect the conference to produce any decisions. This conference was scheduled months before the Mannheim party convention, in order to prevent surprises there and neutralize any potential Juso opposition. Instead, the Jusos at the January conference had an opportunity to voice their critical views (favoring increased cooperation between European socialist parties, a breakup of the two military blocs, reductions of troops). The criticisms had little effect on the other delegates; all were warned by Schmidt at the beginning of the proceedings that there could be no "pure Social Democratic" foreign policy and that the government would reject unacceptable demands. Other leaders noted that top party organs would study the conference views and use them as a base for the convention discussions on foreign policy. The views would then be transmitted formally to the Chancellor, to Genscher, and other cabinet members. [4]

OSTPOLITIK

To what extent the SPD views on foreign policy influenced government policies can be gauged by examining a number of major issues. One was the government policy toward the East (Ostpolitik). When Brandt became foreign minister in the Grand Coalition, he began a new policy of rapprochement with communist nations. Did it have any roots in the SPD? In the early 1960s, left-wing groups, spearheaded by Hesse-South and Schleswig-Holstein, introduced resolutions at conventions calling on the party to press the CDU-led government to normalize relations with the Soviet bloc, in line with the policy of détente initiated by President John F. Kennedy. But the resolutions did not gain a majority. [5] In 1963, Egon Bahr, press secretary to Brandt, then mayor of West Berlin, in an important speech unsuccessfully requested the government to begin a policy of détente with the Soviet Union. Bahr, considered the architect of Ostpolitik, did, however, have great influence on Brandt, who stated before the 1965 election that if he were to become chancellor he would start a dialogue with the Soviet Union on a peace settlement. [6] Thereafter, SPD pressures on the CDU/CSU government had some effect on its adoption of a "policy of small steps" to normalize relations with at least the German Democratic Republic.

Once the SPD joined the Grand Coalition in 1966, Brandt as foreign minister was primarily responsible for foreign policy formulation. Bahr became head of the Foreign Ministry's planning staff and ambassador for special tasks, posts that gave him the opportunity to shape the Ostpolitik's grand design. From 1966 to 1969, Brandt, Bahr, and on occasion Klaus Schütz (SPD), then state secretary in the Foreign Ministry, held a number of private talks with the Soviet ambassador in Bonn. Between November 1967 and spring 1969, SPD leaders conferred secretly with Italian

Communist leaders, who acted as liaison to Soviet leaders. In March 1968, a close aide of Brandt (apparently Bahr) met clandestinely in Vienna with a Polish government representative to discuss a rapprochement between the two countries. At the 1968 Nuremberg SPD convention, Brandt for the first time supported West German recognition of the Oder-Neisse line as the official border between Poland and East Germany--a proposal made years earlier by the party's left wing. The convention adopted a resolution drafted by Eppler and Bahr to this effect. In 1968 and 1969, Brandt and Bahr also met with Soviet Foreign Minister Gromyko in New York on the occasion of United Nations meetings. In June 1969, Schütz and Eugen Selbmann, the Fraktion's foreign policy advisor, at the behest of Brandt, traveled to Poland on separate missions to inform Polish leaders about the party's position on the border question and the advantages to be gained if the two countries were to reestablish contacts. Two months later an SPD delegation, consisting of Schmidt, Möller, and Franke, arrived in Moscow for three days of political conversations with Soviet leaders. FDP leaders, although then in opposition to the CDU-SPD government, concurred with the SPD about the urgency of rapprochement with the East. A number of them had already made a pilgrimage to Moscow in July 1969 and had submitted to the Bundestag earlier that year a draft treaty to normalize relations between the two Germanys. [7]

In sum, Brandt as foreign minister from 1966 to 1969 made ample use of secret or private diplomacy by trusted SPD officials to establish closer links with the Soviet bloc countries. He chose secrecy because the Communist leaders' mistrust, built up by the legacy of the past, could not easily be erased by open diplomacy--which was also used. When Brandt became chancellor he took advantage of the momentum built up in the previous three years to forge ahead with Ostpolitik. Scheel headed the Foreign Ministry but had to play a role secondary to Brandt's, especially until June 1970 when he reorganized his ministry. The Chancellor was the key decision maker, advised by a team of specialists headed by Bahr, then state secretary in the Chancellor's Office, who had already made elaborate plans to conclude treaties providing for mutual renunciation of force with the Soviet Union, Poland, Czechoslovakia, and other Eastern countries, as well as a Four Power Agreement on Berlin and a German Basic Treaty to be concluded with the German Democratic Republic.

The FDP, although in accord with the SPD on Ostpolitik, resented that the Foreign Ministry and the cabinet were largely bypassed. Brandt kept top SPD leaders informed of the progress of diplomatic negotiations but gave them no details. The Fraktion and its foreign policy working group had little influence on negotiations, but Wehner and Mischnick (FDP Fraktion head) met weekly in coalition talks with Brandt and other top officials. Wehner was one of the key policy advisors on Ostpolitik, especially in 1969 and 1970, but thereafter was consulted less frequently. [8]

Yet Brandt did authorize Wehner and Mischnick, who had been invited by East German Communist party leaders for a private visit, to proceed to East Berlin and discuss inter-German affairs. Wehner had tried to keep the meeting secret from other SPD leaders, who were angry to hear about it on East German television. [9] The Fraktion chief became embroiled in another dispute when he attempted to influence the direction of government policy: in late 1972, he urged Brandt and other officials to talk privately with Communist officials in order to speedily resolve the problem of consular protection for West Berlin organizations in Czechoslovakia, Hungary, and Bulgaria—a problem which was delaying the signing of treaties with those three countries. But progress was slow, and the impatient Wehner, while in Moscow on an official visit in September 1973, denounced his own government for demanding too many concessions from Eastern countries (see chapter 4). His remarks infuriated Brandt and other government leaders. Since then Brandt's relations with Wehner have remained cool.

Despite this dramatic incident, Ostpolitik cemented rather than fragmented the party factions. In 1970, when a congruence of views emerged at the party convention, SPD leaders accepted pleas for a rapprochement with the East from the Jusos, who were enthusiastic backers of Ostpolitik. By the time Schmidt became chancellor, the government had signed the most important treaties with the East bloc. He concluded another Polish-West German treaty in 1976 and signed a number of bilateral accords to improve trade, cultural, scientific, and technological exchanges with East Bloc countries. But the élan of the Brandt years disappeared as Schmidt had to tackle other pressing problems.

Brandt thought that with the international prestige he had achieved as chancellor he would still as SPD leader be able to make a contribution in foreign policy. Hence Schmidt and Foreign Minister Genscher permitted him to represent the Federal Republic abroad on a number of trips, but not in an official capacity. Brandt made these trips because he was worried that the successes he had achieved in Ostpolitik might be dissipated by Schmidt and Genscher, whose interest in it did not match his own. He was, of course, aware that conflicts might arise with the Foreign Ministry, which did not want to share its responsibilities with him. To neutralize the hostility, while on a trip to Moscow in July 1975, Brandt sent daily telegrams to the Ministry to keep it informed of his talks with Soviet leaders. On his return he met with Schmidt and Genscher for the same purpose. He told Schmidt that Soviet leaders were eager to have close contacts with the SPD, especially if it were less hostile to West European communist parties. On the other hand, Brandt also knew that he had to keep a distance from Soviet leaders in order to prevent the Christian Democrats from accusing the SPD of flirting with Communists. [10] To quiet any fears in the United States that the Federal Republic would move closer to the Soviet Union, Schmidt told an American audience in June 1979 that his country would not proceed unilaterally to change its course vis-à-vis the East. Although some West German groups were urging the government to be more independent in foreign policy to speed up reunification, he rejected that advice. [11]

THE SOCIALIST INTERNATIONAL

The SPD was interested not only in producing détente with the Soviet bloc but in establishing closer transnational relations between the West and the Third World. It made effective use of one international nongovernmental organization, the Socialist International (SI), which comprised more than sixty socialist and social democratic parties in the noncommunist world. Founded in Frankfurt in July 1951 as the successor to the Labor and Socialist International (1923 to World War II), the SI goals were to set the broad guidelines of democratic socialism, provide linkage for the autonomous member parties, aid in founding new socialist parties, and influence national policies. [12]

The SPD has had considerable weight in the SI. Brandt as chancellor resented the power of what they labeled the "Mafia" and the "Nordic Trio" of Palme, Brandt, and Kreisky. [13]

Despite these tensions within the SI, delegates at the 1976 congress elected Brandt to the SI presidency. He called for a drive for peace, human rights, and closer links between the affluent northern and poorer southern countries and warned that "what we work for and struggle for is the survival of man and humanity." [14] Political democracy must be safeguarded, but the European parties should realize that there is no single universal solution to the problems confronting mankind.

Chancellor Schmidt's keynote address at the same congress was more controversial than Brandt's speech. Schmidt resented the British and French barbs at the SPD's role in the SI and disagreed with a congress resolution, introduced by thirty-seven parties, which pinpointed the source of the world's economic crisis as the "manifest breakdown of international capitalism" and called for more public property and control of giant private firms. He maintained that the crisis was caused by governments (including socialist) managing their economies poorly and living beyond their means and by structural problems in industry. Moreover, there were no easy ideological solutions. Government initiation of public works programs to achieve full employment was inviting aggravated inflation. He proposed instead that the amount of money in circulation be curbed to limit inflation.

Other socialist leaders at the congress were upset by Schmidt's nonideological analysis of the economic crisis and his failure to put priority on the creation of jobs. Kreisky, who normally supported the SPD, sharply attacked Schmidt's views. The Austrian leader contended that capitalism was an issue, as exemplified by the oil price hikes and price speculation on raw materials. Brandt, however, said that Schmidt's remarks should be viewed solely as a base for discussion and not as a directive. [15] These divergent views were symptomatic of the SI's difficulty in producing accord on an important programmatic issue and in developing a supranational consciousness among the member parties.

Left-center SPD leaders assiduously made contacts with as many socialist parties as possible in the hope of cementing an international social democratic bloc to act as a third force between the capitalist and communist worlds. Brandt's reelection in the late 1970s as SI president facilitated this objective, although the SPD has not officially endorsed the third force concept. Despite the links between the socialist parties, the power of the SI in the international arena has remained limited.

RELATIONS WITH FOREIGN SOCIALIST PARTIES

The attempt of the SPD to maintain fraternal relations with other socialist and social democratic parties failed most often in the case of the French Socialist Party (PSF). The PSF, reconstituting itself in 1971, attempted to maintain a distance from the SPD because it equated the ideology of the German party with the failed reform policy of the earlier French Socialist Party (SFIO). Relations improved in 1973 and early 1974 when Mitterrand and Brandt met in Bonn, Paris, or at SI conferences. But when Schmidt became chancellor, his undisguised preference, based on economic ideological reasons, for the conservative Giscard d'Estaing over Mitterrand in the French presidential campaign caused resentment within the PSF. One of its leaders wrote in _Vorwärts_ that such a bias was intolerable and that it might be better if the PSF restricted its links to the SPD's left wing, with which it was in ideological accord. [16]

Thereafter Mitterrand attacked Schmidt publicly. He said on one occasion in 1976 that Schmidt governed "from the right" and on another occasion that the Federal Republic "does not represent the type of society to which we aspire, despite the very laudable and sometimes remarkable efforts of the German Social Democrats," who are nonetheless obliged to rely on the support of their conservative coalition partners. [17] The cool relations between Mitterrand and Schmidt were caused not only by ideological differences but also by differing perceptions of working with communist parties (see below) and by personal dislike of each other. Relations reached a low point in May 1976 when Mitterrand announced at the PSF convention the creation of a French committee to defend the rights of German radicals to public employment. Schmidt considered this move as crass interference in German domestic affairs; Brandt, who was on good terms with Mitterrand, acted as a pacifier in the dispute.

While Mitterrand and Schmidt feuded publicly (but not after Mitterrand's election to the French presidency in 1981), Brandt and Mitterrand agreed in 1976 to bring their policies into closer alignment by setting up joint commissions to study economic and social policies, the future of Europe, and Third World problems. In addition, the PSF supported the SPD call for direct elections to the European Parliament (see below).

Despite this accord, SPD relations with the PSF dipped again over another issue—socialist party links with communist parties. In May 1975, Mitterrand invited "Southern" or "Mediterranean" socialist leaders, heading the Italian, Spanish, Greek, Portuguese, and Belgian parties, to a conference in Latche (France). They agreed to support alliances with strong communist parties as a way of gaining political power within their countries. [18] At another time, Mitterrand assailed Schmidt, who had remonstrated with him for entering an electoral alliance and concluding a common program with the French Communist Party. Mitterrand contended that it was easy for Schmidt to take such a position because Hitler had destroyed the German Communist Party, leaving few Communists in the Federal Republic to challenge the SPD. If Schmidt had as many Communists to deal with as had the PSF, he might better understand the PSF's difficult situation. [19]

In May 1975, at a Vienna meeting of the "Northern" Socialists (Swedish, German, Austrians), Brandt rejected "any kind of community" between the SPD and Communists other than Federal Republic diplomatic links with Communist-ruled countries. [20] In January 1976, the Southern and Northern Socialist leaders met to discuss the question of linkage to communist parties but, as expected, could not reach an accord. Mitterrand argued that the Communists were too powerful to be ignored in France, Italy, Portugal, Finland, and Spain. Schmidt maintained that he saw no reason to engage in any kind of cooperation with Communists which could endanger a nation's international and contractual commitments, such as membership in NATO and the European Community. Both sides knew that their differences could not be bridged and decided that each socialist party would have to act on its own. [21]

The SPD position was taken partly for domestic consumption. Schmidt and Brandt did not want to appear conciliatory toward communism, especially in the 1976 election year. On April 16, in a lively television discussion, Schmidt pointed out that in countries ruled by social democratic parties there was no communist problem. But in Italy, where the Christian their differences could not be bridged and decided that each socialist party would have to act on its own. [21]

The SPD position was taken partly for domestic consumption. Schmidt and Brandt did not want to appear conciliatory toward communism, especially in the 1976 election year. On April 16, in a lively television discussion, Schmidt pointed out that in countries ruled by social democratic parties there was no communist problem. But in Italy, where the Christian Democrats had ruled for thirty years, the Communists, capitalizing on the poor social conditions, had made gains. The West German Christian Democrats, sensitive to an attack on Christian Democrats anywhere, retorted that socialists in other countries were ready to make popular front pacts with communists, which in turn would lead to an end of Western European security. [22] This debate, too, proved inconclusive because it did not consider the varying political circumstances in each country. (Schmidt also failed to mention that in 1975 he had advanced a sizable credit to the Italian government, but with strings attached, which irritated the Italian Socialist and Social Democratic parties.)

Brandt was primarily responsible for aiding Socialist parties in Spain and Portugal, where fascist dictatorships had governed for a long time and where help would strengthen the parties against the threat of competing Communist parties. In April 1973, when Portugal was still governed by a dictatorship, Brandt invited his friend Mario Soares, leader of the illegal Portuguese Socialist cadres, to Munstereifel in West Germany. There the party was officially created, and from then on received substantial financial and material aid to establish itself when the dictatorship was overthrown in 1974. In August 1975, Soares appealed for further help from West European socialist leaders assembled in Stockholm. Brandt, in accord, requested Palme to organize a "committee for solidarity and support of democratic socialism in Portugal." In addition, Brandt and Schmidt informed conservative Portuguese government leaders that any return to dictatorship would mean the immediate cutoff of economic aid from the Federal Republic. [23] On April 24, 1976, a few weeks before a scheduled election in Portugal, the West European social democratic leaders met in the country to demonstrate their continuing support for the Socialist Party.

EUROPEAN COMMUNITY

In its supranational activities the SPD could not neglect the European Community (EC), which has played an important role in decisions affecting citizens of the member states. In 1958 the SPD and its brethren Eurosocialist parties opened a Liaison Bureau in Brussels. The aim was to strengthen lobbying efforts and coordinate the diverging policies of the West German, Belgian, Dutch, Luxemburg, French, and Italian parties. The Bureau, however, never became very active, especially when those socialist parties that gained governmental power devoted more energy to pressing domestic issues. From 1971 on, impulses for Western European integration increased in the wake of demands for an economic and monetary union. Yet a schism between the socialist parties developed at the same time that could not be bridged, despite valiant efforts by working groups. The Dutch Socialists urged the creation of a federally organized Eurosocialist party, but the SPD especially opposed the idea, fearing that such a new party might want to create an electoral alliance with communist parties and might restrict the SPD's freedom of action.

On the other hand, the SPD and other socialist parties had no objection to a more pragmatic integration and a harmonization of programs between them. Accordingly, on April 5, 1974, the Liaison Bureau was transformed into the more formal League of Socialist Parties in the European Community. The League's policy has been made by its bureau, whose members, representing the nine parties, have to unanimously concur on the decisions. (By then the EC had been enlarged to nine members; of the nine socialist parties, six were in control of their national governments or shared power in coalition cabinets.) The League congress, meeting periodically, has set broad guidelines and has ratified the bureau decisions by a two-thirds vote, making them binding on members. The League, however, has not had a strong influence on the EC or been able to integrate the diverse views of the member parties. [24] Wilhelm Dröscher (SPD) headed the League from 1974 until his death in 1977. (Robert Pontillon, a French Socialist Party leader, succeeded him.)

In January 1976, the League prepared a joint election platform for the projected direct election of European Parliament members by voters in the EC states. At the time, Parliament members were still appointed by their home governments but formed transnational party caucuses to arrive at a common position on issues. The socialist caucus in 1973 had forty-three members, of whom seventeen belonged to the SPD, the largest national group by far (other groups ranged from one to four members). The caucus, even though weaker numerically than the Christian Democratic one, had some influence on the work of the Parliament because of its greater cohesion than other caucuses. The SPD set up a liaison office to facilitate communication between its Bundestag Fraktion and the socialist caucus in the European Parliament. [25]

To draw up a common election platform, the League formed four working groups (economic, social, foreign affairs, and the democratization of institutions). Months of preparatory work were filled with tension and differences. The left-leaning socialist parties, especially the French, wanted to include class-struggle slogans, a plan for more nationalization of industry, and a statement that Europe should serve as a third force to mediate the discords between the superpowers. The SPD argued instead for a mixed economic system and emphasis on the NATO alliance as a safeguard of Western interests against the Warsaw Pact. Because of these clashing views, the controversial proposals were not included in a compromise draft accepted by the League bureau in mid-1977.

The bureau's approval of the draft did not lead to immediate acceptance by left-leaning parties, which opposed the concessions to the SPD point of view and wanted more time for consultation. The SPD leaders were disappointed; they had hoped that a joint transnational program could be formulated that would erase the differences at the national level. [26]

The pressure for an accord mounted, however, partly because the caucus of liberal parties was preparing an election platform. Hence on June 23, 1978, the chairmen of the socialist parties concurred on a joint political declaration that was not binding on any party. It called, among many other things, for full employment, close links with the trade unions, public control of nuclear energy firms, a supranational energy policy, détente, harmonizing policy toward the Third World, securing peace, and expanding the EC. [27] Once again, the declaration represented a minimum consensus among the socialist parties.

On January 12, 1979, at their tenth congress, the League members agreed unanimously on an electoral manifesto based to a great extent on the political declaration. It, too, was a compromise at the lowest common denominator and was not even viewed any longer as an electoral platform. It emphasized economic and social themes, among them a thirty-five-hour week and an end to discrimination, especially against women. The more left socialist parties had reduced the dominance of the SPD in this latest version of a common program. The congress delegates agreed that the member parties were free to accept all or any part of the manifesto.

During the socialist parties' deliberations, the Jusos, in sympathy with the Dutch, Belgian, French, and other left socialist parties, challenged the SPD position. They supported West European integration if it would lead to supranational democratic socialism. Such a model would be an important alternative to American capitalism and communist state capitalism. The model, however, could be realized only if the statutory powers of the European Parliament, hitherto weak, were strengthened, an anticapitalist policy was pursued, and a political union was established. The Jusos also called for an increase in international youth exchanges and the establishment of a youth lobby in Brussels to put pressure on the EC. [28]

The SPD executive, in response, reminded them that the party had been a staunch supporter of the EC and that in some of their positions, the Jusos had strayed from the SPD position. It also noted that they were looking at the EC from too narrow a perspective when they claimed that West European capital interests dominated the EC. The Jusos should remember that the EC has also benefited the workers, especially because of trade union pressures. [29]

Despite this intraparty schism, in August 1978 in the SPD commission for European policy headed by Bruno Friedrich, the SPD executive and Jusos agreed on an SPD program draft for the direct election of deputies to the European Parliament. Carefully prepared by five subcommissions, the program, accepted by a special SPD convention in December 1978, demanded that the Parliament's powers be increased to serve as a check on the European bureaucrats in Brussels, to decide on EC expenditures, and to initiate EC legislation on its own. It also demanded a progressive EC structural policy to restore full employment, framework planning to link public and private investments, a mixed economic system in the member states, and ratification of the EC human rights charter. [30]

The program included left-wing and union planks—investment controls on multinational companies, a thirty-five-hour week, prohibition of employer lockouts—that the SPD had hardly dared adopt in its domestic program for fear of scaring off potential SPD voters. The leaders made these concessions to convince the other socialist parties that the SPD was willing to meet them part way in a common program and to show them that it was not a "pliant auxiliary of European capitalism." [31] It also hoped, on the basis of its call for a stronger EC, to convince the British, Danish, and French Socialists who were reluctant to endorse the EC that the organization constituted one building block of European unity. At the convention, Wehner admitted, however, that the SPD did not suffer great illusions concerning the difficulty of "selling" Europe and of achieving integration quickly. According to him, many steps would have to be taken before social democrats achieved their program. [32]

The convention delegates, acting on the recommendations from the party's district and national bodies, also voted on the federal list of eighty-one SPD candidates to run for the same number of European Parliament seats allocated to the Federal Republic. (The Christian Democrats and Free Democrats performed the same task.) The SPD hoped to win from thirty-five to forty seats. Brandt was nominated to head the list, but he agreed only on the condition that the names of at least three prominent union leaders were on the ten top slots and that 20 percent of the first forty places on the list be given to women. His wish was granted: DGB President Vetter, Metal Workers Union President Eugen Loderer, and Chemical Workers Union President Karl Hauenschild represented the unions; former minister of health Katherina Focke and former Juso chairwoman Heidemarie Wieczorek-Zeul topped the list of women. [33]

In the months preceding the election of June 10, 1979, the SPD mounted a major, expensive campaign to mobilize its own members in local branches, normally not much interested in European questions, and to convince the West German voters to support its candidates. But the accent was less on program than on candidates. Typical of the politically bland but pictorially colorful campaign was one of the SPD's posters decorated with pictures of the Eiffel tower, the Cologne cathedral, the European Parliament building, and a bouquet of flowers, inscribed "Germans, Say Yes to Europe." (The CDU countered with "Write Freedom Big—the CDU for Europe.") [34]

On election day, held simultaneously throughout the EC countries, the conservative parties fared well. In the Federal Republic, the CDU/CSU won 49.2 percent of the vote and 42 seats; the SPD, 40.8 percent and 35 seats; and the FDP 6 percent and 4 seats. The SPD was disappointed by the results; it had lost nearly 2 percent of the 1976 vote, most of it to the Greens who, in the wake of the Three Mile nuclear accident, received 3.2 percent of the national vote. Socialist candidates throughout the EC area gained 112 seats out of 410 to form the largest bloc—although they had expected more seats. The People's Party (Christian Democrats) received 108 seats; the European Democratic Group, 64; the Communists and allies, 44; the Liberals and Democrats, 40; the European Progressive Group, 22; and other parties 20. [35]

Despite the publicity for the first election of European Parliament members, the locus of EC decision making has remained in Brussels, where West German government leaders have exerted more influence than the SPD on EC Commission and Council decisions affecting member countries. [36] While Schmidt continued to support the principle of European integration, he was often involved in EC budgetary problems that tested his commitment to further enlargement of the organization. The SPD left-wing's vision of a socialist West Europe came no nearer to realization in the 1970s, because the EC concentrated its attention on immediate budgetary, economic, and social problems and because the European socialists were too weak in the EC.

DEFENSE POLICY

Since 1949, few issues have aroused as much passion within the SPD as defense. As noted in chapter 1, the party opposed West German rearmament in the early 1950s because it feared that Germany's reunification would then become impossible. By 1958, SPD defense spokesman Erler and other chiefs approved the establishment of the army (Bundeswehr) to protect the country's security but insisted that there must be strict civilian and parliamentary control. [37] They tried to win over army officers and enlisted men to the SPD cause, but with little success. Surveys showed that a high percent of the Bundeswehr professional personnel voted for other parties, partly because of their resentment against the SPD opposition to emergency legislation, which was based, among other reasons, on its fear of the army's role in a crisis. [38]

During the Grand Coalition period, the CDU/CSU and SPD concurred on the need for full support of the Bundeswehr. In 1969, at an SPD-sponsored defense policy forum and in the programmatic "Social Democratic Perspectives in Transition to the 1970s," the party reaffirmed its commitment to the Bundeswehr, close security ties to the West, and a defensive military buildup. It also called for an end to the arms race and a reduction of arms and troops in the East and West. [39]

Once Brandt became chancellor, he appointed Schmidt as minister of defense. Schmidt had been one of the party's military experts, a member of the Bundestag defense committee, and chairman of the subcommittee on rearmament and procurement. He had written two books on defense, one in 1961 in which he supported the country's remilitarization, and the other in 1969 in which he supported the strategy of flexible response. [40] Schmidt attempted to modernize the army, improve its management, and make it more efficient. He took no action against the politically conservative officers and supported a Bundeswehr study that demanded restrictions on conscientious objectors.

Schmidt's approval of the study galvanized the SPD's left wing, led by Hesse-South, to publicize its opposition to various aspects of defense policy. As early as 1951 it had demanded an initiative to schedule a Land referendum on remilitarization. Having lost that battle, in 1970 and 1973 it introduced party convention resolutions which demanded arms reduction, freezing or reducing the defense budget, a volunteer army rather than compulsory service (or at least a choice between army and nonmilitary service, rather than the existing restrictive conscientious objector alternative), an end to offset payments to the United States for the stationing of American troops on West German territory, and a call for West Germany to distance itself from NATO.

The left had no chance to win approval for most of its resolutions once the SPD high command, led by Brandt, Schmidt and Wehner, opened a counterattack. The troika maintained that NATO was an instrument not only of collective defense but of détente and arms control and that the U.S. military presence in the Federal Republic was necessary to maintain a balance between East and West. [41] Yet when half the delegates at the 1973 convention supported the resolution to freeze defense expenditures, the party leaders had to pass it on to the Fraktion for its consideration. Minister of Defense Leber (who had succeeded Schmidt in 1972) convinced the Fraktion, however, to support the government defense budget of 26.5 billion DM as the minimum cost to maintain the nation's security. In the June 1973 Bundestag vote, nine left-wing SPD deputies abstained because they wanted the defense budget reduced, with the savings to be used for education and social improvements.

In 1976, when the Jusos, who disliked Minister Leber's right-wing politics, stopped his constituency renomination for the Bundestag, party leaders put him on the Hesse Land list. The Jusos also tried to prevent his reelection to the party presidium. Knowing that he was in difficulty, he did not seek reelection; indeed, without Brandt's assistance he would have had difficulty being elected to the party executive. In an interview with Der Spiegel, Leber admitted that he had had his share of troubles with the party, although it allowed him to do his job as minister. The SPD did not identify itself much with defense policy and its successes, he maintained.

For instance, in the Orientation Framework for 1985 there was hardly any mention of defense policies. Yet, he contended, because the SPD's foreign policies had reduced international tensions, which could have led to military confrontations, the nation's security had increased. [42]

In 1976, Leber's troubles mounted. The party's left accused him of having been too lenient in the past about permitting Nazi veterans' organizations to hold reunions and to contact young Bundeswehr officers. It cited the case of two generals who had defended the presence of a former Nazi top pilot at a veterans rally. (He had said that there were former communists holding seats in the Bundestag—implicitly including Wehner.) As a result, Leber dismissd the generals, but with great reluctance. He gave the impression that he took the action only because of pressure from the party's left wing. [43]

Despite Leber's problems with the party, his unswerving support for a strong defense posture undercut the Christian Democrats' argument that the SPD, plagued by Juso objections to the defense policy, was unreliable on this issue. True, the Jusos remained lukewarm toward the army and continued to call for long-range cuts in defense expenditures, withdrawal of foreign troops from German soil, and the disbanding of military blocs in Europe. Yet they also realized that the Bundeswehr was not going to be disbanded and that they should become active in it rather than leave political recruitment to the Christian Democrats. In 1974, the Jusos urged their members in the Bundeswehr to discuss socialist goals with their fellow soldiers and officers. They urged the creation of a soldiers' parliament and the appointment of more ombudsmen with power to settle disputes. Schmidt considered the latter proposals not relevant enough to be presented to the cabinet. [44] But Leber, after meeting with the Jusos in 1976, agreed that soldiers should share more in the decision-making process in the Bundeswehr.

In July 1977, a major controversy erupted in Western Europe when President Carter urged the U.S. Congress to vote funds for the development of neutron bombs, which would be deployed in Western Europe, including the Federal Republic. The first SPD reaction to the news came from Egon Bahr, then party secretary, who wrote in Vorwärts that the bomb was a symbol of perverted thinking in which the machine rather than the human being was to be preserved in an emergency. He opposed the construction of the bomb as did the Jusos, who maintained that it would lower the nuclear threshold. [45]

Chancellor Schmidt, contradicting Bahr, noted that the bomb was no more terrible a weapon than earlier ones. Yet he announced that he would remain uncommitted, that the United States would have to make a preliminary decision on the bomb, and that NATO would eventually have to hold extensive discussions on its deployment. In the Bundestag, Leber favored a study of whether the weapon was a worthwhile addition to deterrent strategy.

At the November party convention, the left wing urged the delegates to vote for a ban on the bomb's deployment in the Federal Republic. Although unsuccessful, the proposal received enough support from delegates to convince the party chiefs to draft a compromise resolution: "The federal government is invited, within the framework of its security and disarmament policy, to create the political and strategic prerequisites so that a stationing of the neutron weapon upon the territory of the Federal Republic will not be necessary." [46] The party leaders, including Bahr by then, wanted to avoid giving a negative answer, in order to provide another option for the government—to use the threat of production as a negotiating counter in disarmament talks between the Soviet Union and the United States.

CDU chief Kohl accused Schmidt of not clearly stating his pro-bomb position for fear of a left-wing reaction within his own party. Kohl contended that Schmidt's hesitancy was an important factor in Carter's sudden decision in April 1978 to indefinitely postpone production of the bomb. Kohl's statements were made to take advantage of Schmidt's embarrassing position in a year in which four important Länder elections were taking place. The Chancellor could not afford to be tagged as too conciliatory toward the Soviet Union, but for internal SPD reasons, he also could not afford to state that he had communicated to Carter his basic agreement to deploy the weapon on West German territory. Carter's reversal came as a shock to Schmidt, who had gone out on a limb to support the President when he initially made the announcement. [47]

In 1977 and 1978 a number of SPD leaders, including Wehner, were critical of the slow pace of the Vienna negotiations on "mutual balanced force reductions" (MBFR) in Central Europe. Brandt suggested that the Federal Republic seriously consider the Soviet proposal to set a ceiling on the size of the West German army, but Schmidt was noncommittal—another instance of the two SPD leaders' discord on a defense matter. Alfons Pawelczyk, the SPD Fraktion disarmament expert, said that the West should respond to other Soviet proposals at Vienna, but once again Schmidt disagreed on the timing.

In addition, Wehner and other SPD chiefs criticized the cautiousness with which Genscher and the Foreign Ministry handled the theme of arms control and urged them to galvanize NATO into action. Koschnick renewed an earlier SPD demand for the creation of a disarmament office to be attached to the Chancellor's Office. But the proposal had no chance in the face of Genscher's opposition to losing authority over the arms control issue to an office dominated by Schmidt. [48]

Protests from the Jusos and left-wing deputies had occasional success. In May 1977, they convinced the Foreign Ministry to withdraw the credentials of the Chilean military attaché in Bonn, who had been accused of responsibility for the earlier torture of political opponents in Chile. But on the matter of arms exports to Third World countries, they had less immediate success. SPD dissident deputies in the Bundestag queried the government in 1977 on why two West German submarines had been delivered to Indonesia in February and why on November 30 the cabinet had agreed to let Argentina receive one submarine to be built in the Federal Republic, when the cabinet had promised in 1971 not to send arms to Third World countries. An SPD Fraktion group on weapons exports called the November 1977 cabinet decision a "political scandal." The government responded that the building of a submarine would create jobs in the economically depressed shipbuilding industry and in a structurally weak coastal area. [49]

The Fraktion group was not convinced by the government's argument. When it heard in early 1978 that the government had agreed to deliver four naval boats to Iran, it drafted a resolution on March 14 demanding that the government abide by the agreement that arms sales be made to NATO partners only and that parliamentary committees be notified of any exceptions. It also insisted that any new defense contracts not lead to an enlarged defense capacity and that a yearly report on arms control be issued. The resolution had an effect on the Chancellor, who authorized

State Minister Wischnewski to keep the Fraktion informed about weapons exports. [50]

From 1979 on, the SPD was sharply divided on whether it should support the U.S. and NATO plan to deploy in Western Europe, including the Federal Republic, intermediate-range nuclear missiles (Pershing 2 and cruise missiles) intended to counter the build-up of Soviet SS-20 missiles aimed at Western Europe. In January 1979, Wehner, Bahr, Ehmke, and Pawelczyk opposed the Western plan, which at that time called for a missile build-up first and then talks with Moscow for arms control. They contended that their government had neglected to cultivate ties with the East and was not sufficiently interested in détente. Wehner also argued that new American missiles should not be deployed on West German territory and again criticized Genscher for not accelerating the Vienna MBFR talks. [51]

Wehner was worried that the NATO plan would lead to escalation in the arms race and deeper mistrust between the two blocs that could only damage détente and the legitimacy of the Bonn coalition. He was also worried that an arms race would shatter any hope for a confederation or economic unity with the German Democratic Republic. [52] He viewed the Soviet arms build-up as defensive rather than offensive, an opinion shared by the Jusos, who noted that the U.S. plan would disequilibrate the military power relationship in Europe and stop progress on the SALT II arms control negotiations.

Chancellor Schmidt and Defense Minister Apel, disagreeing with Wehner, cautiously supported the U.S. decision. Schmidt was worried about the growing Soviet arsenal of SS-20 missiles but expressed his concern about American missiles being stationed on West German soil and possibly not in other NATO countries. He admitted that the West's rearmament as a prerequisite for disarmament had not been successful in the past. From the CSU came the sharpest criticism of Wehner, who was accused of being a "security risk" for the West. Even though most SPD presidium members disagreed with Wehner's position, they defended him against the CSU accusation. [53]

In May 1979, the SPD sponsored a conference on security policy in Bremen. Top SPD and government leaders tried to paper over their differences but were not always successful. Wehner, backtracking from his earlier position, expressed concern over the level and offensive nature of Soviet armaments and concurred with Schmidt and Apel that the West must not disarm unilaterally in the hope that the Soviet Union would follow suit. But he stated again that the Soviet Union had no aggressive design to invade Western Europe, and that the major powers must proceed more swiftly toward disarmament. Koschnick, concurring in part with Wehner, also contended that nearly any weapons system was offensive and defensive, that détente could not be achieved by forcing the opponent into a weakened position, and that the Soviet Union had historical reasons to feel threatened by the West. [54] Schmidt, this time more conciliatory, supported the concepts of a military balance of power and a defense policy within the European context.

In September, the party executive accepted a security policy resolution drafted by a committee of specialists, to be submitted to the December convention. The resolution underlined the importance of arms control measures but urged that an option be kept open to rearm if talks with the Soviet Union were to fail. Designed to reconcile the SPD factions, it also called on the government to seize the initiative in the MBFR talks on parity in conventional weapons. In addition, the SPD lobbied in Washington, where its Fraktion expert on foreign policy, Peter Corterier, appeared at a Senate hearing on SALT II. He urged its ratification, partly because progress at the MBFR talks depended on its approval. [55]

The SPD left was dissatisfied with the party executive resolution and with the pending "double" NATO decision to station 572 missiles in Western Europe by 1983 unless arms limitation talks were successful by then. At the December 1979 convention in Berlin, left-wing speakers reiterated their mistrust of NATO, their worry about a new spiral in rearmament, and their opposition to deployment of new weapons. Schmidt once again took a hawkish line, not ready to make any concessions to the opposition. After reminding the delegates how often he had been the spokesman for arms limitation and détente at East-West conferences, he insisted that the West must have a bargaining counter in the form of the NATO decision when negotiations with the Soviets began. He warned delegates that if the defense resolution did not pass, the government might resign. [56]

His threat to resign convinced a number of left delegates to vote (but reluctantly) for the resolution. About 20 percent of the delegates remained opposed, even though Wehner and Brandt had also swung over to support Schmidt. Brandt assured delegates before the vote that the founders of Ostpolitik would not become its destroyers. The delegates, regardless of their vote, were uneasy about a possible loss of détente and their party's tarnished disarmament image.

Despite passage of the resolution, intraparty discords surfaced again over defense matters in 1980 and thereafter. The critics were reluctant to let the Federal Republic become too close an ally of the United States in order not to jeopardize détente with the East. At a Juso congress in June 1980, Schröder voiced his mistrust of a U.S.-dominated NATO and criticized Genscher's "vassal loyalty" to the United States. On the other hand, Brandt defended NATO as an element of European stability, although he considered the Juso critique "serious and important." Schmidt contended that the Jusos could not be taken seriously as discussion partners for security matters when they assailed those responsible for the country's defense. [57] Apel, at an earlier party executive meeting, had warned the left to refrain from criticizing the United States in order not to give the Christian Democrats an opportunity to talk in the election campaign about a "Moscow faction" within the SPD. [58]

While the Jusos remained highly critical of the NATO double decision and condemned the Bundeswehr for maintaining its militaristic recruiting pledge (which led in June to violent confrontations between demonstrators and police in Bremen), the more moderate SPD faction began to hedge about the NATO decision. Karsten Voigt, who became the Fraktion's foreign policy spokesman, contended in late 1980 that if the U.S. Senate did not ratify SALT II, the NATO decision should be reconsidered. He argued that negotiations with the Soviets must have "absolute priority" over the missile deployment and that the West must maintain a balance of power rather than military dominance. [59]

After 1980 Juso criticism of the NATO decision gathered more support within the party and among many pacifist and church groups. The peace movement supporters worried about the spiraling arms race on both sides and the danger that West Germany would become a pawn in a superpower confrontation. They feared that stationing more nuclear weapons in Western Europe could increase the risk of limited nuclear war. In October 1981, the largest demonstration in the history of the Federal Republic took place in Bonn to protest the government's backing of the 1979 decision. The Jusos and about one-fourth of the SPD Bundestag deputies supported the demonstration, at which Erhard Eppler, among other speakers, attacked Schmidt's decision.

Later on, Schmidt, in an attempt to stem the tide within the SPD against the missile decision, warned his party opponents that he would resign as chancellor if the party did not back him on the nuclear issue at the 1982 convention. He received such backing by about 2 to 1, but the party decided to review the issue, including a possible moratorium, at a 1983 special convention.

RELATIONS WITH THE THIRD WORLD

The Brandt and Schmidt administrations were sympathetic to Third World countries' aspirations to statehood and requests for economic assistance, but cold war considerations were usually more important. For instance, the Vietnam war had repercussions in West Germany. In the early 1970s, Chancellor Brandt—unlike Palme in Sweden—remained officially noncommittal because he did not want to lose the American government's friendship if he condemned its involvement in the war. Nevertheless, at the 1970, 1971, and 1973 SPD conventions, Hesse-South delegates and others, representing 10 to 20 percent of those in attendance, requested the Brandt government to denounce the American "brutal and imperialist" war of annihilation against the Vietnamese people. At a Frankfurt rally in early 1973, Mayor Arndt condemned the United States' "genocidal" actions. The Jusos were angry that Brandt had not devoted a single sentence in his official New Year's speech to an attack on President Nixon's Christmas bombing of North Vietnam. They demanded that the Federal Republic recognize the North Vietnamese government, stop all aid to the South Vietnamese government, and encourage immediate troop withdrawals. [60]

In January 1973, top party organs, in response to the left criticism, called on the Vietnamese combatants to forget a military solution and seek a political solution. SPD spokesmen welcomed the resumption of talks between the United States and North Vietnam. Yet deputies in the Fraktion still demanded an explanation from Brandt for his earlier silence. He contended that West German interests were paramount but backed Minister Schmidt's remarks (which probably would not have been made without Juso pressure) that the Germans found the war "deeply disturbing" and that if it was not ended soon, Europe might become more alienated from the United States.

Despite Schmidt's mild criticism of U.S. policy, made incidentally on a visit to the United States, the Jusos remained critical of Brandt's equivocal attitude and the SPD presidium warning that they should not burden the search for peace "with actions that benefit no one." [61] A number of SPD leaders welcomed the Juso criticisms but did not dare say so publicly. Although the Jusos maintained their position after 1973, they were not able to convince the West German government to take a more activist position on the Vietnam issue.

The Jusos were also hostile to West German business links with authoritarian and fascist governments in Latin America and South Africa. In such areas, the Jusos insisted, the West German government must support the liberation movements battling the entrenched elite, rather than the German business search for a favorable investment climate. In 1973, the Jusos denounced the bloody terror perpetrated by the Chilean military dictatorship and demanded that the German government take the initiative to halt World Bank credits, impose international sanctions against the Chilean junta, and not recognize it diplomatically. [62] But their demands were not heeded by the government, even though its sympathies lay with opponents of the junta regime.

A similar gap between party and government developed over South Africa. For instance, the 1979 SPD convention passed a resolution welcoming the executive's recognition of the liberation movement as the sole representative of the people and criticizing the German government's failure to back the movement. The delegates knew that the government was reluctant to take a position contrary to the South African regime because of West Germany's dependence on South African raw materials and its desire for trade. In July 1978, on a visit to Nigeria and Zambia, Schmidt bluntly said: "The Federal Republic has no intention of stopping trade with South Africa or starting military aid to . . . black nationalist guerilla movements." [63]

On the same visit to Zambia Schmidt met with Rhodesian Joshua Nkomo, then coleader of the Patriotic Front guerilla movement battling Ian Smith's government. After the meeting, held to show the German government's disapproval of the Smith regime and to pacify the SPD left wing, a German spokesman announced that the Nkomo movement would receive medical and sanitary supplies and refugee aid. Such aid, however, would be administered by the SPD foundation rather than the government. [64]

The Soviet invasion of Afghanistan in 1979 produced another rift between SPD elements and the Schmidt government, which supported (unenthusiastically) President Carter's retaliatory actions, such as the Olympic Game boycott. It did not associate itself with Wehner's statement that one reason for the invasion was fear that the Soviet Moslem population would sympathize with developments in the Islamic world. Nor did the government associate itself with the statements by Voigt and Juso leaders criticizing Carter's retaliatory moves as another danger to détente—although they also denounced the invasion. [65]

Finally, a persistent rift between party and government occurred over the extent of economic aid to be given to Third World countries. In the 1969 government declaration, Chancellor Brandt supported in principle the United Nations program for the second development decade, which called on the industrial nations to give yearly a minimum of 0.7 percent of their gross social product for public development aid and set 1979 as the target date for reaching that level. The West German government did not, however, agree to any date, because it considered 1979 premature. In disagreement, the SPD, at its 1973 and 1975 conventions, requested the government to increase aid in order to decrease the gap between wealthy and poor nations. Party leaders Schlei, Eppler, and Bahr drafted a position paper to be discussed at a September 1977 forum on development aid and at the November 1977 convention. It called for a gradual step-up in aid to 0.7 percent and for a greater orientation toward development policies. But it did not propose how the money would be raised, other than to say that German workers would not lose their jobs. Minister Wischnewski announced at the forum that the government intended to increase development aid by nearly 20 percent, partly by helping to stimulate the purchasing power of Third World countries, which in turn would help German export industries. A 20 percent increase would boost aid from an annual 3.2 billion DM to more than 3.8 billion DM in 1978 and would correspond to the average of other western industrial states.

Wischnewski's arguments were not very convincing to the critics within the party and the cabinet. Bahr insisted that the German contribution was not as high as the average in other western industrial countries and did not correspond to the country's potential. Minister for Economic Cooperation Schlei asserted that German aid amounted to only 0.31 percent of the gross national product. The cabinet had rejected her proposal to provide enough credits to Third World countries to enable them to place orders worth 1 billion DM with German industry. [66]

At the 1979 convention, party organs introduced a number of resolutions criticizing the government's failure to help the poorest countries and its development policy based on narrow economic self-interest. According to the delegates, the Federal Republic should be a model for other industrial countries instead of being condemned at international conferences for its development policies. Despite the resolutions to set a goal of 0.7 percent by the end of the 1980s, and the effort of new Minister for Economic Cooperation Offergeld to continue aid increases by 20 percent a year, Schmidt and Minister of Finance Matthöfer did not concur for fiscal reasons. They averred that a massive transfer of resources would mean an end to the country's welfare growth. In 1980, party organs urged that the target date be set at 1985, to be reached in stages. (That target year was recommended by Brandt's North-South Commission, which also recommended a boost to 1 percent by the end of the century.) The government promised that the target of 0.7 percent would be reached "as soon as possible," but most observers doubted this. [67] The gap between party and government remained as wide as ever on this issue.

CONCLUSION

The SPD played only a limited role in the formulation of foreign policy, which showed remarkable continuity from one administration to the next. True, party initiatives helped shape Ostpolitik, and party specialists were active in the executive branch to provide linkage between party and government. But on the major direction of policy—say, the alliance with the West, support for the Common Market and NATO, reaction to U.S. intervention in Vietnam or the Soviet invasion of Afghanistan, and the level of economic aid to the Third World—the chancellor and the cabinet members were clearly in control. On rare occasions, such as on aspects of defense policy, their freedom of action was constrained by massive opposition within the SPD. Indeed, the Juso and left opposition to the neutron bomb and the missiles played a key role in policy formulation not only within the Federal Republic but in Western Europe as well. It also had an effect on the U.S. response to the growing fear about nuclear rearmament that swept Western Europe in the early 1980s.

The SPD developed transnational links to other socialist parties in the Socialist International and Western European organizations. But the French Socialists, especially, challenged its power and policies. The parties therefore decided to maintain a modus vivendi on such ideological and tactical issues as nationalization and cooperation with communist parties. They realized that a programmatic rapprochement would not occur in the immediate future, given the "north-south" schism between them and the weakness of supranational organizations. If the European Parliament, for instance, had more statutory powers, their case for supranational decision making would be more compelling. Yet they have cooperated on a number of issues and may even occasionally be dreaming of an international socialist order that may some day supplant the present neocapitalist order.

NOTES

1. For surveys of the SPD's foreign policies, primarily before 1969, see Claudia von Braunmühl, Kalter Krieg und friedliche Koexistenz (Frankfurt/Main: Suhrkamp, 1973); Kurt Thomas Schmitz, Deutsche Einheit und Europäische Integration (Bonn: Neue Gesellschaft, 1978); Rudolf Hrbek, Die SPD--Deutschland und Europa (Bonn: Europa-Union, 1972); Abraham Ashkenasi, Reformpartei und Aussenpolitik (Cologne, Opladen: Westdeutscher Verlag, 1968); Reinhold Roth, Parteiensystem und Aussenpolitik (Meisenheim am Glan: Anton Hain, 1973); Gordon D. Drummond, The German Social Democrats in Opposition, 1949-1960: The Case against Rearmament (Norman, Okla.: The University of Oklahoma Press, 1982).

2. Personal interview, SPD Fraktion staff specialist, Bonn, Jan. 15, 1975.

3. Ibid.

4. Vorwärts, Jan. 16, 1975; Süddeutsche Zeitung, Jan. 20, 1975. See also SPD, Internationale Politik, Sozialdemokratische Fachkonferenz, 9./10.4. 1976, Bonn (Bonn, 1976).

5. Lutz-Dieter Behrendt, "Die Führung der westdeutschen Sozialdemokratie und die 'neue' Bonner Ostpolitik," Jahrbuch für Geschichte der sozialistischen Länder Europas, XIII/1 (1969); SPD, Parteitag 1962, p. 584; Parteitag 1964, pp. 943, 946, 949 ff.

6. Vorwärts, July 24, 1963; New York Times, Aug. 4, 1965; SPD, press release, 320/70, Aug. 9, 1970.

7. See Reinhold Roth, Aussenpolitische Innovation und politische Herrschaftssicherung (Meisenheim am Glan: Anton Hain, 1976), pp. 41 ff; Günther Schmid, Entscheidung in Bonn: Die Entstehung der Ost- und Deutschlandpolitik 1969/1970 (Cologne: Wissenschaft und Politik, 1979), pp. 19-22.

8. Ibid., pp. 230-232, 263, 340-342. The Berlin Agreement guaranteed, inter alia, Western access to Western Berlin and permitted the Soviet Union the right to open a consulate in West Berlin. The German Basic Treaty provided for closer diplomatic relations, respect for each other's territorial integrity and sovereignty, enhanced cooperation in such fields as science and transport, and easing of border crossings for West Germans to visit East Germany.

9. Süddeutsche Zeitung, June 1, 1973; June 2/3, 1973.

10. Der Spiegel, July 14, 1975.

11. New York Times, June 8, 1979.

12. For a history of the SI, see Julius Braunthal, History of the International (Vols. I, II, New York: Praeger, 1967; Vol. III, Boulder, Col.: Westview Press, 1981; trans. of Geschichte der Internationale (Hannover: Dietz, 1961, 1963, 1971); Karl-Ludwig Günsche and Klaus Lantermann, Kleine Geschichte der Sozialistischen Internationale (Bonn-Bad Godesberg: Neue Gesellschaft, 1977).

13. Ibid., p. 144.

14. *New York Times*, Nov. 27, 1976.

15. Ibid.; *Süddeutsche Zeitung*, Nov. 29, 1976.

16. *Vorwärts*, June 6, 1974; Jan. 16, 1975. The PSF left wing (CERES) at a PSF colloquium in 1977 spoke of a "Bonn-Washington axis" domination of Europe (*Vorwärts*, Apr. 14, 1977).

17. *New York Times*, Apr. 18, 1976; June 2, 1976; *Der Spiegel*, May 31, 1976. See also Gerhard Kiersch, "Konflikt, Kooperation and strukturelle Dominanz: Frankreichs Sozialisten und die SPD," *Eurosozialismus: Die demokratische Alternative*, eds. Gerhard Kiersch and Reimund Seidelmann (Cologne: Europäische Verlagsanstalt, 1979), pp. 132-144.

18. *New York Times*, May 25, 1975.

19. *Christian Science Monitor*, Apr. 18, 1979.

20. *New York Times*, May 25, 1975.

21. Ibid., Jan. 20, 1976; *Vorwärts*, Jan. 22, 1976.

22. *Stuttgarter Zeitung*, Apr. 17, 1976; *Die Zeit*, Apr. 23, 1976.

23. *New York Times*, Aug. 29, 1975.

24. William E. Paterson, "Social Democratic Parties of the European Community," *Journal of Common Market Studies*, XIII, No. 4 (June 1975), 416-417.

25. Ibid., p. 180 ff; Norbert Gresch, "Der Bund Sozialdemokratischer Parteien in der EG," *Eurosozialismus*, eds. Kiersch and Seidelmann, pp. 126-130.

26. *Der Spiegel*, Sept. 27, 1976; June 13, 1977; SPD, *Sozialdemokraten Service, Presse, Funk, TV*, No. 276/77, June 10, 1977.

27. Guntram von Schenck, "Die sozialdemokratischen Parteien der EG vor den Direktwahlen," *Aus Politik und Zeitgeschichte*, Beilage, *Das Parlament*, B 14/79, Apr. 7, 1979, pp. 29-30. For text of declaration, see SPD, *Politik*, No. 5, July 1978.

28. Ibid., pp. 30-31. For text of manifesto, see SPD, *Politik*, No. 2, Jan. 1979. See also Juso-Argumente, Problem 22, *Jungsozialisten und Europa*, n.d.; *Juso*, 1974/2, pp. 37, 40-41.

29. SPD, Reihe Jugend, Heft 2, j2, *Stellungnahmen des SPD-Parteivorstandes zu den Beschlüssen des Bundeskongresses der Jungsozialisten in Bremen vom 11.-13. Dez. 1970* (Bonn, 1971).

30. For full text, see SPD, executive, Materialen, *Programm der SPD für die erste europäische Direktwahl, Soziale Demokratie für Europa* (1978). See also SPD, *Dokumente zur Europapolitik* (June 1978); *Parteiarbeit: Handbuch für die Arbeit in sozialdemokratischen Ortsvereinen, Europa 79, Daten, Dokumente, Materialen* (June 1978).

31. *Die Zeit*, Dec. 15, 1978.

32. SPD, *Parteitag 1978*, pp. 265-279.

33. Ibid., pp. 45-49.

34. See SPD, executive, *Argumente für Europa, Europa-Informationen* (Bonn, 1979).

35. *New York Times*, June 17, 1979; *Statesman's Year Book 1980-1981* (New York: St. Martin's Press, 1980), p. 47.

36. William E. Paterson, "The German Social Democratic Party, "*Social Democratic Parties in Western Europe*, eds. Paterson and Alastair H. Thomas (London: Croom Helm, 1977), pp. 199-200. For surveys of the SPD and the EC, see Juliet Lodge, *European Policy of the SPD* (Beverly Hills, Calif.: Sage, 1976); Paterson, *The SPD and European Integration* (Westmead: Saxon House, 1974).

37. For SPD views on defense while in opposition, see Udo F. Loewke, *Die SPD und die Wehrfrage, 1949-1955* (Bonn-Bad Godesberg: Neue

Gesellschaft, 1976); Lothar Wilker, Sicherheitspolitik der SPD, 1956-1966 (Bonn-Bad Godesberg: Neue Gesellschaft, 1977); SPD, Sozialdemokratie und Bundeswehr (Berlin, Hannover: Dietz, 1957); Joachim Hütter, SPD und nationale Sicherheit: Internationale und innenpolitische Determinanten des Wandels der sozialdemokratischen Sicherheitspolitik, 1959-1961 (Meisenheim am Glan: Anton Hain, 1975).

38. Martin Kempe, SPD und Bundeswehr: Studien zum militärisch-industriellen Komplex (Cologne: Pahl-Rugenstein, 1973), p. 146.

39. SPD, executive, Reihe Sicherheitsfragen, y 1, Grundsätze Sozialdemokratischer Wehrpolitik (Bonn, 1970). See also y 2, Bundeswehr in der Gesellschaft: Wehrpolitische Tagung der SPD am 20./21. Juni 1970 in Bremen zum "Weissbuch 1970" (Bonn, 1970).

40. Helmut Schmidt, Defense or Retaliation: A German View, trans. Edward Thomas (New York: Praeger, 1962); The Balance of Power: Germany's Peace Policy and the Super Powers, trans. Edward Thomas (London: Kimber, 1971).

41. Arend, pp. 97-104.

42. Der Spiegel, Sept. 15, 1975.

43. New York Times, Nov. 10, 1976.

44. Stuttgarter Zeitung, Jan. 18, 1974; June 18, 1975; Juso, 2/1975; Juso Informationsdienst, No. 10/Oct. 1976.

45. Frankfurter Rundschau, July 20, 1977; Vorwärts, July 21, 1977.

46. Die Welt, Nov. 18, 1977.

47. New York Times. Apr. 6, 1978.

48. Ibid., Jan. 20, 1977; Süddeutsche Zeitung, Mar. 25. 1977; July 13, 1978.

49. Vorwärts, Dec. 15, 1977.

50. Ibid., Mar. 23, 1978.

51. Der Spiegel, Jan. 29, 1979; Feb. 12, 1979; Mar. 12, 1979.

52. Vorwärts, Feb. 15, 1979; Hannoversche Allgemeine, Mar. 22, 1979.

53. Frankfurter Allgemeine Zeitung, Feb. 2, 1979; Süddeutsche Zeitung, Feb. 6, 1979; dpa press release, Feb. 6, 1979.

54. Stuttgarter Zeitung, May 21, 1979; Frankfurter Rundschau, May 21, 1979.

55. Frankfurter Allgemeine Zeitung, Sept. 12, 1979. See also SPD, Materialen, Sicherheitspolitik, "Leitantrag des Parteivorstandes für den Parteitag in Berlin beschlossen am 10.9.79."

56. SPD, Parteitag 1979, pp. 253 ff.

57. SPD, Dokumente, "Beschlüsse zur Aussen-, Deutschland-, Friedens- und Sicherheitspolitik, Nord-Süd-Politik;" Politik, No. 15, Dec. 1979; Berliner Morgenpost, Dec. 3, 1979. See also Juso, No. 3/80, pp. 9-10; Juso Schüler-Express, 4/80.

58. Der Spiegel, May 12, 1980.

59. New York Times, Jan. 6, 1981.

60. Arend, pp. 101-102; Süddeutsche Zeitung, Jan. 3, 1973.

61. New York Times, Jan. 16, 1973; Neue Zürcher Zeitung, Jan. 5, 1973; Jan. 19, 1973.

62. Juso Informationsdienst, No. 10, 1973; Süddeutsche Zeitung, Jan. 28, 1974.

63. New York Times, July 6, 1978.

64. Ibid.

65. ppp, XXXI, No. 17, Jan. 24, 1980; Juso Schüler-Express, 2/80; Bonner General-Anzeiger, Apr. 25, 1980.

66. Handelsblatt, Aug. 3, 1977; Stuttgarter Nachrichten, Sept. 3,

1977; Lübecker Nachrichten, Sept. 2, 1977; Die Welt, Sept. 3, 1977. See SPD, Materialen, Entwicklungspolitik: Die soziale Frage des 20. Jahrhunderts; Forum SPD (Aug. 1977).

67. SPD, "Sitzung der Antragskommission I (Oct. 12-14, 1979)" (mimeo.); SPD, Parteitag 1979, p. 353 ff.; Frankfurter Allgemeine Zeitung, Dec. 6, 1979; Vorwärts, June 5, 1980; July 24, 1980.

15
Conclusion

The profile of the SPD changed significantly from 1969 to 1982, a period during which it reached the pinnacle of political power. One central theme of this study is that external factors caused changes in the party's organization, membership, ideology, and voter support as well as in its imprint on the country's domestic and foreign policies. These changes, producing mounting difficulties for the SPD during a period of fluidity in the party system, must be assessed within the broader framework of West European social democratic developments.

A glance back at the period since World War II indicates that the SPD was in the mainstream of the European movement toward more social reform, although late to achieve political power. Social democrats in Western Europe had gained additional legitimacy during the war, when they were well represented in the leadership and cadres of the resistance movement. After the war they gained control of the British government, maintained power in Scandinavia, and shared power in France, Austria, and other small European democracies. At the time, it seemed as if the social democrat-governed countries would become the dominant third force between the American capitalist and Soviet communist powers, but the rise of strong conservative and Christian Democratic parties in Western Europe, among many other factors, soon limited their growth. To overcome the obstacles and bring theory into line with reality, the SPD and other social democratic parties shed their Marxist ideology and widened their electoral base to include not only the working class but also the growing middle class of salaried employees and civil servants.

During the 1960s, social democratic participation in governments increased again. But the governments' difficulties in translating demands into policy dampened the hopes of members who had anticipated the emergence of socialist economies. After the worldwide recession of 1973, social democratic governments were increasingly on the defensive, trying to maintain the modest gains of earlier decades. [1] The electoral defeat of the Swedish Social Democratic Party in 1976, after it had held power since 1932, symbolized the difficulties being encountered by social democratic governments even in their Scandinavian citadel. (Yet in 1982 the Swedish Social Democrats triumphed again when most voters turned against the incumbent conservative government for its poor performance.)

Despite its venerable history, the SPD had to overcome more hurdles to gain governmental power than some of the other West European social democratic parties. Its early neo-Marxist programmatic stance, abandoned only in 1959, alienated potential voters who had not sharply differentiated Soviet communism from western social democracy, who had benefited from the CDU/CSU-inspired "economic miracle," and who had backed Chancellor Adenauer's foreign policy. But the SPD finally rose to power as the major governing party in 1969 when its domestic and foreign policy planks appealed to an increasing number of voters, when Brandt and other SPD ministers received credit for their accomplishments while in office from 1966 to 1969, and when the party was perceived by the voters to be the most effective in solving current problems.

THE SPD PROFILE CHANGES

But to return to one of our central themes, just when the SPD did gain political power—the chief ambition of any political party—its structural base was coincidentally rocked by external factors. A youth rebellion against the establishment caused a shift in the country's political, social, and cultural infrastructure. It had a spillover effect on the parties, but especially the SPD, which was closest ideologically to the left-leaning students spearheading the rebellion. When the SPD proceeded to integrate the young people into its ranks, profound changes took place within the organization that in turn affected its relations with other organizations and the government. In a cyclical pattern, in the late 1970s and early 1980s, the growth of the ecology and antinuclear movements had a similar, although milder, effect on the party's development.

Within the SPD, still the model of a mass party and the focus of political socialization for its members, the leadership was unable in 1969 to heal a strong factionalism. The well-educated Young Socialists were pitted against a less educated working class, with relatively conservative cultural values and politics. When the Jusos increasingly dominated local branches, the workers became more apathetic and withdrew from active participation. Acting as gadflies, the Jusos demanded more intraparty democracy on Rousseau's model, an effort to be welcomed in any organization with democratic goals. They successfully challenged the theory of democratic centralism sometimes practiced by the entrenched oligarchy, which Robert Michels had criticized decades earlier. More recently, Ralph Miliband may have had the Jusos, among others, in mind when he wrote: "If socialist democracy is [the party's] aspiration for tomorrow, so must internal socialist democracy be its rule today." [2]

The Jusos reached their peak strength in the early 1970s but were unable to steer the party into a system-transcendent socialist direction. Despite this major setback they succeeded in making an imprint on a limited number of domestic and foreign policy planks. The Jusos' internal ideological clashes weakened their position vis-à-vis the rest of the party; yet even if they had been more united they would have been able to make little headway against the power of the party's right wing, concentrated especially in the party's middle and upper echelons and its Fraktionen in the legislatures.

As a result of the Juso challenge to the party establishment for more group autonomy, and of their increased power within the party, the Association of Workers was founded to represent the interests of blue- and white-collar workers, to maintain close links with the DGB, and to recruit more unionists into the party. The Association often conflicted with the Jusos over ideological issues and with government policymakers over economic and social issues. The Association of Social Democratic Women, becoming more assertive as a result of the growing feminist movement (another external influence), had its main quarrel with the male party leaders over insufficient female representation in party councils. SPD leaders found it difficult to accede to the claims of these and other organized groups, especially if the claims conflicted with party or government policy, and to simultaneously preserve centralized control and cohesion of the organization.

The leaders' difficulties were compounded by the rapidly changing party membership, mirroring a trend visible in most other social democratic parties and constituting another external factor affecting the party. The party became more "new" middle class, as salaried employees and civil servants joined in great numbers while the percentage of blue-collar workers continued to decline. The party's younger members became interested in such "new politics" issues as participatory democracy, the quality of life, and other postbourgeois (or postmaterialist) values, while its older members retained their "acquisitive" (or materialist) values relating to such "old politics" issues as job security and adequate incomes.

To what extent the new politics group will expand within the SPD is difficult to forecast. Expansion would cease if a major crisis should threaten its economic welfare or if new alternative movements should attract some of its members. [3] When these movements surfaced in the late 1970s, the old politics group was more easily able to dominate the party's policymaking councils. In turn, this development hindered the party's efforts to attract more youth as members and voters. Such youth would join the party if (as C.A.R. Crosland notes, looking at British Labour) the social democrats turned their attention to the spheres of "personal freedom, happiness, and cultural endeavor" once the traditional objectives were gradually fulfilled. [4]

The party's shift in membership, with all the resultant dilemmas, was paralleled by a renaissance of ideology, with equally positive and negative consequences. This renaissance, sparked by the Jusos, must be applauded because it ended the purely pragmatic course followed by the party since 1959. It produced discord on means and goals, a healthy development unless it leads to irreconcilable factional disputes or even to the losing faction leaving the party and forming a new one—unlikely in the SPD, given a new party's need to gain 5 percent of the national vote in order to be represented in the Bundestag.

In the party's ideological debate, the right wing, on the defensive, had to find a theoretical basis to justify its actions. It began a campaign against the neo-Marxist theory propounded by the Jusos and for a renewal of the Godesberg program. The left-center group urged the party to remain on a reformist course within the neocapitalist system that would produce incremental democratization of the political and economic centers of power and an eventual democratic socialist order. To find a measure of agreement among the diverse groups on how to achieve a better society, the party leaders agreed with the demand of the groups for a long-range economic-political framework (OR '85). Despite the monumental task of writing such a comprehensive blueprint for the future, OR '85—and the reports of the party's basic values commission—had little effect on the immediate problems the party and the social-liberal coalition government were facing. Chancellor Schmidt attempted to solve the problems by pursuing a pragmatic, crisis management course of action. His policy was not acceptable to the party ideologues; they urged their party and government to continue making domestic reforms in order to reenergize the party.

While the party from 1969 to 1982 attempted to arrive at a consensus on doctrinal positions, it had to court key target groups for membership and electoral support. But the SPD, like any major governing party, soon discovered that once it was holding power, its public policymakers could not satisfy fully the aspirations of each group—it had to consider broader national interests. Inevitably, this led to clashes between the groups and the government, although the SPD tried strenuously to minimize them.

The repeated electoral victories of the party at the national level showed that both its mobilization of various groups and voter coalition building had paid off, even though after each national election in which it failed to get 50 percent of the vote, it could not have become the senior governing party without the FDP's willingness to join it in a coalition cabinet. The SPD won elections because of its campaign strategies, relative voter satisfaction with the performance of the government and its chancellor, and the inability of the CDU/CSU (remaining the strongest party except for 1972) to win back the FDP and resume their former coalition until 1982. At the Länder level, the SPD fared quite well during the 1969-1982 period when measured against the normal increase in protest votes directed at the governing parties during national election intervals. However, at the local level, the SPD's strength declined precipitously in a number of cities because of intraparty feuds, financial scandals, and other factors, causing grave concern among the party's policymakers.

The party's electoral fortunes and misfortunes were evidence that Otto Kirchheimer's prediction of the 1960s that the SPD and other West European parties were becoming nonideological catch-all parties had not yet materialized entirely—at least for the SPD. The trend was in that direction, but the party, despite its more heterogeneous membership and voting composition, still failed to receive adequate support from a number of important groups—churchgoers, upper-income salaried employees and civil servants, farmers, professional soldiers, and others. Thus those social scientists who espouse "the end of ideology," "the politics of consensus," and "the politics of postindustrialism" themes, in which they speak of rising economic affluence eroding class distinctions, are not quite accurate if they include the West German party system in their model—as they normally do. The neo-Marxist prediction that the middle class will become radicalized also has not yet become a reality, although there are tendencies in both radical and conservative directions. [5] Rather, in the case of the SPD, its capture of a sizable liberal segment of the new middle class has shown a narrowing but not the elimination of class differences.

One result has been to weaken the voters' attachment to and identification with political parties. Consequently the SPD must attract the floating voters, who are just as likely to cast their ballots for another party, because their votes often spell the difference between victory and defeat. However, unlike France, Italy, and other countries where the left bloc is fragmented, in the Federal Republic the SPD need not worry about the sizable loss of votes to any left splinter party, although it had cause to worry about the growing Green and alternative movements at the end of the 1970s. These movements were able to draw a considerable number of voters away from the SPD, thereby producing political instability and new alignments at the Länder level—with similar possibilities at the national level.

SPD IMPRINT ON POLICIES

Despite such problems, the SPD's capacity to win elections and govern the nation was demonstrated repeatedly from 1969 until its fall in 1982. But questions have to be asked relating to the second major theme of this study: what use did the SPD make of its power and did it leave an imprint on the country's development? To ask such questions is to raise the broader question whether parties matter in the formulation of domestic and foreign policies. As noted earlier, scholars have been unable to agree about whether policy output, especially in social welfare, is dependent on the ideological coloration of a government.

The basis for an eventual consensus might be a European Consortium of Political Research Project "Party Differences and Public Policy," which surveyed twenty-one advanced industrial democracies. It concluded in 1981 that social democratic parties in power tried to introduce a greater measure of social welfare and income equalization into capitalist systems than did bourgeois governments, especially in periods of economic prosperity. Moreover, social democratic governments, such as Sweden's (until 1976), Norway's, and Austria's (since 1970), increased the state's involvement in economic affairs appreciably more than bourgeois governments, such as in the United States, Japan, and Switzerland. However, when policy was at stake that affected the ownership of private enterprises and the distribution of private capital, or the police and the military, the differences among governments disappeared, except for the few instances in which social democrats governed alone (or with communists, as in France since 1981). Similarly, on macroeconomic questions—inflation, price control, unemployment rate—which party was in power mattered less than the strength of employers and unions, the amount of class conflict, and the power distribution between left and right voting blocs. [6]

This definitive study must be supplemented with a careful review of the differences between social democratic parties in power. Then it can be shown that policy outputs will reflect historical, cultural, and structural differences as well as the constraints of the national political, economic, and social environment. When the accomplishments of the Social Democrats while in power in, say, Sweden and the Federal Republic are compared, the differences in setting become crucial. In Sweden, for decades the Social Democrats were able to gain more than 40 percent of the vote, to which must be added a smaller Communist vote to bring the combined total over 50 percent. Thus the Swedish Social Democrats had less difficulty in translating their program of making significant social changes into practice than the SPD, whose leaders were more conservative in their approach to social change and more worried about maintaining a coalition with the Free Democrats.

Whether policy changes in the Federal Republic were made or not depended, of course, on a number of other factors: structural constraints, such as the CDU/CSU-dominated upper house and the Constitutional Court; historical and cultural constraints, such as a bias toward conservatism and against radical experiments among many SPD members and voters; financial constraints during periods of recession; and political constraints, such as the timidity of the SPD governing elite, especially after 1973, to embark on social experiments that might endanger stability or security. These factors explain why the SPD leaders were reluctant, for example, to increase the income tax for wealthy persons and to make abortion reforms that would alienate Catholic voters, but not reluctant to issue a decree against radicals in public employment. Although they made a number of significant reforms in many areas of domestic policy, they had to contend with other structural constraints such as an entrenched bureaucracy, an industrial elite, and competing parties unsympathetic to major changes. Hence, the extent of SPD input into government decisions varied considerably. Because the inputs were system-sustaining, the SPD could not claim to have appreciably moved the country in a socialist direction during the years of its governance.

In foreign policy, the record of the SPD was equally mixed. It had an effect on the grand design of Ostpolitik, but relatively little on government policy toward the European Community, defense, and relations with the Third World. Because of its limited influence on domestic and foreign policies, in the late 1970s and 1980s SPD leaders and members became increasingly dissatisfied with Schmidt's implicit position that the party should primarily be the intermediary between the public and the government. They insisted that, on the contrary, the party must act as a beacon to the government by formulating long-range programmatic goals to which the government should pay more attention.

The party's frequent frustration by its own cabinet ministers, in spite of its repeated assertions that it be counted as a principal political actor in the decision-making process, is another indication that its role was limited. On the other hand, because it had at least a minimum effect on most legislation stemming from the executive branch and supported by the Fraktion, we conclude that German parties do matter, even if in a minor way, in shaping the grand design of government policy.

A party's limited share in policymaking does not contradict the thesis that established parties are on the decline in Western democracies or that they are facing a crisis of legitimacy. In 1979, Suzanne Berger, for instance, argued: "Among the institutional failures of the past decade, those of political parties stand out as critical." [7] She maintained that parties were unable to absorb the rising political mobilization of a segment of the population in the late sixties and seventies and to make major reforms that would be acceptable to all groups. Furthermore, left parties were unable to link their "transformative vision to contemporary social conflicts and to define alternative strategies and outcomes." As a result, new political movements emerged with antiparty and antistate values. [8]

Scholars studying neocorporatist movements contended that the party systems and parliaments no longer function as effective instruments for fulfilling democratic aspirations, partly because governments are overburdened with unfulfillable demands. The parties are too weak to integrate their members, screen demands, and propose realistic alternatives. A convergence of their programs means that parties compete for the same groups and offer little choice to the voters. As a result, economic interest groups become the principal political actors. [9]

Claus Offe wrote that in countries with coalition governments, parties no longer made programmatic policy decisions as they once did. Intraparty deliberations and consensus building had been replaced by interparty negotiations, hence, decisions were made at the coalition government level (or at the party faction level) because of the catch-all parties' inability to aggregate policy options stemming from their heterogeneous base. [10]

These authors concurred in the thesis that parties had stopped performing their traditional functions as vigorously as even a decade earlier. There was a decline in the parties' links between the rulers and the ruled; in their ability to serve as an emotional base for members, to aggregate interests, and to structure political attitudes; and in their intention when in government to set policy. This development reflected a crisis of legitimacy and questioning of values among an increasing number of people.

Are these views of a decline or crises of parties applicable to the West German party system and more specifically, to the SPD? The answer is yes if applied to the period 1969 to 1982, but with qualifications. First, let us look at the affirmative side. Factional disputes weakened the SPD's electoral appeal. Dissidents in the Fraktion, breaking party discipline, voted against government bills. Strains between the SPD and the DGB increased the longer the party was in office and continued to make concessions to the FDP on workers' demands. International financial crises and a national recession contributed to the virtual abandonment of reforms and a specific social democratic profile. The SPD—and FDP—found it difficult to cope with tough economic problems.

In addition, a case can be made that the West German parties, despite political rhetoric to the contrary, have increasingly concurred on basic matters of political substance. Hence, as Peter Katzenstein notes, there was "an increase in the irresponsibility and irrelevance of partisan politics in the Federal Republic. The transformation of the West German party system to a bloc system in the 1970s has made intrabloc politics (within the SPD-FDP government and [within] the CDU-CSU opposition) more important to the process of policy initiation than inter-party competition (between SPD-FDP and CDU-CSU)." [11]

The cyclical rise of protest movements—many, antiestablishment—adds substance to the argument that the German parties experience periodic crises because they are unable or unwilling to provide a conduit for single-issue claims made upon them. In the 1950s, a protest movement, in part supported by the SPD, questioned rearmament and nuclear weapons; in the 1960s, an extraparliamentary opposition and a rising student movement questioned emergency legislation and the Grand Coalition; and in the 1970s, citizens' initiatives, the Greens, and alternative groups, which represented a "new politics" rather than a left-right dimension, emerged as a potent political force. [12] Although earlier protest movements rose and fell, those of the 1970s were strong enough to last into the 1980s and cause instability in the country's two-and-a-half-party system.

On the other hand, the end of the present West German party system is not in sight. The SPD, despite its internal crises and loss of power in 1982, retains its mammoth organization and most of its membership. It will continue to play an important role on the political stage, present policy alternatives while in opposition, and contribute to the legitimacy of the system. The party has gone through earlier crises and surfaced again. Not only the SPD but the other parties still perform such essential functions as interest aggregation, mobilization of voters, leadership selection, participation in governments, and articulation of policy. Although some of the neocorporatist forces—the government bureaucrats and interest group leaders—wield a good deal of power, the parties have not abandoned the political arena to them. The German party system is in a process of flux but is not doomed to obscurity.

THE END OF THE SPD IN POWER

The premature end in September 1982 of the SPD-FDP coalition, breaking up over economic, fiscal, and social policy differences, exemplified West Germany's unstable political condition. Though the SPD knew since the 1980 election that its tenure as a governing party was threatened, the end made it aware that no party can claim a monopoly of power in a democratic system. Relegated once again to the opposition, the party has had to examine the underlying causes of its loss of power and discuss strategy for an electoral comeback.

What were these causes, many dating back to at least 1980 and many reflecting similar difficulties encountered by other social democratic parties in advanced industrial states? An assessment might illuminate problems that have transcended national boundaries and have produced governmental crises elsewhere. One cause has been popular dissatisfaction about economic problems that makes the "ins" in government, especially if they have been in power for a long time, vulnerable to the "outs." Regardless of whether left or right governments are in power, they are not immune to popular pressures for a change—as seen in the almost simultaneous downfall of the West German social-liberal and Danish Social Democratic governments and the Swedish Social Democrats' assumption of power in 1982. For the SPD, the difficulties in governing had already increased after the 1980 election. At that time, the new Schmidt government was facing the same serious economic crises confronting other advanced industrial states—persistent high unemployment, low economic growth, and sectoral and structural weaknesses in industry as well as budgetary difficulties with the social security and health systems, resistance to nuclear energy and defense policies, and worry about the future of détente between East and West. Such an overload of difficult problems heaped on the SPD-led government made it even harder for the SPD to think about the long-range future and increased the frustration and "civic sulkiness" (Staatsverdrossenheit) among many of its leaders and members.

The party's inability to attract enough voters in Länder elections from 1980 to 1982 contributed to its problems. As noted earlier, voters in a number of Länder turned away from the strife-torn party, blaming it for failing to solve problems ranging from unemployment to environmental pollution. Instead, many people abstained, voted for the CDU/CSU, or voted for the Green/alternative parties which capitalized on the dissatisfaction within SPD ranks about the government's controversial positions on nuclear energy and NATO missile modernization.

At the time, Chancellor Schmidt contended that the government must not change its course just because a minority in his party did not concur with it. He knew that most of the trade unions and the Fraktion would maintain their support of his policies, partly because the alternative would be the coming to power of the CDU/CSU. Brandt, on the other hand, strenuously attempted to integrate the warring factions within the SPD and to instill perspective and hope among the members. He made repeated efforts to regain the support of youth, which made up much of the burgeoning ecology and peace movements. But he encountered resistance among conservative SPD leaders (as reflected in a position paper written by Richard Löwenthal) who were afraid that a new influx of youth would radicalize the party, which in turn would lead to further electoral losses. They pointed to the rapidly waning strength of the SPD in major cities, where many workers, normally pro-SPD, were turning away from the party. Brandt, not denying the political difficulties, insisted that if the party relied only on the support of workers, it would be doomed once more to a 33 percent vote. It needed also the backing of youth if it was to maintain a minimum of 40 percent voting strength. [13] Needless to say, Brandt's argument became more compelling when the SPD was ousted in 1982—the party cannot afford to alienate any major voting group if it expects to regain power.

Another cause for the downfall was the strained relationship between Chancellor Schmidt and the party dating back many years. His government statement of November 1980, in which he made no promises for the future but merely outlined in somber terms the immediate tasks ahead, had not been the kind of message to pacify the restless groups in the SPD seeking to rekindle a vision of change and social commitment. Afraid that the party was losing its main purpose, the groups had again insisted that it be one programmatic step ahead of the government. Such a proposal was not realizable as long as the Chancellor kept making costly concessions to the FDP in the cabinet. The groups noted that the protracted wrangle between the coalition partners over the 1982 and 1983 budgets meant that the SPD had had to scrap a proposed supplementary tax to help create more jobs in return for an FDP concession not to cut social programs. But as a result of other SPD concessions to the FDP, the SPD groups felt that the SPD was no longer governing with the FDP but was being governed by it. Even though the Chancellor strenuously denied that charge, the groups remained uneasy until the coalition's end about the program of the government, in which the social democratic reform component kept vanishing and in which concessions to the business leaders (with whom Schmidt was on good terms) were being made. [14] Contributing to the problem was the cabinet's signs of fatigue and listlessness, which prevented the adoption of a more dynamic policy, despite Schmidt's appointment to the cabinet of young SPD leaders whose sympathies lay with a technocratic, problem-solving approach within the neocapitalist system. Perhaps feeling uncomfortable being tagged defenders of such a system, the Schmidt team contended that given the existing circumstances there was no other course to be pursued, while at the same time it professed commitment to the tenets of social democracy.

Critics within the SPD were more doubtful about a technocratic approach to political problems; they preferred the party to embark on low-cost reforms which would give it the reputation of being concerned with the citizens' welfare rather than being just another party receiving and sorting out claims on the state. [15] They admitted that reforms can fail if they are deficient in conceptions; have structural political weaknesses (such as not fitting into one ministry or being stymied by bureaucratic immobilism); are subject to financial constraints; have not sparked the people's consciousness because of fear of change, apathy, or fatalism; are challenged by powerful reform opponents whose prerogatives would be endangered; or run counter to the country's international obligations. But none of these obstacles are insurmountable—they can be solved on an evolutionary path, especially if the party receives support for its reform programs from a broad coalition of "structural" conservatives (who are concerned with the decay of cities and of the landscape), liberals, practicing Christians, and women's groups. Such a coalition is especially important in a period when the political right takes advantage of the limited economic growth to mount a campaign of antireformism and law and order and seeks to dismantle the democratic edifice. The critics called on Social Democratic policymakers to push for a new, less bureaucratic and costly but more effective social policy and a new economic order in which central planning is complemented by greater public ownership and income redistribution (even within the working class). [16] The critics, worried that the SPD program hardly differed from that of the CDU/CSU, would have agreed with Otto Kirchheimer, who wrote in 1966: "Major interparty differences lose their raison d'être when overriding technological, international, and military problems are not debated among the parties." [17] To the discomfort of the critics tactical questions had become more important to SPD leaders than long-range ideological goals.

A final cause of the SPD's end as a governing party was the CDU/CSU's strategy for the 1980s of presenting itself to the voters as a politically moderate party that could be trusted to effectively govern the nation once again. Deemphasizing its own conservatism, the CDU/CSU pledged not to dismantle the welfare system or to weaken the rights of trade unions. In attacking the SPD, it contended that the SPD was sliding toward the left (as evident in OR '85 and the European Parliament electoral program), was wracked by internal struggles, and lacked any orientation toward solving the problems of the 1980s. [18] Even though up to 1982 the CDU/CSU failed to present clear alternatives to the SPD-FDP government program and lacked a leader whose popularity matched Schmidt's, in October 1982 it triumphally returned to power in a new coalition with the FDP, because it was still the largest party in the Bundestag. This transfer of power reinforced the thesis that the Federal Republic has a stable turnover system, in which the major parties are bound to gain and lose power as they contend for the support of the voters at the political center. With the CDU/CSU in power again, it is unlikely that there will be a significant shift in policies, other than the rhetoric about the need to preserve the free enterprise system and the family. To be sure, the party will make limited cuts in the welfare system, allow business more freedoms, and emphasize cultural conservatism, but such a shift will not be radical. In short, the major parties will continue the trend toward consensus politics, with only some—although important—differences separating them.

FUTURE AGENDA

In opposition once again, the SPD leaders will have to confront the aspirations of new voters and the disillusionment among a growing segment of the population with all political parties. Most of the leaders agree that the program for the 1980s must not be restricted to the theme of economic security—of concern especially to the disadvantaged lower-income groups, which still suffer from monotonous work, poor old-age protection, low educational levels, unsatisfactory living conditions, and insufficient health care. The program must also encompass the "postmaterial" or "new politics" themes of concern to the young generation and the new middle class: self-realization, political participation, decentralization, social justice, and an improved quality of life.

In short, the party, according to most of its leaders, must mesh the needs of its diverse subcultures and develop a long-range agenda that would set sights beyond the immediate future. When the SPD regains governmental power, this agenda may include the resumption of domestic reforms—providing for full employment and codetermination, humanizing the work setting, alleviating the energy crisis and environmental problems, improving housing, seeking more equality for women, improving the pension system, lowering subsidies for farmers and civil servants, defending civil liberties, and integrating foreign workers and their families into the political and social life of the nation. The foreign policy agenda probably will emphasize maintenance of peace, arms control and disarmament, détente between East and West, new political and economic relationships between North and South, and restructuring of the international monetary system.

After the 1980 election, SPD leaders set up six commissions to study some of these agenda items and come up with recommendations. They began to hold regular meetings with Jusos and scheduled periodic "future forums" where controversial problems were discussed with political opponents and the public. They also urged party organs to consider increasing the number of labor representatives and works councillors in subdistrict councils, to simplify the structures of the constituent associations, to change the selection procedures for major public office holders, and to set up a historical commission which would publish local and regional party histories.

The agenda for the future and possible structural changes indicate that party leaders have given thought to new directions for the SPD, but the malaise among Jusos, the Association of Social Democratic Women, and intellectuals has not been overcome. These groups, especially, feel that the agenda has not set enough imaginative sights to provide benchmarks for the next two decades and that the failure of OR '85 to be seriously considered by the SPD leaders while in the government was symptomatic of their pragmatic, nondoctrinaire approach. Whether the potential top leaders (Hans-Jochen Vogel and Johannes Rau, Minister-President of North-Rhine Westphalia, among others) who will succeed Schmidt, Brandt, and Wehner will be able to set new goals remains problematic because they have been identified too much with the party's old policies. Missing among most leaders is intellectual vitality—partly the result of having been in power for so long. [19]

Even the Jusos have lost their intellectual élan, not least because they were unable to move the SPD in a socialist direction. They have retained the vision of a millenium but realize that it will not be achieved in their lifetime, when ideologies are near exhaustion. In their program, they remain committed to more economic planning, income redistribution, and social controls of industry (including the multinationals), an end to the privileges of the upper strata, the democratization of society, and renewed emphasis on the basic values of freedom, equality, and justice. [20] Most SPD leaders do not disagree with these goals but give them lower priority. The discord between the two camps also continues to center on the leaders' preference for making only cosmetic changes in the capitalist system to restrict its excesses and the Jusos' preference for transcending it.

As Ralph Miliband notes in writing about West European countries ruled by social democratic coalitions:

> Social-democratic ministers have generally been able to achieve little inside these hybrid (coalition government) formations. Far from presenting a threat to the established order, their main function has been to contain their own parties and to persuade them to accept the

essentially conservative policies which they themselves have sanctioned. For the most part, participation on this basis has been a trap not a springboard. [21]

Michael Harrington comes to the same conclusion when he writes that the Godesberg program of the SPD put an unprecedented emphasis on the virtues of the free market. He contends that social democrats in many countries have opted for "socialist capitalism":

> In redeeming their pledges of social property, the socialists unwittingly turned out to be among the best doctors that capitalism could find. They modernized, rationalized and helped plan capitalist economies. In the process they succeeded in their immediate goal of providing an infinitely more decent and humane life for the great mass of people. But public property seemed destined either to subsidize, or to imitate, private property, and that was not what socialists had intended at all. For socialist capitalism was, and is, a variant of capitalism: more human and infinitely preferable to the sweatshop version of the system but capitalism nevertheless. [22]

Certainly, as Frank Parkin has argued, the SPD and other social democratic and socialist parties are still committed to the material and social improvement of the lower-income groups, to improvements in the welfare system, and to greater educational opportunities for children of working-class families. Yet these moderate reforms are carried out only within the framework of the existing system, partly for fear that radical reforms would alienate the politically middle bloc of voters and cause the business community to sabotage them. [23]

Since the SPD lost political power in Bonn in 1982, much soul searching will need to take place over the direction the party should take. As Francis Castles notes (in discussing social democratic parties in general): ". . . to pursue their social reform aims requires a radical rethinking of the policy options open to a democratic socialist party in the latter decades of the twentieth century." [24] But can a radical rethinking be expected of most SPD leaders who make policy within the organization? Bernard Brown, surveying the Eurosocialist scene and not the SPD specifically, has doubts:

> It is possible that the task is beyond the power of the left to accomplish, or that novelty is not required. It may well be that the left can do no more, in democratic polities, than provide a somewhat more humane administration of capitalism or the market economy than can the center or the right. In effect, that has been the historic mission of social democracy. [25]

Clearly, the malaise among many SPD members and leaders about the direction of policy indicates that more is needed than a humane administration of capitalism. For a role model they look to the Scandinavian countries, where the Social Democrats have pioneered in major social welfare reforms designed to produce a more egalitarian society, and to France, where Mitterrand's left government embarked in 1981 on major domestic reforms, such as more nationalization of industry and banking, an increase in the minimum wage, and structural reforms.

For the SPD, which rejects further nationalization at present, the direction for rejuvenation in its new opposition role could lie rather in an espousal of more political and economic decentralization; income redistribution; egalitarianism; participatory democracy; and, as Alan Wolfe in a survey of capitalism and socialism puts it, "democratic dreams" and pressures from below "to prevent the capitalist state from serving as a mechanism of accumulation pure and simple." [26] This means that the SPD should move leftward if it expects to gain more of the crucial youth vote, that it should formulate not only Keynesian but socialist solutions to the current economic crisis, and that it should abandon a moderate posture that hardly differs from that of its archrival, the CDU/CSU. Only then can this tradition-laden yet resilient party move to the cutting edge of the international socialist movement, where other social democratic parties already have embarked on some audacious economic and social experiments.

NOTES

1. William E. Paterson and Alastair H. Thomas, "Introduction," Social Democratic Parties in Western Europe, eds. Paterson and Thomas (London: Croom Helm, 1977), pp. 13-16.
2. Ralph Miliband, The State in Capitalist Society (London: Wiedenfeld and Nicolson, 1969), p. 275.
3. John Clayton Thomas, The Decline of Ideology in Western Political Parties: A Study of Changing Policy Orientations (London: Sage, 1975), pp. 48-49; Inglehart, "Post-Materialism in an Environment of Insecurity," pp. 880-881. James D. Wright, on the other hand, calculates that the postmaterialist majority "will arrive in West Germany sometime around the year 2015" ("The Political Consciousness of Post-Industrialism," p. 272).
4. C.A.R. Crosland, The Future of Socialism (New York: Schocken, 1963), p. 353.
5. Kirchheimer, "The Transformation of the Western European Party Systems," pp. 181-195, 198-200. James D. Wright and Daniel Holub, "Social Cleavage and Party Affiliation Revisited: A Comparison of West Germany and the United States," Sociology and Social Research, LXIII, No. 4 (July 1979), 671-697; Feist et al., "Structural Assimilation Versus Ideological Polarisation," p. 175.
6. See Manfred G. Schmidt, "Politische Parteien und staatliche Politik in 21 bürgerlichen Demokratien—Ein internationaler Vergleich," Politische Vierteljahresschrift, XXII, No. 4 (Dec. 1981), 440-442; Francis G. Castles, ed., The Impact of Parties: Politics and Policies in Democratic Capitalist States (Beverly Hills, Calif.: Sage, 1982).
7. Berger, "Politics and Antipolitics," p. 27.
8. Ibid., p. 30.
9. E.g., Pizzorno, pp. 253, 268-272.
10. Claus Offe, "The Attribution of Public Status to Interest Groups: Observations on the West German Case," Organizing Interests in Western Europe, ed. Berger, p. 142.
11. Peter J. Katzenstein, "West Germany in the 1980s: Problem or Model?" World Politics, XXXII, No. 4 (July 1980), 589.
12. Ibid.; Max Kaase and Samuel H. Barnes, "In Conclusion: The Future of Political Protest in Western Democracies," Political Action: Mass Participation in Five Western Democracies, eds. Barnes and Kaase et al.

(Beverly Hills, Calif.: Sage, 1979), pp. 523-534; Wilhelm P. Bürklin, "Die Grünen und die 'Neue Politik,' Abschied vom Dreiparteiensystem?" Politische Vierteljahresschrift, XXII, No. 4 (1981), 359-382; Hermann Scheer, Parteien kontra Bürger?: Die Zukunft der Parteiendemokratie (Munich: Piper, 1979); Joachim Raschke, ed., Bürger und Parteien: Ansichten und Analysen einer schwierigen Beziehung (Opladen: Westdeutscher Verlag, 1982).

13. Richard Löwenthal, "Identität und Zukunft der SPD," Neue Gesellschaft, XXVIII, No. 12 (Dec. 1981), 1085-1089; replies by primarily left-center leaders in Neue Gesellschaft, XXIX, No. 1 (Jan. 1982), 4-5, 21-31. See also Stuttgarter Zeitung, June 29, 1981; Frankfurter Allgemeine Zeitung, June 4, 1981; Dec. 5, 1981.

14. Alan Wolfe, "Has Social Democracy a Future?," Comparative Politics, XI, No. 1 (Oct. 1978), 100-125.

15. Kirchheimer, "Germany: The Vanishing Opposition," pp. 253-257.

16. See, e.g., Johano Strasser, Die Zukunft der Demokratie: Grenzen des Wachstums—Grenzen der Freiheit? (Reinbek: Rowohlt, 1977).

17. Kirchheimer, "Germany: The Vanishing Opposition," p. 248.

18. CDU-Bundesgeschäftsstelle, Argumente 80, Machterhalt statt Politik: Die Konfliktlinien in der SPD/FDP Koalition (Bonn, Oct. 1979); Handbuch für die innenpolitische Argumentation (Bonn, Feb. 1980).

19. Norman Birnbaum, "Showdown Time for Schmidt," The Nation, June 20, 1981; Martin Greiffenhagen, "Aussichten der Parteien: Die SPD," Vorwärts, Dec. 11, 1980. In March 1983, Wehner did not seek reelection to the Bundestag; thus giving up his long-held post as Fraktion chairman.

20. Strasser, Die Zukunft der Demokratie, passim.

21. Miliband, p. 98. For views by European and U.S. socialist leaders, see Nancy Lieber, ed., Eurosocialism and America: Political Economy For the 1980s (Philadelphia: Temple University Press, 1982).

22. Michael Harrington, Socialism (New York: Bantam Books, 1973), p. 248.

23. Parkin, pp. 104 ff. See also M. Donald Hancock, "Productivity, Welfare and Participation in Sweden and West Germany: A Comparison of Social Democratic Reform Prospects," Comparative Politics, XI, No. 1 (Oct. 1978), 4-23.

24. Castles, p. 8.

25. Brown, p. 396.

26. Alan Wolfe, The Limits of Legitimacy: Political Contradictions of Contemporary Capitalism (New York: Free Press, 1977), p. 341.

Bibliography

GOVERNMENT PUBLICATIONS

Deutscher Bundesrat. 30 Jahre Bundesrat, 1949-1979. Bonn, 1979.

Deutscher Bundestag. 30 Jahre Deutscher Bundestag: Dokumentation, Statistik, Daten. Bonn, 1979.

----. Verhandlungen des Deutschen Bundestages. Stenographische Berichte. Band 134. Bonn, 1969 and ff.

Inter Nationes. "The Federal Republic of Germany elects the German Bundestag on 5 October 1980: Procedures, Programmes, Profiles." Bonn, 1980.

Presse- und Informationsamt. Bulletin.

----. Gesellschaftliche Daten, 1979.

Statistisches Bundesamt. Statistisches Jahrbuch für die Bundesrepublik Deutschland, 1970. Stuttgart: W. Kohlhammer, 1970 (and later eds.).

SOCIAL DEMOCRATIC PARTY PUBLICATIONS

ASF—das sind wir Frauen in der SPD. Bonn, n.d.

Argumente

Die Aufgabe der Partei. Bonn-Bad Godesberg: Neue Gesellschaft, 1974.

Auslandsbrief

Basic Programme of the SPD. Bonn, n.d. (1959).

"Befragung Junger Sozialdemokraten: Ergebnisse einer Erhebung bei SPD Mitgliedern unter 35 Jahren, Juni 1970" (hectographed)

Bestandsaufnahme 1966: Eine Dokumentation. Bonn, 1967.

Bundestagsfraktion. 147 mal Soll und Haben: Zwischenergebnisse sozialdemokratischer Politik in der Grossen Koalition. Bad Godesberg, 1968.

----. Soll und Haben: Bilanz sozialdemokratischer Bundespolitik in Regierung und Parlament von 1966 bis 1969. Bonn, 1969.

Bundestagswahlkampf 1969: Ein Bericht der SPD. Bonn: Neuer Vorwärts, 1970.

Bundestagswahlkampf 1972: Ein Bericht der SPD. Bonn-Bad Godesberg: Vorwärts-Druck, 1973.

Dokumente

Frau und Gesellschaft

Informationsdienst: intern, intern-dokumente

Jahrbuch der SPD. Bonn, various dates.

Jusos. Bundeskongressbeschlüsse: Jungsozialisten in der SPD, 1969-1976. Bonn-Bad Godesberg, 1978.

----. Handbuch für die Jungsozialistenarbeit. Bonn, 1971.

----. Informationsdienst

----. JS-magazin

----. Juso

----. Organisations Leitfaden. Bonn, n.d.

----. Problem 8, Langzeitprogramm. Bonn, c. 1972.

----. "Rechenschaftsbericht des Bezirksvorstandes der Jungsozialisten in der SPD, Bezirk Niederrhein. Zeitraum: April 1978 bis Mai 1979" (hectographed).

----. Richtlinien der Jungsozialisten. Bonn, 1975.

Materialen zum Parteitag vom 28.11 bis 2.12.1972, Hannover. Entworf eines ökonomisch-politischen Orientierungsrahmen für die Jahre 1973-1985. Bonn, 1972.

Mitbestimmung. Sozialdemokratische Fachkonferenz. Bonn, 1976.

Neue Gesellschaft

Organisationsstatut, Wahlordnung, Schiedsordnung der SPD. Dec. 18, 1971 (rev. Apr. 12, 1973; Nov. 15, 1975; Dec. 10, 1978; Dec. 7, 1979). Bonn, various years.

Orientierungsrahmen '85. Die Anträge zum Parteitag 1973—Synoptischer Überblick. Bonn, n.d.

Parteiarbeit

Parteitag der SPD: Protokoll der Verhandlungen. Bonn, various years.

ppp (news service)

Pressemitteilungen und Informationen

Politik: Aktuelle Informationen der SPD

Reihe Jugend

Reihe Parteien

Reihe Theorie und Grundwerte

Selbständige in der SPD. Geschäftsbericht für die Jahre 1978-1980. Bonn, n.d.

Service. Presse, Funk, TV

Sicherheit für Deutschland: Wahlprogramm 1980. Cologne: Deutz, 1980.

Sozialdemokratie und Bundeswehr. Berlin, Hannover: Dietz, 1957.

"Sozialdemokratie und Protestantismus. Christen in der Tradition der Arbeiterbewegung—Christen in der SPD (1830-1979)" (hectographed).

Sozialdemokratische Perspektiven im Übergang zu den siebziger Jahren. Bonn, 1968.

Sozialdemokrat Magazin

"Vorlage für die gemeinsame Sitzung von Parteirat, Parteivorstand und Kontrollkommission am 22./23. Juni 1979 in Bonn, Bundeshaus" (Junker-Scherf report) (hectographed).

BOOKS AND ARTICLES

Abendroth, Wolfgang. Aufstieg und Krise der deutschen Sozialdemokratie. Frankfurt: Stimme, 1964.

Ackermann, Paul. "Die Jugendorganisationen der politischen Parteien," Demokratisches System und politische Praxis der Bundesrepublik, eds. Gerhard Lehmbruch, Klaus von Beyme, and Iring Fetscher. Munich: Piper, 1971.

Adolph, Hans J. L. Otto Wels und die Politik der deutschen Sozialdemokratie, 1894-1933: Eine politische Biographie. Berlin: de Gruyter, 1971.

Anderson, Evelyn. Hammer or Anvil: The Story of the German Working-Class Movement. London: Gollancz, 1945.

Apel, Hans. "Die Willensbildung in den Bundestagsfraktionen--Die Rolle der Arbeitsgruppen und Arbeitskreise," Zeitschrift für Parlamentsfragen, I, No. 2 (1969-1970), 223-229.

Arend, Peter. Die innerparteiliche Entwicklung der SPD, 1966-1975. Bonn: Eichholz, 1975.

Ashkenasi, Abraham. Reformpartei und Aussenpolitik: Die Aussenpolitik der SPD, Berlin-Bonn. Cologne, Opladen: Westdeutscher Verlag, 1968.

Bahr, Egon, ed. SPD--Porträt einer Partei. Munich: Günter Olzog, 1980.

Baker, Kendall L., Russell J. Dalton, and Kai Hildebrandt. Germany Transformed: Political Culture and the New Politics. Cambridge: Harvard University Press, 1981.

Baring, Arnulf. Machtwechsel: Die Ära Brandt-Scheel. Stuttgart: Deutsche Verlags-Anstalt, 1982.

Bayertz, Kurt. "Der Popper-Boom in der SPD oder die theoretische Offensive des Reformismus," Blätter für deutsche und internationale Politik, No. 3 (1976), pp. 278-289.

Bebel, August. Die Frau und der Sozialismus. Zurich: Volksbuchhandlung, 1879 (and later eds.).

Behrendt, Lutz-Dieter. "Die Führung der westdeutschen Sozialdemokratie und die 'neue' Bonner Ostpolitik," Jahrbuch für Geschichte der sozialistischen Länder Europas. XIII/1 (1969). Berlin: VEB Deutscher Verlag der Wissenschaften, 1969.

Beinert, Heinz, et al. Zwischen Anpassung und politischen Kampf: Zur Geschichte der organisierten Arbeiterjugendbewegung in Deutschland, 1904-1974. Bonn-Bad Godesberg: Vorwärts-Druck, 1974.

Bell, Daniel. The End of Ideology. New York: Free Press, 1960.

Belloni, Frank P., and Dennis C. Beller, eds. Faction Politics: Political Parties and Factionalism in Comparative Politics. Santa Barbara, Calif.: ABC-Clio, 1978.

Berger, Manfred, et al. "Bundestagswahl 1976: Politik und Sozialstruktur," Zeitschrift für Parlamentsfragen, VIII, No. 2 (Aug. 1977), 197-231.

Berger, Suzanne, ed. Organizing Interests in Western Europe: Pluralism, Corporatism, and the Transformation of Politics. Cambridge, England: Cambridge University Press, 1981.

----. "Politics and Antipolitics in Western Europe in the Seventies," Daedalus, CVIII, No. 1 (Winter 1979), 27-50.

Berlau, A. Joseph. The German Social Democratic Party, 1914-1921. New York: Columbia University Press, 1949.

Bermbach, Udo. "Stationen der Regierungsbildung 1969," Zeitschrift für Parlamentsfragen, I, No. 1 (June 1970), 5-23.

----. "Stationen der Regierungs- und Oppositionsbildung 1976," Zeitschrift für Parlamentsfragen, VIII, No. 2 (Aug. 1977), 159-182.

Bernstein, Eduard. Evolutionary Socialism. New York: Huebsch, 1909.

Beyme, Klaus von. Die politische Elite in der Bundesrepublik Deutschland. Munich: Piper, 1971.

----. "Do parties matter? Der Einfluss der Parteien auf politische Entscheidungen," Politische Vierteljahresschrifft, XXII, N. 4 (1981), 343-358.

----. "Regierungswechsel 1969: Zum Wandel der Karrieremuster der politischen Führung," Demokratisches System und politische Praxis der

Bundesrepublik, eds. Gerhard Lehmbruch, Klaus von Beyme, and Iring Fetscher. Munich: Piper, 1971.
----. "The Changing Relations between Trade Unions and the Social Democratic Party in West Germany," Government and Opposition, XIII, No. 4 (1978), 399-415.
Bilstein, Helmut, et al. Organisierter Kommunismus in der Bundesrepublik Deutschland. Opladen: Leske and Budrich, 1975.
Binder, David. The Other German: Willy Brandt's Life and Times. Washington, D.C.: New Republic Book Co., 1975.
Blondel, Jean. Political Parties: A Genuine Case for Discontent. London: Wildwood House, 1978.
Böhm, Walter. "Gewerkschafter im Deutschen Bundestag," Zeitschrift für Parlamentsfragen, V, No. 1 (Mar. 1974), 17-23.
Böhret, Carl, et al., eds. Transfer 2: Wahlforschung Sonden im politischen Markt. Cologne, Opladen: Westdeutscher Verlag, 1976.
Börnsen, Gert. Innerparteiliche Opposition (Jungsozialisten und SPD). Hamburg: Runge, 1969.
Brandt, Hugo, ed. Hoffen, zweifeln, abstimmen. Seit 1969 im Bundestag. Reinbek: rororo, 1980.
Brandt, Willy. My Road to Berlin. Garden City, N.Y.: Doubleday, 1960.
----. People and Politics: The Years 1960-1975. Boston: Little, Brown, 1978.
Brauer, Angela. "Zu den Bedingungen von Reformpolitik am Beispiel Berufsbildungsreform," Unfähig zur Reform? Eine Bilanz der inneren Reformen seit 1969, eds. Christian Fenner, Ulrich Heyder, and Johano Strasser. Cologne: Europäische Verlagsanstalt, 1978.
Braunmühl, Claudia von. Kalter Krieg und friedliche Koexistenz. Frankfurt: Suhrkamp, 1973.
Brauns, Hans Jochen, et al. Die SPD in der Krise: Die deutsche Sozialdemokratie seit 1945. Frankfurt/Main: Fischer, 1976.
Braunthal, Gerard. "Codetermination in West Germany," Cases in Comparative Politics, eds. James B. Christoph and Bernard E. Brown. Boston: Little, Brown, 1976.
----. "Emergency Legislation in the Federal Republic of Germany," Festschrift für Karl Loewenstein, eds. Henry Steele Commager, et al. Tuebingen: J.C.B. Mohr, 1971.
----. "The 1976 West German Election Campaign," Polity, X, No. 2 (Winter 1977), 147-167.
----. "The Policy Function of the German Social Democratic Party," Comparative Politics, XIX, No. 2 (Jan. 1977), 127-145.
----. Socialist Labor and Politics in Weimar Germany: The General Federation of German Trade Unions. Hamden, Conn.: Archon Books, 1978.
----. "Willy Brandt: Politician and Statesman," Governments and Leaders: An Approach to Comparative Politics, eds. Edward Feit. Boston: Houghton Mifflin, 1978.
Braunthal, Julius. History of the International. 3 vols. Vols. I, II: New York: Praeger, 1967; Vol. III: Boulder, Colo.: Westview Press, 1980.
Breitman, Richard. German Socialism and Weimar Democracy. Chapel Hill: University of North Carolina Press, 1981.
Bretschneider, Michael. "Mitgliederzahlen der Parteien und ihre raumliche Verteilung 1977." Deutsches Institut für Urbanistik, n.d. (c. 1978) (hectographed).
Brown, Bernard E., ed. Eurocommunism and Eurosocialism: The Left

Confronts Modernity. New York: Cyrco Press, 1979.

Browne, Eric C., and John Dreijmanis, eds. Government Coalitions in Western Democracies. New York: Longman, 1982.

Bürklin, Wilhelm P. "Die Grünen und die 'Neue Politik,' Abschied vom Dreiparteiensystem?" Politische Vierteljahresschrift, XXII, No. 4 (1981), 359-382.

Bunce, Valerie. Do New Leaders Make a Difference? Executive Succession and Public Policy under Capitalism and Socialism. Princeton: Princeton University Press, 1981.

Burkett, Tony. "Developments in the West German Bundestag in the 1970s," Parliamentary Affairs, XXXIV, No. 3 (Summer 1981), 291-307.

Buschfort, Hermann, Heinz Ruhnau, and Hans-Jochen Vogel, eds. Godesberg und die Gegenwart: Ein Beitrag zur innerparteilichen Diskussion über Inhalte und Methoden sozialdemokratischer Politik. Bonn: Neue Gesellschaft, 1975.

Butterwegge, Christoph. "Der Bernstein Boom in der SPD," Blätter für deutsche und internationale Politik, XXIII, No. 5 (May 1978), 579-592.

----. Juso und SPD. Hamburg: Runge, 1975.

----. Parteiordnungsverfahren in der SPD. Berlin: Demokratische Verlags-Kooperative, 1975.

Cameron, David R. "The Expansion of the Public Economy: A Comparative Analysis," American Political Science Review, LXII, No. 4 (Dec. 1978), 1243-1261.

Canaris, Ute. "Orientierungsrahmen und Frauenfrage," Neue Gesellschaft, XXII, No. 11 (Nov. 1975), 888-891.

Castles, Francis G., ed. The Impact of Parties: Politics and Policies in Democratic Capitalist States. Beverly Hills, Calif.: Sage, 1982.

----. The Social Democratic Image of Society: A Study of the Achievements and Origins of Scandinavian Social Democracy in Comparative Perspective. London: Routledge and Kegan Paul, 1978.

Cerny, Karl H., ed. Germany at the Polls: The Bundestag Election of 1976. Washington, D.C.: American Enterprise Institute for Public Policy Research, 1978.

Chalmers, Douglas A. The Social Democratic Party of Germany: From Working-Class Movement to Modern Political Party. New Haven: Yale University Press, 1964.

Childs, David. From Schumacher to Brandt: The Story of German Socialism, 1945-1965. Oxford: Pergamon Press, 1966.

Coates, David. Labour in Power? A Study of the Labour Government, 1974-1979. London: Longman, 1980.

Cohen, James H. "Political Candidate Nominations: A Comparative Study of the Law of Primaries and German Party Nominating Procedures," Jahrbuch des öffentlichen Rechts der Gegenwart, XVIII (1969), 491-538.

Conradt, David P. The German Polity. New York: Longman, 1978 (2d ed., 1982).

----. "The 1976 Campaign and Election: An Overview," Germany at the Polls: The Bundestag Election of 1976, ed. by Karl H. Cerny. Washington, D.C.: American Enterprise Institute for Public Policy Research, 1978.

----. The West German Party System: An Ecological Analysis of Social Structure and Voting Behavior, 1961-1969. Beverly Hills, Calif.: Sage, 1972.

----, and Dwight Lambert. "Party System, Social Structure, and

Competitive Politics in West Germany," Comparative Politics, VII, No. 1 (Oct. 1974), 61-86.

----, and Ferdinand F. Mueller. "West Germany's Social Democrats since 1969: Factions, Policies, and Electoral Development." Paper read at the annual meeting of the American Political Science Association, Chicago, 1976.

Crosland, C.A.R. The Future of Socialism. New York: Schocken Books, 1963.

Culver, Lowell W. "Land Elections in West German Politics," Western Political Quarterly, XIX, No. 2 (June 1966), 304-336.

Daalder, Hans. "Parties, Elites and Political Developments in Western Europe," Political Parties and Political Development, eds. Joseph LaPalombara and Myron Weiner. Princeton, N.J.: Princeton University Press, 1966.

Deppe, Rainer, Richard Herding, and Dietrich Hoss. Sozialdemokratie und Klassenkonflikte. Frankfurt: Campus, 1978.

Dexheimer, Wolfgang F. Koalitionsverhandlungen in Bonn, 1961-1965-1969: Zur Willensbildung in Parteien und Fraktionen. Bonn: Eichholz, 1973.

Diederich, Nils. "Zur Mitgliederstruktur von CDU and SPD," Parteiensystem in der Legitimationskrise, eds. Jürgen Dittberner and Rolf Ebbighausen. Cologne, Opladen: Westdeutscher Verlag, 1973.

Dittberner, Jürgen. "Die Bundesparteitage der Christlich-Demokratischen Union und der Sozialdemokratischen Partei Deutschlands von 1946 bis 1968: Eine Untersuchung der Funktionen von Parteitagen." Unpublished Ph.D. dissertation, Free University, Berlin, 1969.

----. "The Role of the Party Congress in the Inner Party Process of Policy Making," German Political Studies, Vol. I, 1974, ed. Klaus von Beyme. London: Sage Publications, 1974.

----, and Rolf Ebbighausen, eds. Parteiensystem in der Legitimationskrise: Studien und Materialen zur Soziologie der Parteien in der Bundesrepublik Deutschland. Cologne, Opladen: Westdeutscher Verlag, 1973.

Döring, Herbert, and Gordon Smith, eds. Party Government and Political Culture in Western Germany. London: Macmillan, 1982.

Dohnanyi, Klaus von. "Beispiele aus der Bundespolitik," Was sind der SPD die Selbständigen wert?, ed. Wolfgang Roth. Bonn: Neuer Vorwärts-Verlag, 1979.

Dolive, Linda. Electoral Politics at the Local Level in the German Federal Republic. Gainesville: The University Presses of Florida, 1976.

Downs, Anthony. An Economic Theory of Democracy. New York: Harper, 1957.

Drath, Viola Herms. Willy Brandt: Prisoner of His Past. Radnor, Penn.: Chilton Book Co., 1975.

Drummond, Gordon D. The German Social Democrats in Opposition, 1949-1960: The Case against Rearmament. Norman, Okla.: The University of Oklahoma Press, 1982.

Duverger, Maurice. Political Parties: Their Organization and Activity in the Modern State. Rev. 2d ed. New York: John Wiley, 1959.

Dyson, Kenneth H. F. "The Ambiguous Politics of Western Germany: Politicization in a 'State' Society," European Journal of Political Research, VII, No. 4 (1979), 375-396.

----. Party, State and Bureaucracy in Western Germany. Beverly Hills, Calif.: Sage, 1977.

----. "The Politics of Economic Management in West Germany," West

European Politics, IV, No. 2 (May 1981), 35-55.

Easton, David. A Systems Analysis of Political Life. Chicago: University of Chicago Press, 1979.

Eckhard, Jesse. "Die Bundestagswahlen von 1953 bis 1972: Im Spiegel der repräsentativen Wahlstatistik. Zur Bedeutung eines Schlüsselinstruments der Wahlforschung," Zeitschrift für Parlamentsfragen, VI, No. 3 (1975), 310-322.

Edinger, Lewis J. German Exile Politics and the Social Democratic Executive Committee in the Nazi Era. Berkeley: University of California Press, 1956.

——. Kurt Schumacher: A Study in Personality and Political Behavior. Stanford: Stanford University Press, 1965.

——. "Political Change in Germany: The Federal Republic after the 1969 Election," European Political Processes: Essays and Readings. Boston: Allyn and Bacon, 1974.

——, and Paul Luebke, Jr. "Grass-Roots Electoral Politics in the German Federal Republic: Five Constituencies in the 1969 Election," Comparative Politics, III, No. 4 (July 1971), 463-498.

Ehmke, Horst. "Demokratischer Sozialismus und demokratischer Staat," Beiträge zur Theoriediskussion, ed. Georg Lührs. Vol. II. Berlin, Bonn-Bad Godesberg, 1974.

——. "Perspektiven der 80er Jahre," Was sind der SPD die Selbständigen wert? ed. Wolfgang Roth. Bonn: Neuer Vorwärts-Verlag, 1979.

——, ed. Perspektiven—Sozialdemokratische Politik im Übergang zu den siebziger Jahren, erläutert von 21 Sozialdemokraten. Reinbek: rororo, 1969.

Eichler, Willi. Zur Einführung in den demokratischen Sozialismus. Bonn-Bad Godesberg: Neue Gesellschaft, 1972.

Eldersveld, Samuel J. Political Parties: A Behavioral Analysis. Chicago: Rand McNally, 1964.

Eppler, Erhard. Ende oder Wende? Von der Machbarkeit des Notwendigen. Stuttgart: Kohlhammer, 1975.

——. "Politik nach der Zäsur," Mitte-Links: Energie, Umwelt, ed. Harry Ristock. Bonn-Bad Godesberg: Neue Gesellschaft, 1977.

Erler, Hans. Fritz Erler contra Willy Brandt. Stuttgart: Seewald, 1976.

Evans, Richard J. "Liberalism and Society: The Feminist Movement and Social Change," Society and Politics in Wilhelmine Germany, ed. Richard J. Evans. London: Croom Helm, 1978.

Fabritius, Georg. "Sind Landtagswahlen Bundesteilwahlen?" Aus Politik und Zeitgeschichte, Beilage zu Das Parlament, B 21/79, May 26, 1979.

Farthmann, Friedhelm. "Gewerkschafter und Parlamentarier: Loyalitätskonflikt unvermeidbar?" Gewerkschaftliche Monatshefte, XXV, No. 4 (Apr. 1974), 248-249.

Feist, Ursula. "Unterwegs zur politischen Identität: die Jungwähler," Transfer 2: Wahlforschung Sonden im politischen Markt, eds. Carl Böhret, et al. Cologne, Opladen: Westdeutscher Verlag, 1976.

——, Manfred Güllner, and Klaus Liepelt. "Structural Assimilation Versus Ideological Polarisation: On Changing Profiles of Political Parties in West Germany," Elections and Parties, eds. Max Kaase and Klaus von Beyme. London, Beverly Hills, Calif.: Sage, 1978.

——, and Klaus Liepelt. "Stärkung and Gefährdung der sozial-liberalen Koalition: Das Ergebnis der Bundestagswahl vom 5. Oktober 1980," Zeitschrift für Parlamentsfragen, XII, No. 1 (Apr. 1981), 34-58.

——, and Klaus Liepelt. "Vom Mehrparteien- zum Zweiblocksystem:

Veränderungen in der Wähler- und Sozialstruktur der Bundesrepublik Deutschland," Revue d'Allemagne, IX, No. 2 (April-June 1977), 207-219.

Fenner, Christian. Demokratischer Sozialismus und Sozialdemokratie: Realität und Rhetorik der Sozialismusdiskussion in Deutschland. Frankfurt/Main, New York: Campus, 1977.

-----. "Das Parteiensystem seit 1969—Normalisierung und Polarisierung," Parteiensystem der Bundesrepublik, ed. Dietrich Staritz. Opladen: Leske and Budrich, 1976.

-----, Ulrich Heyder, and Johano Strasser, eds. Unfähig zur Reform? Eine Bilanz der inneren Reformen seit 1969. Cologne: Europäische Verlagsanstalt, 1978.

-----, et al. (Arbeitsteam der HDS). Zur Einführung in die Theorie des Demokratischen Sozialismus. Frankfurt/Main and Cologne: Europäische Verlagsanstalt, 1977.

Flechtheim, Ossip K. Innerparteiliche Auseinandersetzungen. Part II, Vol. VII. Dokumente zur parteipolitischen Entwicklung in Deutschland seit 1945. Berlin: Dokumenten-Verlag Wendler, 1969.

Fliedner, Ortlieb. "Probleme der Organisation und Arbeitsweise von Fraktionen (I), (II), (III)," VOP (Verwaltungsführung Organisation Personalwesen), 3/1979, pp. 144-149; 4/1979, pp. 228-233; 5/1979, pp. 295-298.

Forschungsgruppe Wahlen. "Politik in der Bundesrepublik vor und nach der Bundestagswahl 1972" (hectographed, Dec. 1972).

Freudenhammer, Alfred. Herbert Wehner: Ein Leben mit der Deutschen Frage. Munich: Bertelsmann, 1978.

Frey, Rainer, ed. Kommunale Demokratie. Bonn-Bad Godesberg: Neue Gesellschaft, 1976.

Fried, Robert C. "Party and Policy in West German Cities," American Political Science Review, LXX, No. 1 (Mar. 1976), 11-24.

Friedrich, Bruno. "Godesberger Erneuerung: Überlegungen zum Standort der SPD," c. 1974 (hectographed).

Friedrich-Ebert-Foundation. Framework of Economic and Political Orientation of the Social Democratic Party of Germany for the Years 1975-1985. Bonn-Bad Godesberg, 1976.

Fromme, Friedrich Karl. Gesetzgebung im Widerstreit: Wer beherrscht den Bundesrat? Die Kontroverse seit 1969. 2d ed., Stuttgart: Bonn Aktuell, 1980.

Fülberth, Georg, and Jürgen Harrer. Die deutsche Sozialdemokratie, 1890-1933, Vol. I, Arbeiterbewegung und SPD. Darmstadt: Luchterhand, 1974.

Gay, Peter. The Dilemma of Democratic Socialism. New York: Columbia University Press, 1952.

Giddens, Anthony. The Class Structure of the Advanced Societies. New York: Harper and Row, 1975.

Glotz, Peter. "Anatomie einer politischer Partei in einer Millionenstadt," Aus Politik und Zeitgeschichte, Beilage zu Das Parlament, No. 41, Oct. 11, 1975.

-----. Die Innenstattung der Macht: Politisches Tagebuch, 1976-1978. Munich: Steinhausen, 1979.

-----. "Systemüberwindende Reformen," Aus Politik und Zeitgeschichte, Beilage zu Das Parlament, No. 17/1972.

-----. Der Weg der Sozialdemokratie: Der historische Auftrag des Reformismus. Vienna, Munich, Zurich: Fritz Molden, 1975.

Gluchowski, Peter, and Hans-Joachim Veen. "Nivellierungstendenz in den

Wählern und Mitgliedschaften von CDU/CSU und SPD, 1959 bis 1979," Zeitschrift für Parlamentsfragen, X, No. 3 (Sept. 1979), 312-331.

Graf, William D. German Left since 1945. Cambridge (England): Oleander Press, 1976.

Grasmann, Peter. Sozialdemokraten gegen Hitler, 1933-1945. Munich: Olzog, 1976.

Grebing, Helga. The History of the German Labour Movement. London: Oswald Wolff, 1969.

Gresch, Norbert. "Der Bund Sozialdemokratischer Parteien in der EG," Eurosozialismus: Die demokratische Alternative, eds. Gerhard Kiersch and Reimund Seidelmann. Cologne: Europäische Verlagsanstalt, 1979.

Grube, Frank, and Gerhard Richter, eds. Der SPD-Staat. Munich: Piper, 1977.

----, Gerhard Richter, and Uwe Thaysen. Politische Planung in Parteien und Parlamentsfraktionen. Göttingen: Otto Schwartz, 1976.

Grunenberg, Nina. Vier Tage mit dem Bundeskanzler. Hamburg: Hoffmann and Campe, 1976.

Güllner, Manfred. "Daten zur Mitgliederstruktur der SPD: Von der Arbeiterelite zu den Bourgeoissöhnchen," Transfer 2: Wahlforschung Sonden im politischen Markt, ed. Carl Böhret. Cologne, Opladen: Westdeutscher Verlag, 1976.

----, and Dwaine Marvick. "Aktivisten in einer Parteihochburg: Zum Beispiel Dortmund," Transfer 2: Wahlforschung Sonden im politischen Markt, ed. Carl Böhret. Cologne, Opladen: Westdeutscher Verlag, 1976.

Günsche, Karl-Ludwig, and Klaus Lantermann. Kleine Geschichte der Sozialistischen Internationale. Bonn-Bad Godesberg: Neue Gesellschaft, 1977.

Günther, Klaus. Sozialdemokratie und Demokratie, 1946-1966: Die SPD und das Problem der Verschränkung innerparteilicher und bundesrepublikanischer Demokratie. Bonn-Bad Godesberg: Neue Gesellschaft, 1979.

----, and Kurt Thomas Schmitz. SPD, KPD/DKP, DGB in den Westzonen und in der Bundesrepublik Deutschland, 1945-1973: Eine Bibliographie. Bonn-Bad Godesberg: Neue Gesellschaft, 1976.

Guggenberger, Bernd. Bürgerinitiativen in der Parteiendemokratie: Von der Ökologiebewegung zur Umweltpartei. Stuttgart: Kohlhammer, 1980.

Gunlicks, Arthur B. "Intraparty Democracy in Western Germany: A Look at the Local Level," Comparative Politics, II, No. 2 (Jan. 1970), 229-249.

Guttsman, W. L. The German Social Democratic Party, 1875-1933: From Ghetto to Government. Winchester, Mass.: Allen and Unwin, 1981.

Habermas, Jürgen, et al., eds. Student und Politik. Berlin: Luchterhand, 1969.

Hancock, M. Donald. "Productivity, Welfare and Participation in Sweden and West Germany: A Comparison of Social Democratic Reform Prospects," Comparative Politics, XI, No. 1 (Oct. 1978), 4-23.

----, and Gideon Sjoberg, eds. Politics in the Post-Welfare: Responses to the New Individualism. New York: Columbia University Press, 1972.

Hanrieder, Wolfram, ed. Helmut Schmidt: Perspectives on Politics. Boulder, Colo.: Westview Press, 1982.

Harpprecht, Klaus. Willy Brandt: Portrait and Self-Portrait. Los Angeles: Nash, 1974.

Harrington, Michael. Socialism. New York: Bantam Books, 1973.

Hartweg, Frédéric. "Les églises, les partis et les élections de 1976," Revue d'Allemagne, XI, No. 2 (Apr.-June 1977), 231-254.

Hartwich, Hans-Hermann, "Gewerkschaften und Parteien—Die aktuellen Probleme im Licht politikwissenschaftlicher Untersuchungen und Konzeptionen," Gewerkschaftliche Monatshefte, XXV (Apr. 1974), 225-238.

Haungs, Peter. "Die Bundesrepublik—ein Parteienstaat? Kritische Anmerkungen zu einem wissenschaftlichen Mythos," Zeitschrift für Parlamentsfragen, IV, No. 4 (Dec. 1973) , 502-524.

Heidermann, Horst, ed. Langzeitprogramm 2, Kritik; 3, Jungsozialisten; 4, Kommentare. Bonn-Bad Godesberg: Neue Gesellschaft, 1972.

Heimann, Horst. Theoriediskussion in der SPD. Frankfurt/Main, Cologne: Europäische Verlagsanstalt, 1975.

----, and Thomas Meyer, eds. Bernstein und der demokratische Sozialismus: Bericht über den Wissenschaftlichen Kongress, die Historische Leistung und Aktuelle Bedeutung Eduard Bernsteins. Berlin, Bonn: Dietz, 1978.

Heimann, Klaus, Hans-Peter Altrogge, and Jochen Stemplewski, "Arbeitsgemeinschaften benötigen politischen Spielraum," Neue Gesellschaft, XXII, No. 9 (1975), 714-720.

Hemmer, Hans-O. "Jungsozialisten und Gewerkschaften," Gewerkschaftliche Monatshefte, XXV, No. 4 (Apr. 1974), 256-257.

Hempel-Soos, Karin. "Die AsF zwischen SPD und Frauenbewegung," Neue Gesellschaft, XXVII, No. 2 (Feb. 1980), 111-114.

Hennis, Wilhelm. Grosse Koalition ohne Ende? Die Zunkunft des parlamentarischen Regierungssystems und die Hinauszögerung der Wahlrechtsreform. Munich: Piper, 1968.

----. Organisierter Sozialismus: Zum "strategischen" Staats- und Politikverständnis der Sozialdemokratie. Stuttgart: Klett, 1977.

Hereth, Michael. Die parlamentarische Opposition in der Bundesrepublik Deutschland. Munich: Olzog, 1969.

Herz, John H. "Social Democracy Versus Democratic Socialism: An Analysis of SPD Attempts to Develop a Party Doctrine," Eurocommunism and Eurosocialism, ed. Bernard E. Brown. New York: Cyrco Press, 1979.

Herzog, Dietrich. "Partei und Parlamentskarrieren im Spiegel der Zahlen für die Bundesrepublik Deutschland," Zeitschrift für Parlamentsfragen, VII, No. 1 (Apr. 1976), 25-34.

Hibbs, Douglas A., Jr. "Political Parties and Macroeconomic Policy," American Political Science Review, LXXI, No. 4 (Dec. 1977), 1467-1487.

Hirche, Kurt. "Gewerkschafter im VI. Deutschen Bundestag," Gewerkschaftliche Monatschefte,XX, No. 12 (Dec. 1969), 716-723.

Hirsch, Helmut, ed., Eduard Bernstein: Ein revisionistisches Sozialismusbild. Berlin, Bonn-Bad Godesberg: Neue Gesellschaft, 1976.

Hofmann, Joachim. Die Schülerarbeit der Jungsozialisten. Bonn-Bad Godesberg: Neue Gesellschaft, 1976.

Hofschen, Heinz-Gerd, and Hans Karl Rupp. SPD im Widerspruch: Zur Entwicklung und Perspektive der Sozialdemokratie im System der BRD. Cologne: Pahl-Rugenstein, 1975.

Holzer, Horst. "Medienpolitik der SPD," Der SPD-Staat, eds. Frank Grube and Gerhard Richter. Munich: Piper, 1977.

Horn, Hannelore, Alexander Schwan, and Thomas Weingartner, eds. Sozialismus in Theorie und Praxis: Festschrift für Richard Löwenthal zum 70. Geburtstag am 15. April 1978. Berlin: Walter de Gruyter, 1978.

Hrbek, Rudolf. Die SPD—Deutschland und Europa. Bonn: Europa-Union, 1972.

Hübner, Emil. Partizipation im Parteienstaat. Munich: Ehrenwirth, 1976.

Hütter, Joachim. SPD und nationale Sicherheit: Internationale und innenpolitische Determinanten des Wandels der sozialdemokratischen Sicherheitspolitik, 1959-1961. Meisenheim am Glan: Anton Hain, 1975.

Hunt, Richard N. German Social Democracy, 1918-1933. New Haven: Yale University Press, 1964.

Infas. "Infas-Report: Parteisoziologische Untersuchungen 1977—Zusammenfassung der Ergebnisse." Bonn-Bad Godesberg, 1978 (hectographed).

Infratest. "Infratest Sozialforschung, Kommunikationsstudie zur SPD-Organisation--Zusammenfassung," n.p., n.d. (c. 1978) (hectographed).

Inglehart, Ronald. "Post-Materialism in an Environment of Insecurity," American Political Science Review, LXXV, No. 4 (Dec. 1981), 880-900.

----. The Silent Revolution: Changing Values and Political Styles Among Western Publics. Princeton: Princeton University Press, 1977.

----. "The Silent Revolution in Europe: Intergenerational Change in Post-Industrial Societies," American Political Science Review, LXV, No. 4 (Dec. 1971), 991-1017.

Institut für Marxistische Studien und Forschungen. Der SPD Orientierungsrahmen '85. Frankfurt: Verlag Marxistische Blätter, 1975.

Institut für politische Planung und Kybernetik. "P/A/P, Politische Analyse und Prognose, Folgen 1 bis 9," n.d. (hectographed).

Jahn, Gerhard, ed. Herbert Wehner: Beiträge zu einer Biographie. Cologne: Kiepenheuer and Witsch, 1976.

Jochimsen, Luc. Sozialismus als Männersache oder Kennen Sie "Bebels Frau"?: Seit 100 Jahren ohne Konsequenz. Reinbek: Rowohlt, 1978.

Just, Dieter and Lothar Romain, eds. Auf der Suche nach dem mündigen Wähler: Die Wahlentscheidung 1972 und ihre Konsequenzen. Berlin: Köllen, 1974.

Kaack, Heino. "Die Basis der Parteien. Struktur und Funktion der Ortsvereine," Zeitschrift für Parlamentsfragen, II, No. 1 (1971), 23-38.

----. Geschichte und Struktur des deutschen Parteiensystems. Cologne, Opladen: Westdeutscher Verlag, 1971.

----. "Parteien und Wählergemeinschaften auf kommunaler Ebene," Aspekte und Probleme der Kommunalpolitik, eds. Heinz Rausch and Theo Stammen. Munich: Ernst Vogel, 1974.

----. "Zur Struktur der politischen Führungselite in Parteien, Parlamenten und Regierung," Handbuch des deutschen Parteiensystems, eds. Heino Kaack and Reinhold Roth. Vol. I. Opladen: Leske, 1980.

----. and Reinhold Roth, eds. Parteien-Jahrbuch 1976. Meisenheim am Glan: Anton Hain, 1979.

Kaase, Max. "Determinanten des Wahlverhaltens bei der Bundestagswahl 1969," Politische Vierteljahresschrift, XI, No. 1 (Mar. 1970), 46-110.

----. "Informationen zur Bundestagswahl 1969, I, II" (hectographed).

----, and Samuel H. Barnes. "In Conclusion: The Future of Political Protest in Western Democracies," Political Action: Mass Participation in Five Western Democracies, eds. Samuel H. Barnes and Max Kaase, et al. Beverly Hills, Calif.: Sage, 1979.

----, and Klaus von Beyme, eds. Elections and Parties. Beverly Hills, Calif.: Sage, 1978.

Kahn, Helmut Wolfgang. Helmut Schmidt: Fallstudie über einen Populären. Hamburg: Holsten, 1974.

Kaltefleiter, Werner. Vorspiel zum Wechsel: Eine Analyse der

Bundestagswahl 1976. Berlin: Duncker and Humblot, 1977.

----, and Hans-Joachim Veen. "Zwischen freiem und imperativem Mandat," Zeitschrift für Parlamentsfragen, II, No. 2 (July 1974), 246-267.

----, et al. Im Wechselspiel der Koalitionen: Eine Analyse der Bundestagswahl 1969. Cologne: Carl Heymanns, 1970.

Kastendiek, Hella. Arbeiternehmer in der SPD: Herausbildung und Funktion der Arbeitsgemeinschaft für Arbeitnehmerfragen (AfA). Berlin: Die Arbeitswelt, 1978.

Katz, Richard S. A Theory of Parties and Electoral Systems. Baltimore: Johns Hopkins University Press, 1980.

Katzenstein, Peter J. "West Germany in the 1980s: Problem or Model?" World Politics, XXXII, No. 4 (July 1980), 577-598.

Keefe, William J. Parties, Politics, and Public Policy in America. 3d ed., New York: Holt, Rinehart and Winston, 1980.

Kellerman, Barbara. "Willy Brandt: Portrait of the Leader as Young Politician." Unpublished Ph.D. dissertation, Yale University, 1975.

Kempe, Martin. SPD und Bundeswehr: Studien zum militärisch-industriellen Komplex. Cologne: Pahl-Rugenstein, 1973.

Kiersch, Gerhard. "Konflikt, Kooperation und strukturelle Dominanz: Frankreichs Sozialisten und die SPD," Eurosozialismus: Die demokratische Alternative, eds. G. Kiersch and Reimund Seidelmann. Cologne: Europäische Verlagsanstalt, 1979.

----, and Reimund Seidelmann, eds. Eurosozialismus: Die demokratische Alternative. Cologne: Europäische Verlagsanstalt, 1979.

King, Anthony. "Political Parties in Western Democracies," Polity, II (Winter 1969), 111-141.

Kirchheimer, Otto. "Germany: The Vanishing Opposition," Political Oppositions in Western Democracies, ed. Robert A. Dahl. New Haven: Yale University Press, 1966.

----. "The Transformation of the Western European Party Systems," Political Parties and Political Development, eds. Joseph LaPalombara and Myron Weiner. Princeton, N.J.: Princeton University Press, 1966.

Klingemann, Hans D., and Franz Urban Pappi. "Die Wählerbewegungen bei der Bundestagswahl am 28. September 1969," Politische Vierteljahresschrift, XI, No. 1 (Mar. 1970), 111-138.

----, and Charles Taylor. "Partisanship, Candidates and Issues: Attitudinal Components of the Vote in West German Federal Elections," Elections and Parties, eds. Max Kaase and Klaus von Beyme. Beverly Hills, Calif.: Sage, 1978.

Klotzbach, Kurt. Bibliographie zur Geschichte der deutschen Arbeiterbewegung, 1914-1945. 2d.ed., Bonn-Bad Godesberg: Neue Gesellschaft, 1974.

----. "Die Programmdiskussion in der deutschen Sozialdemokratie, 1945-1959," Archiv für Sozialgeschichte, XVI (1976), 469-483.

Koepcke, Cordula. Sozialismus in Deutschland. Munich, Vienna: Olzog, 1970.

Kohnen, Peter. Deutschland, deine SPD: Die Frustrierten und die Manipulierten. Munich: Politisches Archiv, 1972.

Kommers, D. P. Judicial Politics in West Germany: A Study of the Federal Constitutional Court. Beverly Hills, Calif.: Sage, 1976.

Kowalski, Werner, and Johannes Glasneck. Die Sozialistische Internationale: Ihre Geschichte und Politik. Berlin: VEB Deutscher Verlag der Wissenschaften, 1977.

Kralewski, Wolfgang, and Karlheinz Neunreither. Oppositionelles Verhalten im ersten Deutschen Bundestag, 1949-1953. Cologne and Opladen: Westdeutscher Verlag, 1963.

Kramm, Lothar. Stamokap—eine kritische Abgrenzung. Bonn-Bad Godesberg: Neue Gesellschaft, 1974.

Kremendahl, Hans. Nur die Volkspartei ist mehrheitsfähig: Zur Lage der SPD nach der Bundestagswahl 1976. Bonn-Bad Godesberg: Neue Gesellschaft, 1977.

Kühn, Heinz. "Zum Verhältnis zwischen der Sozialdemokratischen Partei und den Gewerkschaften," Gewerkschaftliche Monatshefte, XXV, No. 10 (Oct. 1974), 614-620.

Küpper, Jost. Die SPD und der Orientierungsrahmen '85. Bonn-Bad Godesberg: Neue Gesellschaft, 1977.

Kürschners Volkshandbuch, Deutscher Bundestag, 6. Wahlperiode, 1969. Darmstadt: Neue Darmstädter Verlagsanstalt, 1970 (and later editions).

Lange, Rolf-Peter. "Auslesestrukturen bei der Besetzung von Regierungsämtern," Parteiensystem in der Legitimationskrise, eds. Jürgen Dittberner and Rolf Ebbighausen. Cologne, Opladen: Westdeutscher Verlag, 1973.

Langzeitprogramm 1, Texte. Bonn-Bad Godesberg: Neue Gesellschaft, 1972.

LaPalombara, Joseph, and Myron Weiner, eds. Political Parties and Political Development. Princeton, N. J.: Princeton University Press, 1966.

Laufer, Heinz. "Der Bundesrat als Instrument der Opposition," Zeitschrift für Parlamentsfragen, I, No. 3 (Oct. 1970), 318-341.

Lauterbach, Albert. "Socialism and Social Democracy: An Exercise in Concepts and Semantics," Association for Comparative Economic Studies Bulletin, XX, No. 1 (Spring 1978), 1-36.

Laux, William E. "West German Political Parties and the 1972 Bundestag Election," Western Political Quarterly, XXIII, No. 3 (Sept. 1973), 507-528.

Lawson, Kay, ed. Political Parties and Linkage: A Comparative Perspective. New Haven: Yale University Press, 1980.

Lechner, Hans, and Klaus Hülshoff. Parlament und Regierung. 2d ed., Munich, Berlin: C. H. Beck'sche Verlagsbuchhandlung, 1958.

Lehmann, Hans-Georg. "Schulreform und Politik," Aus Politik und Zeitgeschichte, Beilage zu Das Parlament, B 36/78, Sept. 9, 1978.

Lehmbruch, Gerhard. "The Ambiguous Coalition in West Germany," Government and Opposition, III, No. 2 (Spring 1968), 181-204.

——. "Party and Federation in Germany: A Developmental Dilemma," Government and Opposition, XIII, No. 2 (Spring 1978), 151-177.

——, Klaus von Beyme, and Iring Fetscher, eds. Demokratisches System und politische Praxis der Bundesrepublik. Munich: Piper, 1971.

Leibfried, Stephen. "Public Assistance in the United States and Federal Republic of Germany: Does Social Democracy Make a Difference?" Comparative Politics, XI. No. 1 (Oct. 1978), 59-76.

Leibholz, Gerhard. Strukturprobleme der modernen Demokratie. 3d. ed., Karlsruhe: C. F. Müller, 1967.

Lidtke, Vernon L. The Outlawed Party: Social Democracy in Germany, 1878-1890. Princeton, N.J.: Princeton University Press, 1966.

Lieber, Nancy, ed. Eurosocialism and America: Political Economy for the 1980s. Philadelphia: Temple University Press, 1982.

Liepelt, Klaus, and Alexander Mitscherlich. Thesen zur Wählerfluktuation. Frankfurt/Main: Europäische Verlagsanstalt, 1968.

——, and Hela Riemenschnitter. "Die Wähler-Wanderungsbilanz," Auf der

Suche nach dem mündigen Wähler, eds. Dieter Just and Lothar Romain. Berlin: Köllen, 1974.
Lodge, Juliet. European Policy of the SPD. Beverly Hills, Calif.: Sage, 1976.
Loewenberg, Gerhard. "The Remaking of the German Party System," Polity, I, No. 1 (1968), 87-113.
Löwenthal, Richard. Sozialismus und aktive Demokratie: Essays zu ihren Voraussetzungen in Deutschland. Frankfurt/Main: S. Fischer, 1974.
Loewke, Udo F. Die SPD und die Wehrfrage, 1949-1955. Bonn-Bad Godesberg: Neue Gesellschaft, 1976.
Lohmar, Ulrich. Innerparteiliche Demokratie. Stuttgart: Ferdinand Enke, 1963.
Lompe, Klaus. "Bilanz der Politik, Innerer Reformen," Die Mitarbeit, No. 2/3, 1979.
----, and Lothar F. Neumann, eds. Willi Eichlers Beiträge zum demokratischen Sozialismus: Eine Auswahl aus dem Werk. Berlin, Bonn: Dietz, 1979.
Lührs, Georg, ed. Beiträge zur Theoriediskussion. 2 vols. Berlin, Bonn-Bad Godesberg: Dietz, 1973, 1974.
----, Thilo Sarrazin, Frithjof Spreer, Manfred Tietzel, eds. Kritischer Rationalismus und Sozialdemokratie. Berlin, Bonn: Dietz, 1975.
----, Thilo Sarrazin, Frithjof Spreer, Manfred Tietzel, eds. Theorie und Politik aus kritisch-rationaler Sicht. Berlin, Bonn: Dietz, 1978.
Marcuse, Herbert. One-Dimensional Man: Studies in the Ideology of Advanced Industrial Society. Boston: Beacon Press, 1966.
Markovits, Andrei S., ed. The Political Economy of West Germany: Modell Deutschland. New York: Praeger, 1982.
Marsh, M. A. "European Social Democratic Party Leaders and the Working Class: Some Linkage Implications of Trends in Recruitment," Political Parties and Linkage: A Comparative Perspective, ed. Kay Lawson. New Haven: Yale University Press, 1980.
Marx, Karl, and Friedrich Engels. Selected Works. New York: International Publishers, 1968.
Matthias, Erich. Sozialdemokratie und Nation: Ein Beitrag zur Ideengeschichte der sozialdemokratischen Emigration in der Prager Zeit des Parteivorstandes 1933-1938. Stuttgart: Deutsche Verlags-Anstalt, 1952.
Mayntz, Renate. "Executive Leadership in Germany: Dispersion of Power or 'Kanzlerdemokratie'?" Presidents and Prime Ministers, eds. Richard Rose and Ezra N. Suleiman. Washington, D.C.: American Enterprise Institute, 1980.
McKenzie, R. T. British Political Parties: The Distribution of Power within the Conservative and Labour Parties. 2d ed., New York: Praeger, 1964.
Mehring, Franz. Geschichte der Deutschen Sozialdemokratie. 2 vols. Berlin: Dietz, 1960 (reprint of 1897 and 1898 editions).
Meng, Richard. Juso-Hochschulgruppen: Geschichte, Praxis, Perspektiven. Giessen: Focus, 1979.
Merkl, Peter. "Factionalism: The Limits of the West German Party-State," Faction Politics: Political Parties and Factionalism in Comparative Perspective, eds. Frank P. Belloni and Dennis C. Beller. Santa Barbara, Calif.: ABC-Clio, 1978.
----, ed. West European Party Systems: Trends and Prospects. New York: Free Press, 1980.
Mettke, Jörg R., ed. Die Grünen: Regierungspartner von morgen? Reinbek:

Rowohlt, 1982.
Meyenberg, Rüdiger. SPD in der Provinz. Frankfurt/Main: R. G. Fischer, 1978.
Meyer, Armin. "Parteiaktivitäten und Einstellungen von CDU- und SPD-Mitgliedern," Parteiensystem in der Legitimationskrise, eds. Jürgen Dittberner and Rolf Ebbighausen. Cologne, Opladen: Westdeutscher Verlag, 1973.
Meyer, Thomas. Grundwerte und Wissenschaft im Demokratischen Sozialismus. Berlin, Bonn: Dietz, 1978.
Michels, Robert. Political Parties: A Sociological Study of the Oligarchical Tendencies of Modern Democracy. New York: Collier Books, 1962. Trans. and reprint of Zur Soziologie des Parteiwesens in der modernen Demokratie Leipzig: W. Klinkhardt, 1911.
Miliband, Ralph. Marxism and Politics. London: Oxford University Press, 1977.
----. The State in Capitalist Society. London: Wiedenfeld and Nicolson, 1969.
Miller, Susanne. Burgfrieden und Klassenkampf: Die deutsche Sozialdemokratie im ersten Weltkrieg. Düsseldorf: Droste, 1974.
----. "Frauenfrage und Sexismus in der deutschen Sozialdemokratie," Sozialismus in Theorie und Praxis, eds. Hannelore Horn, et al. Berlin: Walter de Gruyter, 1978.
----. "Frauenrecht ist Menschenrecht," Frauen heute—Jahrhundertthema Gleichberechtigung, ed. Willy Brandt. Cologne, Frankfurt/Main: Europäische Verlagsanstalt, 1978.
----. Die SPD vor und nach Godesberg. Bonn-Bad Godesberg: Neue Gesellschaft, 1974.
Müller, Emil-Peter. Juso-Sozialismus: Programm und Strategie der Jungsozialisten in der SPD. Cologne: Deutsche Industrieverlags-GmbH, 1972.
----. Die sozio-ökonomische und verbandliche Struktur des VIII. Deutschen Bundestages. Cologne: Deutscher Instituts-Verlag, 1977.
----. "Vertreter der gewerblichen Wirtschaft im VIII. Deutschen Bundestag," Zeitschrift für Parlamentsfragen, VIII, No. 4 (Dec. 1977), 422-428.
----. "Vertreter von Arbeitnehmerorganisationen im 8. Deutschen Bundestag," Zeitschrift für Parlamentsfragen, VIII, No. 2 (Aug. 1977), 184-188.
Müller, Ute. Die demokratische Willensbildung in den politischen Parteien. Mainz: von Hase and Koehler, 1967.
Müller-Rommel, Ferdinand. Innerparteiliche Gruppierungen in der SPD: Eine empirische Studie über informell-organisierte Gruppierungen von 1969-1980. Opladen: Westdeutscher Verlag, 1982.
Narr, Wolf-Dieter, ed. Auf dem Weg zum Einparteienstaat. Cologne and Opladen: Westdeutscher Verlag, 1977.
----, Hermann Scheer, and Dieter Spöri. SPD—Staatspartei oder Reformpartei. Munich: Piper, 1976.
Nassmacher, Karl-Heinz, ed. Kommunalpolitik und Sozialdemokratie. Bonn-Bad Godesberg, 1977.
Nemitz, Manfred, ed. Machtwechsel in Bonn. Gütersloh: Bertelsmann-Sachbuchverlag, 1970.
Noelle-Neumann, Elisabeth. "Wahlentscheidung in der Fernsehdemokratie," Auf der Suche nach dem mündigen Wähler, eds. Dieter Just and Lothar Romain. Berlin: Köllen, 1974.
----. "Zum Einfluss des Meinungsklimas auf das Wahlverhalten," Union

alternativ, eds. Gerd Mayer-Vorfelder and Hubertus Zuber. Stuttgart: Seewald, 1976.

----, ed. The Germans. Westport, Conn.: Greenwood, 1981.

Noller, Gerhard. Die Veränderung der SPD. Reutlingen: Siegfried Noller, 1977.

Norpoth, Helmut. "The German Federal Republic: Coalition Goverment at the Brink of Majority Rule," Government Coalitions in Western Democracies, eds. Eric C. Browne and John Dreijmanis. New York: Longman, 1982.

----. "Party Identification in West Germany," Comparative Political Studies, XI, No. 1 (Apr. 1978), 36-61.

Nowka, Harry. Das Machtverhältnis zwischen Partei und Fraktion in der SPD. Cologne, Berlin: Carl Heymanns, 1973.

Oberndörfer, Dieter, ed. Wählerverhalten in der Bundesrepublik Deutschland: Studien zu ausgewählten Wahlforschung aus Anlass der Bundestagswahl 1976. Berlin: Duncker and Humblot, 1978.

Oertzen, Peter von. Die Aufgabe der Partei. Bonn-Bad Godesberg: Neue Gesellschaft, 1974.

----. "Die Gewerkschaften in der Sicht der SPD," Gewerkschaftliche Monatshefte, XXVII, No. 4 (Apr. 1976), 210-216.

----. "Die innerparteiliche Diskussion zum Orientierungsrahmen '85," Neue Gesellschaft, XXII, No. 11 (1975), 882-884.

----. Thesen zur Strategie und Taktik des demokratischen Sozialismus in der Bundesrepublik Deutschland: Diskussionsthesen zur Arbeit der Partei. Issued by SPD. Bonn, 1974.

----. "Die Zukunft des Godesberger Programms. Zur innerparteilichen Diskussion der SPD," Freiheitlicher Sozialismus, eds. Heiner Flohr, et al. Bonn-Bad Godesberg: Neue Gesellschaft, 1973.

----, Horst Ehmke, and Herbert Ehrenberg, eds. Orientierungsrahmen '85—Text und Diskussion. Bonn-Bad Godesberg: Neue Gesellschaft, 1976.

Offe, Claus. "The Attribution of Public Status to Interest Groups: Observations on the West German Case," Organizing Interests in Western Europe, ed. Suzanne Berger. Cambridge, England: Cambridge University Press, 1981.

Osterroth, Franz, and Dieter Schuster. Chronik der deutschen Sozialdemokratie. 3 vols. Berlin, Bonn: Dietz, 1975-1978.

Pachter, Henry. "The Ambiguous Legacy of Eduard Bernstein," Dissent, Spring 1981, pp. 203-216.

Panitch, Leo. "Trade Unions and the Capitalist State," New Left Review, No. 125 (Jan.-Feb. 1981), pp. 21-43.

Pappi, Franz Urban. "Parteiensystem und Sozialstruktur in der Bundesrepublik," Politische Vierteljahresschrift, XIV, No. 2 (May 1973), 191-213.

Parkin, Frank. Class Inequality and Political Order. New York: Praeger, 1971.

Paterson, William E. "The German Social Democratic Party," Social Democratic Parties in Western Europe, eds. W. E. Paterson and Alastair H. Thomas. London: Croom Helm, 1977.

----. "Political Parties and the Making of Foreign Policy—The Case of the Federal Republic," Review of International Studies, No. 7 (1981), pp. 227-235.

----. "Problems of Party Government in West Germany—A British Perspective." Unpublished paper, 1980.

----. "Social Democratic Parties of the European Community," Journal of Common Market Studies, XIII, No. 4 (June 1975), 415-418.

----. The SPD and European Integration. Westmead (England): Saxon House, 1974.

Pirker, Theo. Die SPD nach Hitler: Die Geschichte der Sozialdemokratischen Partei Deutschlands, 1945-1954. Munich: Rütten and Loening, 1965.

Pizzorno, Alessandro. "Interests and Parties in Pluralism," Organizing Interests in Western Europe, ed. Suzanne Berger. Cambridge, England: Cambridge University Press, 1981.

Popper, Karl. The Open Society and Its Enemies. London: G. Routledge, 1945.

Pore, Renate. A Conflict of Interest: Women in German Social Democracy, 1919-1933. Westport, Conn.: Greenwood Press, 1981.

Potthoff, Heinrich. Die Sozialdemokratie von den Anfängen bis 1945. Bonn-Bad Godesberg: Neue Gesellschaft, 1974.

Pozzoli, Claudio, ed. Die Linke in der Sozialdemokratie, Jahrbuch 3, Arbeiterbewegung, Theorie und Geschichte. Frankfurt/Main: Fischer, 1975.

Preece, R.J.C. 'Land' Elections in the German Federal Republic. London: Longmans, 1968.

Pridham, Geoffrey. "A 'Nationalization' Process? Federal Politics and State Elections in West Germany," Government and Opposition, VIII, No. 4 (Autumn 1973), 455-472.

----. "The 1980 Bundestag Election: A Case of 'Normality'," West European Politics, IV, No. 2 (May 1981), 112-123.

Prittie, Terence. Willy Brandt: Portrait of a Statesman. New York: Schocken Books, 1974.

Przeworski, Adam. "Social Democracy as a Historical Phenomenon," New Left Review, No. 122 (July-Aug. 1980), pp. 27-58.

Pulzer, Peter. "The German Party System in the Sixties," Political Studies, XIX, No. 1 (Mar. 1971), 1-17.

Pruys, Karl Hugo, and Volker Schulze. Macht und Meinung: Aspekte der SPD Medienpolitik. Cologne: Wissenschaft und Politik, 1975.

Pumm, Günter. Kandidatenauswahl und innerparteiliche Demokratie in der Hamburger SPD. Frankfurt/Main: Lang, 1977.

Putnam, Robert D. "The Political Attitudes of Senior Civil Servants in Britain, Germany, and Italy," The Mandarins of Western Europe: The Political Role of Top Civil Servants, ed. Mattei Dogan. New York: John Wiley, 1975.

Quataert, Jean. Reluctant Feminists in German Social Democracy, 1885-1917. Princeton, N.J.: Princeton University Press, 1979.

Rabe, Bernd. Der Sozialdemokratische Charakter: Drei Generationen aktiver Parteimitglieder in einem Arbeiterviertel. Frankfurt/Main, New York: Campus, 1978.

Rapp, Heinz. "Gründen und Überleben," Was sind der SPD die Selbständigen wert? ed. Wolfgang Roth. Bonn: Neuer Vorwärts, 1979.

----. "Zwischen Tagespolitik und Grundsatzprogramm—Die Arbeit der Grundwertekommission der SPD," Neue Gesellschaft, XXVIII, No. 2 (Feb. 1981), 138-144.

Raschke, Joachim. Innerparteiliche Opposition: Die Linke in der Berliner SPD. Hamburg: Hoffmann and Campe, 1974.

----, ed. Bürger und Parteien: Ansichten und Analysen einer schwierigen Beziehung. Opladen: Westdeutscher Verlag, 1982.

Rau, Johannes, and Franz Böckle. Sozialdemokratie und Kirchen. Bonn: Neue Gesellschaft, 1979.

Rausch, Heinz, and Theo Stammen, eds. Aspekte und Probleme der Kommunalpolitik. Munich: Ernst Vogel, 1974.

Rauscher, Anton. Kirche—Partei—Politik. Cologne: J. P. Bachem, 1974.

Reichard, Richard W. Crippled from Birth: German Social Democracy, 1844-1870. Ames, Iowa: Iowa State University Press, 1969.

Rejai, M. ed. Decline of Ideology. Chicago, New York: Aldine-Atherton, 1971.

Reuter, Lutz-Rainer. "Kommunalpolitk im Parteienvergleich," Aus Politik und Zeitgeschichte, Beilage zu Das Parlament, B 34/76, Aug. 21, 1976.

Riedel-Martiny, Anke. "Genosse Hinderlich und die Frauen—Die Situation weiblicher Mitglieder der SPD," Neue Gesellschaft, XXII, No. 9 (1975), 731-734.

Riemer, Jeremiah M. "Alterations in the Design of Model Germany: Critical Innovations in the Policy Machinery for Economic Steering," The Political Economy of West Germany: Modell Deutschland, ed. Andrei S. Markovits. New York: Praeger, 1982.

Riker, William H. The Theory of Political Coalitions. New Haven: Yale University Press, 1962.

Ristock, Harry, ed. Mitte-Links: Energie, Umwelt. Bonn-Bad Godesberg: Neue Gesellschaft, 1977.

Rose, Richard. Do Parties Make a Difference? Chatham, N.J.: Chatham House Publishers, 1980.

Roth, Guenther. The Social Democrats in Imperial Germany: A Study in Working-Class Isolation and National Integration. Totowa, N.J.: The Bedminster Press, 1963.

Roth, Reinhold. Aussenpolitische Innovation und politische Herrschaftssicherung. Meisenheim: Anton Hain, 1976.

——. Parteiensystem und Aussenpolitik. Meisenheim: Anton Hain, 1973.

Roth, Wolfgang, ed. Kommunalpolitik—für wen? Arbeitsprogramm der Jungsozialisten. Frankfurt/Main: Fischer, 1971.

——, ed. Was sind der SPD die Selbständigen wert? Bonn: Neuer Vorwärts, 1979.

Rovan, Joseph. Histoire de la Social-Démocratie Allemande. Paris: Éditions du Seuil, 1978. Trans. by Charlotte Roland into Geschichte der deutschen Sozialdemokratie. Frankfurt/Main: Fischer, 1980.

Russell, Bertrand. German Social Democracy. New York: Simon and Schuster, 1965 (reprint of 1896 edition).

Rustin, Michael. "Different Conceptions of Party: Labour's Constitutional Debates," New Left Review, No. 126 (Mar.-Apr. 1981), 17-42.

Sarcinelli, Ulrich. Das Staatsverständnis der SPD. Meisenheim am Glan: Anton Hain, 1979.

Sarrazin, Thilo, ed. Investitionslenkung: "Spielwiese" oder "vorausschauende Industriepolitik." Bonn-Bad Godesberg: Neue Gesellschaft, 1976.

Sartori, Giovanni. "European Political Parties: The Case of Polarized Pluralism," Political Parties and Political Development, eds. Joseph LaPalombara and Myron Weiner. Princeton, N.J.: Princeton University Press, 1966.

——. Parties and Party Systems: A Framework for Analysis. Cambridge, England: Cambridge University Press, 1976.

Savramis, Demosthenes. Das Christliche in der SPD. Munich: List, 1976.

Scarrow, Howard A. "The Function of Political Parties: A Critique of the Literature and the Approach," Journal of Politics, XXIX (Nov. 1967),

770-790.
Scase, Richard. Social Democracy in Capitalist Society: Working-Class Politics in Britain and Sweden. London: Croom Helm, 1977.
Scharping, Rudolf, and Friedhelm Wollner, eds. Demokratischer Sozialismus und Langzeitprogramm. Reinbek: Rowohlt, 1973.
Schauer, Helmut. "Critique of Co-determination," Workers' Control: A Reader on Labor and Social Change, eds. Gerry Hunnius, G. David Garson, and John Case. New York: Vintage Books, 1973.
Scheer, Hermann. Parteien kontra Bürger?: Die Zunkunft der Parteiendemokratie. Munich: Piper, 1979.
----, Johano Strasser, and Heidemarie Wieczorek-Zeul. "Zehn Jahre Juso-Doppelstrategie," Forum d s, No. 8 (1979), pp. 33-46.
Scheer-Pontenagel, Irm. "Gegenargumente zur 'Frauenquote'," Die Neue Gesellschaft, XXVI, No. 2 (Feb. 1979), 151-153.
Schellenger, Harold K., Jr. The SPD in the Bonn Republic: A Socialist Party Modernizes. The Hague: Nijhoff, 1968.
Schenck, Guntram von. "Die sozialdemokratischen Parteien der EG vor den Direktwahlen," Aus Politik und Zeitgeschichte, Beilage zu Das Parlament, B 14/79, Apr. 7, 1979.
----. Das Hochschulrahmengesetz. Bonn-Bad Godesberg: Neue Gesellschaft, 1976.
Scherf, Henning. "Notwendige Fragen," Die Neue Gesellschaft, XXVI, No. 8 (Aug. 1979), 659-662.
Schell, Marie, and Joachim Wagner. Freiheit--Gerechtigkeit--Solidarität: Grundwerte und praktische Politik. Bonn-Bad Godesberg, 1976.
Schleth, Uwe. Parteifinanzen. Meisenheim am Glan: Anton Hain, 1973.
Schmid, Günther. Entscheidung in Bonn: Die Entstehung der Ost- und Deutschlandpolitik 1969/1970. Cologne: Wissenschaft und Politik, 1979.
Schmidt, Helmut. Als Christ in der politischen Entscheidung. Gütersloh: Gütersloher Verlagshaus, 1976.
----. Strategie des Gleichgewichts: Deutsche Friedenspolitik und die Weltmächte. Stuttgart-Degerloch: Seewald, 1969 (trans. Edward Thomas; The Balance of Power: Germany's Peace Policy and the Super Powers. London: Kimber, 1971).
----. Verteidigung oder Vergeltung: ein deutscher Beitrag zum strategischen Problem der NATO. Stuttgart-Degerloch: Seewald, 1961 (trans. Edward Thomas; Defense or Retaliation: A German View. New York: Praeger, 1962).
Schmidt, Manfred G. CDU und SPD an der Regierung: Ein Vergleich ihrer Politik in den Ländern. Frankfurt: Campus, 1980.
----. "Die 'Politik der inneren Reformen' in der Bundesrepublik seit 1969," Unfähig zur Reform?, eds. Christian Fenner, et al. Cologne: Europäische Verlagsanstalt, 1978. Translated into "The Politics of Domestic Reform in the Federal Republic of Germany," Politics and Society, VIII, No. 2 (1978), 165-200.
----. "Politische Parteien und staatliche Politik in 21 bürgerlichen Demokratien--ein internationaler Vergleich," Politische Vierteljahresschrift, XXII, No. 4 (Dec. 1981), 440-442.
Schmitz, Kurt Thomas. Deutsche Einheit und Europäische Integration: Der sozialdemokratische Beitrag zur Aussenpolitik der Bundesrepublik Deutschland unter besonderer Berücksichtigung des programmatischen Wandels einer Oppositionspartei. Bonn: Neue Gesellschaft, 1978.
Schmollinger, Horst W. "Abhängig Beschäftigte in Parteien der Bundesrepublik: Einflussmöglichkeiten von Arbeitern, Angestellten und

Beamten," Zeitschrift für Parlamentsfragen, V, No. 1 (Mar. 1974), 58-90.

----. "Gewerkschafter in der SPD—Ein Fallstudie," Parteiensystem in der Legitimationskrise, eds. Jürgen Dittberner and Rolf Ebbighausen. Cologne, Opladen: Westdeutscher Verlag, 1973.

----, and Peter Müller. Zwischenbilanz: 10 Jahre sozialliberale Politik, Anspruch und Wirklichkeit. Hannover: Fackelträger, 1980.

----, and Richard Stöss. Die Parteien und die Presse der Parteien und Gewerkschaften in der Bundesrepublik Deutschland, 1945-1974. Munich: Dokumentation, 1975.

----, and Richard Stöss. "Sozialstruktur und Parteiensystem," Das Parteiensystem der Bundesrepublik, ed. Dietrich Staritz. Opladen: Leske and Budrich, 1976.

Schöfberger, Rudolf. "Die Jungsozialisten sind die SPD der achtziger Jahre," Quo vadis SPD? ed. Rolf Seeliger. Munich: Seeliger, 1971.

Scholz, Arno. Turmwächter der Demokratie: Ein Lebensbild von Kurt Schumacher. 2 vols. Berlin: Arani, 1952.

Schorske, Carl E. German Social Democracy 1905-1917: The Development of the Great Schism. Cambridge: Harvard University Press, 1955.

Schüttemeyer, Suzanne S. "Ergebnisse der Landtagswahlen in den Bundesländern 1946-1979," Zeitschrift für Parlamentsfragen, XI, No. 2 (July 1980), 250-255.

Schütz, Klaus. "Die Sozialdemokratie im Nachkriegsdeutschland," Parteien in der Bundesrepublik. By Max Gustav Lange, Gerhard Schulz, and Klaus Schütz. Stuttgart, Düsseldorf: Ring, 1955.

Schultze, Rainer-Olaf. "Nur Parteiverdrossenheit und diffuser Protest? Systemfunktionale Fehlinterpretationen der grünen Wahlerfolge," Zeitschrift für Parlamentsfragen, XI, No. 2 (July 1980), 293-313.

Schumpeter, Joseph A. Capitalism, Socialism and Democracy. New York: Harper, 1947.

Schwan, Alexander, and Gesine Schwan. Sozialdemokratie und Marxismus: Zum Spannungsverhältnis von Godesberger Programm und Marxistischer Theorie. Hamburg: Hoffmann and Campe, 1974.

Schwan, Gesine, ed. Demokratischer Sozialismus für Industriegesellschaften. Cologne: Europäische Verlagsanstalt, 1979.

See, Hans. "Strukturwandel und Ideologieprobleme der SPD—eine empirische Studie," Auf dem Weg zum Einparteienstaat, ed. Wolf-Dieter Narr. Cologne, Opladen: Westdeutscher Verlag, 1977.

Seeliger, Rolf, ed. Bonns Graue Eminenzen: Aktuelle Beiträge zum Thema Ministerialbürokratie und sozialdemokratische Reformpolitik. Munich: Seeliger, 1970.

----. SPD 72: Neue Beiträge zur Mobilisierung der Sozialdemokratie. Munich: Seeliger, 1972.

Siebeck, Werner. "Demokratisierung oder Machtkampf? Studien zur innerparteilichen Demokratie am Beispiel der jüngeren Entwicklung der Münchner SPD." Unpublished Master's thesis, University of Munich, 1977.

Soell, Hartmut. "Fraktion und Parteiorganisation: Zur Willensbildung der SPD in den sechziger Jahren," Politische Vierteljahresschrift, X, No. 4 (Dec. 1969), 604-626.

Sontheimer, Kurt. "The Campaign of the Social Democratic Party," Germany at the Polls: The Bundestag Election of 1976, ed. Karl H. Cerny. Washington, D.C.: American Enterprise Institute for Public Policy Research, 1978.

——. The Government and Politics of West Germany. New York: Praeger, 1973.

Sorg, Richard. Marxismus und Protestantismus in Deutschland. Cologne: Pahl-Rugenstein, 1974.

Spotts, Frederic. The Churches and Politics in Germany. Middletown, Conn.: Wesleyan University Press, 1973.

Stamokap und Godesberg: Auseinandersetzung und sozialdemokratische Praxis und Theorie. Bonn-Bad Godesberg: Neuer Vorwärts, 1977.

Staritz, Dietrich, ed. Das Parteiensystem der Bundesrepublik. Opladen: Leske and Budrich, 1976.

Steffen, Jochen. Strukturelle Revolution. Hamburg: Reinbek, 1974.

Steinberg, Hans-Josef. Die deutsche sozialistische Arbeiterbewegung bis 1914: Eine bibliographische Einführung. Frankfurt/Main: Campus, 1945.

——. Sozialismus und deutsche Sozialdemokratie: Zur Ideologie der Partei vor dem I. Weltkrieg. Hannover: Verlag für Literatur und Zeitgeschichte, 1967 (reprint: Bonn: Dietz, 1979).

Steinkemper, Bärbel. Klassische und politische Bürokraten in der Ministerialverwaltung der Bundesrepublik Deutschland. Cologne: Carl Heymanns Verlag, 1974.

Stephan, Dieter. Jungsozialisten: Stabilisierung nach langer Krise? Theorie und Politik 1969-1979—Eine Bilanz. Bonn: Neue Gesellschaft, 1979.

Stephens, John D. The Transition from Capitalism to Socialism. Atlantic Highlands, N.J.: Humanities Press, 1981.

Strasser, Johano. "Grenzen des Sozialstaats oder Grenzen kompensatorischer Sozialpolitik," Unfähig zur Reform? eds. Christian Fenner, Ulrich Heyder, and Johano Strasser. Cologne: Europäische Verlagsanstalt, 1978.

——. Die Zukunft der Demokratie: Grenzen des Wachstums—Grenzen der Freiheit? Reinbek: Rowohlt, 1977.

Streeck, Sylvia, and Wolfgang Streeck. Parteiensystem und Status quo: Drei Studien zum innerparteilichen Konflikt. Frankfurt/Main: Suhrkamp, 1972.

Streithofen, Heinrich B. SPD und Katholische Kirche. Stuttgart: Seewald, 1974.

Szabo, Stephen F. "Party Permeability: The SPD and the Young Socialists." Paper read at the American Political Science Association convention, Washington, D.C., Aug. 31-Sept. 3, 1979.

Thielemann, Holger. "Neuere Daten zur Sozialstruktur von CDU und SPD," Gegenwartskunde SH '79, pp. 81-86.

Thönnessen, Werner. The Emancipation of Women: The Rise and Decline of the Women's Movement in German Social Democracy, 1863-1933. Trans. Joris de Bres. London: Pluto Press, 1973.

Thomas, John Clayton. The Decline of Ideology in Western Political Parties: A Study of Changing Policy Orientations. London: Sage, 1975.

Troitzsch, Klaus G. "Die Herausforderung der 'etablierten' Parteien durch die Grünen," Handbuch des deutschen Parteiensystems, eds. Heino Kaack and Reinhold Roth. Vol. II. Opladen: Leske, 1980.

Tufte, Edward R. Political Control of the Economy. Princeton: Princeton University Press, 1978.

Urwin, Derek W. "Germany: Continuity and Change in Electoral Politics," Electoral Behavior: A Comparative Handbook, ed. Richard Rose. New York: The Free Press, 1974.

Veen, Hans-Joachim. Die CDU/CSU-Opposition im Parlamentarischen Entscheidungsprozess. Munich: V. Ernst Vögel, 1973.

Vilmar, Fritz. Strategien der Demokratisierung. Darmstadt: Neuwied, 1973.

Vogel, Hans-Jochen. Grundfragen des demokratischen Sozialismus. SPD, executive, Theorie und Grundwerte series, Bonn, 1974.

Wachenheim, Hedwig. Die deutsche Arbeiterbewegung, 1844-1914. Cologne, Opladen: Westdeutscher Verlag, 1967.

Walkhoff, Karl-Heinz. "Parlamentarismus kritisch betrachtet," Quo vadis SPD? ed. Rolf Seeliger. Munich: Seeliger, 1971.

Wallach, Hans Gert Peter. "Leadership Styles in West German Political Parties." Paper read at the American Political Science Association convention, New Orleans, September 4-8, 1973.

Waxman, Chaim I., ed. The End of Ideology Debate. New York: Funk and Wagnalls, 1968.

Weber, Max. Max Weber on Charisma and Institution-Building, ed. S. N. Eisenstadt. Chicago: University of Chicago Press, 1968.

Wehner, Herbert. Politik für Arbeitnehmer: Reden und Beiträgen, 1973-1979. Issued by AfA, Bonn, n.d.

----, Bruno Friedrich, and Alfred Nau. Parteiorganisation. Bonn: Neue Gesellschaft, 1969.

Wilensky, Harold L. "Leftism, Catholicism, and Democratic Corporatism: The Role of Political Parties in Recent Welfare State Development," The Development of Welfare States in Europe and America, eds. Peter Flora and Arnold J. Heidenheimer. New Brunswick, N.J.: Transaction Books, 1981.

----. The Welfare State and Equality: Structural and Ideological Roots of Public Expenditures. Berkeley: University of California Press, 1975.

Wilker, Lothar. Sicherheitspolitik der SPD, 1956-1966. Bonn-Bad Godesberg: Neue Gesellschaft, 1977.

Willey, Richard J. "Trade Unions and Political Parties in the Federal Republic of Germany," Industrial and Labor Relations Review, XXVIII, No. 1 (Oct. 1974), 38-59.

Wilson, Frank L. The French Democratic Left, 1963-1969: Toward a Modern Party System. Stanford: Stanford University Press, 1971.

Wolf, Klaus-Peter. "Die SPD-Bildungspolitik am Beispiel der Gesamtschule," Sozialistische Tribüne, 2/1980, pp. 92-107.

Wolf, Werner. Der Wahlkampf: Theorie und Praxis. Cologne: Wissenschaft und Politik, 1980.

Wolfe, Alan. "Has Social Democracy a Future?" Comparative Politics, XI, No. 1 (Oct. 1978), 100-125.

----. The Limits of Legitimacy: Political Contradictions of Contemporary Capitalism. New York: Free Press, 1977.

Wright, James D. "The Political Consciousness of Post-Industrialism," Contemporary Sociology, VII, No. 3 (May 1978), 270-273.

----, and Daniel Holub. "Social Cleavage and Party Affiliation Revisited: A Comparison of West Germany and the United States," Sociology and Social Research, LXIII, No. 4 (July 1979), 671-697.

Zeuner, Bodo. Innerparteiliche Demokratie. Berlin: Colloquium, 1969.

----. "'Solidarität' mit der SPD oder Solidarität der Klasse? Zur SPD-Bindung der DGB-Gewerkschaften," Prokla, VII, No. 1 (1977), 3-32.

----. "Wahlen ohne Auswahl: Die Kandidatenaufstellung zum Parlament," Parlamentarismus ohne Transparenz, ed. Winifried Steffani. Cologne/Opladen: Westdeutscher Verlag, 1971.

Index

D1524345

Rethinking Homeostasis

Allostatic Regulation in Physiology and Pathophysiology

Jay Schulkin

A Bradford Book
The MIT Press
Cambridge, Massachusetts
London, England

This book was set in Palatino by Achorn Graphic Services, Inc., on the Miles 33 system, and was printed and bound in the United States of America.

Library of Congress Cataloging-in-Publication Data

Schulkin, Jay.
Rethinking homeostasis : allostatic regulation in physiology and pathophysiology / Jay Schulkin.
p. cm.
"A Bradford book."
Includes bibliographical references and index.
ISBN 0-262-19480-5 (hc. : alk. paper)
1. Homeostasis. 2. Neuroendocrinology. 3. Psychophysiology. 4. Biological control systems. I. Title.

QP90.4 .S38 2003
612'.022—dc21

2002071839

Dedicated to Kent Berridge, Bruce McEwen, and Peter Sterling; thank you for the friendship.

Contents

Preface

My scientific activities within biological inquiry have focused on the concept of homeostatic systems—specifically the craving for sodium and calcium. But early on it became apparent that the concept of homeostasis, rich as it is, was not sufficient to account for the diverse behavioral and physiological adaptations that are observed. That is, even within the study of homeostatic systems such as sodium, when one starts to think about its regulation in terms of neural integration, it becomes clear that animals are anticipatory, make adjustments, and have seasonal variation in response to metabolic and other bodily requirements. The brain is vitally involved in the regulatory responses to systemic physiological requirements.

When my research moved from bodily tissue needs to avoidance of fearful events, the concept of homeostasis was less appropriate. In what way is fear linked to homeostatic regulation? This was not obvious. However, evaluating the physical limits of a system's functioning is quite different from evaluating the specific point of regulation that a system is trying to maintain. But in both cases hormonal mechanisms are critical to behavioral and physiological regulation.

The concept of allostasis, for me, is a heuristic for generating research. I offer the concept as a humble suggestion. As in previous books, I apologize in advance to those investigators and their research that I may have omitted from this book. And I thank my family, friends, and colleagues. In particular, I thank Barbara Bettes, George Chrousos, Kristine Erickson, Phil Gold, David Goldstein, Lauren Hill, George Koob, E. E. Krieckhaus, Joe Majzoub, Jamie McGregor, Mike Power, Jeff Rosen, Louis Schmidt, Pathik Wadhwa, Alan Watts, and John Wingfield for their encouragement and help.

Introduction

Evolution provided a rich set of mechanisms to maintain internal stability, which includes both local (e.g., kidney, heart) and broadly coordinated (e.g., brain) functions (Boyd and Noble, 1993). One essential concept to account for physiological stability is that of *homeostasis* (Cannon, 1932). *Homeostasis* is a common term within the biological sciences. A variety of well-known examples of behavioral and biological regulation to maintain homeostasis have been characterized. The maintenance of the internal environment by both physiological and behavioral means is a fundamental component in the well-being of complex animals like ourselves (both short- and long-term prospects). The concept of homeostasis is linked to mechanisms for maintaining internal viability and the defense of physiological events essential for bodily well-being. Some of the more obvious examples are: temperature, pH, glucose, protein, oxygen, sodium, and calcium.

But within considerations of homeostatic regulation, certain limitations of the concept have emerged (see Toates, 1979; Stricker, 1990). While homeostasis is the regulation of a set point in the body (e.g., glucose or oxygen in the blood or pH—as noted above), even that characterization is too rigid and perhaps misleading. For example, body temperature can vary to a certain degree (seasonal differences) and can be both reactive and predictive (Moore-Ede, 1986; Mrosovsky, 1990; Wingfield and Ramenofsky, 1999). There are both anticipatory responses to possible predictable events and reactive responses to unpredictable changes. These events are expressed both in terms of behavior and of physiology. There thus emerged implicit in the

homeostatic literature a conceptual expansion that required something more than simply a set point regulatory system (Nelson and Drazen, 2000).

Evolution favored a number of selected behavioral (Barkow et al., 1992) and physiological mechanisms designed to maintain internal viability. It is also apparent that the central nervous system plays an important role by superceding local physiological function in the maintenance of bodily tissue. In other words, the central nervous system is helping to orchestrate bodily stability (e.g., ingestion of sodium, water, etc.; Denton et al., 1996; Fitzsimons, 1999). This has added a new level of complexity to regulatory events. The central state reflects the balancing of a number of factors essential for maintaining physiological and behavioral viability. Within this context, in part, a new concept emerged.

Less well known is a recently coined term, *allostasis* (Sterling and Eyer, 1988). The term was introduced to take account of regulatory systems in which (1) there is no clear set point, (2) there are individual differences in expression (McEwen and Stellar, 1993), (3) the behavioral and physiological responses are anticipatory (Sterling and Eyer, 1988; Schulkin et al., 1994), and (4) there was a vulnerability to physiological overload and the breakdown of regulatory capacities (bone demineralization, brain deterioration, etc. from, for example, high levels of cortisol for long, unrestrained periods; McEwen, 1998a, b).

Allostasis is essential in maintaining internal viability amid changing conditions (Sterling and Eyer, 1988; McEwen and Stellar, 1993; Schulkin et al., 1994). What is similar about both concepts (homeostasis and allostasis) is the coordinated response to maintain internal stability (Langley, 1973).

The contents of the book are as follows:

The first chapter suggests that, from within considerations of homeostatic regulation, there was a search for a broader term (or a better definition of homeostasis) that could account for variation in response during the defense of the internal milieu, and also for the variation in response to the breakdown of bodily defenses when under chronic duress (figure I.1; Selye, 1982; Goldstein, 1995a, b; Chrousos, 1998).

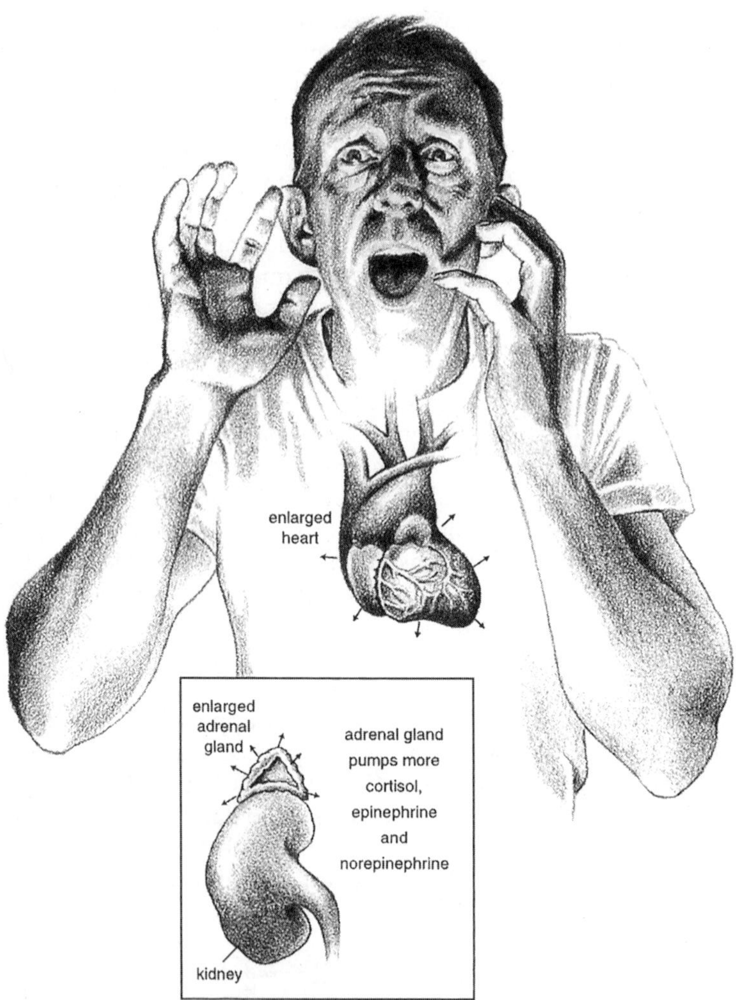

Figure I.1
Neuroendocrine alarm response (Yansen and Schulkin, unpublished).

The concept of allostasis is tied to the fact that one primary role for the central nervous system is to coordinate some of the regulator responses. Therefore in chapter 2, I discuss the hormonal / allostatic regulation of central motive states and the anticipatory nature of them in the organization of behavior. Specifically, I provide a neuroendocrine perspective in which central motive states (e.g., craving water, sodium, food, sex, cocaine, etc.) can be understood. A wide range of instances in which feedforward neuroendocrine mechanisms have functional consequences for behavior and physiological regulation is described. Central motive states (in suitable environments), in part, are sustained and generated by the actions of steroids and the positive induction they have on neuropeptides / neurotransmitters (Pfaff, 1999; Schulkin, 1999a).

One example can do: The secretion of adrenal steroids has diverse effects on neuropeptide systems, depending upon the ecological context and biological needs of the animal. When animals are in need of water or sodium (following blood loss, water deprivation, excessive heat), the adrenal steroid hormone facilitates water and sodium ingestion via the effects on angiotensinergic pathways in the brain (Sumners et al., 1991; chapter 2 of this book).

It is important to note, even in what appears to be a paradigmatic homeostatic system—maintaining body fluid and sodium balance through physiological and behavioral means—a variety of animals that have been tested to date, particularly the omnivorous rat, ingest more sodium than they need (e.g., Denton, 1982; Schulkin, 1991). Moreover, animals are opportunistic in that they ingest what they can when they find it. Nonetheless, sodium ingestion remains one among many outstanding examples of a behavioral and physiological regulatory system.

Chapter 3 describes the behavioral and neuroendocrine regulation of fear and adversity and the consequences that they have on the body. The chapter builds on chapter 2 with regard to the positive induction (or feedforward mechanism) of a neuropeptide corticotropin releasing hormone (CRH) playing a functional role for a motivational state (Swanson and Simmons, 1989;

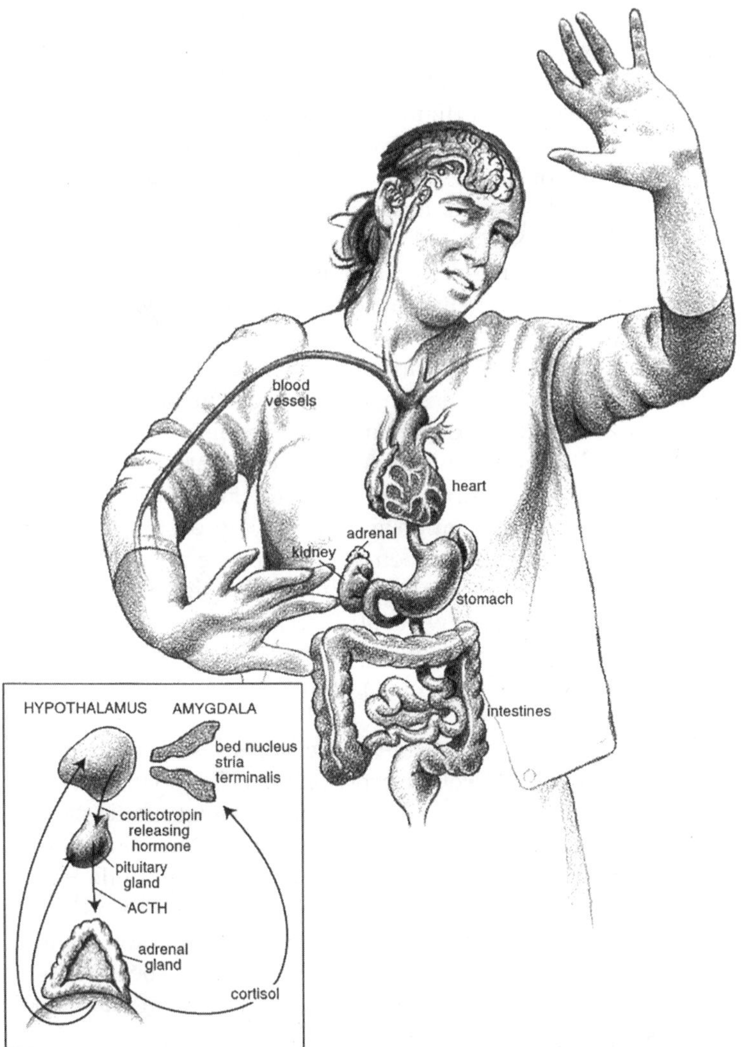

Figure I.2
Neuroendocrine fear response (Yansen and Schulkin, unpublished).

Watts and Sanchez-Watts, 1995). This chapter provides a neuroendocrine perspective on the mechanisms that underlie fear and adversity in terms of both homeostatic and allostatic regulation, and allostatic overload (figure I.2; Schulkin et al., 1994, 1998).

Evolution has selected mechanisms that are not only reflected in neural function but also in the placenta. The placenta is not different from the central nervous system with regard to feedforward endocrine regulatory mechanisms. In chapter 4, I discuss the endocrine regulation of normal birth and birth that is preterm as a result of maternal stress, the breakdown of normal regulatory processes, and the production of preterm babies. The normal example is another instance in which steroids facilitate the expression of peptides to promote a functional relationship—parturition (Majzoub et al., 1999; Challis et al., 2000; King et al., 2001). But under duress (psychosocial stress, risk behaviors) or adversity (bacterial infections), the facilitation may represent an emergency situation and a pathological state (allostatic overload by the overexpression of peptides—e.g., CRH) by steroids and the onset of early parturition (Petraglia et al., 1995a,b; Challis et al., 2000; Wadhwa et al., 2001). Moreover, these endocrine events during pregnancy can have long-term effects on physiological and behavioral expression in the infant (Welberg and Seckl, 2001).

Last, a chronic overextension of the stress system in the brain can characterize the street addict (Koob and Le Moal, 2001). For addicted people, the range of their focus narrows, while the potential events that the drugs are associated with increases. A state of chronic "wanting" pervades the addicted state (Berridge and Robinson, 1998). In chapter 5, I discuss the neuroendocrine and behavioral mechanisms that underlie drug cravings and the compromise it has on bodily functions. A neuroendocrine/behavioral perspective that is outlined in detail in chapters 2 and 3 is extended into chapter 5.

Rethinking Homeostasis

Chapter 1

Allostasis: The Emergence of a Concept

The logic of this chapter is to begin with a brief discussion of the evolution of thinking about homeostatic systems; that is, historical and contemporary perspectives on maintaining internal physiological stability, and its breakdown during duress. One outcome of thinking about homeostatic systems has been the recognition that a concept was needed to explain how the animal *anticipates* and / or reacts to unpredictable change as a function of internal regulation of physiological events. Finally, I introduce the concept of allostasis and present its use in explaining regulatory physiological and pathological events. Thus this chapter should provide first an orientation to how we arrived at perhaps the need to develop a concept in addition to that of homeostasis in accounting for regulatory physiology and, second, to a consideration of allostasis, a concept to account for central nervous system influences on systemic physiological regulation.

The Defense of the Internal Milieu: Homeostasis

Two key concepts have been in our scientific lexicon for some time. Both have to do with bodily regulation: the defense of the internal milieu (Bernard, 1852, 1859) and homeostatic regulation (Cannon, 1915, 1929a).

Bernard offered two clear ideas in his studies on the regulation of the internal milieu. One is the whole-body physiological regulation of internal stasis, and that states can change if the animal is to be evolutionarily viable. The other is breakdown of tissue under duress—the failure of short-term physiological

solutions to resolve the "problem." These two themes would then resonate for those that came after (Goldstein, 1995a, b; Chrousos and Gold, 1998).

Consider the process of digestion. Bernard (1856, 1878) understood that the salivary glands and pancreas worked in unison in the process of digestion. Both served to incorporate needed nutrients into working physiological systems to maintain those systems. He observed the function of this system and searched for "juices" that are secreted. One of his interests was the digestion of fat. He inserted a fistula into the pancreas to determine what was secreted in the process of digestion. Bernard believed that the salivary gland, pancreas, brain, and other organs were in the service of maintaining the internal milieu.

Bernard also studied the breakdown of normal pancreatic function and morphological expression with metabolic stress (see 1856). Interested in understanding glucose homeostasis, he investigated the physiological mechanisms that render internal constancy possible, and then the breakdown of physiology under duress (e.g., extreme hunger, figure 1.1).[1]

Now consider the other key idea of homeostatic regulation. Cannon is associated with the concept of "the wisdom of the body," but the phrase was actually coined by the British physiologist Ernest Starling in 1923. In his paper, Starling referred to hormones as chemical messengers, to their overproduction in pathology (as in Graves' disease and thyroid dysfunction), and to "harmonic relationships" in maintaining bodily health. These physiological events represented "reservoirs of power" (Cannon, 1915, 1929b, p. 22).

Physiological analysis and better understanding of the maintenance of the internal system were coming into their own by the time Cannon arrived (Pfluger, 1877; Fredericq, 1885), and there was the perspective that "living entities seek equilibrium" (Richet, 1900; see Langley, 1973).

1. Nonetheless, he overstated the absolute separation of the internal milieu from the wider environmental contexts of the external world (Holmes, 1986; Sullivan, 1990).

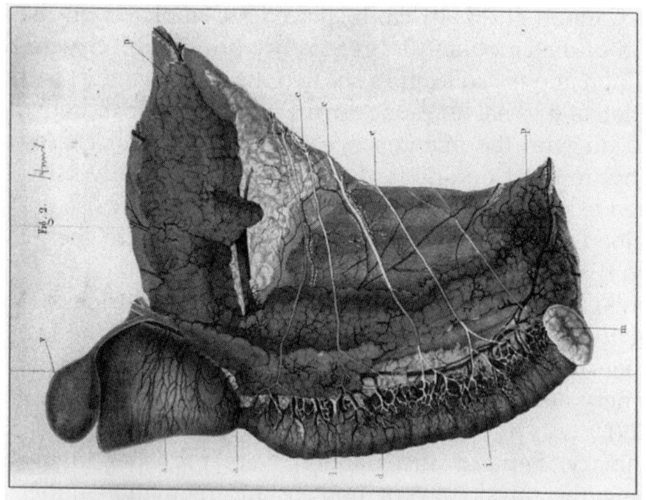

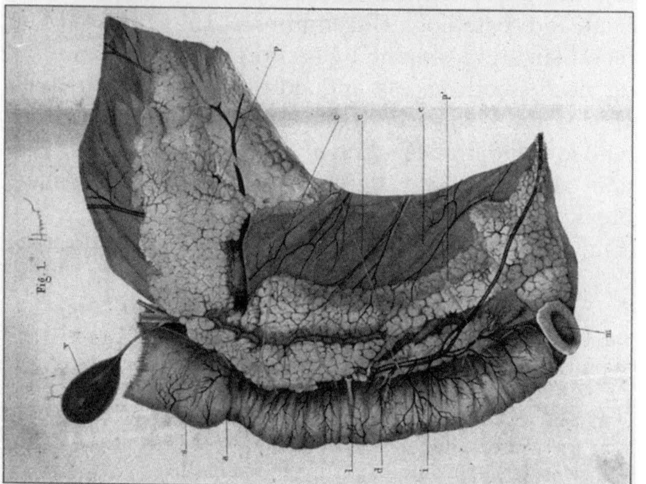

Figure 1.1
Pancreatic morphology of a dog that has not eaten for 36 hours (*left*) and a dog that has eaten (*right*) (Bernard 1856/1985).

Walter Cannon (1915, 1929a, b) placed an emphasis on the interaction of the emotions and regulatory physiology. Specifically, Cannon and his colleagues studied the digestive tract and the secretion of adrenal hormone during a number of conditions having to do with the maintenance and utilization of energy balance (figure 1.2). Conditions of normal adaptation, adversity, and excited extended activity result in increased energy use. Increased blood sugar was seen as essential for short-term energy regulation (Sapolsky, 1992; Dallman et al., 1995).[2]

Cannon's early work focused on adrenal secretion during conditions of duress. He suggested that there were limits to the system. Soldiers during the Great War, he noted, were being beaten down by nervous exhaustion (see Flemming, 1984; see also Haldane, 1929).

In summary, Bernard and Cannon were prescient in understanding the physiology of homeostatic regulation under both normal and pathological conditions. They focused, in part, on blood sugar, its storage by end-organ systems, and its use during need—both excess and normal. Both understood that stability is the key, in both the short and long term, in terms of both low and high taxation of the body's resources. The body's main defense is through physiological mechanisms, and the breakdown of regulatory mechanisms emerges when the organism is pushed beyond regulatory and compensatory capacities.

2. The chemicals secreted in the alimentary system, Cannon suggested (1927, 1931), would provide evidence for the theory that James and Lange suggested for the emotions. Cannon was looking largely at the sympathetic innervation of the adrenal gland and alimentary organs (i.e., perfusion of sugar into the liver) under a variety of conditions. Cannon's theory of the emotions was set in the context of emergency conditions. We recognize now that it is too limited a conception of the emotions to continue to entertain seriously (e.g., LeDoux, 1996; Berridge, 1996; Rosen and Schulkin, 1998; Panksepp, 1998; Lane and Nadel, 1999; Davidson et al., 2000), but what Cannon did capture was an understanding that fatigue, exhaustion, and going beyond what the body could sustain posed a danger to homeostatic regulatory balance (see also Goldstein, 2000).

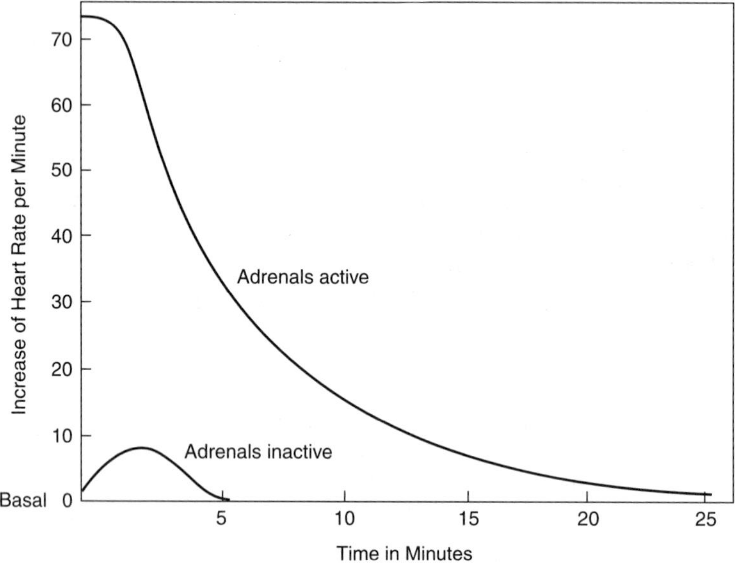

Figure 1.2
Adrenal activation and heart rate: greater response and longer persistence of heart rate in cats whose adrenals were active (Cannon, 1932, 1967).

Stress as a Deviation from Homeostatic Balance: Attempts to Expand the Concept of Homeostasis

Hans Selye of Montreal (1956, 1974, 1982), as is well known, helped establish the scientific study of stress and biological adaptation to everyday adversity. He set out to study the normal "wear and tear" on the body to determine when this stress becomes pathological. Stress turns to distress when the body is no longer able to tolerate the events to which it is subjected and begins to recede into compromised and deteriorating function.

Selye (1956, 1974) integrated his theory of stress with the findings of Bernard and Cannon and the concept of homeostasis, which he called normal adaptation or "general adaptation syndrome." He called it a general syndrome because many parts of

the body were involved and affected. The body's reactions were all in the service of maintaining equilibrium. Viability is endangered when, as Selye understood, one "subtracts" stabilization from the reaction response to the specific event. This can be seen, for example, in "the increased production of adrenocortical hormones, the involution of the lymphatic organs or the loss of weight" (figure 1.3; 1956, 1976, p. 17). Regarding stress, the adaptation syndrome ranges from alertness to fatigue (Goldstein, 2000). The alarm response has endocrine and other bodily consequences. Selye went to great lengths to identify these responses. He argued that stress is a basic physiological event.[3]

Selye, like Cannon, focused on the hypothalamic-pituitary-adrenal (HPA) axis, which, in addition to the immune physiology, is an important regulator in coping with adverse events (Richter, 1942; Mason, 1975a, b). Selye understood that inflammation and the immunological response were essential for adaptation. He postulated that they have long-term costs for bodily health. However, they remain important for short-term viability; evolution does not design immortal organisms (at least not many). He cataloged the range of disease states that can occur from exhaustion and stress (e.g., from nervous tics, sleep disturbances, feeding abnormalities, gastrointestinal disturbances, and migraine headaches to disturbances of the heart and hypertension). He speculated that chronic psychologic worry might be important for the etiology of physiological pathology.

Selye was searching for a concept beyond homeostasis and its link to stress and described what he called *heterostasis* (1956, 1976, p. 85). He stated, "When faced with unusually heavy demands, however, ordinary homeostasis is not enough" (p. 85), because the "homeostat" has been raised to a level beyond its capacity, perhaps to a higher level (e.g., increased production)

3. Many investigators have pointed out the limitations of Selye's view (e.g., Mason, 1971a,b, 1975; McCarty and Pacak, 2000; Goldstein, 2000; McEwen, 2001) with regard to the fact that a variety of neuronal and hormonal responses participate in the response to stress, and the responses are not always nonspecific in the context of the general adaptation syndrome.

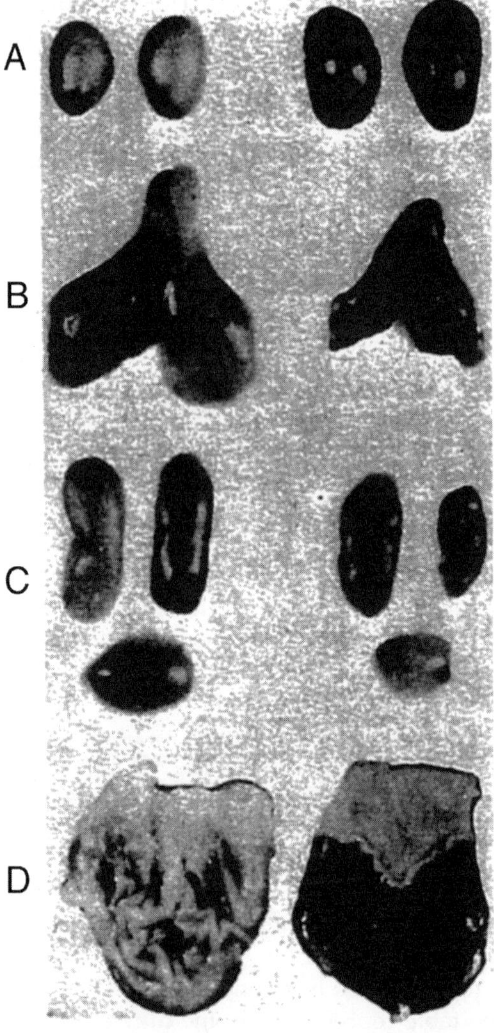

Figure 1.3
The biological alarm reaction. (*A*) Adrenals. (*B*) Thymus. (*C*) A group of the three lymph nodes. (*D*) Inner surface of the stomach. Organs in the left column are from unstressed rats; organs in the right column are from stressed rats (Seyle, 1956, 1976).

of function (see also Goldstein, 1995a, b, 2000). The major difference between the two states of bodily regulation is that one relates to maintaining normal balance, while the other relates to heightened activity with an accelerated rate of defense of bodily viability.

Many investigators have expanded on the insights of Bernard, Cannon, and Selye (e.g., Mason, 1975a, b; Goldstein, 1995a, b, 2000; Chrousos, 1996, 1998; McCarty and Pacak, 2000). One just has to look at the *Encyclopedia of Stress* (Fink, 2000) and the rich assortment of bodily events that are characterized to understand the impact of Selye. Often a critical feature of stress is that it is a threat to homeostasis and that discrepancies of expected outcome result in adaptive physiological responses (Goldstein, 1995a, b). Real stress occurs when expected measures far exceed what the physiological systems can tolerate (Goldstein, 1995a, b, 2000). Complex physiological systems designed to maintain internal stability use common effector systems; when there is a breakdown in one system, there are compensatory responses in others. Moreover, nature has insured safety valves in common effector systems (Goldstein, 1995a, b; Fink, 2000).

"Resetting" of homeostatic systems is an essential function for long-term survival (Goldstein, 1995a, b, 2000; Bauman, 2000). Selye argued that prediction and action in the face of discrepancy were indicative of both physiological and behavioral responses. Distress and defensive behaviors, used to accommodate the stress, have fundamental links to homeostatic regulation (table 1.1).

Of course, the continued elevation of the HPA axis will eventually compromise a number of normal functions (Chrousos, 1996, 1998). Not only are the classical stress systems (including the immune system) of concern to Selye (1982), but so are the profound changes in reproductive hormones. Table 1.1 should be read in context; the table represents chronic duress. This is not a pervasive biological phenomenon (Wingfield and Romero, 2001). In a variety of species, social stress in subordinates decreases levels of reproductive hormones and increases cortisol levels (Sapolsky, 1992, 1995, 1996; Herbert, 1996a). These events

Table 1.1
Behavioral and physical adaptations during acute stress

Behavioral Adaptation	Physical Adaptation
Increased arousal and alertness	Oxygen and nutrients directed to the CNS and stressed body site(s)
Increased cognition, vigilance, and focused attention	Altered cardiovascular tone, increased blood pressure and heart rate
Euphoria or dysphoria	Increased respiratory rate
Suppression of appetite and feeding behavior	Increased gluconeogenesis and lipolysis
Suppression of reproductive behavior	Detoxification from endogenous or exogenous toxic products
Containment of the stress response	Inhibition of growth and reproductive systems
	Inhibition of digestion-stimulation of colonic motility
	Containment of the inflammatory/immune response
	Containment of the stress response

Adapted from Chrousos, 1998

in turn decrease levels of oxytocin and prolactin as neuropeptides and increase corticotropin-releasing hormone (CRH) in extrahypothalamic sites (see chapters 3–5). This results in decreased reproductive fitness and may represent a short-term phenomenon, as the animal utilizes strategies to increase its likelihood of reproductive success by removing itself from the environment and placing itself in a more habitable one.

Homeostatic systems are typically couched, from an endocrine point of view, in terms of negative feedback (Goldstein, 1995a, b, 2000). The classic example is the restraint of the HPA axis and its attendant long-term effects on bodily tissue (see, e.g., Chrousos, 1997, 1998). Most regulatory systems have a way to decrease or inhibit the activation of physiological and

behavioral systems (see Le Magnen, 1984; Smith, 1997a). It is a mistake, however, to assert that one should be suspicious of "any hypothesis that includes a positive feedback loop" (Goldstein, 1995a, p. 28) or to suggest that positive feedback loops are "inherently unstable and rare" (Wingfield and Ramenofsky, 1999). In fact, both negative and positive feedback loops interact in the regulation of the internal milieu. Positive feedback loops or feed forward mechanisms are an important part of allostatic regulation (chapters 2–5) but they are nested within restraining physiological systems.[4]

Perhaps it is more correct to suggest that, in the context of homeostatic systems, positive feedback is less common than negative feedback (Fink, 1997, 2000; but see Kalra, 1993 for a discussion of both positive and negative feedback). One might want to distinguish, as I would (see also Pfaff, 1980, 1999; Herbert, 1993; Schulkin, 1999a) between systemic physiological regulation and the induction of neuropeptides (positive induction by steroid hormones) and the expression of central states that serve regulatory needs. Indeed, many of the regulatory events that underlie behavior, such as water and sodium ingestion, food ingestion, sex, and other appetitive behaviors, all have positive feedback loops (see chapters 2–5). The animal is changing state in order to change its behavior. If the change in behavior satisfies the "need," then the animal will change the state again.

It is important to note that prediction and anticipation of adverse events and behavioral adaptation by external cues (Miller, 1957, 1959; Weiss, 1970, 1971; Weiss et al., 1981) avert physiological pathology. For example, gastric ulceration can be prevented by the prediction of aversive events, which also reduces the elevation of the hormones of stress (Mason, 1971, 1975a, b). In other words, when uncertainty is pervasive, predictability has real consequences for both physiological regulation and behavioral expression (Miller, 1957, 1959; Weiss, 1970, 1971). Mason and his colleagues (1957, 1975a, b), for example, provided contexts

4. I appreciate very much the conversations I have had with Dave Goldstein on this issue.

in which predictability had real consequences on the activation of the HPA axis. Let's turn to Pavlov to consider anticipatory, prediction, and cephalic response to maintain homeostatic balance.

Cephalic Regulatory Responses: Expanding Homeostasis to the Anticipatory

The brain is intimately involved in regulatory events. Pavlov (1927) and many other investigators (see Stellar, 1954, 1960; Kuenzel et al., 1999) have expanded the notion of homeostasis toward the neural/behavioral regulation of local physiological regulation (see Smith's 1995, 1997a, b, 2000 informative depiction of Pavlov's work). The digestive reflexes are biological events through which to understand the relationship between an animal and its external environment. Pavlov noted (1894, 1895, p. 82), "the digestive canal, in respect to its chief function in the organisms" is like "a chemical factory where the raw material—food—undergoes a predominantly chemical treatment; this makes possible its absorption by the juices of the organism and its utilization by the organism for the maintenance of the vital processes." Pavlov, like Bernard, believed salivary secretion to be continuous with gastric secretion. Both serve the same end—namely, the utilization of food sources for bodily needs. Pavlov went on to demonstrate differential salivary secretion to different food sources. Dry food, for example, evokes greater salivary secretion than wet food.

Pavlov realized that a reflex could be associated not only with the sight and sound of food, but with other stimuli, and those other stimuli can elicit food-related physiological responses. A conditioned response to an arbitrary buzzer, for instance, prompted a salivary secretion of 16.5 ml (Pavlov, 1927, 1960). In other words, an arbitrary stimulus could elicit the "conditional" salivary reflex (Todes, 1997a, b; Rescorla, 1988).

Also of importance, Pavlov introduced the concept of *cephalic phase* in the process of digestion (see Powley, 1977, 2000; Mattes, 2000). The cephalic phase is an *anticipatory* response that

prepares the digestive tract to absorb and utilize nutrients essential for bodily maintenance and function (Grill and Berridge, 1985; Powley and Berthoud, 1985). The cephalic response has been demonstrated in several species, including humans, and in various hormonal systems (Teff, 2000; Mattes, 2000; Nederkoorn et al., 2000). The secretion of insulin, for example, to utilize nutrients also plays a functional role to minimize perturbations in homeostatic imbalance by the ingestion of the meal (Woods, 1991)—eating, digestion, and absorption provide the necessary nutrients to keep the organism viable; homeostatic mechanisms operate to keep tissue and fluid balance within viable limits. These events are mediated by vagal and brainstem function (figure 1.4; Powley, 1977). In other words, anticipatory and physiological homeostatic responses are invoked to minimize internal disruption, in terms of both low sources and excess sources (Solomon, 1980; Siegal and Allan, 1998). Compensatory responses are elicited in both contexts to minimize internal disruption. Exaggerated cephalic phase insulin secretory responses have been linked to obesity and conditioned hypoglycemia in animal models (Woods, 1991). It is important to note that a wide range of hormonal secretions that play a role in the regulation of the internal milieu can be elicited not only by stimuli that are inherently linked to what needs to be regulated, but also by arbitrary stimuli associated with them (Konturek and Konturek, 2000; Katschinski, 2000)—part of the evidence for the central nervous system involvement in the regulation of the internal milieu.

Neural/Behavioral Influences on Homeostasis

States of the brain profoundly influence regulatory physiology and behavior. The interactions between behavioral and physiological mechanisms in the maintenance of the internal milieu are widely accepted in many other domains—for example, thermal regulation. Temperature regulation has been under investigation for several hundred years (Blagden, 1775; Hunter, 1778; Langley, 1973), ever since the discovery of the means to mea-

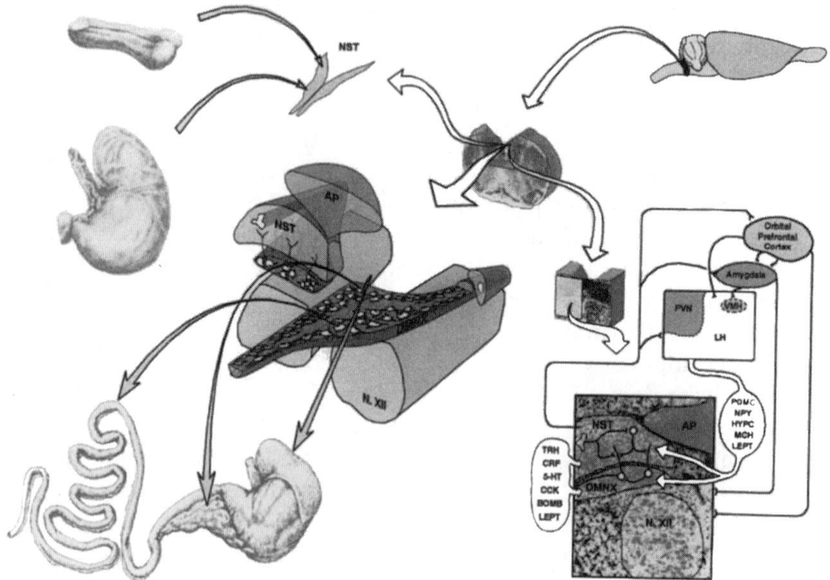

Figure 1.4
The organization of the dorsal vagal complex. The dorsal vagal complex (*center of figure*) is located in medulla oblongata (*upper right*). The complex consists of the dorsal motor nucleus (DMNX), nucleus of the solitary tract (NST), and area postrema (AP). Primary afferents from the different organs of the gastrointestinal tract, e.g., the tongue and stomach, project topographically to different regions of the NST (*upper left*). Preganglionic motor neurons of the DMNX project topographically to the organs of the gastrointestinal tract, e.g., the stomach, pancreas, and intestines (*lower left*). The neurons of the NST and DMNX are distributed in an organization that provides the architecture of the cephalic and other vagal reflexes (*lower right*). This circuitry of the dorsal vagal complex receives projections from more rostral limbic sites and contains dense concentrations of binding sites for different metabolic peptides and hormones (*lower right*). LH, lateral hypothalamus; N. XII, nucleus of 12 or the hypoglossal nucleus; PVN, paraventricular nucleus; VMH, ventromedial hypothalamus (Powley, 2000).

sure temperature (Galileo). Most mammals maintain internal or core temperature at a steady state internally; birds achieve thermal regulation by both physiological and behavioral means (Schmidt-Nielson, 1975). There is some variability in temperature regulation. Mammals also maintain thermal homeostasis by regulating body temperature using both external and internal means (Schmidt-Nielson, 1975; Gisolfi and Mora, 2000).

A variety of animals make nests for safety, reproduction, and warmth (figure 1.5). Curt Richter (1942–43) demonstrated in the laboratory what had been noted in the field—the behavioral regulation of thermal physiology by showing that rats will build nests under cold conditions. He later showed that these regulatory behaviors depend upon an intact hypothalamic pituitary adrenal axis.

Various investigators have demonstrated that a number of species (e.g., rats, goldfish, humans) will perform operant-conditioned behaviors such as bar pressing to gain access to something that would help them return their temperature to

Figure 1.5
Behavioral regulation of temperature—building a nest (Richter, 1942, 1976).

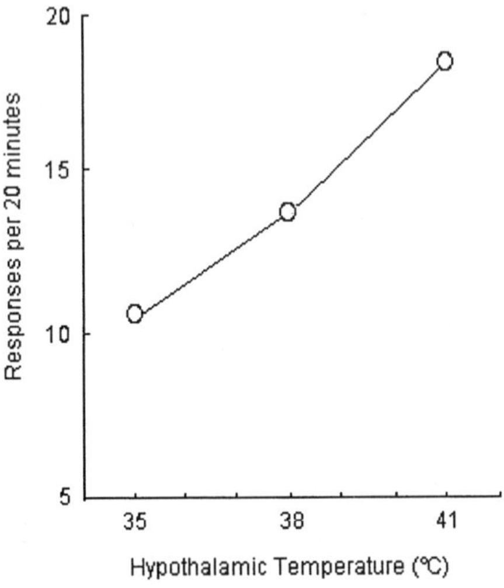

Figure 1.6
Bar pressing to regulate the temperature of hypothalamic neurons (adapted from Corbit, 1973).

within a tolerable range (Rozin, 1961, 1965, 1968; Stellar and Corbit, 1973). Of importance, regions of the hypothalamus respond to changes in thermal temperature, which results in behavioral changes (Satinoff, 1964, 1978). Rats, for example, under excess heat can perform operants to cool the hypothalamus directly (figure 1.6; Corbit, 1973; Cabanac and Dib, 1983). In humans, this regulatory behavioral response is associated with pleasure and / or the easing of discomfort (Cabanac, 1971, 1973, 1979; Stellar and Corbit, 1973).

Circadian Rhythms: Reactive and Predictive Homeostasis

Circadian or other rhythmic pattern regulation of bodily needs reveals diverse regulation of the internal milieu (see Richter, 1922, 1957a, 1965; Moore-Ede et al., 1982; Moore-Ede, 1986;

Wingfield and Romero, 2001). Adaptation is pervasive. Great variation in, for example, cortisol secretion reflects seasonal breeding, hibernation, and the ability to alter metabolic rates.

Thus a term called *predictive homeostasis* was coined by Moore-Ede (1986; Moore-Ede et al., 1982). Predictive homeostasis is an anticipatory adaptation and is to be distinguished from what he called *reactive homeostasis*. This distinction arose in the context of considerations of circadian timing systems in the brain and their role in behavioral and physiological regulation in the anticipation of future needs when they appear (Rosenwasser et al., 1988; Mistlberger, 1994).

Of importance in ethological and laboratory contexts, the circadian clock has been shown to play a role in helping the animal predict what time objects such as food, water, and sodium may appear. This is what Moore-Ede (1986) linked to predictive homeostasis (see also Henen, 1997). In other words, to be able to predict, one has to have a sense of time and be able to detect rhythmic events (Gallistel, 1992).

But the capacity to anticipate events is not just related to a circadian clock; the anticipatory secretion of insulin to food sources is not time-locked to a twenty-four-hour period (Woods, 1970). Behavioral and physiological anticipation in the service of maintaining internal stability is an evolutionary advance in the regulation of the internal milieu (see also Nicolaidis, 1977; Fitzsimons, 1979; Bauman and Currie, 1980; Mrosovsky, 1990).

Rheostasis was a term coined by Mrosovsky (1990) to account for the wide range of biological systems that are regulated differentially depending upon the context, the season, and the external competition. Set-point parameters in a number of systems demonstrate wide variation depending upon the context. Rheostasis was invented as a concept to account for the "physiology of change" (Mrosovsky, 1990).

Both reactive and predictive homeostasis underlie the behavioral and physiological regulation of the internal milieu. It is clear in the literature of appetite regulation, fear, delivery of babies, and even addictions that both are operative. Allostasis brings a whole new dimension, perhaps, to predictive homeo-

stasis in terms of emphasizing the extensive nature in which the central nervous system is involved in behavioral and physiological regulation.

We now turn to consider allostasis.

Origins of the Concept of Allostasis

Allostasis (Sterling and Eyer, 1981, 1988) was introduced to refer to the process of insuring viability in the face of challenge and change. Allostasis means achieving viability through change of state (bodily variation). It refers in part to the process of increasing sympathetic and HPA activity to promote adaptation and to reestablish internal stability (Sterling and Eyer, 1981; McEwen and Stellar, 1993). At the heart of the concept is the depiction of change in order to maintain (or achieve) a state appropriate to the circumstances. Allostasis also highlights our ability to anticipate, adapt to, or cope with impending future events (Schulkin et al., 1994).

For Sterling and Eyer (1988), "allostasis . . . involves whole brain and body rather than simply local feedback," and this is "a far more complex form of regulation than homeostasis" (p. 637). Sterling and Eyer focused on several systems, principally cardiovascular and immunological regulation. In their view, normal regulation for viability is one thing, long term overuse is another. For example, chronic arousal has potential long-term effects on normal renal/cardiovascular function (figure 1.7). These physiological changes are cephalic in nature; they are driven by the brain's attempt to maintain internal viability amid changing circumstances in diverse environments. But they can also reflect the failure of short-term solutions to solve a continuing problem. Allostatic overload (see below) is expressed when the renin-angiotensin-corticosteroids are elevated for long periods of time, during which sodium is ingested (chapter 2) but perhaps not sufficiently excreted. At these times, hypertension may emerge and compromise bodily health (Denton, 1982; Denton et al., 1996).

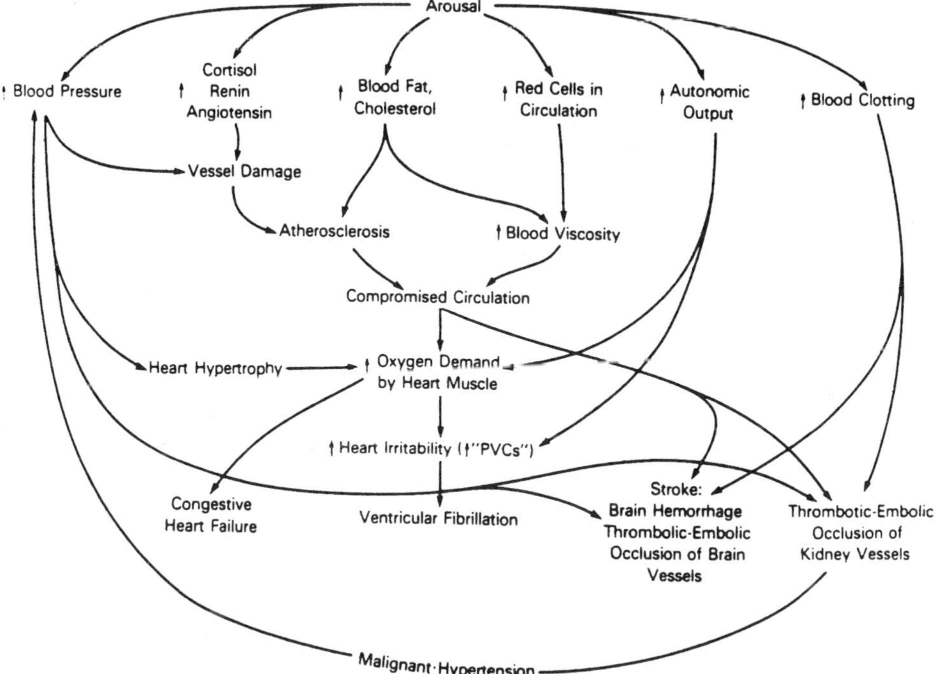

Figure 1.7
Renal-cardiovascular pathology from chronic arousal (Sterling and Eyer, 1981).

Consider another example, that of phosphate regulation of cephalic influence on physiological regulation. The kidney increases phosphate absorption when the animal is deprived of phosphate; the effects are seen within twenty-four hours. A behavior, increased phosphate ingestion, emerges to complement the actions of the kidney in the conservation and maintenance of phosphate levels in the body (Sweeny et al., 1998; Mulroney et al., 2000). It is important to note that the brain itself, in addition to affecting behavior, influences the phosphate regulatory function of the kidney. In phosphate-deprived rats, infusions of phosphate into the third ventricle reduced the expression of

phosphate transporter at the level of the kidney and the brain (figure 1.8), despite the fact that the plasma phosphate remained low (Mulroney et al., 2000).[5] The brain, in other words, has a profound (anticipatory) effect on systemic (kidney) physiological regulation (e.g., Matsui et al., 1995). In fact, the brain receives and sends neural projections directly to most peripheral organs (Powley, 2000) and therefore is involved in most local homeostatic functions.

Chronic arousal, or what Sterling and Eyer referred to as "arousal pathology," is one of the primary features of the modern age. In a carefully presented argument, Eyer and Sterling (1977) reviewed the comparative cultural literature and found dramatic differences in blood pressure that reflected the extent to which chronic arousal was a real everyday factor. This reflects diet, level of exercise, and biological vulnerability. But let us not mythologize the past as peaceful and the present as contaminated by overstimulation. There was overstimulation in the past; nonetheless, examples of physiological responses related to chronic arousal are elevated use of energy; cardiovascular activity; decreases in reproductive function, growth, and appetite; and strain on the immune responses and the aging process (Sapolsky, 1992, 1995; Seeman et al., 1997; Johnston-Brooks et al., 1998).

Sterling and Eyer (1981, 1988) thought major causes of death were linked to arousal pathology: Too much excitement, too much light, too much salt and consumption led to premature death. Fluctuations dominate in systemic physiological stability, and it is the organismic response by the brain that they (Sterling and Eyer, 1988) thought necessitated the invention of the term *allostasis.* "Feedforward" mechanisms induced in the brain by steroid activation of neuropeptides—or neurotransmitter systems, for example—may have an impact on the cardiovascular system, where blood pressure rises in the context of chronic arousal (see Goldstein, 1995a, b, 2000).

5. See Mrosovsky's (1990) discussion on calcium regulation.

NAPi-2 Immunofluorescence in the Amygdaloid Area of the Brain

Low Pi diet + 3V Vehicle **Low Pi Diet + 3V Pi**

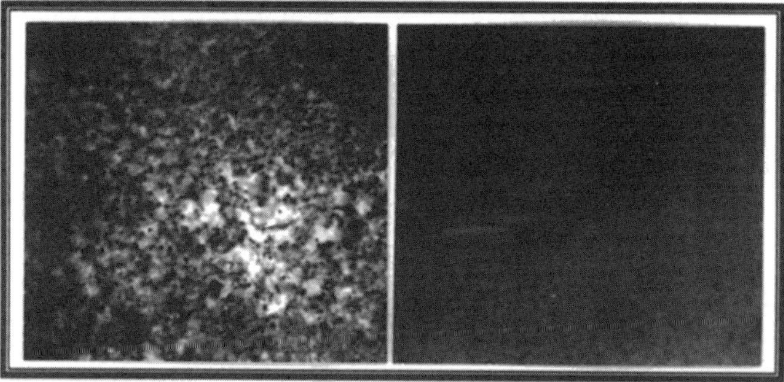

NAPi-2 Immunofluorescence in Cortical Renal Tubules

Low Pi diet + 3V Vehicle **Low Pi Diet + 3V Pi**

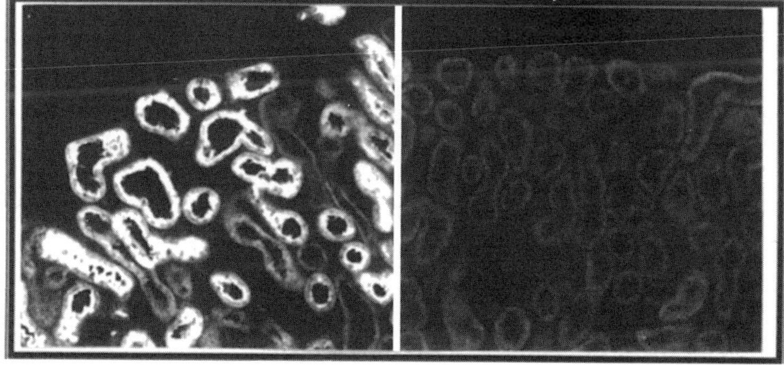

Figure 1.8
Renal and central nucleus phosphate transporter changes in response to central infusions of phosphate in phosphate deficient rats (Mulroney et al., 2000).

Consider several meanings associated with the concept of allostasis (see Sterling and Eyer, 1988; McEwen, 1999; Koob and LeMoal, 2001).

1. *Allostasis:* The process by which an organism achieves internal viability through bodily change of state. Allostasis comprises both behavioral and physiological processes that maintain internal parameters within the limits essential for life.
2. *Allostatic State:* Chronic overactivation of regulatory systems and the alterations of body set points.
3. *Allostatic Overload:* The expression of pathophysiology by the chronic overactivation of regulating systems.

Common physiological mediators include glucocorticoids, DHEA, catecholamines, pituitary hormones, neuropeptides, and cytokines (McEwen, 1998a, b, 2001). In the short term, these mediators serve as beneficial. The immune mediators, in the short term, are boosted in defense of bodily viability, but in the long term, they tend to be compromised in function, both in the periphery and the central nervous system (Sapolsky et al., 2000; Dorries, 2001). The same holds for cardiovascular and metabolic function (Sapolsky et al., 2000), which is why it is important to consider both short-term adaptations and long-term allostatic overload.

Sapolsky and colleagues (2000), in a nice review of the literature on glucocorticoid hormones and stress, suggested that we try to understand the glucocorticoid actions in the following four contexts:

1. Their permissive actions
2. Their suppressive actions
3. Their stimulating actions
4. Their preparative actions

This is a useful way in which to envision glucocorticoid hormones in regulatory physiology. I am mainly focused on their stimulating and preparative actions, of the cephalic role in

regulatory physiology. In part, this occurs through a feedforward mechanism (one form of allostatic regulation), which I assume would be glucocorticoids stimulating and inducing preparative actions (see chapters 2 and 3).

What we can say is that when the physiological mediators, such as cortisol, are overexpressed for long periods of time, pathology can emerge. Examples of allostatic overload include loss of bone mass in people with depression, which is associated with moderately elevated levels of glucocorticoids (Michelson et al., 1996; chapter 4 of this book), and atrophy of neurons in the hippocampus as a result of recurrent depression (Sheline et al., 1996; Bremner et al., 2000). By compromising hippocampal function, allostatic overload impairs normal HPA function as well as memory processes (Axelson et al., 1993; Starkman et al., 1993; Sheline et al., 1996; McEwen, 1997, 1998a, b). Prolonged exposure to glucocorticoids can result in deterioration of the hippocampus in several species (Sapolsky, 1992, 1995; McEwen and Sapolsky, 1995). Prolonged glucocorticoid secretion can compromise glucose transport and utilization, energy store, and use; it can potentiate neuronal toxicity via excitatory amino acids, atrophy of dendrites, reduce neurogenesis (Sapolsky, 1992, 2000). That is, high levels of glucocorticoids (from Cushing's syndrome, from depression, from initial trauma in posttraumatic stress disorder) can have potentially damaging effects on hippocampal tissue and on cognitive functions (figure 1.9; McEwen and Sapolsky, 1995; Bremner et al., 1995, 2000; Sapolsky, 2000).

There are three types of allostatic overload: (1) overstimulation by frequent stress, resulting in excessive stress hormone exposure; (2) failure to inhibit allostatic responses when they are not needed or an inability to habituate to the same stressor, both of which result in overexposure to stress hormones; and (3) inability to stimulate allostatic responses when needed, in which case other systems (e.g., inflammatory cytokines) become hyperactive and produce other types of wear and tear (figure 1.10; McEwen, 1998a, b, 2001).

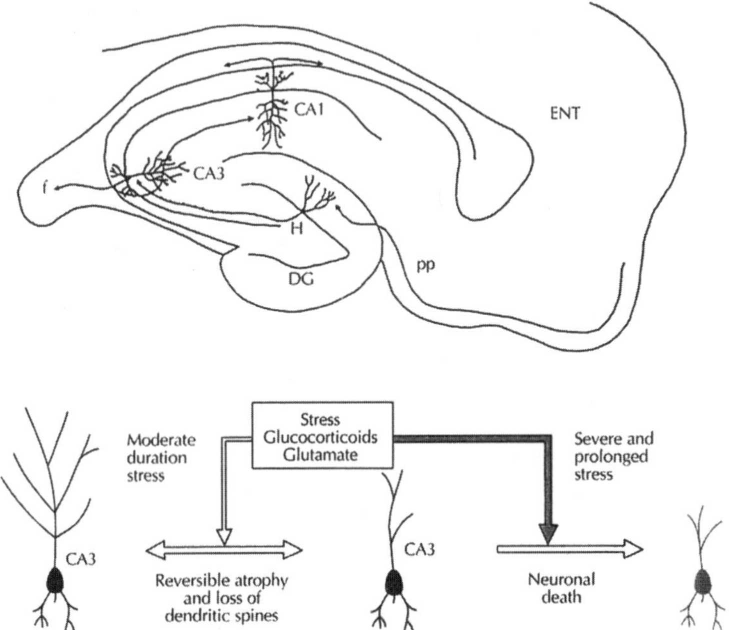

Figure 1.9
Hippocampal neuronal changes in stressed animals (McEwen, 1999).

Indicators of allostatic overload include the following (adapted from McEwen, 1998):

- Cardiovascular pathology
- Metabolic deterioration
- Brain atrophy
- Immune dysfunction and vulnerability to viral impact
- Bone demineralization
- Vulnerability to preterm delivery
- Changes in the sensitization processes

Thus susceptibility to disease is a feature of allostatic overload. The cumulative effect of allostatic overload may be subtle and

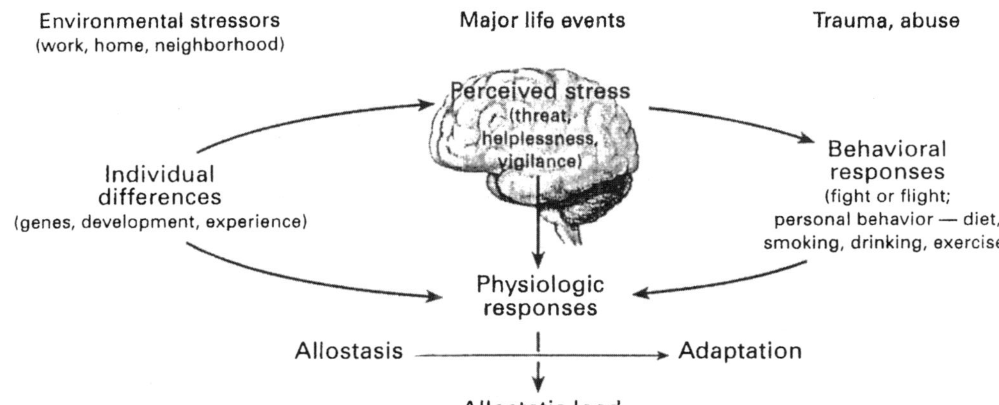

Figure 1.10
The stress response and development of allostatic load as depicted by McEwen (1998).

gradual (e.g., accumulation of body fat and atherosclerotic plaques; McEwen, 2001) or not subtle, as in obesity and change in fat deposition.

Levels of cortisol that are higher during the evening than in the morning, when the hormone is usually elevated, produce greater metabolic costs on the body (e.g., glucose tolerance and insulin regulation; see Plat et al., 1999). Failure to decrease levels of cortisol during the dark phase of circadian rhythm, for example, may reflect both an allostatic state and a vulnerability to physiological deterioration (McEwen, 1999; Van Cauter et al., 2000).

Consider the expression of corticotropin-releasing hormone (CRH) in the brain, something that will be discussed in more detail in later chapters. The overactivation of CRH expression may be one example of allostatic overload (chapters 3–5). What does this mean? Under extremely adverse conditions, such as during chronic anticipatory angst, CRH, the major molecule of duress (Nemeroff et al., 1984; Gold et al. 1988a, b), is overexpressed in regions of the brain linked to fear and anxiety (Koob et al., 1993; Kalin et al., 1994; Makino et al., 1994a, b). When this occurs under extreme conditions, both autonomic and behavioral functions related to fear and anxiety are exacerbated. If these conditions persist over long periods of time (i.e., chronic stress), decay of bodily organs emerges (McEwen and Stellar, 1993; McEwen, 1997, 1998a, b).

Along with compromised HPA function, possibly mediated in part by a damaged hippocampus, there is heightened vigilance incurred by amygdala stimulation to perceive fearful events (Schulkin et al., 1994). This heightened and perhaps chronic vigilance is sustained by high glucocorticoid levels and by the induction of elevated CRH production in the central nucleus of the amygdala and the bed nucleus of the stria terminalis (Swanson and Simmons, 1989; Makino et al., 1994a, b; Watts and Sanchez-Watts, 1995; see chapter 3 of this book). This is not necessarily a pathological state, but an adaptation. An adaptation turns into a pathology, however, when it continues for too long (Rosen and Schulkin, 1998).

Conclusion

Homeostasis is a familiar term in our scientific lexicon; *allostasis* is not. However, there do seem to be physiological and behavioral events that fall outside of a single concept of homeostasis. One can understand that the concept of homeostasis, when expanded from a rather rigid fixed beginning, could perhaps account for allostasis. I would suggest that the concept of allostasis is useful in reorganizing our thinking and facilitating research into understanding regulatory physiology. Part of what allostasis adds is that regulatory events are both behavioral and physiological, and furthermore, that such events are reactive and anticipatory (Moore-Ede, 1986; see Sterling and Eyer, 1988; Schulkin et al., 1994) and that a brain with feedforward mechanisms is one mechanism toward this end.

Allostatic regulation in part reflects cephalic (anticipatory to systemic physiological regulation) involvement in primary regulatory events (Sterling and Eyer, 1988). Evolution selected an important adaptive feature in animals: the anticipation of events. In emergency situations (Wingfield and Ramenofsky, 1999; Wingfield and Romero, 2001), for example, animals with great diversity can increase or decrease, in anticipation of metabolic requirements, the rate of their own regulatory events. Animals anticipate events and modify their physiology accordingly, both daily and seasonally (Nelson and Drazen, 2000). The strategy in environmental contexts for regulation depends on the hormonal and physiological mechanisms that maintain stability and underlie energy expenditure. For example, glucocorticoid hormones are secreted to maintain internal stability in changing environments with regard to nutrient availability and energy homeostasis (Dallman et al., 2000).

Multiple mechanisms are at play at both behavioral and physiological levels of analysis. This all leads to the animal maintaining bodily viability. The route from Bernard to Richter bridges physiological and behavioral mechanisms serving to maintain internal viability. There is no one path to survival, because the world is complex and changing.

The concept of allostasis figures prominently in the recognition of the changing world in which animals like ourselves are constantly adapting, or trying to adapt. With this, the central nervous system involvement with systemic physiological regulation has evolved. Animals need to change state and coordinate a number of competing drives to remain viable. Homeostatic mechanisms tend to resist change of state; allostatic mechanisms were designed to adapt to change. Allostatic mechanisms—both behavioral and physiological—are responsive to anticipatory needs within changing contexts. Like homeostasis, allostasis serves to maintain internal stability.

Allostasis works well when the systems are turned on only when needed and turned off again when no longer in use. However, when allostatic systems remain active, they can cause wear and tear on tissues and accelerate pathophysiology—a phenomenon called *allostatic overload* (McEwen and Stellar, 1993; Schulkin et al., 1994; McEwen, 1997, 1998a, b; Schulkin et al., 1998).

Chapter 2

Central Motive States: Feedforward Neuroendocrine Systems in the Brain

Motivational states are generated by the brain. As my deceased colleague Alan Epstein would say when discussing central motive states and drinking behavior, "Thirst is a state of the brain" (Epstein et al., 1973). However, the acceptance of concepts such as motivation has declined in some intellectual traditions. They warrant resurrection, particularly in the context of the hormonal regulation of behavior, and in the context of allostatic regulation of behavioral and physiological events.

This chapter begins with a discussion of the concept of motivation—its relationship to the central nervous system function and specific hormonal systems. I give some of the logical reasons why the concept of motivation is required in our explanation of behavior. I suggest that the behavioral expression of central motive states (e.g., craving sodium, cocaine, etc.) is coded by neuropeptide expression in the brain and regulated by steroids, that is, positive regulation of neuropeptide expression typically, but not exclusively, by steroids (see Herbert, 1993; Schulkin, 1999a; Pfaff, 1999). Recall that allostatic regulation is anticipatory-cephalic (Sterling and Eyer, 1988; Schulkin et al., 1994). Although homeostatic explanations tend to emphasize negative restraint (Goldstein, 1995a, b; Fink, 1997, 2000), central motive states of the brain are, in part, regulated by steroids in a feedforward fashion, nested within restraining systems.

The concept of allostasis is particularly germane in the analysis of regulatory systems. Many kinds of adaptive responses are not strictly linked to homeostatic regulation. Animals are optimizing their regulatory requirements relative to the season and

Table 2.1
Effects of glucocorticoid hormones

Short-Term Adaptation	Long-Term Disruption
Inhibition of sexual motivation	Inhibition of reproduction
Regulate immune system	Suppress immune system
Increase glucogenesis	Promote protein loss
Increase foraging behavior	Suppress growth

Adapted from Wingfield and Romero, 2001.

the context in which they find themselves (Bauman and Currie, 1980; Wingfield and Romero, 2001). Glucocorticoids are elevated under diverse conditions and are not strictly relegated to the management of stress (table 2.1). But, consider the diverse roles they play in what Wingfield and Romero (see also Sapolsky et al., 2000) termed "contexts of duress."

These effects have relevance for our consideration of motivational systems. Cortisol can facilitate motivational behaviors essential to maintain water and sodium balance and energy balance (for the preparatory role of glucocorticoids, see Sapolsky et al., 2000). These are two systems in which feedforward mechanisms are known to play somewhat of a role in the regulation of appetitive motivational systems. Allostasis is perhaps a more useful concept than traditional homeostatic concepts (which were good for the kidney) but not for the role of motivated behaviors and functional roles in maintaining physiological viability.

Let us turn first to a consideration of the concept of motivation and then to feedforward systems (one kind of allostatic regulation). Thus I begin with a general discussion of the concept of motivation and central motive states of the brain, general features in the brain that underlie central motive states, and then a description of allostatic regulation via feedforward neuroendocrine mechanisms that underlie several central motive states.

The Concept of Motivation

The concept of motivation has figured in the explanation of human behavior throughout recorded history. It may have, in part, evolved as a cognitive ability that was selected to facilitate the prediction and explanation of goal-directed behavior.

Freud (1924), for example, understood that the concept of drive, or libido, generated by the brain was fundamental to explain behavior. But both his drive-reduction model and his singular focus on sexual behavior limited his vision. Although he started out studying the brain to help explain motivated behavior, he abandoned that approach by the turn of the century.

The concepts of motivation and drive were also fundamental in the scientific lexicon of psychology and ethology (Lashley, 1938; Hebb, 1949; Tinbergen, 1951). Unfortunately, however, motivational systems have always had a tendency to multiply like instincts. Of course, that is no different from the unrestrained multiplication of the newest peptide receptor sites (note the proliferation of serotonin, angiotensin, and CRH receptor sites).

Here are some questions to consider:

1. The concept of motivation is bedeviled by questions such as: How many kinds of motivational explanations are there? There are several, and they are not necessarily mutually exclusive. They include drive reduction or homeostatic theories, incentive theories, hedonic theories. For example, when food is attractive, it can be attractive because the animal is hungry (internally pushed); the food is interesting and salient (externally pulled toward an object); or the food is pleasing and hedonistically satisfying (see Toates, 1986; Berridge, 1996), or some combination of all three.
2. Is there a family of core motivational states? Yes. There are core motivational states that subserve the health and reproductive fitness of the animal (Pfaff, 1999; Schulkin, 1999a).

3. What constraints are there in the legitimate use of the term? The constraints come from both psychobiological and neuroscientific levels of analysis (Nader et al., 1997; Swanson, 2000).
4. When is it legitimate to invoke a motivational explanation? It emerges when the concept of motivation provides a definite context and legitimate scientific function in the explanation of animal and human behavior (Hinde, 1968; Toates, 1986).

Motivational systems have long been understood in the context of anticipatory systems generated in the brain (Stellar and Corbit, 1973; Epstein, 1982) that function along with local physiological systems to maintain bodily viability. Perhaps this is why the concept of allostasis may be particularly important to motivational systems that have relevance to bodily viability.

Eliot Stellar (1954) formulated a view held by a generation of investigators about the general mechanism that underlies motivational states. In his classic paper, "The Physiology of Motivation," Stellar suggested that the hypothalamus played a fundamental role in the regulation of excitatory and inhibitory central states (figure 2.1; Stellar, 1954; see also Hebb, 1949). The framework was one in which both internal physiological changes and sensory detection mediated by central hypothalamic sites resulted in behavioral adaptation. Although often construed as merely under hypothalamic control, other regions of the brain are obviously involved in the expression of motivated behaviors, including the cortex and brainstem.

Experiments using electrical (Olds, 1958) and chemical self-stimulation of the hypothalamus and other forebrain sites (Miller, 1957; Grossman, 1968) suggested that stimulation of specific systems in the brain could result in the expression of specific behavior. This result was subsequently challenged by findings that the same site in the hypothalamus, when stimulated, could elicit a range of behaviors such as thirst, hunger, or sex drive, depending upon the context (Valenstein et al., 1970; Valenstein, 1973; see also Wise, 1971). One reasonable explana-

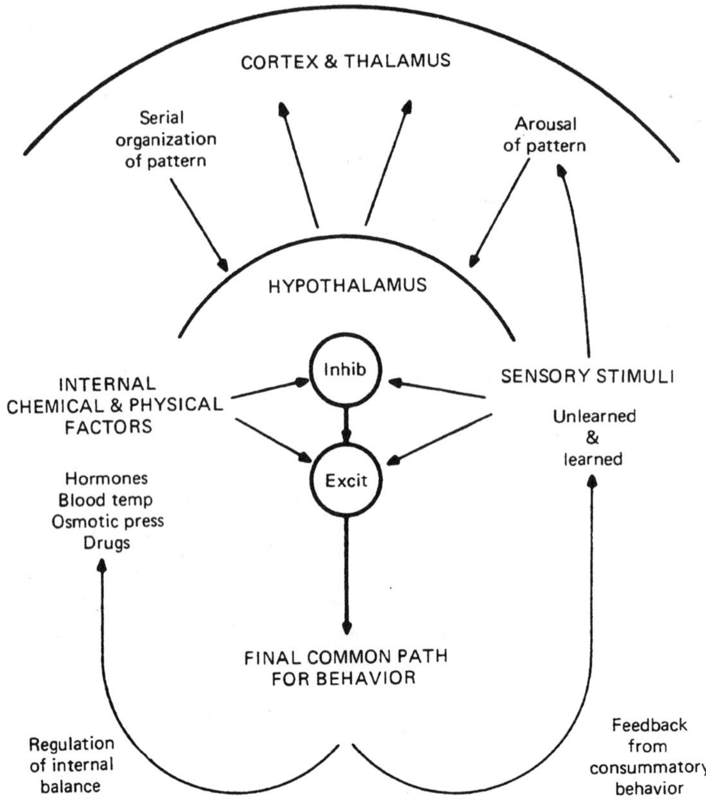

Figure 2.1
The physiological control of motivated behavior (Stellar, 1954).

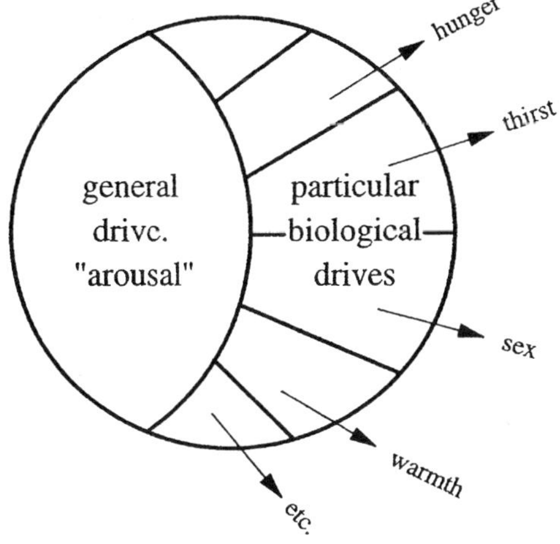

Figure 2.2
The concept of drive or motivation has at least two types of components. There is a component necessary for the *energization* of behavior—arousal—that is general across motivational states. There are also mechanisms that respond to humoral and other particular physiological signals arising from specific biological needs, such as hunger, thirst, sex hormones, temperature changes, and the like. This type of component gives *direction* to motivated behavior (Pfaff, 1999).

tion for the effects of electrical self-stimulation on behavior is that the stimulation increases the salience of environmental stimuli (Berridge and Valenstein, 1991). In retrospect, the expression of behavior by the activation of neural circuits depends upon context or ecological conditions. Behavior does not occur in a vacuum.

This idea that there are no specific signals for the elicitation of behavior also does not always hold. There are both general and specific mechanisms that underlie motivated behaviors (Pfaff, 1999; figure 2.2). Neuropeptides, for example, play specific roles in the expression of motivated behaviors (see Pfaff, 1999; Schulkin, 1999a), in which there are a number of examples of feedforward allostatic regulation. But neuropeptides may also play diverse roles in both physiological and behavioral

regulation, where they have specific physiological functions (e.g., angiotensin, oxytocin, vasopressin; see Herbert, 1993; see below).

Thus motivational states should be characterized as the readiness to behave adaptively in suitable environments (Hinde, 1968, 1970). Motivational behaviors are best understood in the context of being directed toward a certain goal or set of goals in a certain trajectory (Tinbergen, 1951). Neural systems potentiate or depotentiate the readiness for behavioral expression (von Holst and St. Paul, 1963; Gallistel, 1980). Also note, however, that the thirst the animal is trying to quench at the water hole occurs in the context of the fear of possible predation and the need to detect danger signals. The hunger may be related to a specific nutrient or mineral. Motivational systems compete for expression (see McFarland, 1991).

Figure 2.3 depicts one of the ways in which Neil Miller and his colleagues and students understood motivation (Miller, 1957, 1959). For Miller, motivation was an essential category in experimental design; the physiological and neural levels of analysis were linked to the behavioral level of analysis. The behav-

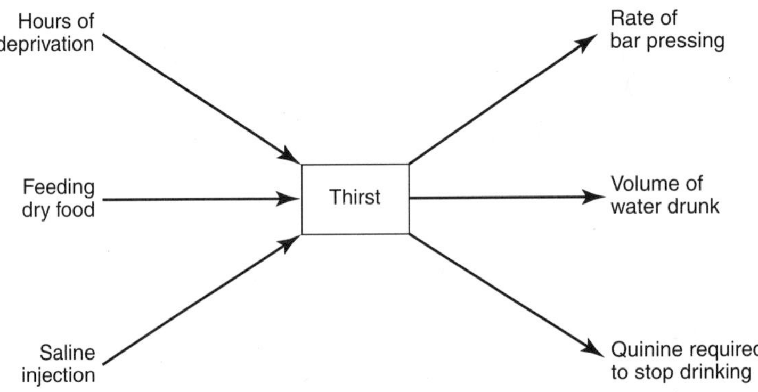

Figure 2.3
The instrumental way in which Neil Miller characterized drive states and in this case the state of thirst (Miller, 1959; Toates, 1986).

iors in the laboratory often reflected the degree of deprivation (water), the ability to undergo travail to approach or avoid a set of environmental conditions, and attractiveness of the water source. I would also add some additional factors to the figure: incentives, genetic and temperamental features, competition with other drives.

At a psychological level, motivational states were analyzed in the context of behavioral flexibility to attain a goal—the range of behavioral options that could be employed toward an end and reflected in a motivated animal (e.g., Tinbergen, 1951; Teitelbaum, 1967, 1977; Epstein, 1982). The concepts of goal and behavioral flexibility figured as criteria for motivation, and a range of physiological responses is essential to *allostatic regulation,* which is why the concept of allostasis may be of importance in the consideration of motivational systems that subserve regulatory physiology.

Limitations of the Homeostatic View of Central States

The concept of motivation is linked to those of drive, energy (e.g., Freud, 1924; Hull, 1943; Lorenz, 1981). The metaphor of motivation is hydraulic in nature. No doubt, the degree of food deprivation and the degree of decrease in glucose levels result in the search for food and instrumental behaviors to procure the required nutrients. The homeostasis model, linked to depletion and repletion of energy and the use of energy, is part of the consideration of a motivational state. But it is neither a necessary nor a sufficient condition (Toates, 1986; Stricker, 1990). The ingestion of food depends upon a number of factors, including the palatability of the food (Young, 1941, 1966) and the assessment of danger in the environment in which the food is located.

The drive-reduction model of learning was impoverished. Many animals can learn about where sources of food or water or salt are at a time when they may not be in any of these central motivation states (Tolman, 1932). One example will suffice. Rats can learn where salt is and how to acquire it even when they are not hungry for sodium (Krieckhaus and Wolf, 1968; Schul-

kin, 1991). Information processing about objects at locations, how to acquire a substance, and even what time of day a particular nutrient might appear (Rosenwasser et al., 1988) occurs with or without sodium hunger at a particular time. Two points stand out from these observations: central motivation states are a larger class than simple drive-reinforcement categorization (see also Tolman, 1932). The simple drive-reduction models of learning (in which there is no clear set point) (see also Hull, 1943; Miller, 1959) were placed in a larger behavioral context in which learning about objects was much broader (Shettleworth, 1998).

In fact, Miller (1959) helped introduce an information-processing model to the study of animal learning, broadening the narrow behavioristic conception that had limited the study of animal behavior. Some years later, behavioristic studies would themselves become part of the cognitive revolution that eventually swept through psychology, including behaviorism (see Rescorla and Wagner, 1972; Dickinson, 1980).

Information-processing systems that represent objects are integral to motivational systems, complex or simple. The brain is an information-processing organ; motivation represented in neural circuits is coded by neuropeptides or neurotransmitters (Herbert, 1993; Pfaff, 1999; Schulkin, 1999a). Thus the concept of motivation is tied to function and evolution and needs a regulatory construct, such as allostasis, which emphasizes anticipatory, reactive, and feedforward regulatory systems in the brain that underlie behavior. It plays an important epistemological role in the explanation of behavior; that is, the logical status of motivation in our scientific lexicon. Motivation predisposes animals to behave "predictably" within an internal and external context and under conditions within the evolutionary context of the organism.

Central Motive States

The concept of a central state is relatively modern and more linked to allostatic regulation (central nervous system involvement in systemic physiological regulation rather than

homeostasis). It is clearly stated in the works of Lashley (1938), Tinbergen (1951), Hinde (1970), Hebb (1949), Morgan (1966), Beach (1942) and Stellar (1954). A central motive state is a state of the brain (Lashley, 1938; Beach, 1942) that is often expressed in terms of two central tendencies toward objects that are either attractive and approached or aversive and avoided (table 2.2; Konorski, 1967; Lang et al., 1998).

For example, there are two prominent features of the central motive state of hunger. The first is the appetitive phase—the search for the desired entity—and the second is the consummatory phase—actually ingesting the desired item or otherwise fulfilling a need. This distinction was expressed early on by the American naturalist Wallace Craig (1918) and later by the pragmatist philosopher John Dewey (1925). Within a short period of time, it was incorporated within ethology (Tinbergen, 1951; Marler and Hamilton, 1966; Hinde, 1970), psychobiology (Beach, 1942), and physiological psychology (Hebb, 1949; Stellar, 1954).

Sodium appetite, as I previously mentioned, is a good model of a motivational system (see Wolf, 1969; Denton, 1982; Schulkin, 1991). On the appetitive side, salt-hungry rats or sheep will press a bar for salt in relation to the degree of sodium they need (Quartermain and Wolf, 1967; Denton, 1982). Salt-hungry rats are also willing to run down an alley for very small quantities of salt (about 0.1 ml for each run; Zhang et al., 1984; Schulkin et al., 1985). Moreover, the intensity of running is related to the strength of the sodium hunger induced by mineralocorticoids alone or by the combination of angiotensin and mineralocorticoid hormones (figure 2.4).

Next, consider the consummatory phase. Infusions into the oral cavity reveal a pattern of facial responses linked to ingestion or rejection (Grill and Norgren, 1978a) that are in fact governed by the caudal brainstem (Steiner, 1973; Grill and Norgren, 1978b). A sweet taste usually, though not always, elicits an ingestive sequence, a bitter taste, a rejection sequence. Hypertonic sodium chloride elicits a mixed ingestive-rejection sequence in a rat that is in sodium balance. But when rats are salt-hungry, the oral-facial response to sodium chloride changes. The re-

Table 2.2
The essential phases of central motive states

Initiation Phase
Deficit signals
Incentive and exteroceptive sensory information
Cognitive information (conditioning, anticipatory)
Circadian influences
Long-term memory
Procurement Phase
Arousal (general)
Foraging behavior
Locomotion
Sensory integration
Previous experience
Short-term or long-term memory
Incentives
Visceral integration
External cues
Consummatory Phase
Programmed motor responses
Discriminatory factors
Satiety mechanisms
Reinforcement
Hedonic motivation
Competition for Behavioral Expression
Multiple motivational states
Environmental factors
Assessment of success / failure

Adapted from Swanson, 1988.

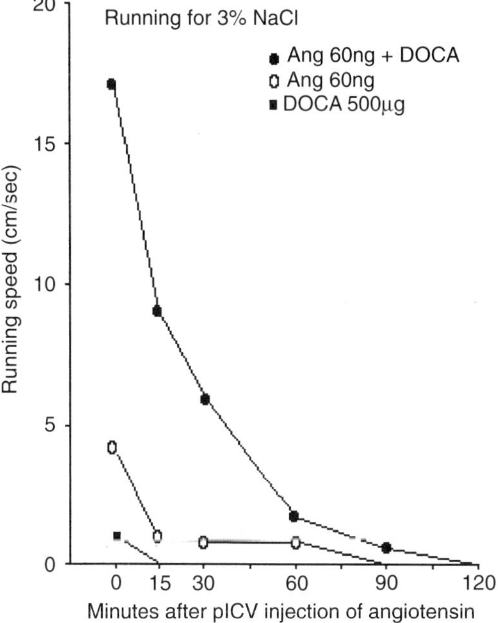

Figure 2.4
Running speed for 3% NaCl of rats that were treated with only DOCA (deoxycorticosterone), only angiotensin, or with both DOCA and angiotensin (adapted from Zhang et al., 1984).

sponse is now largely ingestive; the rejection response decreases (Berridge et al., 1984; Berridge and Schulkin, 1989). This effect, at least in rats, is specific. Other tastants (e.g., hydrogen chloride) elicit equally mixed ingestive-aversive responses that are not changed when the rat is salt hungry (Berridge et al., 1984). Moreover, the oral-facial change to intraoral infusion of hypertonic sodium chloride is not dependent upon experience. The phenomenon is demonstrated the first time rats are sodium depleted (Berridge et al., 1984), and this hedonic shift can be associated with arbitrary gustatory stimuli that have been associated with sodium (Berridge and Schulkin, 1989) (figure 2.5).

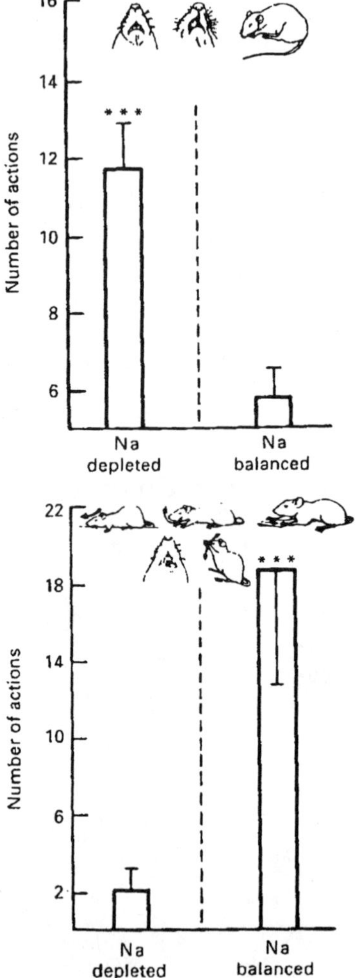

Figure 2.5
Taste reactivity profiles of rats to intraoral infusions of hypertonic NaCl (sea water) when sodium hungry (Na depleted) and when not hungry for sodium (Na balanced). The top panel represents positive facial responses to the intraoral infusions, and the bottom panel represents negative or rejection responses to the infusions (Berridge et al., 1984; Berridge and Schulkin, 1989).

Palatability Judgments

Palatability information processing, in this case of hypertonic sodium (sea water), underlies central motive states such as the tendency to ingest sodium (Berridge et al., 1984; Berridge and Schulkin, 1989). The behavioral and neural mechanisms that underlie palatability are unconscious, and the overuse of these reward mechanisms (e.g., during addictions) have been linked to a form of *allostatic dysregulation* (Koob and LeMoal, 2001).

The facial patterns depicted in figure 2.6 are widespread in a number of primates to sweet stimuli and acceptance, to aversions and rejection to bitter substances (Steiner et al., 2001). Palatability judgments are not the same as the acceptance of a

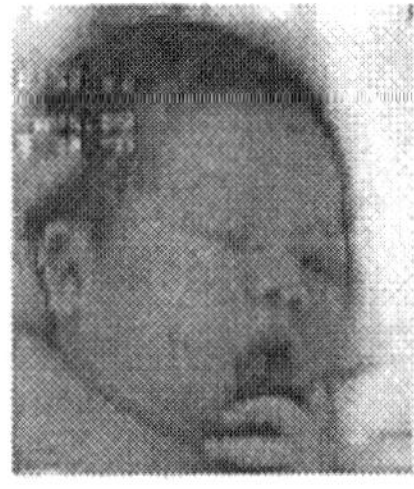

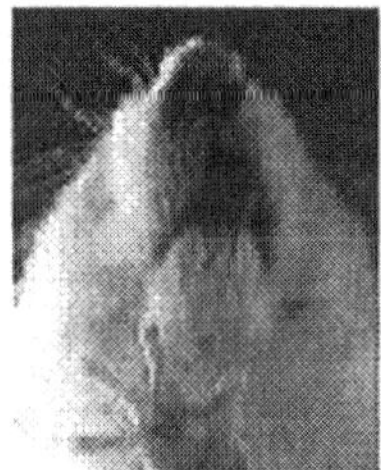

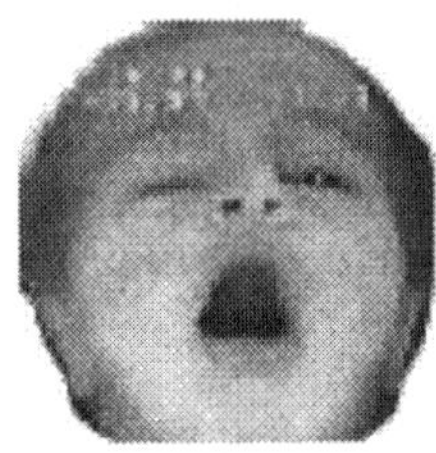

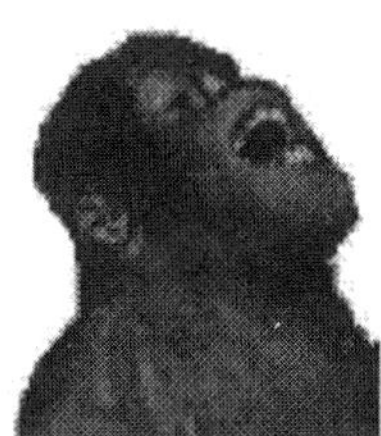

Figure 2.6
Facial expressions to infusions of bitter and sweet tasting substances (from Berridge, 2000; Steiner et al., 2001).

substance or the sensory characteristics (Berridge and Grill, 1983; Berridge and Schulkin, 1989).

Allesthesia is a more physiological term that has been used (Cabanac, 1971, 1979) to depict the regulatory role of hedonics in behavior. Like the example above with regard to sodium hunger, shifts in everything from temperature to sexual attraction underlie hedonic judgments. In fact, one of the more interesting examples is the motivational behaviors that are revealed with regard to cooling the brain: Rats will press a bar to alter their brain temperature (Corbit, 1973; Stellar and Corbit, 1973). Key features of central states are the appetitive behaviors and their diverse expression and consummatory behaviors.

Central states are again wider than this class. Central states can also be depicted as remaining in states of ease and comfort (e.g., the cat's seductive peering behavior and grooming behaviors of social animals).

The ingestion of sodium, like the attraction to a number of appetitive and subsequent consummatory objects, is determined by salience, interests (Bindra, 1969, 1978; Berridge, 1996; 2000), hedonic attractiveness (Young, 1949), and sensory stimulation (Beebe-Center, 1932; Schneirla, 1959, 1965). The influence through hedonic stimuli is an ancient theme in what renders animals attracted to and repelled from objects.

In the literature of ingestion, one distinguishes preference from appetite (Young, 1959) and liking from wanting (Berridge, 1996). The concept of central motive state serves as an umbrella term in accounting for a number of different functions. In other words, central motive states reflect the interactions between the state of the animal, its prior associations, drive state, hedonic judgments about events, and the incentives that are evaluated in suitable environmental contexts (Bindra, 1969; Bolles, 1975; Toates, 1986; Mook, 1987). To the sodium-hungry animal, the hypertonic salt stands out, is hedonic, and is positive. Sources where sodium was located are recalled in memory, objects associated with sodium are salient, (Krieckhaus and Wolf, 1968; Schulkin, 1991). Central motive states reflect the

activation of brain function and the orientation to objects in one's environment.

Similar scenarios hold for most hormonally induced central motive states. Such motivational states result in behaviors that include the craving for and ingestion of food and water, sex behavior as well as social attachments (including parental behavior), fear, and addictive drug use (see Koob et al., 1989; see chapter 5 on addiction). And in each of these examples, feedforward *allostatic* regulatory mechanisms are at play.

The idea of the simple motivational system is that it is tractable at many levels of analysis (Wolf, 1969). This is part of the excitement in studying phenomena such as sodium hunger or thirst, which are less sexy examples when compared with sex behavior, parental behavior, and drug cravings. All these behaviors result from central motive states induced and sustained by hormonal mechanisms. They all feature appetitive as well as consummatory phases of motivation and include salience or interest in various objects. The behaviors linked to hormonal effects on neuropeptides or neurotransmitters are particularly amenable in the analysis of the central mechanisms underlying motivated behavior (Schulkin, 1999a; Pfaff, 1999).

The roots of motivational systems are found within a biological perspective (Sober and Wilson, 1998); behavior evolved to serve animal reproductive ability and fitness (figure 2.7). Motivational states often cause a state change, but are also designed to maintain internal viability and to navigate external circumstances (see Gallistel, 1975, 1980).

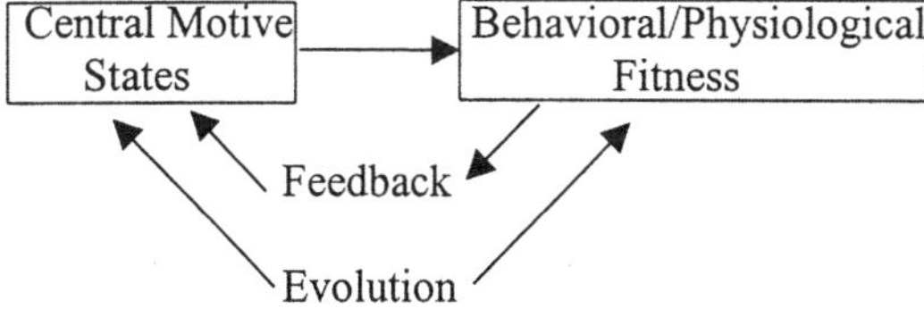

Figure 2.7
Evolution, central states and behavioral adaptation.

The issue of flexibility as the cardinal feature of a motivational system may not be correct (James, 1890; Epstein, 1982). That is, I suspect the contrast between motivation and instinct (Epstein, 1982) is somewhat misleading. In this view, instinct is blind and dumb. Motivation, by contrast, is replete with representations of objects and their importance and behavioral options to attain the goal. Surely the concept of representation figures significantly in understanding the brain as an information-processing system independent of whether the animal is limited in its behavioral options. Something can be instinctual and be fixed, and something can be motivated and be fixed. They are not exclusive. But the intuition that Alan Epstein adumbrated was that motivational systems are flexible and opportunistic, resourceful in the achievement of the goal. This no doubt captures an important element of central motive states.

In debates about the usefulness of the concept of motivation, it has been noted that representations of goal objects are neither necessary nor sufficient for motivated behavior (see also Dethier, 1966; Stellar and Stellar, 1985). The hungry fly may be a machine, narrow in purpose, with few behavioral options and still have representations of goal objects.

Neural Circuits and Motivational States

General Neural Circuits Underlying Motivational States

The reticular formation was envisioned to underlie arousal, as was later the activation of catecholamines (Palkovits, 1981; Stricker and Zigmond, 1986). We now know that a number of neurotransmitter systems (e.g., serotonin, dopamine) that project widely throughout the brain serve to arouse and placate neuronal systems that underlie central motive states (Hoebel, 1988). These systems play an important role in motivated behaviors. For example, ascending noradrenergic pathways from the brainstem to the forebrain are essential for alertness and attention, and serotonergic pathways are essential for mood states (Stellar and Stellar, 1985; Hoebel, 1988).

Consider the central gustatory/visceral system in the brain. At the turn of the century, C. Judson Herrick (1905) described a pathway in the catfish from the solitary nucleus to the amygdala, which later Carl Pfaffmann and his colleagues (Pfaffmann et al., 1977) and others (see Spector, 1995) thought might underlie motivated behavior. The seventh, ninth, and tenth cranial nerves transmit visceral information to the central nervous system and terminate in the rostral portion of the solitary nucleus. Gustatory and other visceral information are then transmitted to the medial region of the parabrachial nucleus (Norgren, 1984, 1995). From this region, there are two main projection systems: a dorsal projection to the ventral basal thalamus and insular cortex and a ventral projection, which crosses through the lateral hypothalamus into the central nucleus of the amygdala, in addition to the bed nucleus of the stria terminalis (Norgren, 1984). It was suggested (Pfaffmann et al., 1977; Spector, 2000) that the sensory evaluation of a food or fluids—whether sweet or salty—is made by the dorsal projection and that the organization of the drive, and the hedonic value of the stimulation, are made by the ventral projection. Interestingly, many of the neuropeptides, or their receptor sites and steroid receptor sites that are linked to central states, are localized within these regions (figure 2.8).

Angiotensin is one peptide that is localized in many of the regions of this visceral pathway in the brain (see Lind et al., 1984). A number of neuropeptides are also distributed along the central visceral axis (e.g., Swanson et al., 1983; Swanson, 2000). This axis includes the central nucleus of the amygdala, the bed nucleus of the stria terminalis, the paraventricular nucleus (PVN) of the hypothalamus, and brainstem sites such as the parabrachial and solitary nuclei (Gray, 1990). This is the same pathway that organizes motivated behaviors in general (Pfaffmann et al., 1977; Stellar and Stellar, 1985). It is part of the neural system—described by Herrick (1905) and expanded upon by Walle Nauta (1961)—that underlies central excitatory states.

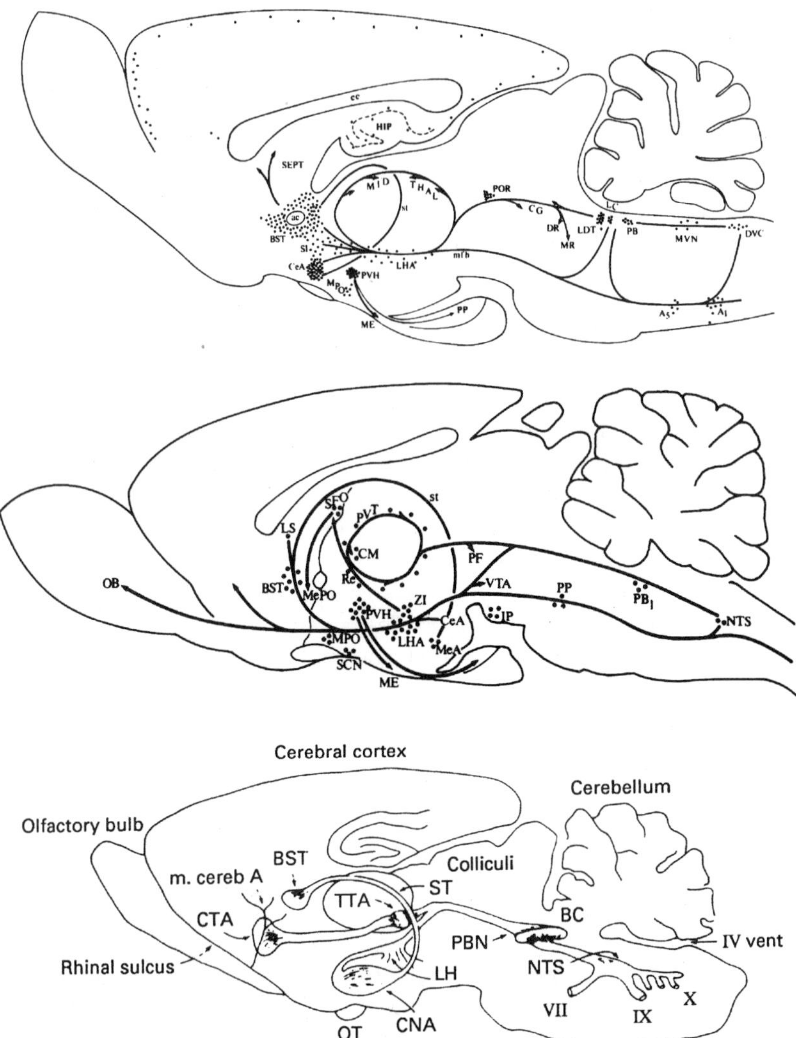

Figure 2.8
From top to bottom the figures depict corticotropin releasing hormone in the brain (Swanson et al., 1983), angiotensin sites in the brain (Lind et al., 1985) and the central gustatory neural axis (Norgren, 1995). One should note that many of the peptide sites overlap with gustatory sites in the brain.

Walle Nauta noted that the concept of the limbic system should include motor regions of the basal ganglia (see Mogenson and Huang, 1973; Mogenson and Yang, 1991; Alheid et al., 1996, 1998). The basal ganglia form an essential link in translating motivational signals from the amygdala and hypothalamus into the organization of action (Swanson and Mogenson, 1981; Kelley, 1999a, b) via the activation of brainstem sites (e.g., Pfaff, 1999). Specialized motor pathways emerged to translate motivational desires into organized goal-directed action (Swanson, 2000).

Since Nauta's original suggestion, research has substantiated that regions of the basal ganglia do in fact seem to underlie a variety of motivated behaviors, including addiction (Koob and LeMoal, 2001). For example, damage to the ventral palladium interferes with the "liking" system underlying the palatability processing of food sources (Berridge, 1996, 2000).

The nucleus accumbens, via glutamate receptors within the accumbens, may underlie appetitive instrumental learning and may be an important link in translating limbic functions into functional action (Kelley, 1999a, b). The range of action or motivational signals is quite diverse and will figure prominently for the rest of this chapter and in subsequent chapters. Let us now turn specifically to the hormonal regulation of motivational states, in which there are a variety of examples of feedforward neuroendocrine systems.

Positive Induction of Neuropeptide Gene Expression by Steroids and the Expression of Central States: An Example of Allostatic Regulation

Steroids, by facilitating neuropeptide expression and regulation in the brain, increase the likelihood of motivational states, both sustaining them and decreasing their expression (e.g., Herbert, 1993; Pfaff, 1999; Schulkin, 1999a). By influencing central states, hormones and their actions in the brain prepare an animal to perceive stimuli and behave in certain characteristic ways; they

increase the likelihood of responding "appropriately" to environmental signals (e.g., Gallistel, 1980; Mook, 1987).

There are a variety of contexts in which steroids and peptides interact to regulate behavior (e.g., Hoebel, 1988; Herbert, 1993). They range from ingesting food, water, and sodium to maternal behavior, fear, and aggression. Nature uses the same hormones to generate a variety of different central states. These, in turn, generate behaviors that, through both anticipatory and reactive mechanisms, help the organism maintain internal stability and external coherence to internal demands (McEwen and Stellar, 1993; Schulkin et al., 1994, 1998; McEwen, 1998a, b). This represents a form of allostatic regulation. Steroids and peptides or neuropeptides interact to influence behavior by their actions in the brain. There are many examples in which hormones that regulate physiology also affect behaviors that serve the same goal.

Steroid hormones such as estrogen, progesterone, aldosterone, corticosterone, testosterone, and vitamin 1,25D3 are widely distributed in the brain (e.g., Pfaff, 1980; Stumpf and O'Brien, 1987; McEwen and Alves, 1999). They have profound effects, for example, on the induction or inhibition of neuropeptide gene expression and subsequent central states and behavioral output (Herbert, 1993; Herbert and Schulkin, 2002).

Consider another fact about peptides and neuropeptides; consider oxytocin. Oxytocin plays multiple roles in facilitating physiological regulation of milk production during lactation and water homeostasis (Kaufman, 1981). But oxytocin expression in the brain underlies behavioral functions such as maternal attachment (see, e.g., Insel, 1992; Carter et al., 1999; Kendrick, 2000), and perhaps more generally for social recognition that underlies attachment behaviors (Ferguson et al., 2001). Oxytocin is both a pituitary peptide linked to milk production and a neuropeptide linked to a variety of central states in which behavior serves physiological regulation and reproductive fitness. The central motivational state that underlies parental behavior is rich and behaviorally diverse (Marler and Hamilton, 1966; Hinde, 1970), and goes beyond anything homeostatic.

Or consider angiotensin, a peptide produced in both the brain and the periphery that has a major impact on the cravings for both water and sodium. Injected centrally, angiotensin-II increases both water intake and sodium intake, independent of sodium loss (see Fitzsimons, 1979, 1999). The behavior of water and sodium ingestion complements the regulatory effects of angiotensin at the level of the kidney and other systemic organ systems (e.g., the heart) linked to body fluid homeostasis. The central motive state of thirst, a state in which feedforward allostatic mechanisms are operative in the brain, is one of several phenomena to which we now turn.

Mineralocorticoids, Glucocorticoids, and Angiotensin: Cravings for Water and Sodium

The adrenal steroid hormones play a profound role in the regulation of body fluid balance. At the level of systemic physiology, both steroids facilitate sodium reabsorption and distribution in the maintenance of sodium and body fluid balance. Of course, aldosterone is a dominant hormone for the regulation of fluid balance (Fitzsimons, 1979, 1999; Denton, 1982; Schulkin, 1991).

Mineralocorticoid hormones increase sodium ingestion (Richter, 1942–43; Wolf, 1964). In part, they do so via changes in angiotensin expression in the brain. For example, mineralocorticoids increase angiotensin-II receptors in the brain and in cell-line cultures. The same treatment is known to increase angiotensin messenger RNA (mRNA) in cell-line cultures in addition to mobilizing intracellular calcium and second-messenger systems (S. J. Fluharty, unpublished observations). Mineralocorticoids also potentiate angiotensin-II-induced sodium intake (Fluharty and Epstein, 1983; Sakai, 1986). This is a feedforward regulatory system that subserves adequate sodium ingestion, but is nested in a larger physiological system that then constrains the levels of natriorexegenic hormones, once sodium and water are ingested and balance is achieved.

It is possible that the overexaggeration activation of this neuroendocrine system underlies some forms of hypertension (Denton, 1982; Watt et al., 1992). In fact, we know that in various

animal models in which angiotensin or mineralocorticoids are overexpressed, there is both an exaggerated sodium consumption and a vulnerability to hypertension (Denton, 1982). The normal regulatory systems to maintain water and sodium balance, when coupled with vulnerable genetic susceptibility and sodium ingestion, can result in allostatic overload.

Interestingly, a key example emphasized by Sterling and Eyer (1981, 1988; Eyer and Sterling, 1977) in one of their original papers was the exaggerated sodium consumption, vulnerability to hypertension, and chronic elevation of the renin-angiotensin-adrenal steroid systems. In cultures in which there was low sodium consumption and less chronic worry, there was little incidence of hypertension and increased mortality (see also Denton, 1982). Chronic stress (allostatic overload) creates a context of reduced life span. By their actions in the brain, the hormones of sodium homeostasis create an environment that results in enhanced sodium consumption—and along with the sodium retention, it results in a greater vulnerability to life-threatening situations.

Consider glucocorticoids, and recall that they, either through their permissive, stimulatory, or preparative functions, play a fundamental role in blood pressure regulation (Sapolsky et al., 2000). And, of importance, elevated glucocorticoids potentiate angiotensin-II-induced drinking. The background of glucocorticoids that are normally elevated following depletion of the body's fluids induces angiotensin-II cells, thereby potentiating the hormone's dipsogenic (Ganesan and Sumners, 1989; Sumners et al., 1991) and natriorexegenic actions. This interaction generates the central states of thirst and sodium hunger, in which both appetitive and consummatory behaviors are expressed. Both behaviors serve the same end point as the renin-angiotensin-aldosterone system—namely, the body's fluid homeostasis (figure 2.9).

More generally, one should note that while sodium depletion (or fluid volume depletion) may be the initial trigger for the hormones linked to sodium and water appetite (Fitzsimons, 1979, 1999; Denton, 1982; Denton et al., 1996), the appetitive and con-

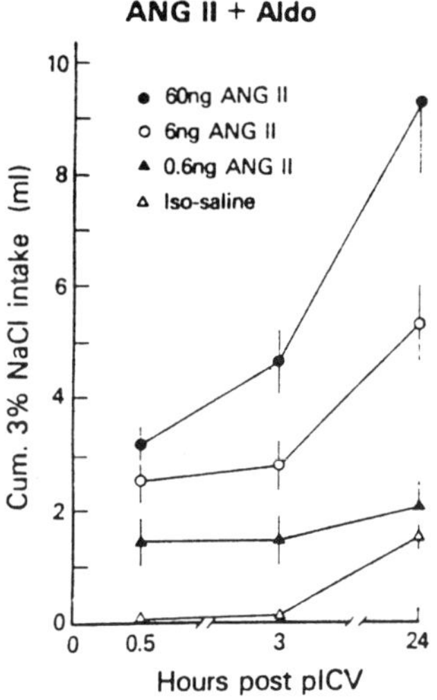

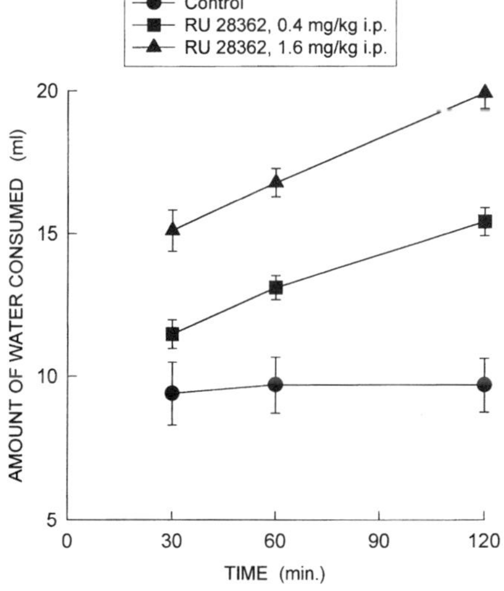

Figure 2.9
(*Top*) Sodium ingestion in rats following daily injections of aldosterone (40 μg) followed by central injection of angiotensin (Sakai, 1986). (*Bottom*) Water ingestion following systemic daily injections of the glucocorticoid agonist followed by a central injection of angiotensin II (10n) (Sumners et al., 1991).

summatory behaviors reflect the expression of the hormonal activation, the effects of aldosterone and corticosterone on central angiotensin (Fluharty and Epstein, 1983; Epstein, 1991; Sumners et al., 1991; Fluharty and Sakai, 1995), and perhaps the decreases in oxytocin expression (see Stricker, 1990; Verbalis et al., 1993).

Homeostatic mechanisms mediated by negative restraint (volume and osmotic receptors) exist alongside allostatic mechanisms (the positive induction of the neuropeptides) and the expression of central motive states of the brain and resultant behavior. The allostatic state can lead, however, to allostatic overload (e.g., chronic activation of the renin-angiotensin-aldosterone system) and vulnerability to excessive sodium consumption, hypertension, and congestive heart failure (Weaber, 2001).

Glucocorticoids and Neuropeptide Y: Food Intake

In the mobilization to procure adequate food sources, glucocorticoids are elevated under conditions in which hunger is a central state of the brain (Dallman et al., 2000). The glucocorticoids have wide and diverse effects on many regulatory systems in the brain and in peripheral end-organ systems that subserve bodily viability. Here again it is useful to break glucocorticoid function down in terms of long- and short-term effects, and whether the actions are permissive, suppressive, stimulatory, or preparative (Sapolsky et al., 2000). One also has to ask what the environmental contexts are in which a wide variety of needs are appraised for bodily viability, including seasonal variations (Wingfield and Romero, 2001).

The context that I want to draw the reader's attention to is one in which low but nonetheless elevated levels of corticosterone can stimulate food intake (Leibowitz, 1995; Bell et al., 2000; Dallman et al., 2000). This situation appears to do so, in part, through activation of neuropeptide Y in the brain, in addition to a variety of other known effects (Dallman et al., 2000). Produced in gastrointestinal sites as well as the central nervous system, neuropeptide Y is activated functionally in the arcuate nucleus and the PVN by food deprivation and corticosterone

(Brady et al., 1990; Dallman et al., 1994, 1995). This increase in food intake depends on an intact adrenal gland and an activation of type-2-corticosteroid receptors (Lebowitz, 1995). Long-term activation of the glucocorticoids (allostatic overload) has significant implications for body fat distribution (Dallman et al., 2000).

Importantly, low doses of glucocorticoids or food deprivation can potentiate neuropeptide-Y-induced food ingestion (Heinrichs et al., 1992); specifically, corticosterone and neuropeptide Y generate carbohydrate ingestion, or fast energy pickups (Leibowitz, 1995). This steroid and neuropeptide hormone facilitates the central motive state of craving carbohydrates (figure 2.10). (Of course, these findings apply to rats; in species that are indifferent to sweet tastes, this phenomenon might not occur.) Adrenalectomy abolishes these effects, and corticosterone will restore them. But without a suitable context in which other concerns are made prevalent in the information-processing systems in the brain (predator detection, conflict with conspecifics, etc.), eating may or may not take place.

Food intake is mediated by mechanisms for short- and long-term regulation that utilize diverse mechanisms (e.g., insulin, leptin; see Dallman et al., 2000). I have focused on a putative feedforward mechanism that may underlie the motivation to search and ingest food sources. This, of course, is but one mechanism at play in food procurement, a positive feedforward system (allostatic)—glucocorticoid potentiation of neuropeptide Y. The overexaggeration of this system, allostatic overload, perhaps could lead to a wide variety of metabolic disturbances (obesity, heart disease, etc.).

Estrogen, Oxytocin, and Prolactin: Sex and Attachment

An example of steroids and peptides acting together to generate central motive states that underlie successful reproduction is that of estrogen-primed rats given progesterone and oxytocin to induce sexual receptivity (Pfaff, 1980, 1999). These events do not occur in a vacuum, despite our laboratory attempts to sim-

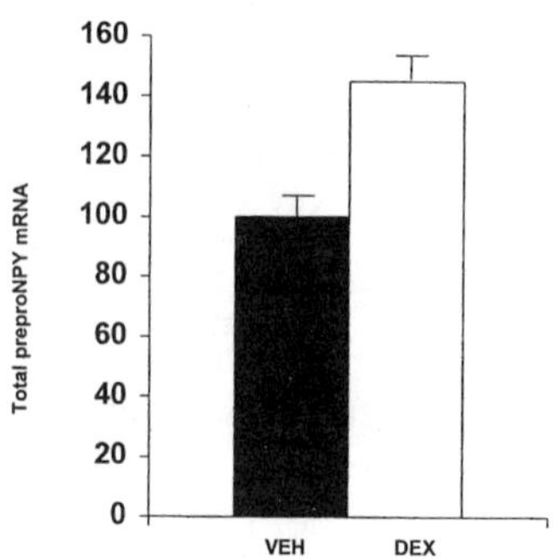

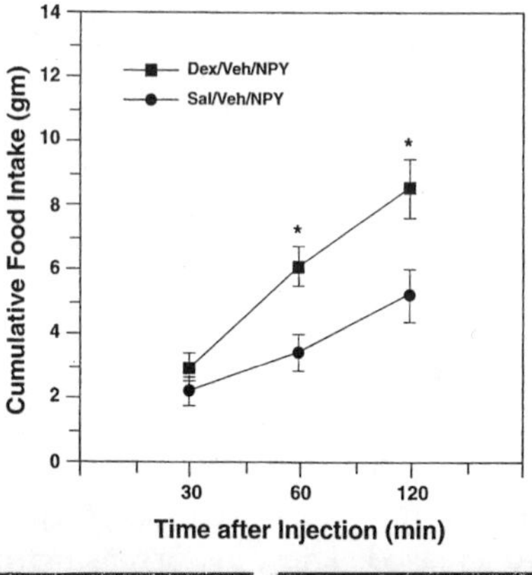

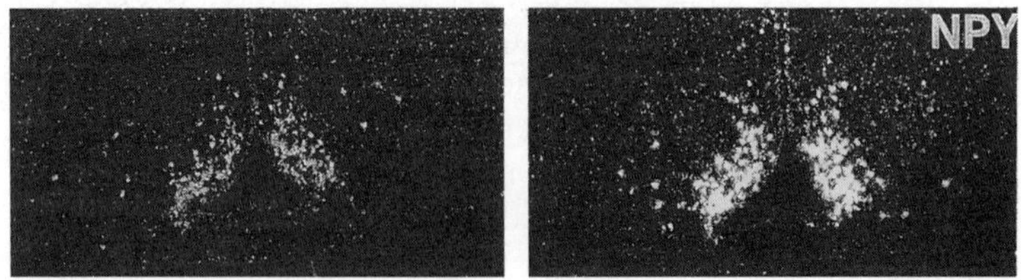

Figure 2.10
(*Top*) Total hybridization pre-pro-neuropeptide Y (preproNPY) mRNA in the arcuate nucleus in vehicle-injected controls (VEH) and hamsters injected daily for 28 days with dexamethasone (DEX) (adapted from Mercer et al., 1996). (*Middle*) Cumulative food intake following pretreatment with dexamethasone (100 µg/kg) or vehicle following 6 hours later by central injection of a vehicle or neuropeptide Y (500 ng Heinrichs et al., 1992). (*Bottom*) Darkfield photomicrographs of neuropeptide-Y mRNA in the arcuate nucleus in sated (A) and food-deprived (B) rats (from L. S. Brady et al., 1990).

plify the context in order to understand the mechanisms. Sex and attachment in a wide variety of animals takes place amid competing interests, competing hormonal influences, and numerous other factors (Wingfield and Romero, 2001).

For example, many of the events during reproduction are demanding on energy resources. Anticipatory mechanisms for predictable events predominate, particularly for seasonal breeding animals (Bauman and Currie, 1980; Wingfield and Romero, 2001). Under duress by what Wingfield and Romero have characterized as a context of emergency life situation, the mechanisms that underlie reproduction can be altered. Reactive mechanisms are operative in these emergency situations, where, for example, reproduction might not be possible (too cold, not enough food, no outlet for reproductive expression, etc.).

In the laboratory a variety of animals treated with systemic estrogen and then with progesterone demonstrate similar sexual receptivity (Wade and Crews, 1991; Pfaff, 1999). Estrogen increases oxytocin expression in cells in the ventral medial hypothalamus. Without sufficient estrogen, oxytocin levels decline and are restored only when estrogen is again elevated (e.g., Schumacher et al., 1990). Oxytocin infused within this region of the brain elicits sexual receptivity, and in estrogen- and progesterone-primed rats, the dose of oxytocin needed to elicit the behavior is decreased. Thus, by increasing oxytocin expression in the brain's ventral medial hypothalamus, estrogen facilitates the likelihood of sexual motivation and receptivity.

In other words, by facilitating the expression of neuropeptides (e.g., oxytocin) and/or receptor sites (e.g., progestin), the gonadal steroid hormones lower the threshold at which a sexual response to environmental stimuli will be elicited by inducing central states in the brain (e.g., Pfaff, 1999). But one should note and consider the multiple effects of estrogen on neuropeptides and neurotransmitters in the brain (figure 2.11; Pfaff, 1999). Within this context, well-known appetitive and consummatory expressions of central states are seen (see Beach, 1942, 1947; Everitt, 1990). But the behavioral expression is not axiomatic and varies with the environmental circumstances and the competi-

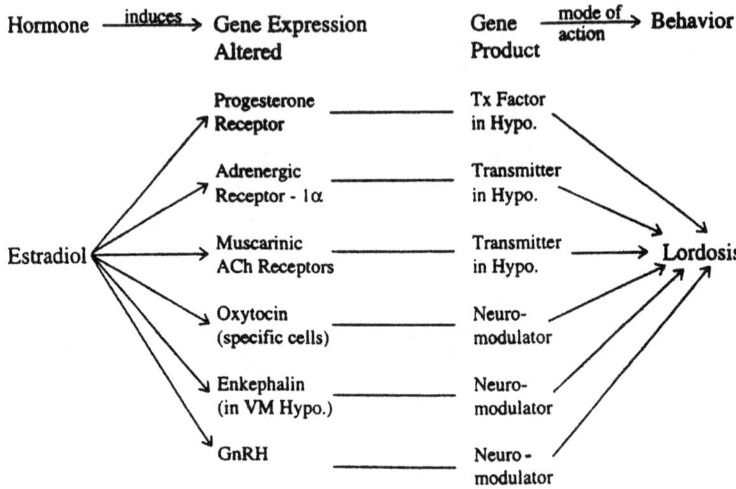

Figure 2.11
Diverse effects of estrogen on the brain essential for reproductive behavior (Pfaff, 1999).

tion with other internal needs or competing motivations (Hinde, 1968, 1970). Motivation figures in determining the direction that behavior will take. An allostatic mechanism is in the induction and sustaining the neuropeptide and neurotransmitters in functional circuits in the brain that underlies the behavior.

Now consider the relationship between estrogen, prolactin, and maternal behavior. Like oxytocin and a number of other peptides, prolactin is both a pituitary hormone and a neuropeptide with a diversity of functions. Central infusions of prolactin facilitate maternal behavior (Bridges and Freemark, 1995)—but only if there is a sufficient level of background estrogen. In other words, as is the case with oxytocin, estrogen facilitates the likelihood of maternal behavior by increasing prolactin expression in the brain (Bridges et al., 2001). The potentiation of the prolactin effects is another example of a feedforward, or allostatic, neuroendocrine system that underlies behavior. Prolactin stimulates maternal central states through both physiological and behavioral mechanisms.

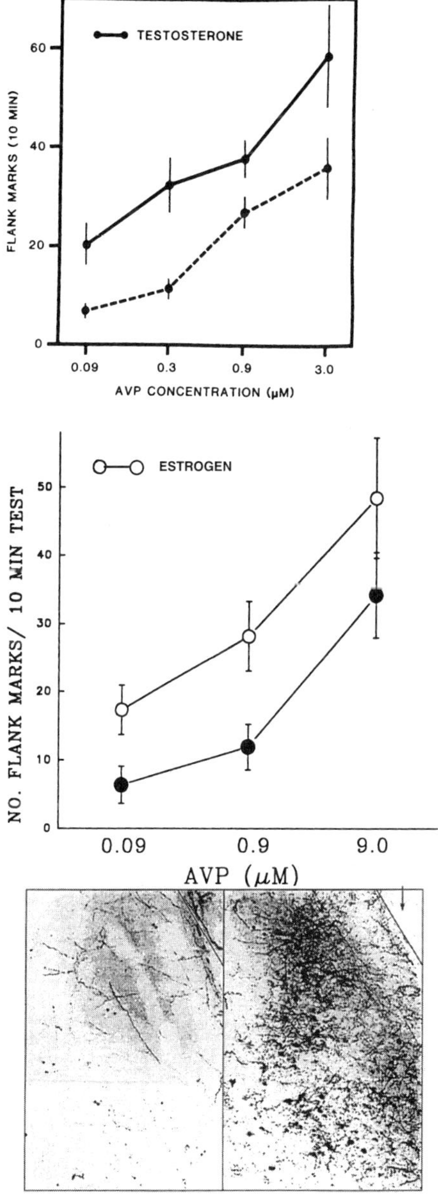

TESTOSTERONE
FLANK MARKS (10 MIN)
60
40
20
0
0.09
0.3
0.9
3.0
AVP CONCENTRATION (μM)
ESTROGEN
NO. FLANK MARKS/ 10 MIN TEST
50
40
30
20
10
0
0.09
0.9
9.0
AVP (μM)

Gonadal Steroids and Vasopressin or Vasotocin: Territory and Kin Relations

In many animals, testosterone concentrations vary with the seasons (e.g., Wingfield et al., 1999). One testosterone-mediated behavior linked to territorial behavior that is well known in a wide variety of mammals is scent marking. It occurs via the gonadal steroid's activation of vasopressin in the brain, particularly in the bed nucleus of the stria terminalis. Infused into this region, vasopressin facilitates the expression of scent marking. A background treatment of testosterone, providing a sustaining mechanism for vasopressin regulation in the brain, enhances this response (figure 2.12; Albers et al., 1988). The same holds for male parental behavior among prairie voles. Presumably, testosterone facilitates this behavior by sustaining and increasing central vasopressin or vasotocin synthesis (DeVries et al., 1995; see also Moore et al., 1992; Goodson and Bass, 2001). This central state does not occur in a vacuum and competes internally for expression.

The vasopressin gene appears to be significantly involved in affiliation (Pitkow et al., 2001). Without testosterone, for example, vasopressinergic neurons are severely depleted in specific regions of the brain that underlie parental behavioral and territorial aggression (DeVries et al., 1995; Albers et al., 1988; Albers and Cooper, 1995). For example, regions of the medial amygdala are significantly involved in flank-marking behavior. Testosterone facilitates flank marking via the induction of vasopressin expression in the medial amygdala (DeVries et al., 1995). The removal of testosterone reduces vasopressin gene expression in this region of the brain and reduces flank-marking behavioral expressions.

Figure 2.12
Flank-marking reaction to central administration of AVP in testosterone-treated or estrogen-treated and control hamsters (Albers et al., 1988; Huhman and Albers, 1993) and vasopressin-immunoreactive cells and fibers in the medial nucleus of the amygdala in castrated (*left*) and control (*right*) rats (courtesy of G. J. DeVries, 1995).

Conclusion: Allostatic Feedforward Mechanisms and Central Motive States

Steroids, by facilitating neuropeptides or neurotransmitters or receptor sites, can influence central states that are typically, though not exclusively, linked to functional requirements. Feedforward systems that underlie central states are nested in negative restraint of those systems; the animals ingest sodium and the natriorexegenic hormones are decreased. Furthermore, central motive states do not exist in a vacuum; they depend upon the environment and other cognitive (including other central motive states) and physiological events. Adaptation reflects an environment in which an animal is trying to cope and provide frameworks of coherence. Central motive states serve bodily viability both in the short and the long term through feedforward allostatic regulation. The state of craving sodium reflects the positive relationship between the activation of adrenal steroids and the induction of central angiotensin (Epstein, 1991).

In fact, what has been emphasized in this chapter is the steroid facilitation of neuropeptide expression and regulation. This is one central feature in the regulation of central motive states. Each of the examples serve important roles in the maintenance of the internal milieu. The events are anticipatory, reflecting the brain's influence over behavioral and physiological events. They reflect cephalic regulation of the internal milieu. These events are linked to adaptive events, including the pleasure of remaining in a state of ease, the satiety sequence associated with satiety (Smith, 1997a), and the states that animals are contented to stay in.

The more general question about the concept of motivation and drive is trying to use the terms in nonviciously circular senses and where it is not clear that it serves a scientific role (Wise, 1987). I would suggest that motivation is both a biological function and a core concept in our sense of ourselves and our representational abilities. It is a piece of cognitive adaptation that is fundamental to a theory of the direction of behav-

ior (Hebb, 1949; Lakoff and Johnson, 1999). Models of motivation include specific behavioral profiles (Oatley, 1970) and reflect both specific motivation and nonspecific mechanisms (Grossman, 1968, 1979). I suggest that we not look for one definition but rather to instrumental use and characterization of the information-processing systems in the brain. Putting the concept of motivation in the context of the circuitry and problem solving that the brain generates in suitable environmental climates renders the concept meaningful in a neuroscience context.

Core motivational states are biological functions that serve the animal in the organization of behavior and the adaptation to changing environmental demands. Functional circuits in the brain underlie both specific and nonspecific aspects of motivational states. Steroids, by the positive induction and regulation of neuropeptides, play an essential role in the expression of motivational states and provide one mechanism in the cephalic involvement in the regulation of the internal milieu and to long-term reproductive success. Thus these feedforward *allostatic* regulatory systems are an essential expression of the nervous system.

Central motive states serve to keep the organism viable by regulating homeostatic mechanisms that try to keep an organism within a state. Allostatic mechanisms drive the animal into a state appropriate (at best) to the challenge and to the environmental context. These states can be high energy, short term, and not desirable to stay in, but they are necessary for viability.

Chapter 3

Anticipation, Angst, Allostatic Regulation: Adrenal Steroid Regulation of Corticotropin-Releasing Hormone

The emotion of fear is regulated by neuroendocrine events in neural circuits that underlie fear-related behavioral and autonomic responses. One brain region critical in the regulation of fear is the amygdala. I suggest that one function of glucocorticoid hormones is to facilitate the synthesis of the neuropeptide CRH in this nucleus (along with the lateral bed nucleus of the stria terminalis). CRH aids in maintaining and coping with events that are perceived as frightening. Elevated levels of glucocorticoids, secreted by the adrenal gland, act on the amygdala and bed nucleus of the stria terminalis to facilitate CRH gene expression (feedforward allostatic mechanisms) and to sustain the central motive state of fear. In this model, long-term fear (chronic angst) is an allostatic state.

This chapter extends (more detail about the behavior and the neuroendocrine regulation of the central state) the feedforward allostatic framework discussed in chapter 2. I begin with an overview of the central motive state of fear and its biological basis. I then discuss the neural circuitry that underlies the perception of fearful events. Next, I describe the neuroendocrine basis of fear and discuss the role of glucocorticoids and CRH in sustaining fear-related behaviors. In each section, I indicate that the same neural and endocrine system underlies pathological states associated with excessive fear that perhaps underlie allostasis and allostatic overload. Certainly fear is the sort of central state in which no constant set point is regulated. I end with a brief discussion of the logical status of the concept of fear in our scientific lexicon.[1]

1. Fear, one should note at the onset, is not synonymous with freezing or startle behaviors. They are, however, useful behavioral measures in the context of

Central Motive State of Fear

Fear is a prototypical exemplar of a central state —a state of the brain. Although systemic physiological changes influence the state of fear (James, 1884, 1890), peripheral changes are not sufficient for the emotional expression of motivated behaviors such as fear (Cannon, 1915, 1929a; Bard, 1939). It is the physiological change in the brain that is linked to the state of fear. We are afraid when we perceive danger, but bodily events influence and reinforce this state (James, 1890; Damasio, 1994). For example, changes in heart rate, blood pressure, respiration, facial muscles, and catecholamines, both peripheral and central (e.g., Yank et al., 1990), influence the state of fear (see LeDoux, 1996, 2000; Rosen and Schulkin, 1998).

The central state of fear is tied to attention and learning as well as to the assessment of relevant information (Dickinson, 1980), which is important in predicting future outcomes (Miller, 1959; Rescorla and Wagner, 1972). The central state of fear is linked to action tendencies (Frijda, 1986), attention (Lang et al., 1998), and appraisals more generally of environmental stimuli (Lazarus, 1984, 1991; Rosen and Schulkin, 1998; Lane and Nadel, 1999).

Fear is also linked to an appetitive system (which includes consummatory behaviors) and an aversive system, such as withdrawal and protectiveness (Konorski, 1967; Davidson et al., 2000). In Konorski's terms (1967), the former is preservative and the latter is protective. Fear maps onto approach/appetitive and avoidance/withdrawal mechanisms influenced by sensory stimulation (Schneirla, 1959; Konorski, 1967).

Fear is an adaptive response to the perception of danger, and it is fundamental in problem solving and survival. In fact, fear as an emotion evolved as a part of problem solving (Darwin, 1872). Fear prepares an animal to respond to danger by height-

---

studying fear-related behavioral responses, just as one should note that the amygdala is not just involved in the regulation of negative events (e.g., Galaverna et al., 1993; Gallagher and Holland, 1994; Baron-Cohen et al., 1999; Davis and Whalen, 2001).

ening vigilant attention (Gallagher and Holland, 1994) and motivating behavior (Bindra, 1978), such as defensive behaviors (Bolles and Fanselow, 1980). The state of fear is one in which there is a readiness to perceive events as dangerous or alarming (LeDoux, 1995, 1996; Rosen et al., 1996). The state is knotted to learning about what is safe and what is not (Miller, 1959), as well as the informational value of stimuli that has predictive value to the animal (Rescorla and Wagner, 1972; Dickinson, 1980).

The physiological and behavioral responses aroused by fear are rooted in our evolutionary past. Fear is an adaptation (Lazarus, 1991), but fear certainly is not always part of our everyday life. Moreover, there are no clear set points in known physiological parameters that underlie the central state of fear, and therefore it is easily understood in the context of allostasis, allostatic state, and allostatic overload.

Emotions like fear are linked to action tendencies (Frijda, 1986) and motivate behavior in response to danger (Rosen and Schulkin, 1998). Behaviors such as startle and freezing are expressions of fear across many species; fear is linked to defensive behavior, but they are not the same. Fear functions to alert the animal to danger, preparing the animal to freeze or flee (Bolles and Fanselow, 1980). The motivated animal seeks relief from this allostatic state, and, with the elimination of fear, there is the sense of relief (Miller, 1959). In other words, fear functions as a central motive state in threatening contexts, resulting in behaviors that serve to alleviate the state, resulting in reducing or warding off harm. Put another way, from an "internal" perspective, fear is typically an aversive state of the mind—the animal acts in ways to reduce this aversive state of mind. Externally, those behaviors serve to reduce or eliminate threats to the animal. The perception of fearful events may be constrained by neuronal processing of information. The vigilance that is required during fear limits the attentional mechanisms that might normally be used elsewhere (Davis et al., 1993; Rosen and Schulkin, 1998). The central state of fear, and there is more than one kind (Hebb, 1946; Kagan and Schulkin, 1995), embodies an

elaborate and complex organization of behavior that includes social signals that reduce fighting and maintain alliances (Marler and Hamilton, 1966; Hauser, 1996).

Neural Circuits Mediating Fear

Amygdala

The amygdala found in vertebrates is centered in the temporal region of mammals (Herrick, 1905). It is almond-shaped and was originally called the *smell brain.* It has long been considered part of the limbic system in the organization of emotional responses (e.g., Papez, 1937; Bard, 1939; MacLean, 1955; LeDoux, 1995; Swanson, 2000).

Regions of the amygdala have been characterized as a *sensory gateway* (Aggleton and Mishkin, 1986; LeDoux et al., 1990) because the amygdala receives information from both cortical and subcortical regions (Krettek and Price, 1978). Specifically, the lateral and basal lateral regions are richly innervated by neocortical and subcortical sites, which relay information to the central nucleus (e.g., Krettek and Price, 1978; Swanson and Petrovich, 1998; Stefanacci and Amaral, 2000). The central nucleus also receives visceral information from brainstem sites that include the solitary and parabrachial nuclei (Norgren and Leonard, 1973) and reciprocally project to these brainstem regions (e.g., Schwaber et al., 1982). The amygdala's direct link to the nucleus accumbens led Nauta (1961, 1972) to suggest an anatomical route by which motivation and motor control action are linked in the organization of behavior (see also Mogenson, 1987; Swanson and Petrovich, 1998; Kelley, 1999a, b; Gray, 1999; Swanson, 2000).

Damage to the amygdala interferes with fear-related behavioral responses. In the past 10 years, evidence has converged to show particularly that the central nucleus within the amygdala orchestrates the behavioral responses related to fear (LeDoux, 1995, 1996, 2000). Lesions or stimulation of the central and lateral nuclei are known to influence behaviors associated with fear (Kapp et al., 1979; LeDoux et al., 1990; Roozendaal and

McGaugh, 1997a, b). Stimulation of the central nucleus of the amygdala, for example, activates the neural circuitry underlying the startle response and amplifies this reaction (Rosen and Davis, 1988). Stimulation of the amygdala heightens attention toward events that are perceived as fearful (Gallagher and Holland, 1994; Rosen et al., 1996). In other words, amygdala activation increases the likelihood that an event will be perceived as threatening, uncertain, or unusual (Gallagher and Holland, 1994; Rosen and Schulkin, 1998; LeDoux, 2000; Dolan et al., 2000) and can lead to anticipatory angst (Schulkin et al., 1994). Infusions of *N*-methyl-D-aspartate (NMDA) antagonists into the central or lateral nuclei interfere with fear-related conditioning (Davis et al., 1993). Neurons within the amygdala are activated by fearful signals (LeDoux, 2000) and are influenced by prefrontal cortex activity (Davidson et al., 2000; figure 3.1).

In elegant detail, LeDoux and his colleagues (e.g., LeDoux et al., 1990; LeDoux, 1995, 1996, 2000) have outlined an anatomical circuit in rats underlying conditioned freezing to an auditory cue. It consists, in part, of pathways from the medial geniculate nucleus en route to the lateral and central nuclei of the amygdala. In addition, projections from the auditory and perirhinal regions of the neocortex, through the lateral nucleus en route to the central nucleus of the amygdala, convey information about acoustic conditioning. Interruption to this input, to the lateral and central nucleus of the amygdala, impairs the fear conditioning. The central nucleus, through its projections to the central gray, regulates freezing and escape behaviors (LeDoux, 1996).

The neural circuitry for conditioned freezing, for conditioned startle (Rosen et al., 1991), and for unconditioned fear require the lateral region of the amygdala to receive information and the central region to orchestrate the behavioral and autonomic responses. Other regions in the forebrain that organize fear include the prefrontal cortex (Morgan and LeDoux, 1995), the perirhinal cortex, and the bed nucleus of the stria terminalis, which, as I will describe, may be linked to the neuroendocrine regulation of anxiety (see Davis et al., 1997; Rosen and Schulkin, 1998).

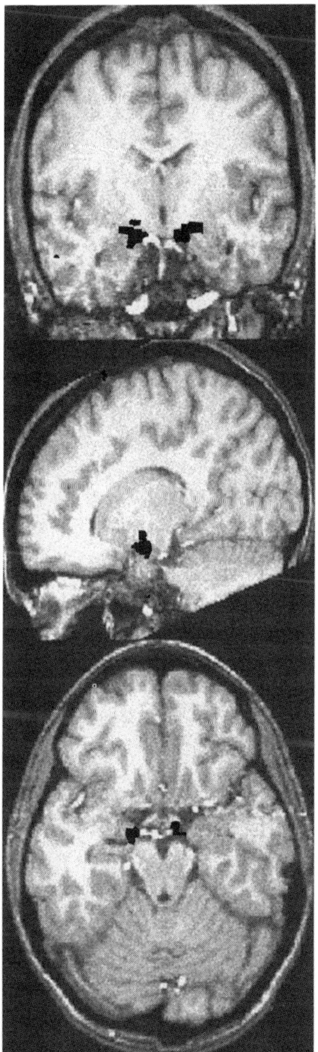

Figure 3.1
Activation of the amygdala in normal subjects to fear-eliciting stimuli (Irwin et al., 1996).

There is also a good deal of evidence in humans that the amygdala is linked to fear (e.g., Aggleton, 1992, 1995, 2000; LeDoux, 1996; Morris et al., 1996; Calder et al., 2001). For example, recently it has been observed that lesions of the amygdala impair fear-related behavior and autonomic responses to conditioned stimuli (e.g., LeDoux, 2000). Several studies have found that lesions of the amygdala interfere with the recognition of fearful facial expression (Adolphs et al., 1995). Also, positron emission tomography (PET) imaging studies have shown greater activation of the amygdala during fear and anxiety-provoking stimuli (Ketter et al., 1996). Such PET studies have also revealed that the amygdala is activated when presented with fearful versus happy faces (Morris et al., 1996; Dolan et al., 2000; Wright et al., 2001). With the use of functional magnetic resonance imaging (MRI), it has further been shown that the amygdala is activated and then habituates when shown fearful in contrast to neutral or happy faces (Breiter et al., 1996), but the amygdala is also responsive to a variety of facial responses (Lane et al., 1999; Dolan et al., 2000; Wright et al., 2001).

Clinically, some forms of depression (anxious) are associated with fear (Gold et al., 1988a, b). Elevated blood flow to the amygdala has been observed using PET in patients who are both fearful and depressed. Many of these patients tend to have higher levels of cortisol than normal controls (Drevets et al., 1992; Drevets, 2001). The metabolic rate of the human amygdala (and neocortical areas) has also been used to predict both depression and negative affect (figure 3.2; Ketter et al., 1996; Davidson et al., 1999).

A hyperexcitable state of the amygdala has been suggested by a number of authors that may underlie excessive fear, chronic arousal, and chronic angst (Kagan et al., 1988; LeDoux, 1996; Rosen and Schulkin, 1998). In animal models, kindling is a way to excite the brain via electrodes targeted to an anatomical site using electrical current delivered to the targeted brain region (see, e.g., Adamec, 1997). In other words, the result of this experimental manipulation is a putative hyperexcitable state in the brain that creates an experimental form of chronic arousal

A

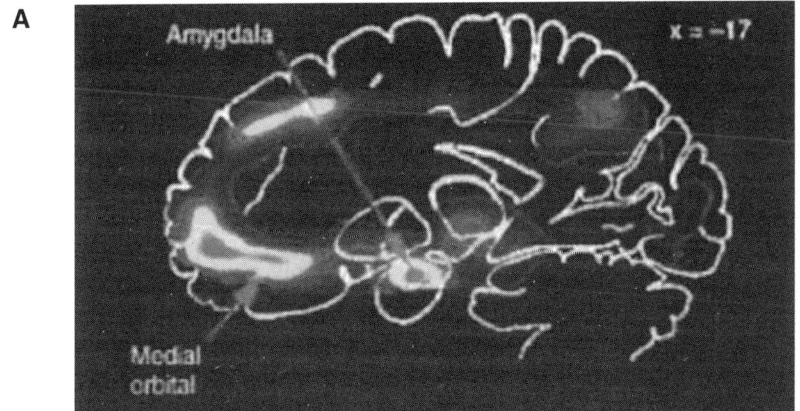

B

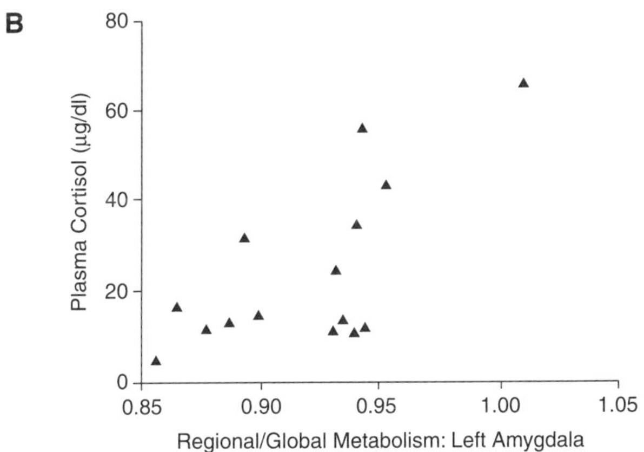

Figure 3.2
(*A*) Activation of the amygdala and medial frontal/orbital cortex in depressed subjects (Drevets, 1999). (*B*) Relationship between plasma cortisol concentrations measured immediately prior to the PET radiotracer injection and normalized glucose metabolism in the left amygdala for the depressed subject (Drevets et al., 2002).

(allostatic). In that study, the idea was that partial amygdala kindling would potentiate fear-related behavioral responses but that dorsal hippocampal kindling would not. Rats were conditioned to be fearful to a light paired with a foot shock. During the next several days, they received partial kindling of the amygdala or of the dorsal hippocampus. Rats were then presented with an auditory startle stimulus with or without light. Fear-potentiated startle was tested one week later (Rosen et al., 1996). The group that underwent amygdala kindling displayed elevated startle amplitude; they were more readily prepared to startle, to perhaps perceive an event as fearful.

Frontal Cortex

One interesting set of observations is that while the amygdala tends to have higher metabolic activity associated with depression and fear (Morris et al., 1996; Drevets, 2001; Drevets et al., 2002), the subgenual prefrontal cortex tends to have decreased metabolic activity (Drevets et al., 1999). Regions of the frontal cortex are fundamental for the emotions, including fear (e.g., Davidson et al., 1990, 1999, 2000; Quirk et al., 2000; Posner and Rothbart, 2000).

Building on the work of Schneirla (1959, 1965), a number of investigators have shown that the representation of emotional events is differentially expressed within this large region of the brain. Right neocortical activation is linked to more negative emotions and withdrawal, whereas the left side of the frontal region is linked to more positive emotions (Davidson et al., 1999, 2000). For example, lesions of the left region are more closely associated with states of depression; the converse holds with damage to the right region (Davidson et al., 1990, 2000). In functional brain-imaging studies, the elicitation of positive emotions is closely linked to left frontal neocortical activation (central states that we prefer to stay in) and negative emotions are closely linked to right neocortical activation (states that we want to remove; Schmidt et al., 1999a; Davidson et al., 2000). In a number of contexts, activation of the left frontal cortex is tied to positive representations, experiences, and contexts; the converse

holds true for negative representations (Davidson and Sutton, 1995; Davidson, 1998). Moreover, this cortical activation is associated with affective states; patients who are depressed have greater relative activation of right frontal cortex than those who are not (Davidson et al., 1999).

The frontal neocortical activation is stable and appears in ontogeny. Young children who are fearful have greater relative activation of the right frontal cortex (Schmidt et al., 1999a). This event is linked to elevated levels of cortisol (Kagan et al., 1988; Gunnar et al., 1989; see Gunnar and Davis, 2001 for a full discussion of cortisol under a variety of central states). In monkeys, this differential representation of cortical function is linked to CRH expression (see below). Some of the key areas linked to the expression of fear and CRH are depicted in figure 3.3.

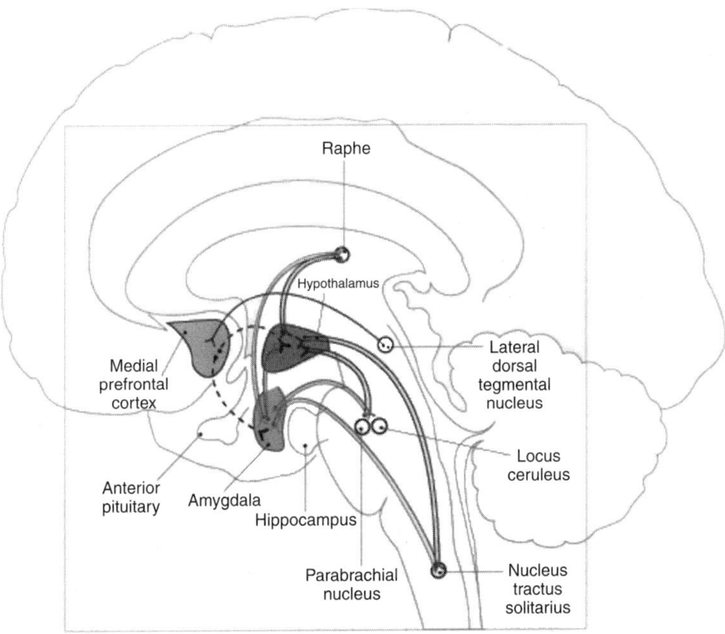

Figure 3.3
Some of the key areas in the brain that underlie fear.

From Normal Fear to Anticipatory Angst and Allostasis

Understanding human anxiety disorders lies in the study of normal fear and its associated behaviors. This includes not only the fear-related autonomic and behavioral responses that are activated during pathological anxiety but, also important, the perceptual fear response of greater vigilance. Unraveling the mechanisms of the perceptual fear response may lead researchers to a greater understanding of pathological anxiety because dysfunction or overactivation of the perception of fear can lead to anxious thought and maladaptive behavior (e.g., Rosen and Schulkin, 1998; Davis and Whalen, 2001).

Animals are ready to respond to external stimuli and, in many cases, in a prepotent or fixed manner (Tinbergen, 1951; Lorenz, 1981). This seems to be particularly true of fear responses (Bolles, 1962). If the perceptual-response system is primed and more sensitive or excitable, then there is a greater tendency for action. Increases in the readiness to respond would produce greater or exaggerated responses to stimulation and would allow for these responses to be elicited with lower intensity stimulation (Arnold, 1969; Frijda, 1986). The various cognitive biases (e.g., interpretive, attention, or memorial) and increased startle responses (Morgan et al., 1995; Grillon et al., 1996) demonstrated by anxiety disorder patients in response to threatening stimuli indicate that neural fear systems are hyperexcitable in anxiety disorders. Neurologically, this can be conceptualized as hyperexcitability of brain structures that evaluate (exteroceptive, interoceptive, and proprioceptive) stimuli as dangerous. Thus external as well as internal autonomic and muscular events are evaluated more readily as signaling danger in a hyperexcitable fear evaluation system.

Trauma at an early age, particularly infant-mother separations, has a detrimental effect on emotional development (Bowlby, 1977). Numerous animal studies have demonstrated that maternal separation or deprivation can have prolonged effects on the behavior and on the physiology of the offspring. Brief, repeated separations may actually immunize for later stress, whereas longer periods of maternal deprivation can

increase later responses to stress (e.g., Levine, 1975, 2000; Meaney et al., 1993). Interestingly, studies throughout several decades demonstrate that maternal behavior can ameliorate the effects of early stress on later behavioral and physiological responses to stress (Levine, 1975; Liu et al., 1997; Van Oers et al., 1998; Caldji et al., 1998). Lack of such ameliorative maternal behavior may sensitize the offspring to stressors.

Glucocorticoids, CRH, and the Allostatic Regulation of Fear

Fear is sustained by neuroendocrine events in most vertebrates that have been studied (Jones et al., 1988; Sapolsky, 1992; Jones and Satterlee, 1996), and there is no clear physiological set point that underlies the states of fear. Under threat, the HPA axis is activated (e.g., Cannon, 1915, 1929a; Selye, 1956; Dallman et al., 2000), as are sites in the brain that participate in the regulation of fear. Let us consider the glucocorticoids first. The secretion of glucocorticoids helps to sustain a number of behavioral responses including fear-related behaviors (Richter, 1949; see review by Korte, 2001). Without glucocorticoids, as Richter (1949) noted, animals die under (conditions of extreme) duress (see also Ingle, 1954; Selye, 1956). Adrenalectomized animals are unable to tolerate fear, duress, or chronic stress and suffer fatally. Glucocorticoids prepare the animal to cope with emergency and taxing environmental contexts (Cannon, 1915, 1929a; Richter, 1949).

Glucocorticoids are also essential in the development of fear (Takahashi, 1995). Removal of corticosterone in rats before (but not after) 14 days of age impairs fear of unfamiliar objects. In other words, there is a critical period in neonatal development in which glucocorticoids facilitate the normal expression of fear of unfamiliar objects (Takahashi, 1995). These events are centrally mediated (Takahashi and Kim, 1994). There are also periods in development that have been characterized as the "stress-hyporesponsive period" (Levine et al., 2000).

Glucocorticoids are secreted under a number of experimental conditions in which fear, anxiety, novelty, and uncertainty are

experimental manipulations (Mason et al., 1957; Mason, 1975a, b; Breier et al., 1988). In contexts in which there is loss of control, or the perception of control (worry is associated with the loss of control), glucocorticoids are secreted. This fact holds across a number of species, including humans (e.g., Breier et al., 1988). Perceived control reduces the levels of glucocorticoids that circulate. In rats, for example, predicting the onset of an aversive signal reduces the level of circulating glucocorticoids (Kant et al., 1992). Within the clinical sphere, one of the most consistent findings in fearful, depressed patients is elevated levels of cortisol and an enlarged adrenal cortex (Sachar et al., 1970; Carroll et al., 1976; Nemeroff et al., 1992). These findings are congruent with those of Richter (1949), who observed an enlarged adrenal gland in stressed, fearful wild rats when compared to unstressed laboratory analogs (figure 3.4).

From a biological view, the chronic activation of glucocorticoid hormones is costly. The subordinate male macaque has elevated cortisol levels but lower levels of testosterone than the dominant one (Sapolsky, 1992, 2000). The lower level of testosterone decreases its reproductive fitness in the short term. The cost of chronic subordination is perhaps more fearfulness and uncertainty of attack as well as a further decrease in the likelihood of successful reproduction. This phenomenon of high corticosterone and low testosterone has been demonstrated in a number of species (see, e.g., Lance and Elsey, 1986).

Sustained fear is also metabolically costly. Although glucocorticoids are essential in the development of neuronal tissue and in adapting to duress, if the elevation of glucocorticoids is sustained over time, tissue (e.g., brain and bone) will begin to deteriorate (Sapolsky, 1992; McEwen, 1997). Chronic glucocorticoid activation, for example, increases the likelihood of neurotoxicity and neural endangerment through the loss of glucocorticoid receptors.

Perhaps to avoid this deterioration, negative regulation of the HPA axis evolved to restrain the stress response. In other words, glucocorticoids restrain the output of the PVN of the hypothalamus and pituitary gland, decreasing CRH and

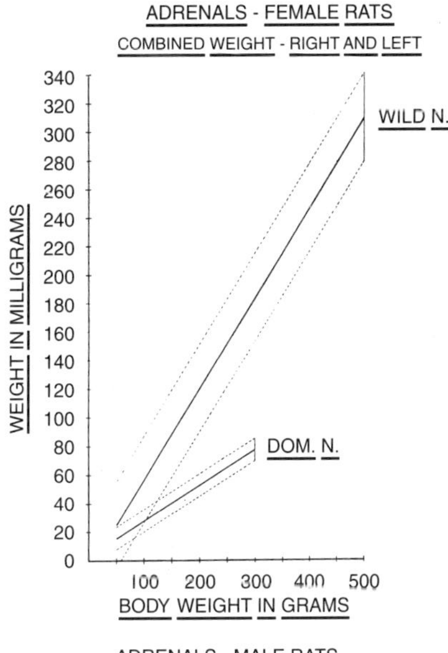

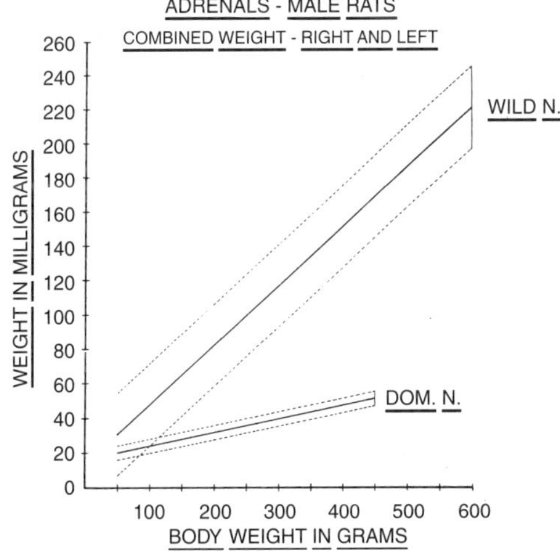

Figure 3.4
Weight of adrenal glands of wild and domestic (DOM) rats (Richter, 1949).

adrenocorticotropic hormone (ACTH) and thereby limiting their own production (Munck et al., 1984; Sawchenko, 1987; Dallman et al., 1987, 1992, 2000). This is classic negative feedback, one mechanism to restrain the activation of the HPA (Munck et al., 1984; Kovacs and Sawchenko, 1996; Dallman et al., 2000). The restraint of CRH, at the level of the PVN, is profound and sustained over time. The restraint of HPA function appears to be regulated in part through glucocorticoid activation of the hippocampus and bed nucleus of the stria terminalis (Beaulieu et al., 1987; Sapolsky et al., 1991; Cullinan et al., 1993). This occurs through efferent control of the PVN by gamma-aminobutyric acid (GABA)-mediated inhibitory neurons (Herman and Cullinan, 1997).

Glucocorticoids play a fundamental role in energy balance (hence their name). They are secreted in young children that are energetic (Gunnar, 1998), they can play a role in attachment behaviors in humans and other animals (DeVries et al., 1995; Fleming et al., 1997; Carter et al., 1999), and they facilitate a number of behavioral events (e.g., Denton, 1982; Schulkin, 1991; Sumners et al., 1991; Wingfield and Ramenofsky, 1997; Dallman et al., 2000) by their actions in the brain and the induction of neuropeptides and neurotransmitters (Herbert and Schulkin, 2002). Glucocorticoids are also important in sustaining a fear response. Fear is a state that is energy expensive (Sapolsky, 1992) and can go on for long periods of time in anticipation of events that may or may not occur. In order to understand the impact of fear on the body and brain, a new conceptual framework that involves two concepts, allostasis and allostatic overload, can serve a conceptual role in our understanding the state of fear, a chronic state, and the eventual breakdown of biological tissue and function.

Corticotropin-Releasing Systems in the Brain

Corticotropin-releasing hormone is now well known to be both a peptide that regulates pituitary and adrenal function and an extrahypothalamic peptide hormone linked to a number of

behaviors, including behavioral expressions of fear (Tarjan et al., 1992; Koob et al., 1993; Kalin et al., 1994).

Corticotropin-releasing hormone is a 41 amino acid peptide hormone initially isolated from the PVN of the hypothalamus that facilitates ACTH secretion from the anterior pituitary (Saffran et al., 1955; Guillemin and Rosenberg, 1955; Vale et al., 1981). In addition, CRH is linked to immune, sleep, and appetitive functions (Owens and Nemeroff, 1991).

Corticotropin-releasing hormone cell bodies are widely distributed in the brain (Swanson et al., 1983; Palkovits et al., 1983; Gray, 1990). The majority of CRH neurons within the PVN are clustered in the parvicellular division. Other regions with predominant CRH-containing neurons are the lateral bed nucleus of the stria terminalis and the central region of the central nucleus of the amygdala. To a lesser degree, there are CRH cells in the lateral hypothalamus, prefrontal, and cingulate cortex. In brainstem regions, CRH cells are clustered near the locus coeruleus (Barrington's nucleus) (Valentino et al., 1994, 1995), parabrachial region, and regions of the solitary nucleus (see figure 2.8).

The CRH receptor has been cloned and contains a 451 amino acid protein (Chen et al., 1993; Perrin et al., 1993; Lovenberg et al., 1995). Activation of the CRH receptor is linked to a G protein and activates adenylate cyclase cascade and an increase in intracellular cyclic adenosine monophosphate (cAMP) and calcium levels (Perrin and Vale, 1999). The distribution of CRH receptor sites includes regions of the hippocampus, septum, and amygdala (medial and lateral region), and neocortex, ventral thalamic, and medial hypothalamic sites, and sparse receptors are located in the PVN and the pituitary gland. The distribution is widespread in cerebellum in addition to brainstem sites such as major sensory nerves and the solitary nucleus (Potter et al., 1994).

In both rodents and primates, further studies have revealed that there are at least two distinct CRH receptor subtypes (Lovenberg et al., 1995; Aguilera et al., 2001; Dautzenberg et al., 2001). The CRH 1 subtype is prominent in limbic regions such

as the amygdala, and the CRH 2 subtype is more widely distributed throughout the brain (Potter et al., 1994). It is the CRH 1 receptor subtype that has been linked to both the regulation of the HPA axis and in extrahypothalamic sites to the reduction of fear and the sense of adversity (Smith et al., 1998; Arborelius et al., 2001; Bale et al., 2001a), and perhaps even a reduction of depression (see below). The regulation of both types of receptors has been linked to allostatic regulation (Coste et al., 2001).

Negative Restraint of PVN CRH Gene Expression by Glucocorticoids: Homeostatic Regulation

Glucocorticoid hormones have one well-known function—namely, to restrain the HPA axis by negative feedback mechanisms (Munck et al., 1984). This negative feedback is a fundamental way in which the HPA axis is restrained during stress and activity (Munck et al., 1984) and is understood in the context of negative feedback regulation (e.g., Goldstein, 1995a, b, 2000). One should also note that recent evidence suggests that negative restraint of CRH may not be confined solely to the PVN; it may also appear in the locus coeruleus (Pavcovich and Valentino, 1997).

The restraint of HPA activation by glucocorticoids is rapid and profound (Dallman et al., 1987). It is also specific; mineralocorticoids do not produce these effects (Sawchenko, 1987; Watts and Sanchez-Watts, 1995). Moreover, glucocorticoids directly control neuronal excitability (Joels and DeKloet, 1994). Given that some of the glucocorticoid effects on the brain are quite rapid, it is possible that corticosterone has nongenomic membrane effects via GABAergic mechanisms (Orchinik et al., 1994), in addition to its genomic effects.

The degree of the HPA activation is coordinated by both humoral and neural mechanisms. Efferent pathways from the hippocampus and amygdala regulate the expression of CRH in the PVN (Sapolsky et al., 1991; Herman and Cullinan, 1997). For example, lesions or stimulation of the central nucleus of the amygdala either decrease or increase HPA activation,

respectively (Beaulieu et al., 1987). Furthermore, neurons within the lateral bed nucleus of the stria terminalis may activate or inhibit PVN function via GABAergic mechanisms (Cullinan et al., 1993; Herman and Cullinan, 1997).

While the profound effect of inhibition is indisputable, there are neuronal populations within the PVN that project to the brainstem that are not decreased by glucocorticoids and some of which are actually enhanced (Swanson and Simmons, 1989; Tanimura and Watts, 1998). That is, CRH neurons en route to the pituitary are restrained by glucocorticoids, but CRH en route to other regions of the brain appears not to be restrained (Swanson and Simmons, 1989; Watts and Sanchez-Watts, 1995; Watts, 1996; Palkovits et al., 1998b).

Positive Induction of CRH Gene Expression in the Central Nucleus of the Amygdala and Bed Nucleus of the Stria Terminalis by Corticosterone: Allostatic Regulation

Several colleagues and I (Schulkin et al., 1994) suggested that corticosterone could restrain one set of CRH-producing cells, namely, that system linked to HPA function, while initiating amygdala production of CRH for fear-related behaviors (Schulkin, 1994; Schulkin et al., 1994). We suggested that there might be this disassociation within the endocrine literature on glucocorticoid regulation of CRH expression on these two different sites. There were intimations of this in the literature (Young and Akil, 1988; Bagdy et al., 1990; Frim et al., 1990; Owens et al., 1990; Imaki et al., 1991). These results have direct relevance for the concept of allostasis and feedforward neuroendocrine systems.

Swanson and Simmons (1989) demonstrated that replacement of corticosterone in adrenalectomized rats would decrease hypothalamic CRH in the parvicellular PVN while it restored and even increased CRH in the central nucleus of the amygdala. This differential regulation of PVN CRH neurons, from central nucleus CRH neurons, in adrenalectomized rats was then extended explicitly and more broadly tested by others (Watts and Sanchez-Watts, 1995; Palkovits, et al., 1998b). It was also noted that within magnicellular neurons within the PVN that pro-

jected to the brainstem there was an actual increase in CRH, and no change in CRH neurons in the lateral hypothalamus (Swanson and Simmons, 1989; Imaki et al., 1991; Watts and Sanchez-Watts, 1995; Tanimura and Watts, 1998). Watts and Sanchez-Watts (1995) also reported that in adrenalectomized rats, aldosterone can increase CRH gene expression in the central nucleus of the amygdala in the absence (but not the presence) of corticosterone, and mineralocorticoid receptor levels are increased by CRH infusions in the brain (Gesing et al., 2001) and thus important interactions exist between both adrenal steroid hormones and CRH. Interestingly, while adrenalectomy results in increases in CRH expression in the paraventricular nucleus, it reduces CRH expression in the central nucleus of the amygdala (Palkovits et al., 1998b).

Makino and colleagues (1994a, b) demonstrated that when adrenally intact rats were treated with high levels of corticosterone for extended periods of time (4 days–2 weeks), there was a decrease of CRH mRNA from the PVN, but an increase in CRH mRNA, or protein, from the central nucleus of the amygdala. In other words, corticosterone could decrease the expression of CRH in the PVN (restraint of HPA axis) while it simultaneously increased CRH gene expression in the central nucleus of the amygdala (Thompson et al., 2000). However, in cell culture CRH neurons of the amygdala, dexamethasone had no effect (Kasckow et al., 1997).

When we (Makino et al., 1995) looked at changes in CRH receptor levels following corticosterone treatment in regions of the amygdala where they are located (basal lateral region), we found at best a modest change in receptor distribution. We found a slight decrease of CRH receptor levels in the basal lateral region of the amygdala following high levels of corticosterone treatment. Dexamethasone pretreatment produced no such effect in extrahypothalamic sites such as the amygdala (Zhou et al., 1996a, b). There are few, if any, CRH receptor sites in the central nucleus of the amygdala (Makino et al., 1995), although CRH receptors have been reported to be altered by high levels of glucocorticoids in tree shrews under chronic psychosocial stress (Fuchs and Flugge, 1995).

Turn now to the bed nucleus of the stria terminalis. The bed nucleus of the stria terminalis plays a fundamental role in the regulation of the HPA axis during stress, and it is the major relay to the PVN from the amygdala and the hippocampus (Herman and Cullinan, 1997; Gray, 1999). Both the central nucleus of the amygdala and ventral subiculum influence HPA function (Beaulieu et al., 1987; Cullinan et al., 1993; Herman et al., 1998) and perhaps do so via the bed nucleus of the stria terminalis.

During fear / anxiety states, the bed nucleus of the stria terminalis may regulate systemic physiological responses. Thus one way in which to envision the hippocampus and the amygdala is through their influence on the bed nucleus of the stria terminalis function and subsequently upon the PVN. The bed nucleus of the stria terminalis may act as the *head ganglia* of the HPA axis in the regulation of systemic physiology as it transduces information from both the hippocampus and the amygdala. The bed nucleus of the stria terminalis is therefore positioned to exert control over output measures from both the hippocampus and the amygdala in the regulation of fear / anxiety-related responses.

The lateral region of the bed nucleus of the stria terminalis contains CRH-producing neurons (Ju et al., 1989; Gray, 1990; Makino et al., 1994b; Watts and Sanchez-Watts, 1995). Corticotropin-releasing hormone gene expression within this region of the bed nucleus of the stria terminalis is increased following corticosterone treatment. In the laboratory, this held for both adrenalectomized rats treated with corticosterone (Watts and Sanchez-Watts, 1995) and adrenally intact rats also treated with corticosterone (Makino et al., 1994b; see chapter 5).

Taken together, these results are examples of allostatic regulation. Now let's see how they underlie a fearful state.

Central CRH, Angst, Allostasis, and the Amygdala

Central CRH and central amygdala activation are linked to the induction of fear in animal studies (Kalin and Takahashi, 1990; Koob et al., 1993). Central infusions of CRH potentiate a number

of fear-related behavioral responses (Takahashi et al., 1989), and infusion of CRH antagonists both within the amygdala and outside of it reduce fear-related responses (Swiergel et al., 1992; Koob et al., 1993). Of importance, infusions of CRH into the ventricles are known to access to CRH receptor sites (Bittencourt and Sawchenko, 2000).

Startle responses are enhanced by CRH infusions (Swerdlow et al., 1989). It is important to note that lesions of the central nucleus of the amygdala, and not the PVN, disrupt CRH-potentiated conditioned fear responses (Liang et al., 1992). That is, only lesions of the amygdala and not the hypothalamus disrupt the behavioral response. Moreover, peripheral blockade of ACTH/glucocorticoids does not disrupt central CRH-related fear responses (Pich et al., 1993a). It is central CRH that is the critical neuroendocrine factor.

Corticosterone Facilitation of CRH and Behavioral Activation of Fear

As I have indicated, high levels of systemic glucocorticoids are associated with fear (or the perception of adverse events) in a number of species (Mason et al., 1957; Jones et al., 1988; Breier, 1989; Takahashi and Kim, 1994; Kalin et al., 1998a, b; Buchanan et al., 1999; see review by Korte, 2001). In one set of experiments, in collaboration with Keith Coordimas and Joe LeDoux (Coordimas et al., 1994), rats (adrenally intact) were pretreated with corticosterone to investigate whether it facilitated conditioned fear-induced freezing. All rats received conditioning trials in which the unconditioned stimulus (foot shock) was presented concurrently with the conditioned stimulus (auditory tone). Several days after the trials, the rats were treated with corticosterone (Coordimas et al., 1994). We found that the same treatment of corticosterone that increased CRH gene expression in the central nucleus of the amygdala and bed nucleus of the stria terminalis also facilitated conditioned fear-induced freezing in rats (Coordimas et al., 1994).

As noted above, CRH facilitates startle responses. This response does not depend on the adrenal glands, because centrally delivered CRH facilitates startle responses in the absence of the adrenal glands (Lee et al., 1994). In their study, Lee and colleagues demonstrated that high chronic plasma levels of corticosterone in adrenally intact rats facilitated CRH-induced startle responses (Lee et al., 1994). Perhaps what occurs normally is that the glucocorticoids, by increasing CRH gene expression, increase the likelihood that something will be perceived as a threat, which results in a startle response. Thus a dose of CRH, given intraventricularly, did not produce a startle response, but when the adrenally intact rats were maintained at high levels of corticosterone for several days prior to the CRH injection, the same dose did produce a startle response.

Corticotropin-releasing hormone centrally infused at high doses into the lateral ventricle facilitates seizures linked to amygdala function (Weiss et al., 1986). In a collaboration with Rosen and his colleagues, we found that a dose of CRH by itself does not induce kindling but does so with a background of high glucocorticoid levels. That is, instead of reducing seizures as was predicted by corticosterone's restraint on the HPA axis, it actually potentiated the seizures in adrenally intact rats (Rosen et al., 1994). One way to understand these findings is that by increasing CRH expression in the brain, the glucocorticoids lower the threshold for the induced seizure. It is now known that long-term effects on CRH gene expression result from adverse experiences (Bruihnzeel et al., 2001) creating perhaps a long-term allostatic state.

In a later study, we looked at contextual fear conditioning in groups of rats that were treated with corticosterone as above and given a vehicle treatment. We replicated our original finding that CRH expression was differentially regulated in the central nucleus of the amygdala and the parvicellular region of the PVN (Thompson et al., 2000; figure 3.5, below). One week after the completion of the conditioning and the last corticosterone injection, the rats were tested for the retention of conditioned

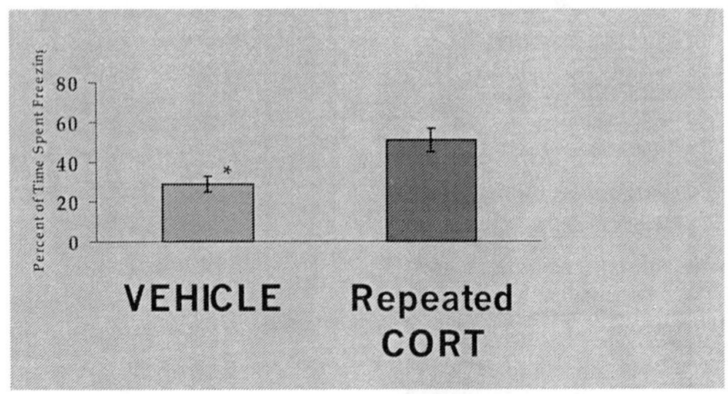

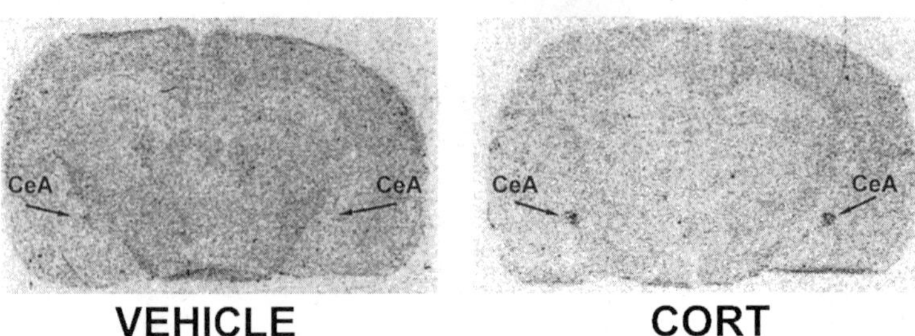

Figure 3.5
Digitized images of CRH mRNA in the central nucleus of the amygdala (CeA) in corticosterone (CORT) (4 mg) or vehicle treated rats (after Thompson et al., 2001). Freezing responses of rats in the retention test in corticosterone treated (5 mg per day for 4 days) or vehicle treated (adapted from Thompson et al., 2000).

fear. The corticosterone-treated rats displayed more fear conditioning than the vehicle-treated rats. The data suggest that repeated high levels of corticosterone can facilitate the retention of contextual fear conditioning, perhaps by the induction of CRH gene expression in critical regions of the brain such as the amygdala.

In an important experiment, Shepard et al. (2000) demonstrated that implants of corticosterone directly into the amygdala resulted in an increase in CRH expression in the central

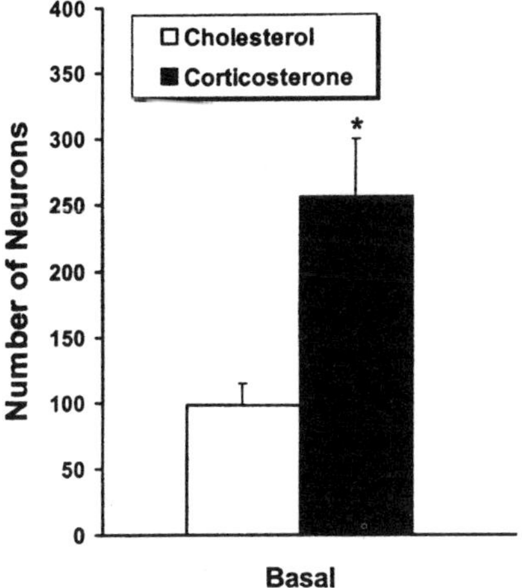

Figure 3.6
Increases in CRH mRNA to injections of corticosterone directly to the central nucleus of the amygdala (Shepard et al., 2000).

nucleus of the amygdala and a reduction in open-field exploratory behavior (figure 3.6). Rats are typically hesitant at first to explore new environments, and this was exacerbated with the induction of CRH in the central nucleus when corticosterone was directly delivered into the amygdala (rats remained in the open chamber for 22.6 sec vs. 67.3 sec for controls). In addition, corticosterone implants directly into the central nucleus increased levels of CRH expression, without affecting AVP levels, in the parvicellular region of the paraventricular nucleus of the hypothalamus (Shepard et al., 2003). Moreover, gastric pathology, one consequence of allostatic overload (colon distension), was apparent as a result of the corticosterone. In further tests, pretreatment with the type-1 receptor CRH antagonist abolished these effects (see also for the role of the CRH type-1 receptor, Smith et al., 1998; Arborelius et al., 2000; and the role for the type-II receptor, Bale et al., 2000; Bakshi et al., 2002).

A Possible Role for Glucocorticoids and CRH within the Bed Nucleus of the Stria Terminalis for Fear-Related Context Learning and Anxiety

Context learning (no one specific cue associated with an event) and uncertainty are known to elevate glucocorticoid levels in a number of species (Mason et al., 1957; Mason, 1975a, b). Uncertainty that stems from environmental context influences CRH expression. For example, in macaques, uncertainty of food availability during development results in elevated levels of cortisol, in addition to increases in the expression of CRH in the cerebrospinal fluid when they are adults (Coplan et al., 1996, 2001).

Corticosterone is also essential in the normal development of fear (Takahashi, 1995) and for context-related fear learning. For example, blocking corticosterone secretion impairs long-term consolidation of context-dependent fear conditioning. Replacement of corticosterone in adrenalectomized rats returns this function to normal (Fleshner et al., 1997; Pugh et al., 1997). These effects are specific for context-dependent fear, as there were no decrements in conditioned fear to a specific stimulus.

The above effects on fear may be mediated by central CRH. In fact, CRH is known to facilitate nonspecific fear conditioning (Davis et al., 1997). Perhaps corticosterone acts to increase CRH gene expression in certain regions of the brain and thereby increases the likelihood of context-dependent fear conditioning.

The bed nucleus of the stria terminalis has been linked to context-dependent learning (Lee and Davis, 1997b), to general anxiety associated with drug abuse (Erb and Stewart, 1999; Koob and LeMoal, 2001; see chapter 5 of this book), and to symptoms associated with generalized anxiety (Stout et al., 2000). Perhaps some of the effects on context-related fear conditioning seen in hippocampal lesions studies (Phillips and LeDoux, 1992; Kim et al., 1993) may be mediated by regions of the bed nucleus of the stria terminalis (Davis et al., 1997; Lee and Davis, 1997a), while the specific conditioned fear state depends upon the amygdala (LeDoux, 1996; Rosen and Schulkin, 1998; Davis and Whalen, 2001).

Lesions of the bed nucleus of the stria terminalis do not interfere with conditioned fear-related responses, unlike lesions of regions of the amygdala, which interfere with fear-potentiated startle or freezing (Hitchcock and Davis, 1991; LeDoux, 1995; Lee and Davis, 1997a, b). Nor does stimulation of this region facilitate fear-potentiated startle responses, whereas stimulation of the central nucleus of the amygdala does (Rosen et al., unpublished observations; Davis et al., 1993). However, lesions of the bed nucleus of the stria terminalis can interfere with basic unconditioned startle responses (Gray et al., 1993; Gray and Bingaman, 1996) and with long-term CRH effects on behavior (Davis et al., 1997).

Of importance, infusions of CRH directly into the bed nucleus of the stria terminalis facilitate fear/anxiety-related behavioral responses; antagonists of CRH into this region do the converse (Davis et al., 1997; Lee and Davis, 1997a; see chapter 5 for a discussion of the effects of drug addiction). This theory of the role of glucocorticoids in facilitating CRH gene expression in several sites in the brain would suggest that pretreatment with glucocorticoids should further potentiate this effect, but this is not known. This again suggests an allostatic mechanism of regulation.

Experiment of Nature: Elevated Cortisol and Central CRH—Inhibited Children and Macaques and Their Fear of the Unfamiliar

A subset of excessively shy and/or fearful children are known to have had, at some point in their developmental history, higher levels of cortisol in several contexts than normal controls (Kagan et al., 1988; Gunnar et al., 1989; Schmidt et al., 1997; Dettling et al., 2000). Interestingly, young children who demonstrate high motor and negative emotional responses at 9 months of age tend to be behaviorally inhibited at 4 and 7 years old. They also tend to have higher cortisol levels. The amount of time that shy and fearful children spend cowering and worrying suggests that the behavioral inhibition is an active process, a metabolically expensive event (figure 3.7).

Figure 3.7
Shy fearful child (Schmidt and Schulkin, 1999).

Although cortisol is certainly not the molecule of fear and anxiety, it is the molecule of energy metabolism; fear, anxiety, and trauma are metabolic events. With this caveat, extremely shy, socially withdrawn children may be vulnerable to anxiety disorders and perhaps depression throughout their lives (Hirshfield et al., 1992; Kagan and Snidman, 1999). They should be vulnerable to allostatic load—for example, vulnerability to allergic symptoms (Kagan et al., 1991) and vascular disease (Bell et al., 1993) perhaps because of the chronic worry that they experience in social contexts or in unfamiliar environments. Interestingly, high cortisol levels have been linked not only to fearfulness in childhood but to repression in adulthood (Brown et al., 1996).

An analogous phenomenon to that of shyness and fearful behavior in children has been observed in a subset of young, fearful rhesus monkeys that have high levels of cortisol. This subset also freezes for longer periods of time than other rhesus monkeys (Champoux et al., 1989). In adult rhesus monkeys, high levels of cortisol, in addition to high levels of CRH from the cerebrospinal fluid, is associated with behavioral inhibition (Kalin et al., 2000; Habib et al., 2000). In addition, when faced with an unknown intruder in an adjacent cage, macaques increase their CRH expression (figure 3.8; Habib et al., 2000). Increases (or sensitization) of CRH in the brain occurs after stress, abuse, and maternal deprivation in macaques (Habib et al., 1999, 2000). Interestingly, the converse holds for neuropeptide Y, a neuropeptide linked to reward, food intake, and positive emotions (e.g., Heinrichs et al., 1992; Wahlestedt et al., 1993).

A subset of these macaques not only have higher levels of CRH and cortisol than normals, but also demonstrate greater fearful temperament and greater activation of right-hemispheric activation which has been linked to withdrawal and negative perception of events (figure 3.9; Davidson et al., 1990, 1999; Habib et al., 1999, 2000; Kalin et al., 2000). Differences in temperamental expression to a number of unconditioned fear-related stimuli may reflect frontal neocortical activation (Kalin et al.,

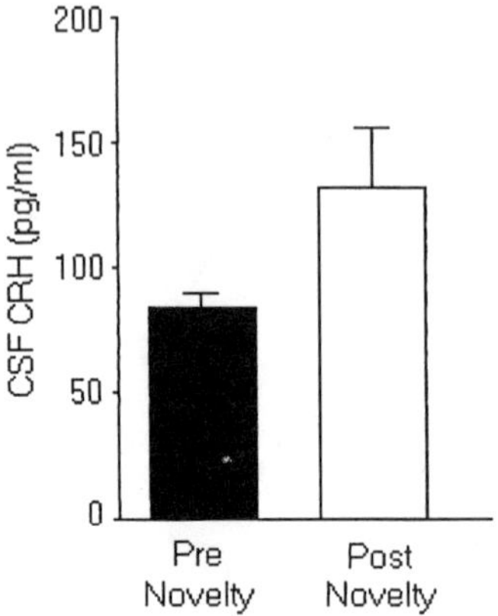

Figure 3.8
Levels of corticotropin releasing hormone in the cerebrospinal fluid of macaques in response to a familiar (prenovelty) and unfamiliar (postnovelty) object (adapted from Habib et al., 1999, 2000).

2001), because ibitenic acid lesions (cell body destroyed and fibers left intact) of the macaque amygdala left a number of unconditioned behavioral traitlike responses intact (Kalin et al., 2001), in addition to the normal asymmetry associated with traitlike dispositions.

Perhaps these excessively shy, fearful children and monkeys reflect differences in endogenous production of CRH. For example, rats that tend to have higher levels of CRH expression in the central nucleus of the amygdala may be more vulnerable to exaggerated fear responses (Altemus et al., 1994). Transgenic mice that overproduce CRH have greater fear-related responses in unfamiliar environments (Stenzel-Poore et al., 1994) in addition to other behavioral abnormalities such as sexual inhibition (Heinrichs et al., 1997; but see also Weninger et al., 1999, or Bakshi and Kalin, 2000, for discussions of the role of the CRH receptor subtypes and the behavioral responses associated with CRH). These same animals also have high levels of corticosterone.

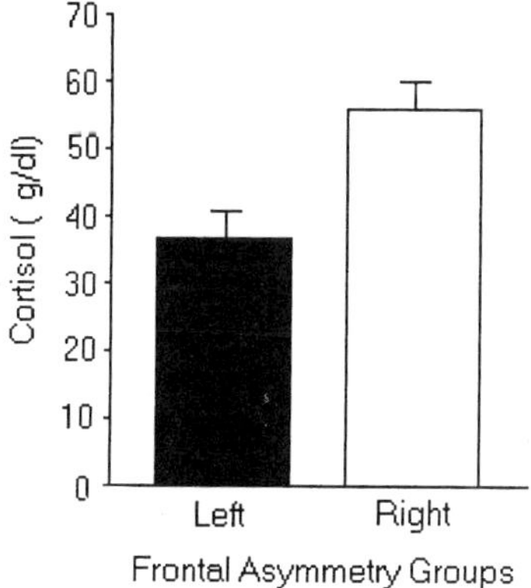

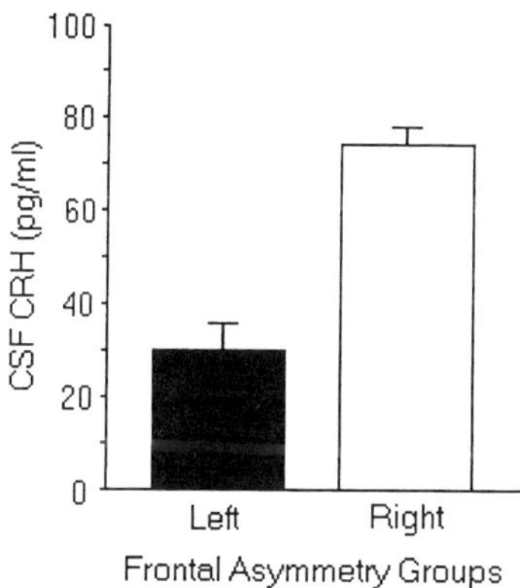

Figure 3.9
Levels of CSF CRH and systemic cortisol in left and right frontal brain activation in macaques (adapted from Kalin et al., 1998a, b, 2000).

Anxious or Melancholic Depression: CRH and Cortisol and Allostatic Overload

Unipolar depression is a major health concern that can affect up to 10–15 percent of the population at any point in time. It is generally held that there is a greater incidence of depression in women than men. There are several types of depression (e.g., seasonal, postpartum, anxious, or melancholic; Nemeroff, 1992, 1999; Gold and Chrousos, 1998). For example, melancholic depression reflects a hyperaroused state—a state of vigilance. This state is marked by a profound sense of chronic angst, decreased pleasure, sleep abnormalities, and alterations of appetite, sense of pleasure, and libido (Nemeroff et al., 1992, 1999; Gold and Chrousos, 1998). Decreased libido and lethargy can be pervasive, with clear decreases in reproductive functions (Chrousos et al., 1998). A number of neurotransmitters and neuropeptides are altered during episodes of melancholic depression, including altered levels of adrenergic and serotinergic functions (e.g., Bunney and Davis, 1965; Gold et al., 1988a, b; Drevets et al., 1999; Lambert et al., 2000; Wong et al., 2000; Caberlotto and Hurd, 2001).

Interestingly, both atypical and seasonal depression are characterized by decreases in arousal, lethargy, a tendency to eat and sleep more, and decreased hypothalamic function (e.g., reduced levels of CRH; Vanderpool et al., 1991; Gold and Chrousos, 1998). As we will see below, anxious depression reflects a tendency for altered levels of both CRH and cortisol (cf. Gold et al., 1984; Nemeroff et al., 1984; Roy et al., 1987, 1988; Geracioti et al., 1997).

A significant subset of patients with agitated depression have elevated levels of cortisol (Sachar et al., 1970; Carroll et al., 1976; Roy et al., 1988; Kling et al., 1991; Nemeroff et al., 1992; Gold and Chrousos, 1998; see also Young et al., 2001). Yet levels of CRH are also elevated in the cerebrospinal fluid of such individuals (Nemeroff et al., 1984; Nemeroff, 1992, 1999, but see review by Kasckow et al., 2001 for the range of studies on levels of CRH

in the cerebrospinal fluid). Interference with the type-1 CRH receptor may reduce some of the symptoms associated with clinical depression (Zobel et al., 2000). This clinical finding forms a basis in which to envision that cortisol might increase extrahypothalamic CRH gene expression when pushed to extreme adverse conditions, such as that of depression. In other words, elevated levels of systemic cortisol in addition to altered levels of central CRH are a feature of melancholic depression (Gold et al., 1984, 1988a, b; Holsboer et al., 1984; Nemeroff et al., 1984, 1992; Holsboer, 2000). Moreover, levels of cortisol in depressed patients are correlated with enhanced amygdala activation (Drevets et al., 2002; see bottom of figure 3.2).

In addition to the overactivation of CRH and cortisol, there is the overactivation of the amygdala and the right frontal cortex in depressed and anxious people (Drevets et al., 1992). Moreover, we know that chronic anxious depression takes its toll on the body. Three examples I mentioned earlier are the demineralization of bone (Michelson et al., 1996), the reduction of hippocampal size and function (Sheline et al., 1996), and prefrontal cell pathology (Rajkowska et al., 1999). In fact, a number of pathophysiological events can occur that are associated with anxious depression. Coronary heart disease and regional fat content have also been linked to anxious depression (Negro et al., 2003). Of importance, CRH and its analogs, in addition to other adrenal hormones (Goldstein, 1995a, b; 2000), are linked to cardiovascular regulation and pathology (Parkes et al., 2001).

Consider another physiological event: bone density changes in depression (Michelson et al., 1996; Robbins et al., 2001; Negro et al., 2003). In one study, for example, people with current major depression, compared to nondepressed controls, had bone mineral density decreases at a number of sites including the hip, spine, and neck (figure 3.10; table 3.1). Cortisol was elevated in the depressed group. When compared with matched controls, for example, the bone density was between 7 and 14 percent lower at various places. Interestingly, vitamin D and parathy-

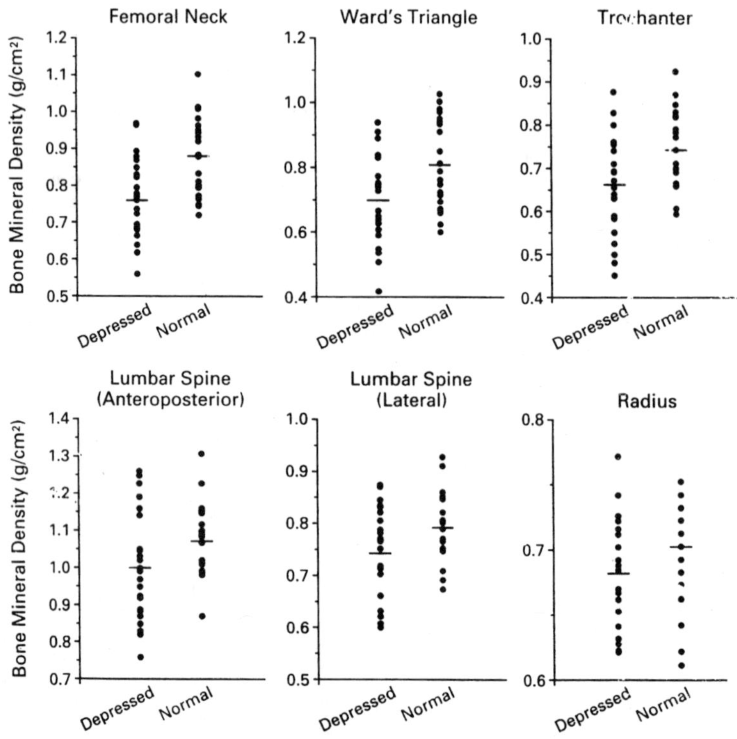

Figure 3.10
Bone mineral density in depressed and normal subjects (Michelson et al., 1996).

roid levels were equivalent in the two groups. Hypercortisol secretion is known to have consequences on bone metabolism and to facilitate bone loss over time (Canalis and Giustina, 2001). In addition to creating a vulnerability to other central and systemic disorders (e.g., cardiovascular pathology; Aromaa et al., 1994; Roy et al., 2001), it increases the likelihood of premature cardiovascular disease. These are examples of the manifestation of physiological/allostatic overload (Cizza et al., 2001).

Table 3.1
Bone mineral density in 24 depressed and 24 normal women

Bone Measurement	Depressed Women	Normal Women	Mean Difference (95% CI)
Lumbar spine (anteroposterior)			
Density (g/cm)	1.00 ± 0.15	1.07 ± 0.09	0.08 (0.02–0.14)
SD from expected peak	−0.42 ± 1.28	0.26 ± 0.82	0.68 (0.13–1.23)
Lumbar spine (lateral)			
Density (g/cm)	0.74 ± 0.09	0.79 ± 0.07	0.05 (0.00–0.09)
SD from expected peak	−0.88 ± 1.07	−0.36 ± 0.80	0.50 (0.04–1.30)
Femoral neck			
Density (g/cm)	0.76 ± 0.11	0.88 ± 0.11	0.11 (0.06–0.17)
SD from expected peak	−1.30 ± 1.07	−0.22 ± 0.99	1.08 (0.55–1.61)
Ward's triangle			
Density (g/cm)	0.70 ± 0.14	0.81 ± 0.13	0.11 (0.06–0.17)
SD from expected peak	−0.93 ± 1.24	0.18 ± 1.22	1.11 (0.60–1.62)
Trochanter			
Density (g/cm)	0.66 ± 0.11	0.74 ± 0.08	0.08 (0.04–0.13)
SD from expected peak	−0.70 ± 1.22	0.26 ± 0.91	0.97 (0.46–1.47)
Radius			
Density (g/cm)	0.68 ± 0.04	0.70 ± 0.04	0.01 (−0.01–0.04)
SD from expected peak	−0.19 ± 0.67	0.03 ± 0.67	0.21 (−0.21–0.64)

Michelson et al., 1996

Post-Traumatic Stress Disorder and Allostatic Overload

Post-traumatic stress disorder (PTSD) is associated with anxiety, memory impairment, and alterations in the HPA axis (Smith et al., 1989; Yehuda et al., 1995a, 1996; Kanter et al., 2001). PTSD is characterized by a state of hypervigilance, chronic arousal, diminished concentration, and altered sleep patterns. Individuals with PTSD often look "shell shocked." The phenomenon has been studied in veterans, in individuals who have been sexually abused, and in a number of other groups.

Patients with PTSD have been found to demonstrate alterations in fear-related responses (Morgan et al., 1995; Grillon et al., 1996). The syndrome is often (Mason et al., 1988; Yehuda et al., 1995a, b) but not always associated with low basal cortisol (Yehuda, 1997; Carrion et al., 2002). For example, low levels of cortisol have been reported in Vietnam veterans who suffered from

PTSD, but not Vietnam veterans who were traumatized but did not suffer from PTSD (Yehuda, 1997; Carrion et al., 2002). Interestingly, in those subjects who did not suffer from PTSD, there was no difference in cortisol levels when compared to normal controls.

More generally, women who have been raped and holocaust survivors who suffer from PTSD have lowered levels of basal cortisol than controls (Yehuda, et al., 1995a; Yehuda, 1997; Steiger et al., 2001). This phenomenon of low basal cortisol is noted in individuals with PTSD but not in individuals who underwent the same traumatic event but do not have PTSD (Yehuda, 1997, 2002).

Interestingly, these same PTSD patients have heightened reactivity or enhanced negative feedback regulation of the HPA axis (Yehuda et al., 1995b). For example, metyrapone, which reversibly inhibits cortisol synthesis, results in greater ACTH secretion in PTSD patients; this may reflect greater activation of CRH (Yehuda, 1997). In other words, while PTSD patients may have lower basal levels than normal subjects, they actually may be more responsive to the activation of the stress hormones (Mason, 1975a, b).

Glucocorticoids modulate memory, in part, via changes in noradrenergic transmission (McGaugh, 2000). These events are mediated in part by the basal lateral region of the amygdala (Roozendaal, 2000). Glucocorticoids can enhance or degrade long-term memory functions (de Quervain et al., 1998). The memory impairments identified among PTSD patients point to a role of the hippocampus that perhaps depends on transmission from the basal lateral region, in addition to the receptor deterioration that can result from excessive levels of glucocorticoids (Roozendaal, 2000; McGaugh, 2000). Short-term memory deficits in soldiers suffering from PTSD are not uncommon, and MRI studies have shown decreased hippocampal volume in patients who suffer PTSD (Bremner et al., 1995). This latter finding is consistent with animal studies that have demonstrated that chronic stress, or allostatic overload, can have long-term consequences such as memory impairment (McEwen and Sapolsky, 1995; McGaugh, 2000).

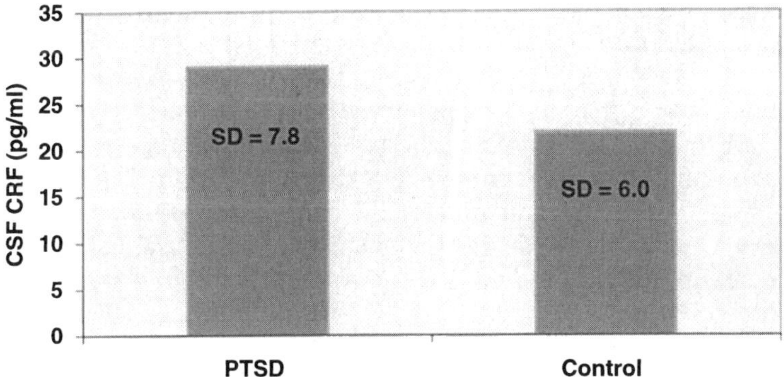

Figure 3.11
Cerebrospinal fluid (CSF) corticotropin releasing hormone levels in post-traumatic stress disorder (PTSD) patients and control subjects (adapted from Bremner et al., 1997).

This finding of low basal cortisol in PTSD patients stands out in contrast to the cortisol levels of people with melancholic depression or excessively shy children. It is important to note that there is some evidence that patients with PTSD have elevated levels of CRH in their cerebrospinal fluid (figure 3.11; Darnell et al., 1994; Bremner et al., 1997; Baker et al., 1999), despite the fact that they have normal levels of cortisol (see also Smith et al., 1989). In other words, patients who suffer from PTSD have elevated CRH levels in the brain under the basal condition, despite the low levels of cortisol that circulate systemically.

One way to understand this phenomenon is that experience with traumatic events induces long-term elevated levels of CRH. As in other contexts in which systemic hormones can have long-term consequences in influencing neuropeptide levels and central states, what matters is not the level of peripheral cortisol or corticosterone, but the induction of a hyperactive CRH system. But the chronic alterations of central CRH and the chronic arousal that is associated with it suggests allostatic dysregulation.

Conclusion: Allostasis and Allostatic Overload

Fear is an adaptation; chronic angst is not. Underlying both, however, is the positive induction of CRH by glucocorticoids in extrahypothalamic sites. I have summarized the evidence that glucocorticoids have differential effects on CRH gene expression in the forebrain. In the parvicellular region of PVN, CRH gene expression is inhibited under some experimental circumstances. In these same contexts, in the central nucleus of the amygdala and the lateral bed nucleus of the stria terminalis, CRH is elevated (Swanson and Simmons, 1989; Makino et al., 1994a, b; Watts and Sanchez-Watts, 1995; Watts, 1996). The elevation of CRH gene expression by glucocorticoids in the central nucleus of the amygdala and lateral bed nucleus of the stria terminalis may underlie a number of fear/anxiety functions as well as pathological states (see Cook, 2002).

I suggested that allostatic regulation is anticipatory and lacks clear set point boundaries—and therefore is not simply reactive to homeostatic imbalances (e.g., restoring plasma levels of sodium in response to alterations of extracellular fluid volume). States of fear and anxiety (or calmness) do not have a simple set point that is maintained and regulated. When elevated in the short term, they may represent an allostatic state (see Koob and LeMoal, 2001 for a discussion of an allostatic state; see chapter 5). Also, I suggested that chronic elevation of corticosterone and central CRH may represent a condition of allostatic overload (Schulkin et al., 1994). Normal fear, unbridled by constraints, can turn into chronic anticipatory angst. In this context, the mechanisms of normal fear are overexpressed, resulting in pathological anxiety (Rosen and Schulkin, 1998; Davis and Whalen, 2001). All of this takes a toll on normal systemic bodily and neural function.

Allostatic overload, as I intimated in the introduction, may reflect the chronic elevation of CRH gene expression in the central nucleus of the amygdala and lateral bed nucleus of the stria terminalis, as well as the concurrent loss of inhibitory CRH gene expression in the PVN by glucocorticoids. In this regard, there

are several experimental contexts in which the effects of restraint stress result in both concurrent elevated levels of corticosterone and CRH gene expression in the central nucleus of the amygdala and the PVN of the hypothalamus. In other words, high levels of corticosterone circulating under restraint stress result in increased levels of CRH release in the central nucleus of the amygdala in addition to the medial basal hypothalamus as measured by microdialysis (Pich et al., 1993b), or increased levels of CRH mRNA in the central nucleus of the amygdala in addition to the PVN measured by in situ hybridization histochemistry (Kalin et al., 1994).

Consider another example: neonatal rats who were stressed during postnatal development are more vulnerable to behavioral expression of helplessness later in life. In this instance, all three classes of CRH mRNA in the central nucleus of the amygdala, the bed nucleus of the stria terminalis, and the PVN of the hypothalamus are elevated when compared to control rats (Plotsky and Meaney, 1996; Caldji et al., 1998; Levine, 2000). These events reflect a compromised inhibitory control over the HPA axis, resulting in greater CRH gene expression at the level of the PVN and concurrent activation of CRH in the central nucleus of the amygdala and lateral bed nucleus of the stria terminalis (Meaney et al., 1993).

In addition, rats injected during this postnatal development with CRH (to create early life adversity) into the third ventricle also resulted in hippocampal cell loss and perhaps dysfunction (Brunson et al., 2001a). The authors suggest that the glucocorticoids are not necessary for this effect, because adrenalectomy did not prevent the neuronal loss. However, by injecting CRH directly into the brain, the authors bypass one normal role of glucocorticoid, namely, regulation of CRH gene expression.

Interestingly, CRH gene expression is elevated in the central nucleus of the amygdala in subordinate adult rats that undergo chronic social stress. There is, however, a concomitant and more varied CRH gene expression in the PVN under these conditions that may reflect the heightened responsiveness to novel stres-

sors and corticosterone secretion in subsets of these subordinate rats (Albeck et al., 1997).

For the depressed person, allostatic overload manifests itself in compromised prefrontal cortex and hippocampal function and chronic amygdala activation (Drevets et al., 1992, 1999, 2002; Davidson, 1998). A depressed person is in a state that he or she has difficulty escaping. Episodic and declarative memory can be impaired, and the individual's perception of the world is colored by the bias of enhanced amygdala activity. For the person suffering from PTSD, there may be highly compromised hippocampal function and deficits of declarative and episodic memory, which may reflect the result of exaggerated levels of glucocorticoids on human performance (e.g., Newcomer et al., 1994, 1999). There may also be hyperactivity of the amygdala (Racuh et al., 2000). For the shy, fearful child or young adult, we do not know definitively about changes in the activation of brain systems, but one hypothesis is a hyperactive amygdala (Kagan et al., 1988) and perhaps some compromised hippocampal function over the long term (McEwen, 2001). There may also be a greater tendency for right frontal activation (Schmidt et al., 1999a).

On the endocrine side, for both the depressed patient and PTSD patient, central CRH is elevated. For the depressed patient and the excessively fearful shy child, cortisol levels are elevated, and for the patient with PTSD, the HPA axis is highly reactive. Each of these situations may reflect allostatic overload. Long-term elevation of central CRH and glucocorticoids can compromise reproductive health, immune function, sleep patterns, feeding, and the general sense of well-being. Chronic worry can compromise metabolic function, rendering one vulnerable to a number of physiological disturbances (McEwen, 1998a, b). Chronic inability to restrain central CRH and systemic glucocorticoids may be an example of allostatic overload.

Richter (1957b) speculated that "voodoo death," being frightened to death, was a state of hopelessness characterized by acute parasympathetic blockage that stops the heart (Goldstein,

1995a, b, 2000). No set point can be found for the chronic fear associated with voodoo death (Schulkin et al., 1994). Chronic fear is a metabolically expensive event; over time, an animal's bodily organs are compromised as the attempt to sustain stability recedes into decreased functional capacity. The body turns frail, stability is compromised, and allostasis, the attempt to maintain stability in diverse circumstances, reaches its limits.

Chapter 4

Normal and Pathological Facilitation of Parturition by a Feedforward Endocrine Mechanism

The emergence of mammals is tied to evolved brains, evolving placental function, and lactation (Easteal, 1999). The placenta is unique in its vast storehouse of biochemical information molecules that are vital to the developing fetus. Nature conserved, extended, and utilized the diverse myriad of information molecules that are well represented in the brain and the placenta and that are fundamental for normal development (Petraglia et al., 1990). Moreover, nature selected a number of endocrine mechanisms to facilitate the viability of fetal development and the progression of a healthy baby; one is an endocrine mechanism that is feedforward. It also provided mechanisms to insure reproductive fitness; for example, extreme nausea during pregnancy may, under some conditions, be a reaction to teratogens (Profet, 1991).

Let me begin with a question: Why the study of preterm delivery of babies in a book on allostatic regulation? There are several reasons. First, placental CRH is elevated during adverse events in pregnancy. It may be a predictor of preterm labor when there are conditions of adversity (see, e.g., Wolfe et al., 1988; Goland et al., 1993; Wadhwa et al., 2001). Second, a positive feedback loop underlies parturition, providing an allostatic mechanism; namely, cortisol increases CRH gene expression in the placenta under normal conditions. And third, this feedback loop may be exaggerated during adverse conditions (*allostatic overload*). In the case of adverse events in pregnancy such as infections, metabolic stress, and social stress, CRH may be overexpressed in the placenta. Similarly, in the case of fear and anxiety, CRH may be altered in the brain (Gold et al., 1984; Nemeroff et al., 1984; Nemeroff, 1992) or with a sense of potential harm (Kalin et al.,

1989; Koob, 1993a; Schulkin et al., 1994). In other words, similar mechanisms that are feedforward (allostatic) endocrine systems underlie the expression of CRH in the brain and CRH in the placenta. This chapter is therefore consistent with the preceding chapters—particularly chapter 3 on fear—with regard to positive feedback endocrine systems. Moreover, these events in utero are known to have long-term physiological and behavioral consequences, including changes in the central nucleus of the amygdala and vulnerability to perceive events as fearful in the infant (Welberg and Seckl, 2001).

Preterm Low-Birth-Weight Babies

Consider the real-world consequences of preterm delivery of babies. Preterm delivery accounts for up to 10 percent of all births and is a leading factor in neonatal morbidity. Consequences of preterm birth include low birth weight and decreased respiratory function (Center for Disease Control, 1997). It accounts for up to 70 percent of newborn deaths (Goldenberg et al., 2000). The rate of preterm delivery has not declined in this country over the past 20 years, but survival of preterm infants has increased.

There are a number of biological and demographic predictors of risk for preterm birth. For example, there are significant differences in the rate of preterm and low-birth-weight infants born to African American women when compared to other racial/ethnic groups. Babies born to African American women are nearly twice as likely as those of any other group to be preterm and have a low birth weight (National Vital Statistics Report, 2000). This difference tends to hold even when one controls for demographic characteristics and the link between infectious diseases and preterm delivery. More generally, a number of infectious diseases (e.g., bacterial vaginosis) increase a woman's vulnerability to preterm delivery (Goldenberg et al., 2000). Levels of CRH, as we will see below, are significantly linked to preterm delivery (Holzman et al., 2001; Wadhwa et al., 2001; figure 4.1).

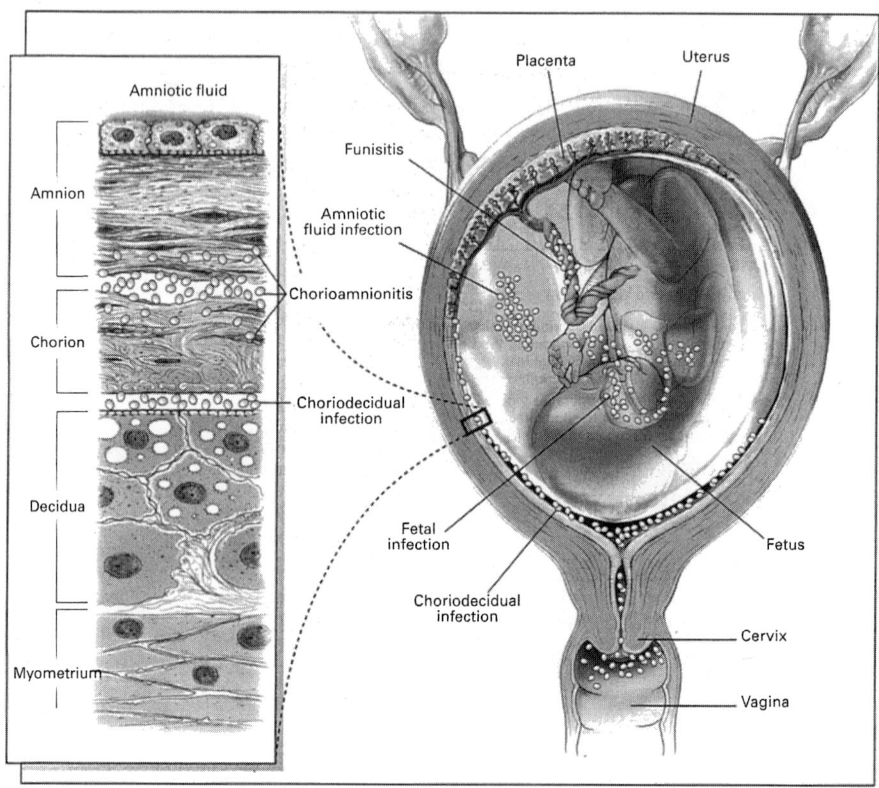

Figure 4.1
Potential sites of bacterial infection within the uterus (Goldenberg et al., 2000).

Placenta and Chemical Messages

Several physiological systems linked to the placenta may play a role in preterm delivery (see, e.g., Goland et al., 1988, 1992a, b, 1995; MacGregor et al., 1994, 1995; Pepe and Albrecht, 1995; Goldenberg et al., 1998). A large number of hormones are produced in the placenta (see, e.g., Ahmed et al., 1992; Lefebvre et al., 1992; Bramley et al., 1994; Petraglia et al., 1990, 1995a, b):

ACTH
Angiotensin
Atrial natriuretic factor
Corticotropin-releasing hormone
Cytokines
Follicle-stimulating hormone
Gonadotropin-releasing hormone
Growth hormone
Growth hormone-releasing hormone
Opioids
Oxytocin
Parathyroid hormone
Parathyroid hormone-related peptide
Prolactin
Prostaglandin
Somatostatin
Thyrotropin-releasing hormone

These placental peptides are homologous in structure to those in the fetal and the mature brain (Challis et al., 1995).

A growing amount of attention in studies of preterm births has focused recently on CRH. Recall that it is a 41-amino acid peptide hormone and a component of the hormonal pathway that regulates the stress response in human beings. Placental CRH is suspected of playing a role in both normal parturition and in preterm birth (Wolfe et al., 1988; Goland et al., 1988). Corticotropin-releasing hormone's role in parturition is therefore especially attractive as a focus of interdisciplinary research for investigators who are working toward an

inclusive central theory of preterm and term labor in human beings.

Discovery of CRH in Human Placenta

Corticotropin-releasing hormone was first isolated from sheep hypothalamus by Vale and colleagues in 1981. A major regulator of the HPA axis, it was named for its ability to stimulate the release of ACTH by the pituitary gland. Corticotropin-releasing hormone was subsequently discovered in extrahypothalamic sites—including the human placenta (figure 4.2), where it was found to have the same structure and bioactivity as hypothalamic CRH (e.g., Sasaki et al., 1987; Robinson et al., 1988).

In the human placenta, CRH is produced exclusively in syncytiotrophoblasts. It is only after cytotrophoblasts fuse into syn-

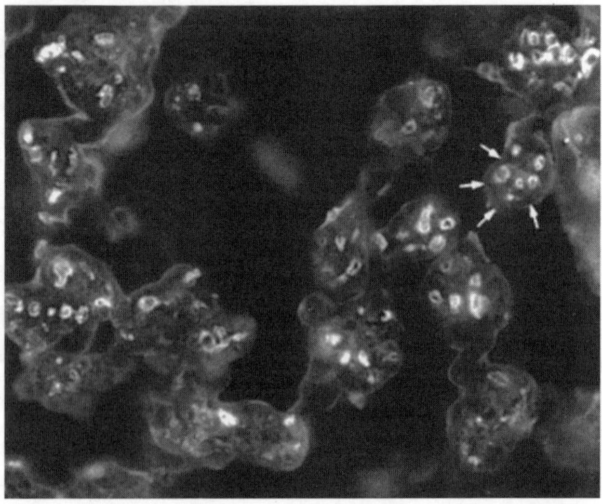

Figure 4.2
Corticotropin-releasing hormone immunostaining in the human placenta (arrows) (courtesy of F. Petraglia and P. Sawchenko).

cytiotrophoblasts that CRH is expressed and secreted into both maternal and fetal circulations (Challis et al., 1995). Levels climb much higher in the maternal than in the fetal circulation, where the upper limit of concentration is in the 300 pg / mL range (Majzoub et al., 1999; Erickson et al., 2001).

Corticotropin-releasing hormone in humans is not detectable in plasma except during pregnancy (Sasaki et al., 1987; Cambell et al., 1987; Goland et al., 1988; Wolfe et al., 1988). During the second and third trimesters of normal pregnancy, CRH (derived from the placenta) is elevated in maternal plasma (figure 4.3). At the same time, both fetal and maternal ACTH and cortisol levels are elevated (Challis et al., 1995; Goland et al., 1995; Erickson et al., 2001). Following parturition, CRH levels in the plasma rapidly decrease to nadir levels. In other words, CRH gene expression in placental trophoblast cells rises during pregnancy in

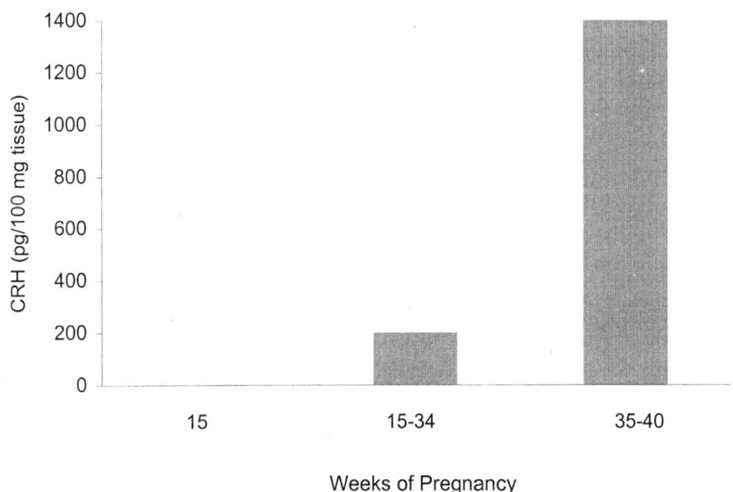

Figure 4.3
Concentrations of immunoreactive corticotropin-releasing hormone (CRH) in placental tissue at various stages of human gestation (adapted from Frim et al., 1988).

several species, including humans (Frim et al., 1988; Riley et al., 1991), gorillas (Robinson et al., 1989), chimpanzees (Smith et al., 1999), and rhesus monkeys (Wu et al., 1995), although there appear to be primate species (Goland et al., 1992a, b; Smith et al., 1993).

It is possible that CRH levels, although low in early gestation, increase at an exponential rate throughout gestation and are detected as rapidly rising only near the end of pregnancy. However, other data suggest that CRH levels are low until the beginning of the third trimester, and only after that do they begin to rise at an accelerated rate. There is large variation, as much as fiftyfold, in maternal CRH concentrations at term among normal pregnancies (Goland et al., 1988; Wolfe et al., 1988; Majzoub et al., 1999; Erickson et al., 2001). The elevation in placental CRH secretion is associated with a surge of fetal glucocorticoids and the production of estriol during the several weeks before normal parturition. This observation, as well as the wide variability in the level of CRH expression seen in different women, has led investigators to speculate that CRH may not be playing an important role in the mother throughout most of gestation but may play a role in initiating parturition (see Wolfe et al., 1988; Goland et al., 1988; Challis et al., 1995).

A parallel rise in fetal cortisol production occurs during the same period, as measured by fetal cortisol sulfated metabolites in maternal blood and urine. The human fetal pituitary system develops early in gestation and responds to low cortisol levels by secreting ACTH. This is best demonstrated in fetuses with enzymatic blocks in cortisol synthesis, resulting in congenital adrenal hyperplasia (Challis et al., 2000). Their systems compensate by increasing the synthesis of all steroids proximal to the enzymatic block, resulting in the virilization of female fetuses by 8 to 10 weeks gestation. Corticotropin-releasing hormone mRNA is also present in placental trophoblast cells by 8 weeks gestation, and CRH levels rise exponentially (as much as 20 times) during the last 6–8 weeks of gestation. Similarly, CRH

peptide levels in maternal blood are quite low until the final 8–10 weeks of gestation (Robinson et al., 1988; Challis et al., 2000).

Role of CRH in Normal Gestation

Feedforward Induction of CRH Gene Expression in the Placenta by Glucocorticoids: Normal Allostatic Regulation

Glucocorticoids are known to restrain CRH production by negative feedback (Munck et al., 1984; Dallman et al., 2000) but, of importance, in one early study it was reported that dexamethasone treatment did not suppress levels of CRH in the plasma of pregnant women (Tropper et al., 1987). It was then demonstrated that glucocorticoids do not inhibit the production of CRH in the placenta as expected; rather, they increase CRH gene expression in the placenta (Robinson et al., 1988; Jones et al., 1989; see also Chan et al., 1988). Glucocorticoids increase CRH gene expression in primary cultures of human placental trophoblasts. These effects are dose related and may be greater in response to dexamethasone than cortisol, suggesting that these effects are dependent upon type-II glucocorticoid receptor sites (Jones et al., 1989; Challis et al., 1995).

Another study demonstrated that pregnant women treated with betamethasone after 30 weeks of gestation had increased CRH levels in both plasma and placental tissue (Marinoni et al., 1998) . An additional study also revealed that pregnant patients at 24 weeks of gestation also have increased levels of plasma CRH following betamethasone treatment (Korebrits et al., 1998). Thus, in marked contrast to glucocorticoids' well-known inhibition of CRH via type-II glucocorticoid receptor sites at the level of the parvicellular region of the PVN of the hypothalamus and the well-known negative restraints (Munck et al., 1984; Sawchenko, 1987; Swanson and Simmons, 1989), glucocorticoids increase CRH gene expression in the placenta (figure 4.4).

This feedforward allostatic regulatory effect on placental expression of CRH represents a mechanism to facilitate normal fetal maturation and eventual parturition. The stimulation of CRH expression by glucocorticoids in placental tissue is via cy-

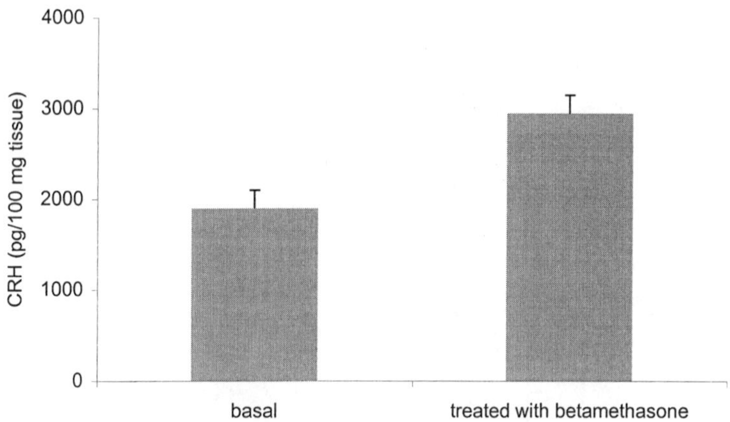

Figure 4.4
Maternal plasma levels of corticotropin-releasing hormone in pregnant women at 35 weeks gestation receiving betamethasone and in control patients (basal) (adapted from Marinoni et al., 1998).

clic adenosine 3,5 monophosphate (Cheng et al., 2000). Primary cultures of human cytotrophoblasts demonstrate increased CRH expression following dexamethasone treatment (figure 4.5). This upregulation of CRH reflects cAMP-mediated CRH promoter activity (Cheng et al., 2000).

One model that seeks to explain the simultaneous rise in CRH and cortisol suggests that, within the placenta, the exponential rate of increase in CRH is positively related to the concentration of cortisol (Majzoub et al., 1999; Challis et al., 2000). Placental CRH, transported through the umbilical vein to the fetus, could stimulate the fetal pituitary-adrenal axis to produce cortisol and cortisol sulfate, which would then be capable of further stimulating placental CRH production, creating a positive feedback loop (figure 4.6). Moreover, the placental production of CRH may in part function for the fetus, reminiscent of neural function, as both a sensory and effector system in providing important sources of adaptation to environmental demands (Wadhwa et al., 2001).

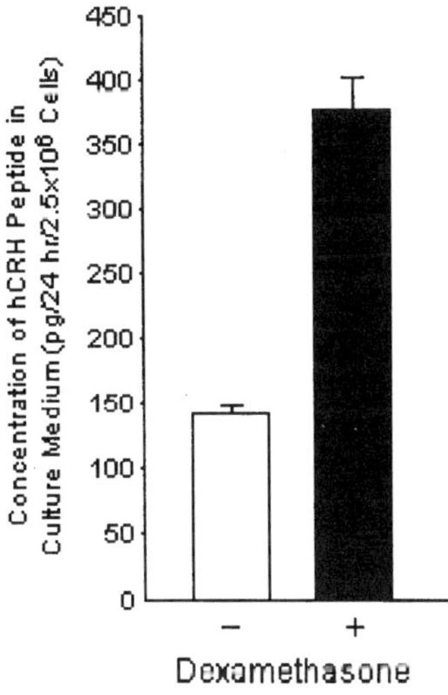

Figure 4.5
Dexamethasone stimulates cAMP-mediated hCRH promoter activity in placental tissue (Cheng et al., 2000).

Again, this model is supported by both in vitro and in vivo data—betamethasone administration to pregnant women results in either no fall in CRH or clear stimulation of placental CRH secretion into the maternal circulation (Majzoub et al., 1999). This placental model is quite different from the regulation of CRH expression in the parvicellular regulation of the PVN of the hypothalamus, which responds to cortisol with downward regulation or negative restraint (Sawchenko, 1987; Swanson and Simmons, 1989; Watts and Sanchez-Watts, 1995).

The Timing of Parturition

The primate placenta is, by its lack of 17-hydroxylase/17–20 lyase, unable to directly synthesize estradiol from progesterone, the only steroid hormone that the primate placenta can synthesize de novo (Pepe and Albrecht, 1995). The fetal adrenal zone therefore serves instead as the predominant source of that

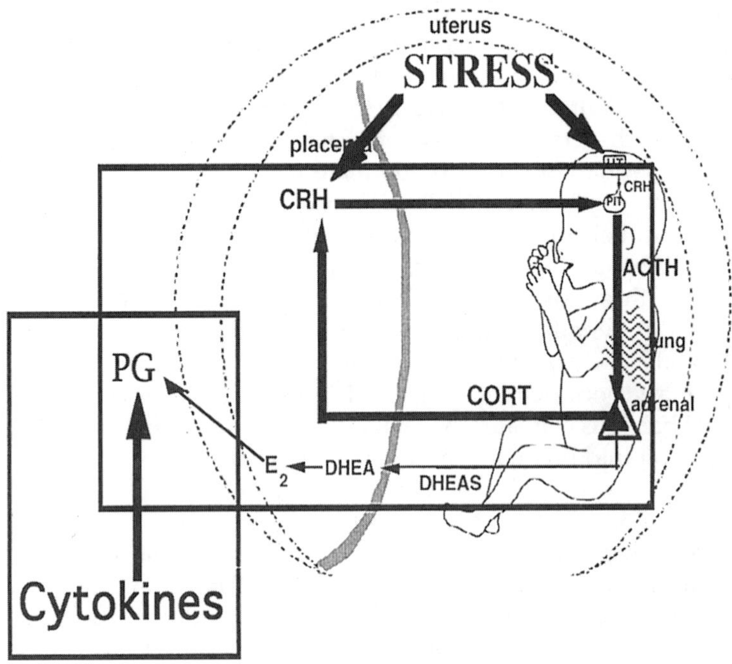

Figure 4.6
The fetopolacental corticotropin-releasing hormone and glucocorticoid positive feedback hypothesis. Corticotropin-releasing hormone, secreted by the placental trophoblasts (T), enters the fetal circulation via the umbilical cord vein and stimulates (+) fetal ACTH release from the fetal pituitary (PIT). Fetal ACTH stimulates secretion of fetal adrenal cortisol sulfate, which enters the placental sulfatase, and cortisol stimulates further placental corticotropin-releasing hormone secretion, thereby completing the positive feedback loop. Fetal corticotropin-releasing hormone, secreted from the fetal hypothalamus (HT), may independently stimulate fetal ACTH release, and placental and fetal hypothalamic corticotropin-releasing hormone may be directly stimulated by environmental stresses (Majzoub et al., 1999).

steroid's precursor, dehydroepiandrosterone (DHEA). Thus placental production of CRH, with its ability to stimulate the fetal adrenal system, may have evolved in primates to stimulate fetal ACTH and ultimately to satisfy the high demand for DHEA synthesis in the fetal adrenal system. This proposed feedback mechanism would function to stimulate a fetal adrenal "factory," contributing to placental estradiol production and to the endocrine sequelae necessary for parturition (Majzoub et al., 1999; Challis et al., 2000). This includes the stimulation of prostaglandin synthesis, oxytocin receptors, and gap junctions. Consistent with this hypothesis are these findings: circulating levels of CRH in fetal blood are similar to those measured in the hypothalamic-pituitary portal circulation; CRH infusion into midgestational fetal baboons activates the fetal HPA axis; and androstenedione infusion into pregnant rhesus females results in preterm delivery. It has also been found that fetal cortisol secretion is tied to maturation of fetal lungs and other systems before birth (Pepe and Albrecht, 1995). Thus, the concomitant stimulation of fetal cortisol and DHEA by placental CRH is of obvious benefit for postnatal survival in that it synchronizes the glucocorticoid effects on fetal organ maturation with the DHEA effects on the timing of parturition.

Moreover, there is some evidence that progesterone may play a role in this differential regulation of CRH in the hypothalamus and placenta—in essence, acting as a brake on the latter system of positive regulation. In vitro studies have shown that when progesterone is added back to placental trophoblast cultures during cortisol stimulation, there is an inhibition of the increases in CRH mRNA and peptide. Furthermore, mifepristone (RU-486), a progesterone / glucocorticoid antagonist, stimulates CRH mRNA. This suggests that a withdrawal of progesterone stimulates CRH effects in the placenta (Karalis et al., 1996; Majzoub and Karalis, 1999).

No progesterone receptors are present in trophoblast cells. Therefore, it is speculated that high levels of placental progesterone early in gestation could compete with cortisol for the glucocorticoid receptors (Falguni and Challis, 2002) inhibiting cortisol

and its effects on CRH synthesis (Majzoub et al., 1999). Because progesterone appears to bind to glucocorticoid receptors about 25–50 percent (as does cortisol), only when levels of cortisol become high enough to effectively block progesterone's inhibitory effect would the CRH elevation occur (Majzoub and Karalis, 1999). Thus progesterone might inhibit the effects of cortisol on placental CRH in a dose-dependent fashion. Inhibition of CRH would be reversed only if the rise in fetal adrenal cortisol secretion in late gestation were late enough to compete with progesterone at the level of the glucocorticoid receptors, essentially causing a functional withdrawal of progesterone at the level of the glucocorticoid receptors. In this way, progesterone might serve as an early brake on the system—a brake that is overridden only after cortisol rises to an appropriately high level (Challis et al., 1995, 2000; Majzoub and Karalis, 1999).

Figure 4.6 shows a schematic representation of leading theories on human parturition. The figure depicts the proposed positive feedback loop responsible for differential regulation of CRH in the fetoplacental axis. In this model, CRH produced in the placenta is secreted into the fetal circulation at a concentration of about 200–300 pg/mL. This is consistent with CRH levels found in the hypothalamic-pituitary portal circulation and sufficient to stimulate corticotropin secretion from the anterior pituitary. Placental CRH, through fetal ACTH or possibly through direct interaction with fetal adrenal CRH receptors, is proposed to stimulate the fetal adrenal system to produce cortisol. Cortisol binds to placental glucocorticoid receptors to block the inhibitory effect of progesterone, which further stimulates CRH production in a positive fashion.

The progressive rise in placental CRH, and concomitant decrease in CRH-binding protein, would stimulate not only fetal cortisol but also the secretion of fetal adrenal DHEA sulfate. This leads to an increase in synthesis of placental estradiol and subsequent factors (prostaglandins, oxytocin, oxytocin receptors, gap junctions) that cause the onset of labor. In this fashion, fetal maturation stimulated by the rise in fetal cortisol secretion, and parturition, stimulated by the rise in fetal DHEA secretion, would

be intimately linked, an obvious benefit for postnatal survival (Nathanielsz, 1998; Challis et al., 2000).

An alternative hypothesis to explain the activation of the fetal HPA axis before primate labor was proposed by Pepe and Albrecht (1995). According to their model, the fetal HPA axis is quiescent during the first half of gestation because of its suppression by the maternal influx of cortisol. During the second half of gestation, the rise in estrogen is hypothesized to stimulate placental 11B-hydroxysteroid dehydrogenase, and this causes cortisol to be converted to its inactive metabolite cortisone. Thus, less cortisol would pass from mother to fetus and negative glucocorticoid feedback on the fetal pituitary gland would be released. As previously mentioned, this would result in an increase in fetal secretion of ACTH, cortisol, and DHEA sulfate, resulting in both fetal maturation and stimulation of parturition.

Allostatic Overload and the Role of CRH in Preterm Labor

From this hypothetical framework of CRH's role in normal parturition, it is relatively easy to make a conjecture regarding its involvement in preterm delivery. The normal feedforward regulatory mechanism is exaggerated under duress (see below) creating an allostatic state and increasing the likelihood of preterm delivery. Much of the groundwork has already been done by several clinical researchers who have demonstrated an association between abnormal, or early elevation in, CRH levels and preterm labor. This is one plausible mechanism, but it is not the only one (see Majzoub et al., 1999; Challis et al., 2000).

Maternal plasma CRH concentrations are also elevated in pregnancy-induced hypertension and intrauterine growth restriction (Wolfe et al., 1988; Goland et al., 1993). In addition, elevation in hypothalamic CRH levels has been demonstrated in response to infection, inflammation, hemorrhage, and stress (Chrousos, 1996, 1998). However, whether the CRH gene in the placenta is similarly regulated is not known. Higher levels of CRH may be associated with intrauterine growth restriction, low birth weight, and preterm birth in the third trimester. In

other words, the most consistent fact about CRH detected in the plasma of pregnant women is its link to both potential maternal-fetal distress and to greater metabolic and physiological demands in women who go on to experience preterm labor (Wolfe et al., 1988; Warren et al., 1990; but see also Berkowitz et al., 1996).

In one early study, diabetics, twin pregnancies, and pregnancy-related hypertension were all associated with CRH levels that were elevated throughout most of the pregnancy (Wolfe et al., 1988). More generally, CRH and glucocorticoid levels are increased following bacterial infectious diseases (Petraglia et al., 1995a, b), preeclampsia (Goland et al., 1995; Leung et al., 2000), diabetes (Wolfe et al., 1988), growth retarded fetal development (Goland et al., 1993), and multiple gestation (Wolfe et al., 1988; Warren et al., 1990; figure 4.7). These events in utero can have long-term impacts on basic physiological functions (Barker, 1997; Seckl, 1997; Martyn et al., 1998; Phillips et al., 1998; Forsen et al., 1999) and perhaps behavioral functions of the neonates (Welberg and Seckl, 2001).

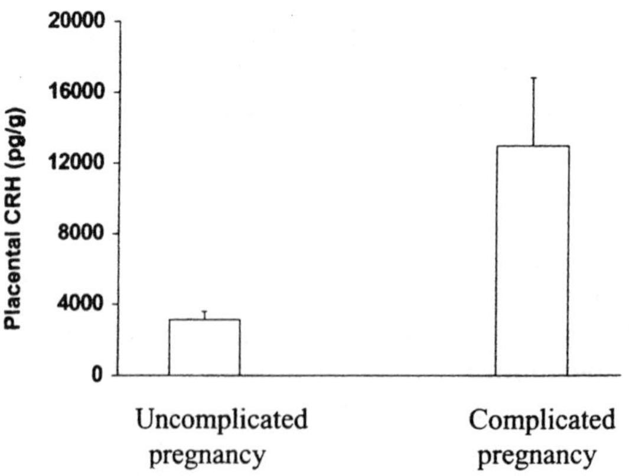

Figure 4.7
Human placental corticotropin-releasing hormone peptide content in pregnancies complicated by pre-eclampsia and uncomplicated pregnancies (adapted from Goland et al., 1995).

It is important to note that at 18–20 weeks of gestation, a subset of women who went into preterm labor, and who reported higher psychosocial stress than controls, also demonstrated higher levels of CRH circulating in the plasma (Hobel et al., 1999b). This was demonstrated in a prospective study of women that controlled for age, previous birth outcome, smoking status, and race. The stress tests were two tests used to assess perceived anxiety about their life and a list of adjectives that depict their situation. Interestingly, while CRH was higher throughout pregnancy for those who went on to deliver preterm, it was only in this first 18–20 weeks that perceived anxiety was correlated with higher CRH levels. But in another study in which CRH and catecholamines were collected at 28 weeks, there was no relationship between psychosocial stress and altered levels of either molecule (Petraglia et al., 2001). The authors suggest that, at this point in the pregnancy, levels of CRH are too high to determine an effect coupled with protective mechanisms to preserve the viability of the healthy fetus.

In this context, the normal feedforward allostatic mechanism is now amplified by the adverse condition. This results in what has been called an "allostatic state" (Koob and LeMoal, 2001), the overactivation of the normal feedforward system. The end point is a baby that is viable, but when the mother is also compromised because of adverse conditions, the fetus perhaps is unloaded.

In another study, preterm birth was associated not only with elevated levels of CRH by 7–23 weeks, but elevated CRH levels were found in women who reported greater risk-related behavior. In this study, this group of risk takers was defined in terms of not buckling their seatbelts while driving (Erickson et al., 2001). A common theme for the exaggerated level of CRH is its link to risk-related events, whether in the brain or in the placenta (figure 4.8).

Pregnancy, however, may also be protective for the mother and the fetus against some of the effects of stress (Wadhwa, 2001). In one study (Glynn et al., 2001), the perceived stress effects from an earthquake were significantly greater in the first

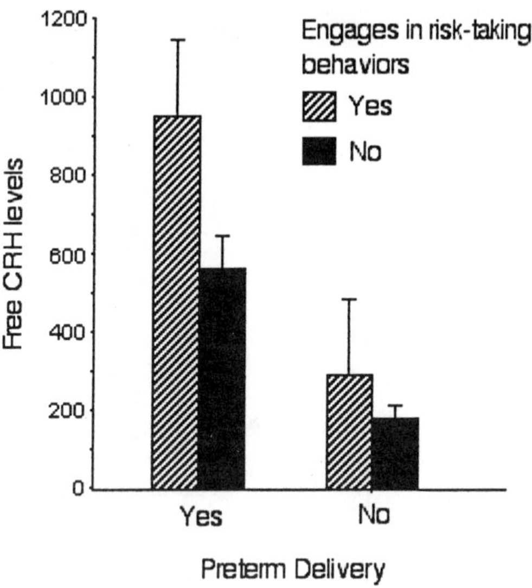

Figure 4.8
Levels of CRH in women who were risk and non-risk takers in midpregnancy and who had or did not have a preterm delivery (adapted from Erickson et al., 2001).

trimester of pregnancy than it was in the second trimester; postpartum women looked like the first trimester women.

Interestingly, in rats, CRH levels in the brain may be reduced by estrogen. The overexpression of central CRH is known to interfere with reproductive function (e.g., Heinrichs et al., 1997). But estrogen does not necessarily reduce fear; mice given estrogen have demonstrated enhanced fear-related behavioral responses (e.g., Morgan and Pfaff, 2001).

Multiple Endocrine Pathways and Parturition

Evolution favored multiple mechanisms underlying parturition, and there appears to be no single path leading to preterm delivery (figure 4.9). Cervical, decidual, and fetal membrane cells

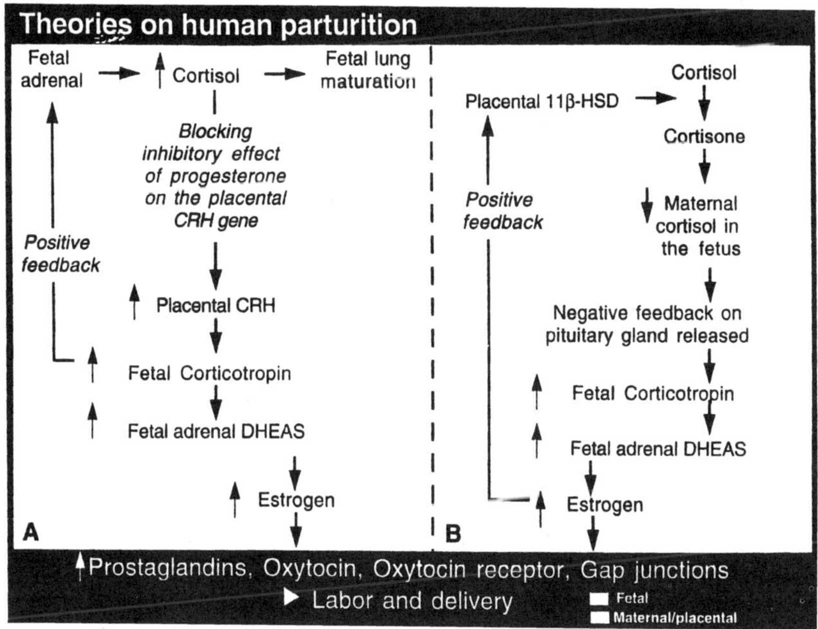

Figure 4.9
Etiological factors promoting preterm delivery (Lockwood, 1994).

may act in concert to promote parturition. Amniochorionic and decidual cells of the placenta, located as they are between the myometrium and fetus, are strategically poised to respond to physiological, hormonal, paracrine, and autocrine regulation. Various influences include stress, infection, and hemorrhage, which trigger prostaglandin and oxytocin secretion and thereby initiate contractions (Lockwood, 1994; McGregor et al., 1995; Goldenberg et al., 1998, 2000; Romero et al., 2001). The same conditions may stimulate production of proteases that degrade the extracellular matrix of cervical and fetal membranes (Challis et al., 2000).

Placental secretion of CRH, possibly triggered further by infection-associated increases in production of inflammatory cy-

tokines (creating an allostatic state, and perhaps allostatic overload), would probably act as a paracrine effector, triggering prostaglandin and endothelin production as well as the production of collagenases that are capable of degrading placental and cervical tissue in preparation for birth (Nathanielsz, 1999a, b; Challis et al., 2000). Recently, decreased inactivation of prostaglandins, through a reduction in prostaglandin dehydrogenase activity, was implicated at the onset of preterm labor (Majzoub et al., 1999; Challis et al., 2000). It is possible that increased CRH, or the resulting rise in fetal cortisol secretion, could contribute to a downward regulation of this enzyme. Immunological and endocrine systems communicate extensively, and within the placenta this might be mediated by interactions between CRH and inflammatory cytokines. Alternatively, hypothalamic CRH might be released by the fetus in response to a physiological stressor, such as hypoxemia caused by uroplacental vascular insufficiency. Finally, maternal stress might activate placental secretion of CRH, leading to preterm delivery.

Corticotropin-releasing hormone is also expressed by amniocytes, cytotrophoblasts, and decidual cells in response to stress, which enhances prostaglandin production by isolated amnion, chorion, and decidual cells. Both prostanoids and oxytocin in turn stimulate CRH release in a cycle that could accelerate toward preterm delivery.

One should note that not all the studies are supportive: One study, although failing to demonstrate a correlation between abnormal CRH elevations and preterm delivery, did show a negative correlation between CRH-binding protein values and gestational age in patients who eventually delivered preterm (Berkowitz et al., 1996). These findings may be interpreted as evidence of the greater bioavailability of CRH-binding protein, which is produced in placental and intrauterine tissues, which may locally counteract the effects of CRH on prostaglandin release and myometrial contractility (Challis et al., 1995, 2000; Lockwood and Kuczynski, 2001). Corticotropin-releasing hormone's link to preterm delivery may not always be reflected by

changes in maternal blood levels (cf. McLean et al., 1995; Coleman et al., 2000; Challis et al., 2000; Erickson et al., 2001).

Placental Clock

A number of organs are organized by biological clocks; circadian, weekly, monthly, and so on. Both peripheral systemic sites and central nervous representations of those sites, and the behavioral and physiological organization reflect the profound effect on bodily regulation of endogenous clocks (Richter, 1965). A further example of a clock is the 9-month gestation. Levels of CRH may be linked to the onset of parturition tied to the placental clock.

A prospective longitudinal study involving nearly 500 women showed that CRH concentrations measured at 16–20 weeks' gestation could predict term, preterm, and postterm birth (Bocking et al., 1999; McLean et al., 1999; McGrath et al., 2002; but see also Coleman et al., 2000; Ellis et al., 2002). The idea that these events are self-contained and self-regulating has been expressed through the analogy of the placental clock, for which the timing is set early in the first trimester of pregnancy, yet remains predictive of later events, including both preterm delivery and postterm birth (McClean et al., 1995; Bocking et al., 1999; Challis et al., 2000). However, it is important to remember that the clock is not self-correcting, and its internal timing may go awry under physiological or psychological duress. At such times, placental CRH secretion may be stimulated by glucocorticoids, inflammatory cytokines, and anoxic conditions to such an extent that it triggers labor prematurely.

Under normal conditions, levels of CRH can be one predictive factor (McClean et al., 1995, 1999; Bocking et al., 1999; Leung et al., 2000), but not always (Berkowitz et al., 1996; Coleman et al., 2000), for women who are vulnerable to preterm delivery. Thus early or abnormal exposure to cortisol may upwardly regulate CRH gene expression in the placenta, prematurely rendering a woman more vulnerable to preterm labor. Abnormal CRH elevation may be a response to inflammatory stress from the decid-

ual or fetal membrane, or from placental infection, or it may be a response to episodic or chronic stressors of a physiological or psychosocial nature (e.g., hypoxia associated with placental insufficiency / allostatic overload). Alternatively, a fast-running placental clock associated with the body's response to a variety of stressors, occurring early in the first trimester, could result in abnormally elevated CRH levels later in pregnancy.

Interestingly, the type-I CRH receptor has been linked to parturition; blockade of this receptor inhibits parturition in sheep (Chan et al., 1998). The type-I receptor antagonist antalarmin was infused into pregnant sheep over a 10-day period, and parturition was delayed (figure 4.10A; Chan et al., 1998). While this same antagonist reduces fear in rats (Deak et al., 1999), a type-I receptor antagonist did not delay parturition in rats (Funai et al., 2000). In monkeys, the Type-I receptor antagonist reduces fear (figure 4.10B; Habib et al., 2000) and the Type-I receptor has also been linked to depression (Zobel et al., 2000).

Childhood Sexual Abuse and Pregnancy

Not to confuse the role of CRH in premature birth from that of its role in early trauma, note that there is some evidence that childhood sexual abuse may have long-term effects on pregnancy-related events. Childhood sexual abuse is defined as an activity that involves inappropriate sexual activities and does not always mean sexual intercourse or physical force (Horan et al., 2000). Childhood sexual abuse is often chronic. Some of the long-term consequences from childhood abuse include chronic pelvic pain; musculoskeletal complaints, gastrointestinal distress, chronic headache, sexual dysfunction; asthma, and other respiratory ailments; in addition to PTSD, depression, vulnerability and thoughts about suicide, drug and alcoholic abuse, and sexual abnormality (McCauley et al., 1997). Moreover, as we will see in the next chapter, drug-abuse-related behaviors are associated with elevated levels of CRH; consumption of high levels of drugs can also be associated with preterm delivery (Kendler et al., 2000). All of this may reflect a vulnerability to allostatic overload.

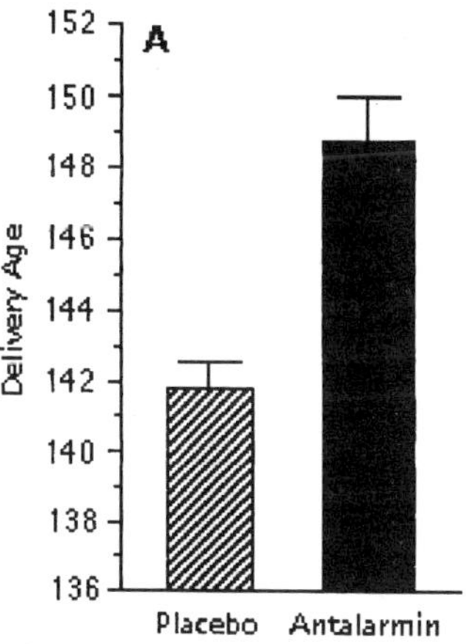

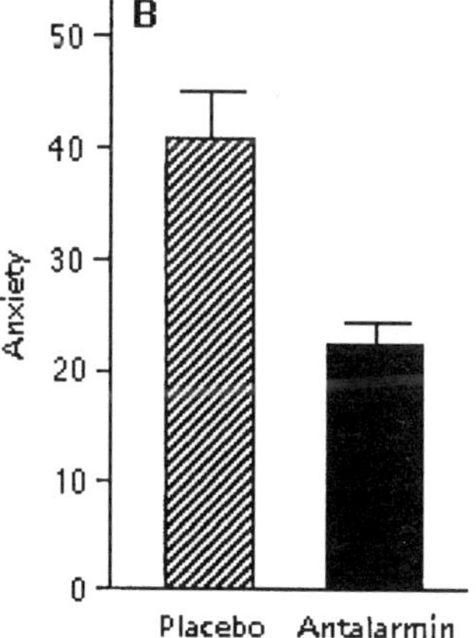

Figure 4.10
(*A*) CRH Receptor type-I antagonist, antalarmin, inhibits parturition in sheep. Six pregnant sheep per group received either an infusion of vehicle (1:1 ethanlo-Cremophor EL mix) or antalarmin (50 g/L in vehicle). The gestational age at delivery is calculated based on the last complete 24 h of gestation (Chan et al., 1998). (*B*) Effect of antalarmin treatment (20 mg/kg orally) on adult male macaques' anxious behaviors to the introduction of two unfamiliar subjects in adjacent cages separated by a transparent Plexiglas plate for 30 min starting 150 min after receiving the drug or placebo in a blind fashion. *, P = 0.04 (Habib et al., 2000).

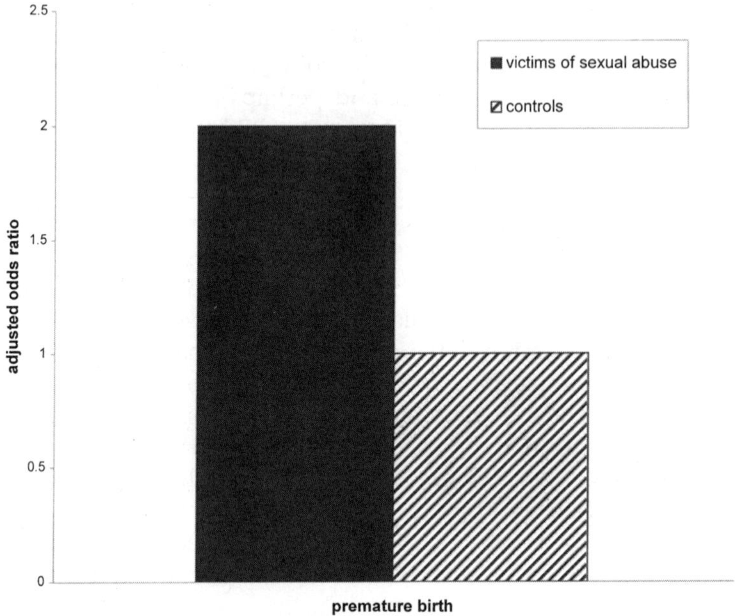

Figure 4.11
Women who were victims of childhood sexual abuse were twice as likely to have a premature infant than were controls. Adjusted odds ratio controlled for severity of abuse, maternal age, poverty, and maternal alcohol use (Evans, 1988).

Pregnancy and childbirth may be a particularly stressful time for survivors of sexual abuse. For example, women who were sexually abused in childhood demonstrate a greater degree of suicidal thoughts during pregnancy (Farber et al., 1996). Although there is a paucity of evidence, one doctoral dissertation by Evans (1988), which controlled for alcohol and tobacco use, demonstrated a relationship between childhood sexual abuse and preterm delivery (figure 4.11). They also had greater medical problems. In another study, survivors of sexual abuse were more likely to have have preterm deliveries and to deliver smaller babies even at full term (Stevens-Simon et al., 1993).

Perhaps—and this is speculative—early sexual abuse or trauma in the life of the mother kindles a vulnerability in the HPA axis to be overactive (Heim et al., 2000, 2001), with perhaps an overactive HPA axis in the fetus, and perhaps at the level of the placenta during pregnancy (Horan et al., 2000).

Conclusion: Allostasis and Allostatic Overload

Glucocorticoid regulation of CRH gene expression in the placenta, in the amygdala, and in the bed nucleus of the stria terminalis look remarkably similar. While glucocorticoids restrain CRH gene expression in the parvicellular region of the PVN of the hypothalamus, they magnify the effects of CRH in these other areas. The induction of CRH gene expression by feedforward mechanisms under certain conditions may contribute to regulatory or allostatic overload. These conditions are wide ranging, and all can compromise reproductive fitness. They include gestational diabetes, multiple births, preeclampsia, bacterial infections, sexually transmitted diseases, and psychosocial stress.

It should be noted that we do not know whether the mechanisms that underlie the placental increase of CRH by glucocorticoids are the same for both the brain and the placenta. Nor do we know whether the induction of CRH gene expression in the placenta originates with the mother, the fetus, or even the placenta itself. What is clear, however, is that, contrary to the belief that glucocorticoids always react to restrain the expression of CRH, glucocorticoids facilitate CRH expression in the placenta and in regions of the brain that underlie the experience of adversity. It is this CRH expression that may be significant in preterm labor (e.g., allostatic overload) at the level of the placenta and in the brain to sustain the experience of adversity. This regulatory response may figure in promoting successful reproductive outcomes, but also in aborting or shortening the gestational expense of ill-fated outcomes.

The concept of allostasis is again tied to systems in which there is no clear physiological set point. That is, the set point

during pregnancy is fluid and changing (Sterling and Eyer, 1988). Allostasis refers to the ability to achieve viability through change. Whereas homeostatic systems such as blood oxygen, blood pH, and body temperature must be maintained within a narrow range, allostatic systems are more labile, allowing them to adjust to external and internal circumstances (McEwen and Stellar, 1993). Both homeostatic (Bernard, 1865; Cannon, 1932; Richter, 1942–43) and allostatic regulation help to maintain the internal milieu (Sterling and Eyer 1988; Schulkin et al., 1994, 1998; McEwen, 1998a, b). It is this latter concept that I hypothesize has relevance to understanding the endocrine mechanisms that may underlie preterm labor induced by maternal-fetal distress.

There is much literature that looks at the effects of prenatal stress in animal models (see review by Takahashi et al., 1998). For example, unpredictable aversive events can result in elevated levels of corticosterone in the mother as well as in the fetus (Takahashi et al., 1998). Alterations of corticosterone in utero in rats have long-term effects on amygdala glucocorticoid mRNA expression in the amygdala and on anxiety-related behavior (Welberg et al., 2000). Prenatal stress can increase the vulnerability to anxiety in the offspring (Vallee et al., 1997). Elevated maternal levels of CRH are thought to affect the human fetus; habituation studies with the fetus provide some evidence (Sandman et al., 1999). Prenatal stress is known to alter levels of CRH expression in the amygdala of neonatal rat pups (Cratty et al., 1995) and to alter biogenic amine levels in primates (Schneider et al., 1998).

The CRH that is hypersecreted in pregnant women following situations of bacterial infectious diseases, preeclampsia or hypertension, multiple gestations, or psychosocial stress may be the result of allostatic overload. Under conditions of allostatic overload, premature parturition may be an adaptive mechanism for both mother and fetus by both reducing stress on the pregnant woman and removing the fetus from an overstressed environment—in other words, making the best of a bad situation (Nathanielsz, 1999a, b, Wadhwa et al., 2001).

One neuroendocrine model has been suggested linking elevated levels of glucocorticoids and amygdala programming in utero (Welberg and Seckl, 2001). Both adrenal steroids (glucocorticoids and mineralocorticoids) compete for access to the receptor sites (de Kloet, 1991); converting enzymes regulate access to the receptor sites (11b-hydroxysteroid dehydrogenase type 2; Seckl, 1997) and both hormones can influence CRH expression (Watts and Sanchez-Watts, 1995)—and perhaps a vulnerability for increased fear/anxiety and decreased reproductive fitness as adults (see review on the role by Korte, 2001; Brunson et al., 2001a, b).

In the species that have been studied, glucocorticoid and CRH elevation decrease reproductive fitness and decrease sexual behavior (e.g., Rivier and Rivest, 1991). When glucocorticoids are elevated under duress, testosterone or estrogen is reduced in most species that have been studied (Sapolsky, 1992; Herbert, 1993; Wingfield and Romero, 2001). But glucocorticoids are also known to be linked to attachment behaviors (Fleming et al., 1997; Carter et al., 1999), and facilitate sexual behavior in some species (e.g., the musk shrew; Schiml and Rissman, 1999). Clearly, one has to consider the degree to which the glucocorticoids are elevated, the functional context, and whether it is a short-term or long-term elevation.

The states of combating disease or experiencing fear (or psychological stress) are metabolically expensive events and thereby reduce the hormones of reproduction and the likelihood of successful reproduction (Sapolsky, 1992; Wingfield and Romero, 2001; see also Sapolsky, 2001). Interestingly, in experiments with subjects that have elevated levels of estrogen, there is a reduction in glucocorticoid receptor binding (Peifer and Barden, 1987; Carey et al., 1995). In addition, an estrogen response has been identified on the CRH gene (Vamvakopoulos and Chrousos, 1993).

Finally, the normal facilitation of parturition reflects in part a feedforward allostatic mechanism: namely, the induction of CRH gene expression by glucocorticoids. This normal mechanism is further augmented under conditions of adversity. For

example, anxiety and depression are linked to preterm labor (Dayan et al., 2002). The underlying hypothesis is that CRH is a signal of danger in both the placenta and in the brain. In the first context, the impact of elevated glucocorticoids on CRH gene expression may render women more vulnerable to preterm labor. In the second, glucocorticoids facilitate the perception of danger and act to magnify or sustain the CRH signal. The physiological events turn into allostatic overload when the normal mechanisms are compromised.

Chapter 5

Addiction to Drugs: Allostatic Regulation under Duress

There are several features of addiction that are relevant to allostasis. The first is the simple elevation in use of a number of neural systems during addiction, both in the appetitive and in the consummatory phases of the central motive state. The second is the dysregulation of the reward system associated with the chronic use of drugs (Koob and Le Moal, 2001). There are indications (for example, in animal models) that drug consumption can have long-term potentiation in specific neurons from cocaine ingestion (e.g., Ungless et al., 2001) and perhaps relapse from association of the drug with environmental events that are linked to this hyperexcitable state of the brain (Stanislav et al., 2001). The third link to allostasis is the long-term consequences of the drug abuse, and the vulnerability to allostatic overload.

This chapter begins with a depiction of the central motive states (linking to chapters 2 and 3) of wanting drugs and some of the neural systems that underlie addictive behaviors. One system underlying drug addiction is extrahypothalamic CRH and HPA regulation. Allostatic feedforward regulation, particularly at the level of the bed nucleus of the stria terminalis, may underlie some of the increased vulnerability for drug consumption. In other words, vulnerability to relapse, in animal studies, is linked to the overexpression of CRH in critical regions of the brain (such as the bed nucleus of the stria terminalis (Shaham et al., 2000; Koob and Le Moal, 2001), in addition to the increase in incentives to an enlarged social context that is associated with a drug culture that reflects dopamine overactivation (Berridge and Robinson, 1998). The addict is trying to maintain internal stability and adapt to an adverse environment (allostasis,

allostatic state) and may eventually slip into allostatic overload (compromised immunological, neural, and bone tissue).

The hypothesis is that the overactivation of central CRH increases the vulnerability for drug use, relapse, and withdrawal. Corticosterone, perhaps by feedforward *allostatic* mechanisms, may facilitate these events. Chronic overactivation of this system can compromise negative inhibition at the level of the PVN, in addition to compromising a number of end-organ systems. The cycle of addiction is an essential obsessive focus on a particular substance, linked to withdrawal and binge-related behaviors (DSM-IV). My focus in this chapter is largely on only part of the neural and physiological systems that underlie addictive behaviors.

I begin with a preliminary discussion of addiction. Cigarettes, alcohol, and other addictive substances are associated with a quarter of all deaths in the United States (McGinnis and Foege, 1999). Substance use also accounts for a large amount of economic burden and social costs to families and communities, including crime, birth defects, family violence, and divorce. The answers to addictive behaviors are not simple. Addictive objects vary considerably; some have properties in common, others do not. Consider the range of objects to which one could become addicted or obsessed with:

Alcohol
Sedatives
Hypnotics
Anxiolytics
Amphetamines
Cocaine
Nicotine
Caffeine

Of course, the range of things for which one can form an obsession or addiction is endless: gambling, work, money, food (see Elster and Skog, 1999). With this great array of candidates, social context matters; addiction takes place in a social milieu

that has consequences for the whole life of the addict, including tolerance, vulnerability to relapse, and overdose (Siegel, 1972, 1975; Woods, 1991).

Central States of Wanting Drugs

An addicted state of mind is one in which the will is compromised. A rape of the will and loss of control are key experiential elements. The focus of the addicted person is narrow and shortsighted (Lowenstein, 1999). Most of the addict's ability to postpone gratification is short-circuited. The greater the addiction, the greater the takeover and loss of control. Addiction is a cycle of increased dysregulation of the reward systems (Koob et al., 1998), and some individuals are at increased risk for long-term substance use and abuse (Koob et al., 1998).

Several emotional states, such as grief and obsessive love, have some of the same properties as addiction (Sabini and Silver, 1998; Elster, 1999). They are conditions in which the individual is overcome with emotion. The root meaning of the passions or the emotions is being overcome, and these states are characterized by the experience of being rendered passive and unable to act effectively. This represents the addicted state but surely does not represent all emotional states (Sabini and Silver, 1998; Elster, 1999). Emotional adaptive behavioral responses evolved, in my view and that of others (e.g., Ekman, 1992; Panksepp, 1998; Lane and Nadel, 1999; Davidson et al., 2000), because they confer cognitive information processing and successful problem solving (Darwin, 1872; Marler and Hamilton, 1966; Schulkin, 2000). They are not just passive confused states that render action incoherent.

Central motive states are states of the brain, linked to a desire, that result in appetitive and consummatory behaviors (Lashley, 1938; chapter 2 of this book). Recall that there are two phases to a central motive state. One is appetitive—the search for the desired object or condition, and the other is the consummation of that desire. In the example of hunger, the state motivates a search for food and, upon finding the food, the state is satisfied

by eating. Addiction is a good example of central motive states (Koob, 1998). Motivational states modulate emotional responses and inherently involve information processing (Lang et al., 1998). Hence motivational states are cognitive. Central motive states underlie our behavioral responses (Lashley, 1938; Stellar, 1954). Furthermore, they are also states of the brain that are constrained by neurobiology (Nader et al., 1997; Swanson, 2000). Hormones associated with a particular central motive state prepare the individual to perceive relevant environmental stimuli necessary for obtaining the desired outcome (Schulkin, 1999a).

Once an individual is caught in the cycle of addiction, this central motive state can become all consuming. Craving motivates the appetitive phase, the search for the object (i.e., the drug), and this search supersedes all else in the addicted person's life. The consummation of this motive state is taking the drug, and the addict is then satisfied for a period of time. Those close to the addicted person are often forced to turn their backs to normalize their own lives, but this has no immediate effect on the addict's lifestyle. The appetitive phase in addiction becomes more important than social interaction, family, friends, personal needs, and obligations.

Many neurotransmitter systems and brain areas are engaged during drug use and abuse (Higley and Bennett, 1999; Koob and Le Moal, 2001). Each drug involves a different constellation of systems (table 5.1). For example, a history of chronic stress interacts with the dopaminergic systems in the brain. An increase in dopamine release occurs in the frontal cortex of rats exposed to chronic stress, while rats without a chronic stress history do not show as much frontal cortex dopamine release when put in the same stressful situation (Cuadra et al., 1999). Chronic stress can also lead to a decrease in dopamine in the nucleus accumbens (Gambarana et al., 1999), and a number of studies have shown that prenatal exposure to, for example, cocaine can have long-term consequences on dopaminergic pathways and the response to duress (e.g., Elsworth et al., 2001).

Conditioned positive and negative reinforcement are both relevant to continued drug abuse and to relapse after prolonged

Table 5.1
Neurobiological substrates for the acute reinforcing effects of drugs of abuse

Drugs of Abuse	Neurotransmitter	Sites
Cocaine and amphetamines	Dopamine Serotonin	Nucleus accumbens Amygdala
Opiates	Dopamine Opioid peptides	Ventral tegmental area Nucleus accumbens
Nicotine	Dopamine Opioid peptides?	Ventral tegmental area Nucleus accumbens Amygdala
Tetrahydro-cannabinol (marijuana)	Dopamine Opioid peptides?	Ventral tegmental area
Ethanol	Dopamine Opioid peptide Serotonin Gamma-aminobutyric acid (GABA) Glutamate	Ventral tegmental area Nucleus accumbens Amygdala

From Koob et al., 1998.

abstinence. If substance use is based purely on unconditioned positive and negative reinforcement (and their underlying neural substrates) then relapse after extended abstinence should not be the social problem that it is in our society. One habit-forming aspect of compulsive drug use is the result of the associated euphoria. Examples of conditioned positive reinforcement exist in the animal and human research literature. Animal research suggests that the amygdala, nucleus accumbens, and ventral striatum are important for associating, acquiring, and responding to the conditioned reinforcing effects of stimuli associated with addiction (Robbins et al., 1989; Altman et al., 1996; Robbins and Everitt, 1999; Ito et al., 2000; Carboni et al., 2000; Thomas and Everitt, 2001). Heroin addicts find injections of saline pleasurable because the conditioned positive reinforcement of the injection is associated with heroin injections. The motivation to continue drug use in order to avoid the negative affective and

physiological consequences of withdrawal is a negatively reinforcing aspect of dependence (Koob, 1998). And, of course, the chronic arousal, the fear, the uncertainty that pervades the heroin or cocaine addict creates a brain state that reflects allostatic overload. Not only are the normal feedforward systems active, but the circuits that underlie a reward, and probably fear, are vulnerable to allostatic overload (see Koob and Le Moal, 2001).

Vulnerability to Drug Abuse: Animal Studies

An individual's inborn characteristics can have mediating effects on both response to stress and reactions to drugs. Animals can be selectively bred to have higher basal levels of corticosterone, and in this context there can be a condition for higher levels of CRH gene expression. Similarly, strains of animals that prefer specific drugs and are more likely to respond to specific drugs can be bred in laboratories. Behavioral and physiological characteristics of selectively bred animals can give insights into characteristics of human vulnerability.

Many studies demonstrate that rats with higher glucocorticoid levels are more likely to self-administer a number of psychotropic agents (figure 5.1; Piazza et al., 1993). In different strains of rats that have different genetically based levels of corticosterone, the corticosterone levels are related to the likelihood of self-administration of psychotropic drugs. Rats with higher levels of corticosterone are more likely to self-administer cocaine, heroin, and amphetamines. In other words, the greater the level of corticosterone that activates the central nervous system, the greater the probability of rats self-administering these agents (Piazza et al., 1989, 1993; Erb et al., 1996). The vulnerability story is more complex than cortisol, corticosterone, or CRH levels, in addition to dopamine levels. Corticosterone also effects dopaminergic expression in several regions of the brain that probably contribute to increased motor behavior (Rouge-Pont et al., 1993, 1998; Lucas et al., 1998a, b), and increased tendency to impulsive choice (Cardinal et al., 2001).

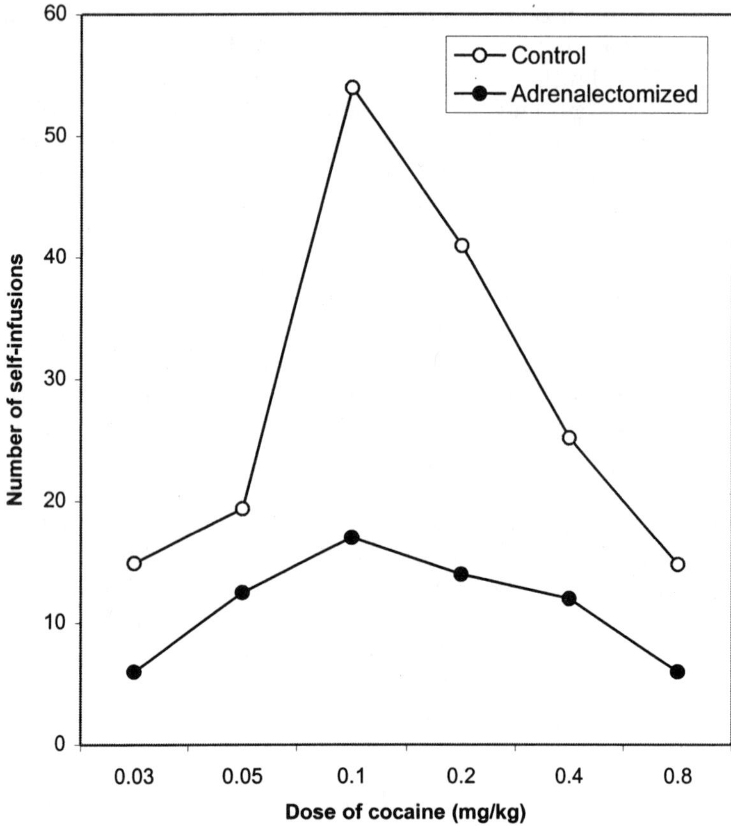

Figure 5.1
Effects of adrenalectomy on cocaine self-administration in rats (after Koob and Le Moal, 1997).

Research suggests that even prenatal stress can have lifelong effects (chapter 4). When cortisol is elevated in both mother and fetus, CRH levels in the amygdala are significantly higher in the offspring when they become young adults (Cratty et al., 1995; Welberg and Seckl, 2001). Additionally, CRH injections to the mother during pregnancy increase the fear responses of the offspring when they are provoked as adults. Prenatal stress can also impair future motor development in primates (Schneider et al., 1992, 1998), and vulnerability to high anxiety and drug use (Vallee et al., 1997).

Parental deprivation is an important variable for predicting later vulnerability to stress among nonhuman primates. Plasma cortisol levels quickly increase in rhesus monkey infants when they are separated from their mothers and peers (Higley et al., 1992). There is a tendency to have higher systemic levels of cortisol in rhesus monkeys maternally deprived during development than in mother-reared monkeys. Rhesus monkey infants subjected to short-term maternal separation and isolation exhibit higher cortisol levels, and perhaps higher levels of central CRH (Kalin et al., 2000). These events create a vulnerability to chronic arousal and a vulnerability to allostatic overload. Rhesus infants reared by surrogate mothers and with limited peer contact do not show as high a cortisol response to isolation (Shannon et al., 1998).

Early life experience with food availability is another stressor with long-lasting consequences. Studies using macaques show that experience of variable food availability during development results in greater CRH levels in the cerebrospinal fluid during adulthood and greater fear-related behavioral responses (Coplan et al., 2001). The changes in the stress system, as a result of early trauma, stems from a lack of predictability and the extreme demands upon the CRH system.

Stressful events, which lead to higher glucocorticoid levels, also induce an increased likelihood of self-administration of drugs at higher rates. When rats are exposed to noncontingent shock, they self-administer cocaine at much higher rates than rats who are exposed to contingent shock or no shock (Goeders,

1998). The noncontingent shock rats were more responsive to lower cocaine doses than the rats in the other shock groups, who required two times the dosage before engaging in significant amounts of cocaine self-administration. Levels of plasma corticosterone in the noncontingent shock rats were much higher than in the other rats.

Maternally deprived macaque monkeys have both higher plasma cortisol concentrations and higher central CRH in the cerebrospinal fluid as young mature adults (Higley et al., 1992, 1996; Habib et al., 1999, 2000). Behaviorally, macaques raised by their peers show higher baseline rates of alcohol consumption when compared with macaques raised by their mothers. However, when subjected to social separation, mother-reared monkeys increase their alcohol consumption during social separation until the consumption is equal to that of peer-reared macaques (Kraemer and McKinney, 1985; Higley et al., 1991). Mother-reared macaques also have larger increases of ACTH than peer-reared macaques during social separation (Clarke, 1993). Macaques separated from their mothers and raised by peers are more socially inept, more aggressive, engage in more deviant behaviors, and consume more alcohol than their mother-reared counterparts (figure 5.2; Higley et al., 1996). Interestingly, in both mother-reared and maternally separated conditions, those macaques that tend to have higher levels of cortisol (and probably higher levels of central CRH) tend to consume more alcohol (Fahlke et al., 2000).

Corticotropin-releasing hormone levels are elevated during both positive and negative experiences (Richter et al., 1995; Merali et al., 1998). Expression of CRH in the brain increases the salience of environmental stimuli (Rosen and Schulkin, 1998) and has implications for situational learning both in addiction and during a child's development. In the case of addiction, this is relevant in terms of the search for and acquisition of the desired object. The actions of glucocorticoids might also be adaptable mechanisms for reducing overactivity of physiological stress systems, allowing the animal to cope more effectively with a stressful situation (Piazza and Le Moal, 1997).

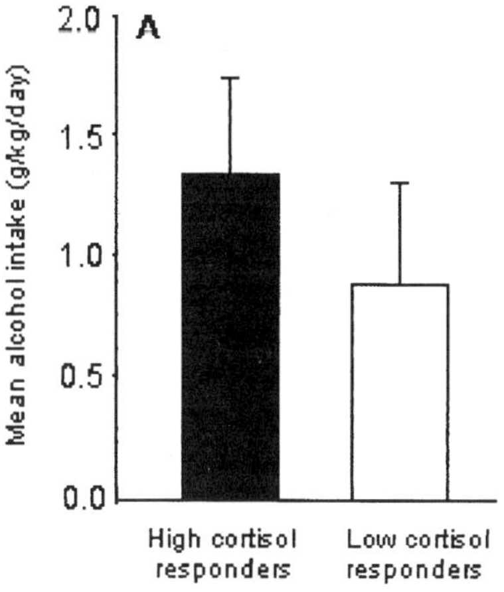

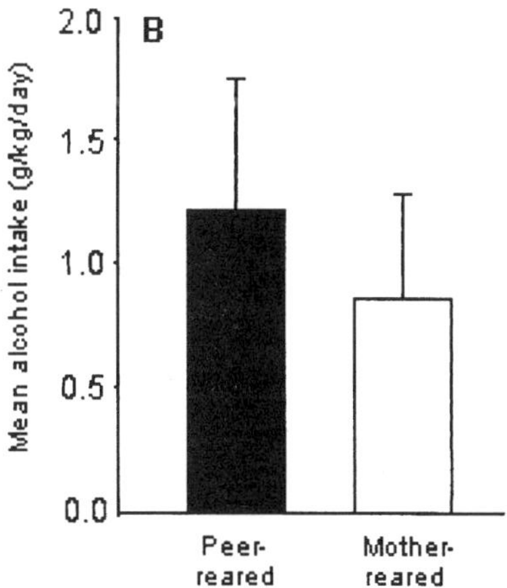

Figure 5.2
High cortisol respondents and low respondent (A) and peer-reared and mother-reared macaques (B) and their ingestion of alcohol. This is the average amount consumed over 10 days (adapted from Higley et al., 1991; Fahlke et al., 2000).

Both glucocorticoids and CRH have psychomotor effects, as does dopamine. Cocaine is considered a psychomotor stimulant. The psychomotor and euphoric effects resulting from cocaine consumption may reflect activation of the neuropeptide CRH and neurotransmitter dopamine as well as their regulation by glucocorticoids (Piazza et al., 1993; Schulkin et al., 1998; Koob, 1998). Cocaine activates the pituitary adrenal axis in both rats and nonhuman primates. Corticotropin-releasing hormone is activated in both hypothalamic and extrahypothalamic areas during cocaine consumption (Koob, 1998). After three weeks of binge cocaine administration, rats show higher basal corticosterone levels when compared with rats in a no-cocaine placebo group (Kreek, 1997; Sarnyai et al., 1998). Increases in CRH activity during cocaine consumption, along with mesolimbic dopaminergic activity, may increase the salience of cocaine and its associated stimuli.

The effects of drug consumption interact with individual stress responses and may be relevant to both the initiation and maintenance of drug abuse. Individual differences in biological responses to stress are measurable in the laboratory. Rats can be categorized as low responders or high responders to stress by measuring corticosterone release and locomotor reactivity in response to a stressful situation. Most animals avoid stressful situations because those situations are unpleasant. However, some animals—and some humans—can be described as stress seeking (Piazza et al., 1993). Animal research shows that these individuals are more likely to self-administer and are more sensitive to the effects of psychostimulants.

Once within the cycle of addiction, individual biology is not as relevant to the animal's interpretation of the environment. One result of cocaine binge administration in rats is the diminution of individual differences in corticosterone hormone response to stress (Sarnyai et al., 1998). Rats that showed high levels of corticosterone release in response to stress and those that showed low levels of release were put in either binge cocaine or saline/control conditions. The individual differences were maintained in animals injected with saline over 3- and

6-week periods. However, the differences in response to stress between low responders and high responders disappeared in the rats treated with cocaine during the same time periods (Sarnyai et al., 1998).

Withdrawal from drug abuse is another aversive condition characterized by elevated glucocorticoid and CRH levels (Koob and LeMoal, 2001). The drugs that produce a pattern of elevated glucocorticoids and CRH in the PVN of the hypothalamus and the central nucleus of the amygdala during withdrawal conditions include ethanol (Pich et al., 1995; Adinoff et al., 1996), cocaine (figure 5.3; Sarnyai et al., 1998; Richter and Weiss, 1999), morphine (Richter et al., 1999, unpublished), cannabis (Rodriguez deFonseca et al., 1997), and even nicotine (Rasmussen, 1998). In rats, alterations of the type-I CRH receptor reduces

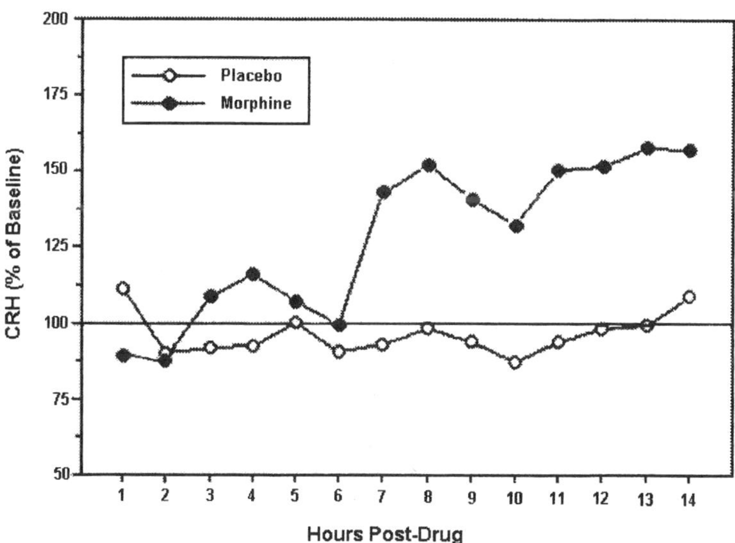

Figure 5.3
Levels of corticotropin releasing hormone (CRH) measured by dialysis following withdrawal from morphine (Richter, Schulkin, and Weiss, 1999, unpublished observations).

the behavioral and endocrine response to morphine and cocaine on alcohol (Skelton et al., 2000; Goeders and Guerin, 2000; Goeders, 2002; Sillaber et al., 2002).

Affectively, anxiety and depression characterize drug withdrawal in humans. In animals, increased reactivity to stress characterizes drug withdrawal. Cerebrospinal fluid concentrations of CRH are elevated during the first day of abstinence from alcohol and decrease over the next three weeks in humans (Adinoff et al., 1996). While CRH is elevated during withdrawal, several neurotransmitters or neuropeptides show decreased expression. Moreover, CRH expression in the brain affects a number of neurotransmitters and neuropeptides (e.g., Swanson, 1991; Watts, 1996; Price and Lucki, 2001).

Feedforward Allostatic Regulation: Vulnerability to Relapse and the Bed Nucleus of the Stria Terminalis

Vulnerability to relapse is a common occurrence for the formerly addicted individual. The best defense for the individual is to remove him or herself from the environment in which he or she might relapse. But that can be very difficult to accomplish. Avoidance behavior is a kind of adaptation, linked perhaps to ensuring internal stability to acquire what is needed and avoid what is not. In both cases, it is anticipatory. With relapse so prominent among those who have been addicted to a substance, what is known about some of the mechanisms of relapse?

Levels of corticosterone are linked to vulnerability to drug administration. This occurs in amphetamine and cocaine self-administration studies in rats, and high responders to amphetamine self-administration have higher levels of circulating corticosterone (Piazza et al., 1989). These levels of corticosterone may increase the salience of objects associated with the drug administration and the sensation of seeking aspects of drug reward (Piazza et al., 1993) by the increased dopamine synthesis facilitated by corticosterone in the nucleus accumbens and the change of state—allostasis.

Various models of stress-related relapse have been studied. Rats that were trained to self-administer cocaine for 12 days, for example, and then withdrawn from the drug use, quickly reinstated their self-administration when they were given a foot shock. This stress-inducing event was more potent than simply being exposed to the cocaine (Erb et al., 1996). This paradigm has been used to assess the relapse for a number of psychotropic drugs of abuse (Erb et al., 2000; Shaham et al., 2000).

While peripheral blockade of corticosterone does not interfere with this effect, interference with central CRH does (Erb et al., 1998). Indeed, CRH is linked to vulnerability to stress-related relapse for former users of heroin (Shaham et al., 1997) and cocaine (Erb et al., 1998). Foot shocking increased relapse, which went on, to some extent, despite the CRH antagonist that was administered (Erb et al., 1998) and was unaffected by dopamine receptor agonist or opioid receptor antagonist (Shaham et al., 2000).

One critical area for this vulnerability, mediated in part by central CRH, appears to be the bed nucleus of the stria terminalis (figures 5.4 and 5.5; Shaham et al., 2000). Recall that this region of the brain is linked to the amygdala (although this is disputed; see Swanson and Petrovich, 1998). Neurons within the lateral region, both dorsal and ventral, contain CRH (Swanson and Simmons, 1989; Makino et al., 1994a, b; Watts and Sanchez-Watts, 1995) and CRH changes within the bed nucleus reflect vagal activation under duress (Nigsen et al., 2001).

The bed nucleus of the stria terminalis, as I indicated in chapter 3, is linked to CRH-related effects on anxiety-like behavioral responses (Davis et al., 1997). Corticotropin-releasing hormone infused into the bed nucleus elicits anxious behavior and an increased tendency to self-administer medication; CRH antagonists in the bed nucleus interfere with foot-shock-related relapse, but this does not occur when the CRH antagonist is infused into the amygdala (Erb and Stewart, 1999). Conversely, when CRH is infused directly in the bed nucleus, cocaine self-administration increases, and this does not occur when CRH is directly infused into the amygdala (figure 5.6).

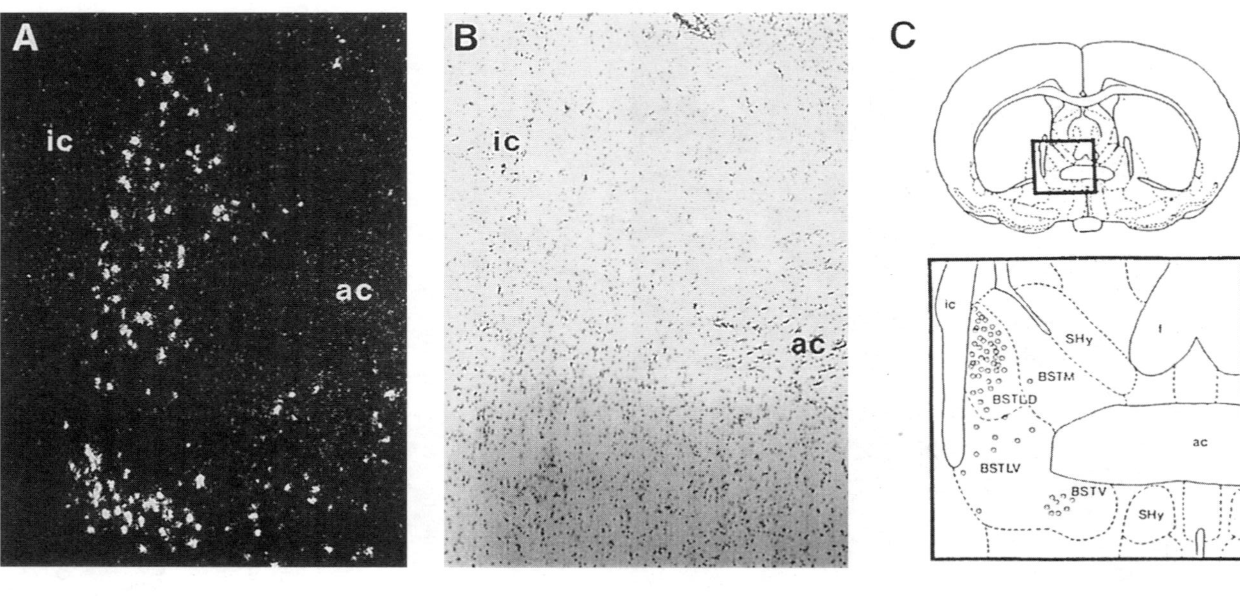

Figure 5.4
(*A*) Dark-field photomicrograph shows localization of CRH mRNA signals in the bed nucleus of the stria terminalis (BNST). Autoradiographic silver grains appear white. CRH mRNA is mainly accumulated in the dorsal part of lateral BNST, and signals are also observed in the ventral part of BNST. (*B*) Cresyl violet stained section corresponding to (*A*) shows cellular architecture of the region. (C) Open circles show the distribution of CRH immunoreactive cell bodies, (*A,B,* original magnification, x 50) BSTLD, dorsolateral BNST; BSTLV, ventrolateral BNST, BSTM, medial BNST, ventral BNST, ventral BNST; ac, anterior commisure; f, fornix, ic, internal capsule; SHy, septohypothalamic nucleus (Makino et al., 1994b).

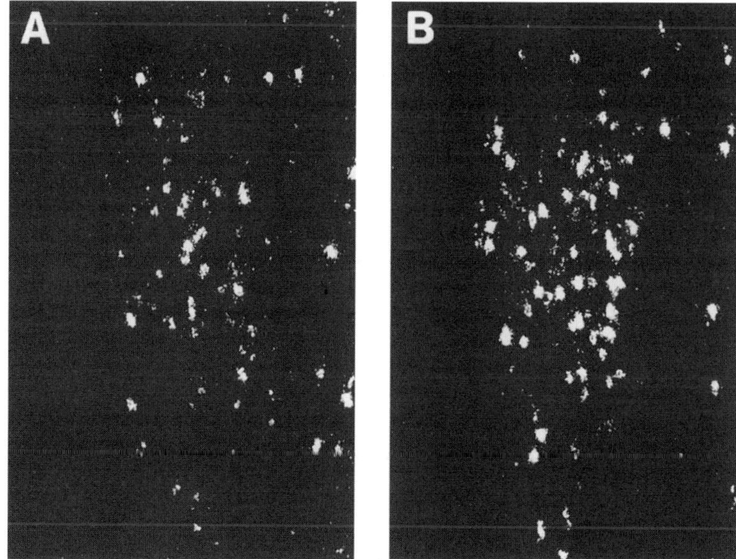

Figure 5.5
Effects of corticosterone (CORT) injection on CRH mRNA levels in the dorsal part of lateral bed nucleus of the stria terminalis (BSTLD). Dark field photomicrographs show the autoradiographic distribution of CRH mRNA in the BNST of control (*A*) and high CORT-treated (*B*, at 4 days) rats. Autoradiographic silver grains appear white. High (CORT) treatment increased CRH mRNA in the BSTLE (original magnification, ×100) (Makino et al., 1994b).

The bed nucleus of the stria terminalis also appears to be linked to some of the withdrawal symptoms experienced when individuals with a past history of drug abuse who are stressed for some reason start to crave the drug again. Thus CRH (in addition to other systems within the bed nucleus of the stria terminalis, e.g., Walker et al., 2000) may contribute to the withdrawal symptoms within the bed nucleus of the stria terminalis which has been linked to a number of biological factors underlying drug abuse (figure 5.7; Koob et al., 1998). But many neural systems are affected by withdrawal. Some of them are depicted in table 5.2.

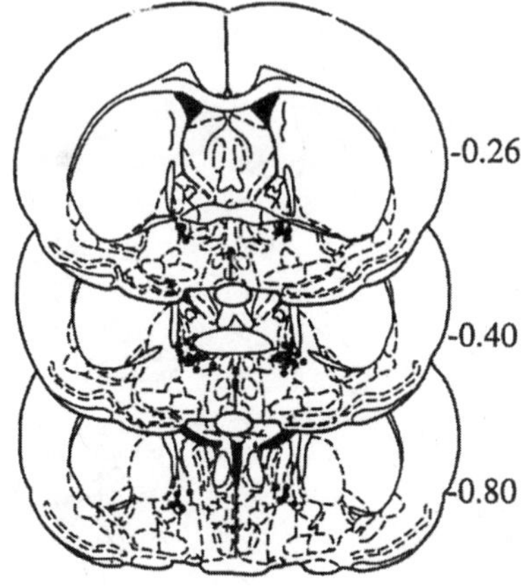

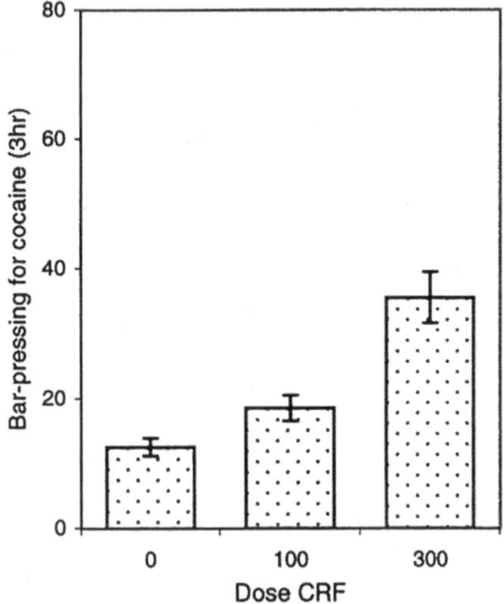

Figure 5.6
CRF injections in the bed nucleus of the stria terminalis and reinstatement of cocaine self-administration (adapted from Erb and Stewart, 1999).

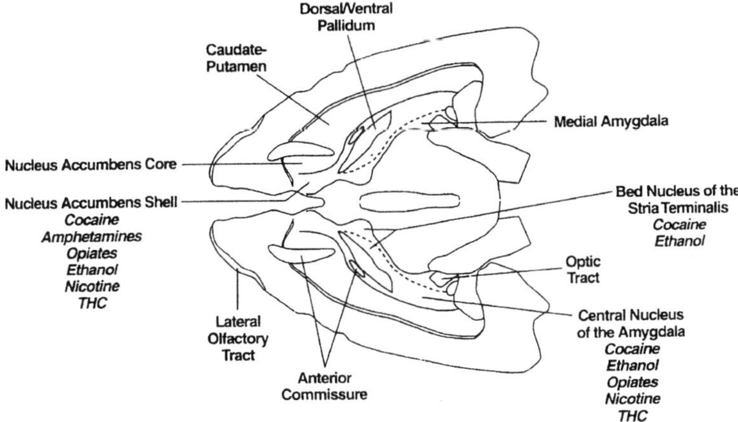

Figure 5.7
Horizontal section of a rat brain depicting some of the principal structures involved in drug use. These structures include the central nucleus of the amygdala, the shell part of the nucleus accumbens, and the bed nucleus of the stria terminalis. The drugs listed below each structure refer to potential sites of action of drug reinforcement during the addiction cycle, either positive or negative. (Koob et al., 1998; see also Alheid et al., 1988; but also Swanson and Petrovich, 1998).

Table 5.2
Some of the neurotransmitters/neuropeptides affected during withdrawal

↓ Dopamine
↓ Opioid peptides
↓ Serotonin
↓ GABA
↑ Corticotropin-releasing factor

Creating a Hyperexcitable State

Neural sensitization means the increased excitability of neurons. The ability of stress hormones and preexposure to psychosocial stressors in animals to precipitate greater stress responses indicates that sensitization processes play a major role in turning normal responses into exaggerated abnormal behavior (Marks and Tobena, 1990; Rosen and Schulkin, 1998). By definition, sensitization implies that the threshold for activation of the system is lower following the presentation of a stimulus. In other words, the system becomes hyperexcitable. The role of sensitization in the development of addiction is not well understood (Koob et al., 1989, 1998; Marks and Tobena, 1990; Robinson and Berridge, 2000). Theoretically, sensitization is an important factor in the etiology of hyperexcitability of the circuits underlying the addict's behavior. However, a number of researchers have linked the sensitization process underlying drug addiction to allostatic regulation (Koob and Le Moal, 2001; see also Rosen and Schulkin, 1998; Cook, 2002) and to CRH regulation (Richter et al., 1995).

Repeated cocaine self-administration in rats, for example, can result in the development of seizures linked to amygdala activation (Weiss et al., 1986), and both CRH and glucocorticoids facilitate cocaine-induced seizures (Weiss et al., 1992; Kling et al., 1993). In one experiment, repeated cocaine administration resulted in the development of seizures that were facilitated by both dexamethasone and, to a lesser extent, corticosterone (figure 5.8; Kling et al., 1993; Lee et al., 1989).

Chronic uncertainty (which can engender hyperexcitablility) can exacerbate the sensitization process. Experimental paradigms, in which an inescapable foot shock is delivered to rats, increase generalized anxiety and can increase the vulnerability of relapse to drug abuse (Erb and Stewart, 1999). The results of sensitization to stressors (i.e., hyperexcitability and pathological anxiety, vulnerability to relapse and allostatic overload) become long lasting and difficult to treat.

Sensitization may produce hyperexcitability by itself or in combination with various learning processes. Simple associative

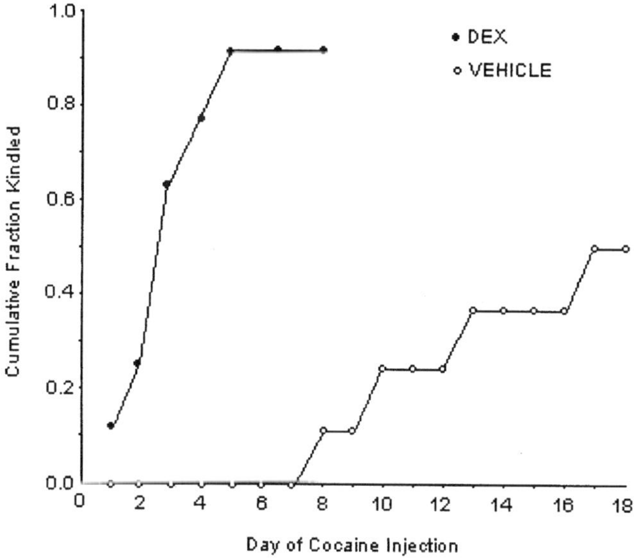

Figure 5.8
Effects of dexamethasone or vehicle administration on the development of kindled seizures to repeated cocaine administration. Rats were pretreated i.p. with dexamethasone (DEX, 250 μg/rat/day), or vehicle daily at 16.00 h beginning 3 days prior to initiating daily i.p. injections of cocaine HCL (40 mg/kg/day) at 09.00 h. Cumulative percentage of rats developing seizures is indicated as a function of days of study. Dexamethasone-treated rats had an increased frequency of kindling compared with controls (adapted from Kling et al., 1993).

conditioning does not explain the development of pathological anxiety. Several factors, including one's history of exposure to uncontrollable and unpredictable stressors, the nature of the stressors and conditioned stimuli (how conditionable they are), and one's temperament all influence learning processes (Rosen and Schulkin, 1998; Bouton et al., 2001). These factors may sensitize neural circuits to associative conditioning processes and thus facilitate responses now associated with the addiction.

Kindling (as in the cocaine example) produces a decrease in threshold and engages the same neural mechanisms in the first

few stimulations as LTP does, but it then recruits additional mechanisms as kindling proceeds further (Rosen and Schulkin, 1998). Thus both LTP and the early stages of kindling may induce similar molecular changes that are important for hyperexcitability. Induction of hyperexcitability from repeated exposure to activation may induce a cascade of biological events that includes the expression of immediate-early genes, such as peptides and structural proteins that render the tissue more sensitive to subsequent stimulation (Rosen and Schulkin, 1998).

Glutamate receptors, particularly the NMDA type, are important for the development of LTP and hyperexcitability in the hippocampus and the amygdala (LeDoux, 2000). Foot-shock-induced sensitization and facilitation of a fear-conditioned response require NMDA activation.

Glutamate, mediated through activation of various second messengers (e.g., calcium and cAMP), is also important for inducing a cascade of genetic transcriptional events. Kindling can also induce the expression of a number of neuropeptides, possibly through mechanisms involving the immediate-early genes. Finally, structural changes also occur in synapses following LTP and kindling (LeDoux 1996, 2000; Adamec, 1997; Rosen and Schulkin, 1998).

These immediate-early genes act as transcriptional factors to induce transcription of other genes, such as neuropeptides that affect behavior and modulate neurotransmission and other processes in the brain. A number of neuropeptides and their mRNA, which also are not normally expressed in fear-related limbic regions or have low levels in these areas, are transiently expressed following kindling (Rosen and Schulkin, 1998). These include peptides that are thought to play roles in pathological anxiety and affect (e.g., CRH, cholecystokinin, thyrotropin-releasing hormone, and neuropeptide Y) (Adamec, 1997). Changes in the expression of other molecules (e.g., growth and neurotrophin factors) that are important for growth and maintenance of neurons may also be affected by fear, stress, and sensitization. Both inescapable stress (restraint) and kindling alter the expression of mRNA for a number of growth factors, including nerve

growth factor, brain-derived neurotrophic factor and neurotrophin-3 (Smith et al., 1995a, b). These factors may be important as a vulnerability for neuronal death (allostatic overload) that may be caused by chronic stress of drug abuse (Sapolsky, 1992; McEwen, 2001).

Overactivity of the amygdala during seizure activity can be translated as a physical metaphor for drug addiction. Addiction is not a pleasurable state and is characterized by overactivity and obsession with the search for and consumption of psychotropic drugs. These are the negative consequences of allostasis. Corticotropin-releasing hormone concentrations are increased during aversive and uncertain events, and the state of addiction is riddled with uncertainty. As I suggested earlier, glucocorticoids are the molecules of energy metabolism, and the addicted person uses all energy to secure the craved substance, to the exclusion of everything else. The states of craving and withdrawal are often characterized by psychomotor overactivity, just as the amygdala becomes overactive when glucocorticoids and CRH levels are elevated—the positive induction of the neuropeptide by this steroid (Cook, 2002).

Corticosterone, CRH, Feedforward Mechanisms, and Self-Administration of Psychotropic Agents

The induction of CRH gene expression in the amygdala, and the bed nucleus of the stria terminalis, by glucocorticoid hormones may also underlie addictive behaviors; these effects appear to be manifested in the anxiety associated with withdrawal. Both high levels of corticosterone and central CRH have been linked to addictive behavior. For example, CRH infusions into the lateral ventricle facilitate amphetamine-induced self-administration (Sarnyai et al., 1993). Corticosterone levels are known to influence the expression of amphetamine self-administration (Piazza et al., 1991; Cador et al., 1993). Systemic injections of corticosterone increase the likelihood of amphetamine self-administration, as do stressful events (Maccari et al., 1991) via activation of glucocorticoid receptor sites (Steckler and Holsboer,

2001)—which increase both corticosterone and central CRH (Heinrichs et al., 1995). Individual differences in levels of corticosterone are correlated with amphetamine self-administration: the higher the level, the greater the self-administration (Piazza et al., 1991).

Corticosterone levels have also been shown to influence dopamine-dependent psychomotor effects of both morphine and cocaine self-administration (Deroche et al., 1994, 1995). Corticosterone is known to influence self-administration of cocaine; the greater the degree of corticosterone that circulates, the greater the probability of self-administration (Goeders and Guerin, 1996). Moreover, changes in dopamine levels in the nucleus accumbens is dependent upon adrenal steroid function (Barrot et al., 2000). The further activation of both CRH and dopaminergic neurons by glucocorticoids from feedforward allostatic mechanisms creates (when the glucocorticoids remain elevated) a vulnerability for drug abuse.

Corticotropin-releasing hormone in the brain has been linked to the anxiety associated with heroin and morphine withdrawal (Sarnyai et al., 1995; Zhou et al., 1996b), alcohol withdrawal (Pich et al., 1995), and cocaine withdrawal (Sarnyai et al., 1992a, b, 1993). In addition, a recent study has demonstrated that cannabinoid withdrawal also elevates CRH in the central nucleus of the amygdala (Rodriguez de Fonseca et al., 1997).

Reducing CRH expression in the amygdala reduces morphine withdrawal systems (Heinrichs et al., 1995). Inhibiting corticosterone synthesis by metyrapone decreases the vulnerability to relapse in cocaine self-administration (Piazza et al., 1994). Corticotropin-releasing hormone is linked to stress-facilitated vulnerability to relapse (Shaham et al., 2000). Perhaps by increasing or decreasing CRH gene expression by corticosterone, these rats are more vulnerable to self-administration of these psychotropic drugs. What this suggests is that the steroid may normally act to facilitate the level of neuropeptide in these extrahypothalamic sites that underlie the behavior. This is similar to the neuroendocrine mechanisms that facilitate and sustain other central motive states discussed in chapter 2.

Conclusion: Allostasis, Allostatic Overload, and Drug Use

The lifestyle of drug abuse, with its health-related consequences, is a run-down state. Addicts spend most of their time thinking of how to procure the next fix. The actual time of pleasure decreases as the addiction takes hold. It requires more drugs to produce the desired effect, the effect may not last very long, and the dominance of the obsession takes hold of the individual.

Homeostasis refers to stability through maintaining constant parameters. Negative feedback mechanisms exist throughout the brain and body in which a change in a system triggers an automatic response, bringing the system back to a basal level of functioning (Goldstein, 1995a, b; Fink, 2000). Allostasis refers to the principal of viability through change; there is no consistent set point (Sterling and Eyer, 1988). The organism responds to the demands of the external environment by changing its internal set points. This is evident in blood pressure changes during the course of an individual day; blood pressure rises in response to stressful, arousing situations that are psychologically experienced as pain, fear, or rage—or the craving for drugs. The chronic overuse of neurotransmitters linked to reward results in their biochemical depletion (Koob and Le Moal, 2001).

Allostasis reflects anticipatory factors (Schulkin et al., 1994), the growth of the associative processes linked to the drug (Berridge and Robinson, 1998; Everitt, 1999), and the long term changes that can occur in both systemic and central systems (Schluger et al., 2001) in biological regulation of the internal milieu. Addiction results in chronic arousal as the individual constantly seeks out the drug—the endless hypervigilant state (Koob and Le Moal, 2001). Brainstem sites such as the locus ceruleus are involved in the interaction of both molecules and interact with forebrain sites such as the amygdala, bed nucleus of the stria terminalis, and the PVN of the hypothalamus (Valentino et al., 1993, 1995). These sites underlie, perhaps, the chronic anxiety of the addict. The positive induction of CRH or dopamine by corticosterone (allostatic mechanism) in regions of the brain that underlie addiction may contribute to the addiction and physio-

logical overload over time along with the input from brainstem feedforward mechanisms of arousal from norepinephrine (Stricker and Zigmond, 1986; Koob and Le Moal, 2001). The changes in excitatory amino acids (e.g., McEwen, 1998a,b) may create a context for vulnerability to relapse and allostatic overload.

When an animal is in a state of relaxation, its body is able to repair damaged tissue and rebuild energy stores. However, when an animal is in a state of psychological arousal, its body begins breaking down metabolic compounds to produce energy. States of arousal are associated with a number of physiological responses, including increased blood pressure, increased breakdown of carbohydrates, fat, and protein, and decreased production of immune system cells. A number of hormone levels increase, including cortisol, vasopressin, angiotensin, and endogenous opiates.

An advantage of allostatic mechanisms is perhaps an increased efficiency in dealing physiologically with changing environmental demands. Moving from a state of complete relaxation to a state of complete alertness is difficult for a homeostatic system because of the great increase in energy demand. When an animal exists in an environment that frequently requires arousal states, allostatic mechanisms allow the body to physiologically change the basal set points of various systems to meet the arousal requirements. This allows the organism to maintain a constant state of alertness. However, there is a price to pay for this allostatic adjustment: increased energy demands on the body compromise other important functions, such as the immune system.

Physiological systems are designed in part to minimize the impact of drastic changes; this holds for situations ranging from the regulation of food to that of drug abuse (Solomon and Corbit, 1974; Woods, 1991; Koob, 1996; Koob and Le Moal, 1997; Siegal and Allan, 1998). Anticipatory responses that serve regulatory physiology can reduce the impact of overingesting as much as underingesting a desired substance—whether it be good or bad for the individual. Anticipatory responses that

serve to reduce the physiological impact of drug use may also hinder the individual.

When allostatic overload is introduced (for example, during the prenatal period or during childhood) by chronic socioeconomic stress or by traumatic experiences, the way in which physiological systems respond later in life can be affected. Multiple adverse events, which can manifest through unpredictable environmental situations, are one type of allostatic overload.

The state of allostasis is the shifting of physiological and behavioral resources in maintaining internal viability. For the addict, stuck in a massive web of salient cues reinforcing the chronic want of the drug, one outcome of allostasis is the possible depletion of a variety of neural systems (e.g., reward; Koob and Le Moal, 2001). A history of chronic drug abuse shifts the reward function (sensitization, tolerance, etc.) with the result of needing more of the drug and gaining less of a high.

Maintaining an addiction, in part, nonetheless, is like maintaining glucose levels or calcium levels. There is a homeostatic element involved in each of these situations (Koob, 1998). The body requires the drug in order to maintain equilibrium and to avoid getting sick, much as the body requires glucose or calcium. The negative reinforcement effects of drugs take hold. Central motive states are elicited, and both appetitive and consummatory behaviors are expressed. Further, as psychological and physical tolerance develops, the consummatory phase is less and less satisfying. When an individual becomes drug dependent, there are changes in the internal drug set points; there is an allostatic reaction to the constant presence of a drug such as cocaine, heroin, or alcohol. In rats, a limited period of daily access to a drug leads to maintaining the same levels of intake from one session to the next. An increased period of daily access (6 hours) leads to increased self-administration of the drug (Ahmed and Koob, 1998). A higher level of intake is required to gain the same hedonic effect from the drug (Koob, 1998).

Again, one way to understand these results is that they represent a shift in sensitivity of the reward function and a varied set point (allostasis) for the drug to have its effects. The drug is now

used more frequently, and physical health deteriorates in the addict because of extended wear and tear on the physical body. At one level, the event is homeostatic (Cannon, 1929a), and the behavior serves the physiology (Richter, 1942–43, 1956). At another level, the behavior is allostatic, a phenomenon that includes anticipatory responses and not just reactive responses (see also Sterling and Eyer, 1981).

It is clear that using drugs is not the same as maintaining sodium or water balance, in which there is a clear set point that has to be maintained. Again, there are physical limits, but that is different from a set point that is actively maintained. The negative aspects of the addiction grow and negative effects accrue while positive effects recede into the background. Yet the addict is enslaved by desire. Allostatic mechanisms, Koob and Le Moal (1997, 2001) suggested, have to do with the normal mechanisms of homeostasis insofar as it relates to reward. But when animals have reached states of dysregulation, the levels of intake are too high. Wanting of the drugs increases, and the addicted person becomes consumed by the desire. The addict's life is replete with endless consumption—and little satisfaction.

The addict's life, characterized by chronic worry, is replete with anticipatory angst, and both glucocorticoids and central CRH are elevated (Schulkin et al., 1998; Koob and Le Moal, 2001). Chronic allostatic overload exists when both glucocorticoids and central CRH are elevated and the body is unable to reduce the levels. There is a breakdown of normal inhibitory response. Maintaining high levels of glucocorticoids for long periods of time, which is the normal state of the addict, has many consequences. The breakdown of tissue, along with the associated addicted lifestyle, leads to an increased risk of many diseases, including human immunodeficiency virus and hepatitis. Compromised immune function, bone deterioration, and impaired memory functions (McEwen, 1998a, b) are a few of the results of maintaining high-energy arousal states over a long period of time.

The molecular substrates underlying craving, reinforcement, and withdrawal are being laid down. However, these

discoveries must be couched in terms of the social milieu in which addicts function. Methadone blocks both reward and withdrawal from opiates, but that is only part of the solution. Thus, CRH blockers will also not solve substance abuse problems. The human connectedness factor must be addressed (Jaspers, 1913). We are social animals, we need each other. Neuroendocrine evidence demonstrates that social adaptation, interacting, and communicating reduces, in suitable environmental conditions, stress hormones and increases the hormones linked to attachment behaviors (oxytocin, prolactin, vasopressin; see Insel, 1992; Bridges and Freemark, 1995; Carter et al., 1999; Bale et al., 2001).

Early life trauma and blunted cortisol response are associated with later substance use as well. However, these studies are necessarily based on clinical populations. Patients being treated for anxiety disorders and substance abuse might only be a subset of those who suffered early life trauma. Relatively large proportions of people who suffer early traumas maintain relatively normal lives, socially and biochemically.

Perhaps consistent and reliable positive human touch and contact can mediate the long-term effects of trauma, and perhaps the pathways influenced are directly related to CRH activity (Liu et al., 1997). It is known that rats who are handled, for example, have reduced levels of stress hormone activation at the level of the PVN production of CRH, pituitary ACTH, and adrenal corticosterone (Levine, 1975; Levine et al., 1989; Meaney et al., 1988, 1989, 1996). They show diminished responsiveness when challenged; it is as if the experience of being cared for or nurtured somewhat enhances the ability to cope with the impact of adversity. This is important for the recovering addict—or for any of us.

Successful drug rehabilitation programs often employ social contact as a vehicle toward mental health (Ouimette et al., 1998). The idea of reaching out to others to maintain abstinence is certainly not new. The effectiveness of this approach might be related to the reduced stress levels and, consequently, reduced CRH levels within the recovering individual. We know that so-

cial contact is an important adaptive behavior, and it is known to reduce stress hormones and to elevate hormones that can enhance well-being—that is, the central state associated with it (Carter et al., 1999). An important strategy, perhaps preferentially expressed as a tendency among the females of our species, and possibly others, is to make contact and sustain meaningful relationships when coping with duress (Taylor et al., 2000). Perhaps those who do not relapse into drug use are those who maintain and strengthen their social contacts, while those who experience relapse are those who refuse social support and are too impulsive to stay on the course of recovery.

Conclusion: Adaptation, Allostasis, and Anticipation

Both homeostasis and allostasis, whole body regulatory concepts, function in our lexicon as integrative terms for understanding physiological/behavioral systems. They reflect our need to understand how internal viability is maintained in a changing environment (see also Mrosovsky, 1990; Bauman, 2000). Allostasis is tied to the central nervous system as it supervenes in the assessment and regulation of bodily states (Sterling and Eyer, 1988; Schulkin et al., 1994).

One impetus for the idea of allostasis was linked to concern about our social world. In a paper by Eyer and Sterling (1977) entitled "Stress-Related Mortality and Social Organization," a major portion was a critique of our society and the onset of a variety of disease states. Sterling and Eyer (1988) and others pointed to the detrimental sequelae of "chronic arousal" (Chrousos and Gold, 1992, 1998; McEwen and Stellar, 1993; Schulkin et al., 1994; Goldstein, 1995a, b). Sterling and Eyer were concerned about widespread chronic fatigue due to overstimulation. They endorsed practices that enhance calmness, such as transcendental meditation and community-based attachments.

One result of chronic arousal is the overactivation of allostatic anticipatory mechanisms, feedforward mechanisms, and eventual allostatic overload (McEwen, 1998a, b; Koob and Le Moal, 2001). The concept of allostasis emphasizes multiple systems in both the adaptive phase and the decline in pathology. The gradual decline of end-organ systems reflects allostatic overload, through their chronic overactivation and exaggerated expression. Moreover, long periods of physiological regulation are emphasized under allostatic regulation, in addition to cephalic

innervation of physiological functions (within the rubric of allostatic regulation). In addition, the concept of allostasis was invoked to account for the way in which one lives; whether one smokes, drinks, or uses psychotropic drugs; how one eats; whether one is defending against deadly viruses.

Allostasis and Cortisol—The Hormone of Energy Metabolism

Cortisol, as I have indicated, has permissive, stimulatory, suppressive, and preparative functions in orchestrating bodily viability to acute challenges (Ingle, 1952; Munck et al., 1984; McEwen, 1998a, b; Sapolsky et al., 2001). Glucocorticoids regulate cardiovascular, metabolic, and neural adaptive functions in the short-term context in a wide variety of ways (Sapolsky et al., 2000).

Social rank is one instance in which cortisol is clearly linked to behavioral expression. Social ranking and attachment have profound effects on internal physiology (Herbert, 1993; Gunnar, 1998; Sapolsky, 2000). In addition, cognitive factors, such as determining what is a real threat from what might not be, can determine cortisol levels; baboons who were less able to determine the real from the not real had higher levels of cortisol and perhaps chronic arousal (figure C.1; Sapolsky, 2000). But more generally, baboons with elevated levels of cortisol were linked to a number of appraisal responses to danger; those with higher cortisol tended to be less likely to differentiate threatening and neutral stimuli, initiate a fight that can be won, differentiating winning and losing a fight, and less likely to express displaced aggression after losing a fight (Sapolsky, 2001). In rats, chronic elevated levels of glucocorticoids along with elevated levels of central CRH are associated with lower social dominance and defeat (Albeck et al., 1997).

Socioeconomic status and a mother's vulnerability to depression affect the levels of cortisol in children (figure C.2; Lupien et al., 2000). For example, children in Montreal with the lowest socioeconomic status had the highest level of cortisol (Lupien et al., 2000). Some factors, however, are unknown, including:

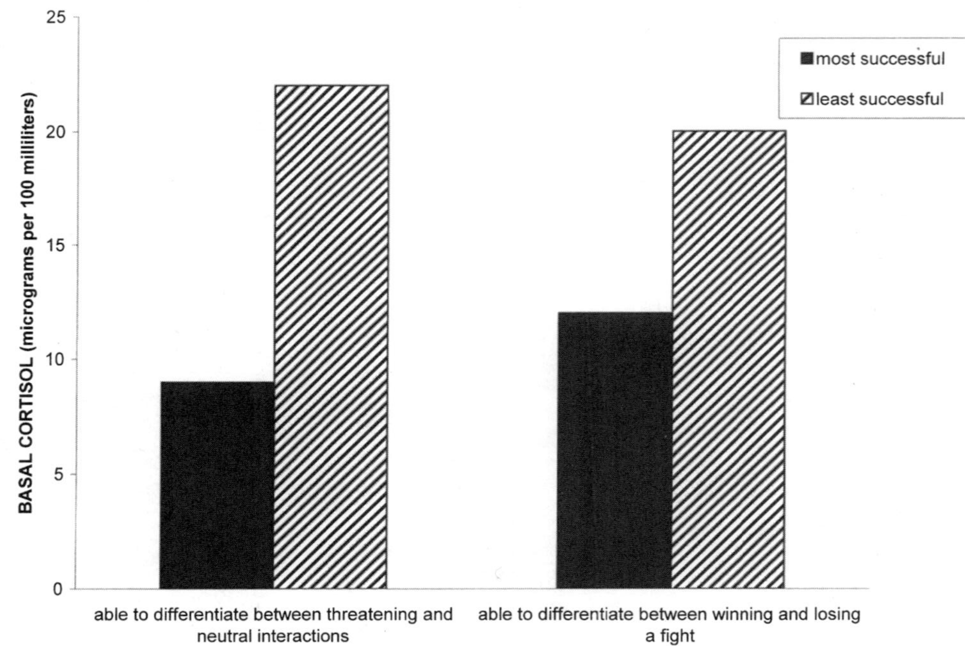

Figure C.1
Male baboons that are less able to determine the reality of a competitive situation have higher basal levels of cortisol (Sapolsky, 2000).

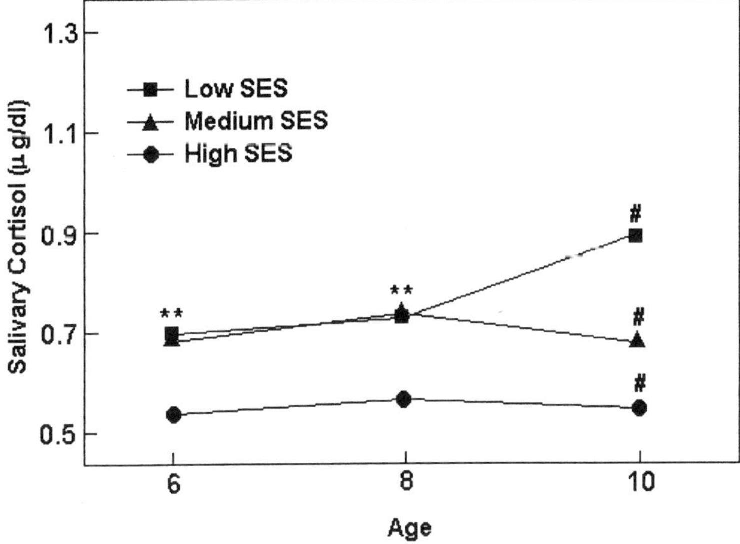

Figure C.2
Cortisol levels in low, medium, and high socioeconomic (SES) groups (Lupien et al., 2000).

nutritional status and fear at home and outside. These may also have an impact on the level of cortisol in this study.

Cortisol is *not* the molecule of fear or stress. Rather, cortisol is the molecule of energy metabolism, and fear is metabolically expensive. Because of its role in energy metabolism, cortisol levels are essential for normal brain function and the regulation of neuropeptides (Herbert, 1993) or neurotransmitters (e.g., Stutzman et al., 1998; Lucas et al., 1998b). In other words, cortisol is released in diverse behavioral, psychological, physiological, and environmental contexts. Cortisol facilitates a wide range of behavioral/psychological events by its effects on the brain (figure C.3) including cognitive functions (Lupien et al., 2002). Understanding these behavioral/psychological events relies on linking the glucocorticoid to the neuropeptides or neurotrans-

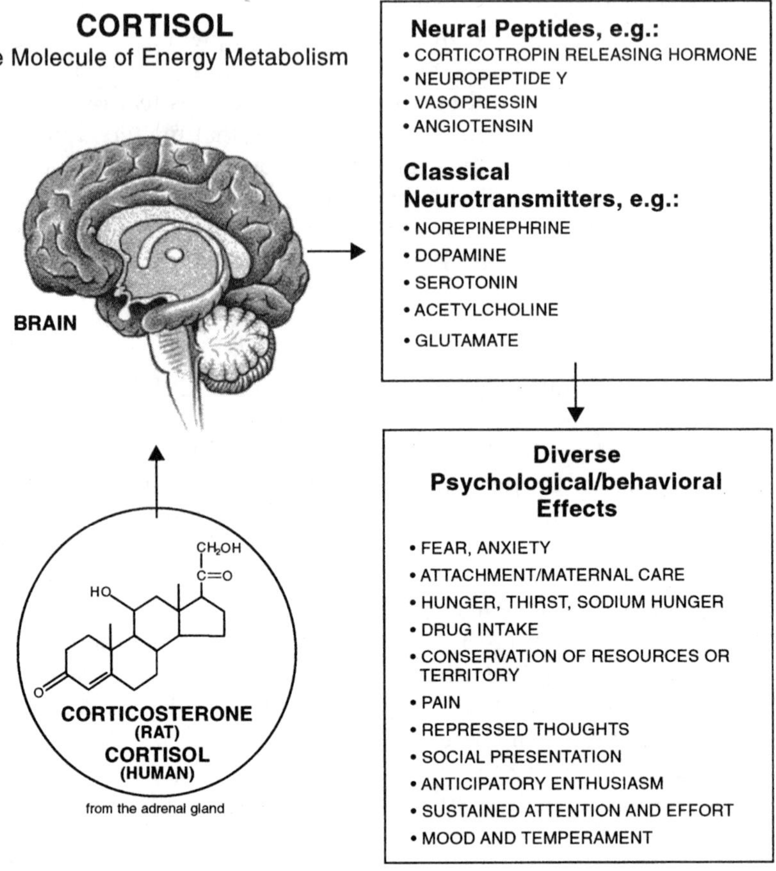

Figure C.3
The diverse effects of glucocorticoids on brain and behavioral/psychological functions. The structural depiction is of the rat's corticosterone (Erickson and Schulkin, unpublished).

mitters that are being synthesized in the brain within the environmental context that the animal is coping with.

Glucocorticoid levels can reflect appetitive states, such as thirst, hunger, sodium hunger, or states such as fear or excitement. It is not the level of cortisol per se that matters, but the effects of cortisol on the brain production of neurotransmitters such as serotonin and dopamine (e.g., Lowry et al., 2001), and neuropeptides such as angiotensin and CRH (e.g., Sumners et al., 1991; Makino et al., 1994a, b) in functional circuits.

Corticotropin-Releasing Hormone and the Amygdala

I have exaggerated the relative importance of CRH. I recognize that it is one peptide among many, and there are compensatory responses that would render CRH unimportant under a number of conditions.[1] Corticotropin-releasing hormone is just one of the peptides that underlie regulatory states such as fear. I have used it to make a point that covers a wide variety of research—fear, trauma, preterm delivery, and addiction. It is one important system among others in maintaining internal stability. A more complete picture will need to embrace the diverse neuropeptides and neurotransmitters that underlie homeostatic and allostatic regulation and that are regulated by internal physiological needs and external contexts.

Moreover, neither glucocorticoids nor CRH (nor the activation of the amygdala) are solely dedicated as signals of fear or adversity. Cortisol is the molecule of energy metabolism and has wide and diverse effects on the brain (see figure C.3). In addition, central CRH can elicit sodium ingestion, and it is important to bear in mind that this peptide is linked to cardiovascular regulation (Denton, 1982; Chrousos et al., 1998). Furthermore, using microdialysis, elevated CRH levels have been discerned in the central nucleus of the amygdala in rats during food ingestion (Merali et al., 1998). Food ingestion places one in

1. In addition, the role of the catecholamines should not be overlooked—see Dave Goldstein's (1995a, 2000) two important books.

a threatening situation—vigilance has to be maintained so as not to become a food source for something else.

That the amygdala is fundamentally tied to vigilance and attention (Whalen, 1998; Gallagher and Holland, 1994; Rosen and Schulkin, 1998; McGaugh, 2000; Davis and Whalen, 2001; Calder et al., 2001) has been recognized by several investigators (see also Flynn, 1972; Baron-Cohen et al., 1999; Schulkin, 2000; Emery et al., 2001). The expression of CRH within this region and others is linked to the animal's sense of adversity and attention to environmental cues (Cook, 2002). Neuropeptides / neurotransmitters regulated by steroid hormones play a fundamental role in the expression of central states.

Chronic Angst, Allostasis, and Pathology

McEwen and his colleagues (McEwen and Stellar, 1993; McEwen, 1998a, b, 1999; McEwen and Seeman, 1999) formulated and developed the terms *allostasis* and *allostatic overload* in an attempt to account for preserving physiological stability amid changing circumstances. For example, when uncertainty persists for long periods or is perceived as going beyond one's control, it results in negative consequences that my colleagues and I called *anticipatory angst* in an earlier paper (Schulkin et al., 1994). There is a plethora of animal and human data on the negative consequences to bodily and psychological health in such a circumstance. This occurs when normal physiological adaptation is run beyond what it was designed to tolerate.

The diverse physiological systems for maintaining bodily viability to acute challenges are reflected in mobilization of cardiovascular function, activation of metabolic fuels, activation of immune defense, and engagement of central nervous systems function (McEwen, 1998a, b; Sapolsky et al., 2000). But the chronic condition (allostatic state; Koob and Le Moal, 2001) can result in allostatic overload and cardiovascular, metabolic, immunological, and neuronal pathology.

Adaptation to uncertainty is a fact of life because uncertainty pervades life. In the short run, allostatic mechanisms can

provide physiological and behavioral resources that help maintain equilibrium. Unfortunately, these resources are finite. Chronic signals from physiological mediators (cytokines, cortisol, catecholamines, etc.) take their toll on bodily function, resulting in vulnerability to a variety of diseases such as those that concerned Sterling and Eyer (1988) and later McEwen and Seeman (1999; including hypertension, diabetes, atherosclerosis, bone loss, sleep disruption, disruption of immune and reproductive functions, inhibition of neurogenesis, aging process; Seeman et al., 2001). Vulnerability to these events can occur from prenatal events (Barker, 1997; Welberg and Seckl, 2001).

Within the literature, something beyond traditional conceptions of homeostasis was needed to account for regulatory events. To Selye and others (Goldstein, 1995a, b, 2000; Chrousos, 1998; Berntson and Cacioppo, 2000), the breakdown of systems was well-known and well-studied. Adaptation can only go so far in the attempt to maintain internal stability amid changing circumstances. The mechanisms for short-term regulation can lead to pathology when pushed beyond their adaptive time frames. To explain wide variation in physiological regulatory events, a biological basis of individual differences was noted.

Anticipatory regulation is a cognitive achievement and built into our brains (Gallistel, 1992; Schulkin, 2000). After all, evolution favored those who could not only react to events but also anticipate them. Thus, it is very reasonable to distinguish reactive from predictive homeostasis (Moore-Ede, 1986). Allostasis accounts for long-term responses—not simply short-term adaptations—and reflects feedforward and cephalic influences over behavioral and physiological events. The concept of allostasis forces one to broaden one's view of maintaining internal viability in changing and uncertain circumstances (but see Goldstein, 2000 for a very detailed depiction of homeostatic systems). But the concept also highlights the regulatory costs, in terms of the initial protective mechanisms and the longer-term damaging consequences of allostatic overload (e.g., the long-term changes in excitatory amino acid by chronic high levels of glucocorticoids; McEwen, 1999, 2001). The time scale in which to envision

regulatory events by the use of the concept of allostasis is expanded quite considerably. What occurs quite naturally is the link between normal variation in use and descent into overload. The mediators of allostasis are different from the standard mediators of homeostasis such as pH, osmolarity, oxygen, and body temperature. Standard homeostatic mediators are less variable in the context of adaptation and bodily viability.

Evolutionary Considerations

Earlier accounts of allostasis overlooked our evolutionary context. When in our evolutionary past have we had prolonged periods of restfulness (Wingfield and Ramenofsky, 1997; Wingfield and Romero, 2001)? We need to take evolution into account as we consider homeostasis, stress, allostasis, and allostatic overload. For example, high levels of corticosterone can favor or support animals in a wide variety of contexts; in a number of species, levels of corticosterone or cortisol can be adjusted in the short term by both behavioral and physiological means (Wingfield and Ramenofsky, 1997). In the short term, glucocorticoids are protective and facilitate normal physiological and behavioral adaptation. But in the long run, high levels of corticosterone interfere with a number of regulatory functions (McEwen, 1998a, b, 2000).

Constant stimulation is not new; our increasing life expectancy is. Tissue declines with age. Rousseau (1762) asked the question, "Why are men in chains when they are born free?" Perhaps an analogous question is, Why is there so much worry when we have so much? One reason is that if we don't find worry, we are very good at constructing it. This is not just a piece of pathology.

The dominant theme that led to the concept of allostasis is that chronic arousal of the brain drives increases in regulatory physiology to a point beyond what is acceptable for normal function. Evolution favored a number of specialized mechanisms in the brain in regulating both behavioral and physiological functions. When activated inappropriately, normal

maintenance turns into pathological vulnerability and expression (figure C.4).

Allostasis—A Plausible Concept

The concept of allostasis has brought about new research under the rubric of a concept that is useful because it provides a plausible hypothesis for connecting what might seem to be unrelated events. For example, we now have discussions about allostasis, allostatic state, and allostatic overload in the context of drug use and sensitization (Koob and Le Moal, 2001) and in preterm delivery of babies (Schulkin, 1999a). The larger rubric is that of regulatory physiology, and both the concepts of homeostasis and allostasis are nominally related to physiological function. There is no isomorphic relationship between the concepts and the regulatory physiological systems.

The induction of neuropeptides by steroids is not an aberration in the behavioral activation that serves physiological and long-term viability. These events, contrary to how positive induction (feedforward mechanisms) is usually or has been construed (Goldstein, 1995a, b, 2000), are not necessarily instances of pathological breakdown and perhaps not any more vulnerable to dysfunction (Korte, 2001) than other regulatory systems. They represent one mechanism by which the brain orchestrates behavioral events that sustain the animal. Negative restraint is only one endocrine mechanism, and positive induction is not an aberration. In a number of regulatory events, there are feedforward mechanisms that underlie the central state.

Allostatic regulation can reflect short-term needs, such as avoiding predators and finding food, as well as intermediate needs, such as conservation of social space or environmental defense. Allostatic regulation is also evident in longer-term needs, such as successful reproduction. In each of these cases, the steroid acts to facilitate or sustain neuropeptide expression—feedforward mechanisms (Pfaff, 1980; Herbert, 1993; Schulkin, 1999a).

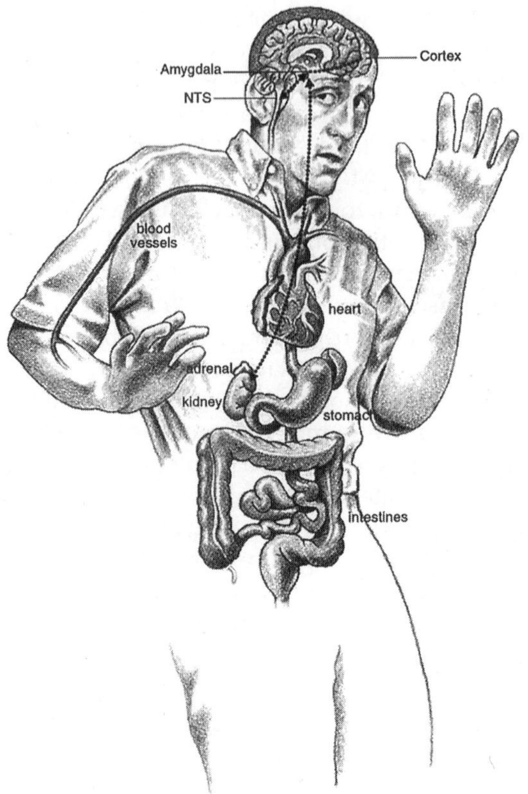

Figure C.4
Cortical, amygdala, brainstem (e.g., solitary nucleus, NTS), and peripheral organs (Yansen and Schulkin, unpublished).

Balancing internal demands with external contexts (what is available, is it safe, what is the probability of being eaten?) is an everyday occurrence for most species. This is achieved by the integration of a number of appraisal mechanisms and balancing competing motivations (McFarland, 1991; Berntson and Cacioppo, 2000) that are then integrated within the nervous system. Social contact, approach, and avoidance mechanisms reflect in part the expression and regulation of neuropeptide and receptor sites by steroid hormones, many of which are important in regulating social behaviors (Insel, 1992; Bridges and Freemark, 1995; Carter et al., 1999). In turn, social behaviors are regulating internal physiology (Hinde, 1968, 1970; Levine, 1975; Levine et al., 1989; Blass et al., 1995; Gunnar and Davis, 2001). The search for social contact and closeness can reduce the level of cortisol and decrease the central nervous system production of CRH, for example, in extrahypothalamic sites. Social engagement is the way by which contact and cooperation serve more than one individual, both in terms of short- and long-term goals (mothers and their offspring; Hofer, 1994; Hofer and Sullivan, 2001). Regulatory physiology is broad in the context of trying to maintain internal viability.

Concluding Remarks

It is beneficial to look at the context in which the terms *homeostasis* and *allostasis* are used in our scientific lexicon. Both homeostasis and allostasis function as heuristics for inquiry, somewhat like other broad biological categories (e.g., *adaptation*). They are scientific concepts, but are not as clear as one would like them to be. Nonetheless, they are useful, for they guide inquiry and provoke a degree of musing.

One could argue that the concept of homeostasis was construed too narrowly, that homeostasis can reflect both predictive and reactive mechanisms (Moore-Ede, 1986), both short-term and long-term regulation of the internal milieu. In fact, it does. The concept of allostasis here is presented in the context of what the philosopher Peirce used to call "a humble argument" (see

the new anthology of his works, 1992–98). One looks at the field and realizes that in the context of what is known about the anatomical connectivity of peripheral sites with the central nervous system (and from brainstem to cortex; Blessing, 1997), that another concept, one expanded beyond what homeostasis has meant to investigators, was necessary to account for emerging data of regulatory systems. It is in this spirit that allostasis is suggested for understanding regulatory physiology and behavioral or systems neuroscience.

Concepts like homeostasis and allostasis function in the context of regulatory physiology. In this great age of molecular biology, whole-body physiological analysis is essential and integrative. These force us to consider end-organ systems together as functioning wholes in maintaining bodily health. They serve to unify and bring into perspective a wide range of physiological data. These concepts play a functional role in biological inquiry and insofar as they further inquiry into understanding bodily stability amid change, they have played an important role.

References

Achermann, P., Borbely, A. A. (1994). Simulation of daytime vigilance by the additive interaction of a homeostatic and a circadian process. *Biol. Cybern.* 71: 115–121.

Achermann, P., Dijk, D. J., Brunner, D. P., and Borbely, A. A. (1993). A model of human sleep homeostasis based on EEG slow-wave activity: quantitative comparison of data and simulations. *Brain Res. Bull.* 31: 97–113.

Adamec, R. (1997). Transmitter systems involved in neural plasticity underlying increased anxiety and defense—Implications for understanding anxiety following traumatic stress. *Neurosci. Biobehav. Rev.* 21: 755–765.

Ader, R., and Grota, L. J. (1969). Effects of early experience on adrenocortical reactivity. *Physiol. Behav.* 4: 303–305.

Adinoff, B., Anton, R., Linnoila, M., Guidotti, A., Nemeroff, C. B., and Bissette, G. (1996). Cerebrospinal fluid concentrations of corticotropin-releasing hormone (CRH) and diazepam-binding inhibitor (DBI) during alcohol withdrawal and abstinence. *Neuropsychopharmacology* 15: 288–295.

Adler, N. E., Boyce, W. T., Chesney, M. A., Folkman, S., and Syme, S. L. (1993). Socioeconomic inequalities in health: No easy solution. *JAMA* 269: 3140–3145.

Adler, N. E., Boyce, T., Chesney, M. A., Cohen, S., Folkman, S., Kahn, R. L., and Syme, L. (1994). Socioeconomic status and health: The challenge gradient. *Am. Psychol.* 49: 15–24.

Adolph, E. F. (1943). *Physiological Regulations.* Lancaster, Pa.: Jaques Cattell Press.

Adolph, E. F. (1947). Urges to eat and drink in rats. *Am. J. Physiol.* 151: 110–125.

Adolphs, R., Tranel, D., Damasio, H., and Damasio, A. (1994). Impaired recognition of emotion in facial expressions following bilateral damage to the human amygdala. *Nature,* 372: 669–672.

Adolphs, R., Tranel, D., Damasio, H., and Damasio, A. R. (1995). Fear and the human amygdala. *J. Neurosci.* 15: 5879–5891.

Aeschbach, D., Cajochen, C., Landolt, H., and Borbely, A. A. (1996). Homeostatic sleep regulation in habitual short sleepers and long sleepers. *Am. J. Physiol.* 270: R41–R53.

Aggleton, J. P. (ed.) (1992). *The Amygdala: Neurobiological Aspects of Emotion, Memory, and Mental Dysfunction.* New York: Wiley-Liss.

Aggleton, J. P. (ed.) (1995/2000). *The Amygdala: A Functional Analysis.* 2nd ed. Oxford: Oxford University Press.

Aggleton, J. P., and Mishkin, M. (1986). The amygdala: Sensory gateway to the emotions. In *Emotion: Theory, Research, and Experience,* edited by R. Plutchik and H. Kellerman. Orlando, Fla.: Academic Press.

Aguilera, G., Diehl, C. R., and Nikodemova, M. (2001). Regulation of pituitary corticotropin releasing hormone receptors. *Peptides* 22: 769–774.

Aguirre, A. A., Balazs, G. H., Sparker, T. R., and Gross, T. S. (1995). Adrenal and hematological responses to stress in juvenile green turtles (*Chelonia mydas*) with and without fibropapillomas. *Physiol. Zool.* 68: 831–854.

Ahmed, S. H., and Koob, G. F. (1997). Cocaine, but not food-seeking behavior is reinstated by stress after extinction. *Psychopharmacology* 32: 289–295.

Ahmed, S. H., and Koob, G. F. (1998). Transition from moderate to excessive drug intake: Change in hedonic set point. *Science* 282: 298–300.

Ahmed, M. S., Cemerkic, B., and Agbas, A. (1992). Properties and functions of human placental opioid system. *Life Sci.* 50: 83–97.

Ahmed, S. H., Walker, J. R., and Koob, G. F. (2000). Persistent increase in the motivation to take heroin in rats with history of drug escalation. *Neuropsychopharmacology* 22: 413–421.

Albeck, D. S., McKittrick, C. R., Blanchard, D. C., Blanchard, R. J., Nikulina, J., McEwen, B. S., and Sakai, R. R. (1997). Chronic social stress alters levels of corticotropin-releasing factor and arginine vasopressin mRNA in rat brain. *J. Neurosci.* 17: 4895–4903.

Albers, H. E., and Cooper, T. T. (1995). Effects of testosterone on the behavioral response to arginine vasopressin microinjected into the central gray and septum. *Peptides* 16: 269–273.

Albers, H. E., and Rawls, S. (1989). Coordination of hamster lordosis and flank marking behavior: Role of arginine vasopressin within the medial preoptic-anterior hypothalamus. *Brain Res. Bull.* 23: 105–109.

Albers, H. E., Liou, S. Y., and Ferris, C. F. (1988). Testosterone alters the behavioral response of the medial preoptic-anterior hypothalamus to microinjection of arginine vasopressin in the hamster. *Brain Res.* 456: 382–386.

Alberts, A. C., Jackintell, L. A., and Phillips, J. A. (1994). Effects of chemical and visual exposure to adults on growth, hormones, and behavior of juvenile green iguanas. *Physiol. Behav.* 55: 987–992.

Alexander, G. M., Packard, M. G., and Hines, M. (1994). Testosterone has rewarding affective properties in male rats: Implications for the biological basis of sexual motivation. *Behav. Neurosci.* 108: 424–428.

Alheid, G. F., De Olmos, J., and Beltramino, C. A. (1996). Amygdala and extended amygdala. In *The Rat Nervous System.* 2nd ed., edited by G. Paxinos. San Diego: Academic Press.

Alheid, G. F., Beltramino, C. A., De Olmos, J. S., Forbes, M. S., Swanson, D. J., and Heimer, L. (1998). The neuronal organization of the supracapsular

part of the stria terminalis in the rat: The dorsal component of the extended amygdala. *Neuroscience* 84: 967–996.

Allen, D. M., and Tarnowski, K. J. (1989). Depressive characteristics of physically abused children. *J. Abnorm. Child Psychol.* 17: 1–11.

Allen, L. H. (1982). Calcium bioavailability and absorption: A review. *Am. J. Clin. Nutr.* 35: 783–808.

Altemus, M., Smith, M. A., Diep, V., Aulakh, C. S., and Murphy, D. L. (1994). Increased mRNA for corticotropin-releasing hormone in the amygdala of fawn-hooded rats: A potential animal model of anxiety. *Anxiety* 1: 251–257.

Altman, J., Everitt, B. J., Glautier, S., Markou, A., Nutt, D., Oretti, R., Phillips, G. D., and Robbins, T. W. (1996). The biological, social, and clinical bases of drug addiction: Commentary and debate. *Psychopharmacology* 125: 285–345.

Altschuler, S. M., Ferenci, D. A., Lynn, R. B., and Miselis, R. R. (1991). Representation of the cecum in the lateral dorsal motor nucleus of the vagus nerve and commissural subnucleus fractus solutarii in the rat. *J. Comp. Neurol.* 283: 261–274.

Anders, T. F., Sachar, E. J., Kream, J., Roffwarg, H. P., and Hellman, L. (1970). Behavioral state and plasma cortisol response in the human newborn. *Pediatrics* 46: 532–537.

Antoch, M. P., Song, E. J., Chang, A. M., Vitaterna, M. H., Zhao, Y., Wilsbacher, L. D., Sangoram, A. M., King, D. P., Pinto, L. H., and Takahashi, J. S. (1997). Functional identification of the mouse circadian clock gene by transgenic BAC rescue. *Cell* 89: 641–653.

Antunes-Rodrigues, J., Favaretto, A. L., Ballejo, G., Gutkowska, J., and McCann, S. M. (1996). ANP as a neuroendocrine modulator of body fluid homeostasis. *Rev. Braz. Biol.* 56: 221–231.

Araneo, B., and Daynes, R. (1995). Dehydropiandrosterone functions as more than an antiglucocorticoid in preserving immunocompetence after thermal injury. *Endocrinology* 136: 393–401.

Arborelius, L., Skelton, K. H., Thruvukraman, K. V., Plotsky, P. M., Schultz, D. W., and Owens, M. J. (2001). Chronic administration of the selective corticotropin-releasing factor 1 receptor antagonist. CP-154.526: Behavioral, endocrine, and neurochemical effect in the rat. *J. Pharm. Exp. Ther.* 294: 588–597.

Arguelles, J., Brime, J. I., Lopez-Sela, P., Perillan, C., and Vijande, M. (2000). Adult offspring long-term effects of high salt and water intake during pregnancy. *Horm. Behav.* 37: 156–162.

Arnold, M. B. (1969). Emotion, motivation, and the limbic system. *Ann. N.Y. Acad. Sci.* 159: 1041–1058.

Aromaa, A., Raitasalo, R., and Reunanen, A. (1994). Depression and cardiovascular diseases. *Acta Psychiatr. Scand. Suppl.* 377: 77–82.

Aronsson, G. (1999). Influence of worklife on public health. *Scand. J. Work Environ. Health* 25: 597–604.

Aschner, M. (1999). Manganese homeostasis in the CNS. *Environ. Res.* 80: 105–109.

Ashby, B. (1998). Co-expression of prostaglandin receptors with opposite effects. *Biochem. Pharmacol.* 55: 239–246.

Axelrod, J., and Reisine, T. D. (1984). Stress hormones: Their interaction and regulation. *Science* 224: 452–459.

Axelson, D. A., Doraiswamy, P. M., McDonald, W. M., Boyko, O. B., Tupler, L. A., Patterson, L. J., Nemeroff, C. B., Ellinwood, E. H. Jr., and Krishman, K. R. (1993). Hypercortisolemia and hippocampal changes in depression. *Psychiatry Res.* 47: 163–173.

Azmitia, E. C. (1999). Serotonin neurons, neuroplasticity, and homeostasis of neural tissue. *Neuropsychopharmacology* 21: 33S–45S.

Baciu, I., and Arama, O. (1994). Integrative cybernetic model of oxygen homeostasis. *Rom. J. Physiol.* 31: 25–45.

Bagdy, G., Calogero, A. E., Szemeredi, K., Chrousos, G. P., and Gold, P. W. (1990). Effects of cortisol treatment on brain and adrenal corticotropin-releasing hormone (CRH) content and other parameters regulated by CRH. *Regul. Peptides* 31: 83–92.

Baker D. G., West, S. A., Nicholson, W. E., Ekhator, N. N., Kasckow, J. W., Hill, K. K., Bruce, A. B., Orth, D. N., and Geracioti, T. D. Jr. (1999). Serial CSF corticotropin-releasing hormone levels and adrenocortical activity in combat veterans with post-traumatic stress disorder. *Am. J. Psychiatry* 156: 585–588.

Bakshi, V. P., and Kalin, N. H. (2000). Corticotropin-releasing hormone and animal models of anxiety: Gene-environment interactions. *Biol. Psychiatry* 48: 1175–1198.

Bakshi, C. P., Smith-Roe, S., Newman, S. M., Grigoriadis, D. E., and Kain, N. H. (2002). Reduction of stress-induced behavior by antagonism of corticotropin releasing hormone CRH receptors in lateral septum or CRH receptors in amygdala. *J. Neurosci.* 22: 2926–2935.

Balasko, M., and Cabanac, M. (1998). Behavior of juvenile lizards *(Iguana iguana)* in a conflict between temperature regulation and palatable food. *Brain Behav. Evol.* 52: 257–262.

Bale, T. L., Contarino, A., Smith, G. W., Chan, R., Gold, L. H., Sawchenko, P. E., Koob, G. E., Vale, W. W., and Lee, K. E. (2000). Mice deficient for corticotropin-releasing hormone receptor-2 display anxiety-like behavior and are hypertensive to stress. *Nat. Genet.* 24: 410–414.

Bale, T. L., Davis, A. M., Auger, A. P., Dorsa, D. M., and McCarthy, M. M. (2001). CNS region-specific oxytocin receptor expression: Importance in regulation of anxiety and sex behavior. *J. Neurosci.* 21: 2546–2552.

Bale, T. L., Picetti, R., Contarino, A., Koob, G. F., Vale, W. W., and Lee, K. (2001). Mice deficient for both corticotropin releasing factor receptor 1 and 2 have

an impaired stress response and display sexually dichotomous anxiety-like behavior. *J. Neurosci.* 22: 193–199.

Balleine, B. W., and Dickinson, A. (1998). Goal-directed instrumental action: Contingency and incentive learning and their cortical substrates. *Neuropharmacology* 37: 407–419.

Balm, P. H. M. (1999). *Stress Physiology in Animals.* Sheffield, UK: Sheffield Academic Press.

Balthazart, J., Reid, J., Absil, P., Foidart, A., and Ball, G. F. (1995). Appetitive as well as consummatory aspects of male behavior in quail are activated by androgens and estrogens. *Behav. Neurosci.* 109: 485–501.

Banki, C. M., Bissette, G., Arato, M., O'Conner, L., and Nemeroff, C. B. (1987). CSF corticotropin-releasing factor-like immunoreactivity in depression and schizophrenia. *Am. J. Psychiatry* 144: 873–877.

Baram, T. Z., Hirsch, E., Snead, O. C., III, and Schultz, L. (1992). Corticotropin-releasing hormone-induced seizures in infant rats originate in the amygdala. *Ann. Neurol.* 31: 488–494.

Bard, P. (1939). Central nervous mechanisms for emotional behavior patterns in animals. *Res. Nerv. Ment. Dis.* 20: 190–216.

Barker, D. J. (1997). The fetal origins of coronary heart disease. *Acta Paediatr. Suppl.* 422: 78–82.

Barkow, J. H., Cosmides, L., and Tooby, J. (1992). *The Adapted Mind.* New York: Oxford University Press.

Barlow, D. H. (1997). Anxiety disorders, comorbid substance abuse, and benzodiazepine discontinuation: Implications for treatment. *NIDA Res. Monogr.* 172: 33–51.

Barnes, G. M., and Windle, M. (1987). Family factors in adolescent alcohol and drug abuse. *Pediatrician* 14(1–2): 13–18.

Baron-Cohen, S., Ring, H. A., Moriatry, J., Schmi, B., Costa, D., and Ell, P. (1999). Social intelligence in the normal and autistic brain. *Br. J. Psychiatry* 4: 113–123.

Barrot, M., Marinelli, M., Abrous, D. N., Rouge-Pont, F., Le Moal, M., and Piazza, P. V. (2000). The dopaminergic hyper-responsiveness of the shell of the nucleus accumbens is hormone-dependent. *Eur. J. Neurosci.* 12: 973–979.

Bartley, S. H. (1970). The homeostatic and comfort perceptual systems. *J. Psychol.* 75: 157–162.

Bauman, D. E. (2000). Regulation of nutrient partitioning during lactation: Homeostasis and homeorhesis revisited. In *Ruminant Physiology: Digestion, Metabolism, Growth and Reproduction,* edited by P. J. Cronje. New York: CABI Publishing.

Bauman, D. E., and Currie, W. B. (1980). Partitioning of nutrients during pregnancy and lactation: A review of mechanisms involving homeostasis and homeorhesis. *J. Dairy Sci.* 63: 1514–1529.

Bayliss, W. M., and Starling, E. H. (1902). The mechanism of pancreatic secretion. *J. Physiol.* 28: 325–353.

Beach, F. A. (1942). Central nervous mechanisms involved in the reproductive behavior of vertebrates. *Psychol. Bull.* 39: 200–206.

Beach, F. A. (1947). A review of physiological and psychological studies of sexual behavior in mammals. *Physiol. Rev.* 27: 240–307.

Beatty, W. W., Katzung, V. M., Moreland, V. J., and Nixon, S. J. (1995). Neuropsychological performance of recently abstinent alcoholics and cocaine abusers. *Drug Alcohol Depend.* 31: 247–253.

Beaulieu, S., DiPaolo, T., Cote, T., and Barden, N. (1987). Participation of the central amygdaloid nucleus in the response to adrenocorticotropin secretion to immobilization stress: Opposing roles of the noradrenergic and dopaminergic systems. *Neuroendocrinology* 45: 37–46.

Beaumont, W. [1833] (1959). *Experiments and Observations on the Gastric Juice and Physiology of Digestion.* Plattsburg: F. P. Allen. Reprint, New York: Dover Publications.

Bechara, A., Damasio, A., and Damasio, H. (2000). Emotion, decision-making, and the orbitofrontal cortex. *Cereb. Cortex.* 10: 295–307.

Beck, M., and Galef, B. G. Jr. (1989). Social influences on the selection of a protein-sufficient diet by Norway rats *(Ratus norvegicus). J Comp. Med.* 103: 132–139.

Becker, J. B., Rudick, C. N., and Jenkins, W. J. (2000). The role of dopamine in the nucleus accumbens and striatum during sexual behavior in the female rat. *J. Neurosci.* 21: 3236–3241.

Beebe-Center, J. G. (1932). *The Psychology of Pleasantness and Unpleasantness.* New York: D. van Nostrand.

Behan, D. P., De Souza, E. B., Lowry, P. J., Potter, E., Sawchenko, P., and Vale, W. W. (1995). Corticotropin-releasing factor (CRF) binding protein: A novel regulator of CRF and related peptides. *Front. Neuroendocrinol.* 16: 362–382.

Behan, D. P., Grigoridalis, D. E., Lovenberg, T., Chalmers, D., Heinrichs, S., Liaw, C., and De Souza, E. B. (1996). Neurobiology of corticotropin-releasing factor (CRF) receptors and CRF-binding protein: Implications for the treatment of CNS disorders. *Mol. Psychiatry* 1: 265–277.

Bell, I. R., Jasnoski, M. L., Kagan, J., and King, D. S. (1990). Is allergic rhinitis more frequent in young adults with extreme shyness? A preliminary study. *Psychosom. Med.* 52: 517–525.

Bell, I. R., Martino, G. M., Meredith, K. E., Schwartz, G. E., Siani, M. M., and Morrow, F. D. (1993). Vascular disease risk factors, urinary free cortisol, and health histories in older adults: Shyness and gender interactions. *Biol. Psychol.* 35: 37–49.

Bell, M. E., Bhatnagar, S., Liang, J., Soriano, L., Nagy, T. R., and Dallman, M. F. (2000). Voluntary sucrose ingestion, like corticosterone replacement, prevents metabolic deficits of adrenalectomy. *J. Neuroendocrinol.* 12: 461–470.

Bell, S. M., Reynolds, J. G., Thiele, T. E., Gan, J., Figlewicz, D. P., and Woods, S. C. (1998). Effect of third intracerebroventricular injections of corticotropin-releasing factor (CRF) on ethanol drinking and food intake. *Psychopharmacology* 139: 128–135.

Benington, J. H., and Heller, H. C. (1995). Restoration of brain energy metabolism as the function of sleep. *Prog. Neurobiol.* 45: 347–360.

Bennett, M. C., Mlady, G. W., Fleshner, M., and Rose, G. M. (1996). Synergy between chronic corticosterone and sodium azide treatments in producing a spatial learning deficit and inhibiting cytochrome oxidase activity. *Proc. Natl. Acad. Sci. USA* 93: 1330–1334.

Beral, V., Bauks, G., Reeves, G., and Wallis, M. (1997). Hormone replacement therapy and high incidence of breast cancer between mammographic screens. *Lancet* 349: 1103–1104.

Berczi, I. (1997). The stress concept: An historical perspective of Hans Selye's contributions. In: *Stress, Stress Hormones, and the Immune System,* edited by J. C. Buckingham, G. E. Gillies, and A. M. Cowell. New York: John Wiley and Sons.

Bergant, A. M., Kirchler, H., Heim, K., Daxenbichler, G., Herold, M., and Schrocksnadel, H. (1998). Childbirth as a biological model for stress? *Gynecol. Obstet. Invest.* 45: 181–185.

Berke, J. D., Paletzki, R. F., Aronson, G. A., Hyman, S. E., and Gerfen, C. R. (1998). A complex program of striatal gene expression induced by dopaminergic stimulation. *Neuroscience* 18: 5301–5310.

Berkowitz, G. S., Lapinski, R. H., Lockwood, C. J., Florio, P., Blackmore-Prince, C., and Petraglia, F. (1996). Corticotropin-releasing factor and its binding protein: Maternal serum levels in term and preterm deliveries. *Am. J. Obstet. Gynecol.* 174: 1477–1483.

Bernal, B., Ardila, A., and Bateman, J. R. (1994). Cognitive impairments in adolescent drug-abusers. *Int. J. Neurosci.* 75: 203–212.

Bernard, C. (1856/1974). Influence du grand sympathique sur la sensibilities et sur la calorification. *C. R. Soc. Biol. (Paris)* 1852: 162–164.

Bernard, C. (1856/1985). *Memoir on the Pancreas.* New York: Academic Press.

Bernard, C. (1859). *Leçons sur les propriétés physiologiques et les alterations pathologiques de l'organisme.* Paris: Ballieres.

Bernard, C. (1865/1957). *An Introduction to the Study of Experimental Medicine.* New York: Dover Press.

Bernard, C. (1878). *Leçons sur les phenomenones de la vie communs aux animaux et aux vegetaux.* Paris: Ballieres.

Bernstein, I. L., and Woods, S. C. (1980). Ontogeny of cephalic insulin release by the rat. *Physiol. Behav.* 24: 529–532.

Berntson, G. G., and Cacioppo, J. T. (2000). From homeostasis to allopdynamic regulation. In *Handbook of Psychophysiology,* edited by J. T. Caccioppo, L. G. Tassinary, and G. G. Bernston. Cambridge: Cambridge University Press.

Berridge, C. W., and Dunn, A. J. (1989). Restraint-stress-induced changes in exploratory behavior appear to be mediated by norepinephrine-stimulated release of CRF. *J. Neurosci.* 9: 3513–3521.

Berridge, K. C. (1996). Food reward: Brain substrates of wanting and liking. *Neurosci. Biobehav. Rev.* 20: 1–25.

Berridge, K. C. (2000). Measuring hedonic impact in animals and infants: Microstructure of affective taste reactivity patterns. *Neurosci. Biobehav. Rev.* 4: 173–198.

Berridge, K. C., and Grill, H. J. (1983). Alternating ingestive and aversive consummatory responses suggest a two-dimensional analysis of palatability in rats. *Behav. Neurosci.* 97: 563–573.

Berridge, K. C., and Robinson, T. E. (1998). What is the role of dopamine in reward: Hedonic impact, reward learning, or incentive salience? *Brain Res. Rev.* 28: 309–369.

Berridge, K. C., and Schulkin, J. (1989). Palatability shift of a salt associated incentive drive associated during sodium depletion. *Q. J. Exp. Psychol.* 41: 121–138.

Berridge, K. C., and Valenstein, E. S. (1991). What psychological process mediates feeding evoked by electricial stimulation of the lateral hypothalamus? *Behav. Neurosci.* 105: 3–14.

Berridge, K. C., Flynn, F. W., Schulkin, J., and Grill, H. J. (1984). Sodium depletion enhances salt palatability in rats. *Behav. Neurosci.* 98: 652–660.

Berry, J., van Gorp, W. G., Herzberg, D. S., Hinkin, C., Boone, K., Steinman, L., and Wilkins, J. N. (1993). Neuropsychological deficits in abstinent cocaine abusers: Preliminary findings after two weeks of abstinence. *Drug Alcohol Depend.* 32: 231–237.

Berthoud, H. R., and Powley, T. L. (1992). Vagal afferent innervation of the rat fundic stomach: Morphological characterization of the gastric tension receptor. *J. Comp. Neurol.* 319: 261–276.

Berthoud, H. R., Bereiter, D. A., Trimble, E. R., Siegel, E. G., and Jeanrenaud, B. (1981). Cephalic phase, reflex insulin secretion. *Diabetologica* 20: 393–401.

Berthoud, H. R., Fox, E. A., and Powley, T. L. (1991). Abdominal pathways and central origin of rat vagal fibers that stimulate gastric acid. *Gastroenterology* 100: 627–637.

Beuving, G., Jones, R. B., and Blokhuis, H. J. (1989). Adrenocortical and heterophil/lymphocyte responses to challenge in hens showing short or long tonic immobility reactions. *Br. Poult. Sci.* 30: 175–184.

Beyenbach, K. W. (1986). Unresolved questions of renal magnesium homeostasis. *Magnesium* 5: 234–247.

Bhatnagar, S., Bell, M. E., Liang, J., Soriano, L., Nagy, T. R., and Dallman, M. F. (2000). Corticosterone facilitates saccharin intake in adrenalectomized rats: Does corticosterone increase stimulus salience? *J. Neuroendocrinol.* 12: 453–460.

Bindra, D. (1969). A unified interpretation of emotions and motivation. *Ann. N.Y. Acad. Sci.* 159: 1071–1083.

Bindra, D. (1978). How adaptive behavior is produced: A perceptual-motivational alternative to response reinforcement. *Behav. Brain Sci.* 1: 41–91.

Bisits, A., Madsen, G., McLean, M., O'Callaghan, S., Smith, R., and Giles, W. (1998). Corticotropin-releasing hormone: A biochemical predictor of preterm delivery in a pilot randomized trial of the treatment of preterm labor. *Am. J. Obstet. Gynecol.* 178: 862–866.

Bittencourt, J. C., and Sawchenko, P. E. (2000). Do centrally administered neuropeptides access cognate receptors? An analysis in the central corticotropin-releasing factor system. *J. Neurosci.* 20: 1142–1156.

Bjorntorp, P. (1990). "Portal" adipose tissue as a generator of risk factors for cardiovascular disease and diabetes. *Atherosclerosis* 10: 493–496.

Black, D. M., Cummings, S. R., Karpf, D. B., Cauley, J. A., Thompson, D. E., Nevitt, M. C., Bauer, D. C., Genault, H. K., Haskell, W. L., Marcus, R., et al. (1996). Randomized trial of effect of alendronate on risk of fracture in women with existing vertebral fractures. Fracture Intervention Trial Research Group. *Lancet* 348: 1535–1541.

Blagden, C. (1775). Experiments and observations in an heated room. *Philos. Trans. R. Soc. Lond. B Biol. Sci.* 65: 11–123.

Blair, R. J., Morris, J. S., Frith, C. D., Perrett, D. I., and Dolan, R. J. (1999). Dissociable neural responses to facial expressions of sadness and anger. *Brain* 122: 883–893.

Blass, E. M. (1976). *The Psychobiology of Curt Richter.* Baltimore: York Press.

Blass, E. M., Shide, D. J., Zaw-Mon, C., and Sorrentino, J. (1995). Mother as shield: Differential effects of contact and nursing on pain responsivity in infant rats: Evidence for nonopioid mediation. *Behav. Neurosci.* 109: 342–353.

Blessing, W. W. (1997). Inadequate frameworks for understanding bodily homeostasis. *Trends Neurosci.* 20: 235–239.

Bloch, H. (1989). François Magendie, Claude Bernard, and the interrelation of science, history, and philosophy. *South. Med. J.* 82: 1259–1261.

Bobak, M., and Marmot, M. (1996). East-West mortality divide and its potential explanations: Proposed research agenda. *Br. Med. J.* 312: 421–425.

Bobak, M., Pikhart, H., Hertzman, C., Rose, R., and Marmot, M. (1998). Socioeconomic factors, perceived control, and self-report health in Russia. A cross-sectional survey. *Soc. Sci. Med.* 47: 269–279.

Bocking, A. D., Challis, J. R., and Korebrits, C. (1999). New approaches to the diagnosis of preterm labor. *Am. J. Obstet. Gynecol.* 180: S247–248.

Boden, S. D., and Kaplan, F. S. (1990). Calcium homeostasis. *Orthop. Clin. North Am.* 21: 31–42.

Bodnar, R., Commons, K., and Pfaff, D. (2002). *Central Neural States Relating Sex and Pain.* Johns Hopkins University Press, in press.

Bolles, R. C. (1962). The readiness to eat and defense: The effect of deprivation conditions. *J. Comp. Physiol. Psychol.* 55: 230–234.

Bolles, R. C. (1975). *Theories of Motivation.* New York: Harper and Row.

Bolles, R. C., and Fanselow, M. S. (1980). A perceptual-defensive-recuperative model of fear and pain. *Behav. Brain Sci.* 3: 291–323.

Bone, H. G., Adami, S., Rizzoli, R., Favus, M., Ross, P. D., Santora, A., Prahalada, S., Daifotis, A., Orloff, J., and Yates, A. J. (2000). Weekly administration of alendronate: Rationale and plan for clinical assessment. *Clin. Ther.* 22: 15–28.

Bonjour, J. P., Caverzasio, J., and Rizzoli, R. (1991). Homeostasis of inorganic phosphate and the kidney. *Nestle Nutr. Workshop Ser.* 21: 35–46.

Borbely, A. A., Achermann, P., Trachsel, L., and Tobler, I. (1989). Sleep initiation and initial sleep intensity: Interactions of homeostatic and circadian mechanisms. *J. Biol. Rhythms* 4: 149–160.

Borecky, L. (1993). Cytokines: The fourth homeostatic system. *Acta Virol.* 37: 276–289.

Boring, E. G. (1942). *Sensation and Perception in the History of Experimental Psychology.* New York: Appleton Century.

Borowsky, B., and Kuhn, C. M. (1991). Chronic cocaine administration sensitizes behavioral but not neuroendocrine responses. *Brain Res.* 543: 301–306.

Bourke, J. F., Iqubal, S. J., and Hutchinson, P. E. (1996). Vitamin D analogues in psoriasis: Effects on systemic calcium. *Br. J. Dermatol.* 135: 347–354.

Bouton, M. E., Mineka, S., and Barlow, D. H. (2001). A modern learning perspective on the etiology of panic disorder. *Psychol. Rev.* 108: 4–32.

Bowen, D. J. (1992). Taste and food preference changes across the course of pregnancy. *Appetite* 19: 233–242.

Bowlby, J. (1977). The making and breaking of affectional bonds. I. Etiology and psychopathology in the light of attachment theory. *Br. J. Psychiatry* 130: 201–210.

Boyd C. A. R., and Noble, D. (1993). *The Logic of Life.* Oxford: Oxford University Press.

Bradberry, C. W., Barrett-Larimore, R. L., Jatlow, P., and Rubino, S. R. (2000). Impact of self-administered cocaine cues on extracellular dopamine in mesolimbic and sensorimotor striatum in rhesus monkeys. *J. Neurosci.* 20: 3874–3883.

Bradbury, M. W., and Sarna, G. S. (1977). Homeostasis of the ionic composition of the cerebrospinal fluid. *Exp. Eye Res.* 25: 249–257.

Brady, L. S., Smith, M. A., Gold, P. W., and Herkenham, M. (1990). Altered expression of hypothalamic neuropeptide mRNAs in food restricted and food deprived rats. *Neuroendocrinology* 52: 441–447.

Brake, W. G., Noel, M. B., Broksa, P., and Gratton, A. (1997). Influence of perinatal factors on the nucleus accumbens dopamine response to repeated stress during adulthood: An electrochemical study in the rat. *Neuroscience* 77: 1067–1076.

Bramley, T. A., McPhie, C. A., and Menzies, G. S. (1994). Human placental gonadotrophin-releasing hormone (GnRH) binding sites: III. Changes in GnRH binding levels with stage of gestation. *Placenta* 15: 733–745.

Brauer, L. H., and de Wit, H. (1997). High dose pimozide does not block amphetamine-induced euphoria in normal volunteers. *Pharmacol. Biochem. Behav.* 56: 265–272.

Breier, A. (1989). Experimental approaches to human stress research: Assessment of neurobiological mechanisms of stress in volunteers and psychiatric patients. *Biol. Psychiatry* 26: 438–462.

Breier, A., Kelsoe, J. R. Jr., Kirwin, P. D., Beller, S. A., Wolkowitz, O. M., and Pickar, D. (1988). Early parental loss and development of adult psychopathology. *Arch. Gen. Psychiatry* 45: 987–993.

Breiter, H. C., Etcoff, N. L., Whalen, P. J., Kennedy, W. A., Rauch, S. L., Buckner, R. L., Strauss, M. M., Hyman, S. E., and Rosen, B. R. (1996). Response and habituation of the human amygdala during visual processing of facial expression. *Neuron* 17: 875–887.

Breiter, H. C., Gollub, R. L., Weisskoff, R. M., Kennedy, D. N., Makris, N., Berke, J. D., Goodman, J. M., Kantor, H. L., Gastfriend, D. R., Riorden, J. P., Mathew, R. T., Rosen, B. R., and Hyman, S. E. (1997). Acute effects of cocaine on human brain activity and emotion. *Neuron* 19: 591–611.

Bremner, J. D., Randall, P., Scott, T. M., Bronen, R. A., Seibyl, J. P., Southwick, S. M., Delaney, R. C., McCarthy, G., Charney, D. S., and Innis, R. B. (1995). MRI-based measurement of hippocampal volume in patients with combat-related posttraumatic stress disorder. *Am. J. Psychiatry* 152: 973–981.

Bremner, J. D., Randall, P., Vermetten, E., Staib, L., Bronen, R. A., Mazure, C., Capelli, S., McCarthy, G., Innis, R. B., and Charney, D. S. (1997). Magnetic resonance imaging-based measurement of hippocampal volume in posttraumatic stress disorder related to childhood physical and sexual abuse—A preliminary report. *Biol. Psychiatry* 41: 23–32.

Bremner, J. D., Narayan, M., Anderson, E. R., Staib, L. H., Miller, H. L., and Charney, D. S. (2000). Hippocampal volume reduction in major depression. *Am. J. Psychiatry* 157: 115–128.

Brett, K. M., and Madans, J. H. (1997). Use of postmenopausal hormone replacement therapy: Estimates from a nationally representative cohort study. *Am. J. Epidemiol.* 145: 536–545.

Bridges, R. S., and Freemark, M. S. (1995). Human placental lactogen infusions into the medial preoptic area stimulate maternal behavior in steroid-primed, nulliparous female rats. *Horm. Behav.* 29: 216–226.

Bridges, R. S., Rigero, B. A., Byrnes, E. N. M., Yang, L., and Walker, A. M. (2001). Central infusions of the recombinant human prolactin receptor antagonist, S179D-PRL, delay the onset of maternal behavior in steroid-primed, nulliparous female rats. *Endocrinology,* 142: 73–79.

Brindley, D. N., and Rolland, Y. (1989). Possible connections between stress, diabetes, obesity, hypertension, and altered lipoprotein metabolism that may result in atherosclerosis. *Clin. Sci.* 77: 453–461.

Britton, D. R., Varela, M., Garcia, A., and Rosenthal, M. (1986). Dexamethasone suppresses pituitary-adrenal but not behavioral effects of centrally administered CRF. *Life Sci.* 38: 211–216.

Brobeck, J. R. (1957). Neural control of hunger, appetite, and satiety. *Yale J. Biol. Med.* 29: 565–574.

Brobeck, J. R., Tepperman, J., and Long, C. N. H. (1943). Experimental hypothalamic hyperphagia in the albino rat. *Yale J. Biol Med.* 15: 837–853.

Brook, J. S., Nomura, C., and Cohen, P. (1989). Prenatal, perinatal, and early childhood risk factors and drug involvement in adolescence. *Genet. Soc. Gen. Psychol. Monogr.* 115: 221–241.

Brook, J. S., Cohen, P., and Jaeger, L. (1998a). Developmental variations in factors related to initial and increased levels of drug involvement. *J. Genet. Psychol.* 159: 179–194.

Brook, J. S., Whiteman, M., Finch, S., and Cohen, P. (1998b). Mutual attachment, personality, and drug use: Pathways from childhood to young adulthood. *Genet. Soc. Gen. Psychol. Monogr.* 124: 492–510.

Brown, J. E., and Toma, R. B. (1986). Taste changes during pregnancy. *Am. J. Clin. Nutr.* 43: 414–418.

Brown, L. L., Tomarken, A. J., Orth, D. N., Loosen, P. T., Kalin, N. H., and Davidson, R. J. (1996). Individual differences in repressive-defensiveness predict basal salivary cortisol levels. *J. Pers. Soc. Psychol.* 70: 362–371.

Brown, M. A., and Gallery, E. D. (1994). Volume homeostasis in normal pregnancy and pre-eclampsia: Physiology and clinical implications. *Ballieres Clin. Obstet. Gynaecol.* 8: 287–310.

Brown, S. A., Vik, P. W., Patterson, T. L., Grant, I., and Schuckit, M. A. (1995). Stress, vulnerability, and adult alcohol relapse. *J. Stud. Alcohol* 56: 538–545.

Brown, S. A., Gleghorn, A., Schuckit, M. A., Myers, M. G., and Mott, M. A. (1996). Conduct disorder among adolescent alcohol and drug abusers. *J. Stud. Alcohol* 57: 314–324.

Browner, W. S., Seeley, D. G., Vogt, T. M., and Cummings, S. R. (1991). Nontrauma mortality in elderly women with low bone mineral density. *Lancet* 338: 355–358.

Bruihnzeel, A. W., Stam, R., Compaan, J. C., and Wiegant, V. M. (2001). Stress-induced sensitization of CRH-ir but p-CREB-ir responsivity in the rat central nervous system. *Brain Res.* 908: 187–196.

Brunner, E. J., Marmot, M. G., Nanchahal, K., Shipley, M. J., Stansfeld, S. A., Juneja, M., and Alberti, K. G. (1997). Social inequality in coronary risk: Central obesity and the metabolic syndrome. Evidence from the Whitehall II Study. *Diabetologica* 40: 1341–1349.

Brunson, K. L., Ahmadi, M. E., Bender, R., Chen, Y., and Baram, T. Z. (2001a). Long-term, progressive hippocampal cell loss and dysfunction induced by early-life administration of corticotropin-releasing hormone reproduce the effects of early-life stress. *Proc. Natl. Acad. Sci.* 98: 8856–8861.

Brunson, K. L., Eliner-Avishai, S., Hatalski, C. G., and Baram, T. Z. (2001b). Neurobiology of the stress response early in life: Evolution of a concept and the role of corticotropin releasing hormone. *Mol. Psychiatry* 6: 647–656.

Buchanan, T. W., Absi, M., and Lovallo, W. R. (1999). Cortisol fluctuates with increases and decreases in negative affect. *Psychoneuroendocrinology* 24: 227–241.

Bunney, W. E., and Davis, J. M. (1965). Norepinephrine in depressive reactions: A review. *Arch. Gen. Psychiatry* 13: 483–494.

Butcher, E. C., and Picker, L. J. (1996). Lymphocyte homing and homeostasis. *Science* 272: 60–66.

Butler, P. D., Weiss, J. M., Stout, J. C., and Nemeroff, C. B. (1990). Corticotropin-releasing factor produces fear-enhancing and behavioral activation effects following infusion into the locus coeruleus. *J. Neurosci.* 10: 176–183.

Byne, W., Kemether, E., Jones, L., Haroutunian, V., and Davis, K. L. (1999). The neurochemistry of schizophrenia. In *Neurobiology of Mental Illness,* edited by D. S. Charney, E. J. Nestler, and B. S. Bunney. New York: Oxford University Press.

Cabanac, M. (1971). Physiological role of pleasure. *Science* 173: 1103–1107.

Cabanac, M. (1973). Hedonic response: Thermal, gustatory, and olfactory. *Neurosci. Res. Prog. Bull.* 11: 329–335.

Cabanac, M. (1979). Sensory pleasure. *Q. Rev. Biol.* 54: 1–29.

Cabanac, M., and Dib, B. (1983). Behavioral responses to hypothalamic cooling and heating in the rat. *Brain Res.* 264: 79–87.

Caberlotto, L., and Hurd, Y. L. (2001). Neuropeptide Y, Y1, and Y2 receptor mRNA expression in the prefrontal cortex of psychiatric subjects. *Neuropsychopharmacology* 25: 91–97.

Cacioppo, J. T., and Bernston, G. G. (2001). Balancing demands of the internal and external milieu. In *Oxford Handbook of Health Psychology,* edited by H. S. Friedman and R. Cohen-Silver. Oxford: Oxford University Press.

Cador, M., Ahmed, S. H., Koob, G. F., Le Moal, M., and Stinus, L. (1992). Corticotropin-releasing factor produces a place aversion independent of its neuroendocrine role. *Brain Res.* 597: 304–309.

Cador, M., Dulluc, J., and Mormede, D. P. (1993). Modulation of the locomotor response to amphetamine by corticosterone. *Neuroscience* 56: 981–988.

Cagnacci, A., Krauchi, K., Wirz-Justice, A., and Volpe, A. (1997). Homeostatic versus circadian effects of melatonin on core body temperature in humans. *J. Biol. Rhythms* 12: 509–517.

Cahill, L., Prins, B., Weber, M., and McGaugh, J. L. (1994). Beta-adrenergic activation and memory for emotional events. *Nature* 371: 702–704.

Caine, S. B., Heinrichs, S. C., Coffin, V. L., and Koob, G. F. (1995). Effects of the dopamine D-1 antagonist SCH 23390 microinjected into the accumbens, amygdala or striatum on cocaine self-administration in the rat. *Brain Res.* 692: 47–56.

Calder, A. J., Lawrence, A. D., and Young, A. W. (2001). Neuropsychology of fear and loathing. *Nat. Neurosci.* 2: 262–283.

Caldji, C., Tannenbaum, B., Sharma, S., Francis, D., Plotsky, P. M., and Meaney, M. J. (1998). Maternal care during infancy regulates the development of neural systems mediating the expression of fearfulness in the rat. *Proc. Natl. Acad. Sci.* 95: 5335–5340.

Campbell, E. A., Linton, E. A., Wolfe, C. D., Scraggs, P. R., Jones, M. T., and Lowry, P. J. (1987). Plasma corticotropin-releasing hormone concentrations during pregnancy and parturition. *J. Clin. Endocrinol. Metab.* 64: 1054–1059.

Canalis, E., and Giustina, A. (2001). Glucocorticoid-induced osteoporosis: Summary of a workshop. *J. Clin. Endocrinol. Metab.* 12: 5681–5687.

Cannon, W. B. (1927). The James-Lange theory of emotions: A critical examination and an alternative theory. *Am. J. Physiol.* 39: 106–124.

Cannon, W. B. (1929a/1915). *Bodily Changes in Pain, Hunger, Fear, and Rage.* New York: D. Appleton.

Cannon, W. B. (1929b). Organization for physiological homeostasis. *Physiol. Rev.* 9: 399–431.

Cannon, W. B. (1931). Again the James-Lange and thalamic theories of emotion. *Psychol. Rev.* 38: 281–295.

Cannon, W. B. (1932/1967). *The Wisdom of the Body.* New York: Norton Press.

Cannon, W. B., and Britton, S. W. (1927). The influence of motion and emotion on medulliadrenal secretion. *Am. J. Physiol.* 79: 433–465.

Cannon, W. B., and de la Paz, D. (1911). Emotional stimulation of adrenal gland secretion. *Am. J. Physiol.* 28: 64–70.

Cannon, W. B., and Washburn, A. L. (1912). An explanation of hunger. *Am. J. Physiol.* 29: 441–454.

Cannon, W. B., Querido, A., Britton, S. W., and Bright, E. M. (1927). The role of adrenal secretion in the chemical control of body temperature. *Am. J. Physiol.* 79: 466–507.

Carafoli, E. (1985). The homeostasis of calcium in heart cells. *J. Mol. Cell. Cardiol.* 17: 203–212.

Carboni, E., Silvagni, S., Rolando, M. T. P., and DiChiara, G. (2000). Stimulation of in vivo dopamine transmission in the bed nucleus of the stria terminalis by reinforcing drugs. *J. Neurosci.* 20: 1–5.

Cardinal, R. N., Pennicott, D. R., Sugathapata, C. L., Robbins, T. W., and Everitt, B. J. (2001). Impulsive choice induced in rats by lesions of the nucleus accumbens core. *Science* 292: 2499–2501.

Care, A. D. (1989). Development of endocrine pathways in the regulation of calcium homeostasis. *Baillieres Clin. Endocrinol. Metab.* 3: 671–688.

Carelli, R. M., Ijames, S. G., and Crumbling, A. J. (2000). Evidence that separate neural circuits in the nucleus accumbens encode cocaine versus "natural" (water and food) reward. *J. Neurosci.* 20: 4255–4266.

Carey, M. P., Deterd, C. H., Koning, J. D., Helmerhorst, F., and de Kloet, E. R. (1995). The influence of ovarian steroids on hypothalamic-pituitary-adrenal regulation in the female rat. *J. Endocrinol.* 144: 311–321.

Carlezon, W. A. Jr., and Wise, R. A. (1996). Rewarding actions of phencyclidine and related drugs in nucleus accumbens shell and frontal cortex. *J. Neurosci.* 16: 3112–3122.

Carrion, V. G., Weems, C. F., Ray, R. D., Glaser, B., Hessi, D., and Reiss, A. L. (2002). Diurnal salivary cortisol in pediatric posttraumatic stress disorder. *Biol. Psychiat.* 51: 575–582.

Carr, D. J., Rogers, T. J., and Weber, R. J. (1996). The relevance of opioids and opioid receptors on immunocompetence and immune homeostasis. *Proc. Soc. Exp. Biol. Med.* 213: 248–257.

Carroll, B. J., Curtis. G. C., Davies, D. M., Mewels, J., and Sugarman, A. A. (1976). Urinal free cortisol excretion in depression. *Psychol. Med.* 6: 43–50.

Carter, C. S. (1992). Oxytocin and sexual behavior. *Neurosci. Bio. Behav. Rev.* 16: 131–144.

Carter, C. S., Lederhendler, I. L., and Kirkpatrick, B. (1999). *The Integrative Neurobiology of Affiliation.* Cambridge: MIT Press.

Cash, W. B., Holberton, R. L., and Knight, S. S. (1997). Corticosterone secretion in response to capture and handling in free-living red-eared slider turtles. *Gen. Comp. Endocrinol.* 108: 427–433.

Casper, R. F., MacLusky, N. J., Vanin, C., and Brown, T. J. (1996). Rationale for estrogen with interrupted progestin as a new low-dose hormonal replacement therapy. *J. Soc. Gynecol. Invest.* 3: 225–234.

Catlin, M. C., Guizzetti, M., and Costa, L. G. (1999). Effects of ethanol on calcium homeostasis in the nervous system: Implications for astrocytes. *Mol. Neurobiol.* 19: 1–24.

Centers for Disease Control. (1997). *Report of Final Statistics* 46: 80 (table 44).

Challis, J. R. G., Matthews, S. G., VanMeir, C., and Ramirez, M. M. (1995). Current topic: The placental corticotropin-releasing hormone-adrenocorticotropin axis. *Placenta* 16: 481–502.

Challis, J. R. G., Matthews, S. G., Gibb, W., and Lye, S. J. (2000). Endocrine and paracrine regulation of birth at term and preterm. *Endocr. Rev.* 21: 514–550.

Champoux, M. B., Coe, C. L., Schanberg, S. M., Kuhn, D. M., and Soumi, S. J. (1989). Hormonal effects of early rearing conditions in infant rhesus monkeys. *Am. J. Primatol.* 19: 111–118.

Champoux, M. B., Zanker, D., and Levine, S. (1993). Food search demand effects on behavior and cortisol in adult female squirrel monkeys. *Physiol. Behav.* 54: 1091–1097.

Chan, E. C., Thompson, M., Madsen, G., Falconer, J., and Smith, R. (1988). Differential processing of corticotropin-releasing hormone by the human placenta and hypothalamus. Biochem. *Biophys. Res. Commun.* 153: 1229–1235.

Chan, E. C., Falconer, J., Madsen, G., Rice, K., Webster, E., Chrousos, G. P., and Smith, R. (1998). A corticotropin-releasing hormone type I receptor antagonist delays parturition in sheep. *Endocrinology* 139: 3357–3360.

Chang, J. Y., Sawyer, S. F., Lee, R. S., and Woodward, D. J. (1994). Electrophysiological and pharmacological evidence for the role of the nucleus accumbens in cocaine self-administration in freely moving rats. *J. Neurosci.* 14: 1224–1244.

Chappell, P., Leckman, J., Goodman, W., Bissette, G., Pauls, D., Anderson, G., Riddle, M., Scahill, L., McDougle, C., and Cohen, D. (1996). Elevated cerebrospinal fluid corticotropin-releasing factor in Tourette's syndrome: Comparison to obsessive-compulsive disorder and normal controls. *Biol. Psychiatry* 39: 776–783.

Chassin, L., Rogosch, F., and Barrera, M. (1991). Substance use and symptomatology among adolescent children of alcoholics. *J. Abnorm. Psychol.* 100: 449–463.

Chattopadhyay, S. C. (1981). Cross-sexual semantic study of Bengali animal abuse: Toward a homeostatic control of the socio-cultural system. *J. Indian Anthropol. Soc.* 16: 45–50.

Chavassieux, P. M., Arlot, M. E., Reda, C., Wiel, A. P., Yates, A. J., and Meunier, P. J. (1997). Histomorphometric assessment of the long-term effects of alendronate on bone quality and remodeling in patients with osteoporosis. *J. Clin. Invest.* 100: 1475–1480.

Cheek, T. R. (1991). Calcium regulation and homeostasis. *Curr. Opin. Cell. Biol.* 3: 199–205.

Chen, D. C., Nommsen-Rivers, L., Dewey, K. G., and Lonnerdal, B. (1998). Stress during labor and delivery and early lactation performance. *Am. J. Clin. Nutr.* 68: 335–344.

Chen, R., Lewis, K. A., Perrin, M. H., and Vale, W. W. (1993). Expression cloning of a human corticotropin-releasing-factor receptor. *Proc. Natl. Acad. Sci. USA* 90: 8967–8971.

Chen, X., and Herbert, J. (1995a). Alterations in sensitivity to intracerebral vasopressin and the effects of a V_{1a} receptor antagonist on cellular, autonomic, and endocrine responses to repeated stress. *Neuroscience* 64: 687–697.

Chen, X., and Herbert, J. (1995b). Regional changes in *c-fos* expression in the basal forebrain and brainstem during adaptation to repeated stress: Correlations with cardiovascular, hypothermic, and endocrine responses. *Neuroscience* 64: 675–685.

Cheng, Y. H., Nicholson, R. C., King, B., Chan, E. C., Fitter, J. T., and Smith, R. (2000). Glucocorticoid stimulation of corticotropin releasing hormone gene expression requires cyclic adenosine 3′,5′-monophosphate regulatory element in human primary placental cytotrophoblast cells. *J. Clin. Endocrinol. Metab.* 85: 1937–1946.

Childress, A. R., Ehrman, R., McLellan, A. T., MacRae, J., Natale, M., and O'Brien, C. P. (1994). Can induced moods trigger drug-related responses in opiate abuse patients? *J. Subst. Abuse Treat.* 11: 17–23.

Cho, K., and Little, H. J. (1999). Effects of corticosterone on excitatory amino acid responses in dopamine-sensitive neurones in the ventral tegmental area. *Neuroscience* 88: 837–845.

Chrischilles, E. A., Butler, C. D., Davis, C. S., and Wallace, R. B. (1991). A model of lifetime osteoporosis impact. *Arch. Intern. Med.* 151: 2026–2032.

Chrousos, G. P. (1996). The hypothalamic-pituitary-adrenal axis and immunomediated inflammation. *N. Engl. J. Med.* 332: 1351–1362.

Chrousos, G. P. (1997). The future of pediatric and adolescent endocrinology. *Ann. N.Y. Acad. Sci.* 816: 4–8.

Chrousos, G. P. (1998). Stressors, stress, and neuroendocrine integration of the adaptive response. The 1997 Hans Selye memorial lecture. *Ann. N.Y. Acad. Sci.* 851: 311–355.

Chrousos, G. P., and Gold, P. W. (1992). The concepts of stress and stress system disorders: Overview of physical and behavioral homeostasis. *JAMA* 267: 1244–1252.

Chrousos, G. P., and Gold, P. W. (1998). A healthy body in a healthy mind and vice-versa: The damaging power of "uncontrollable" stress. *J. Clin. Endocrinol. Metab.* 83: 1842–1845.

Chrousos, G. P., Torpy, D. J., and Gold, P. W. (1998). Interactions between the hypothalamic-pituitary-adrenal axis and the female reproductive system: Clinical implications. *Ann. Intern. Med.* 129: 229–240.

Cicchetti, D., and Walker, E. F. (eds.). (2001). Stress and development: Biological and psychological consequences. *Dev. Psychopathol.* (special ed.) 13: 413–753.

Cizza, G., Ravn, P., Chrousos, G. P., and Gold, P. W. (2001). Depression: A major unrecognized risk factor for osteoporosis? *Trends Endocrinol. Metab.* 12: 198–203.

Clancy, J., and McVicar, A. (1997). Homeostasis—The key concept to physiological control: 8. Wound healing: A series of homeostatic responses. *Br. J. Theatre Nurs.* 7: 25–34.

Clark, D. B., Lesnick, L., and Hegedus, A. M. (1997). Traumas and other adverse life events in adolescents with alcohol abuse and dependence. *J. Am. Acad. Child Adolesc. Psychiatry* 36: 1744–1751.

Clarke, A. S. (1993). Social rearing effects on HPA axis activity over early development and in response to stress in rhesus monkeys. *Dev. Psychobiol.* 26: 433–446.

Clauw, D. J., and Chrousos, G. P. (1997). Chronic pain and fatigue syndromes: Overlapping clinical and neuroendocrine features and potential pathogenic mechanisms. *Neuroimmunomodulation* 4: 134–153.

Cloninger, C. R. (1987). Neurogenetic adaptive mechanisms in alcoholism. *Science* 236: 410–416.

Cochrane, S. W., Gibson, M., Myers, D. A., Schulkin, J., and Greenwood-Van Meerveld, B. (2002). Role of corticotropin-releasing factor-1 (CRF1)-

receptor mediated mechanisms in neural pathways modulating colonic hypersensitivity. Unpublished observations.

Cohen, S., Line, S., Manuck, S. B., Rabin, B. S., Heise, E. R., and Kaplan, J. R. (1997). Chronic social stress, social status, and susceptibility to upper respiratory infections in nonhuman primates. *Psychosom. Med.* 59: 213–221.

Cohen, S., Tyrrell, D. A. J., and Smith, A. P. (1991). Psychological stress and susceptibility to the common cold. *N. Engl. J. Med.* 325: 606–612.

Coldwell, S. E., and Tordoff, M. G. (1996). Immediate acceptance of mineral and HCl by calcium deprived rats: Brief acceptance tests. *Am. J. Physiol.* 271: R11–R17.

Cole, B. J., and Koob, G. F. (1989). Low doses of corticotropin-releasing factor potentiate amphetamine-induced stereotyped behavior. *Psychopharmacology* 99: 27–33.

Coleman, M. A., France, J. T., Schellenberg, J. C., Ananiev, V., Townend, K., Keelan, J. A., Groome, N. P., and McCowan, L. M. (2000). Corticotropin-releasing hormone, corticotropin-releasing hormone binding protein, and activin A in maternal serum: Prediction of preterm delivery and response to glucocorticoids in women with symptoms of preterm labor. *Am. J. Obstet. Gynecol.* 183: 643–648.

Coleman, W. (1985). The cognitive basis of the discipline: Claude Bernard on physiology. *ISIS* 76: 49–70.

Colson, P., Ibarondo, J., Devilliers, G., Balestre, M. N., Duvoid, A., and Guillon, G. (1992). Upregulation of V1a vasopressin receptors by glucocorticoids. *Am. J. Physiol. (Endocrinol Metab.):* 26: E1054–E1062.

Cook, C. J. (2002). Glucocorticoid feedback increases the sensitivity of the limbic system to stress. *Physiol. Behav.* 75: 455–464.

Coordimas, K. J., LeDoux, J. E., Gold, P. W., and Schulkin, J. (1994). Corticosterone potentiation of learned fear. In *Brain Corticosteroid Receptor,* edited by R. de Kloet, E. C. Azmita, and P. W. Landfield. New York: Academic Press.

Coplan, J. D., Andrews, M. W., Rosenblum, L. A., Owens, M. J., Friedman, S., Gorman, J. M., and Nemeroff, C. B. (1996). Persistent elevations of cerebrospinal fluid concentrations of corticotropin-releasing factor in adult nonhuman primates exposed to early-life stressors: Implications for the pathophysiology of mood and anxiety disorders. *Proc. Natl. Acad. Sci. USA* 93: 1619–1623.

Coplan, J. D., Trost, R. C., Owens, M. J., Cooper, T. B., Gorman, J. M., Nemeroff, C. B., and Rosenblum, L. A. (1998). Cerebrospinal fluid concentrations of somatostatin and biogenic amines in grown primates reared by mothers exposed to manipulated foraging conditions. *Arch. Gen. Psychiatry* 55: 473–477.

Coplan, J. D., Smith, E. L. P., Altemus, M., Scharf, B. A., Owens, M. J., Nemeroff, C. B., Gorman, J. M., and Rosenblum, L. A. (2001). Variable foraging de-

mand rearing: Sustained elevations in cisternal cerebrospinal fluid corticotropin releasing hormone factor concentrations in adult primates. *Biol. Psychiatry* 50: 200–204.

Corbit, J. D. (1973). Voluntary control of hypothalamic cooling. *J. Comp. Physiol. Psychol.* 83: 394–411.

Cortright, R. N., Mouoio, D. M., and Dohm, G. L. (1997). Skeletal muscle lipid metabolism: A frontier for new insights into fuel homeostasis. *J. Nutr. Biochem.* 8: 228–245.

Coste, C. S., Murray, S. E., and Stenzel-Poore, M. P. (2001). Animal models of CRH excess and CRH receptor deficiency display altered adaptations to stress. *Peptides* 22: 733–744.

Coustan, D. R. (1993). Gestational Diabetes. *Diabetes Care* 16 (suppl. 3): 8–15.

Cox, V. C., and Valenstein, E. S. (1965). Attenuation of aversive properties of peripheral shock by hypothalamic stimulation. *Science* 149: 323–325.

Craig, W. (1918). Appetites and aversions as constituents of instinct. *Biol. Bull.* 34: 91–107.

Cratty, M. S., Ward, H. E., Johnson, E. A., Azzaro, A. J., and Birkle, D. L. (1995). Prenatal stress increases corticotropin-releasing factor (CRF) content and release in rat amygdala minces. *Brain Res.* 675: 297–302.

Cross, S. J., and Albury, W. R. (1987). Walter B. Cannon, L. J. Henderson, and the organic analogy. *Osiris* 3: 165–192.

Cuadra, G., Zurita, A., Lacerra, C., and Molina, V. (1999). Chronic stress sensitizes frontal cortex dopamine release in response to a subsequent novel stressor: Reversal by naloxone. *Brain Res. Bull.* 48: 303–308.

Cullinan, W. E., Herman, J. P., and Watson, S. J. (1993). Ventral subicular interaction with the hypothalamic paraventricular nucleus: Evidence for a relay in the bed nucleus of the stria terminalis. *J. Comp. Neurol.* 332: 1–20.

Cziko, G. (2000). *The Things We Do.* Cambridge: MIT Press.

Dallman, M. F., and Bhatnager, S. (2000). Chronic stress: Role of the hypothalamo-pituitary-adrenal axis. *Handbook of Physiology,* edited by B. S. McEwen. New York: Oxford University Press.

Dallman, M. F., Akana, S., Cascio, C. S., Darlington, D. N., Jacobson, L., and Levin, N. (1987). Regulation of ACTH secretion: Variations on a theme of B. *Rec. Prog. Horm. Res.* 43: 113–173.

Dallman, M. F., Akana, S. F., Scribner, K. A., Bradbury, M. J., Walker, C. D., Strack, A. M., and Cascio, C. S. (1992). Stress, feedback, and facilitation in the hypothalamic-pituitary-adrenal axis. *J. Neuroendocrinol.* 4: 517–526.

Dallman, M. F., Akana, S. F., Levin, N., Walker, C. D., Bradbury, M. J., Suemaru, S., and Scribner, K. S. (1994). Corticosteroids and the control of function in the hypothalamo-pituitary-adrenal (HPA) axis. *Ann N.Y. Acad. Sci.* 747: 22–31, discussion: 31–32, 64–67.

Dallman, M. F., Akana, S. F., Strack, A. M., Hanson, E. S., and Sebastian, R. J. (1995). The neural network that regulates energy balance is responsive

to glucocorticoids and insulin and also regulates HPA axis responsivity at a site proximal to CRF neurons. *Ann. N.Y. Acad. Sci.* 771: 730–742.

Dallman, M. F., Akana, S. F., Bhatnagar, S., Bell, M. E., and Strack, A. M. (2000). Bottomed out: Metabolic significance of the circadian trough in glucocorticoid concentrations. *Int. J. Obes. Relat. Metab. Disord.* 24 (suppl. 2): S40–S46.

Damasio, A. R. (1994). *Descartes' Error: Emotion, Reason, and the Human Brain.* New York: Plenum Press.

Dao-Castellana, M. H., Samson, Y., Legault, F., Martinot, J. L., Aubin, H. J., Crousel C., Feldman, L., Barrucand, D., Rancurel, G., Feline, A., and Syrota, A. (1998). Frontal dysfunction in neurologically normal chronic alcoholic subjects: Metabolic and neuropsychological findings. *Psychol. Med.* 28: 1039–1048.

Darnell, A., Bremner, J. D., Licinio, J., Krystal, J., Nemeroff, C. B., Owens, M., Erdos, J., and Charney, D. S. (1994). Cerebrospinal fluid levels of corticotropin releasing factor in chronic post-traumatic stress disorder. *Neurosci. Abstr.* 20: 15.

Darwin, C. (1872). *The Expression of the Emotions in Man and Animals.* London: J. Murray.

Dautzenberg, F. M., Kilpatrick, G. J., Hauger, R. L., and Moreau, J. L. (2001). Molecular biology of the CRH receptors—In the mood. *Peptides* 22: 753–760.

Davidson, R. J. (1998). Anterior electrophysiological asymmetries, emotion, and depression: Conceptual and methodological conundrums. *Psychophysiology* 35: 607–614.

Davidson, R. J., and Rickman, M. (1999). Behavioral inhibition and the emotional circuitry of the brain: Stability and plasticity during the early childhood years. In *Extreme Fear, Shyness, and Social Phobia,* edited by L. A. Schmidt and J. Schulkin. New York: Oxford University Press.

Davidson, R. J., and Sutton, S. K. (1995). Affective neuroscience: The emergence of a discipline. *Curr. Opin. Neurobiol.* 5: 217–224.

Davidson, R. J., Ekman, P., Saron, C. D., Senulis, J. A., and Friesnen, W. V. (1990). Approach-withdrawal and cerebral asymmetry: Emotional expression and brain physiology. *Int. J. Pers. Soc. Psychol.* 58: 330–341.

Davidson, R. J., Abercrombie, H., Nitschke, J. B., and Putnam, K. (1999). Regional brain function, emotion, and disorders of emotion. *Curr. Opin. Neurobiol.* 9: 228–234.

Davidson, R. J., Putnam, K. M., and Larson, C. L. (2000). Dysfunction in the neural circuitry of emotion regulation—A possible prelude to violence. *Science* 289: 591–594.

Davis, M., and Whalen, P. J. (2001). The amygdala: Vigilance and emotion. *Mol. Psychiatry* 6: 13–34.

Davis, M., Falls, W. A., Campeau, S., and Kim, M. (1993). Fear-potentiated startle: A neural and pharmacological analysis. *Behav. Brain Res.* 58: 175–198.

Davis, M., Walker, D. L., and Lee, Y. (1997). Amygdala and bed nucleus of the stria terminalis: Differential roles in fear and anxiety measured with the acoustic startle reflex. *Philos. Trans. R. Soc. Lond. B. Biol. Sci.* 352: 1675–1687.

Davis, W. M., and Smith, S. G. (1976). Role of conditioned reinforcers in the initiation, maintenance, and extinction of drug-seeking behavior. *Pavlovian J. Biol. Sci.* 11: 222–236.

Davison, T. F., Rea, J., and Rowell, J. G. (1983). Effects of dietary corticosterone on the growth and metabolism of immature *Gallus domesticus. Gen. Comp. Endocrinol.* 50: 463–468.

Dayan, J., Creveuil, C., Herlicoviez, M., Herbe, C., Baranger, E., Savoye, C., and Thouin, A. (2002). Role of anxiety and depression in the onset of spontaneous preterm labor. *Am. J. Epidemiol.* 155: 293–301.

Deak, T., Nguyen, K. T., Ehrlich, A. L., Watkins, L. R., Spencer, R. L., Maier, S. F., Licino, J., Wong, M. L., Chrousos, G. P., Webster, E., and Gold, P. W. (1999). The impact of a nonpeptide corticotropin-releasing hormone antagonist antalarmin on behavioral and endocrine responses to stress. *Endocrinology* 140: 79–86.

De Bellis, M. D., Chrousos, G. P., Dorn, L. D., Burke, L., Helmers, K., Kling, M. A., Trickett, P. K., and Putnam, F. W. (1994a). Hypothalamic-pituitary-adrenal-axis dysregulation in sexually abused girls. *J. Clin. Endocrinol. Metab.* 78: 249–255.

De Bellis, M. D., Lefter, L., Trickett, P. K., and Putnam, F. W. Jr. (1994b). Urinary catecholamine excretion in sexually abused girls. *J. Am. Acad. Child Adolesc. Psychiatry* 33: 320–327.

De Bellis, M. D., Baum, A. S., Birmaher, B., Keshavan, M. S., Eccard, C. H., Boring, A. M., Jenkins, F. J., and Ryan, N. D. (1999a). Developmental traumatology. Part I: Biological stress systems. *Biol. Psychiatry* 45: 1259–1270.

De Bellis, M. D., Keshavan, M. S., Clark, D. B., Casey, B. J., Giedd, J. N., Boring, A. M., Frustaci, K., and Ryan, N. D. (1999b). Developmental traumatology. Part II: Brain development. *Biol. Psychiatry* 45: 1271–1284.

Deither, V. G. (1982). The contribution of insects to the study of motivation. In *Changing Concepts in the Nervous System,* edited by A. R. Morrison and P. L. Strick. New York: Academic Press.

Deither, V. G., and Stellar, E. (1961). *Animal Behavior.* Englewood Cliffs, N.J.: Prentice Hall.

de Kloet, E.R. (1991). Brain corticosteroid receptor balance and homeostatic control. *Front. Neuroendocrinol.* 12: 95–164.

Dellu, F., Mayo, W., Vallee, M., Le Moal, M., and Simon, H. (1994). Reactivity to novelty during youth as a predictive factor of cognitive impairment in the elderly: A longitudinal study in rats. *Brain Res.* 653: 51–56.

Delmas, P. D., Bjarnason, N. H., Mitlak, B. H., Ravoux, A. C., Shah, A. S., Huster, W. J., Draper, M., and Christiansen, C. (1997). Effects of raloxifene on

bone mineral density, serum cholesterol concentrations, and uterine endometrium in postmenopausal women. *N. Engl. J. Med.* 337: 1641–1647.

DeLuca, H. F. (1988). The vitamin D story: A collaborative effort of basic science and clinical medicine. *FASEBJ* 2: 224–236.

Delville, Y., Mansour, K. M., and Ferris, C. F. (1996). Testosterone facilitates aggression by modulating vasopressin receptors in the hypothalamus. *Physiol. Behav.* 60: 25–29.

Delvin, E. E., Salle, B. L., and Glorieux, F. H. (1991). Vitamin D and calcium homeostasis in pregnancy: Feto-maternal relationships. *Nestle Nutr. Workshop Ser.* 21: 91–105.

Dennett, D. C. (1978). *Brainstorms.* Montgomery, Vt.: MIT Press, Bradford Books.

Denton, D. A. (1982). *The Hunger for Salt.* Berlin: Springer-Verlag.

Denton, D. A., and Sabine, J. R. (1963). The behavior of Na deficient sheep. *Behaviour* 20: 363–376.

Denton, D. A., McKinley, M. J., and Wessinger, R. S. (1996). Hypothalamic integration of body fluid regulation. *Proc. Natl. Acad. Sci. USA* 93: 7397–7404.

Denton, D. A., Shade, R., Zamarippa, F., Egan, G., Blair-West, J., McKinley, M., Lancaster, J., and Fox, P. (1999). Neuroimaging of genesis and satiation of thirst and an interoceptor-driven theory of origins of primary consciousness. *Proc. Natl. Acad. Sci.* 96: 5304-5309.

de Quervain, D. J., Roozendaal, B., and McGaugh, J. L. (1998). Stress and glucocorticoids impair retrieval of long-term spatial memory. *Nature* 394: 787–790.

de Quervain, D. J., Roozendaal, B., Nitsch, R. M., McGaugh, J. L., and Hock, C. (2000). Acute cortisone administration impairs retrieval of long-term declarative memory in humans. *Nat. Neurosci.* 3: 313–314.

Deroche, V., Piazza, P. V., Le Moal, M., and Simon, H. (1994). Social isolation-induced enhancement of the psychomotor effects of morphine depends on corticosterone secretion. *Brain Res.* 640: 136–139.

Deroche, V., Marinelli, M., Maccari, S., Le Moal, M., and Simon, H. (1995). Stress induced sensitization and glucocorticoids. I. Sensitization of dopamine-dependent locomotor effects of amphetamine and morphine depends on stress-induced corticosterone secretion. *J. Neurosci.* 11: 7181–7188.

DeSouza, E. B., Insel, T. R., Perrin, M. H., Rivier, J., Vale, W. W., and Kuhar, M. J. (1985). Corticotropin-releasing factor receptors are widely distributed within the rat central nervous system: An autoradiographic study. *J. Neurosci.* 5: 3189–3203.

Dethier, V. G. (1966). Insects and the concept of motivation. *Nebr. Symp. Motiv.* 14: 105–136.

Dettling, A. C., Parker, S. W., Lane, S., Sebanc, A., and Gunnar, M. R. (2000). Quality of care and temperament determine changes in cortisol concentrations over the day for young children in childcare. *Psychoneuroendocrinology* 25: 819–836.

Deutsch, J. A. (1960). *The Structural Basis of Behavior.* Chicago: University of Chicago Press.

DeVries, A. C., DeVries, M. B., Taymans, S., and Carer, C. S. (1995). Modulation of pair bonding in female voles by corticosterone. *Proc. Natl. Acad. Sci.* 92: 7744–7748.

DeVries, G. J., Buijs, R. M., Van Leeuwen, F. W., Caffe, A. R., and Swaab, D. F. (1985). The vasopressinergic innervation of the brain in normal and castrated rats. *J. Comp. Neurol.* 233: 236–254.

Dewey, J. (1925/1989). *Experience and Nature.* LaSalle, Ill.: Open Court Press.

DeWit, D. J. (1998). Frequent childhood geographic relocation: Its impact on drug use initiation and the development of alcohol and other drug-related problems among adolescents and young adults. *Addict. Behav.* 23: 623–634.

DeWit, D. J., MacDonald, K., and Offord, D. R. (1999). Childhood stress and symptoms of drug dependence in adolescence and early adulthood: Social phobia as a mediator. *Am. J. Orthopsychiatry* 69: 61–72.

de Wit, H., and Stewart, J. (1981). Reinstatement of cocaine-reinforced responding in the rat. *Psychopharmacology* 75: 134–143.

Dhabhar, F. S., and McEwen, B. S. (1996). Moderate stress enhances, and chronic stress suppresses, cell-mediated immunity in vivo. *Soc. Neurosci.* 22: 1350.

Dhabhar, F. S., and McEwen, B. S. (1999). Enhancing versus suppressive effects of stress hormones on skin immune function. *Proc. Natl. Acad. Sci. USA* 96: 1059–1064.

Di Chiara, G., and Imperato, A. (1988). Drugs abused by humans preferentially increase synaptic dopamine concentrations in the mesolimbic system of freely moving rats. *Proc. Natl. Acad. Sci. USA* 85: 5274–5278.

Dickinson, A. (1980). *Contemporary Animal Learning.* Cambridge: Cambridge University Press.

Dilman, V. M., and Blumenthal, H. T. (1981). The law of deviation of homeostasis and diseases of aging. In: *Vladimir M. Dilman,* edited by H. T. Blumenthal. Boston: J. Wright.

Dochir, S., Kadar, T., Robinzon, B., and Levy, A. (1993). Cognitive deficits induced in young rats by long-term corticosterone administration. *Behav. Neural. Biol.* 60: 103–109.

Dolan, R. J., Lane, R., Chua, P., and Fletcher, P. (2000). Dissociable temporal lobe activations during emotional episodic memory retrieval. *Neuroimage* 11: 203–209.

Dorries, R. (2001). The role of T-cell-mediated mechanisms in virus infections of the nervous system. *Curr. Top. Microbiol. Immunol.* 253: 219–245.

Downer, R. G. H. (1983). Ionic and metabolic homeostasis. *Invertebr. Endocrinol.* 1: 409–410.

Drevets, W. C. (1999). Prefrontal cortical-amygdalar metabolism in major depression. *Ann. N.Y. Acad. Sci.* 877: 614–637.

Drevets, W. C. (2001). Neuroimaging and neuropathological studies of depression: Implications for the cognitive-emotional features of mood disorders. *Curr. Opin. Neurobiol.* 11: 240–249.

Drevets, W. C., Videen, T. O., Price, J. L., Preskorn, S. H., Carmichael, S. T., and Raichle, M. E. (1992). A functional anatomical study of unipolar depression. *J. Neurosci.* 12: 3628–3641.

Drevets, W. C., Ongur, D., and Price, J. L. (1998). Neuroimaging abnormalities in the subgenual prefrontal cortex: Implications for the pathophysiology of familial mood disorders. *Mol. Psychiatry* 2: 220–226.

Drevets, W. C., Frank, E., Price, J. C., Kupfer, D. J., Greer, P. J., and Mathis, C. (1999). PET imaging of serotonin 1A receptor binding in depression. *Biol. Psychiatry* 46: 1375–1387.

Drevets, W. C., Price, J. L., Bardgett, M. E., Reich, T., Todd, R. D., and Raichle, M. E. (2002). Glucose metabolism in the amygdala in depression: Relationship to diagnostic subtype and plasma cortisol levels. *Pharm. Biochem. Behav.* 71: 431–447.

Duello, T. M., and Boyle, T. A. (1997). Placental progonadotropin-releasing hormone (pro-GnRH) in the rhesus monkey. *Endocrine* 6: 21–24.

Duffy, V. B., Bartoshuk, L. M., Striegel-Moore, R., and Rodin, J. (1998). Taste changes across pregnancy. *Ann. N.Y. Acad. Sci.* 855: 805–809.

Duncan, R. D., Saunders, B. E., Kilpatrick, D. G., Hanson, R. F., and Resnick, H. S. (1995). Childhood physical assault as a risk factor for PTSD, depression, and substance abuse: Findings from a national survey. *Am. J. Orthopsychiatry* 66: 437–448.

Dunn, A. J., and Berridge, C. W. (1990). Physiological and behavioral responses to corticotropin-releasing factor administration: Is CRF a mediator of anxiety and of stress responses? *Brain Res. Rev.* 15: 71–100.

Eagle, D. M., Humby, T., Dunnett, S. B., and Robbins, T. W. (1999). Effects of regional striatal lesions on motor, motivational, and executive aspects of progressive-ration performance in rats. *Behav. Neurosci.* 113: 718–731.

Easteal, S. (1999). Molecular evidence for the early divergence of placental mammals. *Bioessays* 21: 1052–1058.

Eastell, R., and Riggs, B. L. (1987). Calcium homeostasis and osteoporosis. *Endocrinol. Metab. Clin. North Am.* 16: 829–842.

Eaton, S. B., and Konner, M. (1985). Paleolithic nutrition. A consideration of its nature and current implications. *New Engl. J. Med.* 312: 283–289.

Ebert, B. (1978). Homeostasis. *Fam. Ther.* 5: 171–175.

Edwards, D. A., and Einhorn, L. C. (1986). Preoptic and midbrain control of sexual motivation. *Physiol. Behav.* 37: 329–335.

Ekman, P. (1982). *Emotion and the Human Face.* Cambridge: Cambridge University Press.

Ekman, P. (1992). An argument for basic emotions. *Cogn. Emotion* 6: 169–200.

Ellason, J. W., Ross, C. A., Sainton, K., and Mayran, L. W. (1996). Axis I and II comorbidity and childhood trauma history in chemical dependency. *Bull. Menninger Clin.* 60: 39–51.

Ellis, M. J., Livesey, J. H., Inder, W. J., Prickett, T. C., and Reid, R. (2002). Plasma corticiotropin releasing hormone and unconjugated estriol in human pregnancy: Gestational patterns and ability to predict preterm delivery. *Am. J. Obstet. Gynecol.* 186: 94–99.

Elster, J. (1999). *Strong Feelings.* Cambridge: Cambridge University Press.

Elster, J., and Skog, O.-J. (1999). *Getting Hooked: Rationality and Addiction.* Cambridge: Cambridge University Press.

Elsworth, J. D., Morrow, B. A., and Roth, R. H. (2001). Prenatal cocaine exposure increases mesoprefrontal dopamine neuron responsibility to mild stress. *Synapse* 42: 80–83.

Emery, N. J., and Amaral, D. G. (1999). The role of the amygdala in primate social cognition. In: *Cognitive Neuroscience of Emotion,* edited by R. D. Lane and L. Nadel. Oxford: Oxford University Press.

Emery, N. J., Capitanio, J. P., Mason, W. A., Machado, C. J., Mendoza, S. P., and Amaral, D. G. (2001). The effects of bilateral lesions of the amygdala on dyadic social interactions in rhesus monkeys. *Behav. Neurosci.* 115: 315–334.

Engel, G. L. (1971). Sudden and rapid death during psychological stress: Folklore or folk wisdom? *Ann. Intern. Med.* 74: 771–782.

Epstein, A. N. (1982). Instinct and motivation as explanations for complex behaviour. In *The Physiological Mechanisms of Motivation,* edited by D. W. Pfaff. New York: Springer.

Epstein, A. N. (1991). Neurohormonal control of salt intake in the rat. *Brain Res. Bull.* 27: 315–320.

Epstein, A. N., Fitzsimons, J. T., and Simons, B. J. (1968). Drinking caused by the intracranial injection of angiotensin into the rat. *J. Physiol.* 200: 98P–100P.

Epstein, A. N., Kissileff, H. R., and Stellar, E. (eds.) (1973). *The Neuropsychology of Thirst.* Washington, D.C.: V. H. Winston and Sons.

Epstein, J. N., Saunders, B. E., Kilpatrick, D. G., and Resnick, H. S. (1998). PTSD as a mediator between childhood rape and alcohol use in adult women. *Child Abuse Negl.* 22: 223–234.

Erb, S., and Stewart, J. (1999). A role for the bed nucleus of the stria terminalis, but not the amygdala, in the effects of corticotropin releasing factor on stress-induced reinstatement of cocaine seeking. *J. Neurosci.* 19: 1–6.

Erb, S., Shaham, Y., and Stewart, J. (1996). Stress reinstates cocaine-seeking behavior after prolonged extinction and a drug-free period. *Psychopharmacology* 128: 408–412.

Erb, S., Shaham, Y., and Stewart, J. (1998). The role of corticotropin-releasing factor and corticosterone in stress- and cocaine-induced relapse to cocaine seeking in rats. *Neuroscience* 18: 5529–5536.

Erb, S., Hitchcott, P. K., Rajabi, H., Mueller, D., Shaham, Y., and Stewart, J. (2000). Alpha-2 adrenergic receptor agonists block stress-induced reinstatement of cocaine seeking. *Neuropsychopharmacology* 23: 138–150.

Erecinska, M., Wilson, D. F., and Nishiki, K. (1978). Homeostatic regulation of cellular energy metabolism: Experimental characterization in vivo and fit to a model. *Am. J. Physiol.* 234: C82–C89.

Erickson, C., and Lehrman, D. (1964). Effect of castration of male ring doves upon ovarian activity of females. *J. Comp. Physiol. Psychol.* 58: 164–166.

Erickson, K., Thorsen, P., Chrousos, G., Grigoriadis, D. E., Khongsaly, O., and Schulkin, J. (2001). Preterm birth: Associated neuroendocrine, medical, and behavioral risk factors. *Clin. Endocrinol. Metab.* 86: 2544–2552.

Ericsson, A., Kovacs, K. J., and Sawchenko, P. E. (1994). A functional anatomical analysis of central pathways subserving the effects of interleukin-1 on stress-related neuroendocrine neurons. *J. Neurosci.* 14: 897–913.

Evans, A. E. (1988). Childhood sexual trauma inventory. Unpublished manuscript.

Evans, C. H. (1993). Cytokines: Molecular keys to homeostasis, development, and pathophysiology. *J. Cell. Biochem.* 53: 277–279.

Everitt, B. J. (1990). Sexual motivation: A neural and behavioural analysis of the mechanisms underlying appetitive and copulatory responses of male rats. *Neurosci. Biobehav. Rev.* 14: 217–232.

Everitt, B. J. (1999). Craving cocaine cues: Cognitive neuroscience meets drug addiction research. *Cogn. Sci.* 1: 1–2.

Everitt, B. J., and Herbert, J. (1975). The effects of implanting testosterone propionate into the central nervous system on the sexual behaviour of adrenalectomized female rhesus monkeys. *Brain Res.* 86: 109–120.

Everitt, B. J., Morris, K. A., O'Brien, A., and Robbins, T. W. (1991). The basolateral amygdala-ventral striatal system and conditioned place preference: Further evidence of limbic-striatal interactions underlying reward-related processes. *Neuroscience* 42: 1–18.

Everitt, B. J., Cardinal, R. N., Hall, J., Parkinson, J. A., and Robbins, T. R. (2000). Differential involvement of amygdala subsystems in appetitive conditioning and drug addiction. In *The Amygdala: A Functional Analysis,* edited by J. P. Aggleton. Oxford: Oxford University Press.

Eyer, J., and Sterling, P. (1977). Stress-related mortality and social organization. *Rev. Radical Polit. Econ.* 9: 1–44.

Fabre, V., Boutrel, B., Hanoun, N., Lanfumey, L., Fattaccini, C. M., Demeneix, B., Adrien, J., Hammon, M., and Martres, M. P. (2000). Homeostatic regulation of serotonergic function by the serotonin transporter as revealed by nonviral gene transfer. *J. Neurosci.* 20: 5065–5075.

Fahlke, C., Engel, J. A., Erikson, C. J., Hard, E., and Soderpalm, B. (1994). Involvement of corticosterone in the modulation of ethanol consumption in the rat. *Alcohol* 11: 195–202.

Fahlke, C., Lorenz, J. G., Long, J., Champoux, M., Soumi, S. J., and Higley, J. D. (2000). Rearing experiences and stress-induced plasma cortisol as early risk factors for excessive alcohol consumption in nonhuman primates. *Alcohol. Clin. Exp. Res.* 24: 644–650.

Falguni, P., and Challis, J. R. G. (2002). Cortisol/progesterone antagonism in regulation of 15-hydroxysteroid dehydrogenase activity and mRNA levels in human chorion and placental trophoblast cells at term. *J. Clin. Endocrinol. Metab.* 87: 700–798.

Fant, R. V., Heishman, S. J., Bunker, E. B., and Pickworth, W. B. (1998). Acute and residual effects of marijuana in humans. *Pharmacol. Biochem. Behav.* 60: 777–784.

Farber, E. W., Herbert, S. E., and Reviere, S. L. (1996). Childhood abuse and suicidility in obstetric patients in a hospital-based urban prenatal clinic. *Gen. Hosp. Psychiatry* 18: 56–60.

Favus, M. J. (ed.) (1996). *Primer on the Metabolic Bone Diseases and Disorders of Mineral Metabolism.* New York: Lippincott-Raven.

Feder, H. H. (1965). Feminine behavior in neonatally castrated and estrogen-treated male rats. *Science* 147: 306–307.

Felitti, V. J., Anda, R. F., Nordenberg, D., Williamson, D. F., Spitz, A. M., Edwards, V., Koss, M. P., and Marks, J. S. (1998). Relationship of childhood abuse and household dysfunction to many of the leading causes of death in adults. The adverse childhood experiences (ACE) study. *Am. J. Prev. Med.* 14: 245–258.

Fenster, C. B., and Galloway, L. F. (1992). Developmental homeostasis and floral form: Evolutionary consequences and genetic basis. *Int. J. Plant Sci.* 158: S121–S130.

Ferguson, J. N., Aldag, J. M., Insel, T. R., and Young, L. J. (2001). Oxytocin in the medial amygdala is essential for social recognition in the mouse. *J. Neurosci.* 21: 8278–8285.

Fergusson, D. M., and Horwood, L. J. (1997). Early onset cannabis use and psychosocial adjustment in young adults. *Addiction* 92: 279–296.

Fergusson, D. M., and Lynskey, M. T. (1996). Adolescent resiliency to family adversity. *J. Child Psychol. Psychiatry* 37: 281–292.

Ferin, M. (1995). The antireproductive role of corticotropin releasing hormone and interleukin-1 in the female rhesus monkey. *Ann. Endocrinol. (Paris)* 56: 181–186.

Ferrari, E., Magri, F., Locatelli, M., Balza, G., Nescis, T., Battegazzore, C., Cuzzoni, G., Fioravanti, M., and Solerte, S. B. (1996). Chrono-neuroendocrine markers of the aging brain. *Aging (Milano)* 8: 320–327.

Ferris, C. F., Axelson, J. F., Martin, A. M., and Roberge, L. F. (1989). Vasopressin immunoreactivity in the anterior hypothalamus is altered during the establishment of dominant/subordinate relationships between hamsters. *Neuroscience* 29: 675–683.

Ferris, C. F., Melloni, R. H. Jr., Koppel, G., Perry, K. W., Fuller, R. W., and Delville, Y. (1997). Vasopressin/serotonin interactions in the anterior hypothalamus control aggressive behavior in golden hamsters. *Neuroscience* 17: 4331–4340.

Filip, M., Thomas, M. L., and Cunningham, K. A. (2000). Dopamine D5 receptors in nucleus accumbens contribute to the detection of cocaine in rats. *J. Neurosci.* 20: 1–4.

Findling, J. W., Adams, N. D., Lemann, J. Jr., Gray, R. W., Thomas, C. J., and Tyrrell, J. B. (1982). Vitamin D metabolites and parathyroid hormone in Cushing's syndrome: Relationship to calcium and phosphorus homeostasis. *J. Clin. Endocrinol. Metab.* 54: 1039–1044.

Fink, G. (1997). Mechanisms of negative and positive feedback of steroids in the HPA system. In *Principles of Medical Biology*. Vol. 10, *Molecular and Cellular Endocrinology*, edited by E. E. Bittar and N. Bittar. Greenwich, Conn.: JAI Press, pp. 29–30.

Fink, G. (2000). *Encylopedia of Stress*. New York: Academic Press.

Fischman, A. J., and Moldow, R. L. (1982). Extrahypothalamic distribution of CRF-like immunoreactivity in the rat brain. *Peptides* 1: 149–153.

Fitzsimons, J. T. (1970). Interactions of intracranially administered renin or angiotensin and other thirst stimuli on drinking. *J. Physiol. (Lond.)* 210: 152P–153P.

Fitzsimons, J. T. (1976). The experimental notebooks of Claude Bernard [proceedings]. *J. Physiol. (Lond.)* 263: 37P–41P.

Fitzsimons, J. T. (1979). *The Physiology of Thirst and Sodium Appetite*. Cambridge: Cambridge University Press.

Fitzsimons, J. T. (1999). Angiotensin, thirst, and sodium appetite. *Physiol. Rev.* 76: 583–686.

Fitzsimons, J. T., and Le Magnen, J. (1969). Eating as a regulatory control of drinking. *J. Comp. Physiol. Psychol.* 67: 273–283.

Fleming, A. S., Steiner, M., and Corter, C. (1997). Hormones, hedonics, and maternal responsiveness in human mothers. *Horm. Behav.* 32: 85–98.

Fleming, J., Mullen, P. E., Sibthorpe, B., Atwell, R., and Bammer, G. (1998). The relationship between childhood sexual abuse and alcohol abuse in women—A case-control study. *Addiction* 93: 1787–1798.

Flemming, D. (1984). Walter B. Cannon and homeostasis. *Soc. Res.* 51: 609–640.

Fleshner, M., Pugh, C. R., Tremblay, D., and Rudy, J. W. (1997). DHEA-S selectively impairs contextual-fear conditioning: Support for the antiglucocorticoid hypothesis. *Behav. Neurosci.* 111: 512–517.

Fluharty, S. J., and Epstein, A. N. (1983). Sodium appetite elicited by intracerebroventricular infusion of angiotensin II in the rat: II. Synergistic interaction with systemic mineralocorticoids. *Behav. Neurosci.* 97: 746–758.

Fluharty, S. J., and Sakai, R. R. (1995). Behavioral and cellular studies of corticosterone and angiotensin interaction in brain. In *Progress in Psychobiology and Physiological Psychology*, edited by S. J. Fluharty and A. R. Morrison. New York: Academic Press.

Flynn, J. P. (1972). Patterning mechanisms, patterned reflexes, and attack behavior in cats. *Nebr. Symp. Motiv.* 20: 125–153.

Forsen, T., Eriksson, T.G., Tuomilehto, J., Osmond, C., and Barker, D. J. (1999). Growth in utero and during childhood among women who develop coronary heart disease: Longitudinal study. *BMJ* 319: 1403–1407.

Fossey, M. D., Lydiard, R. B., Ballenger, J. C., Laraia, M. T., Bissette, G., and Nemeroff, C. B. (1996). Cerebrospinal fluid corticotropin-releasing factor concentrations in patients with anxiety disorders and normal comparison subjects. *Biol. Psychiatry* 39: 703–707.

Fowler, J. S., Volkow, N. D., Malison, R., and Gatley, S. J. (1999). Neoroimaging studies of substance abuse disorders. In *Neurobiology of Mental Illness,* edited by D. S. Charney, E. J. Nestler, and B. S. Bunney. New York: Oxford University Press.

Fox, E. A., and Powley, T. L. (1985). Longitudinal columnar organization within the dorsal motor nucleus represents separate branches of the abdominal vagus. *Brain Res.* 341: 269–282.

Fraser, A. F. (1983). Processes of ethological homeostasis. *Appl. Anim. Ethol.* 11: 101–110.

Fraser, D. R. (1991). Physiology of vitamin D and calcium homeostasis. *Nestle Nutr. Workshop Ser.* 21: 23–34.

Frederick, S. L., Reus, V. I., Ginsberg, D., Hal, S. M., Munoz, R. F., and Ellman, G. (1998). Cortisol and response to dexamethasone as predictors of withdrawal distress and abstinence success in smokers. *Biol. Psychiatry* 43: 525–530.

Fredericq, L. (1885). The influence of the environment on the composition of blood of aquatic animals. *Arch. Zool. Exper. Gen.* 3: 34–38.

Fregly, M. J., Katovich, M. J., and Barney, C. C. (1979). Effect of chronic treatment with desoxycorticosterone on the dipsogenic response of rats to isoproterenol and angiotensin. *Pharmacology* 19: 165–172.

Freud, S. [1924] (1960). *A General Introduction to Psychoanalysis,* edited and translated by J. Riviere. New York: Washington Square Press.

Friedman, L. S., Sammett, J. H., Roberts, M. S., Hudlin, M., and Hunts, P. (1992). Inquiry about victimization experiences. A survey of patient preferences and physician practices. *Arch. Intern. Med.* 152: 1186–1190.

Frijda, N. H. (1986). *The Emotions.* Cambridge: Cambridge University Press.

Frim, D. M., Emanuel, R. L., Robinson, B. G., Smas, C. M., Adler, G. K., and Majzoub, J. A. (1988). Characterization and gestational regulation of corticotropin-releasing hormone messenger RNA in human placenta. *J. Clin. Invest.* 82: 287–292.

Frim, D. M., Robinson, B. G., Pasicka, K. B., and Majzoub, J. A. (1990). Differential regulation of corticotropin releasing hormone mRNA in rat brain. *Am. J. Physiol.* 258: 686–692.

Fuchs, E., and Flugge, F. (1995). Modulating of binding sites for corticotropin-releasing factor by chronic psychosocial stress. *Psychoneuroendocrinology* 20: 33–51.

Funai, E. F., O'Neill, L. M., Roque, H., and Finlay, T. H. (2000). A corticotropin releasing hormone receptor antagonist does not delay parurition in rats. *J. Perinat. Med.* 28. 294–297.

Fuster, J. M. (2001). The prefrontal cortex—An update: Time is of the essence. *Neuron* 30: 319–333.

Galaverna, O. G., Seeley, R. J., Berridge, K. C., Grill, H. J., Epstein, A. N., and Schulkin, J. (1993). Lesions of the central nucleus of the amygdala: I. Effects on taste reactivity, taste aversion learning, and sodium appetite. *Behav. Brain Res.* 59: 11–17.

Galef, B. G. Jr. (1996). Food selection: Problems in understanding how we choose foods to eat. *Neurosci. Biobehav. Rev.* 20: 67–73.

Galef, B. G. Jr., and Beck, M. (1990). Diet selection and poison avoidance by mammals individually and in social groups. In *Handbook of Behavioral Neurobiology.* Vol. 10, edited by E. M. Stricker. New York: Plenum.

Gallagher, M., and Holland, P. C. (1994). The amygdala complex: Multiple roles in associative learning and attention. *Proc. Natl. Acad. Sci. USA* 91: 11771–11776.

Gallistel, C. R. (1975). Motivation as central organizing process: The psychophysical approach to its functional and neurophysiological analysis. *Nebr. Symp. Motiv.* 22: 182–225.

Gallistel, C. R. (1980). *The Organization of Action—A New Synthesis.* Hillsdale, N.J.: Erlbaum.

Gallistel, C. R. (1992). *The Organization of Learning.* Cambridge: MIT Press.

Gambarana, C., Ghiglieri, O., Masi, F., Scheggi, S., Tagliamonte, A., and De Montis, M. G. (1999). The effects of long-term administration of rubidium or lithium on reactivity to stress and on dopamine output in the nucleus accumbens in rats. *Brain Res.* 828: 200–209.

Ganesan, R., and Sumners, C. (1989). Glucocorticoids potentiate the dipsogenic action of angiotensin II. *Brain Res.* 449: 121–130.

Garcia, J., and Ervin, F. R. (1968). Gustatory-visceral and telereceptor-cutaneous conditioning-adaptation to internal and external milieus. *Commun. Behav. Biol.* A: 389–415.

Garcia, J., Hankins, W. G., and Rusiniak, K. W. (1971). Behavioral regulation of the milieu interne in man and rat. *Science* 201: 267–269.

Gazmararian, J. A., Adams, M. M., Saltzman, L. E., Johnson, C. H., Bruce, F. C., Marks, J. S., and Zahniser, S. C. (1995). The relationship between pregnancy intendedness and physical violence in mothers of newborns. The Prams Working Group. *Obstet. Gynecol.* 85: 1031–1038.

Gazmararian, J. A., Lazorick, S., Spitz, A. M., Ballard, T. J., Saltzman, L. E., and Marks, J. S. (1996). Prevalence of violence against pregnant women. *JAMA* 275: 1915–1920.

Gendall, K. A., Sullivan, P. F., Joyce, P. R., Fear, J. L., and Bulik, C. M. (1997). Psychopathology and personality of young women who experience food cravings. *Addict. Behav.* 22: 545–555.

George, M. S., Anton, R. F., Bloomer, C., Teneback, C., Drobes, D. J., Lorberbaum, J. P., Nahas, Z., and Vincent, D. J. (2001). Activation of prefrontal cortex and anterior thalamus in alcoholic subjects on exposure to alcohol-specific cues. *Arch. Gen. Psychiatry* 58: 345–352.

Geracioti, T. D., Jr., Loosen, P. T., and Orth, D. N. (1997). Low cerebrospinal fluid corticotropin-releasing hormone concentrations in eucortisolemic depression. *Biol. Psychiatry* 42: 165–174.

Gerin, W., and Pickering, T. G. (1995). Association between delayed recovery of blood pressure after acute mental stress and parental history of hypertension. *J. Hypertens.* 13: 603–610.

Gerra, G., Calbiani, B., Zaimovic, A., Sartori, R., Ugolotti, G., Ippolito, L., Delsigore, R., Rustichelli, P., and Fontanesi, B. (1998). Regional cerebral blood flow and comorbid diagnosis in abstinent opioid addicts. *Psychiatry Res.* 83: 117–126.

Gesing, A., Bieuel, A. B., Droste, S. K., Linthorst, A. C. E., Holsboer, F., and Reul, J. M. (2001). Psychological stress increases hippocampal mineralocorticoid receptor levels: Involvement of corticotropin releasing hormone. *J. Neurosci.* 21: 4822–4829.

Gil-Rivas, V., Fiorentine, R., and Anglin, M. D. (1996). Sexual abuse, physical abuse, and posttraumatic stress disorder among women participating in outpatient drug abuse treatment. *J. Psychoactive Drugs* 28: 95–102.

Gil-Rivas, V., Fiorentine, R., Anglin, M. D., and Taylor, E. (1997). Sexual and physical abuse: Do they compromise drug treatment outcomes? *J. Subst. Abuse Treat.* 14: 351–358.

Gisolfi, C. F., and Mora, F. (2000). *The Hot Brain.* Cambridge: MIT Press.

Glavin, G. B. (1992). Dopamine: A stress modulator in the brain and gut. *Gen. Pharmacol.* 23: 1023–1026.

Glick, S. D., Merski, C., Steindorf, S., Wang, S., Keller, R. W., and Carlson, J. N. (1992). Neurochemical predisposition to self-administer morphine in rats. *Brain Res.* 578: 215–220.

Glickman, S. E., and Schiff, B. B. (1967). A biological theory of reinforcement. *Psychol. Rev.* 74: 81–109.

Glowa, J. R., Barrett, J. E., and Gold, P. W. (1992). Effects of corticotropin releasing hormone on appetitive behaviors. *Peptides* 13: 609–621.

Glynn, L. M., Wadwha, P. D., Dunkel-Schetter, C., Chicz-Demet, A., and Sandman, C. A. (2001). When stress happens matters: Effects of earthquake timing on stress responsitivity in pregnancy. *Am. J. Obstet. Gynecol.* 184: 637–642.

Goeders, N. E. (1997). A neuroendocrine role in cocaine reinforcement. *Psychoneuroendocrinology* 22: 237–259.

Goeders, N. E. (1998). Stress, the hypothalamic-pituitary-adrenal axis, and vulnerability to drug abuse. *NIDA Res. Monogr.* 169: 83–104.

Goeders, N. E. (2002). The HPA axis and cocaine reinforcement. *Psychoneuroendocrinology* 27:13–33.

Goeders, N. E., and Guerin, G. F. (1996). Role of corticosterone in intravenous cocaine self administration in rats. *Neuroendocrinology* 64. 337–348.

Goeders, N. E., and Guerin, G. F. (2000). Effects of the CRH receptor antagonist CP-154,526 on intravenous cocaine self-administration in rats. *Neuropharmacology* 23: 577–586.

Goenjian, A. K., Yehuda, R., Pynoos, R. S., Steinberg, A. M., Tashjian, M., Yang, R. K., Najarian, L. M., and Fairbanks, L. A. (1996). Basal cortisol, dexamethasone suppression of cortisol, and MHPG in adolescents after the 1988 earthquake in Armenia. *Am. J. Psychiatry* 153: 929–934.

Goland, R. S., Wardlaw, S. L., Blum, M., Tropper, P. J., and Stark, R. I. (1988). Biologically active corticotropin-releasing hormone in maternal and fetal plasma during pregnancy. *Am. J. Obstet. Gynecol.* 159: 884–890.

Goland, R. S., Conwell, I. M., Warren, W. B., and Wardlaw, S. L. (1992a). Placental corticotropin-releasing hormone and pituitary-adrenal function during pregnancy. *Neuroendocrinology* 56: 742–749.

Goland, R. S., Wardlaw, S. L., Fortman, J. D., and Stark, R. I. (1992b). Plasma corticotropin-releasing hormone factor concentrations in the baboon during pregnancy. *Endocrinology* 131: 1782–1786.

Goland, R. S., Jozak, S., Warren, W. B., Conwell, I. M., Stark, R. I., and Tropper, P. J. (1993). Elevated levels of umbilical cord plasma corticotropin-releasing hormone in growth-retarded fetuses. *J. Clin. Endocrinol. Metab.* 77: 1174–1179.

Goland, R. S., Jozak, R. N., and Conwell, I. (1994). Placental corticotropin-releasing hormone and the hypercortisolism of pregnancy. *Am. J. Obstet. Gynecol.* 171: 1287–1291.

Goland, R. S., Tropper, P. J., Warren, W. B., Stark, R. I., Jozak, S. M., and Conwell, I. M. (1995). Concentrations of corticotropin-releasing hormone in the umbilical cord blood of pregnancies complicated by pre-eclampsia. *Reprod. Fertil. Dev.* 7: 1227–1230.

Gold, P. W., and Chrousos, G. P. (1998). The endocrinology of melancholic and atypical depression: Relation to neurocircuitry and somatic consequences. *Proc. Assoc. Am. Physicians* 111: 22–34.

Gold, P. W., Chrousos, G. P., Kellner, C., Post, R., Roy, A., Augerinos, P., Schulte, H., Oldfield, E., and Loriaux, D. L. (1984). Psychiatric implications for basic and clinical studies with corticotropin-releasing hormone. *Am. J. Psychiatry* 141: 619–627.

Gold, P. W., Goodwin, F. K., and Chrousos, G. P. (1988a). Clinical and biochemical manifestation of depression: Relation to the neurobiology of stress (part 1). *N. Engl. J. Med.* 319: 348–353.

Gold, P. W., Goodwin, F. K., and Chrousos, G. P. (1988b). Clinical and biochemical manifestation of depression: Relation to the neurobiology of stress (part 2). *N. Engl. J. Med.* 319: 348–353.

Goldenberg, R. L., Iams, J. D., Mercer, B. M., Meis, P. J., Moawad, A. H., Cooper, R. L., Das, A., Thom, E., and Johnson, F. (1998). The preterm prediction

study: The value of new vs. standard risk factors in predicting early and all spontaneous preterm births. *Am. J. Public Health* 88: 233–238.

Goldenberg, R. L., Hauth, J. C., and Andrews, W. W. (2000). Intrauterine infection and preterm delivery. *N. Engl. J. Med.* 342: 1500–1507.

Goldstein, A., and Naidu, A. (1989). Multiple opioid receptors: Ligand selectivity profiles and binding site signatures. *Mol. Pharmacol.* 36: 265–272.

Goldstein, D. S. (1995a). *Stress, Catecholamines, and Cardiovascular Disease.* New York: Oxford University Press.

Goldstein, D. S. (1995b). Stress as a scientific idea: Homeostatic theory of stress and distress. *Homeostasis* 36: 117–215.

Goldstein, D. S. (2000). *The Autonomic Nervous System in Health and Disease.* New York: Marcel Dekker.

Gonzalvez, M. L., Milanes, M. V., Marinez-Pinero, M. G., Marin, M. T., and Vargas, M. L. (1994). Effects of intracerebroventricular clonidine on the hypothalamic noradrenaline and plasma corticosterone levels of opiate naïve rats and after naloxone-induced withdrawal. *Brain Res.* 647: 199–203.

Goodson, J. L., and Bass, A. H. (2001). Social behavior functions and related anatomical characteristics of vasotocin/vasopressin systems in vertebrates. *Brain Res. Rev.* 35: 246–265.

Gortmaker, S. L., Kagan, J., Caspi, A., and Silva, P. A. (1997). Daylength during pregnancy and shyness in children: Results from northern and southern hemispheres. *Dev. Psychobiol.* 31: 107–114.

Gould, E., McEwen, B. S., Tanapat, P., Galea, L. A., and Fuchs, E. (1996). Neurogenesis in the dentate gyrus of the adult tree shrew is regulated by psychosocial stress and NMDA receptor activation. *J. Neurosci.* 17: 2492–2498.

Goya, R. G., and Bolognani, F. (1999). Homeostasis, thymic hormones, and aging. *Gerontology* 45: 174–178.

Grammatopoulos, D. K., and Hillhouse, E. W. (1999). Role of corticotropin-releasing hormone in onset of labour. *Lancet* 354: 1546–1549.

Grant, S., London, E. O., Newlin, D. B., Villemagne, V. L., Liu, X., Contoreggi, C., Phillips, R. L., Kimes, A. S., and Margolin, A. (1996). Activation of memory circuits during cue-elicited cocaine craving. *Proc. Natl. Acad. Sci. USA* 93: 12040–12045.

Gray, J. A. (1987). *The Psychology of Fear and Stress.* 2nd ed. New York: Cambridge University Press.

Gray, T. S. (1990). The organization and possible function of amygdaloid corticotropin-releasing factor pathways. In *Corticotropin-Releasing Factor: Basic and Clinical Studies of a Neuropeptide,* edited by E. B. DeSousa and C. B. Nemeroff. Boca Raton, Fla.: CRC Press.

Gray, T. S. (1999). Functional and anatomical relationships among the amygdala, basal forebrain, ventral stiatum and cortex: An integrative discussion. *Ann. N.Y. Acad. Sci.* 877: 439–444.

Gray, T. S., and Bingaman, E. W. (1996). The amygdala: Corticotropin-releasing factor, steroids, and stress. *Crit. Rev. Neurobiol.* 10: 155–168.

Gray, T. S., Piechowski, R. A., Yracheta, J. M., Rittenhouse, P. A., Bethea, C. L., and Van de Kar, L. D. (1993). Ibotenic acid lesions in the bed nucleus of the stria terminalis attenuate conditioned stress induced increases in prolactin, ACTH, and corticosterone. *Neuroendocrinology* 57: 517–524.

Greenspan, S. L., and Greenspan, F. S. (1999). The effect of thyroid hormone on skeletal integrity. *Ann. Intern. Med.* 130: 750–758.

Greenwood Van Meerveld, B., Gibson, M., Gunter, W., Shepard, J., Foreman, R., and Myers, D. (2001). Stereotaxic delivery of corticosterone to the amygdala modulates colonic sensitivity in rats. *Brain Res.* 893: 135–142.

Grigoriadia, D. E., Dent, G. W., Turner, J. G., Uno, H., Shelton, S. E., De Souza, E. B., and Kalin, N. H. (1995). Corticotropin-releasing factory (CRF) receptors in infant rhesus monkey brain and pituitary gland: Biochemical characterization and autoradiographic localization. *Dev. Neurosci.* 17: 357–367.

Grill, H. J., and Berridge, K. C. (1985). Taste reactivity as a measure of the neural control of palatability. In *Progress in Psychobiology and Physiological Psychology*. Vol. 11, edited by A. N. Epstein and A. R. Morrison. New York: Academic Press, pp. 1–54.

Grill, H. J., and Norgren, R. (1978a). The taste reactivity test. I: Oral facial responses to gustatory stimuli in neurologically normal rats. *Brain Res.* 142: 263–279.

Grill, H. J., and Norgren, R. (1978b). The taste reactivity test. II: Mimetic responses to gustatory stimuli in chronic thalamic and chronic decerebrated rats. *Brain Res.* 143: 281–287.

Grillon, C. C., Morgan, S., Davis, M., and Wouthwick, S. (1996). Preliminary report presented at the Annual Meeting of the Society for Biological Psychiatry, May, New York.

Grinker, R. R., and Spiegel, J. P. (1945). *Men Under Stress.* Philadelphia: Blakiston.

Groenwegen, H. J., Berendse, H. W., Meredith, G. E., Haber, S. N., Voorn, P., Wolters, J. G., and Lohman, A. H. M. (1991). Functional anatomy of the ventral, limbic system-innervated striatum. In *The Mesolimbic Dopamine System: From Motivation to Action.* Edited by P. W. Scheel Kruger. Chichester, UK: Wiley.

Groome, L. J., Loizou, P. C., Holland, S. B., Smith, L. A., and Hoff, C. (1999). High vagal tone is associated with more efficient regulation of homeostasis in low-risk human fetuses. *Dev. Psychobiol.* 35: 25–34.

Grossman, S. P. (1968). The physiological basis of specific and nonspecific motivational processes. *Nebr. Symp. Motiv.* 16: 1–46.

Grossman, S. P. (1979). The biology of motivation. *Annu. Rev. Psychol.* 30: 209–242.

Guillemin, R., and Rosenberg, B. (1955). Humoral hypothalamic control of anterior pituitary: A study with combined tissue cultures. *Endocrinology* 57: 599–607.

Gunnar, M. R. (1998). Quality of early care and buffering or neuroendocrine stress reactions: Potential effects on the developing human brain. *Prev. Med.* 27: 208–211.

Gunnar, M. R., and Davis, E. P. (2001). The developmental psychobiology of stress and emotion in early childhood. In *Comprehensive Handbook of Psychology.* Vol. 6, *Developmental Psychology,* edited by R. M. Lerner, M. A. Easterbrooks, and J. Mistry. New York: Wiley.

Gunnar, M. R., Isensee, J., and Fust, L. S. (1987). Adrenocortical activity and the Brazelton neonatal assessment scale: Moderating effects of the newborn's biomedical status. *Child Dev.* 58: 1448–1458.

Gunnar, M. R., Mangelsdorf, S., Larson, M., and Hertsgaard, L. (1989). Attachment, temperament, and adrenocortical activity in infancy: A study of psychoendocrine regulation. *Dev. Psychol.* 25: 355–363.

Gutman, D. A., Owens, M. J., Skelton, K. H., Knight, D. L., Thrivirkraman, K. V., Plotsky, P. M., and Nemeroff, C. B. (2000). Behavioral, neuroendocrine, and pharmacokinetic observations on CRF1-selective antagonist, R121919 in the rat. *Neuropsychopharmacology* 23: S119–S120.

Guyton, J. R., Foster, R. O., Soeldner, J. S., Tan, M. H., Kahn, C. B., Koncz, L., and Gleason, R. E. (1978). A model of glucose-insulin homeostasis in man that incorporates the heterogeneous fast pool theory of pancreatic insulin release. *Diabetes* 27: 1027–1042.

Habib, K. E., Weld, K. P., Schulkin, J., Pushkas, J., Listwak, S., Champoux, M., Shannon, C., Chrousos, G. P., Suomi, S., Gold, P. W., and Higley, J. D. (1999). Cerebrospinal fluid levels of corticotropin-releasing hormone positively correlate with acute and chronic social stress in non-human primates. Paper presented at Society for Neuroscience Annual Meeting, Miami Beach, Florida.

Habib, K. E., Weld, K. P., Rice, K. C., Pushkas, J., Champoux, M., Listwak, S., Webster, E. L., Atkinson, A. J., Schulkin, J., Contoreggic, C., Chrousos, G. P., McCann, S. M., Soumi, S. J., Higley, J. D., and Gold, P. W. (2000). Oral administration of a corticotropin-releasing hormone receptor antagonist significantly attenuates behavioral, neuroendocrine, and autonomic responses to stress in primates. *Proc. Natl. Acad. Sci. USA* 97: 6079–6084.

Habib, K. E., Pushksas, J. G., Champoux, M., Chrousos, G. P., Rice, K. C., Schulkin, J., Erickson, K., Weld, K. P., Ronsabille, D., McCann, S. M., Soumi, S. J., Gold, P. W., and Higley, J. D. (2002). Sensitization of brain CRH after maternal deprivation and peer separation in juvenile primates. Unpublished.

Haldane, J. S. (1929). Claude Bernard's conception of the internal environment. *Science* 69: 433–454.

Hamberger, L. K., Saunders, D. G., and Hovey, M. (1992). Prevalence of domestic violence in community practice and rate of physician inquiry. *Fam. Med.* 24: 283–287.

Hamilton, R. B., and Norgren, R. (1984). Central projections of gustatory nerves. *J. Comp. Neurol.* 222. 560–577.

Haney, M., Maccari, S., Le Moal, M., Simon, H., and Piazza, P. V. (1995). Social stress increases the acquisition of cocaine self-administration in male and female rats. *Brain Res.* 698: 46–52.

Harding, C., Knox, W. F., Faragher, E. B., Balidam, A., and Bundred, N. J. (1996). Hormone replacement therapy and tumor grade in breast cancer: Prospective study in screening unit. *BMJ* 312: 1646–1647.

Harmon-James, E., and Allen, J. J. (1998). Anger and frontal brain activity: EEG asymmetry consistent with approach motivation despite negative affective valence. *J. Pers. Soc. Psychol.* 74: 1310–1316.

Harris, A. K. (1987). Cell motility and the problem of anatomical homeostasis. *J. Cell. Sci. Suppl.* 8: 121–140.

Harrison, A. A., Liem, Y. T. B., and Markou, A. (2001). Fluoxetine combined with a serotonin-1A receptor antagonist revered reward deficits observed during nicotine and amphetamine withdrawal in rats. *Neuropsychopharmacology* 25: 55–71.

Hartline, K. M., Owens, M. J., and Nemeroff, C. B. (1996). Postmortem and cerebrospinal fluid studies of corticotropin-releasing factor in humans. *Ann. N.Y. Acad. Sci.* 780: 96–105.

Hartmann, P. E., Sherriff, J. L., and Mitoulas, L. R. (1998). Homeostatic mechanisms that regulate lactation during energetic stress. *J. Nutr.* 128 (2 suppl.): 394S–399S.

Hauser, M. D. (1996). *The Evolution of Communication.* Cambridge, Mass.: MIT Press.

Hawley, R. J., Major, L. F., Schulman, E. A., and Lake, C. R. (1981). CSF levels of norepinephrine during alcohol withdrawal. *Arch. Neurol.* 38: 289–292.

Haymond, M. W., and Sunehag, A. (1999). Controlling the sugar bowl. Regulation of glucose homeostasis in children. *Endocrinol. Metab. Clin. North Am.* 28: 663–694.

Hebb, D. O. (1946). Emotion in man and animal: An analysis of the intuitive processes of recognition. *Psych. Rev.* 53: 88–106.

Hebb, D. O. (1949). *The Organization of Behavior: A Neuropsychological Theory.* New York: Wiley.

Hebb, D. O. (1955). Drives and the conceptual nervous system. *Psychol. Rev.* 62: 243–254.

Heggenes, J., Krog, O. M. W., and Lindas, O. R. (1993). Homeostatic behavioural responses in a changing environment: Brown trout *(Salmo trutta)* become nocturnal during winter. *J. Anim. Ecol.* 62: 295–308.

Heilman, K. M. (1997). The neurobiology of emotional experience. *J. Neuropsychiatry Clin. Neurosci.* 9: 439–448.

Heim, C., Ehlert, U., Hanker, J. P., and Hellhammer, D. H. (1998). Abuse-related posttraumatic stress disorder and alterations of the hypothalamic-

pituitary-adrenal axis in women with chronic pelvic pain. *Psychosom. Med.* 60: 309–318.

Heim, C., Newport, D. J., Heit, S., Graham, Y. P., Wilcox, M., Bonsall, R., Miller, A. H., and Nemeroff, C. B. (2000). Pituitary-adrenal and autonomic responses to stress in women after sexual and physical abuse in childhood. *JAMA* 294: 592–597.

Heim, C., Newport, D. J., Bonsall, R., Miller, A. H., and Nemeroff, C. B. (2001). Altered pituitary-adrenal axis responses to provocative challenge tests in adult survivors of childhood abuse. *Am. J. Psychiatry* 158: 575–581.

Heinrichs, S. C., Pich, E. M., Miczek, K., Britton, K. T., and Koob, G. F. (1992). Corticotropin-releasing factor antagonist reduces emotionality in socially defeated rats via direct neurotropic action. *Brain Res.* 581: 190–197.

Heinrichs, S. C., Manzaghi, F., Pich, E. M., Hauger, R. L., and Koob, G. F. (1993). Corticotropin releasing factor in the paraventricular nucleus modulates feeding induced by neuropeptide Y. *Brain Res.* 611: 18–24.

Heinrichs, S. C., Menzaghi, F., Pich, E. M., Baldwin, H. A., Rassnick, S., Britton, K. T., and Koob, G. F. (1994). Anti-stress action of a corticotropin-releasing factor antagonist on behavioral reactivity to stressors of varying type and intensity. *Neuropsychopharmacology* 11: 179–186.

Heinrichs, S. C., Menzaghi, F., Schulteis, G., Koob, G. F., and Stinus, L. (1995). Supression of corticotropin-releasing hormone in the amygdala attenuates aversive consequences of morphine withdrawal. *Behav. Pharmacol.* 6: 74–80.

Heinrichs, S. C., Lapsansky, J., Behan, D. P., Chan, R. K., Sawchenko., P. E., Lorang, M., Ling, N., Vale, W. W., and De Souza, E. B. (1996). Corticotropin-releasing factor-binding protein ligand inhibitor blunts excessive weight gain in genetically obese Zucker rats and rats during nicotine withdrawal. *Proc. Natl. Acad. Sci. USA* 93: 15475–15480.

Heinrichs, S. C., Min, S. C., Tamraz, S., Carmouche, M., Boehme, S. A., and Vale, W. W. (1997). Anti-sexual and anxiogenic behavioral consequences of corticotropin-releasing hormone factor overexpression are centrally mediated. *Psychoneuroendocrinology* 22: 215–224.

Heishman, S. J., Huestis, M. A., Henningfield, J. E., and Cone, E. J. (1990). Acute and residual effects of marijuana: Profiles of plasma THC levels, physiological, subjective, and performance measures. *Pharmacol Biochem. Behav.* 37: 561–565.

Helfer, V., Deransart, C., Marescaux, C., and Depaulis, A. (1996). Amygdala kindling in the rat: Anxiogenic-like consequences. *Neuroscience* 73: 971–978.

Hellstrom, H. R. (1999). The altered homeostatic theory: A holistic approach to multiple diseases, including atherosclerosis, ischemic diseases, and hypertension. *Med. Hypotheses* 53: 194–199.

Henen, B. T. (1997). Seasonal and annual energy budgets of female desert tortoises. *Ecology* 78:283–296.

Henke, P. G., Ray, A., and Sullivan, R. M. (1991). The amygdala: Emotions and gut function. *Dig. Dis. Sci.* 36: 1633–1643.

Henry, J. P., Stephens, P. M., and Ely, D. L. (1986). Psychosocial hypertension and the defence and defeat reactions. *J. Hypertens.* 4: 687–697.

Herbert, J. (1993). Peptides in the limbic system: Neurochemical codes for co-ordinated adaptive responses to behavioral and physiological demand. *Prog. Neurobiol.* 41: 723–791.

Herbert, J. (1996a). Sexuality, stress, and the chemical architecture of the brain. *Annu. Rev. Sex Res.* 7: 1–43.

Herbert, J. (1996). Studying the central actions of angiotensin using the expression of immediate-early genes: Expectations and limitations. *Regul. Pept.* 66: 13–18.

Herbert, J., and Schulkin, J. (2002). Neurochemical coding of adaptive responses in the limbic system. In *Hormones, Brain and Behavior,* edited by D. Pfaff. New York: Elsevier.

Herd, J. A. (1991). Cardiovascular response to stress. *Physiol Rev.* 71: 305–330.

Herman, J. P., and Cullian, W. E. (1997). Neurocircuitry of stress: Central control of the hypothalamic-pituitary-adrenocortical axis. *Trends Neurosci.* 20: 78–84.

Herman, J. P., Dolgas, C. M., and Carlson, S. L. (1998). Ventral subiculum regulates hypothalamic-pituitary-adrenocortical and behavioral responses to cognitive stressors. *Neuroscience* 86: 449–459.

Herrick, C. J. (1905). The central gustatory pathway in the brain of bony fishes. *J. Comp. Neurol.* 15: 375–486.

Heuser, I., Bissette, G., Dettling, M., Schweiger, U., Gotthardt, U., Schmider, J., Lammers, C. H., Nemeroff, C. B., and Holsboer, F. (1998). Cerebrospinal fluid concentrations of corticotropin-releasing hormone, vasopressin, and somatostatin in depressed patients and healthy controls: response to amitriptyline treatment. *Depression Anxiety* 8: 71–79.

Higley, J. D., and Bennett, A. J. (1999). Central nervous system serotonin and personality as variables contributing to excessive alcohol consumption in non-human primates. *Alcohol Alcohol.* 34: 402–418.

Higley, J. D., Hasert, M. F., Suomi, S. J., and Linnoila, M. (1991). Nonhuman primate model of alcohol abuse: Effects of early experiences, personality, and stress on alcohol consumption. *Proc. Natl. Acad. Sci. USA* 88: 7261–7265.

Higley, J. D., Suomi, S. J., and Linnoila, M. (1992). A longitudinal assessment of CSF monoamine metabolite and plasma cortisol concentrations in young rhesus monkeys. *Biol. Psychiatry* 32: 127–145.

Higley, J. D., Thompson, W. W., Champoux, M., Goldman, D., Hasert, M. F., Kraemer, G. W., Scanlan, J. M., Suomi, S. J., and Linnoila, M. (1993). Paternal and maternal genetic and environmental contributions to cerebrospinal fluid monoamine metabolites in rhesus monkeys *(Macaca mulatta). Arch Gen Psychiatry* 50: 615–623.

Higley, J. D., Suomi, S. J., and Linnoila, M. (1996). A nonhuman primate model of type II excessive alcoholism? Part 1. Low cerebrospinal fluid 5-hydroxyindoleacetic acid concentrations and diminished social competence correlate with excessive alcohol consumption. *Alcohol Clin. Exp. Res.* 20: 629–642.

Hill, E. M., Ross, L. T., Mudd, S. A., and Blow, F. C. (1997). Adulthood functioning: The joint effects of prenatal alcoholism, gender, and childhood social-economic stress. *Addiction* 92: 583–596.

Hillier, S. L., Nugent, R. P., Eschenbach, D. A., Krohn, M. A., Gibbs, R. S., Martin, D. H., Cotch, M. F., Edelman, R., Pastorek, J. G. 2nd, Rao, A. V., et al. (1995). Association between bacterial vaginosis and preterm delivery of a low-birth-weight infant. *N. Engl. J. Med.* 333: 1737–1742.

Himpens, B., and Missiaen, L. (1993). [Ca2+ homeostasis in mammalian cells] [Dutch]. *Verh. K. Acad. Geneesk Belg.* 55: 425–456.

Hinde, R. A. (1968). Critique of energy models of motivation. In *Motivation,* edited by D. Bindra and J. Stewart. Baltimore: Penguin Books.

Hinde, R. A. (1970). *Animal Behavior—A Synthesis of Ethology and Comparative Psychology.* 2nd ed. New York: McGraw-Hill.

Hirshfeld, D. R., Dina, R., Rosenbaum, J. F., Biederman, J., Boduc, E. A., and Kagan, J. (1992). Stable behavioral inhibition and its association with anxiety disorder. *J. Am. Acad. Child Adolesc. Psychiatry* 31: 103–110.

Hitchcock, J. M., and Davis, M. (1991). Efferent pathway of the amygdala involved in conditioned fear as measured with the fear-potentiated startle paradigm. *Behav. Neurosci.* 105: 826–841.

Hobel, C. J., Arora, C. P., and Korst, L. M. (1999a). Corticotrophin-releasing hormone and CRH-binding protein. Differences between patients at risk for preterm birth and hypertension. *Ann. N.Y. Acad. Sci.* 897: 54–65.

Hobel, C. J., Dunkel-Schetter, C., Roesch, S. C., Castro, L. C., and Arora, C. P. (1999b). Maternal plasma corticotropin-releasing hormone associated with stress at 20 weeks' gestation in pregnancies ending in preterm delivery. *Am. J. Obstet. Gynecol.* 180: S257–S263.

Hoebel, B. (1988). Neuroscience of motivation: Peptides and pathways that define motivational systems. In: *Handbook of Experimental Psychology,* edited by S. S. Stevens. New York: Wiley Press.

Hofer, M. A. (1973). The role of nutrition in the physiological and behavioral effects of early maternal separation on infant rats. *Psychosom. Med.* 35: 350–359.

Hofer, M. A. (1984). Early stages in the organization of cardiovascular control. *Exp. Biol. Med.* 175: 147–157.

Hofer, M. A. (1994). Early relationships as regulators of infant physiology and behavior. *Acta Paediatr. Suppl.* 397: 9–18.

Hofer, M. A., and Sullivan, R. M. (2001). Toward a neurobiology of attachment. In *Developmental Cognitive Neuroscience,* edited by C. A. Nelson, M. Luciana. Cambridge: MIT Press.

Hollerman, J. R., Tremblay, L., and Schultz, W. (2000). Involvement of basal ganglia and orbitofrontal cortex in goal-directed behavior. *Prog. Brain Res.* 126: 193–215.

Holmes, F. L. (1986). Claude Bernard, the milieu interieur, and regulatory physiology. *Pubbl. Stn. Zool. Napoli [II]* 8: 3–25.

Holsboer, F. (2000). The corticosteroid receptor hypothesis of depression. *Neuropharmacology* 23: 477–501.

Holsboer, F., Muller, O. A., Doerr, H. G., Sippell, W. G., Stalla, G. K., Gerken, A., Sterger, A., Boll, E., and Benkert, O. (1984). ACTH and multi-steroid responses to corticotropin-releasing hormone in depressive illness: Relationship to multi-steroid responses after ACTH stimulation and dexamethasone suppression. *Psychoneuroendocrinology* 9: 147–160.

Holt, D. J., Graybiel, A. M., and Saper, C. B. (1997). Neurochemical architecture of the human striatum. *J. Comp. Neurol.* 384: 1–25.

Holzman, C., Jetton, J., Siler-Khodor, T., Fisher, R., and Rip, T. (2001). Second trimester corticotropin releasing hormone. *Obstetr. Gynecol.* 97: 657–663.

Horan, D. L., Hill, L. D., and Schulkin, J. (2000). Childhood sexual abuse and preterm labor in adulthood: An endocrinological hypothesis. *Womens Health Issues* 10: 27–33.

Horger, B. A., and Roth, R. H. (1996). The role of mesoprefrontal dopamine neurons in stress. *Crit. Rev. Neurobiol.* 10: 395–418.

Horner, M. D., Waid, L. R., Johnson, D. E., Latham, P. K., and Anton, R. F. (1999). The relationship of cognitive functioning to amount of recent and lifetime alcohol consumption in outpatient alcoholics. *Addict. Behav.* 24: 449–453.

Horst, R. L. (1986). Regulation of calcium and phosphorous homeostasis in the dairy cow. *J. Dairy Sci.* 69: 604–616.

Hosking, D., Chilvers, C. E., Christiansen, C., Raun, P., Wasnich, R., Ross, P., McClung, M., Balske, A., Thompson, D., Daley, M., and Yates, A. J. (1998). Prevention of bone loss with alendronate in postmenopausal women under 60 years of age. Early postmenopausal intervention cohort study group. *N. Engl. J. Med.* 338: 485–492.

Housknecht, K. L., and Portocarrero, C. P. (1998). Leptin and its receptors: Regulators of whole-body energy homeostasis. *Domest. Anim. Endocrinol.* 15: 457–475.

Howard, M. O., Kivlahan, D., and Walker, R. D. (1997). Cloninger's tridimensional theory of personality and psychopathology: Applications to substance use disorders. *J. Stud. Alcohol* 58: 48–66.

Hsu, D. T., Chen, F. L., Takahashi, L. K., and Kalin, N. H. (1998). Rapid stress-induced elevations in corticotropin-releasing hormone mRNA in rat central amygdala nucleus and hypothalamic paraventricular nucleus: An in situ hybridization analysis. *Brain Res.* 788: 305–310.

Huether, G. (1996). The central adaptation syndrome: Psychosocial stress as a trigger for adaptive modifications of brain structure and brain function. *Pregnancy Neurobiol.* 48: 569–612.

Hughs, K. M., Popi, L., and Wolgin, D. L. (1999). Loss of tolerance to amphetamine-induced hypophagia in rats: Homeostatic readjustment vs. instrumental learning. *Pharm. Biochem. Behav.* 64: 177–182.

Huhman, K. L., and Albers, H. E. (1993). Estradiol increases the behavioral response to arginine vasopressin (AVP) in the medial preoptic-anterior hypothalamus. *Peptides* 14: 1049–1054.

Hull, C. L. (1943). *Principles of Behavior.* New York: Appleton-Century Crofts.

Hunter, J. (1778). Of the heat of animals and vegetables. *Philos. Trans. R. Soc. Lond. B Biol. Sci.* 68: 7–49.

Hurwitz, S. (1989). Calcium homeostasis in birds. *Vitam. Horm.* 45: 173–221.

Hurwitz, S. (1996). Homeostatic control of plasma calcium concentration. *Crit. Rev. Biochem. Mol. Biol.* 31: 41–100.

Hurwitz, S., Fishman, S., Bar, A., Pines, M., Riesenfeld, G., and Talpaz, H. (1983). Simulation of calcium homeostasis: Modeling and parameter estimation. *Am. J. Physiol.* 245: R664–R672.

Hyman, S. E. (1996). Addiction to cocaine and amphetamine. *Neuron* 16: 901–904.

Ikemoto, S., and Panksepp, J. (1999). The role of the nucleus accumbens dopamine in motivated behavior: A unifying interpretation with special reference to reward-seeking. *Brain Res. Rev.* 31: 6–41.

Illnerova, H., and Vanecek, J. (1982). Two-oscillator structure of the pacemaker controlling the circadian rhythm of N-Acetyltransferase in the rat pineal gland. *J. Comp. Physiol.* 145: 539–548.

Imaki, T., Nahan, J. L., Rivier, C., and Vale, W. (1991). Differential regulation of corticotropin releasing hormone mRNA in rat brain regions by glucocorticoids and stress. *J. Neurosci.* 11: 585–598.

Ingle, D. J. (1952). The role of the adrenal cortex in homeostasis. *J. Endocrinol.* 8: 23–37.

Ingle, D. J. (1954). Permissibility of hormone action: A review. *Acta Endocrinologica* 17: 172–186.

Insel, T. R. (1992). Oxytocin—A neuropeptide for affiliation: Evidence from behavioral, receptor autoradiographic, and comparative studies. *Psychoneuroendocrinology* 17: 3–35.

Insel, T. R., Aloi, J. A., Goldstein, D. S., Wood, J. H., and Jimmerson, D. C. (1978). Plasma cortisol and catecholamine responses to intracerebroventricular administration of CRF to rhesus monkeys. *Life Sci.* 34: 1873–1878.

Ireland, T., and Widom, C. S. (1994). Childhood victimization and risk for alcohol and drug arrests. *Int. J. Addict.* 29: 235–274.

Irwin, W., Davidson, R. J., Lowe, M. J., Mock, B. J., Sorenson, J. A., and Turski, P. A. (1996). Human amygdala activation detected with echo-planar functional magnetic resonance imaging. *Neuroreport* 7: 1765–1769.

Ito, R., Dalley, J. W., Howes, S. R., Robbins, T. W., and Everitt, B. J. (2000). Dissociation in conditioned dopamine release in the nucleus accumbens core

and shell in response to cocaine cues and during cocaine-seeking behavior in rats. *J. Neurosci.* 20: 7489–7495.

Iversen, L. L. (1967). *The Uptake and Storage of Noradrenaline in Sympathetic Nerves.* Cambridge: Cambridge University Press.

Izard, C. E. (1978). Emotions as motivations: An evolutionary-development perspective. *Nebr. Symp. Motiv.* 26: 163–200.

Jackson, J. H. (1958). The Croonian lectures on evolution and dissolution of the nervous system. In *Selected Writings of John Hughlings Jackson,* edited by J. Taylor. London: Staples Press. (Reprinted from *BMJ* 1(1884): 591–593, 660–663, 703–707.)

Jackson, M., and Dudley, D. J. (1998). Endocrine assays to predict preterm delivery. *Clin. Perinatol.* 25: 837–857.

Jacobs, K. M., Mark, G. P., and Scott, T. (1988). Taste responses in the nucleus tractus solitatrious of sodium-deprived rats. *J. Physiol. (Lond.)* 406: 393–410.

Jacobson, L., and Sapolsky, R. (1991). The role of the hippocampus in feedback regulation of the hypothalamic-pituitary-adrenal axis. *Endocr. Rev.* 12: 118–134.

Jaeger, T. V., and van der Kooy, D. (1996). Separate neural substrates mediate the motivating and discriminative properties of morphine. *Behav. Neurosci.* 110: 181–201.

James, W. (1884). What is an emotion? *Mind* 9: 188–205.

James, W. (1890). *Principles of Psychology.* New York: Henry Holt.

Jang, K. L., Livesley, W. J., and Vernon, P. A. (1997). Gender-specific etiological differences in alcohol and drug problems: A behavioral genetic analysis. *Addiction* 92: 1265–1276.

Jaros, G. G., Belonje, P. C., van Hoorn-Hickman, R., and Newman, E. (1984). Transient response of the calcium homeostatic system: Effect of calcitonin. *Am. J. Physiol.* 246: R693–R697.

Jarvinen, M. K., and Powley, T. L. (1999). Dorsal motor nucleus of the vagus neurons: A multivariate taxonomy. *J. Comp. Neurol.* 403: 359–377.

Jaspers, K. [1913] (1997). *Gen. Psychopathol.* Baltimore: Johns Hopkins University Press.

Jennings, H. S. (1906). *Behavior of the Lower Organism.* New York: Columbia University Press.

Joels, M. (1997). Steroid hormones and excitability in the mammalian brain. *Front. Neuroendocrinol.* 18: 2–48.

Joels, M., and de Kloet, R. (1994). Mineralocorticoid and glucocorticoid receptors in the brain: Implications for the permeability and transmitter systems. *Prog. Neurobiol.* 43: 1–36.

Johansson, C., Gardsell, P., Mellstrom, D., Johnell, O., and Nilssen, B. E. (1992). Bone mineral measurement is a predictor of survival. *Bone Miner.* 17: 166.

Johnson, A. E., Barberis, C., and Albers, H. E. (1995). Castration reduces vasopressin receptor binding in the hamster hypothalamus. *Brain Res.* 673: 153–159.

Johnson, A. K., and Gross, P. M. (1993). Sensory circumventricular organs and brain homeostatic pathways. *FASEBJ* 7: 678–686.

Johnson, A. K., and Thunhorst, R. L. (1997). The neuroendocrinology of thirst and salt appetite: Visceral sensory signals and mechanisms of central integration. *Front. Neuroendocrinol.* 18: 292–353.

Johnson, D. E., Waid, L. R., and Anton, R. F. (1997). Childhood hyperactivity, gender, and Cloninger's personality dimensions in alcoholics. *Addict. Behav.* 22: 649–653.

Johnson, E. O., Kamilaris, T. C., Chrousos, G. P., and Gold, P. W. (1992). Mechanisms of stress: A dynamic overview of hormonal and behavioral homeostasis. *Neurosci. Biobehav. Rev.* 16: 115–130.

Johnson, K. G., and Cabanac, M. (1982). Homeostatic competition between food intake and temperature regulation in rats. *Physiol. Behav.* 28: 675–679.

Johnson, P. E., Hunt, C. D., Milne, D. B., and Mullen, L. K. (1993). Homeostatic control of zinc metabolism in men: Zinc excretion and balance in men fed diets low in zinc. *Am. J. Clin. Nutr.* 57: 557–565.

Johnson, V., and Padina, R. J. (1993). A longitudinal examination of the relationships among stress, coping strategies, and problems associated with alcohol use. *Alcohol Clin. Exp. Res.* 17: 696–702.

Johnston, J. B. (1923). Further contributions to the study of the evolution of the forebrain. *J. Comp. Neurol.* 56: 337–381.

Johnston-Brooks, C. H., Lewis, M. A., Evans, G. W., and Whalen, C. K. (1998). Chronic stress and illness in children: The role of allostatic load. *Psychosom. Med.* 60: 597–603.

Johnstone, H. A., Wigger, A., Douglas, A. J., Neumann, I. D., Landgraf, R., Seckl, J. R., and Russell, J. A. (2000). Attenuation of hypothalamic-pituitary-adrenal axis stress responses in late pregnancy: Changes in feedforward and feedback mechanisms. *J. Neuroendocrinol.* 12: 811–822.

Jones, R. B., and Satterlee, D. G. (1996). Threat-induced behavioral inhibition in Japanese quail genetically selected for contrasting adrenocortical response to mechanical restraint. *Br. Poult. Sci.* 37: 465–470.

Jones, R. B., Beuving, G., and Blockhuis, H. J. (1988). Tonic immobility and heterophil/lymphocyte responses of the domestic fowl to corticosterone infusion. *Physiol. Behav.* 42: 249–253.

Jones, R. B., Satterlee, D. G., and Ryder, F. H. (1992). Fear and distress in Japanese quail chicks of two lines genetically selected for low or high adrenocortical response to immobilization stress. *Horm. Behav.* 26: 385–393.

Jones, S. A., Brooks, A. N., and Challis, J. R. G. (1989). Steroids modulate corticotropin-releasing hormone production in human fetal membranes and placenta. *Clin. Endocrinol. Metabol.* 68: 825–830.

Joracsky, D. (1989). *Russian Psychology: A Critical History.* Oxford: Basil Blackwell.

Jordanova, L. J. (1978). The historiography of the Claude Bernard industry. *Hist. Sci.* 16: 214–221.

Joseph-Vanderpool, J. R., Rosenthal, N. E., Chrousos, G. P., Wehr, T. A., Skwerer, R., Kasper, S., and Gold, P. W. (1991). Abnormal pituitary-adrenal responses to corticotropin-releasing hormone in patients with seasonal affective disorder: Clinical and pathophysiological implications. *J. Clin. Endocrinol. Metabol.* 72: 1382–1387.

Joshi, J. G., Dhar, M., Clauberg, M., and Chauthaiwale, V. (1993). Iron and aluminum homeostasis in neural disorders. *Environ. Health Perspect.* 102: 207 213.

Ju, G., Swanson, L. W., and Simerly, R. B. (1989). Studies on the cellular architecture of the bed nuclei of the stria terminalis in the rat: II. Chemoarchitecture. *J. Comp. Neurol.* 280: 603–621.

Jung, S., and Littman, D. R. (1999). Chemokine receptors in lymphoid organ homeostasis. *Curr. Opin. Immunol.* 11: 319–325.

Kagan, J., and Schulkin, J. (1995). On the concepts of fear. *Harvard Rev. Psychiatry* 3: 31–34.

Kagan, J., and Snidman, N. (1999). Early childhood predictors of adult anxiety disorders. *Biol. Psychiatry* 46: 1536–1541.

Kagan, J., Resnick, J. S., and Snidman, N. (1988). Biological bases of childhood shyness. *Science* 240: 167–171.

Kagan, J., Snidman, N., Julia-Sellers, M., and Johnson, M. O. (1991). Temperament and allergic symptoms. *Psychom. Med.* 53: 332–340.

Kalin, N. H. (1985). Behavioral effects of corticotropin releasing hormone administered to rhesus monkeys. *Fed. Proc.* 44: 249–253.

Kalin, N. H., and Shelton, S. E. (1998). Asymmetric frontal brain ontogeny and stability of separation and threat-induced defensive behaviors in rhesus monkeys during the first year of life. *Am. J. Primatol.* 44: 125–135.

Kalin, N. H., and Takahashi, L. K. (1990). Fear-motivated behavior by prior shock experience is mediated by corticotropin-releasing hormone. *Brain Res.* 509: 80–81.

Kalin, N. H., Shelton, S. E., and Barksdale, C. M. (1989). Behavioral and physiologic effects of CRH administered to infant primates undergoing maternal separation. *Neuropsychopharmacology* 2: 97–104.

Kalin, N. H., Takahashi, L. K., and Chen, F. L. (1994). Restraint stress increases corticotropin releasing hormone mRNA content in the amygdala and the paraventricular nucleus. *Brain Res.* 656: 182–186.

Kalin, N. H., Larson, C., Shelton, S. E., and Davidson, R. J. (1998a). Asymmetric frontal brain activity, cortisol, and behavior associated with fearful temperament in rhesus monkeys. *Behav. Neurosci.* 112: 286–292.

Kalin, N. H., Shelton, S. E., Rickman, M., and Davidson, R. J. (1998b). Individual differences in freezing and cortisol in infant and mother rhesus monkeys. *Behav. Neurosci.* 112: 251–254.

Kalin, N. H., Shelton, S. E., and Davidson, R. J. (2000). Cerebrospinal fluid corticotropin-releasing hormone levels are elevated in monkeys with

patterns of brain activity associated with fearful temperament. *Biol. Psychiatry* 47: 579–585.

Kalin, N. H., Shelton, S. E., Davidson, R. J., and Kelley, A. E. (2001). The primate amygdala mediates acute fear but not the behavioral and physiological components of anxious temperament. *J. Neurosci.* 21: 2067–2074.

Kalra, S. P. (1993). Mandatory neuropeptide-steroid signaling for the preovulatory LHRH discharge. *Endocrinol. Rev.* 14: 507–538.

Kalra, S. P., Dube, M. G., Sahu, A., Phelps, C. P., and Kalra, P. S. (1991). Neuropeptide Y secretion increases in the paraventricular nucleus in association with increased appetite for food. *Proc. Natl. Acad. Sci. USA* 88: 10931–10935.

Kant, G. I., Bauman, R. B., Anderson, S. M., and Moughey, E. H. (1992). Effects of controllable vs. uncontrollable chronic stress on stress responsive plasma hormones. *Physiol. Behav.* 51: 1285–1288.

Kanter, E. D., Wilkinson, C. W., Radant, A. D., Petrie, E. C., Dobie, D. J., McFall, M. F., Peskin, E. R., and Raskind, M. A. (2001). Glucocorticoid feedback sensitivity and adrenocortical responsiveness in posttraumatic stress disorder. *Biol. Psychiatry* 50: 238–245.

Kapp, B. S., Frysinger, R. C., Gallagher, M., and Haselton, J. R. (1979). Amygdala central nucleus lesions: Effects on heart rate conditioning in the rabbit. *Physiol. Behav.* 23: 1109–1117.

Karalas, K., Goodwin, G., and Majzoub, J. A. (1996). Cortisol blockade of progesterone: A possible molecular mechanism involved in the initiation of labor. *Nat. Med.* 2: 556–560.

Kardiner, A., and Spiegel, H. (1947). *The Traumatic Neuroses of War.* New York: Paul Hoeber.

Karil, P. (1968). The limbic system and the motivation process. *J. Physiol. (Paris)* 60 (suppl. 1): 3–48.

Karpf, D. B., Shapiro, D. R., Seeman, E., Ensrud, K. E., Johnston, C. C. Jr., Adami, S., Harris, S. T., Santora, A. C. II, Hirsch, J. L., Oppenheimer, L., and Thompson, D. (1997). Prevention of nonvertebral fractures by alendronate. A meta-analysis. Alendronote osteoporosis treatment study group. *JAMA* 277: 1159–1164.

Kasckow, J. W., Regmi, A., Gill, P. S., Parkes, D. G., and Geracioti, T. D. (1997). Regulation of corticotropin-releasing factor (CRF) messenger ribonucleic acid and CRF peptide in the amygdala: Studies in primary amygdalar cultures. *Endocrinology* 138: 4774–4782.

Kasckow, J. W., Baker, D., and Geracioti, T. D. Jr. (2001). Corticotropin releasing hormone in depression and post-traumatic stress disorder. *Peptides* 22: 845–851.

Katschinski, M. (2000). Nutritional implications of cephalic phase gastrointestinal responses. *Appetite* 34: 189–196.

Kaufman, J., Brimaher, B., Perel, J., Dahl, R. E., Moreci, P., Nelson, B., Wells, W., and Ryan, N. D. (1997). The corticotropin-releasing hormone challenge

in depressed abused, depressed nonabused, and normal control children. *Biol. Psychiatry* 42: 669–679.

Kaufman, J., Birmaher, B., Perel, J., Dahl, R. E., Stull, S., Brendt, D., Trubnick, L., al-Shabbout, M., and Ryan, N. D. (1998). Serotonergic functioning in depressed abused children: Clinical and familial correlates. *Biol. Psychiatry* 44: 973–981.

Kaufman, S. (1981). Control of fluid intake in pregnant and lactating rats. *J. Physiol.* 318: 9–16.

Kaufman, S., and MacKay, B. J. (1983). Plasma prolactin levels and body fluid deficits in the rat: Causal interactions and control of water intake. *J. Physiol.* 336: 73–81.

Kaye, W. H., Gwirtsman, H. E., George, D. T., Ebert, M. H., Jimerson, D. C., Tomai, D. T., Chrousos, G. P., and Gold, P. W. (1987). Elevated cerebrospinal fluid levels of immunoreactive corticotropin-releasing hormone in anorexia nervosa: Relation to state of nutrition, adrenal function, and intensity of depression. *J. Clin. Endocrinol. Metab.* 64: 203–208.

Keiger, C. J., O'Steen, W. K., Brewer, G., Sorci-Thomas, M., Zehnder, T. J., and Rose, J. C. (1994). Corticotropin releasing factor mRNA and peptide levels are differentially regulated in the developing ovine brain. *Brain Res. Mol. Brain Res.* 27: 103–110.

Kelley, A. E. (1999a). Neural integrative activities of nucleus accumbens subregions in relation to learning and motivation. *Psychobiology* 27: 198–213.

Kelley, A. E. (1999b). Functional specificity of ventral striatal compartments in appetitive behaviors. *Ann. N.Y. Acad. Sci.* 877: 71–90.

Kellner, M., Holsboer, F., and Heuser, I. (1995). Intermediate glucocorticoid feedback of corticotropin secretion in patients with major depression. *Psychiatry Res.* 59: 157–160.

Kelly, A. B., and Watts, A. G. (1996). Mediation of dehydration-induced peptidergic gene expression in the rat lateral hypothalamic area by forebrain afferent projections. *J. Comp. Neurol.* 370: 231–246.

Kendler, K. S., Heath, A. C., Neale, M. C., Kessler, R. C., and Eaves, L. J. (1992a). A population-based twin study of alcoholism in women. *JAMA* 268: 1877–1882.

Kendler, K. S., Neale, M. C., Kessler, R. C., Heath, A. C., and Eaves, L. J. (1992b). Childhood parental loss and adult psychopathology in women. A twin study perspective. *Arch. Gen. Psychiatry* 49: 109–116.

Kendler, K. S., Neal, M. C., Prescott, C. A., Kessler, R. C., Jeath, A. C., Corey, L. A., and Eaves, L. J. (1996). Childhood parental loss and alcoholism in women: A causal analysis using a twin-family design. *Psychol. Med.* 26: 79–95.

Kendler, K. S., Bulik, C. M., Silberg, J., Hettema, J. M., Myers, J., and Prescott, C. A. (2000). Childhood sexual abuse and adult psychiatric and substance use disorders in women: An epidemiological and co-twin control analysis. *Arch. Gen. Psychiatry* 57: 953–959.

Kendrick, K. M. (2000). Oxytocin, motherhood, and bonding. *Exp. Physiol.* 85: 111S–124S.

Kessler, R. C., Davis, C. G., and Kendler, K. S. (1997). Childhood adversity and adult psychiatric disorder in the U.S. National Comorbidity Survey. *Psychol. Med.* 27: 1101–1119.

Ketter, T. A., Andreason, P. J., George, M. S., Lee, C., Gill, D. S., Parekh, P. I., Willis, M. W., Herscovitch, P., and Post, R. M. (1996). Anterior paralimbic mediation of procaine-induced emotional and psychosensory experiences. *Arch. Gen. Psychiatry* 53: 59–69.

Kiecolt-Glaser, J. K., Glaser, R., Gravenstein, S., Malarkey, W. B., and Sheridan, J. (1996). Chronic stress alters the immune response to influenza virus vaccine in older adults. *Proc. Natl. Acad. Sci. USA* 93: 3043–3047.

Killeen, T. K., Brady, K. T., and Thevos, A. (1995). Addiction severity, psychopathology, and treatment compliance in cocaine-dependent mothers. *J. Addict. Dis.* 14: 75–84.

Kilpatrick, D. G., Acierno, R., Resnick, H. S., Saunders, B. E., and Best, C. L. (1997). A 2-year longitudinal analysis of the relationship between violent assault and substance use in women. *J. Consult. Clin. Psychol.* 65: 834–847.

Kilts, C. D., Schweitzer, J. B., Quinn, C. K., Gross, R. E., Faber, T. L., Muhammad, F., Ely, T. D., Hoffman, J. M., and Drexler, K. P. G. (2001). Neural activity related to drug craving in cocaine addiction. *Arch. Gen. Psychiatry* 58: 334–341.

Kim, J. J., Rison, R. A., and Fanselow, M. S. (1993). Effects of amygdala, hippocampus, and periaqueductal gray lesions on short- and long-term contextual fear. *Behav. Neurosci.* 107: 1093–1098.

King, B. R., Smith, R., and Nicholson, R. C. (2001). The regulation of human corticotropin releasing hormone gene expression in the placenta. *Peptides* 22: 795–801.

Kirby, L. G., Rice, K. C., and Valentino, R. J. (1999). Effects of corticotropin-releasing factor on neuronal activity in the serotonergic dorsal raphe nucleus. *Neuropsychopharmacology* 22: 148–162.

Kirby, R. F., and Johnson, A. K. (1992). Regulation of sodium and body fluid homeostasis during development: Implications for the pathogenesis of hypertension. *Experientia* 48: 345–351.

Kirschbaum, C., Prussner, J. C., Stone, A. A., Federenko, I., Gaab, J., Lintz, D., Schommer, N., and Hellhammer, D. H. (1995). Persistent high cortisol responses to repeated psychological stress in a subpopulation of healthy men. *Psychosom. Med.* 57: 468–474.

Kirschbaum, C., Kudielka, B. M., Gaab, J., Schommer, N. C., and Hellhammer, D. H. (1999). Impact of gender, menstrual cycle phase, and oral contraceptive use on the activity of the hypothalamo-pituitary-adrenal axis. *Psychosom. Med.* 61: 154–162.

Kitraki, E., Alexis, M. N., Papalopoulou, M., and Stylianopoulou, F. (1996). Glucocorticoid receptor gene expression in the embryonic rat brain. *Neuroendocrinology* 63: 305–317.

Klara, S. (1993). Mandatory neuropeptide-steroid signaling for the preovulatory luteinizing hormone-releasing hormone discharge. *Endocr. Rev.* 14: 507–538.

Klerman, E. B., Boulos, Z., Edgar, D. M., Mistlberger, R. E., and Moore-Ede, M. C. (1999). Circadian and homeostatic influences on sleep in the squirrel monkey: Sleep after sleep deprivation. *Sleep* 22: 45–59.

Kling, M. A., Roy, A., Doran, A. R., Calabrese, J. R., Rubinow, D. R., Whitfield, H. J. Jr., May, C., Post, R. M., Chrousos, G. P., and Gold, P. W. (1991). Cerebrospinal fluid immunoreactive corticotropin releasing hormone and ACTH secretion in Cushing's disease and major depression: Potential clinical implications. *J. Clin. Endocrinol. Metab.* 72: 260–271.

Kling, M. A. Smith, M. A., Glowa, J. R., Pluznik, D., Demas, J., DeBellis, M. D., Gold, P. W., and Schulkin, J. (1993). Facilitation of cocaine kindling by glucocorticoids in rats. *Brain Res.* 629: 163-166.

Koegler-Muly, S. M., Owens, M. J., Ervin, G. N., Kilts, C. D., and Nemeroff, C. B. (1993). Potential corticotropin-releasing factor pathways in the rat brain as determined by bilateral electrolytic lesions of the central amygdaloid nucleus and the paraventricular nucleus of the hypothalamus. *J. Neuroendocrinol.* 5: 95–98.

Kolb, B., and Whishaw, I. Q. (1990). *Fundamentals of Human Neuropsychology.* New York: W. H. Freeman and Company.

Konorski, J. (1967). *Integrative Activity of the Brain: An Interdisciplinary Approach.* Chicago: University of Chicago Press.

Konturek, S. J., and Konturek, J. W. (2000). Cephalic phase of pancreatic secretion. *Appetite* 34: 197–205.

Konyshev, V. A. (1980). Information transfer in the systems controlling homeostatic balance in the organism. *Prog. Food Nutr. Sci.* 3: 121–139.

Koob, G. F. (1993). The role of corticotropin-releasing hormone in behavioral responses to stress. In *Corticotropin Releasing Factor,* edited by K. Chadwick, J. Marshj, and K. Ackrill. Wiley: New York.

Koob, G. F. (1996). Drug addiction: The yin and yang of hedonic homeostasis. *Neuron* 16: 893–896.

Koob, G. F. (1998). The role of the striatopallidal and extended amygdala systems in drug addiction. *Ann. N.Y. Acad. Sci.* 877: 445–460.

Koob, G. F., and Bloom, F. E. (1985). Corticotropin releasing hormone and behavior. *Fed. Proc.* 44: 259–263.

Koob, G. F., and Le Moal, M. (1997). Drug abuse: Hedonic homeostatic dysregulation. *Science* 278: 52–58.

Koob, G. F., and Le Moal, M. (2001). Drug addiction, dysregulation of reward, and allostasis. *Neuropsychopharmacology* 24: 94–129.

Koob, G. F., Stinus, L., Le Moal, M., and Bloom, F. E. (1989). Opponent process theory of motivation: Neurobiological evidence from studies of opiate dependence. *Neurosci. Biobehav. Rev.* 13: 135–140.

Koob, G. F., Markou, A., Weiss, F., and Schulteis, G. (1993). Opponent process and drug dependence: Neurobiological mechanisms. *Semin. Neurosci.* 5: 351–358.

Koob, G. F., Caine, B., Markou, A., Pulvirenti, L., and Weiss, F. (1994). Role for the mesocortical dopamine system in the motivating effects of cocaine. *NIDA Res. Monogr.* 145: 1–18.

Koob, G. F., Sanna, P. P., and Bloom, F. E. (1998). Neuroscience of addiction. *Neuron* 21: 467–476.

Korebrits, C., Yu, D. H., Ramirez, M. M., Marinoni, E., Bocking, A. D., and Challis, J. R. (1998). Antenatal glucocorticoid administration increases corticotropin releasing hormone in maternal plasma. *Br. J. Obstet. Gynaecol.* 105: 556–561.

Korner, P. I. (1982). Causal and homeostatic factors in hypertension. *Clin. Sci.* 63 (suppl. 8): S52–S55.

Korte, S. M. (2001). Corticosteroids in relation to fear, anxiety, and psychopathology. *Neurosci. Biobehav. Rev.* 25: 117–142.

Koss, M. P., and Heslet, L. (1992). Somatic consequences of violence against women. *Arch. Fam. Med.* 1: 53–59.

Kovacs, C. S., and Kronenberg, H. M. (1997). Maternal-fetal calcium and bone metabolism during pregnancy, puerperium, and lactation. *Endocr. Rev.* 18: 832–872.

Kovacs, K. J., and Sawchenko, P. E. (1993). Mediation of osmoregulatory influences on neuroendocrine corticotropin-releasing factor expression by the ventral lamina terminalis. *Proc. Natl. Acad. Sci. USA* 90: 7681–7685.

Kovacs, K. J., and Sawchenko, P. E. (1996). Regulation of stress-induced transcriptional changes in the hypothalamic neurosecretory neurons. *J. Mol. Neurosci.* 96: 125–133.

Kovacs, K. J., Foldes, A., and Sawchenko, P. E. (2000). Glucocorticoid negative feedback selectivity targets vasopressin transcription in parvocellular neurosecretory neurons. *J. Neurosci.* 20: 3843–3852.

Kraemer, G. W., and McKinney, W. T. (1985). Social separation increases alcohol consumption in rhesus monkeys. *Psychopharmacology (Berl.)* 86: 182–189.

Kreek, M. J. (1997). Opiate and cocaine addictions: Challenge for pharmacotherapies. *Pharmacol. Biochem. Behav.* 3: 551–569.

Krettek, J. E., and Price, J. L. (1978). Amygdaloid projections to subcortical structures within the basal forebrain and brainstem in the rat and cat. *J. Comp. Neurol.* 178: 225–254.

Krieckhaus, E. E., and Wolf, G. (1968). Acquisition of sodium by rats: Interaction of innate mechanisms and latent learning. *J. Comp. Physiol. Psychol.* 65: 197–201.

Kruesi, M. J., Schmidt, M. E., Donnelly, M., Hibbs, E. D., and Hamburger, S. D. (1989). Urinary free cortisol output and disruptive behavior in children. *J. Am. Acad. Child Adolesc. Psychiatry* 28: 441–443.

Kuenzel, W. J., Beck, M. M., and Teruyama, R. (1999). Neural sites and pathways regulating food intake in birds: A comparative analysis to mammalian systems. *J. Comp. Zool.* 283: 348–364.

Kurki, T., Laatikainen, T., Salminen-Lappalainen, K., and Ylikorkala, O. (1991). Maternal plasma corticotrophin-releasing hormone—Elevated in preterm labour but unaffected by indomethacin or nylidrin. *Br. J. Obstet. Gynaecol.* 98: 685–691.

Kushner, M. G., Sher, K. J., and Beitman, B. D. (1990). The relationship between alcohol problems and the anxiety disorders. *Am. J. Psychiatry* 147: 685–695.

Kvetnansky, R., Fukuhara, K., Pacak, K., Cizza, G., Goldstein, D. S., and Kopin, I. J. (1993). Endogenous glucocorticoids restrain catecholamine synthesis and release at rest and during immobilization stress in rats. *Endocrinology* 133: 1411–1419.

Ladd, C. O., Owens, M. J., and Nemeroff, C. B. (1996). Persistent changes in corticotropin-releasing factor neuronal systems induced by maternal deprivation. *Endocrinology* 137: 1212–1218.

Ladd, C. O., Huot, R. L., Thrivikraman, K. V., Nemereroff, C. B., Meaney, M. J., and Plotsky, P. M. (2000). Long-term behavioral and neuroendocrine adaptations to adverse early experience. *Prog. Brain Res.* 122: 81–103.

Lakoff, G., and Johnson, M. (1999). *Philosophy in the Flesh.* New York: Basic Books.

Lambert, G., Johansson, M., Agren, H., and Friberg, P. (2000). Reduced brain norepinephrine and dopamine in treatment-refractory depression: Evidence in support of the catecholamine hypothesis of mood disorders. *Arch. Gen. Psychiatry* 57: 787–793.

Lambert, P. D., Phillips, P. J., Wilding, J. P., Bloom, S. R., and Herbert, J. (1995). c-fos expression in the paraventricular nucleus of the hypothalamus following intracerebroventricular infusion of neuropeptide Y. *Brain Res.* 670: 59–65.

Lance, V. A., and Elsey, R. M. (1986). Stress-induced suppression of testosterone secretion in male alligators. *J. Exp. Zool.* 239: 241–246.

Lane, R. D., and Nadel, L. (1999). *Cognitive Neuroscience of Emotion.* Oxford: Oxford University Press.

Lane, R.D., Chua, P. M., and Dolan, R. J. (1999). Common effects of emotional valence, arousal and attention on neural activation during visual processing of pictures. *Neuropsychologia* 37: 989–997.

Lang, P. J., Greenwald, M. K., Bradley, M. M., and Hamm, A. O. (1993). Looking at pictures: Affective, facial, visceral, and behavioral reactions. *Psychophysiology* 30: 261–273.

Lang, P. J., Bradley, M. M., and Cuthbert, B. N. (1998). Emotion, motivation, and anxiety: Brain mechanisms and psychophysiology. *Biol. Psychiatry* 44: 1248–1263.

Langley, L. L. (1973). *Homeostasis: Origins of the Concept.* Stroudsburg, Penn.: Dowden, Hutchingson, and Ross.

Lashley, K. S. (1938). An experimental analysis of instinctive behavior. *Psychol. Rev.* 45: 445–471.

Lashley, K. S. (1951). The problem of serial order in behavior. In *Cerebral Mechanisms in Behavior,* edited by L. A. Jeffres. New York: Wiley.

Lashley, K. S. (1966). Drive as facilitation of specific neural mechanisms. In *Motivation,* edited by D. Bindra and J. Stewart. Baltimore: Penguin Books.

Laskey, M. A., Prentice, A., Shaw, J., Zachou, T., Ceesay, S. M., Vasquez-Velasquez, L., and Fraser, D. R. (1990). Breast-milk calcium concentrations during prolonged lactation in British and rural Gambian mothers. *Acta Paediatr. Scand.* 79: 507–512.

Laws, A. (1993). Does a history of sexual abuse in children play a role in women's medical problems? A review. *J. Womens Health* 2: 165–172.

Lazarus, R. S. (1966). *Psychological Stress and the Coping Process.* New York: McGraw-Hill.

Lazarus, R. S. (1984). On the primacy of cognition. *Am. Psychol.* 39: 124–129.

Lazarus, R. S. (1991). *Emotion and Adaptation.* New York: Oxford University Press.

Le, A. D., Harding, S., Juzytsch, W., and Shaham, Y. (2001). The role of corticotropin-releasing factor in stress-induced relapse to alcohol seeking. *Psychopharmacology* 150: 317–324.

LeBlanc, J. (2000). Nutritional implications of cephalic phase thermogenic responses. *Appetite* 34: 214–216.

Lechner, M. E., Vogel, M. E., Garcia-Shelton, L. M., Leichter, J. L., and Steibel, K. R. (1993). Self-report medical problems of adult female survivors of childhood sexual abuse. *J. Fam. Pract.* 36: 633–638.

Lechner, S. M., and Valentino, R. J. (1999). Glucocorticoid receptor-immunoreactivity in corticotropin-releasing factor afferents to the locus coeruleus. *Brain Res.* 816: 17–28.

LeDoux, J. E. (1995). Emotion: Clues form the brain. *Annu. Rev. Psychol.* 46: 209–235.

LeDoux, J. E. (1996). *The Emotional Brain.* New York: Simon and Schuster.

Le Doux, J. E. (2000). Emotion circuits in the brain. *Annu. Rev. Neurosci.* 23: 155–184.

LeDoux, J. E., Cicchetti, P., Xagoraris, A., and Romanski, L. M. (1990). The lateral amygdaloid nucleus: Sensory interface of the amygdala in fear conditioning. *J. Neurosci.* 10: 1062–1069.

Lee, P. H., Zhao, D. Y., Mitchell, C. L., and Hong, J. S. (1987). Effects of corticosterone on shaking and seizure behavior induced by prepyriform cortex kindling. *Neurosci. Lett.* 82: 337–342.

Lee, P. H., Grimes, L., and Hong, J. S. (1989). Glucocorticoids potentiate kainic acid-induced seizures and wet dog shakes. *Brain Res.* 480: 322–333.

Lee, Y., and Davis, M. (1997a). Role of the septum in the excitatory effect of corticotropin-releasing hormone on the acoustic startle reflex. *J. Neurosci.* 17: 6424–6433.

Lee, Y., and Davis, M. (1997b). Role of the hippocampus, the bed nucleus of the stria terminalis, and the amygdala in the excitatory effect of corticotropin-releasing hormone on the acoustic startle reflex, *J. Neurosci.* 17: 6434–6446.

Lee, Y., Schulkin, J., and Davis, M. (1994). Effect of corticosterone on the enhancement of the acoustic startle reflex by corticotropin releasing hormone. *Brain Res.* 666: 93–98.

Leibowitz, S. F. (1995). Brain peptides and obesity: Pharmacological treatment. *Obesity Res.* 3: 573–589.

Le Magnen, J. (1984). Ingestive behavior in the homeostatic control of internal environment. *Appetite* 5: 159–168.

Le Magnen, J. (1985). *Hunger.* Cambridge: Cambridge University Press.

Lemieux, A. M., and Coe, C. L. (1995). Abuse-related posttraumatic stress disorder: Evidence for chronic neuroendocrine activation in women. *Psychosom. Med.* 57: 105–115.

Letchworth, S. R., Nader, M. A., Smith, H. R., Friedman, D. P., and Porrino, L. J. (2001). Progression of changes in dopamine transporter binding site density as a result of cocaine self-administration in rhesus monkeys. *J. Neurosci.* 21: 2799–2807.

Leung, T. N., Chung, T. K., Madsen, G., McLean, M., Chang, A. M., and Smith, R. (1999). Elevated mid-trimester maternal corticotrophin-releasing hormone levels in pregnancies that delivered before 34 weeks. *Br. J. Obstet. Gynaecol.* 106: 1041–1046.

Leung, T. N., Chung, T. K., Madsen, G., Lam, C. W., Lam, P. K., Walters, W. A., and Smith, R. (2000). Analysis of mid-trimester corticotropin releasing hormone and fetoprotein concentrations for predicting pre-eclampsia. *Hum. Reprod.* 15: 1813–1818.

Levin, B. E., Dunn-Meynell, A. A., and Routh, V. H. (1999). Brain glucose sensing and body energy homeostasis: Role in obesity and diabetes. *Am. J. Physiol.* 276: R1223–R1231.

Levine, S. (1975). Psychosocial factors in growth and development. In *Society, Stress, and Disease,* edited by L. Levi. London: Oxford University Press.

Levine, S. (2000). Modulation of CRF gene expression by early experience. *Neuropsychopharmacology* 23: S77.

Levine, S., Coe, C., and Wiener, S. (1989). The psychoneuroendocrinology of stress: A psychobiological perspective. In *Psychoendocrinology,* edited by S. Levine and R. Brush. New York: Academic Press.

Levine, S., Dent, G., and de Kloet, E. R. (2000). Stress-hyporesponsive period. In *Encyclopedia of Stress.* Vol. 3, edited by G. Fink. San Diego: Academic Press, pp. 518–526.

Levitan, R. D., Parikh, S. V., Lesage, A. D., Hegadoren, K. M., Adams, M., Kennedy, S. H., and Goering, P. N. (1998). Major depression in individuals with a history of childhood physical or sexual abuse: Relationship to neurovegetative features, mania, and gender. *Am. J. Psychiatry* 155: 1746–1752.

Levy, J. (1999). Abnormal cell calcium homeostasis in type 2 diabetes mellitus: A new look on old disease. *Endocrine* 10: 1–6.

Liang, K. C., Melia, K. R., Campeau, S., Falls, W. A., Miserendino, M. J., and Davis, M. (1992). Lesions of the central nucleus of the amygdala but not the paraventricular nucleus of the hypothalamus block the excitatory effects of corticotropin-releasing factor on the acoustic startle response. *J. Neurosci.* 19: 2313–2320.

Liberman, U. A., Weiss, S. R., Broll, J., Minne, H. W., Quan, H., Bell, H., Rodrigues, L., Portales, J., Downs, R. W. Jr., Dequeker, J., and Favus, M. (1995). Effect of oral alendronate on bone mineral density and the incidence of fractures in postmenopausal osteoporosis. The alendronate phase III osteoporosis treatment study group. *N. Engl. J. Med.* 333: 1437–1443.

Licinio, J., Gold, P. W., and Wong, M. L. (1995). A molecular mechanism for stress-induced alterations in susceptibility to disease. *Lancet* 346: 104–106.

Lind, R. W., Swanson, L. W., and Ganten, D. (1985). Organization of angiotensin immunoreactive cells and fibers in the rat central nervous system. An immunohistochemical study. *Neuroendocrinology* 40: 2–24.

Lindheimer, M. D., Baron, W. M., Durr, J., and Davison, J. M. (1987). Water homeostasis and vasopressin release during rodent and human gestation. *Am. J. Kidney Dis.* 9: 270–275.

Lindquist, B., and Svenningsen, N. W. (1983). Acid-base homeostasis of low-birth-weight and full term infants in early life. *J. Pediatr. Gastroenterol. Nutr.* 2 (suppl. 1): S99–S107.

Lindsley, D. B. (1960). Attention, consciousness, sleep, and wakefulness. *Handbook Physiol.* 15: 53–93.

Lipsitz, L. A. (1989). Altered blood pressure homeostasis in advanced age: Clinical and research implications. *J. Gerontol.* 44: M179–M183.

Liu D., Diorio, J., Tannenbaum, B., Caldji, C., Francis, D., Freedman, A., Sharma, S., Pearson, D., Plotsky, P. M., and Meaney, M. J. (1997). Maternal care, hippocampal glucocorticoid receptors, and hypothalamic-pituitary-adrenal responses ot stress. *Science* 277: 1659–1662.

Lloyd, I. J. (1990). Is the extracellular matrix an integral and dynamic component of the sodium and water homeostatic system? *Med. Hypotheses* 33: 197–199.

Lobel, M., Dunkel-Schetter, C., and Scrimshaw, S. C. (1992). Prenatal maternal stress and prematurity: A prospective study of socioeconomically disadvantaged women. *Health Psychol.* 11: 32–40.

Lockwood, C. J. (1994). Recent advances in elucidating the pathogenesis of preterm delivery, the detection of patients at risk, and preventative therapies. *Curr. Opin. Obstet. Gynecol.* 6: 7–18.

Lockwood, C. J., and Kuczynski, E. (2001). Risk stratification and pathological mechanisms in preterm delivery. *Paediatr. Perinat. Epidemiol.* 15. 78–89.

London, E. D., Bonson, K. R., Ernst, M., and Grant, S. (1999). Brain imaging studies of cocaine abuse: Implications for medication development. *Crit. Rev. Neurobiol.* 13: 227–242.

Lorenz, K. (1950). The comparative method in studying innate behaviour patterns. *Symp. Soc. Exp. Biol.* 4: 221–268.

Lorenz, K. (1981). *The Foundations of Ethology.* New York: Springer.

Louch, C. D., and Higginbotham, M. (1967) The relation between social rank and plasma corticosterone levels in mice. *Gen. Comp. Endocrinol.* 8: 441–444.

Louie, A. K., Lannon, R. A., and Ketter, T. A. (1989). Treatment of cocaine-induced panic disorder. *Am. J. Psychiatry* 46: 40–44.

Lovenberg, T. W., Liaw, C. W., Gigoriadis, D. E., Clevenger, W., Chalmers, D. T., DeSouza, E. D., and Oltersdorf, T. (1995). Cloning and characterization of a functionally distinct corticotropin-releasing factor receptor subtype from rat brain. *Proc. Natl. Acad. Sci. USA* 92: 836–840.

Lowenstein, G. F. (1999). A visceral account of addiction. In *Getting Hooked: Rationality and Addiction,* edited by J. Elster and O.-J. Skog. Cambridge: Cambridge University Press.

Lowry, C. A., Burke, K. A., Renner, K. J., Moore, F. L., and Orchinik, M. (2001). Rapid changes in momoamine levels following administration of corticotropin releasing factor or corticosterone are localized in the dorsomedial hypothalamus. *Horm. Behav.* 39: 195–205.

Lucas, L. R., Angulo, J. A., Le Moal, M., McEwen, B. S., and Piazza, P. V. (1998a). Neurochemical characterization of individual vulnerability to addictive drugs. *Eur. J. Neurosci.* 10: 3153–3161.

Lucas, L. R., Pompei, P., Ono, J., and McEwen, B. S. (1998b). Effects of adrenal steroids on basal ganglia neuropeptide mRNA and tyrosine hydroxylase radioimmunoreactive levels in the adrenalectomized rat. *J. Neurochem.* 71: 833–843.

Lucas, L. R., Pompei, P., and McEwen, B. S. (2000). Salt appetite in salt-replete rats: Involvement of mesolimbic structures in deoxycorticosterone-induced salt craving behavior. *Neuroendocrinology* 71: 386–395.

Lupien, S. J., and McEwen, B. S. (1997). The acute effects of corticosteroids on cognition: Integration of animal and human model studies. *Brain Res. Rev.* 24: 1–27.

Lupien, S., Lecours, A. R., Lussier, I., Schwartz, G., Nair, N. P., and Meaney, M. J. (1994). Basal cortisol levels and cognitive deficits in human aging. *J. Neurosci.* 14: 2893–2903.

Lupien, S. J., de Leon, M., de Santi, S., Convit, A., Tarshish, C., Nair, N. P., Thakur, M., McEwen, B. S., Hauger, R. L., and Meaney, M. J. (1998). Cortisol levels during human aging predict hippocampal atrophy and memory deficits. *Nat. Neurosci.* 1: 69–73.

Lupien, S. J., Gillin, C. J., and Hauger, R. L. (1999). Working memory is more sensitive than declarative memory to the acute effects of corticosteroids: A dose-response study in humans. *Behav. Neurosci.* 113: 420–430.

Lupien, S. J., King, S., Meaney, M. J., and McEwen, B. S. (2000). Child's stress hormone levels correlate with mother's socioeconomic status and depressive state. *Biol. Psychiatry* 48: 976–980.

Lupien, S. J., Wilkinson, C. W., Briere, S., Menard, C., Kin. N. M. K., and Nair, N. P. V. (2002). The modulatory effects of corticosteroids on cognition. *Psychoneuroendocrinology* 27: 401–416.

Lynch, J. W., Kaplan, G. A., Cohen, R. D., Tuomilehto, J., and Salonen, J. T. (1996). Do cardiovascular risk factors explain the relation between socioeconomic status, risk of all-cause mortality, cardiovascular mortality, and acute myocardial infarction? *Am. J. Epidemiol.* 144: 934–942.

Lynch, J. W., Kaplan, G. A., and Shema, S. J. (1997). Cumulative impact of sustained economic hardship on physical, cognitive, psychological, and social functioning. *N. Engl. J. Med.* 337: 1889–1895.

Lyons, D. M., and Levine, S. (1994). Socioregulatory effects on squirrel monkey pituitary-adrenal activity: A longitudinal analysis of cortisol and ACTH. *Psychoneuroendocrinology* 19: 283–291.

Maas, L. C., Lukas, S. E., Kaufman, M. J., Weiss, R. D., Daniels, S. L., Rogers, V. W., Kukes, T. J., and Renshaw, P. F. (1998). Functional magnetic resonance imaging of human brain activation during cue-induced cocaine craving. *Am. J. Psychiatry* 155: 124–126.

Maccari, S., Piazza, P. V., Deminiere, J. M., Lemaire, V., Mormede, P, Simon, H., Angelucci, L., and Le Moal, M. (1991). Life events-induced decrease of coticosteroid type 1 receptors is associated with reduced corticosterone feedback and enhanced vulnerability to amphetamine self-administration. *Brain Res.* 547: 7–12.

Maclean, P. D. (1955). The limbic system ("visceral brain") and emotional behavior. *Arch. Neurol. Psychiatry* 73: 130–134.

Magarinos, A. M., McEwen, B. S., Flugge, G., and Fuchs, E. (1996). Chronic psychosocial stress causes apical dendritic atrophy of hippocampal CA3 pyramidal neurons in subordinate tree shrews. *J. Neurosci.* 16: 3534–3540.

Magarinos, A. M., Verdugo, J. M., and McEwen, B. S. (1997). Chronic stress alters synaptic terminal structure in hippocampus. *Proc. Natl. Acad. Sci. USA* 94: 14002–14008.

Magiakou, M. A., Mastorakos, G., Rabin, D., Dubbert, B., Gold, P. W., and Chrousos, G. P. (1996a). Hypothalamic corticotropin-releasing hormone suppression during the postpartum period: Implications for the increase in psychiatric manifestations at this time. *J. Clin. Endocrinol. Metabol.* 81: 1912–1917.

Magiakou, M. A., Mastorakos, G., Rabin, D., Margioris, A. N., Dubbert, B., Calogero, A. E., Tsigos, C., Munsen, P. J., and Chrousos, G. P. (1996b). The

maternal hypothalamic-pituitary-adrenal axis in the third trimester of human pregnancy. *Clin. Endocrinol.* 44: 419–428.

Mahon, J. M., Allen, M., Herbert, J., and Fitzsimons, J. T. (1995). The association of thirst, sodium appetite, and vasopressin release with c-fos expression in the forebrain of the rat after intracerebroventricular injection of angiotensin II, angiotensin-(1-7), or carbachol. *Neuroscience* 69: 199–208.

Majzoub, J. A., and Karilis, K. P. (1999). Placental corticotropin releasing hormone: Function and regulation. *Am. J. Obstet. Gynecol.* 180: S242–S246.

Majzoub, J. A., McGregor, J. A., Lockwood, C. J., Smith, R., Taggart, M. S., and Schulkin, J. (1999). A central theory of preterm and term labor: Putative role for corticotropin-releasing hormone. *Am. J. Obstet. Gynecol.* 180: S232–S241.

Makino, S., Gold, P. W., and Schulkin, J. (1994a). Corticosterone effects on corticotropin-releasing hormone mRNA in the central nucleus of the amygdala and the parvocellular region of the paraventricular nucleus of the hypothalamus. *Brain Res.* 640: 105–112.

Makino, S., Gold, P. W., and Schulkin, J. (1994b). Effects of corticosterone on CRH mRNA and content in the bed nucleus of the amygdala and the paraventricular nucleus of the hypothalamus. *Brain Res.* 657: 141–149.

Makino, S., Schulkin, J., Smith, M. A., Pacak, K., Palkorits, M., and Gold, P. W. (1995). Regulation of corticotropin-releasing hormone receptor messenger ribonucleic acid in the rat brain and pituitary by glucocorticoids and stress. *Endocrinology* 136: 4517–4525.

Maney, D. L., and Wingfield, J. C. (1998). Neuroendocrine suppression of female courtship in a wild passerine: Corticotropin-releasing factor and endogenous opioids. *J. Neuroendocrinol.* 10: 593–599.

Mann, K., Gunther, A., Stetter, F., and Ackermann, K. (1999). Rapid recovery from cognitive deficits in abstinent alcoholics: A controlled test-retest study. *Alcohol Alcohol.* 34: 567–574.

Manolagas, S. C., Bellido, T., and Jilka, R. L. (1995). New insights into the cellular, biochemical, and molecular basis of postmenopausal and senile osteoporosis: Roles of IL-6 and gp 130. *Int. J. Immunopharmacol.* 17: 109–116.

Manuck, S. B., Kaplan, J. R., Muldoon, M. F., Adams, M. R., and Clarkson, T. B. (1991). The behavioral exacerbation of athersclerosis and its inhibition by propranolol. In *Stress, Coping, and Disease,* edited by P. M. McCabe, N. Scheiderman, T. M. Field, and J. S. Skyler. London: Lawrence Erlbaum Associates.

Marcilhac, A., and Siaud, P. (1997). Identification of projections from the central nucleus of the amygdala to the paraventricular nucleus of the hypothalamus which are immunoreactive for corticotrophin-releasing hormone in the rat. *Exp. Physiol.* 82: 273–281.

Marcus, R. (1996). The nature of osteoporosis. *J. Clin. Endocrinol. Metab.* 81: 1–5.

Margioris, A. N., Grino, M., Protos, P., Gold, P. W., and Chrousos, G. P. (1988). Corticotropin-releasing hormone and oxytocin stimulate the release of

placental propiomelanocortin peptides. *J. Clin. Endocrinol. Metabol.* 66: 922–926.

Marinoni, E., Korebrits, C., Di Iorio, R., Cosmi, E. V., and Challis, J. R. (1998). Effect of betamethasone in vivo on placental corticotropin-releasing hormone in human pregnancy. *Am. J. Obstet. Gynecol.* 178: 770–778.

Markowe, H. L., Marmot, M. G., Shipley, M. J., Bulpitt, C. J., Meade, T. W., Stirling, Y., Vickers, M. V., and Semmence, A. (1985). Fibrinogen: A possible link between social class and coronary heart disease. *Br. Med. J. (Clin Res. Ed.)* 291: 1312–1314.

Marler, C. A., Boyd, S. K., and Wilczynski, W. (1999). Forebrain arginine vasotocin correlates of alternative mating strategies in cricket frogs. *Horm. Behav.* 36: 53–61.

Marler, C. A., Chu, J., and Wilczynski, W. (1995). Arginine vasotocin injection increases probability of calling in cricket frogs, but causes call changes characteristic of less aggressive males. *Horm. Behav.* 29: 554–570.

Marler, P., and Hamilton, W. J. (1966). *Mechanisms of Animal Behavior.* New York: Wiley.

Marmot, M. G., Smith, G. D., Stansfeld, S., Patel, C., North, F., Head, J., White, I., Brunner, E., and Feeney, A. (1991). Health inequalities among British civil servants: The Whitehall II study. *Lancet* 337: 1387–1393.

Marsden, C. D. (1984). The pathophysiology of movement disorders. *Neurol. Clin.* 2: 435–459.

Martyn, C. N., Hales, C. N., Barker, D. J., and Jespersen, S. (1998). Fetal growth and hyperinsulinaemia in adult life. *Diabetes Med.* 15: 688–694.

Maslow, A. H. (1954). *Motivation and Personality.* New York: Harper and Row.

Mason, J. W. (1971). A re-evaluation of the concept of "non-specificity" in stress theory. *J. Psychiatr. Res.* 8: 323–333.

Mason, J. W. (1975a). A historical view of the stress field. II. *J. Hum. Stress* 1: 6–12, cont.

Mason, J. W. (1975b). Emotions as reflected as patterns of endocrine integration. In *Emotions: Their Parameters and Measurements,* edited by L. Levi. New York: Raven Press.

Mason, J. W., Bra, J. V., and Sidman, M. (1957). Plasma 17-hydroxycorticosteroid levels and conditioned behavior in rhesus monkeys. *Endocrinology* 69: 741–752.

Mason, J. W., Giller, E. L., Kosten, T. R., and Harkness, L. (1988). Elevation of urinary norepinephrine/cortisol ratio in posttraumatic stress disorder. *J. Nerv. Ment. Disord.* 176: 498–502.

Masse, L. C., and Tremblay, R. E. (1997). Behavior of boys in kindergarten and the onset of substance use during adolescence. *Arch. Gen. Psychiatry* 54: 62–68.

Matsui, H., Aou, S., Ma, J., and Hori, T. (1995). Central actions of parathyroid hormone on blood calcium and hypothalamic neuronal activity in the rat. *Am. J. Physiol.* 37: R21–R27.

Mattes, R. D. (2000). Nutritional implications of the cephalic-phase salivary response. *Appetite* 34: 177–183.

Matthew, R. J., and Wilson, W. H. (1991). Substance abuse and cerebral blood flow. *Am. J. Psychiatry* 148: 292–305.

Matthews, S. G., and Challis, J. R. G. (1995). Regulation of CRH and AVP mRNA in the developing ovine hypothalamus: Effects of stress and glucocorticoids. *Am. J. Physiol.* 268: E1096–E1107.

Mattson, M. P. (1998). Modification of ion homeostasis by lipid peroxidation: Roles in neuronal degeneration and adaptive plasticity. *Trends Neurosci.* 21: 53–57.

Mattson, M. P., Mark, R. J., Furukawa, K., and Bruce, A. J. (1997). Disruption of brain cell ion homeostasis in Alzheimer's disease by oxy radicals, and signaling pathways that protect therefrom. *Chem. Res. Toxocol.* 10: 507–517.

May, M., Holmes, E., Rogers, W., and Poth, M. (1990). Protection from glucocorticoid induced thymic involution by dehydroepiandrosterone. *Life Sci.* 46: 1627–1631.

May, M. J., Vernoux, T., Leaver, C., van Montagu, M., and Inze, D. (1998). Glutathione homeostasis in plants: Implications for environmental sensing and plant development. *J. Exp. Botany* 49: 649–667.

McBurnett, K., Lahey, B. B., Frick, P. J., Risch, C., Loeber, R., Hart, E. L., Christ, M. A., and Hanson, K. S. (1991). Anxiety, inhibition, and conduct disorder in children: II. Relation to salivary cortisol. *J. Am. Acad. Child Adolesc. Psychiatry* 30: 192–196.

McCann, S. M., Franci, C. R., and Antunes-Rodrigues, J. (1989). Hormonal control of water and electrolyte intake and output. *Acta Physiol. Scand.* 583 (suppl.): 97–104.

McCarthy, M. M., Curran, G. H., and Siegel, H. L. (1993). Evidence for the involvement of prolactin in the maternal behavior of the hamster. *Physiol. Behav.* 55: 181–184.

McCarty, R., and Pacak, K. (2000). Alarm phase and general adaptation syndrome. *Encylopedia of Stress.* Vol. 1, edited by G. Fink. San Diego: Academic Press, pp. 126–130.

McCauley, J., Kern, D. E., Kolodner, K., Dill, L., Schroeder, A. F., DeChant, H. K., Ryden, J., Derogatis, L. R., and Dass, E. B. (1997). Clinical characteristics of women with a history of childhood abuse. *JAMA* 277: 1362–1368.

McClelland, D. C., Atkinson, J. W., Clark, R. W., and Lowell, E. L. (1976). *The Achievement Motive.* 2nd ed. New York: Irvington.

McEwen, B. S. (1995). Steroid actions on neuronal signalling. *Ernst Schering Research Foundation Lecture Series* 27: 1–45.

McEwen, B. S. (1997). Possible mechanisms for atrophy of the human hippocampus. *Mol. Psychiatry* 2: 255–262.

McEwen, B. S. (1998a). Protective and damaging effects of stress mediators. *New Engl. J. Med.* 338: 171–179.

McEwen, B. S. (1998b). Stress, adaptation, and disease: Allostasis and allostatic load. *Ann. N.Y. Acad. Sci.* 840: 33–44.

McEwen, B. S. (1999). Stress and hippocampal plasticity. *Annu. Rev. Neurosci.* 22: 105–122.

McEwen, B. S. (ed.) (2001). *Coping with the Environment: Neural and Endocrine Mechanisms.* Oxford: Oxford University Press.

McEwen, B. S., and Alves, S. E. (1999). Estrogen actions in the central nervous system. *Endocr. Rev.* 203: 279–306.

McEwen, B. S., and Magarinos, A. M. (1997). Stress effects on morphology and function of the hippocampus. *Ann. N.Y. Acad. Sci.* 21: 271–284.

McEwen, B. S., and Sapolsky, R. M. (1995). Stress and cognitive function. *Curr. Opin. Neurobiol.* 5: 205–216.

McEwen, B. S., and Seeman, T. (1999). Protective and damaging effects of mediators of stress: Elaborating and testing the concepts of allostasis and allostatic load. *Ann. N.Y. Acad. Sci.* 896: 30–47.

McEwen, B. S., and Stellar, E. (1993). Stress and the individual: Mechanisms leading to disease. *Arch. Intern. Med.* 153: 2093–3101.

McEwen, B. S., Lambdin, L. T., Rainbow, T. C., and De Nicola, A. F. (1986). Aldosterone effects on salt appetite in adrenalectomized rats. *Neuroendocrinology* 43: 38–43.

McEwen, B. S., Angulo, J., Cameron, H., Chao, H. M., Daniels, D., Gannon, M. N., Gould, E., Mendelson, S., Sakai, R., Spencer, R., and Woolley, C. (1992). Paradoxical effects of adrenal steroids on the brain: Protection versus degeneration. *Biol. Psychiatry* 31: 177–199.

McEwen, B. S., Biron, C. A., Brunson, K. W., Bulloch, K., Chambers, W. H., Dhabhar, F. S., Goldfarb, R. H., Kitson, R. P., Miller, A. H., Spencer, R. L., and Weiss, J. M. (1997). The role of adrenocorticoids as modulators of immune function in health and disease. *Brain Res. Rev.* 23: 79–133.

McFarland, D. (1991). Defining motivation and cognition in animals. *Int. Stud. Philosophy Sci.* 5: 153–170.

McGaugh, J. L. (2000). Memory—A century of consolidation. *Science* 287: 248–251.

McGinnis, J. M., and Foege, W. H. (1999). Mortality and morbidity attributable to use of addictive substances in the United States. *Proc. Assoc. Am. Physicians* 111: 109–118.

McGinty, J. F. (1999). Advancing from the ventral striatum to the extended amygdala. Implications for neuropsychology and drug abuse. *Ann. N.Y. Acad. Sci.* 877: vii–xv.

McGrath, S., McLean, M., Smith, D., Bistis, A., Giles, W., and Smith, R. (2002). Maternal CRH trajectories vary depending on the cause of preterm delivery. *Am J. Obstet. Gynecol.* 186: 257–269.

McGregor, J. A., French, J. I., Jones, W., Milligran, K., McKinney, P. J., Patterson, E., and Parker, R. (1994). Bacterial vaginosis is associated with prema-

turity and vaginal fluid mucinase and sialidase: Results of a controlled trial of topical clindamycin cream. *Am. J. Obstet. Gynecol.* 170: 1048–1060.

McGregor, J. A., Jackson, M., Lachelin, G. C. L., Goodwin, T. M., Artal, R., Hastings, C., and Dullien, V. (1995). Salivary estriol as risk assessment for preterm labor: A prospective trial. *Am. J. Obstet. Gynecol.* 173: 1337–1342.

McKay, J. R., Murphy, R. T., Rivinus, T. R., and Maisto, S. A. (1991). Family dysfunction and alcohol and drug use in adolescent psychiatric inpatients. *J. Am. Acad. Child Adolesc. Psychiatry* 30: 967–972.

McKibben, L., De Vos, E., and Newberger, E. H. (1989). Victimization of mothers of abused children: A controlled study. *Pediatrics* 84: 531–535.

McLean, M., Bisits, A., Davies, J., Woods, R., Lowry, P., and Smith, R. (1995). A placental clock controlling the length of human pregnancy. *Nat. Med.* 1: 460–463.

McLean, M., Bisits, A., Davies, J., Walters, W., Hackshaw, A., De Voss, K., and Smith, R. (1999). Predicting risk of preterm delivery by second-trimester measurement of maternal plasma corticotropin-releasing hormone and α-fetoprotein concentrations. *Am. J. Obstet. Gynecol.* 181: 207–215.

McVicar, A., and Clancy, J. (1998). Homeostasis: A framework for integrating the life sciences. *Br. J. Nurs.* 7: 601–607.

Meaney, M. J., Aitken, D. H., Sharma, S., Viau, V., and Sarrieau, A. (1989). Neonatal handling increases hippocampal type II glucocorticoid receptors and enhances adrenocortical negative-feedback efficacy in the rat. *Neuroendocrinology* 5: 597–604.

Meaney, M. J., Aitken, D. H., van Berkel, H., Bhatnagar, S., and Sapolsky, R. M. (1988). Effect of neonatal handling of age-related impairments associated with the hippocampus. *Science* 239: 766–768.

Meaney, M. J., Bhatnagar, S., Larocque, S., McCormick, C., Shauks, N., Sharma, S., Smythe, J., Viau, V., and Plotsky, P. M. (1993). Individual differences in the hypothalamic pituitary adrenal stress response and the hypothalamic CRF system. *Ann. N.Y. Acad. Sci.* 697: 70–85.

Meaney, M. J., Diorio, J., Francis, D., Widdowson, J., LaPlante, P., Caldji, C., Sharma, S., Seckl, J., and Plotsky, P. M. (1996). Early environmental regulation of forebrain glucocorticoid receptor gene expression: Implications for adrenocortical responses to stress. *Dev. Neurosci.* 18: 49–72.

Mearns, J., and Lees-Haley, P. R. (1993). Discriminating neuropsychological sequelae of head injury from alcohol-abuse-induced deficits: A review and analysis. *J. Clin. Psychol.* 49: 714–720.

Mehlman, P., Higley, J. D., Faucher, I., Lilly, A. A., Taub, D. M., Vickers, J., Suomi, S. J., and Linnoila, M. (1994). Low CSF 5-HIAA concentrations and severe aggression and impaired impulse control in nonhuman primates. *Am. J. Psychiatry* 151: 1485–1491.

Meier, J., and Stocker, K. (1991). Effects of snake venoms on hemostasis. *Crit. Rev. Toxicol.* 21: 171–182.

Meis, P. J., Goldenberg, R. L., Mercer, B., Moawod, A., Das, A., McNellis, D., Johnson, F., Iams, J. D., Thom, E., and Andrews, W. W. (1995). The preterm prediction study: Significance of vaginal infections. National Institute of Child Health and Human Development Maternal-Fetal Medicine Units Network. *Am. J. Obstet. Gynecol.* 173: 1231–1235.

Meneghini, R. (1997). Iron homeostasis, oxidative stress, and DNA damage. *Free Radic. Biol. Med.* 23: 783–792.

Menzaghi, F., Heinrichs, S. C., Pich, E. M., Tilders, F. J., and Koob, G. F. (1993). Functional impairment of hypothalamic corticotropin-releasing factor neurons with immunotargeted toxins enhances food intake induced by neuropeptide Y. *Brain Res.* 618: 76–82.

Merali, Z., McIntoch, J., Kent, P., Michaud, D., and Anisman, H. (1998). Aversive and appetitive events evoke the release of corticotropin-releasing hormone and bombesin-like peptides at the central nucleus of the amygdala. *J. Neurosci.* 18: 4758–4766.

Mercer, J. G., Lawrence, C. B., and Atkinson, T. (1996). Hypothalamic NPY and CRF expression in the food-deprived hamster. *Physiol. Behav.* 60: 121–127.

Merchenthaler, I., Vigh, S., Petrusz, P., and Schally, A. V. (1982). Immunocytochemical localization of corticotropin-releasing factor (CRF) in the rat brain. *Am. J. Anat.* 165: 385–396.

Merikangas, K. R. (1990). The genetic epidemiology of alcoholism. *Psychol. Med.* 20: 11–22.

Merikangas, K. R., Rounsaville, B. J., and Prusoff, B. A. (1992). Familial factors in vulnerability to substance abuse. In *Vulnerability to Drug Abuse,* edited by M. Glantz and R. Pickens. American Psychiatric Association Press: Washington, D.C.

Mesiano, S., and Jaffe, R. B. (1997). Developmental and functional biology of the primate fetal adrenal cortex. *Endocr. Rev.* 18: 378–403.

Meyer, R. E., and Mirin, S. M. (1979). *The Heroin Stimulus.* New York: Plenum Press.

Michelson, D., Stratakis, C., Hill, L., Reynolds, J., Galliven, E., Chrousos, G., and Gold, P. (1996). Bone mineral density in women with depression. *N. Engl. J. Med.* 335: 1176–1181.

Miles, A. (1982). Reports by Louis Pasteur and Claude Bernard on the organization of scientific teaching and research. *Notes Rec. R. Soc. Lond.* 37: 101–118.

Miles, R. (1999). Neurobiology. A homeostatic switch. *Nature* 397: 215–216.

Miller, B. A., Downs, W. R., Gondoli, D. M., and Keil, A. (1987). The role of childhood sexual abuse in the development of alcoholism in women. *Violence Vict.* 2: 157–172.

Miller, N. E. (1957). Experiments of motivation. Studies combining psychological, physiological, and pharmacological techniques. *Science* 126: 1271–1278.

Miller, N. E. (1959). Liberalization of basic S-R concepts: Extensions to conflict behavior, motivation, and social learning. In *Psychology: A Study of a Science,* vol. 2, edited by S. Koch. New York: McGraw-Hill.

Miller, N. E. (1965). Chemical coding of behavior in the brain. *Science* 148, 328–338.

Miller, N. E., Bailey, C. J., and Stevenson, J. A. F. (1950). Decreased "hunger" but increased food intake resulting from hypothalamic lesions. *Science* 112: 256–259.

Miller-Johnson, S., Lochman, J. E., Coie, J. D., Terry, R., and Hyman, C. (1998). Comorbidity of conduct and depressive problems at sixth grade: Substance use outcomes across adolescence. *J. Abnorm. Child Psychol.* 26: 221–232.

Millerschoen, N. R., and Riggs, D. S. (1969). Homeostatic control of plasma osmolality in the dog and the effect of ethanol. *Am. J. Physiol.* 217: 431–437.

Milner, P. M. (1991). Brain-stimulation reward: A review. *Can. J. Psychol.* 45: 1–36.

Mimura, T. (1995). Homeostasis and transport of inorganic phosphate in plants. *Plant Cell Physiol.* 36: 1–7.

Miner, J. N., Diamond, M. I., and Yamamoto, K. R. (1991). Joints in the regulatory lattice: Composite regulation by steroid receptor-AP 1 complexes. *Cell Growth Differ.* 2: 525–530.

Mistlberger, R. E. (1994). Circadian food-anticipatory activity: Formal models and physiological mechanisms. *Neurosci. Biobehav. Rev.* 18: 171–195.

Mitchell, J. B., and Gratton, A. (1994). Involvement of mesolimbic dopamine neurons in sexual behaviors: Implications for the neurobiology of motivation. *Rev. Neurosci.* 5: 317–329.

Mogenson, G. J. (1987). Limbic-motor integration. In *Progress in Psychobiology and Physiological Psychology,* edited by A. N. Epstein and J. Sprague. New York: Academic Press.

Mogenson, G. J., and Huang, Y. H. (1973). The neurobiology of motivated behavior. *Prog. Neurobiol.* 1: 52–83.

Mogenson, G. J., and Yang, C. R. (1991). The contribution of basal forebrain to limbic-motor integration and the mediation of motivation to action. *Adv. Exp. Med. Biol.* 295: 267–290.

Mogenson, G. J., Jones, D. L., and Yim, C. Y. (1980). From motivation to action: Functional interface between the limbic system and the motor system. *Prog. Neurobiol.* 14: 69–97.

Monk, T. H., Buysse, D. J., Reynolds, C. F. III, Jarrett, D. B., and Kupfer, D. J. (1992). Rhythmic vs. hormonal influences on mood, activation, and performance in young and old men. *J. Gerontol.* 47: 221–227.

Mook, D. (1987). *Motivation.* New York: Norton Press.

Moore, F. L., Wood, R. E., and Boyd, S. K. (1992). Sex steroids and vasotocin interact in a female amphibian *(Taricha granulosa)* to elicit female-like egg-laying behavior or male-like courtship. *Horm. Behav.* 26: 156–166.

Moore-Ede, M. C. (1986). Physiology of the circadian timing system: Predictive versus reactive homeostasis. *Am. J. Physiol.* 250: R737–R752.
Moore-Ede, M. C., Sulzman, F. M., and Fuller, C. A. (1982). *The Clocks that Time Us.* Cambridge: Harvard University Press.
Moran, T. H., and Schulkin, J. (2000). Curt Richter and Regulatory Physiology. *Am. J. Physiol.* 279: R357–R363.
Morgan, C. A. III, Grillon, C., Southwick, S. M., Davis, M., and Charney, D. S. (1995). Fear-potentiated startle in posttraumatic stress disorder. *Biol. Psychiatry* 38: 378–385.
Morgan, C. T. (1966). The central motive state. In *Motivation,* edited by D. Bindra and J. Stewart. Baltimore: Penguin Books.
Morgan, C. T., and Stellar, E. (1950). *Physiological Psychology.* 2nd ed. New York: McGraw-Hill.
Morgan, M. A., and LeDoux, J. E. (1995). Differential contribution of dorsal and ventral medial prefrontal cortex to the acquisition and extinction of conditioned fear in rats. *Behav. Neurosci.* 109: 681–688.
Morgan, M. A., and Pfaff, D. W. (2001). Effects of estrogen on activity and fear-related behaviors in mice. *Horm. Behav.* 40: 472–482.
Morris, C. M., Candy, J. M., Keith, A. B., Oakley, A. E., Taylor, G. A., Pullen, R. G., Bloxham, C. A., Gocht, A., and Edwardson, J. A. (1992). Brain iron homeostasis. *J. Inorg. Biochem.* 47: 257–265.
Morris, J. S., Frith, C. D., Perrett, D. I., Rowland, D., Young, A. W., Calder, A. J., and Dolan, R. J. (1996). A differential neural response in the human amygdala to fearful and happy facial expressions. *Nature* 383: 812–815.
Morse, D. S., Suchman, A. L., and Frankel, R. M. (1977). The meaning of symptoms in 10 women with somatization disorder and a history of childhood abuse. *Arch. Fam. Med.* 6: 468–476.
Moser-Veillon, P. B. (1995). Zinc needs and homeostasis during lactation. *Analyst* 120: 895–897.
Moss, H. B., Kirisci, L., Gordon, H. W., and Tarter, R. E. (1994). A neuropsychologic profile of adolescent alcoholics. *Alcohol Clin. Exp. Res.* 18: 159–163.
Mrosovsky, N. (1990). *Rheostasis: The Physiology of Change.* Oxford: Oxford University Press.
Mullen, P. E., Martin, J. L., Anderson, J. C., Romans, S. E., and Herbison, G. P. (1996). The long-term impact of the physical, emotional, and sexual abuse of children: A community study. *Child Abuse Negl.* 20: 7–21.
Mulroney, S. E., Woda, C. B., Halaihel, N., Louie, B., McDonnell, K., Schulkin, J., and Levi, M. (2000). Regulation of type-II sodium-phosphate (NaPi-2) transporters in the brain: Central control of renal NAPI-2 transporters. *FASEB.*
Munck, A., Guyre, P. M., and Holbrook, N. J. (1984). Physiological functions of glucocorticoids in stress and their relations to pharmacological actions. *Endocr. Rev.* 5: 25–44.

Murphy, E. A., and Pyeritz, R. E. (1986). Homeostasis VII. A conspectus. *Am. J. Med. Genet.* 24: 735–751.

Murphy, E. A., and Renie, W. A. (1984). The dynamics of quantifiable homeostasis. IV. Zero-order homeostasis. *Am. J. Med. Genet.* 18: 99–113.

Musselman, D. L., and Nemeroff, C. B. (2000). Depression really does hurt your heart: Stress, depression, and cardiovascular disease. *Prog. Brain Res.* 122: 43–59.

Nader, K., and van der Kooy, D. (1997). Deprivation state switches the neurobiological substrates mediating opiate reward in the ventral tegmental area. *J. Neurosci.* 17: 383–390.

Nader, K., Bechara, A., and van der Kooy, D. (1997). Neurobiological constraints on behavioral models of motivation. *Annu. Rev. Psychol.* 48: 85–114.

Naisberg, Y. (1996). Homeostatic disruption and depression. *Med. Hypotheses* 47: 415–422.

Nakamura, K., and Norgren, R. (1995). Sodium-deficient diet reduces gustatory activity in the nucleus of the solitary tract of behaving rats. *Am. J. Physiol.* 269: R647–R661.

Nasajon, R. (1999). The homeostatic model of depression applied to a case study. *Dissertation Abstr. Int. Sec. B Sci. Eng.* 60: 1310.

Nathanielsz, P. W. (1998). Comparative studies on the initiation of labor. *Eur. J. Obstet. Gynecol. Reprod. Biol.* 78: 127–132.

Nathanielsz, P. W. (1999a). How far upstream or downstream is corticotropin-releasing hormone in the overall process of parturition in rhesus monkeys? *Am. J. Obstet. Gynecol.* 180: S267–268.

Nathanielsz, P. W. (1999b). *Life in the Womb.* New York: Promethean Press.

National Vital Statistics Report. (2000). No. 46, p. 75.

Nattrass, M. (1991). Abnormalities of glucose homeostasis in diabetes. *Proc. Nutr. Soc.* 50: 577–581.

Nauta, W. J. H. (1961). Fibre degeneration following lesions of the amygdaloid complex in the monkey. *J. Anat.* 95: 516–531.

Nauta, W. J. H. (1963). Central nervous organization and the endocrine motor system. In *Advances in Neuroendocrinology,* edited by A. V. Nalbandov. Urbana: University of Illinois Press.

Nauta, W. J. H. (1972). The central visceromotor system: A general survey. In *Limbic System Mechanisms and Autonomic Function,* edited by C. H. Hockman. Springfield, Ill.: Charles C. Thomas.

Nederkoorn, C., Smulders, F. T., and Jansen, A. (2000). Cephalic phase responses, craving and food intake in normal subjects. *Appetite* 35: 45–55.

Negro, J. N. Jr., Michelson, D., Palladino-Negro, P., Elliott, E. A., Sciullo, D. A., and Gold, P. E. (2003). In press.

Nelson, R. J. (1997). The use of genetic "knockout" mice in behavioral endocrinology research. *Horm. Behav.* 31: 188–196.

Nelson, R. J., and Drazen, D. L. (2000). Seasonal changes in stress responses. *Encyclopedia of Stress.* Vol. 3, edited by G. Fink. San Diego: Academic Press, pp. 402–408.

Nemeroff, C. B. (1992). New vistas in neuropeptide research in neuropsychiatry: Focus on corticotropin-releasing factor. *Neuropsychopharmacology* 6: 69–75.

Nemeroff, C. B. (1999). The preeminent role of neuropeptide systems in the early pathophysiology of Alzheimer disease: Up with corticotropin-releasing factor, down with acetylcholine (comment). *Arch. Gen. Psychiatry* 56: 981–987.

Nemeroff, C. B., Widerlov, E., Bissette, G., Wallens, H., Karlsson, I., Ekluud, K., Kilts, C. D., Loosen, P. T., and Vale, W. (1984). Elevated concentrations of CSF corticotropin releasing factor-like immunoreactivity in depressed outpatients. *Science* 26: 1342–1344.

Nemeroff, C. B., Owens, M. J., Bissette, G., Andorn, A. C., and Stanley, M. (1988). Reduced corticotropin-releasing factor binding sites in the frontal cortex of suicide victims. *Arch. Gen. Psychiatry* 45: 577–579.

Nemeroff, C. B., Krishnan, K. R., Reed, D., Leder, R., Beam, C., and Dunnick, N. R. (1992). Adrenal gland enlargement in major depression: A computed tomographic study. *Arch. Gen. Psychiatry* 49: 384–387.

Nestler, E. J. (1999). Cellular and molecular mechanisms of addiction. In *Neurobiology of Mental Illness,* edited by D. S. Charney, E. J. Nestler, and B. S. Bunney. New York: Oxford University Press.

Nestler, E. J., and Aghajanian, G. K. (1997). Molecular and cellular basis of addiction. *Science* 278: 58–63.

Nestler, E. J., Hope, B. T., and Widnell, K. L. (1993). Drug addiction: A model for the molecular basis of neural plasticity. *Neuron* 11: 995–1006.

Newberger, E. H., Barkan, S. E., Lieberman, E. S., McCormick, M. C., Yllo, K., Gary, L. T., and Schecter, S. (1992). Abuse of pregnant women and adversive birth outcome. Current knowledge and implications for practice. *JAMA* 267: 2370–2372.

Newcomer, J. W., Craft, S., Hershey, T., Askins, K., and Bardgett, M. E. (1994). Glucocorticoid-induced impairment in declarative memory performance in adult humans. *J. Neurosci.* 14: 2047–2053.

Newcomer, J. W., Selke, G., Melson, A. K., Hershey, T., Craft, S., Richards, K., and Alderson, A. L. (1999). Decreased memory performance in healthy humans induced by stress-level cortisol treatment. *Arch. Gen. Psychiatry* 56: 527–533.

Newport, D. J., and Nemeroff, C. B. (2000). Neurobiology of posttraumatic stress disorder. *Curr. Opin. Neurobiol.* 10: 211–218.

Nicholls, P. (1988). "Integrity of structure" and "latent life"—The respiratory chain, Claude Bernard, and David Keilin. *Prog. Clin. Biol. Res.* 274: 65–78.

Nichols, J. R. (1983). The homeostatic reflex and addictive drugs. *Neurobehav. Toxicol. Teratol.* 5: 237–240.

Nicolaidis, S. (1977). Sensory-neuroendocrine reflexes and their anticipatory and optimizing role in metabolism. In *The Chemical Senses and Nutrition,* edited by M. R. Kare and O. Maller. New York: Academic Press.

Nishijo, H., and Norgren, R. (1997). Parabrachial neural coding of taste stimuli in awake rats. *J. Neurophysiol.* 78: 2254–2268.

Norgren, R. (1984). Central gustatory mechanisms of taste. In *Handbook of Physiology and the Nervous System*, edited by J. M. Brookhart and V. B. Mountcastle. Bethesda, MD: American Physiological Society.

Norgren, R. (1995). Gustatory system. In *The Rat Nervous System*, edited by G. Pazinos. New York: Academic Press.

Norgren, R., and Leonard, C. M. (1973). Ascending central gustatory pathways. *J. Comp. Neurol.* 150: 217–238.

Norgren, R., and Smith, G. P. (1988). The central distribution of vagal subdiaphragmatic branches in the rat. *J. Comp. Neurol.* 273: 207–223.

Notzon, F. C., Komarov, Y. M., Ermakov, S. P., Sempos, C. T., Marks, J. S., and Sempos, E. V. (1998). Causes of declining life expectancy in Russia. *JAMA* 279: 793–800.

Oatley, K. (1970). Brain mechanisms and motivation. *Nature* 225: 797–801.

O'Brian, C. P. (1997). A range of research-based pharmacotherapies for addiction: A critical review. *Br. J. Addict.* 82: 127–137.

O'Doherty, F., and Davies, B. J. (1987). Life events and addiction: A critical review. *Br. J. Addict.* 82: 127–137.

Ohuoha, D. C., Maxwell, J. A., Thomson, L. E. III, Cadet, J. L., and Rothman, R. B. (1997). Effect of dopamine receptor antagonists on cocaine subjective effects: A naturalistic case study. *J. Subst. Abuse Treat.* 14: 249–258.

Okamoto, M., and Hayashji, K. (1984). Homeostatic capability of rate-sensitive feedback system: Mathematical model. *Am. J. Physiol.* 247: R927–R931.

Olds, J. (1958). Self-stimulation of the brain: Its use to study local effects of hunger, sex, and drugs. *Science* 127: 315–324.

Olds, J., and Milner, P. (1954). Positive reinforcement produced by electrical stimulation of septal area and other regions of rat brain. *J. Comp. Physiol. Psychol.* 47: 419–427.

Olds, M. E., and Forbes, J. L. (1981). The central basis of motivation: Intracranial self-stimulation studies. *Annu. Rev. Psychol.* 32: 523–574.

Orchinik, M., Murray, T. F., and Moore, F. L. (1994). Steroid modulation of GABA A receptors in an amphibian brain. *Brain Res.* 646: 258–266.

Ornstein, T. J., Iddon, J. L., Baldacchino, A. M., Sahakian, B. J., London, M., Everitt, B. J., and Robbins, T. W. (2000). Profiles of cognitive dysfunction in chronic amphetamine and heroin abusers. *Neuropsychopharmacology* 23: 113–126.

Orrenius, S., and Bellomo, G. (1986). Toxicological implications of perturbation of Ca2+ homeostasis in hepatocytes. *Calcium Cell Funct.* 6: 185–208.

Ouimette, P. C., Ahrens, C., Moos, R. H., and Finney, J. W. (1998). During treatment chances in substance abuse patients with posttraumatic stress disorder. The influence of specific interventions and program environments. *J. Subst. Abuse Treat.* 15: 555–564.

Owens, M. J., and Nemeroff, C. B. (1991). Physiology and pharmacology of corticotropin-releasing hormone. *Pharmacol. Rev.* 43: 425–473.

Owens, M. J., Bartolome, J., Schanberg, S. M., and Nemeroff, C. B. (1990). Corticotropin releasing factor concentrations exhibit an apparent diurnal rhythm in hypothalamic and extrahypothalamic brain regions: Differential sensitivity to corticosterone. *Neuroendocrinology* 52: 626–631.

Ozernyuk, N. D., Dyomin, V. I., Prokofyev, E. A., and Androsova, I. M. (1992). Energy homeostasis and developmental stability. *Acta Zool. Fenn.* 191: 167–175.

Pacak, K., Armando, I., Komoly, S., Fukuhara, K., Weise, V. K., Holmes, C., Kopin, I. J., and Goldstein, D. S. (1992). Hypercortisolemia inhibits yohimbine-induced release of norepinephrine in the posterolateral hypothalamus of conscious rats. *Endocrinology* 131: 1369–1367.

Pacak, K., Kvetnansky, R., Palkovits, M., Fukuhara, K., Yadid, G., Kopin, I., and Goldstein, D. S. (1993). Adrenalectomy augments in vivo release of norepinephrine in the paraventricular nucleus during immobilized stress. *Endocrinology* 133: 1404–1410.

Pacak, K., Palkovits, M., Kvetnansky, R., Matern, P., Hart, C., Kopin, I., and Goldstein, D. S. (1995). Catecholaminergic inhibition by hypercortisolemia in paraventricular nucleus of conscious rats. *Endocrinology* 136: 4814–4819.

Palkovits, M. (1981). Catecholamines in the hypothalamus: An anatomical review. *Neuroendocrinology* 33: 123–128.

Palkovits, M. (1984). Role of the central nervous system neuropeptides in body fluid homeostasis. *J. Physiol.* 79: 428–431.

Palkovits, M. (1999). Interconnections between the neuroendocrine hypothalamus and the central autonomic system. *Front. Neuroendocrinol.* 20: 270–295.

Palkovits, M., Brownstein, M. J., and Vale, W. (1983). Corticotropin releasing hormone immunoreactivity in hypothalamus and extrahypothalamic nuclei of sheep brain. *Neuroendocrinology* 37: 302–305.

Palkovits, M., Baffi, J., Toth, Z. E., and Pacak, K. (1998a). Brain catecholamine systems in stress. *Adv. Pharmacol.* 42: 572–575.

Palkovits, M., Young, W. S. III, Kovacks, K., Toth, Z., and Makara, G. B. (1998b). Alterations in corticotropin releasing hormone gene expression of central amygala neurons following long-term paraventricular lesions and adrenalectomy. *Neuroscience* 85: 135–147.

Palmer, T. N., Cook, E. B., and Drake, P. G. (1991). Alcohol abuse and fuel homeostasis. *NATO Asi Ser. Life Sci.* 206: 223–235.

Panksepp, J. (1998). *Affective Neuroscience: The Foundations of Human and Animal Emotions.* New York: Oxford University Press.

Panzica, G. C., Viglietti-Panzica, C., and Balthazart, J. (1996). The sexually dimorphic medial preoptic nucleus of quail: A key brain area mediating steroid action on male sexual behavior. *Front. Neuroendocrinol.* 17: 51–125.

Papez, J. W. (1937). A proposed mechanism of emotion. *Arch. Neurol. Psychiatry* 38: 725–744.

Parazzini, F., La Vecchia, C., Negri, E., Francheschi, S., Moroni, S., Chatenoud, L., and Bolis, G. (1997). Case-control study of estrogen replacement therapy and risk of cervical cancer. *BMJ* 315: 85–88.

Parker, B., McFarlane, J., and Soeken, K. (1994). Abuse during pregnancy: Effects on maternal complications and birth weight in adult and teenage women. *Obstet. Gynecol.* 84: 323–328.

Parkes, D. G., Weisinger, R. S., and May, C. N. (2001). Cardiovascular actions of CRH and urocortin: An update. *Peptides* 22: 821–827.

Paut-Pagano, L., Roky, R., Valatx, J. L., Kitahama, K., and Jouvet, M. (1993). Anatomical distribution of prolactin-like immunoreactivity in the rat brain. *Neuroendocrinology* 58: 682–695.

Pavcovich, L. A., and Valentino, R. J. (1997). Regulation of putative neurotransmitter effect of corticotropin-releasing factor: Effects of adrenalectomy. *J. Neurosci.* 17: 401–408.

Pavlov, I. P. (1894–1895/1955). Lectures on the work of the principal digestive glands. In *Selected Works,* edited by Kh. S. Koshtoyants. Moscow: Foreign Languages Publishing House.

Pavlov, I. P. (1897/1902). *The Work of the Digestive Glands,* translated by W. H. Thompson. London: Griffin.

Pavlov, I. P. (1927/1960). *Conditional Reflexes. An Investigation of the Physiological Activity of the Cerebral Cortex.* London: Oxford University Press.

Pavlov, I. P. (1928). *Lectures on Conditioned Reflexes: Twenty-five Years of Objective Study of the Higher Nervous Activity,* translated by W. H. Gantt. New York: Liveright Publishing.

Pecina, S., and Berridge, K. C. (1996). Brainstem mediates diazepam enhancement of palatability and feeding: Microinjections into fourth ventricle versus lateral ventricle. *Brain Res.* 727: 22–30.

Pecina, S., and Berridge, K. C. (2000). Opioid eating site in accumbens shell mediates eating intake and hedonic "liking" for food: Map based on microinjection Fos plumes. *Brain Res.* 863: 71–86.

Pedersen, W., and Skrondal, A. (1996). Alcohol and sexual victimization: A longitudinal study of Norwegian girls. *Addiction* 91: 565–581.

Peifer, A., and Barden, N. (1987). Estrogen-induced decrease of glucocorticoid receptor messenger ribonucleic acid concentration in rat anterior pituitary gland. *Mol Endocrinol.* 1: 435–440.

Peirce, C. S. (1992–98). *The Essential Peirce,* edited by N. Houser. Bloomington: Indiana University Press.

Pena, M. M., Lee, J., and Thiele, D. J. (1999). A delicate balance: Homeostatic control of copper uptake and distribution. *J. Nutr.* 129: 1251–1260.

Pepe, G. J., and Albrecht, E. D. (1995). Actions of placental and fetal adrenal steroid hormones in primate pregnancy. *Physiol. Rev.* 16: 608–648.

Perkonigg, A., Lieb, R., and Wittchen, H. U. (1998). Prevalence of use, abuse, and dependence of illicit drugs among adolescents and young adults in a community sample. *Eur. Addict. Res.* 4: 58–66.

Perrin, M. H., and Vale, W. W. (1999). Corticotropin-releasing factor receptors and their ligand family. *Ann. N.Y. Acad. Sci.* 885: 312–328.

Perrin, M. H., Donaldson, C. J., Chen, R., Lewis, K. A., and Vale, W. W. (1993). Cloning and functional expression of a rat brain corticotropin releasing hormone receptor. *Endocrinology* 6: 3058–3061.

Perry, B. D., and Pollard, R. (1998). Homeostasis, stress, trauma, and adaptation: A neurodevelopment view of childhood trauma. *Child Adolesc. Psychiatric Clin. North Am.* 7: 33–51, viii.

Peters, K. R., Maltzman, I., and Villone, K. (1994). Childhood abuse of parents of alcohol and other drug misusing adolescents. *Int. J. Addict.* 29: 1259–1268.

Petit, A. (1987). Claude Bernard and the history of science. *ISIS* 78: 201–219.

Peto, C. A., Arias, C., Vale, W. W., and Sawchenko, P. E. (1999). Ultrastructural localization of the corticotropin-releasing hormone binding protein in rat brain and pituitary. *J. Comp. Neurol.* 413: 241–254.

Petraglia, F., Volpe, A., Genazzani, A. R., Rivier, J., Sawchenko, P. E., and Vale, W. (1990). Neuroendocrinology of the human placenta. *Front. Neuroendocrinol.* 11: 6–37.

Petraglia, F., Coukos, G., Volpe, A., Genazzani, A. R., and Vale, W. (1991). Involvement of placental neurohormones in human parturition. *Ann. N.Y. Acad. Sci.* 622: 331–340.

Petraglia, F., Aguzzoli, L., Florio, P., Baumann, P., Genazzani, A. D., Di Carlo, C., and Romero, R. (1995a). Maternal plasma and placental immunoreactive corticotropin-releasing factor concentrations in infection-associated term and pre-term delivery. *Placenta* 16: 157–164.

Petraglia, F., Benedetto, C., Florio, P., D'Ambrogio, G., Genazzani, A. D., Marozio, L., and Vale, W. (1995b). Effect of corticotropin-releasing factor-binding protein on prostaglandin release from cultured maternal decidua and on contractile activity of human myometrium in vitro. *J. Clin. Endocrinol. Metab.* 80: 3073–3076.

Petraglia, F., Hatch, M. C., Lapinski, R., Stomati, M., Reis, F. M., Cobellis, L., and Berkowitz, G. S. (2001). Lack of effect of psychosocial stress on maternal corticotropin releasing factor and catecholamine levels at 28 weeks' gestation. *J. Soc. Gyn. Invest.* 8: 83–88.

Pettifor, J. M. (1990). Recent advances in pediatric metabolic bone disease: The consequences of altered phosphate homeostasis in renal insufficiency and hypophosphemic vitamin D-resistant rickets. *Bone Miner.* 9: 199–214.

Pettit, H. O., Ettenberg, A., Bloom, F. E., and Koob, G. F. (1984). Destruction of dopamine in the nucleus accumbens selectively attenuates cocaine but not heroin self-administration. *Psychopharmacology* 84: 167–173.

Pfaff, D. W. (1980). *Estrogens and Brain Function.* New York: Springer-Verlag.

Pfaff, D. W. (1982). Neurobiological mechanisms of sexual motivation. In *The Physiological Mechanisms of Motivation,* edited by D. S. Pfaff. New York: Springer-Verlag.

Pfaff, D. W. (1999). *Drive.* Cambridge: MIT Press.

Pfaffmann, C. (1960). The pleasures of sensation. *Psychol. Rev.* 67: 253–268.

Pfaffmann, C. (1982). Taste: A model of incentive motivation. In *The Physiological Mechanisms of Motivation,* edited by D. W. Pfaff. New York: Springer-Verlag.

Pfaffmann, C., Norgren, R., and Grill, H. J. (1977). Sensory affect and motivation. In *Tonic Function of Sensory Systems,* edited by B. M. Wenzel and H. P. Ziegler. New York: New York Academy of Sciences.

Pfluger, E. (1877). The telegogic mechanisms of living nature. *Plfugers Arch.* 15: 57–103.

Phillips, D. I., Barker, D. J., Fall, C. H., Seckl, J. R., Whorwood, C. B., Wood, P. J., and Walker, B. R. (1998). Elevated plasma cortisol concentrations: A link between low birth weight and the insulin resistance syndrome? *J. Clin. Endocrinol. Metab.* 83: 757–760.

Phillips, G. D., Robbins, T. W., and Everitt, B. J. (1994). Bilateral intra-accumbens self-administration of d-amphetamine: Antagonism with intra-accumbens SCH-23390 and sulpiride. *Psychopharmacology* 114: 477–485.

Phillips, R. G., and LeDoux, J. E. (1992). Differential contribution of amygdala and hippocampus to cued and contextual fear conditioning. *Behav. Neurosci.* 106: 274–285.

Phillips, R. J., Baronowsky, E. A., and Powley, T. L. (1997). Afferent innervation of gastrointestinal tract smooth muscle by the hepatic branch of the vagus. *J. Comp. Neurol.* 384: 248–270.

Piazza, P. V., and Le Moal, M. (1997). Glucocorticoids as a biological substrate of reward: Physiological and pathophysiological implications. *Brain Res. Brain Res. Rev.* 25: 359–372.

Piazza, P. V., Deminiere, J. M., Le Moal, M., and Simon, H. (1989). Factors that predict individual vulnerability to amphetamine self-administration. *Science* 245: 1511–1513.

Piazza, P. V., Maccari, S., Deminiere, J. M., Le Moal, M., Mormede, P., and Simon, H. (1991). Corticosterone levels determine individual vulnerability to amphetamine self-administration. *Proc. Natl. Acad. Sci. USA* 88: 2088–2092.

Piazza, P. V., Deroche, V., Deminiere, J. M., Maccari, S., Le Moal, M., and Simon, H. (1993). Corticosterone in the range of stress-induced levels possesses reinforcing properties: Implications for sensation-seeking behaviors. *Proc. Natl. Acad. Sci. USA* 90: 11738–11742.

Piazza, P. V., Marinelli, M., Iodogne, C., Deroche, V., Rouge-Pont, F., Maccari, S., Le Moal, M., and Simon, H. (1994). Inhibition of corticosterone synthesis by Metyrapone decreases cocaine-induced locomotion and relapse of cocaine self-administration. *Brain Res.* 658: 259–264.

Piazza, P. V., Deroche-Gamonent, V., Rouge-Pont, F., and Le Moal, M. (2000). Vertical shifts in self-administration dose-response functions predict a drug-vulnerable phenotype predisposed to addiction. *J. Neurosci.* 20: 4226–4232.

Pich, E. M., Heinrichs, S. C., Rivier, C., Miczek, K. A., Fisher, D. A., and Koob, G. F. (1993a). Blockade of pituitary-adrenal axis activation induced by peripheral immunoneutralization of corticotropin-releasing factor does not affect the behavioral response to social defeat stress in rats. *Psychoneuroendocrinology* 18: 495–507.

Pich, E. M., Koob, G. F., Heilig, M., Menzaghi, F., Vale, W., and Weiss, F. (1993b). Corticotropin-releasing factor release from the mediobasal hypothalamus of the rat as measured by microdialysis. *Neuroscience* 55: 695–707.

Pich, E. M., Lorang, M., Yeganeh, M., Rodriguez de Fonseca, F., Raber, J., Koob, G. F., and Weiss, F. (1995). Increase of extracellular corticotropin releasing factor-like immunoreactivity levels in the amygdala of awake rats during restraint stress and ethanol withdrawal as measured by microdialysis. *J. Neurosci.* 15: 5439–5447.

Pihoker, C., Owens, M. J., Khun, C. M., Schanberg, S. M., and Nemeroff, C. B. (1993). Maternal separation in neonatal rats elicits activation of the hypothalamic-pituitary-adrenocortical axis: A putative role for corticotropin-releasing factor. *Psychoneuroendocrinology* 18: 485–493.

Pike, M. C., Peters, R. K., Cozen, W., Probst-Hensch, N. M., Felix, J. C., Wan, P. C., and Mack, T. M. (1997). Estrogen-progestin replacement therapy and endometrial cancer. *J. Natl. Cancer Inst.* 89: 1110–1116.

Pike, R. L., and Yao, C. (1971). Increased sodium chloride appetite during pregnancy in the rat. *J. Nutr.* 101: 169–176.

Pine, D. S., Coplan, J. D., Wasserman, G. A., Miller, L. S., Fried, J. E., Davies, M., Cooper, T. B., Greenhill, L., Shaffer, D., and Parsons, B. (1998). Neuroendocrine responses to fenfluramine challenge in boys. Associations with aggressive behavior and adverse rearing. *Arch. Gen. Psychiatry* 54: 839–846.

Pitkow, L. J., Sharer, C. A., Ren, X., Insel, T. R., Terwillinger, E. F., and Young, L. J. (2001). Facilitation of affiliation and pair-bond formation by vasopressin receptor gene transfer into the ventral forebrain of a monogamous vole. *J. Neurosci.* 15: 7392–7396.

Pitman, D. L., Natelson, B. H., Ottenweller, J. E., McCarty, R., Pritzel, T., and Tapp, W. N. (1995). Effects of exposure to stressors of varying predictability on adrenal function in rats. *Behav. Neurosci.* 109: 767–776.

Pitman, R. K. (1989). Post-traumatic stress disorder, hormones and memory. *Biol. Psychiatry* 26: 221–223.

Pitman, R. K., and Orr, S. P. (1990). Twenty-four hour urinary cortisol and catecholamine excretion in combat-related posttraumatic stress disorder. *Biol. Psychiatry* 27: 245–247.

Pittendrigh, C. S., and Caldarola, P. C. (1973). General homeostasis of the frequency of circadian oscillations. *Proc. Natl. Acad. Sci. USA* 70: 2697–2701.

Plat, L., Leproult, R., L'Hermite-Baleriaux, M., Fery, F., Mockel, J., Polousky, K.S., and Van Cauter, E. (1999). Metabolic effects of short-term elevations of plasma cortisol are more pronounced in the evening than in the morning. *J. Clin. Endocrinol. Metab.* 84: 3082–3092.

Plihal, W., Krug, R., Pietrowsky, R., Fehm, H. L., and Born, J. (1996). Corticosteroid receptor mediated effects on mood in humans. *Psychoneuroendocrinology* 21: 515–523.

Plotsky, P. M., and Meaney, M. J. (1993). Early, postnatal experiences alters hypothalamic corticotropin-releasing factor (CRF) mRNA, median eminence CRF content and stress-induced release in adult rats. *Brain Res. Mol. Brain Res.* 18: 195–200.

Plotsky, P. M., and Meaney, M. J. (1996). Neonatal rearing conditions alter HPA axis function, central CRF mRNA, CSF CRF levels, and behavior: Reversal by SSRI treatment. Abstract for the twenty-sixth ISPNE congress.

Plummer, J. P. (1981). Acupuncture and homeostasis: Physiological, physical (postural), and psychological. *Am. J. Chin. Med.* 9: 1–14.

Porrino, L. J., and Lyons, D. (2000). Orbital and medial prefrontal cortex and psychostimulant abuse: Studies in animal models. *Cereb. Cortex* 10: 326–333.

Posner, M., and Rothbart, M. (2000). Developing mechanisms of self-regulation. *Dev. Psychopathol.* 12: 427–442.

Potter, E., Sutton, S., Donaldson, C., Chen, R., Perrin, M., Lewis, K., Sawchenko, P. E., and Vale, W. (1994). Distribution of corticotropin-releasing factor receptor mRNA expression in the rat brain and pituitary. *Proc. Natl. Acad. Sci. USA* 91: 8777–8781.

Poulos, C. X., and Cappell, H. (1991). Homeostatic theory of drug tolerance: A general model of physiological adaptation. *Psychol. Rev.* 98: 390–408.

Poulos, C. X., and Hinson, R. E. (1984). A homeostatic model of Pavlovian conditioning: Tolerance to scopolamine-induced adipsia. *J. Exp. Psychol. Anim. Behav. Process* 10: 75–89.

Poulos, C. X., Wilkinson, D. A., and Cappell, H. (1981). Homeostatic regulation and Pavlovian conditioning in tolerance to amphetamine-induced anorexia. *J. Comp. Physiol. Psychol.* 95: 735–746.

Pounds, J. G. (1984). Effect of lead intoxication on calcium homeostasis and calcium-mediated cell function. *Neurotoxicology* 5: 295–332.

Powley, T. L. (1977). The ventromedial hypothalamic syndrome, satiety, and cephalic phase. *Psychol. Rev.* 84: 89–126.

Powley, T. L. (2000). Vagal circuitry mediating cephalic-phase responses to food. *Appetite* 34: 184–188.

Powley, T. L., and Berthoud, H.-R. (1985). Diet and cephalic phase insulin responses. *Am. J. Clin. Nutr.* 42: 991–1002.

Praemer, A., Funer, S., and Rice, D. (1992). *Musculoskeletal Conditions in the United States.* Park Ridge, Ill.: American Academy of Orthopedic Surgeons.

Price, D. D. (2000). Psychological and neural mechanisms of the affective dimension of pain. *Science* 288: 1769–1772.

Price, J. L. (1999). Prefrontal cortical networks related to visceral function and mood. *Ann. N.Y. Acad. Sci.* 877: 383–396.

Price, J. S. (1991). Change or homeostasis? A systems theory approach to depression. *Br. J. Med. Psychol.* 64: 331–344.

Price, M. L., and Lucki, I. (2001). Regulation of serotonin release in the lateral septum and striatum by corticotropin releasing factor. *J. Neurosci.* 21: 2833–2841.

Profet, M. (1991). The function of allergy: Immunological defense against toxins. *Q. Rev. Biol.* 66: 23–62.

Pugh, C. R., Tremblay, D., Fleshner, M., and Rudy, J. W. (1997). A selective role for corticosterone in fear conditioning. *Behav. Neurosci.* 111: S303–S311.

Putilov, A. A. (1995). Timing of sleep modelling: Circadian modulation of the homeostatic process. *Biol. Rhythm Res.* 26: 1–19.

Quartermain, D., and Wolf, G. (1967). Drive properties of mineralocorticoid-induced sodium appetite. *Physiol. Behav.* 2: 261–263.

Quirarte, G. L., Roozendaal, B., and McGaugh, J. L. (1997). Glucocorticoid enhancement of memory storage involves noradrenergic activation in the basolateral amygdala. *Proc. Natl. Acad. Sci. USA* 94: 14048–14053.

Quirk, G. J., Russo, G. K., Barron, J. L., and Lebron, K. (2000). The role of ventromedial prefrontal cortex in the recovery of extinguished fear. *J. Neurosci.* 20: 6225–6231.

Raadsheer, F. C., van Heerikhuize, J. J., Lucassen, P. J., Hoogendijk, J. G., Tilders, F. J., and Swaab, D. F. (1995). Corticotropin-releasing hormone mRNA levels in the paraventricular nucleus of patients with Alzheimer's disease and depression. *Am. J. Psychiatry* 152: 1372–1376.

Rabinowitz, L. (1989). Homeostatic regulation of potassium excretion. *J. Hypertens.* 7: 433–442.

Racuh, C. L., Whalen, P. J., Shin, L. M., McInerney, S. C., Macklin, M. L., Lasko, N. B., Orr, S. P., and Pitman, R. K. (2000). Exaggerated amygdala response to masked facial stimuli in posttraumatic stress disorder: A functional MRI study. *Biol. Psychiatry* 47: 769–776.

Rajakumar, P. A., He, J., Simmons, R. A., and Devaskar, S. U. (1998). Effect of uteroplacental insufficiency upon brain neuropeptide Y and corticotropin-releasing factor gene expression and concentrations. *Pediatr. Res.* 44: 168–174.

Rajkowska, G., Miguel-Hidalgo, J., Wei, J., Dilley, G., Pittman, S. D., Meltzer, H. Y., Overholser, J. C., Roth, B. L., and Stockmeier, C. A. (1999). Morphometric evidence for neuronal and glial prefrontal cell pathology in major depression. *Biol. Psychiatry* 45: 1085–1098.

Ramesh, B. (1996). Dietary management of pancreatic beta-cell homeostasis and control of diabetes. *Med. Hypotheses* 46: 357–361.

Ramsay, D., and Thrasher, T. N. (1989). Homeostatic mechanisms in the regulation of plasma osmolality. *Acta Physiol. Pol.* 40: 275–281.

Ramsay, D. S., and Woods, S. C. (1997). Biological consequences of drug administration: Implications for acute and chronic tolerance. *Psychol. Rev.* 104: 170–193.

Ramsay, D. S., Seeley, R. J., Bolles, R. C., and Woods, S. C. (1996). Ingestive homeostasis: The primacy of learning. In *Why We Eat What We Eat: The Psychology of Eating,* edited by E. D. Capaldi. Washington, D.C.: American Psychological Association.

Ramsay, T. G., Kasser, T. R., Hausman, G. J., and Martin, R. J. (1986). Metabolic development of the porcine placenta in response to alterations in maternal or fetal homeostasis. In *Swine in Biomedical Research,* edited by M. E. Tumbleson. New York: Plenum Press.

Rand, M. J., and Majewski, H. (1984). Adrenaline mediates a positive feedback loop in noradrenergic transmission: Its possible role in development of hypertension. *Clin. Exp. Hypertens.* A6: 347–370.

Rasmussen, D. D. (1998). Effects of chronic nicotine treatment and withdrawal on hypothalamic propiomelanocortin gene expression and neuroendocrine regulation. *Psychoneuroendocrinology* 23: 245–259.

Ravn, P., Bidstrup, M., Wasnich, R. D., Davis, J. W., McClung, M. R., Balske, A., Coupland, C., Sahota, O., Kaur, A., Daley, M., and Cizza, G. (1999). Alendronate. *Ann. Intern. Med.* 131: 935–942.

Recordati, G. (1984). The functional role of the visceral nervous system: A critical evaluation of Cannon's "homeostatic" and "emergency" theories. *Arch. Ital. Biol.* 122: 249–267.

Reeves, J. P., Chernaya, G., and Condrescu, M. (1996). Sodium-calcium exchange and calcium homeostasis in transfected Chinese hamster ovary cells. *Ann. N.Y. Acad. Sci.* 779: 73–85.

Refinetti, R., and Menaker, M. (1997). Is energy expenditure in the hamster primarily under homeostatic or circadian control? *J. Physiol.* 501: 449–453.

Reid, I. R., Chin, K., Evans, M. C., and Jones, J. G. (1994). Relation between increase in length of hip axis in older women between 1950s and 1990s and increase in age specific rates of hip fracture. *Br. Med. J.* 309: 508–509.

Reiman, E. M., Fusselman, M. J., Fox, P. T., and Raichle, M. E. (1989). Neuroanatomical correlates of anticipatory anxiety. *Science* 243: 1071–1074.

Reinhardt, T. A., Horst, R. L., and Goff, J. P. (1988). Calcium, phosphorus, and magnesium homeostasis in ruminants. *Vet. Clin. North Am. Food Anim. Pract.* 4: 331–350.

Renie, W. A., and Murphy, E. A. (1984). The dynamics of quantifiable homeostasis. III. A linear model of certain metrical diseases. *Am. J. Med. Genet.* 18: 25–37.

Reoetti, R. L., Taylor, S., and Seeman, T. (1999). Risky families: Family social environments and the mental and physical health of offspring. Submitted.

Rescorla, R. A. (1988). Pavlovian conditioning: It's not what you think it is. *Am. Psychol.* 43: 151–160.

Rescorla, R. A., and Wanger, A. R. (1972). A theory of Pavlovian conditioning: Variations in the effectiveness of reinforcement and non-reinforcement. In *Classical Conditioning,* edited by A. H. Black and W. F. Prokasy. New York: Appleton-Century Crofts.

Resnick, H. S., Yehuda, R., Pitman, R. K., and Foy, D. W. (1995). Effect of previous trauma on acute plasma cortisol level following rape. *Am. J. Psychiatry* 152: 1675–1677.

Richet, C. (1900, 1973). Functions of defense. In *Homeostasis: Origins of the Concept,* edited by L. L. Langley. Stroudsburgh, Pa.: Dowden, Hutchinson and Ross.

Richter, C. P. (1922). A behavioristic study of the activity of the rat. *Comp. Psychol. Mongr.* 1: 1–55.

Richter, C. P. (1936). Increased salt appetite in adrenalectomized rats. *Am. J. Physiol.* 115: 155–161.

Richter, C. P. (1942–43). Total self-regulatory functions in animals and human beings. *Harvey Lect.* 38: 63–103.

Richter, C. P. (1949). Domestication of the Norway rat and its implications for the problem of stress. *Proc. Assoc. Res. Nerv. Ment. Dis.* 29: 19–30.

Richter, C. P. (1953a). Experimentally produced behavior reactions to food poisoning in wild and domesticated rats. *Ann. N.Y. Acad. Sci.* 556: 225–239.

Richter, C. P. (1953b). Free research versus design research. *Science* 118: 91–92.

Richter, C. P. (1956). Salt appetite of mammals: Its dependence on instinct and metabolism. In *L'Instince dans le Comportement des Animaux et de l'Homme.* Paris.

Richter, C. P. (1957a). Hormones and rhythms in man and animals. *Recent Prog. Horm. Res.* 13: 105–159.

Richter, C. P. (1957b). Phenomena of sudden death in animals and man. *Psychosom. Med.* 19: 191–198.

Richter. C. P. (1959). Rats, man, and the welfare state. *Am. Psychol.* 14: 18–28.

Richter, C. P. (1965). *Biological Clocks in Medicine and Psychiatry.* Springfield, Ill.: Charles C. Thomas.

Richter, C. P., and Barelare, B. Jr. (1938). Nutritional requirements of pregnant and lactating rats studied by the self-selection method. *Endocrinology* 23: 15–24.

Richter, C. P., and Eckert, J. F. (1937). Increased calcium appetite of parathyroidectomized rats. *Endocrinology* 21: 50–54.

Richter, C. P., and Eckert, J. F. (1939). Mineral appetite of parathyroidectomized rats. *Am. J. Med. Sci.* 198: 9–16.

Richter, R. M., and Weiss, F. (1999). In vivo CRF release in rat amygdala is in-

creased during cocaine withdrawal in self-administering rats. *Synapse* 32: 254–261.

Richter, R. M., Pich, E. M., Koob, G. F., and Weiss, F. (1995). Sensitization of cocaine-stimulated increase in extracellular levels of corticotropin-releasing factor from the rat amygdala after repeated administration as determined by intracranial microdialysis. *Neurosci. Lett.* 187: 169–172.

Riggs, B. L., and Melton, L. J. III (1986). Involutional osteoporosis. *N. Engl. J. Med.* 314: 1676–1686.

Riley, S. C., Walton, J. C., Herlick, J. M., and Challis, J. R. (1991). The localization and distribution of corticotropin-releasing hormone in the human placenta and fetal membranes throughout gestation. *J. Clin. Endocrinol. Metab.* 72: 1001–1007.

Rinomhota, A. S., and Cooper, K. (1996). Homeostasis: Restoring the internal well-being in patient/clients. *Br. J. Nurs.* 5: 1100–1104, 1106–1108.

Risch, H. A. (1996). Estrogen replacement therapy and risk of epithelial ovarian cancer. *Gynecol Oncol.* 63: 254–257.

Ritz, P., and Elia, M. (1999). The effect of inactivity on dietary intake and energy homeostasis. *Proc. Nutr. Soc.* 58: 115–122.

Rivier, C. (1996). Alcohol stimulates ACTH secretion in the rat: Mechanisms of action and interactions with other stimuli. *Alcohol Clin. Exp. Res.* 20: 240–254.

Rivier, C., and Rivest, S. (1991). Effect of stress on the activity of the hypothalamic-pituitary-gonadal axis: Peripheral and central mechanisms. *Biol. Reprod.* 45: 523–532.

Robbins, J., Hirsch, C., Whitmer, R., Cauley, J., and Harris, T. (2001). The association of bone mineral density and depression in an older population. *J. Am. Geriatr. Soc.* 49: 732–736.

Robbins, T. W., and Everitt, B. J. (1999). Interaction of dopaminergic system with mechanisms of associative learning and cognition: Implications for drug abuse. *Psychol. Sci.* 10: 199–202.

Robbins, T. W., Cador, M., Taylor, J. R., and Everitt, B. J. (1989). Limbic-striatal interactions in reward-related processes. *Neurosci. Biobehav. Rev.* 13: 155–162.

Roberts, A. J., Heyser, C. J., Cole, M., Griffin, P., and Koob, G. F. (2000). Excessive ethanol drinking following a history of dependence: Animal model of allostasis. *Neuropsychopharmacology* 22: 581–594.

Robin, E. D. (1979). Claude Bernard. Pioneer of regulatory behavior. *JAMA* 21: 1283–1284.

Robinson, B. G., Arbiser, J. L., Emanuel, R. L., and Majzoub, J. A. (1989). Species-specific placental corticotropin releasing hormone messenger RNA and peptide expression. *Mol. Cell. Endocrinol.* 62: 337–341.

Robinson, B. G., Emanuel, R. L., Frim, D. M., and Majzoub, J. A. (1988). Glucocorticoid stimulates expression of corticotropin-releasing hormone gene in human placenta. *Proc. Natl. Acad. Sci. USA* 85: 5244–5248.

Robinson, J. L., Kagan, J., Reznick, J. S., and Corely, R. (1992). The heritability of inhibited and uninhibited behaviors. *Dev. Psychol.* 28: 1030–1037.

Robinson, T. E., and Berridge, K. C. (1993). The neural basis of drug craving: An incentive-sensitization theory of addiction. *Brain Res. Rev.* 18: 247–291.

Robinson, T. E., and Berridge, K. C. (2000). The psychology and neurobiology of addiction: An incentive-sensitization view. *Addiction* 95: S91–S117.

Robinson, T. E., and Kolb, B. (1997). Persistent structural modifications in nucleus accumbens and prefrontal cortex neurons produced by previous experience with amphetamine. *J. Neurosci.* 17: 8491–8497.

Robinson, T. E., Browman, K. E., Crombag, H. S., and Badiani, A. (1998). Modulation of the induction of expression of psychostimulant sensitization by the circumstances surrounding drug administration. *Neurosci. Biobehav. Rev.* 22: 347–354.

Rocha, B. A., Scearce-Levie, K., Lucas, J. J., Hiroi, N., Castanon, N., Crabbe, J. C., Nestler, E. J., and Hen, R. (1998). Increased vulnerability to cocaine in mice lacking the serotonin-1B receptor. *Nature* 393: 175–178.

Rochford, J., Grant, I., and LaVigne, G. (1977). Medical students and drugs: Further neuropsychological and use pattern considerations. *Int. J. Addict.* 12: 1057–1065.

Rodriguez de Fonseca, F., Carrera, M. R. A., Navarro, M., Koob, G. F., and Weiss, F. (1997). Activation of corticotropin-releasing factor in the limbic system during canabinoid withdrawal. *Science* 276: 2050–2054.

Rodriguez-Soriano, J. (1995). Potassium homeostasis and its disturbances in children. *Pediatr. Nephrol.* 9: 364–374.

Rohsenow, D. J., Corbett, R., and Devine, D. (1988). Molested as children: A hidden contribution to substance abuse? *J. Subst. Abuse Treat.* 5: 13–18.

Roll-Hansen, N. (1976). Critical teleology: Immanuel Kant and Claude Bernard on the limitations of experimental biology. *J. Hist. Biol.* 9: 59–91.

Rolls, B. J., Wood, R. J., and Stevens, R. M. (1978). Palatability and body fluid homeostasis. *Physiol. Behav.* 20: 15–19.

Rolls, B. J., Rolls, E. T., and Rave, E. A. (1982). The influence of variety on human food selection and intake. In *The Psychobiology of Human Food Selection,* edited by L. M. Barker. Westport, Conn.: AVI.

Rolls, E. T. (2000). The orbitofrontal cortex and reward. *Cereb. Cortex* 10: 284–294.

Romani, A., Marfella, C., and Scarpa, A. (1993). Cell magnesium transport and homeostasis: Role of intracellular compartments. *Miner. Electrolyte Metab.* 19: 282–289.

Romero, R., Gomez, R., Chaiworapongsa, T., Conoscenti, G., Kim, J. C., and Kim, Y. M. (2001). The role of infection in preterm labour and delivery. *Paediatr. Perinat. Epidemiol.* 15: 41–56.

Roozendaal, B. (2000). Glucocorticoids and the regulation of memory consolidation. *Psychoneuroendocrinology* 25: 213–238.

Roozendaal, B., and McGaugh, J. L. (1997a). Basolateral amygdala lesions block the memory-enhancing effect of glucocorticoid administration in the dorsal hippocampus of rats. *Eur. J. Neurosci.* 9: 76–83.

Roozendaal, B., and McGaugh, J. L. (1997b). Glucocorticoid receptor agonist and antagonist administration into the basolateral but not central amygdala modulates memory storage. *Neurobiol. Learn. Mem.* 67: 176–179.

Roozendaal, B., Carmi, O., and McGaugh, J. L. (1996a). Adrenocortical suppression blocks the memory-enhancing effects of amphetamine and epinephrine. *Proc. Natl. Acad. Sci. USA* 93: 1429–1433.

Roozendaal, B., Portillo-Marquez, G., and McGaugh, J. L. (1996b). Basolateral amygdala lesions block glucocorticoid-induced modulation of memory for spatial learning. *Behav. Neurosci.* 110: 1074–1083.

Roozendaal, B., de Quervain, D. J. F., Ferry, B., Setlow, B., and McGaugh, J. L. (2001). Basolateral amygdala-nucleus accumbens interactions in mediating glucocorticoid enhancement of memory consolidation. *J. Neurosci.* 21: 2518–2525.

Rosen, J. B., and Davis, M. (1988). Enhancement of acoustic startle by electrical stimulation of the amygdala. *Behav. Neurosci.* 102: 195–202.

Rosen, J. B., and Schulkin, J. (1998). From normal fear to pathological anxiety. *Psychol. Rev.* 105: 325–350.

Rosen, J. B., Hitchcock, J. M., Sahanes, C. B., Miserandino, M. J., and Davis, M. (1991). A direct projection from the central nucleus of the amygdala to the acoustic startle pathway: Anterograde and retrograde tracing studies. *Behav. Neurosci.* 105: 817–825.

Rosen, J. B., Pishevar, S. K., Weiss, S. R., Smith, M. A., Kling, M. A., Gold, P. W., and Schulkin, J. (1994). Glucocorticoid potentiation of CRH-induced seizures. *Neurosci Lett.* 174: 113–116.

Rosen, J. B., Hamerman, E., Sitcoske, M., Glowa, J. R., and Schulkin, J. (1996). Hyperexcitability: Exaggerated fear-potentiated startle produced by partial amygdala kindling. *Behav. Neurosci.* 110: 43–50.

Rosenwasser, A. M., Schulkin, J., and Adler, N. T. (1988). Anticipatory appetitive behavior of adrenalectomized rats under circadian salt-access schedules. *Anim. Learn. Behav.* 16: 324–329.

Rouge-Pont, F., Piazza, P. V., Kharouby, M., Le Moal, M., and Simon, H. (1993). Higher and longer stress-induced increase in dopamine concentrations in the nucleus accumbens of animal predisposed to amphetamine self-administration. A microdialysis study. *Brain Res.* 602: 169–174.

Rouge-Pont, F., Deroche, V., Le Moal, M., and Piazza, P. V. (1998). Individual differences in stress-induced dopamine release in the nucleus accumbens are influenced by corticosterone. *Eur. J. Neurosci.* 10: 3903–3907.

Rourke, S. B., and Grant, I. (1999). The interactive effects of age and length of abstinence on the recovery of neuropsychological functioning in chronic male alcoholics: A 2-year follow-up study. *J. Int. Neuropsychol. Soc.* 5: 234–246.

Rousseau, J. J. (1762/1947). *The Social Contract.* New York: Hafner Press.

Rowland, N. E. (1998). Brain mechanisms of mammalian fluid homeostasis: Insights from use of immediate early gene mapping. *Neurosci. Biobehav. Rev.* 23: 49–63.

Roy, A., Pickar, D., Paul, S., Doran, A., Chrousos, G. P., and Gold, P. W. (1987). CSF corticotropin-releasing hormone in depressed patients and normal control subjects. *Am. J. Psychiatry* 144: 641–645.

Roy, A., Linnoila, M., Karoum, F., and Pickar, D. (1988). Urinary-free cortisol in depressed patients and controls: Relationships to urinary indices of noradrenergic function. *Psychol. Med.* 18: 93–98.

Roy, M. P., Kirschbaum, C., and Steptoe, A. (2001). Psychological, cardiovascular, and metabolic correlates of individual differences in cortisol stress recovery in young men. *Psychoneuroendocrinology* 26: 375–391.

Rozin, P. (1961). Thermal reinforcement and thermoregulatory behavior in the goldfish, *Carassius auratus. Science* 134: 942–943.

Rozin, P. (1965). Temperature independence of an arbitrary temporal discrimination in the goldfish. *Science* 149: 561–563.

Rozin, P. (1968). The use of poikilothermy in the analysis of behavior. In *The Central Nervous System and Fish Behavior,* edited by D. Ingle. Chicago: University of Chicago Press.

Rozin, P., and Kalat, J. (1971). Specific hungers and poison avoidance as adaptive specializations of learning. *Psychol. Rev.* 78: 459–486.

Ruby, N. F., and Zucker, I. (1992). Daily torpor in the absence of the suprachiasmatic nucleus in Siberian hamsters. *Am. J. Physiol.* 263: R353–R362.

Ryan, K. (1996). The chronically traumatized child. *Child Adolesc. Soc. Work J.* 13: 287–310.

Ryan, M. P. (1993). Interrelationships of magnesium and potassium homeostasis. *Miner. Electrolyte Metab.* 19: 290–295.

Saag, K. G., Emkey, R., Schitzer, T. J., Brown, J. P., Hawkins, F., Goemaere, S., and Thomsborg, G. (1998). Alendronate for the prevention and treatment of glucocorticoid-induced osteoporosis. *New Engl. J. Med.* 339: 292–299.

Sabini, J., and Silver, M. (1998). *Emotion, Character, and Responsibility.* London: Oxford University Press.

Sachar, E. J., Hellman, L., Fukushima, D. K., and Gallagher, T. F. (1970). Cortisol production in depressive illness: A clinical and biochemical clarification. *Arch. Gen. Psychiatry* 23: 289–298.

Sacher, G. A. (1977). Life table modification and life prolongation. In *Handbook of the Biology of Aging,* edited by C. E. Finch and L. Hayflick. New York: Van Nostrand Reinhold.

Saeed, B. O., Weightman, D. R., and Self, C. H. (1997). Characterization of corticotropin-releasing hormone binding sites in the human placenta. *J. Recept. Signal Transduct. Res.* 17: 647–666.

Saffran, M., Schally, A. V., and Bentey, B. G. (1995). Stimulation of the release of corticotropin from the adenohypophysis by a neurohypophysial factor. *Endocrinology* 57: 439–444.

Sakai, R. R. (1986). The hormones of renal sodium conservation act synergistically to arouse a sodium appetite in the rat. In *The Physiology of Thirst and Sodium Appetite,* edited by G. De Caro, A. N. Epstein, and M. Massi. New York: Plenum Press.

Salamone, J. D. (1994). The involvement of nucleus accumbens dopamine in appetitive and aversive motivation. *Behav. Brain Res.* 61: 117–133.

Sambrook, P., Birmingham, J., and Kelly, P. (1993). Prevention of corticosteroid osteoporosis, a comparison of calcium, calcitriol, and calcitonin. *N. Engl. J. Med.* 328: 1747–1752.

Sanchez, M. M., Young, L. J., Plotsky, P. M., and Insel, T. R. (2000). Distribution of corticosteroid receptors in the rhesus brain: Relative absence of glucocorticoid receptors in the hippocampal formation. *J. Neurosci.* 20: 4657–4668.

Sandman, C. A., Wadhwa, P. D., Chicz-DeMet, A., Porto, M., and Garite, T. J. (1999). Maternal corticotropin-releasing hormone and habituation in the human fetus. *Dev. Psychobiol.* 34: 163–173.

Sandoval, V., Riddle, E. L., Ugarte, Y. V., Hanson, G. R., and Fleckenstein, A. E. (2001). Methamphetamine-induced rapid and reversible changes in dopamine transporter function: An in vivo model. *J. Neurosci.* 21: 1413–1419.

Sapolsky, R. M. (1990). A. E. Bennett Award paper. Adrenocortical function, social rank, and personality among wild baboons. *Biol. Psychiatry* 28: 862–878.

Sapolsky, R. M. (1992). *Stress: The Aging Brain and the Mechanisms of Neuron Death.* Cambridge, Mass.: MIT Press.

Sapolsky, R. M. (1995). Social subordinance as a marker of hypercortisolism. Some unexpected subtleties. *Ann. N.Y. Acad. Sci.* 771: 626–639.

Sapolsky, R. M. (1996). Why stress is bad for your brain. *Science* 273: 749–750.

Sapolsky, R. M. (2000). Glucocorticoids and hippocampal atrophy in neuropsychiatric disorders. *Arch. Gen. Psychiatry* 57: 925–935.

Sapolsky, R. M. (2001). Physiological and pathophysiological implications of social stress in mammals. In *Coping with the Environment: Neural and Endocrine Mechanisms,* edited by B. S. McEwen and H. M. Goodman. New York: Oxford University Press, pp. 517–532.

Sapolsky, R. M., Krey, L. W., and McEwen, B. S. (1986). The neuroendocrinology of stress and aging: The glucocorticoid cascade hypothesis. *Endocr. Rev.* 7: 284–297.

Sapolsky, R. M., Zola-Morgan, S., and Squire, L. R. (1991). Inhibition of glucocorticoid secretion by the hippocampal formation in the primate. *J. Neurosci.* 11: 3695–3704.

Sapolsky, R. M., Romero, M., and Munck, A. U. (2000). How do glucocorticoids influence stress responses? Integrating permissive, suppressive, stimulatory, and preparative actions. *Endocr. Rev.* 21: 55–89.

Sarnyai, Z., Biro, E., Penke, B., and Telegdy, G. (1992a). The cocaine-induced elevation of plasma corticosterone is mediated by endogenous corticotropin-releasing factor (CRF) in rats. *Brain Res.* 489: 154–156.

Sarnyai, Z., Hohn, J., Szabo, G., and Penke, B. (1992b). Critical role of endogenous corticotropin-releasing factor (CRF) in the mediation of the behavioral action of cocaine in rats. *Life Sci.* 51: 2019–2024.

Sarnyai, Z., Biro, E., Gardi, J., Vecsernyes, M., Julesz, J., and Telegdy, G. (1993). Alterations of corticotropin-releasing factor-like immunoreactivity in different brain regions after acute cocaine administration in rats. *Brain Res.* 616: 315–319.

Sarnyai, Z., Biro, E., Gardi, J., Vecsernyes, M., Julesz, J., and Telegdy, G. (1995). Brain corticotropin-releasing factor mediates "anxiety-like" behavior induced by cocaine withdrawal in rats. *Brain Res.* 675: 89–97.

Sarnyai, Z., Dhabhar, F. S., McEwen, B. S., and Kreek, M. J. (1998). Neuroendocrine-related effects of long-term, binge cocaine administration: Diminished individual differences in stress-induced corticosterone response. *Neuroendocrinology* 68: 334–344.

Sasaki, A., Shinkawa, O., Margioris, A. N., Liotta, A. S., Sato, S., Murakami, O., Go, M., Shimizu, Y., Hanew, K., and Yoshinga, K. (1987). Immunoreactive corticotropin-releasing hormone in human plasma during pregnancy, labor, and delivery. *J. Clin. Endocrinol. Metabol.* 64: 224–229.

Satinoff, E. (1964). Behavioral thermoregulation in response to local cooling of the rat brain. *Am. J. Physiol.* 206: 1389–1394.

Satinoff, E. (1978). Neural organization and evolution of thermal regulation in mammals. *Science* 201: 16–22.

Satinoff, E., and Rutstein, J. (1970). Behavioral thermoregulation in rats with anterior hypothalamic lesions. *J. Comp. Physiol. Psychol.* 71: 77–82.

Sawchenko, P. E. (1987). Evidence for local site of action for glucocorticoids in inhibiting CRH and vasopressin expression in the paraventricular nucleus. *Brain Res.* 17: 213–223.

Sawchenko, P. E., and Swanson, L. W. (1982). The organization of noradrenergic pathways from the brainstem to the paraventricular and supraoptic nuclei in the rat. *Brain Res.* 257: 275–325.

Sawchenko, P. E., and Swanson, L. W. (1985). Localization, colocalization, and plasticity of corticotropin-releasing factor immunoreactivity in rat brain. *Fed. Proc.* 44: 221–227.

Sax, K. W., and Strakowski, S. M. (1998). Enhanced behavioral response to repeated d-amphetamine and personality traits in humans. *Biol. Psychiatry* 44: 1192–1195.

Schanberg, S. M., Evoniuk, G., and Kuhn, C. M. (1984). Tactile and nutritional aspects of maternal care: Specific regulators of neuroendocrine function and cellular development. *Proc. Soc. Exp. Biol. Med.* 175: 135–146.

Scheier, L. M., and Botvin, G. J. (1995). Effects of early adolescent drug use on cognitive efficacy in early-late adolescence: A developmental structural model. *J. Subst. Abuse* 7: 379–404.

Scheurink, A. J., Balkan, B., Nyakas, C., van Dijk, G., Steffens, A. B., and Bohus, B. (1995). Energy homeostasis, autonomic activity, and obesity. *Obes. Res.* 3: 721S–727S.

Schiml, P. A., and Rissman, E. F. (1999). Cortisol facilitates induction of sexual behavior in the female musk shrew. *Behav. Neurosci.* 113: 166–175.

Schluger, J. M., Borg, L., Ho, A., and Kreek, M. J. (2001). Altered HPA axis responsivity to metyrapone testing in methadone maintained former heroin addicts with ongoing cocaine addiction. *Neuropsychopharmacology* 24: 568–575.

Schlussman, S. D., Zhou, Y., Johansson, P., Kiuru, A., Ho, A., Nyberg, F., and Kreek, M. J. (2000). Effects of the androgenic anabolic steroid, nandrolone decanoate, on ACTH, corticotropin releasing factor, and corticotropin releasing factor receptor-1 mRNA levels in the hypothalamus, pituitary, and amygdala in the rat. *Brain Res.* 284: 190–194.

Schmidt, L. A., and Schulkin, J. (eds.) (1999). *Extreme Fear, Shyness, and Social Phobia.* Oxford: Oxford University Press.

Schmidt, L. A., Fox, N. A., Rubin, K. J., Sternberg, E. M., Gold, P. W., Smith, C., and Schulkin, J. (1997). Behavioral and neuroendocrine responses in shy children. *Dev. Psychobiol.* 30: 127–140.

Schmidt, L. A., Fox, N. A., Goldberg, M. C., Smith, C. C., and Schulkin, J. (1998). Effects of acute prednisone administration on memory, attention, and emotion in healthy human adults. *Psychoneuroendocrinology* 24: 461–483.

Schmidt, L. A., Fox, N. A., Schulkin, J., and Gold, P. W. (1999a). Behavioral and psychophysiological correlates of self-presentation in temperamentally shy children. *Dev. Psychobiol.* 35: 119–135.

Schmidt, L. A., Fox, N. A., Sternberg, E. M., Gold, P. W., Smith, C. C., and Schulkin, J. (1999b). Adrenocortical reactivity and social competence in seven-year-olds. *Pers. Individual Differences* 26: 977–985.

Schmidt-Nielsen, B. [1975] (1997). *Animal Physiology: Adaptation and Environment.* Cambridge: Cambridge University Press.

Schneider, M. L., Coe, C. L., and Lubach, G. R. (1992). Endocrine activation mimics the adverse effects of prenatal stress on the neuromotor development of the infant primate. *Dev. Psychobiol.* 25: 427–439.

Schneider, M. L., Clarke, A. S., Kraemer, G. W., Roughton, E. C., Lubach, G. R., Rimm-Kaufman, S., Schmidt, D., and Ebert, M. (1998). Prenatal stess alters brain biogenic amine levels in primates. *Dev. Psychopathol.* 10: 427–440.

Schneirla, T. C. (1959). An evolutionary and developmental theory of biphasic processes underlying approach and withdrawal. In *The Nebraska Symposium on Motivation,* edited by M. R. Jones. Lincoln: University of Nebraska Press.

Schneirla, T. C. (1965). Aspects of stimulation and organization in approach/withdrawal processes underlying vertebrate behavioral development. In *Advances in the Study of Behavior,* edited by D. Lehrman, R. Hindle, and E. Shaw. New York: Academic Press.

Schuhr, B. (1987). Social structure and plasma corticosterone level in female albino mice. *Physiol. Behav.* 40: 680–683.

Schulkin, J. (1991). *Sodium Hunger.* Cambridge: Cambridge University Press.

Schulkin, J. (1994). Melancholic depression and the hormones of adversity. *Dir. Psychol. Sci.* 5: 41–44.

Schulkin, J. (1999a). *The Neruroendocrine Regulation of Behavior.* Cambrige: Cambridge University Press.

Schulkin, J. (1999b). Corticotropin-releasing hormone signals adversity in both the placenta and the brain: Regulation by glucocorticoids and allostatic overload. *J. Endocrinol.* 161: 349–356.

Schulkin, J. (2000) *Social Sensibility and Neural Function.* Cambridge: MIT Press.

Schulkin, J. (2001). *Behavioral and Biological Regulation of Calcium.* Cambridge: Cambridge University Press.

Schulkin, J., Arnell, P., and Stellar, E. (1985). Running to the taste of salt in mineralocorticoid treated rats. *Horm. Behav.* 19: 413–425.

Schulkin, J., McEwen, B. S., and Gold, P. W. (1994). Allostasis, amygdala, and anticipatory angst. *Neurosci. Biobehav. Rev.* 18: 385–396.

Schulkin, J., Gold, P. W., and McEwen, B. S. (1998). Induction of corticotropin-releasing hormone gene expression by glucocorticoids. *Psychoneuroendocrinology* 23: 219–243.

Schulteis, G., and Koob, G. F. (1996). Reinforcement processes in opiate addiction: A homeostatic model. *Neurochem. Res.* 21: 1437–1454.

Schultz, W., Dayan, P., and Montague, P. R. (1997). A neural substrate of prediction and reward. *Science* 275: 1593–1599.

Schumacher, M., Coirini, H., Pfaff, D. W., and McEwen, B. S. (1990). Behavioral effects of progesterone associated with rapid modulation of oxytocin receptors. *Science* 250: 691–694.

Schwaber, J. S., Kapp, B. S., Higgins, G. A., and Rapp, P. R. (1982). Amygdaloid and basal forebrain direct connections with the nucleus of the solitary tract. *J. Neurosci.* 2: 1424–1438.

Schwartz, M. W., Dallman, M. F., and Woods, S. C. (1995). Hypothalamic response to starvation: Implications for the study of wasting disorders. *Am. J. Physiol.* 269: R949–R957.

Schwartz, R. H., Gruenewald, P. J., Klitzner, M., and Fedio, P. (1989). Short-term memory impairment in cannabis-dependent adolescents. *Am. J. Dis. Child.* 143: 1214–1219.

Seasholtz, A. F., Burrows, H. L., Karolyi, I. J., and Camper, S. A. (2001). Mouse models of altered CRH-binding protein expression. *Peptides* 22: 743–751.

Seckl, J. R. (1997). Glucocorticoids, feto-placental 11 beta-hydroxysteroid dehydrogenase type 2, and the early life origins of adult disease. *Steroids* 62: 89–94.

Seeley, R. J., Payne, C. J., and Woods, S. C. (1995). Neuropeptide Y fails to increase intraoral intake in rats. *Am. J. Physiol.* 268: R423–R427.

Seely, E. W., and Graves, S. W. (1993). Calcium homeostasis in normotensive and hypertensive pregnancy. *Compr. Ther.* 19: 124–128.

Seeman, T. E., McEwen, B. S., Singer, B. H., Albert, M. S., and Rowe, J. W. (1997a). Increase in urinary cortisol excretion and memory declines: MacArthur studies of successful aging. *J. Clin. Endocrinol. Metab.* 82: 2458–2465.

Seeman, T. E., Singer, B. H., Rowe, J. W., Horwitz, R. I., and McEwen, B. S. (1997). Price of adaptation—Allostatic load and its health consequences. MacArthur studies of successful aging. *Arch. Intern. Med.* 157: 2259–2268.

Seeman, T. E., McEwen, B. S., Rowe, J. W., and Singer, B. H. (2001). Allostatic load as a marker of cumulative biological risk: MacArthur studies of successful aging. *Proc. Nat. Acad. Sci.* 98: 4770–4775.

Selby, M. J., and Azrin, R. L. (1998). Neuropsychological functioning in drug abusers. *Drug Alcohol Depend.* 50: 39–45.

Self, D. W., and Nestler, E. J. (1998). Relapse to drug-seeking: Neural and molecular mechanisms. *Drug Alcohol Depend.* 51: 49–69.

Self, D. W., Barnhart, W. J., Lehman, D. A., and Nestler, E. J. (1996). Cocaine-seeking behavior is suppressed by D1-like and induced by D2-like dopamine receptor agonists. *Science* 271: 1586–1589.

Self, D. W., Genova, L. M., Hope, B. T., Barnhart, W. J., Spencer, J. J., and Nestler, E. J. (1998). Involvement of cAMP-dependent protein kinase in the nucleus accumbens in cocaine self-administration and relapse of cocaine-seeking behavior. *J. Neurosci.* 18: 1848–1859.

Seligman, M. E. P. (1970). On generality of the laws of learning. *Psychol. Rev.* 77: 406–418.

Seligman, M. E. P., and Maier, S. F. (1967). Failure to escape traumatic shock. *J. Exp. Psychol.* 74: 1–9.

Sell, L. A., Morris, J., Bearn, J., Frackowiak, R. S., Friston, K. J., and Dolan, R. J. (1999). Activation of reward circuitry in human opiate addicts. *Eur. J. Neurosci.* 11: 1042–1048.

Sell, L. A., Morris, J. S., Bearn, J., Frackowiak, R. S., Friston, K. J., and Dolan, R. J. (2000). Neural responses associated with cue evoked emotional states and heroin in opiate addicts. *Drug Alcohol Depend.* 60: 207–216.

Sellers, T. A., Mink, P. J., Cerhan, J. R., Zheng, W., Anderson, K. E., Kushi, L. H., and Folsom, A. R. (1997). The role of hormone replacement therapy in the risk for breast cancer and total mortality in women with a family history of breast cancer. *Ann. Intern. Med.* 127: 973–980.

Selye, H. (1956/1976). *The Stress of Life.* New York: McGraw-Hill.

Selye, H. (1974). *Stress Without Distress.* New York: New American Library.

Selye, H. (1982). Stress: Eustress, distress, and human perspectives. In *Life Stress.* Vol. 3, *Companion to the Life Sciences,* edited by S. B. Day. New York: Van Nostrand Reinhold.

Setlow, B., Roozendaal, B., and McGaugh, J. L. (2000). Involvement of a basolateral amygdala complex-nucleus accumbens pathway in glucocorticoid-

induced modulation of memory consolidation. *Eur. J. Neurosci.* 12: 367–375.

Shaham, Y., and Stewart, J. (1995). Stress reinstates heroin self-administration behavior in drug-free animals: An effect mimicking heroin, not withdrawal. *Psychopharmacology* 119: 334–341.

Shaham, Y., and Stewart, J. (1996). Effects of opioid and dopamine receptor antagonists on relapse induced by stress and re-exposed to heroin in rats. *Psychopharmacology* 125: 385–391.

Shaham, Y., Rajabi, H., and Stewart, J. (1996). Relapse to heroin-seeking in rats under opioid maintenance: The effects of stress, heroin priming, and withdrawal. *J. Neurosci.* 16: 1957–1963.

Shaham, Y., Funk, D., Erb, S., Brown, T. J., Walker, C. D., and Stewart, J. (1997). Corticotropin-releasing factor, but not corticosterone, is involved in stress-induced relapse to heroin-seeking rats. *Neuroscience* 17: 2605–2614.

Shaham, Y., Erb, S., and Stewart, J. (2000). Stress-induced relapse to heroin and cocaine seeking in rats: A review. *Brain Res.* 33: 13–33.

Shannon, C., Champoux, M., and Suomi, S. J. (1998). Rearing condition and plasma cortisol in rhesus monkey infants. *Am. J. Primatol.* 46: 311–321.

Shapiro, R. E., and Miselis, R. R. (1985). The central organization of the vagus nerve innervating the stomach of the rat. *J. Comp. Neurol.* 238: 473–488.

Sheline, Y. I., Wang, P. W., Gado, M. H., Csernansky, J. G., and Vannier, W. W. (1996). Hippocampal atrophy in recurrent major depression. *Proc. Natl. Acad. Sci.* 93: 3908–3913.

Shepard, J. D., Barron, K. W., and Myers, D. A. (2000). Corticosterone delivery to the amygdala increases corticotropin-releasing hormone mRNA in the central nucleus of the amygdala and anxiety-like behavior. *Brain Res.* 861: 288–295.

Shepard, J. D., Barron, K. W., and Myers, D. A. (2003). Sterotaxic localization of corticosterone to the amygdala enhances hypothalamo-pituitary adrenal responses to behavioral stress. *Brain Res.*

Sherrington, C. [1906] (1948). *The Integrative Action of the Nervous System.* New Haven: Yale University Press.

Shettleworth, S. J. (1971). Constraints on learning. In *Advances in the Study of Behavior,* edited by D. S. Lehrman, R. A. Hinde, and E. Shaw. New York: Academic Press.

Shettleworth, S. J. (1998). *Cognition, Evolution, and Behavior.* Oxford: Oxford University Press.

Shrivastava, A., and Aggarwal, B. B. (1998). Cytokines as biological regulators of homeostasis. *J. Biol. Regul. Homeost. Agents* 12: 1–24.

Siegel, G. J., Agranoff, B. W., Albers, R. W., Fisher, S. K., and Uhler, M. D. (1999). *Basic Neurochemistry.* 6th ed. New York: Lippincott-Raven.

Siegel, S. (1972). Conditioning of insulin-induced glycemia. *J. Comp. Physiol. Psychol.* 78: 233–241.

Siegel, S. (1975). Evidence from rats that morphine tolerance is a learned response. *J. Comp. Physiol. Psychol.* 89: 498–506.

Siegel, S., and Allan, L. G. (1998). Learning and homeostasis: Drug addiction and the McCollough effect. *Psychol. Bull.* 124: 230–239.

Sillaber, I., Rammes, G., Zimmerman, S., Mahal, B., Zieglgansberger, W., Wurst, W., Holsboer, F., and Spangel, R. (2002). Enhanced and delayed stress-induced drinking in mice lacking functional CRH1 receptors. *Science* 296: 931–933.

Silverman, A. B., Reinherz, H. Z., and Giaconia, R. M. (1996). The long-term sequelae of child and adolescent abuse: A longitudinal community study. *Child Abuse Negl.* 20: 709–723.

Simon, E., Brummermann, M., Erbe, K. H., and Simon-Oppermann, C. (1989). Homeostatic actions of osmoregulatory hormones: Clues derived from studies on avian osmoregulation. *Acta Physiol. Pol.* 40: 338–346.

Sim-Selley, L. J., Selley, D. E., Vogt, L. J., Childers, S. R., and Martin, T. J. (2000). Chronic heroin self-administration desensitizes μ opioid receptor-activated G-proteins in specific regions of rat brain. *J. Neurosci* 201: 4555 4562.

Skelton, K. H., Owens, M. J., Gutman, D. A., O'Brien, D., Oren, D., Thrivilaaman, K. V., Easterling, K. W., Holtzmans, G., Knight, D. L., and Nemeroff, C. B. (2000). The corticotropin-releasing factor $(CRF)_1$, receptor antagonist, R121919, attenuates the behavioral and neuroendocrine response to precipitated morphine or lorazepam withdrawal in the rat. *Neuropsychopharmacology* 23: S149.

Skinner, B. F. (1938). *The Behavior of Organisms.* New York: Appleton-Century.

Slotkin, T. A., Zhang, J., McCook, E. C., and Seidler, F. J. (1998). Glucocorticoid administration alters nuclear transcription factors in fetal rat brain: Implications for the use of antenatal steroids. *Dev. Brain Res.* 111: 11–24.

Smagin, G. N., Heinrichs, S. C., and Dunn, A. J. (2001). The role of CRH in behavioral responses to stress. *Peptides* 22: 713–724.

Smith, G. P. (1995). Pavlov and appetite. *Integr. Physiol. Behav. Sci.* 30: 169–174.

Smith, G. P. (1997a). *Satiation from Gut to Brain.* Oxford: Oxford University Press.

Smith, G. P. (1997b). Eating and the American zeitgeist. *Appetite* 29: 191–200.

Smith, G. P. (2000). Pavlov and integrative physiology. *Am. J. Physiol. Regul. Integr. Comp. Physiol.* 279: R743–R755.

Smith, G. W., Aubry, J. M., Dellu, F., Contarino, A., Bilezkiianl, M., Gold, L. H., Chen, R., Marchuk, Y., Hauser, C., Bentley, C. A. Sawchenko, P. E., Koob, G. F., Vale, W., and Lee, K. F. (1998). Corticotropin releasing factor receptor 1-deficient mice display decreased anxiety, impaired stress response, and aberrant neuroendocrine development. *Neuron* 20: 1093–1102.

Smith, M. A., Davidson, J., Ritchie, J. C., Kudler, H., Lipper, S., Chappell, P., and Nemeroff, C. B. (1989). The corticotropin-releasing hormone test in patients with posttraumatic stress disorder. *Biol. Psychiatry* 26: 349–355.

Smith, M. A., Weiss, S. R. B., Abedin, T., Kim, H., Post, R. M., and Gold, P. W. (1991). Effects of amygdala kindling and electroconvulsive seizures on the expression of corticotropin-releasing hormone in the rat brain. *Mol. Cell. Neurosci.* 2: 103–116.

Smith, M. A., Makino, S., Altemus, M., Michelson, D., Hong, S.-K., Kvetnansky, R., and Post, R. M. (1995a). Stress and antidepressants differentially regulate neurotrophin 3 mRNA expression in the locus coeruleus. *Proc. Natl. Acad. Sci. USA* 92: 8788–8792.

Smith, M. A., Makino, S., Kim, S.-Y., and Kvetnansky, R. (1995b). Stress increases brain-derived neurotropic factor messenger ribonucleic acid in the hypothalamus and pituitary. *Endocrinology* 136: 3743–3750.

Smith, M. A., Makino, S., Kvetnansky, R., and Post, R. M. (1995c). Stress and glucocorticoids affect the expression of brain-derived neurotrophic factor and neurotrophin-3 mRNAs in the hippocampus. *J. Neurosci.* 15: 1768–1777.

Smith, M. A., Kim, S-Y., van Oers, H. J., and Levine, S. (1997). Maternal deprivation and stress induce immediate early genes in the infant rat brain. *Endocrinology* 138: 4622–4628.

Smith, O. A., DeVito, J. L., and Astley, C. A. (1990). Neurons controlling cardiovascular responses to emotion are located in lateral hypothalamus-perifornical region. *Am. J. Physiol.* 259: R943–R954.

Smith, R., Chan, E. C., Bowman, M. A., Harewood, W. J., and Phippard, A. F. (1993). Corticotropin-releasing hormone in baboon pregnancy. *J. Clin. Endocrinol. Metabol.* 76: 1063–1068.

Smith, R., Wickings, J. E., Bowman, M. E., Belleoud, A., Dubreuil, G., Davies, J. J., and Madsen, G. (1999). Corticotropin-releasing hormone in chimpanzee and gorilla pregnancies. *J. Clin. Endocrinol. Metab.* 84: 2820–2825.

Smith, T., and Cuzner, M. L. (1994). Neuroendocrine-immune interactions in homeostasis and autoimmunity. *Neuropathol. Appl. Neurobiol.* 20: 413–422.

Snowdon, C. T., and Epstein, A. N. (1970). Oral and intragastric feeding in vagotomized rats. *J. Comp. Physiol. Psychol.* 71: 59–67.

Sober, E., and Wilson, D. S. (1998). *Unto Others: The Evolution and Psychology of Unselfish Behavior.* Cambridge, Mass.: Harvard University Press.

Solomon, R. L. (1980). The opponent process theory of acquired motivation. *Am. Psychol.* 35: 691–712.

Solomon, R. L., and Corbit, J. D. (1974). An opponent-process theory of motivation: Temporal dynamics of affect. *Psychol. Rev.* 81: 119–145.

Solter, M., and Sekso, M. (1983). Effect of fasting on posthyperglycemic glucose homeostasis in obesity—Experimental model for reactive hypoglycemia. *Exp. Clin. Endocrinol.* 81: 33–40.

Southwick, S. M., Bremner, D., Krystal, J. H., and Charney, D. S. (1994). Psychobiologic research in post-traumatic stress disorder. *Psychiatr. Clin. North Am.* 17: 251–264.

Spak, L., Spak, F., and Allebeck, P. (1998) Sexual abuse and alcoholism in a female population. *Addiction* 93: 1365–1373.

Spanagel, R., and Weiss, R. (1999). The dopamine hypothesis of reward: Past and current status. *Trends in Neurosci.* 22: 521–527.

Spector, A. C. (1995). Gustatory functions of the parabrachial nuclei: Implications from lesion studies in the rat. *Rev. Neurosci.* 6: 143–175.

Spector, A. C. (2000). Linking gustatory neurobiology to behavior in vertebrates. *Neurosci. Biobehav. Rev.* 24: 391–416.

Stacy, A. W., and Newcomb, M. D. (1999). Adolescent drug use and adult drug problems in women: Direct, interactive, and mediational effects. *Exp. Clin. Psychopharmacol.* 7(2): 160–173.

Stanford, S. C., and Salmon, F. (1993). *Stress: Free Synapse and Syndrome.* San Diego: Academic Press.

Stanislav, V., Liu, R., Hayes, R. J., Spector, J. A., and Gardner, E. L. (2001). Relapse to cocaine-seeking after hippocampal theta burst stimulation. *Science* 292: 1175–1178.

Starkman, M. N., Gebarski, S. S., Berent, S., and Schteingart, D. E. (1993). Hippocampal formation volume, memory dysfunction, and cortisol levels in patients with Cushing's syndrome. *Biol. Psychiatry* 32: 756–765.

Starling, E. H. (1923). *The Wisdom of the Body.* London: H. K. Lewis.

Steckler, T., and Holsboer, F. (2001). Conditioned activity to amphetamine in transgenic mice expressing an antisense RNA against the glococorticoid receptor. *Behav. Neurosci.* 15: 207–219.

Stefanacci, L., and Amaral, D. G. (2000). Topographic organization of cortical inputs to the lateral nucleus of the macaque monkey amygdala: A retrograde tracing study. *J. Comp. Neurol.* 42: 52–79.

Steffens, A. B. (1976). Influence of the oral cavity on insulin release in the rat. *Am. J. Physiol.* 230: 1411–1415.

Steiger, H., Gauvin, L., Israel, M., Koerner, N., Ng Ying Kin, N. M., Paris, J., and Young, S. N. (2001). Association of serotonin and cortisol indices with childhood abuse in bulimia nervosa. *Arch. Gen. Psychiatry* 58: 837–843.

Stein, M. B., Yehuda, R., Koverola, C., and Hanna, C. (1997). Enhanced dexamethasone supression of plasma cortisol in adult women traumatized by childhood sexual abuse. *Biol. Psychiatry* 42: 680–686.

Steiner, J. E. (1973). The gustofacial response: Observation on normal and anencephalic newborn infants. *Sens. Percep.* 4: 254–278.

Steiner, J. E., Glaser, D., Hawilo, M. E., and Berridge, K. C. (2001). Comparative expression of hedonic impact: Affective reactions to taste by human infants and other primates. *Neurosci. Biobehav. Rev.* 25: 53–74.

Stellar, E. (1954). The physiology of motivation. *Psychol. Rev.* 61: 5–22.

Stellar, E. (1960). Drive and motivation. In *Handbook of Physiology,* Vol. 3, sec. 1, *Neurophysiology,* edited by H. W. Magoun. Washington, D.C.: American Physiological Society.

Stellar, E., and Corbit, J. D. (1973). Neural control of motivated behavior: A report based on an NRP work session. *Neurosci. Res. Prog. Bull.* 11: 295–410.

Stellar, J. R., and Stellar, E. (1985). *The Neurobiology of Motivation and Reward.* New York: Springer-Verlag.

Stenzel-Poore, M. P., Heinrichs, S. C., Rivest, S., Koob, G. F., and Vale, W. W. (1994). Overproduction of corticotropin-releasing hormone in transgenic mice: A genetic model of anxiogenic behavior. *J. Neurosci.* 14: 2579–2584.

Steptoe, A., Cropley, M., and Joekes, K. (1999). Job strain, blood pressure, and response to uncontrollable stress. *J. Hypertens.* 17: 193–200.

Sterling, P., and Eyer, J. (1981). Biological basis of stress-related mortality. *Soc. Sci. Med.* 15: 3–42.

Sterling, P., and Eyer, J. (1988). Allostasis: A new paradigm to explain arousal pathology. In *Handbook of Life Stress, Cognition, and Health,* edited by S. Fisher and J. Reason. New York: John Wiley and Sons.

Stern, N., and Tuck, M. L. (1986). Homeostatic fragility in the elderly. *Cardiol. Clin.* 4: 201–211.

Sternberg, E. M. (1997). Neural-immune interactions in health and disease. *J. Clin. Invest.* 100: 2641–2647.

Stevens-Simon, C., Kaplan, D. W., and McAnarey, E. R. (1993). Factors associated with pretem delivery among pregnant adolescents. *J. Adolesc. Health* 14: 340–342.

Stewart, J., and Vezina, P. (1988). A comparison of the effects of intra-accumbens injections of amphetamine and morphine on reinstatement of heroin intravenous self-administration behavior. *Brain Res.* 457: 287–294.

Stewart, J., and Wise, R. A. (1992). Reinstatement of heroin self-administration habits: Morphine prompts and naltrexone discourages renewed responding after extinction. *Psychopharmacology* 108: 79–84.

Stoff, J. S. (1982). Phosphate homeostasis and hypophosphatemia. *Am. J. Med.* 72: 489–495.

Stout, S. C., Mortas, P., Owens, M. J., Nemeroff, C. B., and Moreau, J. (2000). Increased corticotropin-releasing factor concentrations in the bed nucleus of the stria terminalis of anhedonic rats. *Eur. J. Pharmacol.* 401: 39–46.

Stout, S. C., Owens, M. J., Lindsey, K. P., Knight, D. L., and Nemeroff, C. B. (2001). Effects of sodium valproate on corticotropin-releasing factor systems in rat brain. *Neuropsychopharmacology* 24: 624–631.

Strand, F. L. (1999). *Neuropeptides: Regulators of Physiological Processes.* Cambridge, MIT Press.

Stricker, E. M. (1990). Homeostatic origins of ingestive behavior. In *Neurobiology of Food and Fluid Intake.* New York: Plenum Press.

Stricker, E. M., and Wolf, G. (1969). Behavioral control of intravascular fluid volume: Thirst and sodium appetite. *Ann. N.Y. Acad. Sci.* 157: 553–568.

Stricker, E. M., and Zigmond, M. J. (1986). Brain monoamines, homeostasis, and adaptive behavior. In *Handbook of Physiology.* Sec. 1, *The Nervous System,*

edited by V. B. Mountcastle. Bethesda, Md.: American Physiological Society.

Stricker, E. M., Rowland, N., Saller, C. F., and Friedman, M. I. (1977). Homeostasis during hypoglycemia: Central control of adrenal secretion and peripheral control of feeding. *Science* 196: 79–81.

Stricker, E. M., Vagnucci, A. H., McDonald, R. H., Jr., and Leenen, F. H. (1979). Renin and aldosterone secretions during hypovolemia in rats: Relation to NaCl intake. *Am. J. Physiol.* 237: R45–R51.

Stumpf, W. E., and O'Brien, L. P. (1987). 1,25 (OH) vitamin D sites of action in the brain. *Histochemistry* 87: 393–406.

Stutzmann, G. E., McEwen, B. S., and LeDoux, J. E. (1998). Serotonin modulation of sensory inputs to the lateral amygdala: Dependency on corticosterone. *J. Neurosci.* 18: 9529–9538.

Suchecki, D., Nelson, D. Y., Van Oers, H. J., and Levine, S. (1995). Activation and inhibition of the hypothalamic-pituitary-adrenal axis of the neonatal rat: Effects of maternal deprivation. *Psychoneuroendocrinology* 20: 169–182.

Sudakov, K. V. (1996). Motivation and reinforcement in the systemic mechanisms of behavior: Dynamic reinforcement engrams. *Neurosci. Behav. Physiol.* 26: 445–453.

Sullivan, M. D. (1990). Reconsidering the wisdom of the body: An epistemological critique of Claude Bnernard's concept of the internal environment. *J. Med. Philos.* 15: 493–514.

Sumners, C., Gault, T. R., and Fregly, M. J. (1991). Potentiation of angiotensin II-induced drinking by glucocorticoids is a specific glucocorticoid type II receptor (GR)-mediated event. *Brain Res.* 552: 283–290.

Suomi, S. J. (1997). Early determinants of behaviour: Evidence from primate studies. *Brit. Med. Bull.* 53: 170–184.

Sutton, M. A., Karanian, D. A., and Self, D. W. (2000). Factors that determine a propensity for cocaine-seeking behavior during abstinence in rats. *Neuropsychopharmacology* 22: 626–641.

Swanson, L. W. (1987). The hypothalamus. In *Handbook of Chemical Neuroanatomy.* Vol. 5, *Integrated Systems of the CNS,* part I, Hypothalamus, Hippocampus, Amygdala, Retina, edited by A. Bjorklund, T. Hokfelt, and L. W. Swanson. New York: Elsevier Science.

Swanson, L. W. (1988). The neural basis of motivated behavior. *Acta Morphol. Neurol. Scand.* 26: 165–176.

Swanson, L. W. (1991). Biochemical switching in hypothalamic circuits mediating responses to stress. *Prog. Brain Res.* 87: 181–200.

Swanson, L. W. (2000). Cerebral hemisphere regulation of motivated behavior. *Brain Res.* 886: 113–164.

Swanson, L. W., and Mogenson, G. J. (1981). Neural mechanisms for the functional coupling of autonomic, endocrine, and somatomotor responses in adaptive behavior. *Brain Res.* 228: 1–34.

Swanson, L. W., and Petrovich, G. D. (1998). What is the amygdala? *Trends Neurosci.* 21: 323–331.

Swanson, L. W., and Simmons, D. M. (1989). Differential steroid hormone and neural influences on peptide mRNA levels in CRH cells of the paraventricular nucleus: A hybridization histochemical study in the rat. *J. Comp. Neurol.* 285: 413–435.

Swanson, L. W., Sawchenko, P. E., Rivier, J., and Vale, W. W. (1983). Organization of ovine corticotropin releasing hormone immunoreactive cells and fibers in the rat brain: An immunohistochemical study. *Neuroendocrinology* 36: 165–186.

Sweeny, J. M., Seibert, H. E., Woda, C., Schulkin, J., Haramati, A., and Mulroney, S. E. (1998). Evidence for induction of a phosphate appetite in juvenile rats. *Am. J. Physiol.* 275: R1358–R1365.

Swerdlow, N. R., Briton, K. T., and Koob, G. F. (1989). Potentiation of acoustic startle by corticotropin-releasing factor (CRF) and by fear are both reversed by alpha-helical CRF (9-41). *Neuropsychopharmacology* 2: 285–292.

Swiergel, A. H., Takahashi, L. K., Rubin, W. W., and Kalin, N. H. (1992). Antagonism of corticotropin-releasing factor receptors in the locus coeruleus attenuates shock-induced freezing in rats. *Brain Res.* 587: 263–268.

Szabo, S. (1998). Hans Selye and the development of the stress concept. Special reference to gastroduodenal ulcerogenesis. *Ann. N.Y. Acad. Sci.* 851: 19–27.

Szczepanska-Sadowska, E. (1989). Mechanisms subserving brain water-electrolyte homeostasis. *Acta Physiol. Pol.* 40: 301–318.

Takahashi, L. K. (1995). Glucocorticoids, the hippocampus, and behavioral inhibition in the preweanling rat. *J. Neurosci.* 15: 6023–6034.

Takahashi, L. K. (2001). Role of CRF receptors in fear and anxiety. *Neurosci. Biobehav. Rev.* 25: 627–636.

Takahashi, L. K., and Kim, H. (1994). Intracranial action of corticosterone facilitates the development of behavioral inhibition in the adrenalectomized preweanling rat. *Neurosci. Lett.* 176: 272–276.

Takahashi, L. K., Kalin, N. H., Vanden-Burgt, J. A., and Sherman, J. E. (1989). Corticotropin-releasing hormone modulates defensive-withdrawal and exploratory behavior in rats. *Behav. Neurosci.* 3: 648–654.

Takahashi, L. K., Turner, J. G., and Kalin, N. H. (1998). Prolonged stress-induced elevation in plasma corticosterone during pregnancy in the rat: Implications for prenatal stress studies. *Psychoneuroendocrinology* 23: 571–581.

Tamura, R., and Norgren, R. (1997). Repeated sodium depletion affects gustatory neural responses in the nucleus of the solitary tract of rats. *Am. J. Physiol.* 273: R1381–R1391.

Tanimura, S. M., and Watts, A. G. (1998). Corticosterone can facilitate as well as inhibit corticotropin-releasing hormone gene expression in the rat hypothalamic paraventricular nucleus. *Endocrinology* 139: 3830–3836.

Tarjan, E., Denton, D. A., Ferraro, T., and Weissinger, R. S. (1992). Effect of CRF, ACTH, and adrenal steroids on sodium intake and excretion in rabbits. *Kidney Int.* 37: S97–S101.

Tarpret, S. F., and Brown, S. A. (1999). Neuropsychological correlates of adolescent substance abuse: Four-year outcomes. *J. Int. Neuropsychol. Soc.* 5: 481–493.

Tattersall, R. (1997). Frederick Pavy (1829–1911) and his oppositions to the glycogenic theory of Claude Bernard. *Ann. Sci.* 54: 361–374.

Taylor, S. E., Klein, L. T., Lewis, B. P., Gruenwald, T. L., Gurung, R. A., and Updegraff, J. A. (2000). Biobehavioral responses to stress in females: Tend and befriend, not fight or flight. *Psychol. Rev.* 107: 411–429.

Teff, K. (2000). Nutritional implications of the cephalic-phase reflexes: Endocrine responses. *Appetite* 34: 206–213.

Teitelbaum, P. (1967). The biology of drive. In *The Neurosciences: A Study Program,* edited by G. Quarton, T. Melnechuk, and F. D. Schmidt. New York: The Rockefeller Press.

Teitelbaum, P. (1971). The encephalization of hunger. *Prog. Physiol. Psychol.* 4: 319–350.

Teitelbaum, P. (1977). Levels of integration of the operant. In *Handbook of Operant Behavior,* edited by W. K. Honig and J. E. R. Staddon. Englewood Cliffs, N.J.: Prentice-Hall.

Tennes, K., and Kreye, M. (1985). Children's adrenocortical responses to classroom activities and tests in elementary school. *Psychosom. Med.* 47: 451–460.

Thomas, K. L., and Everitt, B. J. (2001). Limbic-cortical-ventral striatal activation during retrieval of a discrete cocaine-associated stimulus: A cellular imaging study with protein kinase c expression. *J. Neurosci.* 21: 2526–2535.

Thompson, B. L., Schulkin, J., and Rosen, J. B. (2000). Chronic corticosterone enhances contextual fear conditioning and CRH mRNA expression in the amygdala. *Neurosci. Abst.*

Thorndike, E. L. (1911). *Animal Intelligence.* New York: Macmillan.

Thorpe, S. J., Rolls, E. T., and Maddison, S. (1983). The orbitofrontal cortex: Neuronal activity in the behaving monkey. *Exp. Brain Res.* 49: 93–115.

Thrivikraman, K. V., Nemeroff, C. B., and Plotsky, P. M. (2000). Sensitivity to glucocorticoid-mediated fast-feedback regulation of the hypothalamic-pituitary-adrenal axis is dependent upon stressor specific neurocircuitry. *Brain Res.* 980(1–2): 87–101.

Thunhorst, R. L., and Johnson, A. K. (1994). Renin-angiotensin, arterial blood pressure, and salt appetite in rats. *Am. J. Physiol.* 266: R458–R465.

Tinbergen, N. (1951/1969). *The Study of Instinct.* Oxford: Oxford University Press.

Toates, F. M. (1979). Homeostasis and drinking. *Behav. Brain Sci.* 2: 95–136.

Toates, F. M. (1986). *Motivational Systems.* Cambridge: Cambridge University Press.

Todes, D. P. (1997a). From the machine to the ghost within. *Am. Psychol.* 52: 947–955.

Todes, D. P. (1997b). Pavlov's physiology factory, 1891–1904. *ISIS* 88: 204–246.

Tolman, E. C. (1932). *Purposive Behavior in Animals and Men.* New York: The Century Company.

Tolman, E. C., and Gleitman, H. (1949). Studies in learning and motivation: I. Equal reinforcements in both end-boxes, followed by shock in one end-box. *J. Exp. Psychol.* 39: 810–819.

Tordoff, M. G., Ulrich, P. M., and Schulkin, J. (1990). Calcium deprivation increases salt intake. *Am. J. Physiol.* 259: R411–R419.

Trachsel, L., Edgar, D. M., Seidel, W. F., Heller, H. C., and Dement, W. C. (1992). Sleep homeostasis in suprachiasmatic nuclei-lesioned rats: Effects of sleep deprivation and triazolam administration. *Brain Res.* 589: 253–261.

Tranel, D. (2000). Electrodermal activity in cognitive neuroscience: Neuroanatomical and neurophysiological correlates. In *Cognitive Neuroscience of Emotion,* edited by R. D. Lane and L. Nadel. Oxford: Oxford University Press.

Triffleman, E. G., Marmar, C. R., Delucchi, K. L., and Ronfeldt, H. (1995). Childhood trauma and posttraumatic stress disorder in substance abuse inpatients. *J. Nerv. Ment. Dis.* 183: 172–176.

Tropper, P. J., Goland, R. S., Wardlaw, S. L., Fox, H. E., and Frantz, A. G. (1987). Effects of betamethasone on maternal plasma corticotropin releasing factor, ACTH and cortisol during pregnancy. *J. Perinatal Med.* 15: 221–225.

Tropper, P. J., Warren, W. B., Jozak, S. M., Conwell, I. M., Stark, R. I., and Goland, R. S. (1992). Corticotropin releasing hormone concentrations in umbilical cord blood of preterm fetuses. *J. Dev. Physiol.* 18: 81–85.

Tupala, E., Hall, H., Bergwtrom, K., Sarkloja, T., Rasanen, P., Mantere, T., Callaway, J., Hiltunen, J., and Tihonen, J. (2001). Dopamine D2/D3 receptor and transporter densities in nucleus accumbens and amygdala of type 1 and 2 alcoholics. *Mol. Psychiatry* 6: 261–267.

Turnbull, A. V., and Rivier, C. (1997). Corticotropin-releasing factor (CRF) and endocrine responses to stress: CRF receptors, binding protein, and related peptides. *Exp. Biol. Med.* 215: 1–10.

Turnbull, J. E. (1994). Early background variables as predictors of adult alcohol problems in women. *Int. J. Addict.* 29: 707–728.

Turrigiano, G. G. (1999). Homeostatic plasticity in neuronal networks: The more things change, the more they stay the same. *Trends Neurosci.* 22: 221–227.

Tzchentke, T. M. (2001). Pharmacology and behavioral pharmacology of the mesocortical dopamine system. *Prog. Neurobiol.* 63: 241–320.

Ungless, M. A., Whistler, J. L., Malonka, R. G., and Bonci, A. (2001). *Nature* 411: 863–867.

Unterwald, E. M., Rubenfeld, J. M., and Kreek, M. J. (1994). Repeated cocaine administration upregulates kappa and mu, but not delta, opioids. *Neuroreport* 5: 1613–1616.

Vale, W., Spiess, J., Rivier, C., and Rivier, J. (1981). Characterization of a 41-residue ovine hypothalamic peptide that stimulates the secretion of corticotropin releasing hormone and beta-endorphin. *Science* 213: 1394–1397.

Valenstein, E. S. (1973). History of brain stimulation: Investigations into the physiology of motivation. In *Brain Stimulation and Motivation: Research and Commentary*, edited by E. S. Valenstein. Glenview, Ill.: Scott, Foresman, and Company.

Valenstein, E. S., Cox, V. C., and Kakolewski, J. K. (1970). Reexamination of the role of the hypothalamus in motivation. *Psychol Rev.* 77: 16–31.

Valentino, R. J., Foote, S. L., and Page, M. E. (1993). The locus coeruleus as a site for integrating corticotropin-releasing factor and noradrenergic mediation of stress responses. *Ann N.Y. Acad. Sci.* 697: 173–188.

Valentino, R. J., Pavcovich, L. A., and Hirata, H. (1995). Evidence for corticotropin-releasing hormone projections from Barrington's nucleus to the periaqueductal gray and dorsal motor nucleus of the vagus in the rat. *J. Comp. Neurol.* 363: 402–422.

Vallee, M., Mayo, W., Dellu, F., Le Moal, M., Simon, H., and Maccari, S. (1997). Prenatal stress induces high anxiety and postnatal handling induces low anxiety in adult offspring: Correlation with stress induced corticosterone secretion. *J. Neurosci.* 17: 2626–2636.

Vamvakopoulos, N. C., and Chrousos, G. P. (1993). Evidence of direct estrogenic regulation of human coritotropin releasing hormone gene expression. *J. Clin. Invest.* 2: 1896–1902.

Van Cauter, E., LeProult, R., and Plat, L. (2000). Age-related changes in slow wave sleep and REM sleep and relationship with growth hormone and cortisol levels in healthy men. *JAMA* 284: 861–868.

Van Cauter, E., Polonsky, K. S., and Scheen, A. J. (1997). Roles of circadian rhythmicity and sleep in human glucose regulation. *Endocrinol. Rev.* 18: 716–738.

Van de Kar, L. D., Javed, A., Zhang, Y., Serres, F., Raap, D. K., and Gray, T. S. (2001). 5-HT2A receptors stimulate ACTH, corticosterone, oxytocin, renin, and prolactin release and activate hypothalamic CRF and oxytocin-expressing cells. *J Neurosci.* 21: 3572–3579.

Van den Bree, M. B., Johnson, E. O., Neale, M. C., and Pickens, R. W. (1998). Genetic and environmental influences on drug use and abuse/dependence in male and female twins. *Drug Alcohol Depend.* 52: 231–241.

Van den Buuse, M. (1997). Pressor responses to brain dopaminergic stimulation. *Clin. Exp. Pharmacol. Physiol.* 24: 764–769.

Van Der Leder, M.E., and Raskin, V. D. (1993). Psychological sequelae of childhood sexual abuse: Relevant in subsequent pregnancy. *Am. J. Obstet. Gynecol.* 168: 1336–1337.

Vanderpool, J. R. J., Rosenthal, N. R., Chrousos, G. P., Wehr, T. A., Skwerer, R., Kasper, S., and Gold, P. W. (1991). Abnormal pituitary-adrenal responses to corticotropin releasing hormone in patients with seasonal affective dis-

order: Clinical and pathophysiological implications. *J. Clin. Endocrinol. Metabol.* 72: 1382–1387.

Vanderschuren, L. J., Schmidt, E. D., de Vries, T. J., Van Moorsel, C. A., Tilders, F. J., and Schoffelmeer, A. N. (1999). A single exposure to amphetamine is sufficient to induce long-term behavioral, neuroendocrine, and neurochemical sensitization in rats. *J. Neurosci.* 19: 9579–9586.

Vanderwolf, C. H., Kelly, M. E., Kraemer, P., and Streather, A. (1988). Are emotion and motivation localized in the limbic system and nucleus accumbens? *Behav. Brain Res.* 27: 45–58.

Van Gorp, W. G., Wilkins, J. N., Hinkin, C. H., Moore, L. H., Hull, J., Horner, M. D., and Plotkin, D. (1999). Declarative and procedural memory functioning in abstinent cocaine abusers. *Arch. Gen. Psychiatry* 56: 85–89.

Van Oers, H. J., de Kloet, E. R., Li, C., and Levine, S. (1998). The ontogeny of glucocorticoid negative feedback: Influence of maternal deprivation. *Endocrinology* 139: 2838–2846.

Van Parijs, L., and Abbas, A. K. (1998). Homeostasis and self-tolerance in the immune system: Turning lymphocytes off. *Science* 280: 243–248.

Vazquez, D. M., Van Oers, H. J., Levine, S., and Akil, H. (1996). Regulation of glucocorticoid and mineralocorticoid receptor mRNAs in the hippocampus of the maternally deprived infant rat. *Brain Res.* 731: 79–90.

Verbalis, J. G., Blackburn, R. E., Olsen, B. R., and Sticker, E. M. (1993). Central oxytocin inhibition of food and salt ingestion: A mechanism for intake regulation of solute homeostasis. *Regul. Peptides* 45: 149–154.

Virtanen, R. (1986). Calude Bernard's prophecies and the historical relation of science to literature. *J. Hist. Ideas* 47: 275–286.

Volkow, N. D., Mullani, N., Gould, L., Adler, S. S., Guynn, R. W., Overall, J. F., and Dewey, S. (1988). Effects of acute alcohol intoxication on cerebral blood flow measured with PET. *Psychiatry Res.* 24: 201–209.

Volkow, N. D., Fowler, J. S., Wolf, A. P., Hitzeman, R., Dewey, S., Bendriem, B., Alpert, R., and Hoff, A. (1991). Changes in brain glucose metabolism in cocaine dependence and withdrawal. *Am. J. Psychiatry* 148: 621–626.

Volkow, N. D., Hitzemann, R., Wang, G. J., Fowler, J. S., Burr, G., Pascani, K., Dewey, S. L., and Wolf, A. P. (1992). Decreased brain metabolism in neurologically intact healthy alcoholics. *Am. J. Psychiatry* 149: 1016–1022.

Volkow, N. D., Wang, G. J., Fischman, M., Foltin, R. W., Fowler, J. S., Abumrad, N. N., Vitkun, S., Logan, J., Gatley, S. J., Pappas, N., Hitzemann, R., and Shea, C. F. (1997). Relationship between subjective effects of cocaine and dopamine transporter occupancy. *Nature* 386: 827–830.

von Holst, E., and St. Paul, U. (1963). On the functional organization of drives. *Anim. Behav.* 11: 1–20.

Voorhuis, T. A., De Kloet, E. R., and De Wied, D. (1991). Effect of a vasotocin analog on singing behavior in the canary. *Horm. Behav.* 25: 549–559.

Waddell, B. J. (1993). The placenta as hypothalamus and pituitary: Possible impact on maternal and fetal adrenal function. *Reprod. Fertil. Dev.* 5: 479–497.

Wade, G. N., and Schneider, J. E. (1992). Metabolic fuels and reproduction in female mammals. *Neurosci. Biobehav. Rev.* 16: 235–272.

Wade, J., and Crews, D. (1991). The effects of intracranial implantation of estrogen on receptivity in sexually and asexually reproducing female whiptail lizards, *Cnemidophorus inornatus* and *Cnemidophorus uniparens*. *Horm Behav.* 25: 342–353.

Wadhwa, P. D. (2001). Stress, infection, and preterm birth: A biobehavioral perspective. *Paediatr. Perinat. Epidemiol.* 15: 17–29.

Wadhwa, P. D., Sandman, C. A., Porto, M., Dunkel-Schetter, C., and Garite, T. J. (1993). The association between prenatal stress and infant birth weight and gestational age at birth: A prospective investigation. *Am. J. Obstet. Gynecol.* 169: 858–865.

Wadhwa, P. D., Dunkel-Schetter, C., Chicz-DeMet, A., Porto, M., and Sandman, C. A. (1996). Prenatal psychosocial factors and the neuroendocrine axis in human pregnancy. *Psychosom. Med.* 58: 432–446.

Wadhwa, P. D., Sandman, C. A., Chicz-DeMet, A., and Porto, M. (1997). Placental CRH modulates maternal pituitary-adrenal function in human pregnancy. *Ann. N.Y. Acad. Sci.* 814: 276–281.

Wadhwa, P. D., Porto, M., Garite, T. J., Chicz-DeMet, A., and Sandman, C. A. (1998). Maternal corticotropin-releasing hormone levels in the early third trimester predict length of gestation in human pregnancy. *Am. J. Obstet. Gynecol.* 179: 1079–1085.

Wadwha, P. D., Sandman, C. A., and Garite, T. J. (2001). The neurobiology of stress in human pregnancy: Implications for development of the fetal central nervous system. *Prog. Brain Res.* 133: 1–12.

Wahlestedt, C., Pich, E. M., Koob, G. F., Yee, F., and Heilig, M. (1993). Modulation of anxiety and neuropeptide Y-Y1 receptors by antisense oligodeoxynucleotides. *Science* 259: 528–531.

Walker, J. R., Ahmed, S. H., Gracy, K. N., and Koob, G. F. (2000). Microinjections of an opiate receptor antagonist into the bed nucleus of the stria terminalis suppress heroin self-administration in dependent rats. *Brain Res.* 854: 85–92.

Wallace, K. J., and Rosen, J. B. (2001). Neurotoxic lesions of the lateral nucleus of the amygdala decrease conditioned fear but not unconditioned fear of a predator odor: Comparison with electrolytic lesions. *J. Neurosci.* 21: 3619–3627.

Wang, S., Mason, J., Charney, D., Yehuda, R., Riney, S., and Southwick, S. (1997). Relationships between hormonal profile and novelty seeking in combat-related posttraumatic stress disorder. *Biol. Psychiatry* 41: 145–151.

Wang, Z., Smith, W., Major, D. E., and De Vries, G. J. (1994). Sex and species differences in the effects of cohabitation on vasopressin messenger RNA expression in the bed nucleus of the stria terminalis in prairie voles *(Microtus ochrogaster)* and meadow voles *(Microtus pennsylvanicus)*. *Brain Res.* 650: 212–218.

Warren, W. B., and Goland, R. S. (1995). Effects of parturition on corticotropin releasing hormone and products of the pituitary and adrenal in term fetuses at delivery. *J. Perinat. Med.* 23: 453–458.

Warren, W. B., Goland, R. S., Wardlaw, S. L., Stark, R. I., Fox, H. E., and Conwell, I. M. (1990). Elevated maternal plasma corticotropin releasing hormone levels in twin gestation. *J. Preinat. Med.* 18: 39–44.

Wasserman, R. H. (1989). Physiological mechanisms of calcium absorption and homeostasis, with emphasis on vitamin D action. *Curr. Topics Nutr. Dis.* 21: 105–134.

Wasserstein, A. G. (1996). Death and the internal milieu: Calude Bernard and the origins of experimental medicine. *Perspect. Biol. Med.* 39: 313–326.

Watt, G. C., Harrap, S. B., Foy, C. J., Holton, D. W., Edwards, H. V., Davidson, H. R., Connor, J. M., Lever, A. F., and Fraser, R. (1992). Abnormalities of glucocorticoid metabolism and the renin-angiotensin system: A four-corners approach to the identification of genetic determinants of blood pressure. *J. Hypertens.* 10: 473–482.

Watts, A. G. (1996). The impact of physiological stimuli on the expression of corticotropin-releasing hormone (CRH) and other neuropeptide genes. *Front. Neuroendocrinol.* 17: 281–326.

Watts, A. G. (2000). Understanding the neural control of ingestive behaviors: Helping to separate cause from effect with dehydration-associated anorexia. *Horm. Behav.* 37: 261–283.

Watts, A. G., and Sanchez-Watts, G. (1995). Region-specific regulation of neuropeptide mRNAs in rat limbic forebrain neurones by aldosterone and corticosterone. *J. Physiol. (Lond.)* 484: 721–736.

Watts, A. G., Sanchez-Watts, G., and Kelly, A. B. (1999). Distinct patterns of neuropeptide gene expression in the lateral hypothalamic area and arcuate nucleus are associated with dehydration-induced anorexia. *J. Neurosci.* 19: 6111–6121.

Weaber, K. L. (2001). Aldosterone in congestive heart failure. *N. Engl. J. Med.* 345: 1689–1697.

Weaver, D. R., Liu, C., and Reppert, S. M. (1996). Nature's knockout: The Mel_{1b} receptor is not necessary for reproductive and circadian responses to melatonin in Siberian hamsters. *Mol. Endocrinol.* 10: 1478–1487.

Wehling, M., Eisen, C., and Christ, M. (1992). Aldosterone-specific membrane receptors and rapid non-genomic actions of mineralocorticoids. *Mol. Cell. Endocinol.* 90: C5–C9.

Weir, M. R. (1997). Non-diuretic-based antihypertensive therapy and potassium homeostasis in elderly patients. *Coron. Artery Dis.* 8: 499–504.

Weisfeld, G. E. (1982). An extension of the stress-homeostasis model based on ethological research. *Perspect. Biol. Med.* 26: 79–97.

Weisinger, R. S., Blair-West, J. R., Denton, D. A., and McBurnie, M. I. (1999). Angiotensin II stimulates intake of etanol in C57BL/6J mice. *Physiol. Behav.* 67: 369–376.

Weisinger, R. S., Blair-West, J. R., Burns, P., Denton, D. A., McKinley, M. J., Purcell, B., Vale, W., Rivier, J., and Sunagawa, K. (2000). The inhibitory effect of hormones associated with stress on Na appetite of sheep. *Proc. Natl. Acad. Sci. USA* 97: 2922–2927.

Weiss, E. L., Longhurst, J. G., and Mazure, C. M. (1999). Childhood sexual abuse as a risk factor for depression in women: Psychosocial and neurobiological correlates. *Am. J. Psychiatry* 156: 816–828.

Weiss, F., Markou, A., Lorang, M. T., and Koob, G. F. (1992). Basal extracellular dopamine levels in the nucleus accumbens are decreased during cocaine withdrawal after unlimited-access self-administration. *Brain Res.* 593: 314–318.

Weiss, F., Parsons, L. H., Schulteis, G., Hyytia, P., Lorang, M. T., Bloom, F. E., and Koob, G. F. (1996). Ethanol self-administration restores withdrawal-associated deficiencies in accumbal dopamine and 5-hydroxytryptamine release in dependent rats. *J. Neurosci.* 16: 3474–3485.

Weiss, J. M. (1970). Somatic effects of predictable and unpredictable shock. *Psychosom. Med.* 32: 397–408.

Weiss, J. M. (1971). Effects of coping behavior in different warning signal conditions on stress pathology in rats. *J. Comp. Physiol. Psychol.* 77: 1–13.

Weiss, J. M., Goodman, P. A., Losito, B. G., Corrigan, S., Charry, J. M., and Bailey, W. H. (1981). Behavioral depression produced by an uncontrollable stressor: Relationship to norepinephrine, dopamine, and serotonin levels in various regions of the brain. *Brain Res. Rev.* 3: 167–205.

Weiss, S. R., Post, R. M., Gold, P. W., Chrousos, G., Sullivan, T. L., Walker, D., and Pert, A. (1986). CRF-induced seizures and behavior: Interaction with amygdala kindling. *Brain Res.* 372: 345–351.

Weiss, S. R., Nierenberg, J., Lewis, R., and Post, R. M. (1992). Corticotropin-releasing hormone: Potentiation of cocaine-kindled seizures and lethality. *Epilepsia* 33: 248–254.

Weissman, M. (1988). Anxiety and alcoholism. *J. Clin. Psychiatry* 49 (suppl.): 17–19.

Welberg, L. A., and Seckl, J. R. (2001). Prenatal stress, glucocorticoids, and the programming of the brain. *J. Neuroendocrinol.* 13: 113–128.

Welberg, L. A., Seckl, J. R., and Holmes, M. C. (2000). Inhibition of 11 beta-hydroxysteroid dehydrogenase, the foeto-placental barrier to maternal glucocorticoids, permanently programs amygdala GR mRNA expression and anxiety-like behavior in the offspring. *Eur. J. Neurosci.* 12: 1047–1054.

Weninger, S. C., Dunn, A. J., Muglia, L. J., Dikkes, P., Miczekk, A., Swiergie, A. U., Berridge, C. W., and Majzoub, J. A. (1999). Stress-induced behaviors require the corticotropin-releasing hormone (CRH) receptor, but not CRH. *Proc. Natl. Acad. Sci.* 96 (July): 8283–8299.

Wert, R. C., and Raulin, M. L. (1986). The chronic cerebral effects of cannabis use: II. Psychological findings and conclusions. *Int. J. Addict.* 21: 629–642.

Westbrook, S. L., and Marek, E. A. (1992). A cross-age study of student understanding of the concept of homeostasis. *J. Res. Sci. Teaching.* 29: 51–61.

Whalen, P. J. (1998). Fear, vigilance, and ambiguity: Initial neuroimaging studies of the human amygdala. *Curr. Dir. Psychol. Sci.* 7: 177–188.

Widdowson, P. S., Ordway, G. A., and Halaris, A. E. (1992). Reduced neuropeptide Y concentrations in suicide brain. *J. Neurochem.* 59: 73–80.

Wiers, R. W., Sergeant, J. A., and Gunning, W. B. (1994). Psychological mechanisms of enhanced risk of addiction in children of alcholics: A dual pathway? *Acta Paediatr. Suppl.* 404: 9–13.

Wiersma, A., Konsman, J. P., Knollema, S., Bohus, B., and Koolhaas, J. M. (1998). Differential effects of CRH infusion into the central nucleus of the amygdala in the Roman high-avoidance and low-avoidance rats. *Psychoneuroendocrinology* 23: 261–274.

Wilkins, L., and Richter, C. P. (1940). A great craving for salt by a child with corticoadrenal insufficiency. *JAMA* 114: 866–868.

Willard, M. D. (1989). Disorders of potassium homeostasis. *Vet. Clin. North Am. Small Anim. Pract.* 19: 241–263.

Wills, M. R., Bruns, D. E., and Savory, J. (1982). Disorders of calcium homeostasis in the fetus and neonate. *Ann. Clin. Lab. Sci.* 12: 79–88.

Wills, T. A., Windle, M., and Cleary, S. D. (1998). Temperament and novelty seeking in adolescent substance use: Convergence of dimensions of temperament with constructs from Cloninger's theory. *J. Pers. Soc. Psychol.* 74: 387–406.

Wilsnack, S. C., Vogeltanz, N. D., Klassen, A. D., and Harris, T. R. (1997). Childhood sexual abuse and women's substance abuse: National survey findings. *J. Stud. Alcohol.* 58: 264–271.

Windle, M. (1994). Temperamental inhibition and activation: Hormonal and psychosocial correlates and associated psychiatric disorders. *Pers. Individual Diff.* 17: 61–70.

Wingfield, J. C., and Ramenofsky, M. (1997). Corticosterone and facultative dispersal in response to unpredictable events. *Ardeam* 85: 155–166.

Wingfield, J. C., and Ramenofsky, M. (1999). Hormones and the behavioral ecology of stress. In *Stress Physiology in Animals,* edited by P. H. M. Balm. Sheffield, UK: Sheffield Academic Press.

Wingfield, J. C., and Romero, L. M. (2001). Adrenocortical responses to stress and their modulation in free-living vertebrates. In *Coping with the Environment: Neural and Endocrine Mechanisms,* edited by B. S. McEwen. Oxford: Oxford Unversity Press.

Winslow, J. T., Hastings, N., Carter, C. S., Harbaugh, C. R., and Insel, T. R. (1993). A role for central vasopressin in pair bonding in monogamous prairie voles. *Nature* 365: 545–548.

Wise, R. A. (1971). Individual differences in effects of hypothalamic stimulation: The role of stimulation locus. *Physiol. Behav.* 6: 569–572.

Wise, R. A. (1987). Sensorimotor modulation and the viable action pattern: Toward a noncircular defination of drive and motivation. *Psychobiology* 15: 7–20.

Wise, R. A. (1996). Neurobiology of addiction. *Curr. Opin. Neurobiol.* 6: 243–251.

Wise, R. A., and Bozarth, M. A. (1987). A psychomotor stimulant theory of addiction. *Psychol. Rev.* 94: 469–492.

Wise, R. A., and Rompre, P. P. (1989). Brain dopamine and reward. *Ann. Rev. Psychol.* 40: 191–225.

Wise, R. A., Spindler, J., deWit, H., and Gerberg, G. J. (1978). Neuroleptic-induced "anhedonia" in rats: Pimozide blocks reward quality of food. *Science* 201: 262–264.

Wolf, G. (1964). Sodium appetite elicited by aldosterone. *Psychonomic Sci.* 1: 211–212.

Wolf, G. (1969). Innate mechanisms for regulation of sodium appetite. In *Olfaction and Taste,* edited by C. Pfaffmann. New York: Rockefeller University Press.

Wolfe, C. D., Patel, S. P., Linton, E. A., Campbell, E. A., Anderson, J., Dornhorst, A., Lowry, P. J., and Jones, M. T. (1988). Plasma corticotropin-releasing factor (CRF) in abnormal pregnancy. *Br. J. Obstet. Gynaecol.* 95: 1003–1006.

Wolkowitz, O. M., Rubinow, D., Doran, A. R., Breier, A., Berrettini, W. H., Kling, M. A., and Pickar, D. (1990). Prednisone effects on neurochemistry and behavior. Preliminary findings. *Arch. Gen. Psychiatry* 47: 963–968.

Wong, D., Herman, J. P., Pritchard, L. M., Spitzer, R. H., Ahlbrand, R. L., Kramer, G. L., Petty, R., Salle, F. R., and Richtand, N. M. (2001). Cloning, expression, and regulation of glucocorticoid-induced receptor in rat brain: Effect of repetitive amphetamine. *J. Neurosci.* 21: 9027–9035.

Wong, M. L., Bongiorno, P. B., Rettori, V., McCann, S. M., and Licinio, J. (1997). Interleukin (IL) 1β, IL-1 receptor antagonist, IL-10, and IL-13 gene expression in the central nervous system and anterior pituitary during systemic inflammation: Pathophysiological implications. *Proc. Natl. Acad. Sci.* 94: 227–232.

Wong, M. L., Kling, M. A., Munson, P. J., Listwak, S., Licinio, J., Prolo, P., Karp, B., McCutcheon, I. E., Geracioti, T. D. Jr., DeBellis, M. D., Rice, K. C., Goldstein, D. S., Veldhuis, J. D., Chrousos, G. P., Oldfield, E. H., McCann, S. M., and Gold, P. W. (2000). Pronounced and sustained central hypernoradrenergic function in major depression with melancholic features: Relation to hypercortisolism and corticotropin-releasing hormone. *Proc. Natl. Acad. Sci.* 97: 325–330.

Woods, S. C. (1970). Conditioned insulin secretion in the albino rat. *Proc. Soc. Exp. Biol. Med.* 133: 965–968.

Woods, S. C. (1983). Conditioned hypoglycemia and conditioned insulin secretion. *Adv. Metab. Disord.* 10: 485–495.

Woods, S. C. (1991). The eating paradox: How we tolerate food. *Psychol. Rev.* 98: 488–505.

Woods, S. C., and Kenney, N. J. (1979). Alternatives to homeostasis. *Behav. Brain Sci.* 2: 123–124.

Woods, S. C., Seeley, R. J., Porte, D. Jr., and Schwartz, M. W. (1998). Signals that regulate food intake and energy homeostasis. *Science* 280: 1378–1383.

Woolley, C. S., and McEwen, B. S. (1994). Estradiol regulates hippocampal dendritic spine density via an *N*-methyl-D-aspartate receptor-dependent mechanism. *J. Neurosci.* 14: 7680–7687.

Worsley, J. N., Moszczynska, A., Falaradeau, P., Kalasinsky, S. K., Schmunk, G., Guttman, M., Furukawa, Y., Ang, L., Adams, V., Reiber, G., Anthony, R. A., Wickman, D., and Kish, S. J. (2000). Dopamine D1 receptor protein is elevated in nucleus accumbens of human, chronic methamphetamine users. *Mol. Psychiatry* 5: 664–672.

Wren, B. (1996). Hormonal therapy and genital tract cancer. *Curr. Opin. Obstet. Gynecol.* 8: 38–41.

Wright, B. E., Porter, J. R., Browne, E. S., and Svec, F. (1992). Antiglucocorticoid action of dehydroepiandrosterone in young obese Zucker rats. *Int. J. Obes. Relat. Metab. Disord.* 16: 579–593.

Wright, C. L., Fischer, H., Whalen, P. J., McInerney, S. C., Shin, L. M., and Rauch, S. L. (2001). Differential prefrontal cortex and amygdala habituation to repeatedly presented emotional stimuli. *Neuroreport* 12: 379–383.

Wu, Q., Reith, M. E. A., Kuhar, M. J., Carroll, E. I., and Garris, P. A. (2001). Preferential increases in nucleus accumbens dopamine after systemic cocaine administration are caused by unique characteristics of dopamine neurotransmission. *J. Neurosci.* 21: 6338–6347.

Wu, W. X., Unno, S., Giussani, D. A., Mecenas, C. A., McDonald, T. J., and Nathaniels, P. W. (1995). Corticotropin-releasing hormone and its receptor distribution in fetal membranes and placenta of the rhesus monkey in the late gestation and labor. *Endocrinology* 136: 4621–4628.

Wurts, S. W., and Edgar, D. M. (2000). Circadian and homeostatic control of rapid eye movement (REM) sleep: Promotion of REM tendency by the suprachiasmatic nucleus. *J. Neurosci.* 20: 4300–4310.

Wyell, C.L., and Berridge, K. C. (2000). Intra-accumbens amphetamine increases the conditioned incentive salience of sucrose reward: Enhancement of reward "wanting" without enhanced "liking" of response reinforcement. *J. Neurosci.* 20: 8122–8130.

Xu, Z., and Herbert, J. (1994). Regional supression by water intake of *c-fos* expression induced by intraventricular infusions of angiotensin II. *Brain Res.* 659: 157–168.

Yama, M. F., Tovey, S. L., Fogas, B. S., and Teegarden, L. A. (1992). Joint consequences of parental alcoholism and childhood sexual abuse, and their partial mediation by family environment. *Violence Vict.* 7: 313–325.

Yamada, K., Duong, D. T., Scott, D. K., Wang, J. C., and Granner, D. K. (1999). CCAAT/enhancer-binding protein is an accessory factor for the gluco-

corticoid response from the cAMP response element in the rat phosphoenolpyruvate carboxykinase gene promoter. *J. Biol. Chem.* 274: 5880–5887.

Yeh, C. W., and McKnight, S. L. (1995). Regulation of adipose maturation and energy homeostasis. *Curr. Opin. Cell Biol.* 7: 885–890.

Yehuda, R. (1997). Sensitization of the hypothalamic-pituitary-adrenal axis in posttraumatic stress disorder. In *Psychobiology of Posttraumatic Stress Disorder,* edited by R. Yehuda and A. C. McFarlane. New York: Academic Press.

Yehuda, R. (2002). Post-traumatic stress disorder. *N. Engl. J. Med.* 346: 108–114.

Yehuda, R., Kahana, B., Binder-Brynes, K., Southwick, S. M., Mason, J. W., and Giller, E. L. (1995a). Low urinary cortisol excretion in Holocaust survivors with posttraumatic stress disorder. *Am. J. Psychiatry* 152: 982–986.

Yehuda, R., Boisoneau, D., Lowy, M. T., and Giller, E. L. Jr. (1995b). Dose-response changes in plasma cortisol and lymphocyte glucocorticoid receptors following dexamethasone administration in combat veterans with and without posttraumatic stress disorder. *Arch. Gen. Psychiatry* 52: 583–593.

Yehuda, R., Teicher, M. H., Trestman, R. L., Levengood, R. A., and Siever, L. J. (1996). Cortisol regulation in posttraumatic stress disorder and major depression: A chronobiological analysis. *Biol. Psychiatry* 40: 79–88.

Yehuda, R., Resnick, H. S., Schmeidler, J., Yang, R. K., and Pitman, R. K. (1998). Predictors of cortisol and 3-methoxy-4-hydroxyphenylglycol responses in the acute aftermath of rape. *Biol. Psychiatry* 43: 855–859.

Young, E. A., and Akil, J. (1988). Paradoxical effect of corticosteroids on pituitary ACTH/beta-endorphin release in stressed animals. *Psychoneuroendocrinology* 13: 317–323.

Young, E. A., Abelson, J. L., Curtis, G. C., and Nesse, R. M. (1997). Childhood adversity and vulnerability to mood and anxiety disorders. *Depression Anxiety* 5: 66–72.

Young, E. A., Carlson, N. E., and Brown, M. B. (2001). Twenty-four-hour ACTH and cortisol pulsatility in depressed women. *Biol. Psychiatry* 25: 267–276.

Young, P. T. (1941). The experimental analysis of appetite. *Psychol. Bull.* 38: 129–164.

Young, P. T. (1949). Studies of food preference, appetite, and dietary habit. *Comp. Psychol. Monogr.* 19: 1–74.

Young, P. T. (1959). The role of affective processes in learning and motivation. *Psychol. Rev.* 66: 104–125.

Young, P. T. (1966). *Motivation and Emotion.* New York: Wiley.

Young, R. C., Gibbs, J., Antin, J., Holt, J., and Smith, G. P. (1974). Absence of satiety during sham feeding in the rat. *J. Comp. Physiol. Psychol.* 87: 795–800.

Zaslav, M. R. (1994). Psychology of comorbid posttraumatic stress disorder and substance abuse: Lessons from combat veterans. *J. Psychoactive Drugs* 26: 393–400.

Zhang, D.-M., Stellar, E., and Epstein, A. N. (1984). Together intracranial angiotensin and systemic mineralocorticoid produce avidity for salt in the rat. *Physiol. Behav.* 32: 677–681.

Zhou, Y., Spangler, R., LaForge, K. S., Maggos, C. E., Ho, A., and Kreek, M. J. (1996a). Modulation of CRF-R1 mRNA in rat anterior pituitary by dexamethasone: Correlation with POMC mRNA. *Peptides* 17: 435–441.

Zhou, Y., Spangler, R., LaForge, K. S., Maggos, C. E., Ho, A., and Kreek, M. J. (1996b). Corticotropin-releasing factor and type 1 corticotropin-releasing factor receptor messenger RNAs in rat brain and pituitary during "binge"-pattern cocaine administration and chronic withdrawal. *J. Pharmacol. Exp. Ther.* 279: 351–358.

Ziegler, D. R., Cass, W. A., and Herman, J. P. (1999). Excitatory influence of the locus coeruleus in hypothalamic-pituitary-adrenocortical axis responses to stress. *J. Neuroendocrinol.* 11: 361–369.

Zigmond, M. J. (1994). Chemical transmission in the brain: Homeostatic regulation and its functional implications. *Prog. Brain Res.* 100: 115–122.

Zobel, A. W., Nickel, T., Kunzel, J. E., Ackl, N., Sonntag, A., Ising, M., and Holsboer, F. (2000). Effects of the high-affinity corticotropin-releasing hormone receptor l antagonist R121919 in major depression: The first 20 patients treated. *J. Psychiatr. Res.* 34: 171–181.

Name Index

Subject Index